WORDSWORTH CLASSICS
OF WORLD LITERATURE

General Editor: Tom Griffith

THE CONCISE PEPYS

The Concise Pepys

❖

With an Introduction by Stuart Sim

WORDSWORTH CLASSICS
OF WORLD LITERATURE

This edition published 1997 by Wordsworth Editions Limited
8b East Street, Ware, Hertfordshire SG12 9HJ

ISBN 1 85326 478 4

Text © Wordsworth Editions Limited 1997
Introduction © Stuart Sim 1997

Wordsworth® is a registered trademark of
Wordsworth Editions Limited

2 4 6 8 10 9 7 5 3 1

Typeset by Antony Gray
Printed and bound in Great Britain by
Mackays of Chatham plc, Chatham, Kent.

INTRODUCTION

Samuel Pepys's *Diary* is rightly celebrated as one of the most fascinating documents in the English language, from both an historical and a literary point of view. In almost a decade of diary-keeping between 1660 and 1669 Pepys provides us with a unique insight into daily life in the seventeenth century, including first-hand accounts of such momentous events as the Restoration of the Stuart monarchy in 1660, the dreadful plagues of the 1660s, and the Great Fire of London in 1666. Pepys himself was a figure of some significance in the political life of the period, working his way up the ladder as a civil servant ultimately to become Secretary of the Admiralty, and his diary offers us a tantalising glimpse into the world of later seventeenth-century English power politics.

The diary also offers us a tantalising glimpse into personal life, with Pepys recording his social – and, somewhat notoriously, his love – life in some detail. He most certainly had an active social life, and his gregarious nature reveals itself at every turn, whether he is simply delighting in the company of friends, enjoying a visit to the theatre or recording with relish the meals he had eaten and the wine he had drunk that day (feminists will find his treatment of women harder to forgive, one suspects). In modern terms of reference Pepys was a very 'clubbable' man, one who was never so happy as when in the company of his friends and acquaintances. And his circle of friends and acquaintances did seem to be very wide – Pepys rarely lacked companions:

> At home to look after things for dinner. And anon at noon comes Mr Creed by chance, and by and by the three young ladies: and very merry we were with our pasty, very well baked; and a good dish of roasted chickens; pease, lobsters, strawberries. And after dinner to cards: and about five o'clock, by water down to Greenwich; and up to the top of the hill, and there played upon the ground at cards.[1]

It is a pattern of events which is to be repeated over and again throughout the diary's narrative of the decade.

The diary is a work of literature as well as an historical record. Pepys writes well, in a simple, unaffected manner that draws the reader effortlessly into his concerns, and the diary has something of the impact of a

1 June 15th, 1664, p. 289.

novel, with Pepys himself as its hero. Certainly the diary works well as a narrative, and Pepys's adventures prove to be as absorbing as those of any fictional creation of the time. Long as the complete work is (about one and a quarter million words), most readers come out of the diary sad that Pepys was forced to abandon keeping it because of the deteriorating condition of his eyes in the late 1660s.

Life and Career

Samuel Pepys was born in London in 1633, and lived an eventful life until his death in 1703 from the effects of the kidney stone ('my old pain'[2]) which had troubled him so much throughout his life. He was educated at St Paul's School, London and Magdalene College, Cambridge, where he took his degree in 1654. Married in 1655, Pepys and his wife had no children, which, as the diary makes clear, was a source of much regret to both of them in an age which set so much store by family life. Although an adulterous husband – and on a very regular basis too, it should be said – there is nevertheless much evidence from the diary to suggest that Pepys had great affection for his wife, and after her death in 1669, shortly after he ceased to keep the diary, he never remarried.

Family connections led to Pepys becoming secretary to Sir Edward Montagu, commander of the Commonwealth fleet under Oliver Cromwell in the 1650s, and then to his entry into the Navy Office, where Pepys became Clerk of the Acts in 1660, and finally in 1673 Secretary of the Admiralty. Becoming such a high public official in this period meant gaining the opportunity to secure one's position financially, and Pepys ended his life a comparatively wealthy man; although it is worth stating that his standards of probity were probably higher than most of his contemporaries in similar positions. Christopher Hill has dubbed him 'the first modern civil servant'[3] in this respect, and David Ogg has gone so far as to call Pepys 'the greatest of civil servants'.[4] The diary provides us with frequent reports on the author's financial state, and he clearly took considerable relish in this side of his life as well, happily recording the progressively improving condition of his estate over the course of the 1660s: 'Yet, blessed be God! and I pray God make me thankful for it, I do find myself worth in money, all good, above £6200: which is above £1800 more than I was the last year'.[5]

2 1659–60, p. 5.

3 Christopher Hill, *The Century of Revolution, 1603–1714*, Van Nostrand Reinhold, Wokingham, Berkshire 1961, p. 244.

4 David Ogg, *England in the Reign of Charles II*, Oxford University Press, 1964, pp. 737–8.

5 December 31st, 1666, p. 479.

Pepys was Secretary to the Admiralty from 1673 to 1679, but by 1679 he had made enough enemies (not a difficult thing to do as a public official in this era) to end up imprisoned in the Tower for six weeks on suspicion of being involved in the Popish plot. Although acquitted in the courts he did not return to public life in the Navy Office until 1684, subsequently retiring for good during the 'Glorious Revolution' of 1688–89 that expelled the Stuart monarchy from the English throne for the last time. Pepys spent the remainder of his life as a patron of the arts and sciences (having already been President of the Royal Society in 1684 and 1685). He also expended considerable time and effort in putting together a library, which he bequeathed to his old college, Magdalene.

The Restoration Period

Pepys's *Diary* provides us with an invaluable record of a momentous period in English history, and its reports of the Restoration, the Plague of 1665, and the Great Fire of London in 1666, as well as of the wars with the Dutch that saw enemy ships raiding up the Medway on occasion, adds immeasurably to our understanding of the culture and everyday life of seventeenth-century England. We are presented with those events as they were experienced on the ground, by an interested party eager to register his impressions of what he realised were culturally very significant happenings.

Pepys was heavily involved in the public life of the 1660s and 1670s, and the diary charts his rise to a position of some influence in the state. We see Pepys engaged in the reorganisation, and indeed professionalisation, of the Navy Office, which he clearly left in a far healthier state in the late 1680s when he retired than when he entered it; we see him wheeling and dealing with some of the major political players of the day; giving evidence to parliamentary committees (he was to become an MP himself in the 1670s): and generally entering with gusto into the turbulent and faction-ridden political life of Restoration England. For all his socialising it has to be said that Pepys was a hard worker, who achieved his position of eminence in the Restoration political world more by his diligence and capacity for sustained effort than by his family connections (his career has been described as a tribute to the effectiveness of the Protestant work ethic). We might say of him, in modern parlance, that he worked hard and played hard, taking full, and enthusiastic, advantage of the many opportunities opened up by the new socio-political climate of the 1660s. The sheer excitement of this fascinating period is well caught by Pepys's chatty and often breathless prose, with what David Ogg has called the author's 'thirst for information'[6] well to the fore.

6 *England in the Reign of Charles II*, p. 736.

Diary-Keeping

Diary-keeping is very much a seventeenth-century phenomenon, and it serves notice of the growing importance of the individual in the cultural scheme of things. Pepys's efforts in this direction, with the wealth of information they provide about the minutiae of individual daily existence, constitute valuable evidence for the rise of individualism, which cultural historians see as such a notable feature of the period. The contemporary concern, even obsession, with individual experience can be seen in several other literary forms, most notably perhaps in the spiritual autobiography. Spiritual autobiographies were, in effect, spiritual diaries, where individuals charted their personal progress (often a psychologically tortuous one) to a state of grace in which personal salvation could be assumed as all but certain. Religion at the time, particularly in its sectarian manifestations (the Baptists, for example), encouraged this process of close scrutiny of one's personal behaviour in the search for signs of God's grace, and a host of spiritual autobiographies were written over the course of the seventeenth century. The form rapidly became very conventionalised, with a set narrative pattern of events (sin to repentance and back again several times until one reached the desired state of grace), and, with the exception of John Bunyan's *Grace Abounding to the Chief of Sinners*, they are little read today; but they remain of considerable interest to the cultural historian for what they tell us of the rise of individualism.

The diary can be seen as a secular equivalent of the spiritual auto-biography, of interest precisely because of the fact that it places the individual at the centre of events, and presents him or her as a focal point of the social process. We take diary-keeping for granted nowadays, but it is worth remembering just how recent is the assumption that the individual's daily affairs are a matter worth recording. Pepys, in common with other contemporary diary-keepers such as his friend John Evelyn, is a very modern figure in this regard.

The Diary

One of the first points that needs to be made about the *Diary* is that the original is in shorthand, which means that Pepys scholars are required to decode the work. (It is possible that Pepys felt the need to write in 'characters' given the political uncertainty of the period, and the intense nature of Restoration censorship.) Decoding causes certain problems since the shorthand Pepys used is not as precise as its modern counterparts, and in some cases there is a degree of ambiguity as to meaning. The original manuscript consists of six bound volumes, held in the Pepys Library at Magdalene College. It was not decoded and published until

1825. Publication initially was in abridged form, and various other abridged editions followed over the course of the nineteenth century, until the Henry R. Wheatley edition of 1893–99, which was the most comprehensive until modern times.[7] The first complete edition did not appear until the 1970s.[8] It is the original edition of 1825, deciphered by John Smith and edited by Lord Braybrooke, that we reproduce here.

The abridgements betray a reticence about Pepys's account of his sexual life, about which he was relatively uninhibited – at least within the confines of his coded diary entries. At any one time over the course of the 1660s Pepys had several mistresses, although he sometimes displays a sense of remorse over his sexual conduct (as he does also over his theatre-going). His seduction of the family servant girl Deb Willett is a rather sordid affair which shows him in a very poor light, and there is no doubt that in today's terms of reference Pepys was a predatory male who used his position to exploit women sexually. The Restoration was, notoriously, a period of male sexual licence (the image of the 'Restoration rake' has long since passed into popular legend) and Pepys was by no means the worst offender. Nevertheless, this aspect of his life can still cause us some qualms today (a recent biographer speaks distastefully of 'the computerised lechery'[9] of Pepys's affair with a subordinate's wife, for example), and it is not surprising that the Victorians saw fit to censor him on this topic. As several commentators have remarked, it would be interesting to have a diary by Mrs Pepys recording *her* view of her husband's sexual adventurism.

While their inclusion gives us a fuller picture of Pepys, warts and all as it were, it has to be said that the absence of the sexual passages does not necessarily have a very detrimental effect on the overall work. It should be pointed out too that even Pepys himself can be somewhat reticent over such matters, often lapsing into foreign languages to describe the sexual act (sometimes even a jumble of foreign languages), and that he does not dwell on these episodes salaciously; they are simply recorded as part and parcel of his daily round – of no greater or lesser importance, it would seem, than any other activity in his hectic social life.

The Diary as a Literary Artefact

The Diary is now generally recognised to be a considerable work of literature, both for the narrative that it recounts and for the style in which

7 *The Diary of Samuel Pepys*, vols. I–X, Henry R. Wheatley (ed.), G. Bell and Sons, London 1893–9.

8 *The Diary of Samuel Pepys*, vols. I–XI, Robert Latham and William Matthews (eds), Bell and Hyman, London 1970–83.

9 Richard Ollard, *Pepys: A Biography*, Hodder and Stoughton, London 1974, p. 98.

it is delivered. Pepys has an engaging, button-holing kind of style, which most readers find hard to resist. His recording of the Fire of London is often applauded by critics for the vividness of its description, and shows Pepys to best advantage as an author:

> So near the fire as we could for smoke; and all over the Thames, with one's faces in the wind, you were almost burned with a shower of fire-drops. This is very true: so as houses were burned by these drops and flakes of fire, three or four, nay, five or six houses, one from another. When we could endure no more upon the water, we to a little ale-house on the Bankside, over against the Three Cranes . . . We staid till, it being darkish, we saw the fire as only one entire arch of fire from this to the other side the bridge, and in a bow up the hill for an arch of above a mile long: it made me weep to see it. [10]

This is a masterly piece of observation, which in its juxtaposition of the helpless bystanders and the all-conquering fire sweeping unchecked through the stricken city, captures the scale and dramatic intensity of the event to marvellous effect.

We noted above that we can treat the diary as a novel and Pepys as an engaging fictional creation. The diary is, after all, a compelling piece of narrative which carries the reader along with it, keen to know what will happen to the hero next. It is also a narrative which provides considerable insight into the psychology of its protagonist, and, like Defoe's *Robinson Crusoe* or *Moll Flanders* shortly afterwards, it presents us with a success story which tells us a great deal about the preoccupations of the times – not least, to reiterate the point made earlier, the growing importance of the individual in the cultural scheme of things. Pepys rises in the social scale, has many interesting adventures and encounters on the way, and becomes economically successful by the end of his narrative, accumulating wealth systematically as he goes. We can consider Pepys as one of the great characters of English literature, one whose exploits continue to provide absorbing reading matter right into the present day.

This Edition

The Braybrooke edition constitutes around a quarter of the complete work, and the momentous events of the time – the Restoration, the Plague, the Great Fire of London, and the Dutch Wars – are all included. The episodic nature of the diary means that one can edit it down quite considerably yet still gain a clear picture of the progress of Pepys's life and

10 September 2nd, 1666, pp. 432–33.

career between 1660 and 1669. Abridged or unabridged, Pepys's narrative, this 'cornucopia' as Roger Pooley[11] has so aptly referred to it, retains its considerable power to draw us into its fascinating world.

STUART SIM
University of Sunderland

SUGGESTIONS FOR FURTHER READING

Richard W. Barber, *Samuel Pepys Esquire*, [catalogue of an exhibition at the] National Portrait Gallery, London 1970

Arthur Bryant, *Samuel Pepys: The Man in the Making*, Collins, London 1933.

Arthur Bryant, *Samuel Pepys: The Years of Peril*, Collins, London 1935.

Arthur Bryant, *Samuel Pepys: The Saviour of the Navy*, Collins, London 1938.

John Hearsey, *Young Mr Pepys*, Constable, London 1973.

Helen T. Heath (ed.), *The Letters of Samuel Pepys and his Family Circle*, Oxford University Press, 1955.

Marjory Hope Nicolson, *Pepys' Diary and the New Science*, Virginia University Press, Charlottesville, Va. 1965.

David Ogg, *England in the Reign of Charles II* (2nd edn), Oxford University Press, 1964.

Richard Ollard, *Pepys: A Biography*, Hodder and Stoughton, London 1974.

Roger Pooley, *English Prose of the Seventeenth Century, 1590–1700*, Longman, London and New York 1992.

NOTE ON DATES

Before 1752, when the Gregorian calendar was adopted in England, the year was reckoned, at least for official and fiscal purposes, to begin on March 25 (the Feast of the Annunciation of the Virgin Mary, 'Lady Day'). However, it was also common to treat January 1 as New Year's Day, as we know that Pepys did himself.

With this dual system of reckoning, it was not entirely clear whether the period from January 1 to March 24 belonged to the old year or the new. Hence in this edition, as in the original diary, both dates are given.

---

11 Roger Pooley, *English Prose of the Seventeenth Century, 1590–1700*, Longman, London and New York 1992, p. 83.

HISTORICAL CHRONOLOGY

1633	Pepys born in London.
1640	Parliament recalled after personal rule of Charles I; breakdown of relations between monarchy and Parliament leads to Civil War.
1646–50	Pepys attends St Paul's School, London.
1649	Charles I beheaded; Stuart monarchy deposed until 1660.
1650	Pepys enters Magdalene College, Cambridge as scholar.
1652–54	First Dutch War.
1653	Oliver Cromwell appointed Lord Protector.
1654	Pepys takes degree at Magdalene; becomes Secretary to Sir Edward Montagu.
1655	Pepys marries Elizabeth St Michel.
1658	Cromwell's son, Richard, appointed Lord Protector on his father's death.
1660	Stuart monarchy, in the person of Charles II, recalled to the English throne (the 'Restoration'). Pepys becomes Clerk of the Acts in the Navy Office.
1660–69	Pepys keeps Diary.
1665	Great Plague of London.
1665–67	Second Dutch War.
1666	Great Fire of London.
1667	Dutch fleet raids up the Medway.
1669	Pepys's wife dies.
1673	Third Dutch War. Pepys becomes Secretary of the Admiralty; elected MP for Castle Rising .
1679	Pepys elected MP for Harwich. Popish Plot; Pepys under suspicion of involvement, and imprisoned briefly; resigns post at Admiralty.
1684	Pepys returns as Secretary of the Admiralty.
1688–89	'Glorious Revolution'; Stuart monarchy, in the person of James II, deposed from the English throne for the last time.
1689	Pepys retires from Admiralty.
1703	Pepys dies in London.

PREFACE TO THE ORIGINAL EDITION

In submitting the following pages to the public, I feel that it is incumbent upon me to explain by what circumstances the materials from which the work has been compiled were placed at my disposal. The original diary, comprehending six volumes, closely written in short-hand by Mr Pepys himself, belonged to the valuable collection of books and prints, bequeathed by him to Magdalene College, Cambridge, and had remained there unexamined, till the appointment of my brother, the present Master, under whose auspices the manuscript was deciphered by Mr John Smith, with a view to its publication.

My brother's time, however, being too much engrossed by more important duties to admit of his editing the work, the task of preparing it for the press was undertaken by me at his request.

The Diary commences January 1st, 1659/60, and after being regularly kept for ten years, it is brought to a sudden conclusion, owing to the weak state of Mr Pepys's eyes, which precluded him from continuing or resuming the occupation. As he was in the habit of recording the most trifling occurrences of his life, it became absolutely necessary to curtail the manuscript materially, and in many instances to condense the matter; but the greatest care has been taken to preserve the original meaning, without making a single addition, excepting where, from the short-hand being defective, some alteration appeared absolutely necessary. It may be objected by those who are not aware how little is known from authentic sources of the history of the stage about the period of the Restoration, that the notices of theatrical performances occur too frequently; but as many of the incidents recorded, connected with this subject, are not to be met with elsewhere, I thought myself justified in retaining them, at the risk of fatiguing those readers who have no taste for the concerns of the drama. The general details may also, in some instances, even in their abridged form, be considered as too minute; nor is it an easy task, in an undertaking of this sort, to please everybody's taste: my principal study in making the selection, however, has been to omit nothing of public interest; and to introduce at the same time a great variety of other topics, less important, perhaps, but tending in some degree to illustrate the manners and habits of the age.

In justice to Mr Pepys's literary reputation, the reader is forewarned that he is not to expect to find in the diary accuracy of style or finished composition. He should rather consider the work as a collection of reminiscences hastily thrown together at the end of each succeeding day, for the exclusive perusal of the Author.

The Journal contains the most unquestionable evidences of veracity; and, as the writer made no scruple of committing his most secret thoughts to paper, encouraged no doubt by the confidence which he derived from the use of short-hand, perhaps there never was a publication more implicitly to be relied upon for the authenticity of its statements and the exactness with which every fact is detailed. Upon this point, I can venture to speak with the less hesitation, having, in preparing the sheets for the press, had occasion to compare many parts of the Diary with different accounts of the same transactions recorded elsewhere; and in no instance could I detect any material error or wilful misrepresentation

The notes at the bottom of the pages were introduced to elucidate obscure passages; and I have been tempted occasionally to insert short biographical sketches of the principal persons who are named, accompanied by such references as will enable the curious reader to inform himself more fully respecting them. In some instances I experienced considerable difficulty in identifying the individuals; but I trust that the notices will be found, on the whole, sufficiently correct to answer the object intended.

When the concluding sheets of the Diary were nearly worked off, I was apprised by my friend, Dr Bandinel, that a great mass of original papers formerly belonging to Mr Pepys had been deposited in the Bodleian Library, among Dr Rawlinson's collections; and I immediately proceeded to Oxford to examine them. As I found as many as seventy volumes of different descriptions, put together without any arrangement, and in no one instance furnished with an Index, it was impossible, in the short time allowed, to examine the contents very minutely. I was enabled, however, with the assistance of Mr William Upcott, of the London Institution, who kindly volunteered his services on the occasion, to select a great number of letters, which will be found in the correspondence comprised in the fifth volume of the Memoirs.[1] We could not obtain any conclusive evidence as to the manner in which these papers came into Dr Rawlinson's possession. It appears from the doctor's letters to Mr Rawlins, that although Mr Jackson's widow, who was still living, might have satisfied him more fully concerning the collection which he had acquired, he declined prosecuting the inquiry, sufficiently happy in the idea of having rescued such a prize, as he himself expressed it, '*thus et odores vendentibus*'. I feel convinced myself, that when Mr Pepys removed to Mr Hewer's house at Clapham, a great portion of his familiar letters and other manuscripts remained at his London residence in York Buildings, or in the custody of some friend: for he speaks, in the correspondence, of trusting himself with the company of those papers only which he did not object to have looked into, and Mr Jackson was probably never aware of their existence. At all events, we must consider it as a fortunate circumstance, that so large a mass of original manuscripts should have been saved from destruction, and deposited in a place where the laudable care bestowed upon the literary treasures, and the facilities afforded to those who are desirous of examining them, reflect the highest credit on the University of Oxford and the officers of the Bodleian Library.

The remaining portion of the correspondence has been principally made up from a large collection of letters, discovered by Mr Upcott among the archives of Mr Samuel Pepys Cockerell, the representative of the family of Pepys (as the lineal descendant from the secretary's sister, Mrs Jackson), who kindly permitted them to be copied for publication. They contain many interesting particulars respecting Mr Pepys and his friends – and, though the subjects of which they treat are not of much importance, it is hoped that from their variety, and the celebrity of some of the writers (amongst whom Mr Evelyn should not be forgotten), they will be found worthy of perusal. The correspondence is, generally speaking, autographic, and, like the Diary, entirely new to the public.

It remains for me gratefully to acknowledge the assistance afforded by those gentlemen whom I had occasion to consult whilst employed in arranging the materials for the press.

To Samuel Pepys Cockerell, Esq. of Westbourne, my thanks are, in

---

1 In the original edition a selection from Pepys's correspondence followed the Diary.

the first instance, more particularly due, for the readiness and liberality with which he entrusted to me the original papers before-mentioned, as well as for the information which he was at all times ready to communicate upon every circumstance connected with the history of his family. To Dr Bandinel, and his colleagues, Dr Bliss and Mr Lawrence, I am indebted in no small degree, for their personal attentions to me at Oxford; for the zeal with which they forwarded my researches in the Bodleian Library, and the accuracy and promptitude evinced by them in superintending the task of copying the manuscript letters. Nor should I forget to express my sense of the good offices rendered to me during the progress of the work by Mr William Upcott, of the London Institution; to whom I also owe copies of some interesting letters from the Evelyn Collection. In justice to the Revd John Smith (with whom I am not personally acquainted), it may be added, that he appears to have performed the task allotted to him, of deciphering the short-hand diary, with diligence and fidelity, and to have spared neither time nor trouble in the undertaking.

The best account of Mr Pepys occurs in the supplement to Collier's *Historical Dictionary*, published soon after his death, and written, as I have reason to believe, by his relative Roger Gale. Some particulars may also be obtained from Knight's *Life of Dean Colet*; Chalmers's *Biographical Dictionary*; Cole's manuscripts in the British Museum; the manuscripts in the Bodleian and Pepysian Libraries, and the Cockerell Papers.

BRAYBROOKE
Audley End, May 14, 1825

The Diary

1659/60. Blessed be God, at the end of the last year I was in very good health, without any sense of my old pain, but upon taking of cold. I lived in Axe Yard, having my wife, and servant Jane, and no other in family than us three.

The condition of the State was thus; viz. the Rump, after being disturbed by my Lord Lambert,[1] was lately returned to sit again. The officers of the Army all forced to yield. Lawson[2] lies still in the river, and Monk[3] is with his army in Scotland. Only my Lord Lambert is not yet come into the Parliament, nor is it expected that he will without being forced to it. The new Common Council of the City do speak very high; and had sent to Monk their sword-bearer, to acquaint him with their desires for a free and full Parliament, which is at present the desires, and the hopes, and the expectations of all. Twenty-two of the old secluded members having been at the House-door the last week to demand entrance, but it was denied them; and it is believed that neither they nor the people will be satisfied till the House be filled. My own private condition very handsome, and esteemed rich, but indeed very poor; besides my goods of my house,

1 Sufficiently known by his services as a Major-General in the Parliament forces during the Civil War, and condemned as a traitor after the Restoration; but reprieved and banished to Guernsey, where he lived in confinement thirty years.
2 Sir John Lawson, the son of a poor man at Hull, rose to the rank of Admiral, and distinguished himself during the Protectorate; and, though a republican in his heart, readily closed with the design of restoring the King. He was mortally wounded in the sea fight in 1665.
3 George Monk, afterwards Duke of Albemarle.

and my office, which at present is somewhat certain. Mr Downing[4] master of my office.[5]

January 1st (Lord's day). This morning (we living lately in the garret,) I rose, put on my suit with great skirts, having not lately worn any other clothes but them. Went to Mr Gunning's[6] chapel at Exeter House,[7] where he made a very good sermon upon these words: – 'That in the fulness of time God sent his Son, made of a woman, &c.'; showing, that, by 'made under the law', is meant the circumcision, which is solemnized this day. Dined at home in the garret, where my wife dressed the remains of a turkey, and in the doing of it she burned her hand. I staid at home the whole afternoon, looking over my accounts; then went with my wife to my father's, and in going observed the great posts which the City workmen set up at the Conduit in Fleet-street.

2nd. Walked a great while in Westminster Hall, where I heard that Lambert was coming up to London: that my Lord Fairfax was in the head of the Irish brigade, but it was not certain what he would declare for. The House was to-day upon finishing the act for the Council of State, which they did; and for the indemnity to the soldiers; and were to sit again thereupon in the afternoon. Great talk that many places had declared for a free Parliament; and it is believed that they will be forced to fill up the House with the old members. From the Hall I called at home, and so went to Mr Crewe's[8] (my

4 George Downing, son of Calibute Downing, DD and Rector of Hackney. Wood calls him a sider with all times and changes; skilled in the common cant, and a preacher occasionally. He was sent by Cromwell to Holland as resident there. About the Restoration he espoused the King's cause, and was knighted and elected MP for Morpeth in 1661. Afterwards, becoming Secretary to the Treasury and Commissioner of Customs, he was in 1663 created a Baronet of East Hatley, in Cambridgeshire.

5 The office appears to have been in the Exchequer, and connected with the pay of the army.

6 Peter Gunning, afterwards Master of St John's College, Cambridge, and successively Bishop of Chichester and Ely: died 1684. He had continued to read the Liturgy at the Chapel at Exeter House when the Parliament was most predominant, for which Cromwell often rebuked him. – Wood's *Athenae*.

7 Essex-street in the Strand was built on the site of Exeter House.

8 John Crewe, Esq., created Baron Crewe of Stene at the coronation of Charles II. He married Jemima, daughter and co-heir to Edward Walgrave, Esq., of Lawford, co. Essex.

wife she was to go to her father's), and Mr Moore and I and another gentleman went out and drank a cup of ale together in the new market, and there I eat some bread and cheese for my dinner.

3rd. To White Hall, where I understood that the Parliament had passed the act for indemnity for the soldiers and officers that would come in, in so many days, and that my Lord Lambert should have benefit of the said act. They had also voted that all vacancies in the House, by the death of any of the old members, should be filled up; but those that are living shall not be called in.

4th. Strange the difference of men's talk! Some say that Lambert must of necessity yield up; others, that he is very strong, and that the Fifth-monarchy-men will stick to him, if he declares for a free Parliament. Chillington was sent yesterday to him with the vote of pardon and indemnity from the Parliament. Went and walked in the Hall, where I heard that the Parliament spent this day in fasting and prayer; and in the afternoon came letters from the North, that brought certain news that my Lord Lambert his forces were all forsaking him, and that he was left with only fifty horse, and that he did now declare for the Parliament himself; and that my Lord Fairfax[9] did also rest satisfied, and had laid down his arms, and that what he had done was only to secure the country against my Lord Lambert his raising of money, and free quarter.

5th. I dined with Mr Shepley, at my Lord's[10] lodgings, upon his turkey-pie. And so to my office again; where the Excise money was brought, and some of it told to soldiers till it was dark. Then I went home, after writing to my Lord the news that the Parliament had this night voted that the members that were discharged from sitting in the years 1648 and '49, were duly discharged; and that there should be writs issued presently for the calling of others in their places, and that Monk and Fairfax were commanded up to town, and that the Prince's lodgings were to be provided for Monk at Whitehall. Mr Fage and I did discourse concerning public business; and he told me it is true the City had not time enough to do much, but they had resolved to shake

9 Thomas Lord Fairfax, Generalissimo of the Parliament forces. After the Restoration he retired to his country seat, where he lived in private till his death in 1671.
10 Admiral Sir Edward Montagu, afterwards Earl of Sandwich, uniformly styled 'My Lord' throughout the Diary.

off the soldiers; and that unless there be a free Parliament chosen, he did believe there are half the Common Council will not levy any money by order of this Parliament.

6th. This morning Mr Shepley and I did eat our breakfast at Mrs Harper's, (my brother John being with me,) upon a cold turkey-pie and a goose.

9th. I rose early this morning, and looked over and corrected my brother John's speech, which he is to make the next opposition.[11] I met with W. Simons, Muddiman, and Jack Price, and went with them to Harper's and staid till two of the clock in the afternoon. I found Muddiman a good scholar, an arch rogue; and owns that though he writes new books for the Parliament, yet he did declare that he did it only to get money; and did talk very basely of many of them. Among other things, W. Simons told me how his uncle Scobell[12] was on Saturday last called to the bar, for entering in the journal of the House, for the year 1653, these words: 'This day his Excellence the Lord G. Cromwell dissolved this House'; which words the Parliament voted a forgery, and demanded of him how they came to be entered. He said that they were his own hand-writing, and that he did it by rights of his office, and the practice of his predecessor; and that the intent of the practice was to let posterity know how such and such a Parliament was dissolved, whether by the command of the King, or by their own neglect, as the last House of Lords was; and that to this end, he had said and writ that it was dissolved by his Excellence the Lord G.; and that for the word dissolved, he never at the time did hear of any other term; and desired pardon if he would not dare to make a word himself what it was six years after, before they came themselves to call it an interruption; that they were so little satisfied with this answer, that they did chuse a committee to report to the House, whether this crime of Mr Scobell's did come within the act of indemnity or no. Thence into the Hall, where I heard for certain that Monk was coming to London, and that Bradshaw's[13] lodgings were preparing for him. I

11 Declamations at St Paul's school, in which there were opponents and respondents.
12 H. Scobell, clerk to the House of Commons.
13 John Bradshaw, Serjeant-at-Law, President of the High Court of Justice.

heard Sir H. Vane[14] was this day voted out of the House, and to sit no more there; and that he would retire himself to his house at Raby, as also all the rest of the nine officers that had their commissions formerly taken away from them, were commanded to their furthest houses from London during the pleasure of the Parliament.

10th. To the Coffee-house, where were a great confluence of gentlemen; viz. Mr Harrington,[15] Poultny,[16] chairman, Gold, Dr Petty,[17] &c., where admirable discourse till 9 at night. Thence with Doling to Mother Lam's, who told me how this day Scott[18] was made Intelligencer, and that the rest of the members that were objected against last night were to be heard this day se'nnight.

13th. Coming in the morning to my office, I met with Mr Fage and took him to the Swan. He told me how he, Haselrigge,[19] and Morley,[20] the last night began at my Lord Mayor's to exclaim against the City of London, saying that they had forfeited their charter. And how the Chamberlain of the City did take them down, letting them know how much they were formerly beholding to the City, &c. He also told me that Monk's letter that came by the sword-bearer was a cunning piece, and that which they did not much trust to: but they were resolved to make no more applications to the Parliament, nor to pay any money, unless the secluded members be brought in, or a free Parliament chosen.

14 Son of a statesman of both his names, and one of the most turbulent enthusiasts produced by the Rebellion, and an inflexible republican. His execution, in 1662, for conspiring the death of Charles I was much called in question as a measure of great severity.

15 James Harrington, the political writer, author of *Oceana*, and founder of a club called The Rota, in 1659, which met at Miles's coffee-house in Old Palace Yard, and lasted only a few months. In 1661 he was sent to the Tower, on suspicion of treasonable designs. His intellects appear to have failed afterwards, and he died 1677.

16 Sir William Poultny, subsequently MP for Westminster, and a Commissioner of the Privy Seal under King William. Died 1691.

17 Sir William Petty, an eminent physician, and celebrated for his proficiency in every branch of science. Died 1687.

18 Thomas Scott, MP, made Secretary of State to the Commonwealth Jan. 17th following.

19 Sir Arthur Haselrigge, Bart. of Nosely, co. Leicester, Colonel of a regiment in the Parliament army, and much esteemed by Cromwell. Died 1660.

20 Probably Colonel Morley, Lieutenant of the Tower.

16th. In the morning I went up to Mr Crewe's, who did talk to me concerning things of state; and expressed his mind how just it was that the secluded members should come to sit again. From thence to my office, where nothing to do; but Mr Downing came and found me all alone; and did mention to me his going back into Holland, and did ask me whether I would go or no, but gave me little encouragement, but bid me consider of it; and asked me whether I did not think that Mr Hawley could perform the work of my office alone. I confess I was at a great loss, all the day after, to bethink myself how to carry this business. I staid up till the bell-man came by with his bell just under my window as I was writing of this very line, and cried, 'Past one of the clock, and a cold, frosty, windy morning.'

17th. In our way to Kensington, we understood how that my Lord Chesterfield[21] had killed another gentleman about half an hour before, and was fled. I went to the Coffee Club and heard very good discourse; it was in answer to Mr Harrington's answer, who said that the state of the Roman government was not a settled government, and so it was no wonder that the balance of prosperity was in one hand, and the command in another, it being therefore always in a posture of war; but it was carried by ballot, that it was a steady government, though it is true by the voices it had been carried before that it was an unsteady government; so to-morrow it is to be proved by the opponents that the balance lay in one hand, and the government in another. Thence I went to Westminster, and met Shaw and Washington, who told me how this day Sydenham[22] was voted out of the House for sitting any more this Parliament, and that Salloway[23] was voted out likewise and sent to the Tower, during the pleasure of the House. At Harper's Jack Price told me, among other things, how much the Protector is altered, though he would seem to bear out his trouble very well, yet he is scarce able to talk sense with a man; and how he will say that 'Who should a man trust, if he may not trust to a brother and an uncle'; and 'how much those men have to answer before God Almighty, for their playing the knave with him

---

21 Philip, second Earl of Chesterfield, born 1634, died 1713.
22 Colonel Sydenham had been an active officer during the Civil Wars, on the Parliament side. MP for Dorsetshire, and Governor of Melcombe, and one of the Committee of Safety.
23 In the Journals of that date Major Salwey.

as they did.' He told me also, that there was £100,000 offered, and would have been taken for his restitution, had not the Parliament come in as they did again; and that he do believe that the Protector will live to give a testimony of his valour and revenge yet before he dies, and that the Protector will say so himself sometimes.

18th. All the world is at a loss to think what Monk will do: the City saying that he will be for them, and the Parliament saying he will be for them.

19th. This morning I was sent for to Mr Downing, and at his bed side he told me, that he had a kindness for me, and that he thought that he had done me one; and that was, that he had got me to be one of the Clerks of the Council; at which I was a little stumbled, and could not tell what to do, whether to thank him or no; but by and by I did; but not very heartily, for I feared that his doing of it was only to ease himself of the salary which he gives me. Mr Moore and I went to the French Ordinary, where Mr Downing this day feasted Sir Arth. Haselrigge, and a great many more of the Parliament, and did stay to put him in mind of me. Here he gave me a note to go and invite some other members to dinner tomorrow. So I went to White Hall, and did stay at Marsh's with Simons, Luellin, and all the rest of the Clerks of the Council, who I hear are all turned out, only the two Leighs, and they do all tell me that my name was mentioned last night, but that nothing was done in it.

20th. In the morning I met Lord Widdrington[24] in the street, going to seal the patents for the Judges to-day, and so could not come to dinner. This day three citizens of London went to meet Monk from the Common Council. Received my £25 due by bill for my trooper's pay. At the Mitre, in Fleet-street, in our way calling on Mr Fage, who told me how the City have some hopes of Monk. This day Lenthall[25] took his chair again, and the House resolved a declaration to be brought in on Monday to satisfy the world what they intend to do.

24 Sir Thomas Widdrington, Knight, Serjeant-at-Law, one of Cromwell's Commissioners of the Treasury, appointed Speaker 1656, and first Commissioner for the Great Seal, January, 1659; he was MP for York.
25 William Lenthall, Speaker of the Long or Rump Parliament, and made Keeper of the Great Seal to the Commonwealth, died 1662.

22nd. To church in the afternoon to Mr Herring, where a lazy poor sermon. This day I began to put on buckles to my shoes.

23rd. This day the Parliament sat late, and resolved of the declaration to be printed for the people's satisfaction, promising them a great many good things.

24th. Came Mr Southerne, clerk to Mr Blackburne, and with him Lambert, lieutenant of my Lord's ship, and brought with them the declaration that came out to-day from the Parliament, wherein they declare for law and gospel, and for tythes; but I do not find people apt to believe them. This day the Parliament gave orders that the late Committee of Safety should come before them this day se'nnight, and all their papers, and their model of Government that they had made, to be brought in with them.

25th. Coming home heard that in Cheapside there had been but a little before a gibbet set up, and the picture of Huson[26] hung upon it in the middle of the street. I called at Paul's Churchyard, where I bought Buxtorf's Hebrew Grammar; and read a declaration of the gentlemen of Northampton which came out this afternoon.

26th. Called for some papers at Whitehall for Mr Downing, one of which was an order of the Council for £1800 per annum, to be paid monthly; and the other two, Orders to the Commissioners of Customs, to let his goods pass free. Home from my office to my Lord's lodgings where my wife had got ready a very fine dinner – viz. a dish of marrow bones; a leg of mutton; a loin of veal; a dish of fowl, three pullets, and a dozen of larks all in a dish; a great tart, a neat's tongue, a dish of anchovies; a dish of prawns and cheese. My company was my father, my uncle Fenner, his two sons, Mr Pierce, and all their wives, and my brother Tom.[27] The news this day is a letter that speaks absolutely Monk's concurrence with this Parliament, and nothing else, which yet I hardly believe.

28th. I went to Mr Downing, who told me that he was resolved to be gone for Holland this morning. So I to my office again, and

26 John Hewson, who had been a shoemaker, became a Colonel in the Parliament Army, and sat in judgement on the King: he escaped hanging by flight, and died in 1662, at Amsterdam.
27 Died 1663.

dispatch my business there, and came with Mr Hawley to Mr Downing's lodgings, and took Mr Squib from White Hall in a coach thither with me, and there we waited in his chamber a great while, till he came in; and in the mean time, sent all his things to the barge that lays at Charing-Cross stairs. Then came he in, and took a very civil leave of me, beyond my expectations, for I was afraid that he would have told me something of removing me from my office; but he did not, but that he would do me any service that lay in his power. So I went down and sent a porter to my house for my best fur cap, but he coming too late with it I did not present it to him: and so I returned and went to Heaven,[28] where Luellin and I dined.

29th. In the morning I went to Mr Gunning's, where he made an excellent sermon upon the 2nd of the Galatians, about the difference that fell between St Paul and St Peter, whereby he did prove, that, contrary to the doctrine of the Roman Church, St Paul did never own any dependance, or that he was inferior to St Peter, but that they were equal, only one a particular charge of preaching to the Jews, and the other to the Gentiles.

30th. This morning, before I was up, I fell a-singing of my song, 'Great, good and just', &c.[29] and put myself thereby in mind that this was the fatal day, now ten years since, his Majesty died. There seems now to be a general cease of talk, it being taken for granted that Monk do resolve to stand to the Parliament, and nothing else.

31st. After dinner to Westminster Hall, where all we clerks had orders to wait upon the Committee, at the Star-chamber that is to try

28 A place of entertainment in Old Palace Yard, on the site of which the Committee-Rooms of the House of Commons now stand. It is called in *Hudibras*, 'False Heaven, at the end of the Hall'.

29 This is the beginning of Montrose's verses on the execution of Charles I, which Pepys had probably set to music:

> Great, good, and just, could I but rate
> My grief and thy too rigid fate,
> I'd weep the world to such a strain
> That it should deluge once again.
> But since thy loud-tongued blood demands supplies
> More from Briareus' hands, than Argus' eyes,
> I'll sing thy obsequies with trumpet sounds,
> And write thy epitaph with blood and wounds.

Colonel Jones,[30] and to give an account what money we had paid him; but the Committee did not sit to-day. Called in at Harper's with Mr Pulford, servant to Mr Waterhouse, who tells me, that whereas my Lord Fleetwood[31] should have answered to the Parliament to-day, he wrote a letter and desired a little more time, he being a great way out of town. And how that he is quite ashamed of himself, and confesses how he had deserved this, for his baseness to his brother. And that he is like to pay part of the money, paid out of the Exchequer during the Committee of Safety, out of his own purse again, which I am glad on. I could find nothing in Mr Downing's letter, which Hawley brought me concerning my office; but I could discern that Hawley had a mind that I would get to be Clerk of the Council, I suppose that he might have the greater salary; but I think it not safe yet to change this for a public employment.

February 1st. Took Gammer East, and James the porter, a soldier, to my Lord's lodgings, who told me how they were drawn into the field to-day, and that they were ordered to march away to-morrow to make room for General Monk; but they did shout their Colonel Fitch,[32] and the rest of the officers out of the field, and swore they would not go without their money, and if they would not give it them, they would go where they might have it, and that was the City. So the Colonel went to the Parliament, and commanded what money could be got, to be got against to-morrow for them, and all the rest of the soldiers in town, who in all places made a mutiny this day, and do agree together.

2nd. To my office, where I found all the officers of the regiments in town, waiting to receive money that their soldiers might go out of town, and what was in the Exchequer they had. Harper, Luellin, and I went to the Temple to Mr Calthrop's chamber, and from thence

30 Colonel John Jones, impeached, with General Ludlow and Miles Corbet, for treasonable practices in Ireland.

31 Charles Fleetwood, Lord Deputy of Ireland during the Usurpation, became Cromwell's son-in-law by his marriage with Ireton's widow, and a member of the Council of State. He seems disposed to have espoused Charles II's interests, but had not resolution enough to execute his design. At the Restoration he was excepted out of the Act of Indemnity, and spent the remainder of his life in obscurity, dying soon after the Revolution.

32 Thomas Fitch, Colonel of a regiment of foot in 1658, MP for Inverness.

had his man by water to London Bridge to Mr Calthrop a grocer, and received £60 for my Lord. In our way we talked with our waterman, White, who told us how the watermen had lately been abused by some that had a desire to get in to be watermen to the State, and had lately presented an address of nine or ten thousand hands to stand by this Parliament, when it was only told them that it was a petition against hackney coaches; and that to-day they had put out another to undeceive the world and to clear themselves. After I had received the money we went homewards, but over against Somerset House, hearing the noise of guns, we landed and found the Strand full of soldiers. So I took my money and went to Mrs Johnson, my Lord's sempstress, and giving her my money to lay up, Doling and I went up stairs to a window, and looked out and saw the foot face the horse and beat them back, and stood bawling and calling in the street for a free Parliament and money. By and by a drum was heard to beat a march coming towards them, and they got all ready again and faced them, and they proved to be of the same mind with them; and so they made a great deal of joy to see one another. After all this I went home on foot to lay up my money, and change my stockings and shoes. I this day left off my great skirt suit, and put on my white suit with silver lace coat, and went over to Harper's, where I met with W. Simons, Doling, Luellin and three merchants, one of which had occasion to use a porter, so they sent for one, and James the soldier came, who told us how they had been all day and night upon their guard at St James's, and that through the whole town they did resolve to stand to what they had began, and that to-morrow he did believe they would go into the City, and be received there. After this we went to a sport called, selling of a horse for a dish of eggs and herrings, and sat talking there till almost twelve at night.

3rd. Drank my morning draft at Harper's, and was told there that the soldiers were all quiet upon promise of pay. Thence to St James's Park, back to Whitehall, where in a guard-chamber I saw about thirty or forty 'prentices of the City, who were taken at twelve o'clock last night and brought prisoners hither. Thence to my office, where I paid a little more money to some of the soldiers under Lieut.-Col. Miller (who held out the Tower against the Parliament after it was taken away from Fitch by the Committee of Safety, and yet he continued in his office). About noon Mrs Turner came to speak with me and Joyce, and I took them and shewed them the manner of the Houses sitting, the door-keeper very civilly opening the door for us. We went walking all over White Hall, whither General Monk was newly come, and we saw all his forces march by in very good plight and stout officers. After dinner I went to hear news, but only found that the Parliament House was most of them with Monk at White Hall, and that in his passing through the town he had many calls to him for a free Parliament, but little other welcome. I saw in the Palace Yard how unwilling some of the old soldiers were yet to go out of town without their money, and swore if they had it not in three days, as they were promised, they would do them more mischief in the country than if they had staid here; and that is very likely, the country being all discontented. The town and guards are already full of Monk's soldiers.

4th. All the news to-day is, that the Parliament this morning voted the House to be made up four hundred forthwith.

6th. To Westminster, where we found the soldiers all set in the Palace Yard, to make way for General Monk to come to the House. I stood upon the steps and saw Monk go by, he making observance to the judges as he went along.

7th. To the Hall, where in the Palace I saw Monk's soldiers abuse Billing and all the Quakers, that were at a meeting-place there, and indeed the soldiers did use them very roughly and were to blame. This day Mr Crew told me that my Lord St John is for a free Parliament, and that he is very great with Monk, who hath now the absolute command and power to do any thing that he hath a mind to do.

8th. Before I was out of my bed, I heard the soldiers very busy in the morning, getting their horses ready when they lay at Hilton's, but I knew not then their meaning in so doing. In the Hall I understand how Monk is this morning gone into London with his army; and Mr Fage told me that he do believe that Monk is gone to secure some of the Common-council of the City, who were very high yesterday there, and did vote that they would not pay any taxes till the House was filled up. I went to my office, where I wrote to my Lord after I had been at the Upper Bench, where Sir Robert Pye this morning came to desire his discharge from the Tower; but it could not be granted. I called at Mr Harper's, who told me how Monk had this day clapt up many of the Common-council, and that the Parliament had voted that he should pull down their gates and portcullisses, their posts and their chains, which he do intend to do, and do lie in the City all night.

To Westminster Hall, where I heard an action very finely pleaded between my Lord Dorset[33] and some other noble persons, his lady and other ladies of quality being there, and it was about £330 per annum, that was to be paid to a poor Spittal, which was given by some of his predecessors; and given on his side.

10th. Mr Fage told me what Monk had done in the City, how he had pulled down the most part of the gates and chains that they could break down, and that he was now gone back to White Hall. The City look mighty blank, and cannot tell what in the world to do; the Parliament having this day ordered that the Common-council sit no more, but that new ones be chosen according to what qualifications they shall give them.

11th. I heard the news of a letter from Monk, who was now gone into the City again, and did resolve to stand for the sudden filling up of the House, and it was very strange how the countenance of men in the Hall was all changed with joy in half an hour's time. So I went up to the lobby, where I saw the Speaker reading of the letter; and after it was read, Sir A. Haselrigge came out very angry, and Billing standing at the door, took him by the arm, and cried, 'Thou man, will thy beast carry thee no longer? thou must fall!' We took coach for the City to Guildhall, where the Hall was full of people expecting Monk and Lord Mayor to come thither, and all very joyfull. Met Monk coming out of the chamber where he had been with the Mayor and Aldermen, but such a shout I never heard in all my life, crying out, 'God bless your Excellence.' Here I met with Mr Lock, and took him to an ale-house: when we were come together, he told us the substance of the letter that went from Monk to the Parliament; wherein after complaints that he and his officers were put upon such offices against the City as they could not do with any content or honour, it states, that there are many members now in the House that were of the late tyrannical Committee of Safety. That Lambert and

33 Richard, 5th Earl of Dorset, died 1677.

Vane are now in town, contrary to the vote of Parliament. That
many in the House do press for new oaths to be put upon men;
whereas we have more cause to be sorry for the many oaths that we
have already taken and broken. That the late petition of the fanatique
people presented by Barebone, for the imposing of an oath upon all
sorts of people, was received by the House with thanks. That
therefore he[34] did desire that all writs for filling up of the House be
issued by Friday next, and that in the mean time, he would retire into
the City and only leave them guards for the security of the House and
Council. The occasion of this was the order that he had last night, to
go into the City and disarm them, and take away their charter;
whereby he and his officers said, that the House had a mind to put
them upon things that should make them odious; and so it would be
in their power to do what they would with them. We were told that
the Parliament had sent Scott and Robinson to Monk this afternoon,
but he would not hear them. And that the Mayor and Aldermen had
offered their own houses for himself and his officers; and that his
soldiers would lack for nothing. And indeed I saw many people give
the soldiers drink and money, and all along the streets cried, 'God
bless them!' and extraordinary good words. Hence we went to a
merchant's house hard by, where I saw Sir Nich. Crisp,[35] and so we
went to the Star Tavern, (Monk being then at Benson's). In
Cheapside there was a great many bonfires, and Bow bells and all the
bells in all the churches as we went home were a-ringing. Hence we
went homewards, it being about ten at night. But the common joy
that was every where to be seen! The number of bonfires, there being
fourteen between St Dunstan's and Temple Bar, and at Strand Bridge
I could at one time tell thirty-one fires. In King-street seven or eight;
and all along burning, and roasting, and drinking for rumps. There
being rumps tied upon sticks and carried up and down. The butchers
at the May Pole in the Strand rang a peal with their knives when they
were going to sacrifice their rump. On Ludgate Hill there was one
turning of the spit that had a rump tied upon it, and another basting
of it. Indeed it was past imagination, both the greatness and the

34 Monk.
35 An eminent merchant and one of the Farmers of the Customs. He had advanced
large sums to assist Charles I, who created him a Baronet. He died February, 1667,
aged 67.

suddenness of it. At one end of the street you would think there was a whole lane on fire, and so hot that we were fain to keep on the further side.

12th. In the morning, it being Lord's day, to White Hall, where Dr Hones preached; but I staid not to hear, but walking in the court, I heard that Sir Arth. Haselrigge was newly gone into the City to Monk, and that Monk's wife removed from White Hall last night. After dinner I heard that Monk had been at Paul's in the morning, and the people had shouted much at his coming out of the church. In the afternoon he was at a church in Broad-street, whereabout he do lodge. To my father's, where Charles Glascocke was overjoyed to see how things are now; who told me the boys had last night broke Barebone's[36] windows.

13th. This day Monk was invited to White Hall to dinner by my Lords; not seeming willing, he would not come. I went to Mr Fage from my father's, who had been this afternoon with Monk, who did promise to live and die with the City, and for the honour of the City; and indeed the City is very open-handed to the soldiers, that they are most of them drunk all day, and had money given them.

14th. To Westminster Hall, there being many new remonstrances and declarations from many counties to Monk and the City, and one coming from the North from Sir Thomas Fairfax.[37] I heard that the Parliament had now changed the oath so much talked of to a promise; and that among other qualifications for the members that are to be chosen, one is, that no man, nor the son of any man that hath been in arms during the life of the father, shall be capable of being chosen to sit in Parliament. This day, by an order of the House, Sir H. Vane was sent out of town to his house in Lincolnshire.

15th. No news to-day, but all quiet to see what the Parliament will do about the issuing of the writs tomorrow for the filling up of the House, according to Monk's desire.

17th. To Westminster Hall, where I heard that some of the members

36 'Praise God' Barebone, an active member of the Parliament called by his name. About this period he had appeared at the head of a band of fanatics, and alarmed Monk, who well knew his influence.
37 Thomas Lord Fairfax, mentioned before.

of the House was gone to meet with some of the secluded members and General Monk in the City. Hence to White Hall, thinking to hear more news, where I met with Mr Hunt, who told me how Monk had sent for all his goods that he had here, into the City; and yet again he told me, that some of the members of the House had this day laid in firing into their lodgings at Whitehall for a good while, so that we are at a great stand to think what will become of things, whether Monk will stand to the Parliament or no.

18th. This day two soldiers were hanged in the Strand for their late mutiny at Somerset-house.

19th (Lord's day). To Mr Gunning's, and heard an excellent sermon. Here I met with Mr Moore, and went home with him to dinner, where he told me the discourse that happened between the secluded members and the members of the House, before Monk last Friday. How the secluded said, that they did not intend by coming in to express revenge upon these men, but only to meet and dissolve themselves, and only to issue writs for a free Parliament. He told me how Haselrigge was afraid to have the candle carried before him, for fear that the people seeing him, would do him hurt; and that he was afraid to appear in the City. That there is great likelihood that the secluded members will come in, and so Mr Crewe and my Lord are likely to be great men, at which I was very glad. After dinner there was many secluded members come in to Mr Crewe, which, it being the Lord's day, did make Mr Moore believe that there was something extraordinary in the business.

20th. I went forth to Westminster Hall, where I met with Chetwind, Simons, and Gregory.[38] They told me how the Speaker Lenthall do refuse to sign the writs for choice of new members in the place of the excluded; and by that means the writs could not go out to-day. In the evening Simons and I to the Coffee House, where I heard Mr Harrington, and my Lord of Dorset and another Lord, talking of getting another place at the Cockpit, and they did believe it would come to something.

21st. In the morning I saw many soldiers going towards Westminster Hall, to admit the secluded members again. So I to Westminster Hall, and in Chancery I saw about twenty of them who had been at White

38 Mr Gregory was, in 1672, Clerk of the Cheque at Chatham.

Hall with General Monk, who came thither this morning, and made a speech to them, and recommended to them a Commonwealth, and against Charles Stuart. They came to the House and went in one after another, and at last the Speaker came. But it is very strange that this could be carried so private, that the other members of the House heard nothing of all this, till they found them in the House, insomuch that the soldiers that stood there to let in the secluded members, they took for such as they had ordered to stand there to hinder their coming in. Mr Prin[39] came with an old basket-hilt sword on, and a great many shouts upon his going into the Hall. They sat till noon, and at their coming out Mr Crewe saw me, and bid me come to his house and dine with him, which I did; and he very joyful told me that the House had made General Monk, General of all the Forces in England, Scotland, and Ireland; and that upon Monk's desire, for the service that Lawson had lately done in pulling down the Committee of Safety, he had the command of the Sea for the time being. He advised me to send for my Lord forthwith, and told me that there is no question that, if he will, he may now be employed again; and that the House do intend to do nothing more than to issue writs, and to settle a foundation for a free Parliament. After dinner I back to Westminster Hall with him in his coach. Here I met with Mr Lock and Pursell,[40] Master of Musique, and went with them to the Coffee House, into a room next the water, by ourselves, where we spent an hour or two till Captain Taylor come and told us, that the House had voted the gates of the City to be made up again, and the members of the City that are in prison to be set at liberty; and that Sir G. Booth's[41] case be brought into the House tomorrow. Here we had variety of brave Italian and Spanish songs, and a canon for eight voices, which Mr Lock had lately made on these words: *Domine salvum fac Regem.* Here out of the window it was a most pleasant sight to see the City from one end to the other with a glory about it, so high was the light of the bonfires, and so thick round the City, and the bells rang every where.

---

39 William Prynne, the lawyer, well known by his voluminous publications, and the persecution which he endured. He was MP for Bath, 1660, and died 1669.
40 Matthew Locke and Henry Purcell, both celebrated Composers.
41 Of Dunham Massey, Bart., created Baron Delamer, 1661, for his services in behalf of the King.

22nd. Walking in the Hall, I saw Major General Brown,[42] who had a long time been banished by the Rump, but now with his beard overgrown, he comes abroad and sat in the House. To White Hall, where I met with Will. Simons and Mr Mabbot at Marsh's, who told me how the House had this day voted that the gates of the City should be set up at the cost of the State. And that Major-General Brown's being proclaimed a traitor be made void, and several other things of that nature. I observed this day how abominably Barebone's windows are broke again last night.

23rd. Thursday, my birth-day, now twenty-seven years. To Westminster Hall, where, after the House rose, I met with Mr Crewe, who told me that my Lord was chosen by 73 voices, to be one of the Council of State. Mr Pierpoint[43] had the most, 101, and himself the next, 100.

24th. I rose very early, and taking horse at Scotland Yard, at Mr Garthwayt's stable, I rode to Mr Pierce's: we both mounted, and so set forth about seven of the clock; at Puckridge we baited, the way exceeding bad from Ware thither. Then up again and as far as Foulmer, within six miles of Cambridge, my mare being almost tired: here we lay at the Chequer. I lay with Mr Pierce, who we left here the next morning upon his going to Hinchingbroke to speak with my Lord before his going to London, and we two come to Cambridge by eight o'clock in the morning. I went to Magdalene College to Mr Hill, with whom I found Mr Zanchy, Burton and Hollins, and took leave on promise to sup with them. To the Three Tuns, where we drank pretty hard and many healths to the King, &c.: then we broke up, and I and Mr Zanchy went to Magdalene College, where a very handsome supper at Mr Hill's chambers, I suppose upon a club among them, where I could find that there was nothing at all left of the old preciseness in their discourse, specially on Saturday nights. And Mr Zanchy told me that there was no such thing now-a-days among them at any time.

---

42 Richard Brown, a Major-General of the Parliament forces, Governor of Abingdon, and Member for London in the Long Parliament. He had been imprisoned by the Rump Faction.
43 William Pierrepont, MP of Thoresby, second son to Robert, first Earl of Kingston, died 1677, aged 71.

26th. Found Mr Pierce at our Inn, who told us he had lost his journey, for my Lord was gone from Hinchingbroke to London on Thursday last, at which I was a little put to a stand.

27th. Up by four o'clock: Mr Blayton and I took horse and straight to Saffron Walden, where at the White Hart, we set up our horses, and took the master of the house to shew us Audly End House, who took us on foot through the park, and so to the house, where the housekeeper shewed us all the house, in which the stateliness of the ceilings, chimney-pieces, and form of the whole was exceedingly worth seeing. He took us into the cellar, where we drank most admirable drink, a health to the King. Here I played on my flageolette, there being an excellent echo. He shewed us excellent pictures; two especially, those of the four Evangelists and Henry VIII. In our going, my landlord carried us through a very old hospital or almshouse, where forty poor people was maintained; a very old foundation; and over the chimneypiece was an inscription in brass: *Orate pro anima Thomae Bird*, &c.[44] They brought me a draft of their drink in a brown bowl, tipt with silver, which I drank off, and at the bottom was a picture of the Virgin with the child in her arms, done in silver. So we took leave, the road pretty good, but the weather rainy to Eping.

28th. Up in the morning. Then to London through the forest, where we found the way good, but only in one path, which we kept as if we had rode through a kennel all the way. We found the shops all shut, and the militia of the red regiment in arms at the old Exchange, among whom I found and spoke to Nich. Osborne, who told me that it was a thanksgiving-day through the City for the return of the Parliament. At Paul's I light, Mr Blayton holding my horse, where I found Dr Reynolds in the pulpit, and General Monk there, who was to have a great entertainment at Grocers' Hall.

29th. To my office. Mr Moore told me how my Lord is chosen General at Sea by the Council, and that it is thought that Monk will be joined with him therein. This day my Lord came to the House, the first time since he come to town; but he had been at the Council before.

---

44 The inscription and the bowl are still to be seen in the alms-house.

March 1st. I went to Mr Crewe's, whither Mr Thomas was newly come to town, being sent with Sir H. Yelverton, my old school-fellow at Paul's School, to bring the thanks of the county to General Monk for the return of the Parliament.

2nd. I went early to my Lord at Mr Crewe's where I spoke to him. Here were a great many come to see him, as Secretary Thurloe,[45] who is now by the Parliament chosen again Secretary of State. To Westminster Hall, where I saw Sir G. Booth at liberty. This day I hear the City militia is put into good posture, and it is thought that Monk will not be able to do any great matter against them now, if he had a mind. I understand that my Lord Lambert did yesterday send a letter to the Council, and that to-night he is to come and appear to the Council in person. Sir Arthur Haselrigge do not yet appear in the House. Great is the talk of a single person, and that it would now be Charles, George, or Richard again. For the last of which my Lord St John is said to speak high. Great also is the dispute now in the House, in whose name the writs shall run for the next Parliament; and it is said that Mr Prin, in open House, said, 'In King Charles's.'

3rd. To Westminster Hall, where I found that my Lord was last night voted one of the Generals at Sea, and Monk the other. I met my Lord in the Hall, who bid me come to him at noon. After dinner I to Warwick House, in Holborne, to my Lord, where he dined with my Lord of Manchester,[46] Sir Dudley North,[47] my Lord Fiennes,[48] and my Lord Barkley.[49] I staid in the great hall, talking with some gentlemen there, till they all come out. Then I, by coach with my Lord, to Mr Crewe's, in our way talking of publick things. He told

45 John Thurloe, who had been Secretary of State to the two Protectors, but was never employed after the Restoration, though the King solicited his services. Died 1668.

46 The Parliamentary General, afterwards particularly instrumental in the King's Restoration, became Chamberlain of the Household, KG, a Privy Counsellor, and Chancellor of the University of Cambridge. He died in 1671, having been five times married.

47 Sir Dudley North, KB, became the 4th Lord North, on the death of his father in 1666. Died 1677.

48 John, third son of William, 1st Viscount Say and Sele, and one of Oliver's Lords.

49 George, 13th Lord Berkeley, created Earl Berkeley 1679. He was a Privy Counsellor, and had afterwards the management of the Duke of York's family. Died 1698.

me he feared there was new design hatching, as if Monk had a mind to get into the saddle. Returning, met with Mr Gifford who told me, as I hear from many, that things are in a very doubtful posture, some of the Parliament being willing to keep the power in their hands. After I had left him, I met with Tom Harper; he talked huge high that my Lord Protector would come in place again, which indeed is much discoursed of again, though I do not see it possible.

4th. Lord's day. To Mr Gunning's, an excellent sermon upon charity.

5th. To Westminster by water, only seeing Mr Pinky at his own house, where he shewed me how he had alway kept the Lion and Unicorne, in the back of his chimney, bright, in expectation of the King's coming again. At home I found Mr Hunt, who told me how the Parliament had voted that the Covenant be printed and hung in churches again. Great hopes of the King's coming again.

6th. Shrove Tuesday. I called Mr Shepley and we both went up to my Lord's lodgings, at Mr Crewe's, where he bid us to go home again and get a fire against an hour after. Which we did at White Hall, whither he came, and after talking with him about our going to sea, he called me by myself into the garden, where he asked me how things were with me; he bid me look out now at this turn some good place, and he would use all his own, and all the interest of his friends that he had in England, to do me good. And asked me whether I could, without too much inconvenience, go to sea as his secretary, and bid me think of it. He also began to talk of things of State, and told me that he should want one in that capacity at sea, that he might trust in, and therefore he would have me to go. He told me also, that he did believe the King would come in, and did discourse with me about it, and about the affection of the people and City, at which I was full glad. Wrote by the post, by my Lord's command, for I. Goods to come up presently. For my Lord intends to go forth with Goods to the *Swiftsure* till the *Nazeby* be ready. This day I hear that the Lords do intend to sit, a great store of them are now in town, and I see in the Hall to-day. Overton at Hull do stand out, but can it is thought do nothing; and Lawson, it is said, is gone with some ships thither, but all that is nothing. My Lord told me, that there was great endeavours to bring in the Protector again; but he told me, too, that he did believe it would not last long if he were brought in; no, nor the King neither, (though he seems to think that he will come in), unless he carry himself very soberly and well. Every body now drink the King's health without any fear, whereas before it was very private that a man dare do it. Monk this day is feasted at Mercers' Hall, and is invited one after another to all the twelve Halls in London. Many think that he is honest yet, and some or more think him to be a fool that would raise himself, but think that he will undo himself by endeavouring it.

7th. Ash Wednesday. Going homeward, my Lord overtook me in his coach, and called me in, and so I went with him to St James's, and G. Montagu[50] being gone to White Hall, we walked over the Park thither, all the way he discoursing of the times, and of the change of things since the last year, and wondering how he could bear with so great disappointment as he did. He did give me the best advice that he could what was best for me, whether to stay or go with him, and offered all the ways that could be, how he might do me good, with the greatest liberty and love. This day, according to order, Sir Arthur[51] appeared at the House; what was done I know not, but there was all the Rumpers almost come to the House to-day. My Lord did seem to wonder much why Lambert was so willing to be put into the Tower, and thinks he had some design in it; but I think that he is so poor that he cannot use his liberty for debts, if he were at liberty; and so it is as good and better for him to be there, than any where else.

8th. To Westminster Hall, where there was a general damp over men's minds and faces upon some of the Officers of the Army being about making a remonstrance upon Charles Stuart or any single person; but at noon it was told, that the General had put a stop to it, so all was well again. Here I met with Jasper who was to bring me to my Lord at the lobby; whither sending a note to my Lord, he comes out to me and gives me directions to look after getting some money for him from the Admiralty, seeing that things are so unsafe, that he would not lay out a farthing for the State, till he had received some

50 George Montagu, afterwards MP for Dover, second son of Edward, second Earl of Manchester, and father of the first Earl of Halifax.
51 Haselrigge.

money of theirs. This afternoon, some of the officers of the Army, and some of the Parliament, had a conference at White Hall to make all right again, but I know not what is done. At the Dog tavern, in comes Mr Wade and Mr Sterry, secretary to the plenipotentiary in Denmark, who brought the news of the death of the King of Sweden[52] at Gottenburgh the 3rd of last month.

9th. To my Lord at his lodging, and came to Westminster with him in the coach; and Mr Dudley and he in the Painted Chamber walked a good while; and I telling him that I was willing and ready to go with him to sea, he agreed that I should, and advised me what to write to Mr Downing about it. This day it was resolved that the writs do go out in the name of the Keepers of the Liberty, and I hear that it is resolved privately that a treaty be offered with the King. And that Monk did check his soldiers highly for what they did yesterday.

13th. At my Lord's lodgings, who told me that I was to be secretary, and Crewe deputy treasurer to the Fleet. This day the Parliament voted all that had been done by the former Rump against the House of Lords be void, and to-night that the writs go out without any qualification. Things seem very doubtful what will be the end of all; for the Parliament seems to be strong for the King, while the soldiers do all talk against.

14th. To my Lord's, where infinity of applications to him and to me. To my great trouble, my Lord gives me all the papers that was given to him, to put in order and to give him an account of them. I went hence to St James's to speake with Mr Clerke, Monk's secretary, about getting some soldiers removed out of Huntingdon to Oundle, which my Lord told me he did to do a courtesy to the town, that he might have the greater interest in them, in the choice of the next Parliament; not that he intends to be chosen himself, but that he might have Mr G. Montagu and my Lord Mandevill chose there in spite of the Bernards. I did promise to give my wife all that I have in the world, but my books, in case I should die at sea. After supper I went to Westminster Hall, and the Parliament sat till ten at night, thinking and being expected to dissolve themselves today, but they did not. Great talk to-night that the discontented officers did think this night to make a stir, but prevented.

52 Charles Gustavus.

16th. To Westminster Hall, where I heard how the Parliament had this day dissolved themselves, and did pass very cheerfully through the Hall, and the Speaker without his mace. The whole Hall, was joyfull thereat, as well as themselves, and now they begin to talk loud of the King. To-night I am told, that yesterday, about five o'clock in the afternoon, one came with a ladder to the Great Exchange, and wiped with a brush the inscription that was on King Charles, and that there was a great bonfire made in the Exchange, and people called out 'God bless King Charles II!'

19th. Early to my Lord, where infinity of business to do, which makes my head full; and indeed, for these two or three days, I have not been without a great many cares. After that to the Admiralty, where a good while with Mr Blackburne, who told me that it was much to be feared that the King would come in, for all good men and good things were now discouraged. Thence to Wilkinson's, where Mr Shepley and I dined; and while we were at dinner, my Lord Monk's life-guard come by with the Serjeant at Armes before them, with two Proclamations, that all Cavaliers do depart the town: but the other that all officers that were lately disbanded should do the same. The last of which Mr R. Creed, I remember, said, that he looked upon it as if they had said, that all God's people should depart the town. All the discourse now-a-day is, that the King will come again; and for all I see, it is the wishes of all; and all do believe that it will be so.

21st. To my Lord's, but the wind very high against us; here I did very much business, and then to my Lord Widdrington's from my Lord, with his desire that he might have the disposal of the writs of the Cinque Ports. My Lord was very civil to me, and called for wine, and writ a long letter in answer.

22nd. To Westminster, and received my warrant of Mr Blackburne, to be Secretary to the two Generals of the Fleet.

23rd. My Lord, Captain Isham, Mr Thomas, John Crewe, W. Howe, and I to the Tower, where the barges staid for us; my Lord and the Captain in one, and W. Howe and I, &c., in the other, to the Long Reach, where the *Swiftsure* lay at anchor; (in our way we saw the great breach which the late high water had made, to the loss of many thousands of pounds to the people about Limehouse.) Soon as my Lord on board, the guns went off bravely from the ships. And a little while after comes the Vice-Admiral Lawson, and seemed very respectful to my Lord, and so did the rest of the Commanders of the frigates that were thereabouts. We were late writing of orders for the getting of ships ready, &c.; and also making of others to all the seaports between Hastings and Yarmouth, to stop all dangerous persons that are going or coming between Flanders and there.

24th. At work hard all the day writing letters to the Council, &c.

25th. About two o'clock in the morning, letters came from London by our Coxon, so they waked me, but I bid him stay till morning, which he did, and then I rose and carried them into my Lord, who read them a-bed. Among the rest, there was the writ and mandate for him to dispose to the Cinque Ports for choice of Parliament-men. There was also one for me from Mr Blackburne, who with his own hand superscribes it to S. P. Esq., of which God knows I was not a little proud. I wrote a letter to the Clerk of Dover Castle to come to my Lord about issuing of those writs.

26th. This day it is two years since it pleased God that I was cut for the stone at Mrs Turner's[53] in Salisbury Court. And did resolve while I live to keep it a festival, as I did the last year at my house, and for ever to have Mrs Turner and her company with me. But now it pleased God that I am prevented to do it openly; only within my soul I can and do rejoice, and bless God, being at this time, blessed be his holy name, in as good health as ever I was in my life. This morning I rose early, and went about making of an establishment of the whole Fleet, and a list of all the ships, with the number of men and guns. About an hour after that, we had a meeting of the principal commanders and seamen, to proportion out the number of these things. All the afternoon very many orders were made, till I was very weary.

27th. This morning the wind came about, and we fell into the Hope. I sat the first time with my Lord at table since my coming to sea. All the afternoon exceeding busy in writing of letters and orders. In the afternoon, Sir Harry Wright[54] come on board us, about his

53 Mrs Turner was the sister of Edward Pepys.
54 MP for Harwich. He married Anne, daughter of Lord Crewe, and sister to Lady Sandwich, and resided at Dagenham, Essex; he was created a Baronet by Cromwell, 1658, and by Charles II, 1660.

business of being chosen a Parliament-man. My Lord brought him to see my cabbin, when I was hard a-writing. At night supped with my Lord too, with the Captain.

28th. This morning and the whole day busy. At night there was a gentleman very well bred, his name was Banes, going for Flushing, who spoke French and Latin very well, brought by direction from Captain Clerke hither, as a prisoner, because he called out of the vessel that he went in, 'Where is your King, we have done our business, *Vive le Roi.*' He confessed himself a Cavalier in his heart, and that he and his whole family, had fought for the King; but that he was then drunk, having been taking his leave at Gravesend the night before, and so could not remember what it was that he said; but in his words and carriage showed much of a gentleman. My Lord had a great kindness for him, but did not think it safe to release him. But a while after, he sent a letter down to my Lord, which my Lord did like very well, and did advise with me that the gentleman was to be released. So I went up and sat and talked with him in Latin and French; and about eleven at night he took boat again, and so God bless him. This day we had news of the election at Huntingdon for Bernard[55] and Pedley, at which my Lord was much troubled for his friends' missing of it.

29th. We lie still a little below Gravesend. At night Mr Shepley returned from London, and told us of several elections for the next Parliament. That the King's effigies was new making to be set up in the Exchange again. This evening was a great whispering that some of the Vice-Admiral's captains were dissatisfied, and did intend to fight themselves, to oppose the General. But it was soon hushed, and the Vice-Admiral did wholly deny any such thing, and protested to stand by the General.

30th. This day, while my Lord and we were at dinner, the *Nazeby* came in sight towards us, and at last came to anchor close by us. My Lord and many others went on board her, where every thing was out of order, and a new chimney made for my Lord in his bed-chamber, which he was much pleased with. My Lord, in his discourse, discovered a great deal of love to this ship.[56]

55 John Bernard and Nicholas Pedley, re-elected in the next Parliament.
56 Lord Sandwich's flag was on board the *Nazeby*, when he went to the Sound.

April 1st (Lord's day). Mr Ibbot[57] preached very well. After dinner my lord did give me a private list of all the ships that were to be set out this summer, wherein I do discover that he hath made it his care to put by as much of the Anabaptists as he can. By reason of my Lord and my being busy to send away the packet by Mr Cooke of the *Nazeby*, it was four o'clock before we could begin sermon again. This day Captain Guy come on board from Dunkirk, who tells me that the King will come in, and that the soldiers at Dunkirk do drink the King's health in the streets.

2nd. Up very early, and to get all my things and my boy's packed up. Great concourse of commanders here this morning to take leave of my Lord upon his going into the *Nazeby*. This morning comes Mr Ed. Pickering,[58] he tells me that the King will come in, but that Monk did resolve to have the doing of it himself, or else to hinder it.

3rd. There come many merchants to get convoy to the Baltique, which a course was taken for. They dined with my Lord, and one of them by name Alderman Wood talked much to my Lord of the hopes that he had now to be settled, (under the King he meant); but my Lord took no notice of it. This day come the Lieutenant of the *Swiftsure* (who was sent by my lord to Hastings, one of the Cinque Ports, to have got Mr Edward Montagu to have been one of their burgesses, but could not, for they were all promised before).

4th. This morning come Colonel Thomson with the wooden leg, and G. Pen, and dined with my Lord and Mr Blackburne, who told me that it was certain now that the King must of necessity come in, and that one of the Council told him there is something doing in order to a treaty already among them. And it was strange to hear how Mr Blackburne did already begin to commend him for a sober man, and how quiet he would be under his government, &c. The Commissioners come to-day, only to consult about a further reducement of the Fleet, and to pay them as fast as they can. At night, my Lord resolved to send the Captain of our ship to Waymouth and promote his being chosen there, which he did put himself into readiness to do the next morning.

57 Minister of Deal, 1676 – Pepys's manuscript letters.
58 Brother to Sir Gilbert Pickering, Bart.

9th. This afternoon I first saw France and Calais, with which I was much pleased, though it was at a distance.

11th. A Gentleman came from my Lord of Manchester to my Lord for a pass for Mr Boyle,[59] which was made him. All the news from London is that things go on further towards a King. That the Skinners' Company the other day at their entertaining General Monk had took down the Parliament Arms in their Hall, and set up the King's. My Lord and I had a great deal of discourse about the several Captains of the Fleet and his interest among them, and had his mind clear to bring in the King. He confessed to me that he was not sure of his own Captain, to be true to him, and that he did not like Capt. Stokes.

14th. This day I was informed that my Lord Lambert is got out of the Tower, and that there is £100 proffered to whoever shall bring him forth to the Council of State. My Lord is chosen at Waymouth this morning; my Lord had his freedom brought him by Capt. Tiddiman of the port of Dover, by which he is capable of being elected for them. This day I heard that the Army had in general declared to stand by what the next Parliament shall do.

15th (Lord's day). To sermon, and then to dinner, where my Lord told us that the University of Cambridge had a mind to choose him for their burgess, which he pleased himself with, to think that they do look upon him as a thriving man, and said so openly at table. At dinner-time Mr Cooke came back from London with a packet which caused my Lord to be full of thoughts all day, and at night he bid me privately to get two commissions ready, one for Capt. Robert Blake to be captain of the *Worcester*, in the room of Capt. Dekings, an anabaptist, and one that had witnessed a great deal of discontent with the present proceedings. The other for Capt. Coppin to come out of that into the *Newbury* in the room of Blake, whereby I perceive that General Monk do resolve to make a thorough change, to make way for the King. From London I hear that since Lambert got out of the Tower, the Fanatiques had held up their heads high, but I hope all that will come to nothing.

59 The celebrated Robert Boyle, youngest son of Richard first Earl of Cork.

17th. All the morning getting ready commissions for the Vice-Admiral and the R. Admiral, wherein my Lord was very careful to express the utmost of his own power, commanding them to obey what orders they should receive from the Parliament, &c., or both or either of the Generals. My Lord told me clearly his thoughts that the King would carry it, and that he did not think himself very happy that he was now at sea, as well for his own sake, as that he thought he might do his country some service in keeping things quiet.

18th. Mr Cooke returned from London, bringing me this news, that the Cavaliers are something unwise to talk so high on the other side as they do. That the Lords do meet every day at my Lord of Manchester's, and resolve to sit the first day of the Parliament. That it is evident now that the General and the Council do resolve to make way for the King's coming. And it is clear that either the Fanatiques must now be undone, or the gentry and citizens throughout England, and clergy must fall, in spite of their militia and army, which is not at all possible I think.

19th. At dinner news brought us that my Lord was chosen at Dover.

20th. This evening come Mr Boyle on board, for whom I writ an order for a ship to transport him to Flushing. He supped with my Lord, my Lord using him as a person of honour. Mr Shepley told me that he heard for certain at Dover that Mr Edw. Montagu[60] did go beyond sea when he was here first the other day, and I am apt to believe that he went to speak with the King. This day one told me how that at the election at Cambridge for knights of the shire, Wendby and Thornton by declaring to stand for the Parliament and a King and the settlement of the Church, did carry it against all expectation against Sir Dudley North and Sir Thomas Willis.[61]

21st. This day dined Sir John Boys[62] and some other gentlemen formerly great Cavaliers, and among the rest one Mr Norwood,[63] for whom my Lord give a convoy to carry him to the *Brill*, but he is

60 Eldest son of Edward, second Lord Montagu, of Boughton, killed at Berghen, 1685.
61 He had represented Cambridgeshire in the preceding Parliament.
62 Gentleman of the Privy-Chamber.
63 A Major Norwood had been Governor of Dunkirk; and a person of the same name occurs, as one of the Esquires of the body at the Coronation of Charles II.

certainly going to the King. For my Lord commanded me that I should not enter his name in my book. My Lord do show them and that sort of people great civility. All their discourse and others are of the King's coming, and we begin to speak of it very freely. And heard how in many churches in London, and upon many signs there, and upon merchants' ships in the river, they had set up the King's arms. This night there came one with a letter from Mr Edw. Montagu to my Lord, with command to deliver it to his own hands. I do believe that he do carry some close business on for the King. This day I had a large letter from Mr Moore, giving me an account of the present dispute at London that is like to be at the beginning of the Parliament, about the House of Lords, who do resolve to sit with the Commons, as not thinking themselves dissolved yet. Which, whether it be granted or no, or whether they will sit or no, it will bring a great many inconveniences. His letter I keep, it being a very well writ one.

22nd. Several Londoners, strangers, friends of the Captains, dined here, who, among other things told us, how the King's Arms are every day set up in houses and churches, particularly in Allhallows Church in Thames-street, John Simpson's church, which being privately done was a great eye-sore to his people when they came to church and saw it. Also they told us for certain, that the King's statue is making by the Mercers' Company (who are bound to do it) to set up in the Exchange.

23rd. In the evening for the first time, extraordinary good sport among the seamen, after my Lord had done playing at nine-pins.

24th. We were on board the *London*, which hath a stateroom much bigger than the *Nazeby*, but not so rich. After that, with the Captain on board our own ship, where we were saluted with the news of Lambert's being taken, which news was brought to London on Sunday last. He was taken in Northamptonshire by Colonel Ingoldsby,[64] in the head of a party, by which means their whole design is broke, and things now very open and safe. And every man begins to be merry and full of hopes.

64 Colonel Richard Ingoldsby had been Governor of Oxford under his kinsman Cromwell, and one of Charles I's Judges; but was pardoned for the service here mentioned, and made KB at the Coronation of Charles II. He afterwards retired to his seat at Lethenborough, Buckinghamshire, and died 1685.

25th. Dined to-day with Captain Clerke on board the *Speaker* (a very brave ship) where was the Vice-Admiral, R. Admiral, and many other commanders. After dinner home, not a little contented to see how I am treated, and with what respect made a fellow to the best commander in the Fleet.

26th. This day come Mr Donne back from London, who brought letters with him that signify the meeting of the Parliament yesterday. And in the afternoon by other letters I hear, that about twelve of the Lords met and had chosen my Lord of Manchester Speaker of the House of Lords (the young Lords that never sat yet, do forbear to sit for the present); and Sir Harbottle Grimstone,[65] Speaker for the House of Commons, which, after a little debate, was granted. Dr Reynolds preached before the Commons before they sat. My Lord told me how Sir H. Yelverton[66] (formerly my schoolfellow) was chosen in the first place for Northamptonshire and Mr Crewe in the second. And told me how he did believe that the Cavaliers have now the upper hand clear of the Presbyterians.

27th. After dinner came on board Sit Thomas Hatton[67] and Sir R. Maleverer,[68] going for Flushing; but all the world know that they go where the rest of the many gentlemen go that every day flock to the King at Breda. They supped here, and my Lord treated them as he do the rest that go thither, with a great deal of civility. While we were at supper a packet came, wherein much news from several friends. The chief is that, that I had from Mr Moore, viz. that he fears the Cavaliers in the House will be so high, that the other will be forced to leave the House and fall in with General Monk, and so offer things to the King so high on the Presbyterian account that he may refuse, and so they will endeavour some more mischief; but when I told my Lord it, he shook his head and told me, that the Presbyterians are deceived, for the General is certainly for the King's interest, and so they will not be able to prevail that way with him. After supper the two knights went on board the *Grantham*, that is to convey them to Flushing. I am informed that the Exchequer is now so low, that there

---

65 He was made Master of the Rolls, November following, and died 1683.
66 Of Easton Mauduit, Bart, grandson to the Attorney General of both his names. Died 1679.
67 Of Long Stanton, co. Cambridge, Bart.
68 Of Allerton Maleverer, Yorkshire, Bart.

is not £20 there, to give the messenger that brought the news of Lambert's being taken; which story is very strange that he should lose his reputation of being a man of courage now at one blow, for that he was not able to fight one stroke, but desired of Colonel Ingoldsby several times to let him escape. Late reading my letters, my mind being much troubled to think that, after all our hopes, we should have any cause to fear any more disappointments therein.

29th. After sermon in the morning Mr Cooke came from London with a packet, bringing news how all the young lords that were not in arms against the Parliament do now sit. That a letter is come from the King to the House, which is locked up by the Council 'till next Thursday that it may be read in the open House when they meet again, they having adjourned till then to keep a fast to-morrow. And so the contents is not yet known. £13,000 of the £20,000 given to General Monk is paid out of the Exchequer, he giving £12 among the teller's clerks of Exchequer. My Lord called me into the great cabbin below, where he told me that the Presbyterians are quite mastered by the Cavaliers, and that he fears Mr Crewe did go a little too far the other day in keeping out the young lords from sitting. That he do expect that the King should be brought over suddenly, without staying to make any terms at all, saying that the Presbyterians did intend to have brought him in with such conditions as if he had been in chains. But he shook his shoulders when he told me how Monk had betrayed him, for it was he that did put them upon standing to put out the lords and other members that come not within the qualifications, which he did not like, but however he had done his business, though it be with some kind of baseness. After dinner I walked a great while upon the deck with the chyrurgeon and purser, and other officers of the ship, and they all pray for the King's coming, which I pray God send.

May 1st. To-day I hear they were very merry at Deale, setting up the King's flags upon one of their Maypoles, and drinking his health upon their knees in the streets, and firing the guns, which the soldiers of the Castle threatened, but durst not oppose.

2nd. Mr Dunne from London, with letters that tell us the welcome news of the Parliament's votes yesterday, which will be remembered for the happiest May-day that hath been many a year to England. The

King's letter was read in the House, wherein he submits himself and all things to them, as to an Act of Oblivion to all, unless they shall please to except any, as to the confirming of the sales of the King's and Church lands, if they see good. The House upon reading the letter, ordered £50,000 to be forthwith provided to send to His Majesty for his present supply; and a committee chosen to return an answer of thanks to His Majesty for his gracious letter; and that the letter be kept among the records of the Parliament; and in all this not so much as one No. So that Luke Robinson[69] himself stood up and made a recantation of what he had done, and promises to be a loyal subject to his Prince for the time to come. The City of London have put out a Declaration, wherein they do disclaim their owning any other government but that of a King, Lords, and Commons. Thanks was given by the House to Sir John Greenville,[70] one of the bedchamber to the King, who brought the letter, and they continued bare all the time it was reading. Upon notice from the Lords to the Commons, of their desire that the Commons would join with them in their vote for King, Lords, and Commons; the Commons did concur and voted that all books whatever that are out against the Government of King, Lords, and Commons, should be brought into the House and burned. Great joy all yesterday at London, and at night more bonfires than ever, and ringing of bells, and drinking of the King's health upon their knees in the streets, which methinks is a little too much. But every body seems to be very joyfull in the business, insomuch that our sea-commanders now begin to say so too, which a week ago they would not do. And our seamen, as many as had money or credit for drink, did do nothing else this evening. This day come Mr North[71] (Sir Dudley North's son) on board, to spend a little time here, which my Lord was a little troubled at, but he seems to be a fine gentleman, and at night did play his part exceeding well at first sight.

3rd. This morning my Lord showed me the King's declaration and his letter to the two Generals to be communicated to the fleet. The

69 Of Pickering Lyth, in Yorkshire, MP for Scarborough ; discharged from sitting in the House of Commons, July 21, 1660.
70 Created Earl of Bath, 1661, son of Sir Bevill Grenville, killed at the battle of Newbury, and said to have been the only person entrusted by Charles II and Monk in bringing about the Restoration.
71 Charles, eldest son of Dudley, afterwards fourth Lord North.

contents of the letter are his offer of grace to all that will come in
within forty days, only excepting them that the Parliament shall
hereafter except. That the sales of lands during these troubles, and all
other things, shall be left to the Parliament, by which he will stand.
The letter dated at Breda, April 4/14th 1660, in the 12th year of his
reign. Upon the receipt of it this morning by an express, Mr Phillips,
one of the messengers of the Council from General Monk, my Lord
summoned a council of war, and in the meantime did dictate to me
how he would have the vote ordered which he would have pass this
council. Which done the Commanders all came on board, and the
council sat in the coach[72] (the first council of war that had been in
my time), where I read the letter and declaration; and while they
were discoursing upon it, I seemed to draw up a vote, which being
offered, they passed. Not one man seemed to say no to it, though I
am confident many in their hearts were against it. After this was
done, I went up to the quarter-deck with my Lord and the
Commanders, and there read both the papers and the vote; which
done, and demanding their opinion, the seamen did all of them cry
out, 'God bless King Charles!' with the greatest joy imaginable. That
being done, Sir R. Stayner,[73] who had invited us yesterday, took all
the Commanders and myself on board him to dinner, which not
being ready, I went with Captain Hayward to the *Plimouth* and
Essex, and did what I had to do and returned, where very merry at
dinner. After dinner, to the rest of the ships quite through the fleet.
Which was a very brave sight to visit all the ships, and to be received
with the respect and honour that I was on board them all; and much
more to see the great joy that I brought to all men; not one through
the whole fleet showing the least dislike of the business. In the
evening as I was going on board the Vice-Admiral, the General
began to fire his guns, which he did all that he had in the ship, and so
did all the rest of the Commanders, which was very gallant, and to
hear the bullets go hissing over our heads as we were in the boat.
This done and finished my Proclamation, I returned to the *Nazeby*,
where my Lord was much pleased to hear how all the fleet took it in
a transport of joy, showed me a private letter of the King's to him,

72 Coach, on board a man-of-war, 'The Council Chamber'.
73 Knighted and made a Vice-Admiral by Cromwell, 1657, and sent by Charles II
to command at Tangier till the Governor arrived.

and another from the Duke of York in such familiar style as their common friend, with all kindness imaginable. And I found by the letters, and so my Lord told me too, that there had been many letters passed between them for a great while, and I perceive unknown to Monk. And among the rest that had carried these letters Sir John Boys is one, and Mr Norwood, which had a ship to carry him over the other day, when my Lord would not have me put down his name in the book. The King speaks of his being courted to come to the Hague, but to desire my Lord's advice where to come to take ship. And the Duke offers to learn the seaman's trade of him in such familiar words as if Jack Cole and I had writ them. This was very strange to me, that my Lord should carry all things so wisely and prudently as he do, and I was over joyful to see him in so good condition, and he did not a little please himself to tell me how he had provided for himself so great a hold on the King.

After this to supper, and then to writing of letters till twelve at night, and so up again at three in the morning. My Lord seemed to put great confidence in me, and would take my advice in many things. I perceive his being willing to do all the honour in the world to Monk, and to let him have all the honour of doing the business, though he will many times express his thoughts of him to be but a thick-skulled fool. So that I do believe there is some agreement more than ordinary between the King and my Lord to let Monk carry on the business, for it is he that can do the business, or at least that can hinder it, if he be not flattered and observed. This, my Lord will hint himself sometimes. My Lord, I perceive by the King's letter, had writ to him about his father, Crewe,[74] and the King did speak well of him; but my Lord tells me, that he is afraid that he hath too much concerned himself with the Presbyterians against the House of Lords, which will do him a great discourtesy.

4th. I wrote this morning many letters, and to all the copies of the vote of the council of war I put my name that if it should come in print my name may be to it. I sent a copy of the vote to Doling, inclosed in this letter:

SIR — He that can fancy a fleet (like ours) in her pride, with

---

74 He had married Jemima, daughter of John Crewe, Esq., created afterwards Baron Crewe of Stene.

pendants loose, guns roaring, caps flying, and the loud '*Vive le Roy's*', echoed from one ship's company to another, he, and he only, can apprehend the joy this inclosed vote was received with, or the blessing he thought himself possessed of that bore it, and is

Your humble servant.

About nine o'clock I got all my letters done, and sent them by the messenger that come yesterday. This morning come Captain Isham on board with a gentleman going to the King, by whom very cunningly, my Lord tells me, he intends to send an account of this day's and yesterday's actions here, notwithstanding he had writ to the Parliament to have leave of them to send the King the answer of the fleete. Since my writing of the last paragraph, my Lord called me to him to read his letter to the King, to see whether I could find any slips in it or no. And as much of the letter as I can remember, is thus: 'it please your Most Excellent Majesty', and so begins: That he yesterday received from General Monk his Majesty's letter and direction; and that General Monk had desired him to write to the Parliament to have leave to send the vote of the seamen before he did send it to him, which he had done by writing to both Speakers; but for his private satisfaction he had sent it thus privately, (and so the copy of the proceedings yesterday was sent him) and that this come by a gentleman that come this day on board, intending to wait upon his Majesty, that he is my Lord's countryman, and one whose friends have suffered much on his Majesty's behalf. That my Lords Pembroke[75] and Salisbury[76] are put out of the House of Lords. That my Lord is very joyful that other countries do pay him the civility and respect due to him; and that he do much rejoice to see that the King do receive none of their assistance (or some such words) from them, he having strength enough in the love and loyalty of his own subjects to support him. That his Majesty had chosen the best place, Scheveling, for his embarking, and that there is nothing in the world of which he is more ambitious, than to have the honour of attending his Majesty, which he hoped would be speedy. That he had commanded the

75 Philip, fifth Earl of Pembroke, and second Earl of Montgomery, died 1669. Clarendon says, 'This young Earl's affections were entire for his Majesty.'
76 Williams, second Earl of Salisbury. After Cromwell had put down the House of Peers, he was chosen a Member of the House of Commons, and sat with them, died 1660.

vessel to attend at Helversluce till this gentleman returns, that so if his Majesty do not think it fit to command the fleete himself, yet that he may be there to receive his commands and bring them to his Lordship. He ends his letter, that he is confounded with the thoughts of the high expressions of love to him in the King's letter, and concludes, 'Your most loyall, dutifull, faithfull and obedient subject and servant, E. M.'

After supper at the table in the coach, my Lord talking concerning the uncertainty of the places of the Exchequer to them that had them now; he did at last think of an office which do belong to him in case the King do restore every man to his places that ever had been patent, which is to be one of the clerks of the signet, which will be a fine employment for one of his sons.

In the afternoon come a minister on board, one Mr Sharpe, who is going to the King; who tells me that Commissioners are chosen both of the Lords and Commons to go to the King; and that Dr Clarges[77] is going to him from the Army, and that he will be here tomorrow. My letters at night tell me, that the House did deliver their letter to Sir John Greenville, in answer to the King's sending, and that they give him £500 for his pains, to buy him a jewel, and that besides the £50,000 ordered to be borrowed of the City for the present use of the King, the twelve companies of the City do give every one of them to his Majesty, as a present, £1000.

5th. All the morning very busy writing letters to London, and a packet to Mr Downing, to acquaint him with what had been done lately in the fleet. And this I did by my Lord's command, who, I thank him, did of himself think of doing it, to do me a kindness, for he writ a letter himself to him, thanking him for his kindness to me. This evening come Dr Clarges to Deale, going to the King; where the townes-people strewed the streets with herbes against his coming, for joy of his going. Never was there so general a content as there is now. I cannot but remember that our parson did, in his prayer to-night, pray for the long life and happiness of our King and dread Soveraigne, that may last as long as the sun and moon endureth.

77 Thomas Clarges, physician to the Army, created a Baronet, 1674, died 1695. He had been previously knighted; his sister Anne married General Monk.

6th. It fell very well to-day, a stranger preached here for Mr Ibbot, one Mr Stanley, who prayed for King Charles, by the Grace of God, &c., which gave great contentment to the gentlemen that were on board here, and they said they would talk of it, when they come to Breda, as not having it done yet in London so publickly. After they were gone from on board, my Lord writ a letter to the King and give it me to carry privately to Sir William Compton,[78] on board the *Assistance*, which I did, and after a health to his Majesty on board there, I left them under sail for Breda.

7th. My Lord went this morning about the flag-ships in a boat, to see what alterations there must be, as to the armes and flags. He did give me orders also to write for silk flags and scarlett waistcloathes.[79] For a rich barge; for a noise of trumpets, and a set of fidlers. Very great deal of company come to-day, among others Mr Bellasses,[80] Sir Thomas Lenthropp, Sir Henry Chichley, Colonel Philip Honiwood, and Captain Titus,[81] the last of whom my Lord showed all our cabbins, and I suppose he is to take notice what room there will be for the King's entertainment.

8th. My letters to-day tell me how it was intended that the King should be proclaimed to-day in London, with a great deal of pomp. I had also news who they are that are chosen of the Lords and Commons to attend the King. And also the whole story of what we did the other day in the fleet, at reading of the King's declaration, and my name at the bottom of it.

9th. Up very early, writing a letter to the King, as from the two Generals of the fleet, in answer to his letter to them, wherein my Lord do give most humble thanks for his gracious letter and declaration; and promises all duty and obedience to him. This letter was carried this morning to Sir Peter Killigrew,[82] who come hither this morning early to bring an order from the Lords' House to my Lord, giving him power to write an answer to the King. This

78 Sir William Compton, third son of Spencer, Earl of Northampton, a Privy Counsellor and Master of the Ordnance, died 1663, aged 39.
79 Clothes hung about the cage-work of a ship's hull to protect the men in action.
80 Henry, eldest son of Lord Bellasis, made KB at Charles II's Coronation.
81 Colonel Silas Titus, Gentleman of the Bedchamber to Charles II, author of *Killing no Murder*.
82 Knight, of Arwenach, Cornwall, MP for Camelford, 1660.

morning my Lord St John and other persons of honour were here to see my Lord, and so away to Flushing. As we were sitting down to dinner, in comes Noble with a letter from the House of Lords to my Lord, to desire him to provide ships to transport the Commissioners to the King, which are expected here this week. He brought us certain news that the King was proclaimed yesterday with great pomp, and brought down one of the Proclamations, with great joy to us all; for which God be praised. This morning come Mr Saunderson, that writ the story of the King, hither, who is going over to the King.

10th. At night, while my Lord was at supper, in comes my Lord Lauderdale[83] and Sir John Greenville, who supped here, and so went away. After they were gone, my Lord called me into his cabbin, and told me how he was commanded to set sail presently for the King, and was very glad thereof. I got him afterwards to sign things in bed.

11th. This morning we began to pull down all the State's arms in the fleet, having first sent to Dover for painters and others to come to set up the King's. There dined here my Lord Crafford[84] and my Lord Cavendish,[85] and other Scotchmen whom I afterwards ordered to be received on board the *Plymouth*, and to go along with us. After dinner we set sail from the Downes. In the afternoon overtook us three or four gentlemen: two of the Berties, and one Mr Dormerhay,[86] a Scotch gentleman, who, telling my Lord that they heard the Commissioners were come out of London today, my Lord dropt anchor over against Dover Castle (which give us about thirty guns in passing), and upon a high debate with the Vice and Rear Admiral whether it were safe to go and not stay for the Commissioners, he did resolve to send Sir R. Stayner to Dover, to enquire of my Lord Winchelsea,[87] whether or no they are come out of London, and then to resolve to-morrow morning of going or not. Which was done.

83 John, second Earl and afterwards created Duke of Lauderdale, Earl of Guilford (in England) and KG. He became sole Secretary of State for Scotland in 1661, and was a Gentleman of His Majesty's Bedchamber, and died in 1682, without issue.
84 John, fourteenth Earl of Crauford, restored in 1661 to the office of High Treasurer of Scotland, which he had held eight years under Charles I.
85 Afterwards fourth Earl and first Duke of Devonshire.
86 Probably Dalmahoy.
87 Heneage, second Earl of Winchelsea, constituted by General Monk, Governor of Dover Castle, July, 1660; made Lord Lieutenant of Kent, and afterwards ambassador to Turkey. Died 1689.

12th. My Lord give me many orders to make for direction for the ships that are left in the Downes, giving them the greatest charge in the world to bring no passengers with them, when they come after us to Scheveling Bay, excepting Mr Edward Montagu, Mr Thomas Crewe, and Sir H. Wright. Sir R. Stayner told my Lord, that my Lord Winchelsea understands by letters, that the Commissioners are only to come to Dover to attend the coming over of the King. So my Lord did give order for weighing anchor, which we did, and sailed all day.

13th. To the quarter-deck, at which the taylors and painters were at work, cutting out some pieces of yellow cloth in the fashion of a crown and C. R. and put it upon a fine sheet, and that into the flag instead of the State's arms, which after dinner was finished and set up. This morn Sir J. Boys and Capt. Isham met us in the *Nonsuch*, the first of whom, after a word or two with my Lord, went forward, the other staid. I heard by them how Mr Downing had never made any address to the King, and for that was hated exceedingly by the Court, and that he was in a Dutch ship which sailed by us, then going to England with disgrace. Also how Mr Morland[88] was knighted by the King this week, and that the King did give the reason of it openly, that it was for his giving him intelligence all the time he was clerk to Secretary Thurloe. In the afternoon a council of war, only to acquaint them that the Harp must be taken out of all their flags, it being very offensive to the King. Late at night we writ letters to the King of the news of our coming, and Mr Edward Pickering[89] carried them. Capt. Isham went on shore, nobody showing of him any respect; so the old man very fairly took leave of my Lord, and my Lord very coldly bid him 'God be with you', which was very strange, but that I hear that he keeps a great deal of prating and talking on shore, on board, at the King's Courts, what command he had with my Lord, &c.

88 Samuel Morland, successively scholar and fellow of Magdalene College, and Mr Pepys's tutor there, became afterwards one of Thurloe's Under Secretaries, and was employed in several embassies by Cromwell, whose interests he betrayed, by secretly communicating with Charles II. In consideration of these services he was created a baronet of Sulhamstead Banister, Berks, after the Restoration. He was an ingenious mechanic, supposed by some persons to have invented the steam engine, and lived to an advanced age.
89 Sir Gilbert Pickering's eldest son.

14th. In the morning the Hague was clearly to be seen by us. My Lord went up in his nightgown into the cuddy, to see how to dispose thereof for himself and us that belong to him, to give order for our removal to-day. Some nasty Dutchmen came on board to proffer their boats to carry things from us on shore, &c. to get money by us. Before noon some gentlemen came on board from the shore to kiss my Lord's hands. And by and by Mr North and Dr Clerke went to kiss the Queen of Bohemia's hands, from my Lord, with twelve attendants from on board to wait on them, among which I sent my boy, who, like myself, is with child to see any strange thing. After noon they came back again after having kissed the Queen of Bohemia's[90] hand, and were sent again by my Lord to do the same to the Prince of Orange.[91] So I got the Captain to ask leave for me to go, which my Lord did give, and I taking my boy and Judge Advocate with me, went in company with them. The weather bad; we were sadly washed when we come near the shore, it being very hard to land there. The shore is so, all the country between that and the Hague, all sand. The Hague is a most neat place in all respects. The houses so neat in all places and things as is possible. Here we walked up and down a great while, the town being now very full of Englishmen, for that the Londoners were come on shore to-day. But going to see the Prince,[92] he was gone forth with his governor, and so we walked up and down the town and court to see the place; and by the help of a stranger, an Englishman, we saw a great many places, and were made to understand many things, as the intention of may-poles, which we saw there standing at every great man's door, of different greatness according to the quality of the person. About ten at night the Prince comes home, and we found an easy admission. His attendance very inconsiderable as for a prince; but yet handsome, and his tutor a fine man, and himself a very pretty boy.

15th. Coming on board we found all the Commissioners of the House of Lords at dinner with my Lord, who after dinner went away for shore. Mr Morland, now Sir Samuel, was here on board, but I do not find that my Lord or any body did give him any respect, he being looked upon by him and all men as a knave.

90 Daughter of James I.
91 Afterwards William III.
92 Henry Duke of Gloucester, Charles II's youngest brother.

Among others he betrayed Sir Rich. Willis that married Dr F. Jones's daughter, who had paid him £1000 at one time by the Protector's and Secretary Thurloe's order, for intelligence that he sent concerning the King. In the afternoon my Lord called me on purpose to show me his fine cloathes which are now come hither, and indeed are very rich as gold and silver can make them, only his sword he and I do not like. In the afternoon my Lord and I walked together in the coach two hours, talking together upon all sorts of discourse: as religion, wherein he is, I perceive, wholly sceptical, saying, that indeed the Protestants as to the Church of Rome are wholly fanatiques: he likes uniformity and form of prayer: about State-business, among other things he told me that his conversion to the King's cause (for I was saying that I wondered from what time the King could look upon him to become his friend,) commenced from his being in the Sound, when he found what usage he was likely to have from a Commonwealth. My Lord, the Captain, and I supped in my Lord's chamber, where I did perceive that he did begin to show me much more respect than ever he did yet. After supper, my Lord sent for me, intending to have me play at cards with him, but I not knowing cribbage, we fell into discourse of many things, and the ship rolled so much that I was not able to stand, and so he bid me go to bed.

16th. Come in some with visits, among the rest one from Admiral Opdam,[93] who spoke Latin well, but not French nor English, whom my Lord made me to entertain. Commissioner Pett[94] was now come to take care to get all things ready for the King on board. My Lord in his best suit, this the first day, in expectation to wait upon the King. But Mr Edw. Pickering coming from the King brought word that the King would not put my Lord to the trouble of coming to him, but that he would come to the shore to look upon the fleet to-day, which we expected, and had our guns ready to fire, and our scarlet waist-cloathes out and silk pendants, but he did not come. This evening came Mr John Pickering on board, like an asse, with his feathers and new suit that he had made at the Hague. My Lord very angry for his staying on shore, bidding me a little before to send for him, telling me that he was afraid that for his father's sake he might

93 The celebrated Dutch Admiral.
94 Naval Commissioner at Chatham.

have some mischief done him, unless he used the General's name.
This afternoon Mr Edw. Pickering told me in what a sad, poor
condition for clothes and money the King was, and all his attendants,
when he came to him first from my Lord, their clothes not being
worth forty shillings the best of them. And how overjoyed the King
was when Sir J. Greenville brought him some money; so joyful, that
he called the Princess Royal[95] and Duke of York to look upon it as it
lay in the portmanteau before it was taken out. My Lord told me,
too, that the Duke of York is made High Admiral of England.

17th. Dr Clerke came to me to tell me that he heard this morning,
by some Dutch that are come on board already to see the ships, that
there was a Portuguese taken yesterday at the Hague, that had a
design to kill the King. But this I heard afterwards was only the
mistake upon one being observed to walk with his sword naked, he
having lost his scabbard. Before dinner Mr Edw. Pickering and I, W.
Howe, Pim, and my boy, to Scheveling, where we took coach, and
so to the Hague, where walking, intending to find one that might
show us the King incognito, I met with Captn. Whittington (that
had formerly brought a letter to my Lord from the Mayor of
London) and he did promise me to do it, but first we went and dined.
At dinner in came Dr Cade, a merry mad parson of the King's. And
they two got the child and me (the others not being able to crowd in)
to see the King, who kissed the child very affectionately. Then we
kissed his, and the Duke of York's, and the Princess Royal's hands.
The King seems to be a very sober man; and a very splendid Court
he hath in the number of persons of quality that are about him;
English very rich in habit. From the King to the Lord Chancellor,
who did lie bed-rid of the gout: he spoke very merrily to the child
and me. After that, going to see the Queen of Bohemia, I met Dr
Fuller, whom I sent to a tavern with Mr Edw. Pickering, while I and
the rest went to see the Queen, who used us very respectfully: her
hand we all kissed. She seems a very debonaire, but a plain lady. In a
coach we went to see a house of the Princess Dowager's[96] in a park
about a mile from the Hague, where there is one of the most

95 Mary, eldest daughter of Charles I, and widow of the Prince of Orange who
died 1646–47. She was carried off by the small-pox, December 1660, leaving a son,
afterwards King William III.
96 Mary, daughter of Charles I.

beautiful rooms for pictures in the whole world. She had here one picture upon the top, with these words, dedicating it to the memory of her husband: *Incomparabili marito, inconsolabilis vidua.*

18th. Very early up, and, hearing that the Duke of York, our Lord High Admiral, would go on board to-day, Mr Pickering and I took waggon for Scheveling. But the wind being so very high that no boats could get off from shore, we returned to the Hague (having breakfasted with a gentleman of the Duke's and Commissioner Pett, sent on purpose to give notice to my Lord of his coming); we got a boy of the town to go along with us, and he showed us the church where Van Trump lies entombed with a very fine monument. His epitaph is concluded thus: *Tandem Bello Anglico tantum non victor, certe invictus, vivere et vincere desiit.* There is a sea-fight cut in marble, with the smoake, the best expressed that ever I saw in my life. From thence to the great church, that stands in a fine great market-place, over against the Stadt-house, and there I saw a stately tombe of the old Prince of Orange, of marble and brass; wherein among other rarities there are the angels with their trumpets expressed as it were crying. Here were very fine organs in both the churches. It is a most sweet town, with bridges, and a river in every street. We met with Commissioner Pett going down to the water-side with Major Harly, who is going upon a dispatch into England.

19th. Up early and went to Scheveling, where I found no getting on board, though the Duke of York sent every day to see whether he could do it or no. By waggon to Lausdune, where the 365 children were born. We saw the hill where they say the house stood wherein the children were born. The basins wherein the male and female children were baptized do stand over a large table that hangs upon a wall, with the whole story of the thing in Dutch and Latin, beginning, '*Margarita Herman Comitissa*', &c. The thing was done about 200 years ago.

20th. Commissioner Pett at last came to our lodging, and caused the boats to go off; so some in one boat and some in another we all bid adieu to the shore. But through the badness of weather we were in great danger, and a great while before we could get to the ship. This hath not been known four days together such weather this time of year, a great while. Indeed our fleet was thought to be in great danger, but we found all well.

21st. The weather foul all this day also. After dinner, about writing one thing or other all day, and setting my papers in order, hearing by letters that came hither in my absence, that the Parliament had ordered all persons to be secured, in order to a trial, that did sit as judges in the late King's death, and all the officers attending the Court. Sir John Lenthall moving in the House, that all that had borne arms against the King should be exempted from pardon, he was called to the bar of the House, and after a severe reproof he was degraded his knighthood. At Court I find that all things grow high. The old clergy talk as being sure of their lands again, and laugh at the Presbytery; and it is believed that the sales of the King's and Bishops' lands will never be confirmed by Parliament, there being nothing now in any man's power to hinder them and the King from doing what they had a mind, but everybody willing to submit to any thing. We expect every day to have the King and Duke on board as soon as it is fair. My Lord does nothing now, but offers all things to the pleasure of the Duke as Lord High Admiral. So that I am at a loss what to do.

22nd. News brought that the two Dukes are coming on board, which, by and by, they did, in a Dutch boat, the Duke of York in yellow trimmings, the Duke of Gloucester in grey and red. My Lord went in a boat to meet them, the Captain, myself, and others, standing at the entering port. So soon as they were entered we shot the guns off round the fleet. After that they went to view the ship all over, and were most exceedingly pleased with it. They seem to be very fine gentlemen. After that done, upon the quarter-deck table, under the awning, the Duke of York and my Lord, Mr Coventry[97] and I, spent an hour at allotting to every ship their service, in their return

97 Sir William Coventry, to whom Mr Pepys became so warmly attached afterwards, was the youngest son of Thomas first Lord Coventry, and Lord Keeper. He entered at Queen's College, Oxford, in 1642: and on his return from his travels was made Secretary to the Duke of York, and elected MP for Yarmouth. In 1662 he was appointed a Commissioner of the Admiralty: in 1665 knighted and sworn a privy Counsellor; and in 1667, constituted a Commissioner of the Treasury, but having been forbid the Court, on account of his challenging the Duke of Buckingham, he retired into the country, nor could he subsequently be prevailed upon to accept of any official employment. Burnet calls Sir W. C. the best speaker in the House of Commons, and a man of great notions and eminent virtues: and Mr Pepys never omits an opportunity of paying a tribute to his public and private worth. Died 1686, aged 60.

to England; which being done, they went to dinner, where the table was very full: the two Dukes at the upper end, my Lord Opdam next on one side, and my Lord on the other. Two guns given to every man while he was drinking the King's health, and so likewise to the Duke's health. I took down Monsieur d'Esquier to the great cabbin below, and dined with him in state along with only one or two friends of his. All dinner the harper belonging to Captain Sparling played to the Dukes. After dinner, the Dukes and my Lord to sea, the Vice and Rear-Admirals and I in a boat after them. After that done, they made to the shore in the Dutch boat that brought them, and I got into the boat with them; but the shore was full of people to expect their coming. When we came near the shore, my Lord left them and come into his own boat, and Pen and I with him; my Lord being very well pleased with this day's work. By the time we came on board again, news is sent us that the King is on shore; so my Lord fired all his guns round twice, and all the fleet after him. The gun over against my cabbin I fired myself to the King, which was the first time that he had been saluted by his own ships since this change; but holding my head too much over the gun, I had almost spoiled my right eye. Nothing in the world but giving of guns almost all this day. In the evening we began to remove cabbins; I to the carpenter's cabbin, and Dr Clerke with me. Many of the King's servants come on board to-night; and so many Dutch of all sorts come to see the ship till it was quite dark, that we could not pass by one another, which was a great trouble to us all. This afternoon Mr Downing (who was knighted yesterday by the King) was here on board, and had a ship for his passage into England, with his lady and servants. By the same token he called me to him when I was going to write the order, to tell me that I must write him Sir G. Downing. My Lord lay in the roundhouse tonight. This evening I was late writing a French letter by my Lord's order to Monsieur Wragh, Embassador de Denmarke à la Haye, which my Lord signed in bed.

23rd. In the morning come infinity of people on board from the King to go along with him. My Lord, Mr Crewe, and others, go on shore to meet the King as he comes off from shore, where Sir R. Stayner, bringing His Majesty into the boat, I hear that His Majesty did with a great deal of affection kiss my Lord upon his first meeting. The King, with the two Dukes and Queen of Bohemia, Princesse

Royalle, and Prince of Orange, come on board, where I in their coming in kissed the King's, Queen's and Princesse's hands, having done the other before. Infinite shooting off of the guns, and that in a disorder on purpose, which was better than if it had been otherwise. All day nothing but Lords and persons of honour on board, that we were exceeding full. Dined in a great deal of state, the Royalle company by themselves in the coach, which was a blessed sight to see. After dinner the King and Duke altered the name of some of the ships, viz. the *Nazeby* into *Charles*;[98] the *Richard*, *James*; the *Speaker*, *Mary*; the *Dunbar* (which was not in company with us), the *Henry*; *Winsly*, *Happy Return*; *Wakefield*, *Richmond*; *Lambert*, the *Henrietta*; *Cheriton*, the *Speedwell*; *Bradford*, the *Successe*. That done, the Queen, Princesse Royalle, and Prince of Orange, took leave of the King, and the Duke of York went on board the *London*, and the Duke of Gloucester, the *Swiftsure*. Which done, we weighed anchor, and with a fresh gale and most happy weather we set sail for England. All the afternoon the King walked here and there, up and down (quite contrary to what I thought him to have been) very active and stirring. Upon the quarter-deck he fell into discourse of his escape from *Worcester*, where it made me ready to weep to hear the stories that he told of his difficulties that he had passed through, as his travelling four days and three nights on foot, every step up to his knees in dirt, with nothing but a green coat and a pair of country breeches on, and a pair of country shoes that made him so sore all over his feet, that he could scarce stir. Yet he was forced to run away from a miller and other company, that took them for rogues. His sitting at table at one place, where the master of the house, that had not seen him in eight years, did know him, but kept it private; when at the same table there was one that had been of his own regiment at Worcester, could not know him, but made him drink the King's health, and said that the King was at least four fingers higher than he. At another place he was by some servants of the house made to drink, that they might know that he was not a Roundhead, which they swore he was. In another place at his inn, the master of the house, as the King was standing with his hands upon the back of a chair by the fire-side, kneeled down and

<hr/>

98   The *Nazeby* now no longer England's shame,
              But better to be lost in Charles his name.

                                  Dryden's *Astraea Redux*.

kissed his hand, privately, saying, that he would not ask him who he was, but bid God bless him whither he was going. Then the difficulties in getting a boat to get into France, where he was fain to plot with the master thereof to keep his design from the foreman and a boy (which was all the ship's company), and so get to Fecamp in France. At Rouen he looked so poorly, that the people went into the rooms before he went away to see whether he had not stole something or other. In the evening I went up to my Lord to write letters for England, which we sent away with word of our coming, by Mr Edw. Pickering. The King supped alone in the coach; after that I got a dish, and we four supped in my cabbin, as at noon. About bed-time my Lord Bartlett[99] (who I had offered my service to before) sent for me to get him a bed, who with much ado I did get to bed to my Lord Middlesex[100] in the great cabbin below, but I was cruelly troubled before I could dispose of him, and quit myself of him. So to my cabbin again, where the company still was, and were talking more of the King's difficulties; as how he was fain to eat a piece of bread and cheese out of a poor body's pocket; how, at a Catholique house, he was fain to lie in the priest's hole a good while in the house for his privacy. After that our company broke up. We have all the Lords Commissioners on board us, and many others. Under sail all night, and most glorious weather.

24th. Up, and made myself as fine as I could, with the linning stockings on and wide canons that I bought the other day at Hague. Extraordinary press of noble company, and great mirth all the day. There dined with me in my cabbin (that is, the carpenter's) Dr Earle[101] and Mr Hollis, the King's Chaplins, Dr Scarborough,[102] Dr Quarterman,[103] and Dr Clerke, Physicians, Mr Daray, and Mr Fox,[104] (both very fine gentlemen) the King's servants, where we had

99 A mistake, for Lord Berkeley, who had been deputed with Lord Middlesex and four other Peers by the House of Lords, to present an address of congratulation to the King.

100 Lionel, third and last Earl of Middlesex. Died 1674.

101 John Earle, Dean of Westminster, successively Bishop of Worcester and Salisbury. Died 1665.

102 Charles Scarborough, MD, principal Physician to Charles II (by whom he was knighted in 1669), James II, and William III, a learned and incomparable anatomist.

103 William Quarterman, MD, of Pembroke College, Oxford.

104 Afterwards Sir Stephen Fox, Knight, Paymaster to the Forces.

brave discourse. Walking upon the decks, were persons of honour all
the afternoon, among others, Thomas Killigrew,[105] (a merry droll,
but a gentleman of great esteem with the King,) who told us many
merry stories. At supper the three Drs. of Physique again at my
cabbin; where I put Dr Scarborough in mind of what I heard him
say, that children do, in every day's experience, look several ways
with both their eyes, till custom teaches them otherwise. And that we
do now see but with one eye, our eyes looking in parallel lynes. After
this discourse I was called to write a pass for my Lord Mandeville[106]
to take up horses to London, which I wrote in the King's name, and
carried it to him to sign, which was the first and only one that ever he
signed in the ship *Charles*. To bed, coming in sight of land a little
before night.

25th. By the morning we were come close to the land, and every
body made ready to get on shore. The King and the two Dukes did
eat their breakfast before they went, and there being set some ship's
diet, they eat of nothing else but pease and pork, and boiled beef. Dr
Clerke, who eat with me, told me how the King had given £50 to
Mr Shepley for my Lord's servants, and £500 among the officers and
common men of the ship. I spoke to the Duke of York about
business, who called me Pepys by name, and upon my desire did
promise me his future favour. Great expectation of the King's making
some Knights, but there was none. About noon (though the
brigantine that Beale made was there ready to carry him) yet he
would go in my Lord's barge with the two Dukes. Our Captn.
steered, and my Lord went along bare with him. I went, and Mr
Mansell, and one of the King's footmen, and a dog that the King
loved, in a boat by ourselves, and so got on shore when the King did,
who was received by General Monk with all imaginable love and
respect at his entrance upon the land of Dover. Infinite the crowd of
people and the horsemen, citizens, and noblemen of all sorts. The
Mayor of the town come and gave him his white staffe, the badge of
his place, which the King did give him again. The Mayor also

105 Thomas Killigrew, younger son of Sir Robert Killigrew, of Hanworth,
Middlesex, Page of Honour to Charles I, and Groom of the Bedchamber to Charles
II, whose fortunes he had followed. He was resident at Venice, 1651; a great
favourite with the King on account of his uncommon vein of humour, and author
of several plays. Died 1682.
106 Eldest son of the Earl of Manchester.

presented him from the town a very rich Bible, which he took and said it was the thing that he loved above all things in the world. A canopy was provided for him to stand under, which he did, and talked awhile with General Monk and others, and so into a stately coach there set for him, and so away through the towne towards Canterbury, without making any stay at Dover. The shouting and joy expressed by all is past imagination. Seeing that my Lord did not stir out of his barge, I got into a boat and so into his barge. My Lord almost transported with joy that he had done all this without any the least blur or obstruction in the world, that could give offence to any, and with the great honour he thought it would be to him. Being overtook by the brigantine, my Lord and we went out of our barge into it, and so went on board with Sir W. Batten[107] and the Vice and Rear-Admirals. At night I supped with the Captn., who told me what the King had given us. My Lord returned late, and at his coming did give me order to cause the marke to be gilded, and a Crowne and C. R. to be made at the head of the coach table, where the King to-day with his own hand did marke his height, which accordingly I caused the painter to do, and is now done as is to be seen.

26th. My Lord dined with the Vice-Admiral to-day (who is as officious, poor man! as any spaniel can be; but I believe all to no purpose, for I believe he will not hold his place); so I dined commander at the coach table to-day, and all the officers of the ship with me, and Mr White of Dover. After a game or two at nine-pins, to work all the afternoon, making above twenty orders. In the evening my Lord having been a-shore, the first time that he hath been a-shore since he come out of the *Hope*, (having resolved not to go till he had brought his Majesty into England,) returned on board with a great deal of pleasure. The Captain told me that my Lord had appointed me £30 out of the 1000 ducats which the King had given to the ship.

27th (Lord's day). Called up by John Goods to see the Garter and Heralds coate, which lay in the coach, brought by Sir Edward Walker, King at Armes, this morning, for my Lord. My Lord had summoned all the Commanders on board him, to see the ceremony,

107 A Commissioner in the Navy, and in 1661 MP for Rochester.

which was thus: Sir Edward putting on his coate, and having laid the George and Garter, and the King's letter to my Lord, upon a crimson cushion, (in the coach, all the Commanders standing by,) makes three congees to him, holding the cushion in his arms. Then laying it down with the things upon it upon a chair, he takes the letter, and delivers it to my Lord, which my Lord breaks open and gives him to read. It was directed to our trusty and well beloved Sir Edward Montagu, Knight, one of our Generals at sea, and our Companion elect of our Noble Order of the Garter. The contents of the letter is to show that the Kings of England have for many years made use of this honour, as a special mark of favour, to persons of good extraction and valour, (and that many Emperors, Kings and Princes of other countries have borne this honour), and that whereas my Lord is of a noble family, and hath now done the King such service by sea, at this time, as he hath done; he do send him this George and Garter to wear as Knight of the Order, with a dispensation for the other ceremonies of the habit of the Order, and other things, till hereafter, when it can be done. So the herald putting the ribbon about his neck, and the Garter on his left leg, he saluted him with joy as Knight of the Garter. And after that was done he took his leave of my Lord, and so to shore again to the King at Canterbury, where he yesterday gave the like honour to General Monk, who are the only two for many years that have had the Garter given them, before they had honours of Earldome, or the like, excepting only the Duke of Buckingham, who was only Sir George Villiers when he was made Knight of the Garter.[108]

29th. Abroad to shore with my Lord, (which he offered me of himself, saying that I had a great deal of work to do this month, which was very true.) On shore we took horses, my Lord and Mr Edward, Mr Hetly and I, and three or four servants, and had a great deal of pleasure in riding. At last we came upon a very high cliffe by the sea-side, and rode under it, we having laid great wagers, I and Dr Mathews, that it was not so high as Paul's; my Lord and Mr Hetly, that it was. But we riding under it, my Lord made a pretty good measure of it with two sticks, and found it to be not thirty-five yards high, and Paul's is reckoned to be about ninety. From thence toward the barge again, and in our way found the people of Deale going to

108 In 1616.

make a bonfire for joy of the day, it being the King's birthday, and had some guns which they did fire at my Lord's coming by. For which I did give twenty shillings among them to drink. While we were on the top of the cliffe, we saw and heard our guns in the fleet go off for the same joy. And it being a pretty fair day we could see above twenty miles into France. Being returned on board, my Lord called for Mr Shepley's book of Paul's, by which we were confirmed in our wager. This day, it is thought, the King do enter the City of London.

30th. All this morning making up my accounts, in which I counted that I had made myself now worth about £80, at which my heart was glad, and blessed God.

June 1st. At night Mr Cook comes from London with letters, leaving all things there very gallant and joyful. And brought us word that the Parliament had ordered the 29th of May, the King's birth-day, to be for ever kept as a day of thanksgiving for our redemption from tyranny, and the King's return to his Government, he entering London that day.

2nd. Being with my Lord in the morning about business in his cabbin, I took occasion to give him thanks for his love to me in the share that he had given me of his Majesty's money, and the Duke's. He told me he hoped to do me a more lasting kindness, if all things stand as they are now between him and the King, but, says he, 'We must have a little patience and we will rise together; in the mean time I will do yet all the good jobs I can.' Which was great content for me to hear from my Lord. All the morning with the Captain, computing how much the thirty ships that come with the King from Scheveling their pay comes to for a month (because the King promised to give them all a month's pay), and it comes to £6538, and the *Charles* particularly £777. I wish we had the money.

3rd. Captaine Holland is come to get an order for the setting out of his ship, and to renew his commission. He tells me how every man goes to the Lord Mayor to set down their names, as such as do accept of his Majesty's pardon, and showed me a certificate under the Lord Mayor's hand, that he had done so.

At sermon in the morning; after dinner into my cabbin, to cast my accounts up, and find myself to be worth near £100 for which I bless Almighty God, it being more than I hoped for so soon, being I believe not clearly worth £25 when I come to sea besides my house and goods.

4th This morning the King's Proclamation against drinking, swearing, and debauchery, was read to our ships' companies in the fleet, and indeed it gives great satisfaction to all.

6th. In the morning I had letters come, that told me among other things, that my Lord's place of Clerke of the Signet was fallen to him, which he did most lovingly tell me that I should execute, in case he could not get a better employment for me at the end of the year. Because he thought that the Duke of York would command all, but he hoped that the Duke would not remove me but to my advantage.

My letters tell me, that Mr Calamy[109] had preached before the King in a surplice (this I heard afterwards to be false); that my Lord, Gen. Monk, and three more Lords, are made Commissioners for the Treasury; that my Lord had some great place conferred on him, and they say Master of the Wardrobe; and the two Dukes do haunt the Park much, and that they were at a play, Madam Epicene,[110] the other day; that Sir Ant. Cooper,[111] Mr Hollis, and Mr Annesly, late Presidents of the Council of State, are made Privy Councillors to the King.

7th. After dinner come Mr John Wright and Mr Moore, with the sight of whom my heart was very glad. They brought an order for my Lord's coming up to London, which my Lord resolved to do to-morrow. All the afternoon getting my things in order to set forth tomorrow. At night walked up and down with Mr Moore, who did give me an account of all things at London. Among others, how the Presbyterians would be angry if they durst, but they will not be able to do any thing.

8th. Out early, took horses at Deale.

9th. To White Hall with my Lord and Mr Edwd. Montagu. Found the King in the Park. There walked. Gallantly great.

---

109 Edward Calamy, the celebrated Nonconformist Divine, born 1616, appointed Chaplain to Charles II 1660. Died 1666.
110 *Epicoene*, or *The Silent Woman*, a comedy by Ben Jonson.
111 Afterwards Chancellor, and created Earl of Shaftesbury.

11th. With my Lord to Dorset House[112] to the Chancellor.

13th. By water with my Lord in a boat to Westminster, and to the Admiralty, now in a new place.

15th. My Lord told me how the King has given him the place of the great Wardrobe.

16th. To my Lord, and so to White Hall with him about the Clerk of the Privy Seale's place, which he is to have. Then to the Admiralty, where I wrote some letters. Here Coll. Thompson told me, as a great secret, that the *Nazeby* was on fire when the King was there, but that is not known; when God knows it is quite false.

17th (Lord's day). To Mr Messinn's; a good sermon. This day the organs did begin to play at White Hall before the King. After dinner to Mr Messinn's again, and so in the garden, and heard Chippell's father preach, that was Page to the Protector.

18th. To my Lord's, where much business. With him to the Parliament House, where he did intend to have made his appearance today, but he met Mr Crewe upon the stairs, and would not go in. He went to Mrs Brown's, and staid till word was brought him what was done in the House. This day they made an end of the twenty men to be excepted from pardon to their estates. By barge to Stepney with my Lord, where at Trinity House we had great entertainment. With my Lord there went Sir W. Pen, Sir H. Wright, Hetly, Pierce, Creed, Hill, I and other servants. Back again to the Admiralty, and so to my Lord's lodgings, where he told me that he did look after the place of the Clerk of the Acts for me.

19th. Much business at my Lord's. This morning my Lord went into the House of Commons, and there had the thanks of the House, in the name of the Parliament and Commons of England, for his late service to his King and Country. A motion was made for a reward for him, but it was quashed by Mr Annesly, who, above most men, is engaged to my Lord's and Mr Crewe's favours. My Lord went at night with the King to Baynard's Castle to supper, and I home.

112 Dorset-House, in Salisbury Court, at this time occupied by the Chancellor, once the residence of the Bishops of Salisbury, one of whom (Jewel) alienated it to the Sackville family. The house being afterwards pulled down, a theatre was built on its site, in which the Duke of York's troop performed.

20th. With my Lord (who lay long in bed this day, because he came home late from supper with the King) to the Parliament House, and, after that, with him to General Monk's, where he dined at the Cockpit. Thence to the Admiralty, and despatched away Mr Cooke to sea; whose business was a letter from my Lord about Mr G. Montagu to be chosen as a Parliament-man in my Lord's room at Dover; and another to the Vice-Admiral to give my Lord a constant account of all things in the fleet, merely that he may thereby keep up his power there; another letter to Captn. Cuttance to send the barge that brought the King on shore, to Hinchingbroke by Lynne.

21st. To my Lord, much business. With him to the Council Chamber, where he was sworne; and the charge of his being admitted Privy Counsellor is £56. To White Hall, where the King being gone abroad, my Lord and I walked a great while discoursing of the simplicity of the Protector, in his losing all that his father had left him. My Lord told me, that the last words that he parted with the Protector with (when he went to the Sound), were, that he should rejoice more to see him in his grave at his return home, than that he should give way to such things as were then in hatching, and afterwards did ruine him: and that the Protector said, that whatever G. Montagu, my Lord Broghill,[113] Jones, and the Secretary, would have him to do, he would do it, be it what it would.

22nd. To my Lord, where much business. With him to White Hall, where the Duke of York not being up, we walked a good while in the Shield Gallery. Mr Hill (who for these two or three days hath constantly attended my Lord) told me of an offer of £500 for a Baronet's dignity, which I told my Lord of in the balcone of this gallery, and he said he would think of it. My dear friend Mr Fuller of Twickenham and I dined alone at the Sun Tavern, where he told me how he had the grant of being Dean of St Patrick's, in Ireland; and I told him my condition, and both rejoiced one for another. Thence to my Lord's and had the great coach to Brigham's, who told me how my Lady Monk deals with him and others for their places, asking him £500 though he was formerly the King's coach-maker, and sworn to it.

113 Roger Boyle, Lord Broghill, created Earl of Orrery, 1660. Died 1679.

23rd. To my Lord's lodgings, where Tom Guy come to me, and there staid to see the King touch people for the King's evil. But he did not come at all, it rayned so; and the poor people were forced to stand all the morning in the rain in the garden. Afterward he touched them in the banquetting-house. With my Lord, to my Lord Frezendorfe's,[114] where he dined today. He told me that he had obtained a promise of the Clerke of the Acts place for me, at which I was glad.

25th. With my Lord at White Hall all the morning. I spoke with Mr Coventry about my business, who promised me all the assistance I could expect. Dined with young Mr Powell, lately come from the Sound, being amused at our great charges here, and Mr Southerne, now Clerke to Mr Coventry, at the Leg in King-street. Thence to the Admiralty, where I met Mr Turner, of the Navy-office, who did look after the place of Clerke of the Acts. He was very civil to me, and I to him, and shall be so. There come a letter from my Lady Monk to my Lord about it this evening, but he refused to come to her, but meeting in White Hall, with Sir Thomas Clarges, her brother, my Lord returned answer, that he could not desist in my business; and that he believed that General Monk would take it ill if my Lord should name the officers in his army; and therefore he desired to have the naming of one officer in the fleete. With my Lord by coach to Mr Crewe's, and very merry by the way, discoursing of the late changes and his good fortune. Thence home, and then with my wife to Dorset-House, to deliver a list of the names of the justices of peace for Huntingdonshire.

26th. My Lord dined at his lodgings all alone today. I went to Secretary Nicholas to carry him my Lord's resolutions about his title, which he had chosen, and that is Portsmouth.

To Backewell[115] the goldsmith's, and there we chose a £100 worth of plate for my Lord to give Secretary Nicholas.

27th. With my Lord to the Duke, where he spoke to Mr Coventry to despatch my business of the Acts, in which place every body gives me joy, as if I were in it, which God send.

114 John Frederic de Friesendorff, Ambassador from Sweden to Charles II, who created him a Baronet 1661.
115 Edward Bakewell, an Alderman of London, and opulent banker, ruined by the shutting up of the Exchequer in 1672, when he retired to Holland, where he died.

28th. To Sir G. Downing, the first visit I have made him since he come. He is so stingy a fellow I care not to see him; I quite cleared myself of his office, and did give him liberty to take any body in. After all this to my Lord, who lay a–bed till eleven o'clock, it being almost five before he went to–bed, they supped so late last night with the King. This morning I saw poor Bishop Wren[116] going to Chappel, it being a thanksgiving day for the King's returne.

29th. Up and to White Hall, where I got my warrant from the Duke to be Clerke of the Acts. Also I got my Lord's warrant from the Secretary for his honour of Earle of Portsmouth, and Viscount Montagu of Hinchingbroke. So to my Lord, to give him an account of what I had done. Then to Sir Geffery Palmer,[117] who told me that my Lord must have some good Latinist to make the preamble to his Patent, which must express his late service in the best terms that he can, and he told me in what high flaunting terms Sir J. Greenville had caused his to be done, which he do not like; but that Sir Richard Fanshawe[118] had done General Monk's very well. Then to White Hall, where I was told by Mr Hutchinson at the Admiralty, that Mr Barlow, my predecessor, Clerke of the Acts, is yet alive, and coming up to town to look after his place, which made my heart sad a little. At night told my Lord thereof, and he bad me get possession of my Patent; and he would do all that could be done to keep him out. This night my Lord and I looked over the list of the Captains, and marked some that my Lord had a mind to put out.

30th. By times to Sir R. Fanshawe to draw up the preamble to my Lord's patent. So to my Lord, and with him to White Hall, where I saw a great many fine antique heads of marble, that my Lord Northumberland[119] had given the King. To White Hall with Mr Moore, where I met with a letter from Mr Turner, offering me £150 to be joined with me in my patent, and to advise me how to improve

---

116 Matthew Wren, Bishop of Ely. Died 1667, aged 82.

117 Sir Geoffrey Palmer, Attorney General, and Chief Justice of Chester, 1660; created a Baronet, 1661. Died 1670.

118 Sir Richard Fanshawe, Knight and Baronet, Secretary to Charles II in Scotland, and after the Restoration employed on several embassies. He was a good linguist, and translated the *Lusiad* and *Pastor Fido*.

119 Algernon Percy, tenth Earl of Northumberland.

the advantage of my place, and to keep off Barlow. This day come Will,[120] my boy, to me: the maid continuing lame.

July 1st. This morning come home my fine Camlett cloak, with gold buttons, and a silk suit, which cost me much money, and I pray God to make me able to pay for it. In the afternoon to the Abbey, where a good sermon by a stranger, but no Common Prayer yet.

2nd. All the afternoon with my Lord, going up and down the town; at seven at night he went home, and there the principal Officers of the Navy,[121] among the rest myself was reckoned one. We had order to meet to-morrow, to draw up such an order of the Council as would put us into action before our patents were passed. At which my heart was glad. At night supped with my Lord, he and I together, in a great dining-room alone by ourselves.

3rd. The Officers and Commissioners of the Navy met at Sir G. Carteret's[122] chamber, and agreed upon orders for the Council to

120 William Hewer, respecting whose origin I can only make out, that he was a nephew to Mr Blackburne, so often mentioned in these pages, where his father's death, of the plague, also occurs. He became afterwards a Commissioner of the Navy, and Treasurer for Tangier ; and was the constant companion of Mr Pepys, who died in his house at Clapham, previously the residence of Sir Dennis Gauden. Mr Hewer was buried in the old Church at Clapham, where there is a large monument of marble in *alto relievo* erected to his memory.

121 A list of the Officers of the Admiralty, 31st May, 1660, from a manuscript in the Pepysian Library.

His Royal Highness James, Duke of York, Lord High Admiral
Sir George Carteret, Treasurer
Sir Robert Slingsby, (soon after) Comptroller
Sir William Batten, Surveyor
Samuel Pepys, Esq., Clerk of the Acts
John, Lord Berkeley ⎫
Sir William Penn ⎬ Commissioners
Peter Pett, Esq. ⎭

122 Sir George Carteret, Knight, had originally been bred to the sea service, and became Comptroller of the Navy to Charles I, and Governor of Jersey, where he obtained considerable reputation by his gallant defence of that Island against the Parliament forces. At the Restoration he was made Vice-Chamberlain to the King, Treasurer of the Navy, and a Privy Councillor, and in 1661 MP for Portsmouth. He continued in favour with his sovereign till 1679, when he died in his 80th year. He married his cousin Elizabeth, daughter of Sir Philip Carteret, Knight, of St Ouen, and had issue three sons and five daughters.

supersede the old ones, and empower us to act. Dined with Mr Stephens, the treasurer of the Navy, and Mr Turner, to whom I offered £50 out of my own purse for one year, and the benefit of a Clerke's allowance beside, which he thanked me for; but I find he hath some design yet in his head, which I could not think of. In the afternoon my heart was quite pulled down, by being told that Mr Barlow was to enquire today for Mr Coventry; but at night I met with my Lord, who told me that I need not fear, for he would get me the place against the world. And when I come to W. Howe, he told me that Dr Petty had been with my Lord, and did tell him that Barlow was a sickly man, and did not intend to execute the place himself, which put me in great comfort again.

4th. To Mr Backewell's, the goldsmith, where I took my Lord's £100 in plate for Mr Secretary Nicholas, and my own piece of plate, being a state dish and cup in chased work for Mr Coventry, cost me above £19. Carried these and the money by coach to my Lord's at White Hall, and from thence carried Nicholas's plate to his house and left it there, intending to speak with him anon. So to my Lord's, and walking all the afternoon in White Hall Court, in expectation of what shall be done in the Council as to our business. It was strange to see how all the people flocked together bare, to see the King looking out of the Council window. At night my Lord told me how my orders that I drew last night about giving us power to act, are granted by the Council. At which I was very glad.

5th. This morning my brother Tom brought me my jackanapes coat with silver buttons. It rained this morning, which makes us fear that the glory of this day will be lost; the King and Parliament being to be entertained by the City today with great pomp. Mr Hater was with me today, and I agreed with him to be my clerke. Being at White Hall, I saw the King, the Dukes, and all their attendants go forth in the rain to the City, and it spoiled many a fine suit of clothes. I was forced to walk all the morning in White Hall, not knowing how to get out because of the rain. Met with Mr Cooling,[123] my Lord Chamberlain's secretary, who took me to dinner among the gentlemen waiters, and

123 Richard Cooling or Coling, AM, of All-Souls College, Secretary to the Earls of Manchester and Arlington, when they filled the office of Lord Chamberlain, and a Clerk of the Privy Council in ordinary. There is a mezzotinto print of him in the Pepysian Collection.

after dinner into the wine-cellar. He told me how he had a project for all us Secretaries to join together, and get money by bringing all business into our hands. Thence to the Admiralty, where Mr Blackburne and I (it beginning to hold up) went and walked an hour or two in the Park, he giving of me light in many things in my way in this office that I go about. And in the evening I got my presents of plate carried to Mr Coventry's. At my Lord's at night comes Dr Petty to me, to tell me that Barlow was come to town, and other things, which put me into a despair, and I went to bed very sad.

6th. In the afternoon my Lord and I, and Mr Coventry and Sir G. Carteret, went and took possession of the Navy-Office, whereby my mind was a little cheered, but my hopes not great. From thence Sir G. Carteret and I to the Treasurer's Office, where he set some things in order.

8th (Lord's day). To White Hall chapel, where I got in with ease by going before the Lord Chancellor with Mr Kipps. Here I heard very good musique, the first time that ever I remember to have heard the organs and singing-men in surplices in my life. The Bishop of Chichester[124] preached before the King, and made a great flattering sermon, which I did not like that the Clergy should meddle with matters of state. Dined with Mr Luellin and Salisbury at a cook's shop. Home, and staid all the afternoon with my wife till after sermon. There till Mr Fairebrother[125] come to call us out to my father's to supper. He told me how he had perfectly procured me to be made Master in Arts by proxy,[126] which did somewhat please me, though I remember my cousin Roger Pepys[127] was the other day persuading me from it.

124 Henry King, Dean of Rochester, advanced to the See of Chichester, 1641. Died 1669.

125 William Fairbrother, in 1661 made DD at Cambridge *per regias litteras*.

126 The Grace which passed the University, on this occasion, is preserved in Kennett's *Chronicle*, and commenced as follows: *Cum Sam Pepys, Coll. Magd. Inceptor in Artibus in Regia Classe existat e Secretis. exindeq. apud mare adeo occupatissimus ut Comitiis proxime futuris interesse non possit; placet vobis ut dictus S. P. admissionem suam necnon creationem recipiat ad gradum Magistri in Artibus sub persona Timothei Wellfit Inceptoris*, &c. &c. – June 26, 1660.

127 Roger Pepys, a Barrister, MP for Cambridge, 1661, and afterwards Recorder of that town.

9th. To the Navy-office,[128] where in the afternoon we met and sat, and there I begun to sign bills in the Office the first time.

10th. This day I put on my new silk suit, the first that ever I wore in my life. Home, and called my wife, and took her to Clodins's to a great wedding of Nan Hartlib to Mynheer Roder, which was kept at Goring House[129] with very great state, cost, and noble company. But among all the beauties there, my wife was thought the greatest. And finding my Lord in White Hall garden, I got him to go to the Secretary's, which he did, and desired the dispatch of his and my bills to be signed by the King. His bill is to be Earle of Sandwich, Viscount Hinchingbroke, and Baron of St Neot's. Home, with my mind pretty quiet: not returning, as I said I would, to see the bride put to bed.

11th. With Sir W. Pen[130] by water to the Navy-office, where we met, and dispatched business. And that being done, we went all to dinner to the Dolphin, upon Major Brown's invitation. After that to the office again, where I was vexed, and so was Commissioner Pett, to see a busy fellow come to look out the best lodgings for my Lord Barkley, and the combining between him and Sir W. Pen; and, indeed, was troubled much at it.

12th. Up early and by coach to White Hall with Commissioner Pett, where, after we had talked with my Lord, I went to the Privy Seale and got my bill perfected there, and at the Signet: and then to the House of Lords, and met with Mr Kipps, who directed me to Mr Beale to get my patent engrossed; but he not having time to get it done in Chancery-hand, I was forced to run all up and down Chancery-lane, and the Six Clerks' Office, but could find none that

128 The Navy Office was erected on the site of Lumley House, formerly belonging to the *Fratres Sanctae Crucis* (or Crutched Friars), and all business connected with Naval concerns was transacted there, till its removal to Somerset House.
129 Goring House was burnt in 1674, at which time Lord Arlington resided in it.
130 Sir William Pen was born at Bristol in 1621; of the ancient family of the Pens of Pen Lodge, Wilts. He was Captain at the age of 21; Rear-Admiral of Ireland at 23; Vice-Admiral of England, and General in the first Dutch war at 32. He was subsequently MP for Weymouth, Governor of Kinsale, and Vice-Admiral of Munster. After the Dutch fight in 1665, where he distinguished himself as second in command under the Duke of York, he took leave of the sea, but continued to act as a Commissioner for the Navy till 1669, when he retired on account of his bodily infirmities to Wanstead, and died there September 16, 1670, aged 49.

could write the hand, that were at leisure. And so in despair went to
the Admiralty, where we met the first time there, my Lord Montagu,
my Lord Barkley, Mr Coventry, and all the rest of the principal
Officers and Commissioners, except only the Controller, who is not
yet chosen.

13th. Up early, the first day that I put on my black camlett coat with
silver buttons. To Mr Spong, whom I found in his night-gown
writing of my patent. It being done, we carried it to Worcester
House,[131] to the Chancellor, where Mr Kipps got me the Chancellor's *recepi* to my bill; and so carried it to Mr Beale for a dockett; but
he was very angry, and unwilling to do it, because he said it was ill
writ, (because I had got it writ by another hand, and not by him); but
by much importunity I got Mr Spong to go to his office and make an
end of my patent; and in the mean time Mr Beale to be preparing my
dockett, which being done, I did give him two pieces, after which it
was strange how civil and tractable he was to me. Met with Mr
Spong, who still would be giving me council of getting my patent
out, for fear of another change, and my Lord Montagu's fall. After
that to Worcester House, where by Mr Kipps's means, and my
pressing in General Montagu's name to the Chancellor, I did, beyond
all expectation, get my seal passed; and while it was doing in one
room, I was forced to keep Sir G. Carteret (who by chance met me
there, ignorant of my business) in talk. I to my Lord's, where I
dispatched an order for a ship to fetch Sir R. Honywood home. Late
writing letters; and great doings of musique at the next house, which
was Whally's; the King and Dukes there with Madame Palmer,[132] a
pretty woman that they had a fancy to. Here at the old door that did
go into his lodgings, my Lord, I, and W. Howe, did stand listening a
great while to the musique.

---

131 The Earls of Worcester had a large house between Durham Place and the
Savoy, which Lord Clarendon rented at £5 per annum, while his own was
building.
132 Barbara Villiers, daughter of William Viscount Grandison, wife of Roger
Palmer, Esq., created Earl of Castlemaine, 1661. She became the King's mistress
soon after the Restoration, and was in 1670 made Duchess of Cleveland. She died
1709, aged 69.

14th Comes in Mr Pagan Fisher,[133] the poet, and promises me what he had long ago done, a book in praise of the King of France, with my armes, and a dedication to me very handsome.

15th. My wife and I mightily pleased with our new house that we hope to have. My patent has cost me a great deal of money; about £40. In the afternoon to Henry VII's Chapel, where I heard a Sermon.

17th. This morning (as indeed all the mornings now-adays) much business at my Lord's. There come to my house before I went out Mr Barlow, an old consumptive man, and fair conditioned. After much talk, I did grant him what he asked, viz. £50 per annum, if my salary be not increased, and £100 per annum, in case it be £350 at which he was very well pleased to be paid as I received my money, and not otherwise, so I brought him to my Lord's and he and I did agree together.

18th. This morning we met at the office: I dined at my house in Seething Lane.

19th. We did talk of our old discourse when we did use to talk of the King, in the time of the Rump, privately; after that to the Admiralty Office, in White Hall, where I staid and writ my late observations for these four days last past. Great talk of the difference between the Episcopal and Presbyterian Clergy, but I believe it will come to nothing.

22nd. After dinner to White Hall, where I find my Lord at home, and walked in the garden with him, he showing me all respect. I left him and went to walk in the inward Park, but could not get in; one

133 Payne Fisher, who styled himself Paganus Piscator, was born in 1616, in Dorsetshire, and removed from Hart Hall, Oxford, of which he had been a commoner, to Magdalene College, Cambridge, in 1634; and there took a degree of BA, and first discovered a turn for poetry. He was afterwards a Captain in the King's service at Marston Moor fight; but leaving his command, employed his pen against the cause which he had supported with his sword, and became a favourite of Cromwell's. After the King's return, he obtained a scanty subsistence by flattering men in power, and was frequently imprisoned for debt. He died in 1693. He published several poems, chiefly in Latin ; and, in 1682, printed a book of Heraldry, with the arms of such of the gentry as he had waited upon with presentation copies. He was a man of talents, but vain, unsteady, and conceited, and a great time-server.

man was basted by the keeper, for carrying some people over on his back, through the water. Home, and at night had a chapter read; and I read prayers out of the Common Prayer Book, the first time that ever I read prayers in this house. So to bed.

23rd. After dinner to my Lord, who took me to Secretary Nicholas;[134] and before him and Secretary Morris,[135] my Lord and I upon our knees together took our oaths of Allegiance and Supremacy; and the Oath of the Privy Seale, of which I was much glad, though I am not likely to get anything by it at present; but I do desire it, for fear of a turn-out of our office.

24th. To White Hall, where I did acquaint Mr Watkins with my being sworn into the Privy Seale, at which he was much troubled, but did offer me a kinsman of his to be my clerk. In the afternoon I spent much time in walking in White Hall Court with Mr Bickerstaffe,[136] who was very glad of my Lord's being sworn, because of his business with his brother Baron,[136] which is referred to my Lord Chancellor, and to be ended to-morrow. Baron had got a grant beyond sea, to come in before the reversionary of the Privy Seale.

25th. I got my certificate of my Lord's and I being sworn. This morning my Lord took leave of the House of Commons, and had the thanks of the House for his great service to his country.[137]

26th. Early to White Hall, thinking to have a meeting of my Lord and the principal officers, but my Lord could not, it being the day that he was to go and be admitted in the House of Lords, his patent being done, which he presented upon his knees to the Speaker; and so it was read in the House, and he took his place. T. Doling carried me to St James's Fair, and there meeting with W. Symons and his wife, and Luellin, and D. Scobell's wife and cousin, we went to Wood's at the Pell Mell (our old house for clubbing), and there we spent till ten at night.

134 Sir Edward Nicholas, many years principal Secretary of State to Charles I and II; dismissed from his office through the intrigues of Lady Castlemaine in 1663, and died 1669, aged 77.
135 Sir William Morris, Secretary of State from 1660 to 1668. Died 1676. He was kinsman to General Monk.
136 They were both clerks of the Privy Seal.
137 In the Journals this is stated to have taken place July 24th.

28th. A boy brought me a letter from Poet Fisher, who tells me that he is upon a panegyrique of the King, and desired to borrow a piece of me; and I sent him half a piece. To Westminster, and there met Mr Henson, who had formerly had the brave clock that went with bullets (which is now taken away from him by the King, it being his goods).

29th. With my Lord to White Hall Chapel, where I heard a cold sermon of the Bishop of Salisbury's, Duppa's,[138] and the ceremonies did not please me, they do so overdo them. My Lord went to dinner at Kensington with my Lord Camden.[139]

30th. This afternoon I got my £50, due to me for my first quarter's salary as Secretary to my Lord, paid to Tho. Hater for me, which he received and brought home to me, of which I felt glad. The sword-bearer of London (Mr Man) came to ask for us, with whom we sat late, discoursing about the worth of my office of Clerke of the Acts, which he hath a mind to buy, and I asked four years' purchase.

31st. To White Hall, where my Lord and the principal officers met, and had a great discourse about raising of money for the Navy, which is in very sad condition, and money must be raised for it. I back to the Admiralty, and there was doing things in order to the calculating of the debts of the Navy and other business, all the afternoon. At night I went to the Privy Seale, where I found Mr Crofts and Mathews making up all their things to leave the office to-morrow, to those that come to wait the next month.

August 1st. In the afternoon at the office, where we had many things to sign: and I went to the Council Chamber, and there got my Lord to sign the first bill, and the rest all myself; but received no money today.

2nd. To Westminster by water with Sir W. Batten and Sir W. Pen, (our servants in another boat) to the Admiralty; and from thence I went to my Lord's to fetch him thither, where we stayed in the morning about ordering of money for the victuallers, and advising

138 Brian Duppa, successively bishop of Chichester, Salisbury, and Winchester. Died 1662.
139 Baptist, second Viscount Campden, Lord Lieutenant of Rutlandshire. Died 1683.

how to get a sum of money to carry on the business of the Navy. From thence W. Hewer and I to the office of Privy Seale, where I stayed all the afternoon, and received about £40 for yesterday and today, at which my heart rejoiced for God's blessing to me, to give me this advantage by chance, there being of this £40 about £10 due to me for this day's work. So great is the present profit of this office, above what it was in the King's time; there being the last month about 300 bills, whereas in the late King's time it was much to have 40. I went and cast up the expense that I laid out upon my former house, (because there are so many that are desirous of it, and I am, in my mind, loth to let it go out of my hands, for fear of a turn). I find my layings-out to come to about £20 which with my fine will come to about £22 to him that shall hire my house of me.

4th. To White Hall, where I found my Lord gone with the King by water to dine at the Tower with Sir J. Robinson,[140] Lieutenant. I found my Lady Jemimah,[141] at my Lord's, with whom I staid and dined, all alone; after dinner to the Privy Seale Office, where I did business. So to a Committee of Parliament, (Sir Hen. Finch,[142] Chairman), to give them an answer to an order of theirs, 'that we could not give them any account of the Accounts of the Navy in the years 36, 37, 38, 39, 40, as they desire.'

6th. This night Mr Man offered me £1000 for my office of Clerke of the Acts, which made my mouth water; but yet I dare not take it till I speak with my Lord to have his consent.

7th. Mr Moore and myself dined at my Lord's with Mr Shepley. While I was at dinner in come Sam. Hartlibb[143] and his brother-in-law, now knighted by the King, to request my promise of a ship for them to Holland, which I had promised to get for them. After dinner to the Privy Seale all the afternoon. At night, meeting Sam. Hartlibb, he took me by coach to Kensington, to my Lord of Holland's; I staid in the coach while he went in about his business.

140 Sir John Robinson, created a Baronet for his services to Charles II, 1660, and had an augmentation to his arms. He was Lord Mayor of London, 1663.
141 Lady Jemimah Montagu.
142 Solicitor-General, 1660; Lord Keeper, 1673; Chancellor, 1675; created Earl of Nottingham, 1681. Died 1682.
143 Samuel Hartlib, son of a Polish merchant, and author of several ingenious Works on Agriculture, for which he had a pension from Cromwell.

9th. With Judge Advocate Fowler, Mr Creed, and Mr Shepley to the Rhenish Wine-house, and Captain Hayward of the *Plymouth*, who is now ordered to carry my Lord Winchelsea, Embassador to Constantinople. We were very merry, and Judge Advocate did give Captain Hayward his Oath of Allegiance and Supremacy.

10th. With Mr Moore and Creed to Hide-parke by coach, and saw a fine foot-race three times round the Park, between an Irishman and Crow, that was once my Lord Claypoole's[144] footman. By the way I cannot forget that my Lord Claypoole did the other day make enquiry of Mrs Hunt, concerning my House in Axe-yard, and did set her on work to get it of me for him, which methinks is a very great change. But blessed be God for my good chance of the Privy Seale, where I get every day I believe about £3. This place my Lord did give me by chance, neither he nor I thinking it to be of the worth that he and I find it to be.

12th (Lord's day). To my Lord, and with him to White Hall Chapel, where Mr Calamy preached, and made a good sermon upon these words 'To whom much is given, of him much is required.' He was very officious with his three reverences to the King, as others do. After sermon a brave anthem of Captain Cooke's,[145] which he himself sung, and the King was well pleased with it. My Lord dined at my Lord Chamberlin's.[146]

14th. To the Privy Seale, and thence to my Lord's, where Mr Pin the taylor, and I agreed upon making me a velvet coat. From thence to the Privy Seale again, where Sir Samuel Morland come with a Baronet's grant to pass, which the King had given him to make money of. Here we staid with him a great while; and he told me the

144 John Lord Claypoole married, in 1645, Mary, second daughter of Oliver Cromwell, to whom he became Master of the Horse, and a Lord of the Bedchamber: he was also placed in his Father-in-Law's Upper House. During Richard Cromwell's time he retained all his places at Court; and at the Restoration, never having made an enemy whilst his relations were in power, he was not molested, and lived till 1688. His father had been proceeded against in the Star Chamber, for resisting the payment of Ship Money, and was by Cromwell constituted Clerk of the Hanaper, and created a Baronet.

145 Henry Cooke, Master of the Children of the Chapel Royal, and an excellent musician. Died 1672.

146 The Earl of Manchester.

whole manner of his serving the King in the time of the Protector; and how Thurloe's bad usage made him to do it; how he discovered Sir R. Willis, and how he had sunk his fortune for the King; and that now the King had given him a pension of £500 per annum out of the Post Office for life, and the benefit of two Baronets; all which do make me begin to think that he is not so much a fool as I took him to be. I did make even with Mr Fairebrother for my degree of Master of Arts, which cost me about £9 16s.

15th. To the office, and after dinner by water to White Hall, where I found the King gone this morning by five of the clock to see a Dutch pleasure-boat below bridge, where he dines and my Lord with him. The King do tire all his people that are about him with early rising since he come.

18th. Captain Ferrers took me and Creed to the Cockpitt play, the first that I have had time to see since my coming from sea, *The Loyall Subject*,[147] where one Kinaston,[148] a boy, acted the Duke's sister, but made the loveliest lady that ever I saw in my life.

20th. This afternoon at the Privy Seale, where reckoning with Mr Moore, he had got £100 for me together, which I was glad of, guessing that the profit of this month would come to £100. With W. Hewer by coach to Worcester House, where I light, sending him home with the £100 that I received today. Here I staid, and saw my Lord Chancellor come into his Great Hall, where wonderful how much company there was to expect him. Before he would begin any business, he took my papers of the state of the debts of the Fleet, and there viewed them before all the people, and did give me his advice privately how to order things, to get as much money as we can of the Parliament.

21st. I met Mr Crewe and dined with him, where there dined one Mr Hickeman, an Oxford man, who spoke very much against the height of the now old clergy, for putting out many of the religious fellows of Colleges, and inveighing against them for their being

147 Tragi-comedy by Beaumont and Fletcher.
148 Edward Kynaston, engaged by Sir W. Davenant in 1660, to perform the principal female characters: he afterwards assumed the male ones in the first parts of tragedy, and continued on the stage till the end of King William's reign. The period of his death is not known.

drunk. It being post-night, I wrote to my Lord to give him notice that all things are well; that General Monk is made Lieutenant of Ireland, which my Lord Roberts[149] (made Deputy) do not like of, to be Deputy to any man but the King himself.

22nd. In the House, after the Committee was up, I met with Mr G. Montagu, and joyed him in his entrance (this being his 3rd day) of Dover. Here he made me sit all alone in the House, none but he and I, half an hour, discoursing how there was like to be many factions at Court between Marquis Ormond,[150] General Monk, and the Lord Roberts, about the business of Ireland; as there is already between the two Houses about the Act of Indemnity; and in the House of Commons, between the Episcopalian and Presbyterian men.

23rd. By water to Doctors' Commons to Dr Walker,[151] to give him my Lord's papers to view over, concerning his being empowered to be Vice-Admiral under the Duke of York. Thence by water to White Hall, to the Parliament House, where I spoke with Colonel Birch,[152] and so to the Admiralty chamber, where we and Mr Coventry had a meeting about several businesses. Amongst others, it was moved that Phineas Pett,[153] (kinsman to the Commissioner,) of Chatham, should be suspended his employment till he had answered some articles put in against him, as that he should formerly say that the King was a bastard and his mother a strumpet.

25th. This night W. Hewer brought me home from Mr Pim's my velvet coat and cap, the first that ever I had.

28th. Colonel Scroope[154] is this day excepted out of the Act of Indemnity, which has been now long in coming out, but it is expected to-morrow. I carried home £80 from Privy Seale, by coach.

149 John, second Lord Robartes, advanced to the dignity of Earl of Radnor, 1679. Died 1685.
150 James, afterwards created Duke of Ormond, and KG and twice Lord Lieutenant of Ireland.
151 One of the Judges of the Admiralty.
152 Colonel John Birch represented Leominster at that time, and afterwards Penryn. He was an active Member of Parliament.
153 Phineas Pett, an eminent ship-builder employed by the Admiralty.
154 Colonel Adrian Scroope, one of the persons who sat in judgement upon Charles I.

30th. To White Hall, where I met with the Act of Indemnity, (so long talked-of and hoped for,) with the Act of Rate for Pole-money, and for judicial proceedings. This the first day that ever I saw my wife wear black patches since we were married.

September 1st. All this afternoon sending express to the fleet, to order things against my Lord's coming; and taking direction of my Lord about some rich furniture to take along with him for the Princesse.[155] And talking after this, I hear by Mr Townsend, that there is the greatest preparation against the Prince de Ligne's coming over from the King of Spain, that ever was in England for their Embassador.

3rd. Up and to Mr —, the goldsmith, and there, with much ado, got him to put a gold ring to the jewell, which the King of Sweden did give my Lord: out of which my Lord had now taken the King's picture, and intends to make a George of it. About noon my Lord, having taken leave of the King in the Shield Gallery, (where I saw with what kindnesse the King did hugg my Lord at his parting,) I went over with him and saw him in his coach at Lambeth, and there took leave of him, he going to the Downes.

5th. Great newes now-a-day of the Duke d'Anjou's[156] desire to marry the Princesse Henrietta. Hugh Peters is said to be taken. The Duke of Gloucester is ill, and it is said it will prove the small-pox.

13th. This day the Duke of Gloucester died of the small-pox by the great negligence of the doctors.

15th. To Westminster, where I met with Dr Castles, who chidd me for some error in our Privy-Seale business; among the rest, for letting the fees of the six judges pass unpaid, which I know not what to say to, till I speak to Mr Moore. I was much troubled, for fear of being forced to pay the money myself. Called at my father's going home, and bespoke mourning for myself, for the death of the Duke of Gloucester.

16th. My Lord of Oxford[157] is also dead of the smallpox; in whom

155 The princess of Orange.
156 The only brother of Louis XIV, became Duke of Orleans on the death of his uncle.
157 This must be a mistake for some other person, Robert, nineteenth Earl of Oxford, having died in 1632, and Aubrey de Vere, his successor, the twentieth Earl, living until 1703.

his family dyes, after 600 years having that honour in their family and name. To the Park, where I saw how far they had proceeded in the Pell-mell, and in making a river through the Park, which I had never seen before since it was begun. Thence to White Hall garden, where I saw the King in purple mourning for his brother.

18th. This day I heard that the Duke of York, upon the news of the death of his brother yesterday, came hither by post last night.

To the Miter taverne in Wood-streete (a house of the greatest note in London,) where I met W. Symons, and D. Scobell, and their wives, Mr Samford Luellin, Chetwind, one Mr Vivion, and Mr White,[158] formerly chaplain to the Lady Protectresse, (and still so, and one they say that is likely to get my Lady Francesse for his wife). Here some of us fell to handycapp, a sport that I never knew before.

20th. To Major Hart's lodgings in Cannon-streete, who used me very kindly with wine and good discourse, particularly upon the ill method which Col. Birch and the Committee use in defending of the army and the navy; promising the Parliament to save them a great deal of money, when we judge that it will cost the King more than if they had nothing to do with it, by reason of their delayes and scrupulous enquirys into the account of both.

21st. Upon the water saw the corpse of the Duke of Gloucester brought down to Somerset House stairs, to go by water to Westminster, to be buried.

22nd. I bought a pair of short black stockings, to wear over a pair of silk ones for mourning; and I met with The. Turner and Joyce, buying of things to go into mourning too for the Duke, which is now the mode of all the ladies in towne. This day Mr Edw. Pickering is come from my Lord, and says that he left him well in Holland, and that he will be here within three or four days.

23rd. This afternoon, the King having news of the Princesse being come to Margatte, he and the Duke of York went down thither in barges to her.

158 According to Noble, Jeremiah White married Lady Frances Cromwell's waiting-woman, in Oliver's life-time, and they lived together fifty years. Lady Frances had two husbands, Mr Robert Rich and Sir John Russell, the last of whom she survived fifty-two years, dying 1721–22.

24th. I arose from table and went to the Temple church, where I had appointed Sir W. Batten to meet him; and there at Sir Heneage Finch Solliciter General's chambers, before him and Sir W. Wilde, Recorder of London (whom we sent for from his chamber) we were sworn justices of peace for Middlesex, Essex, Kent, and Southampton; with which honour I did find myself mightily pleased, though I am wholly ignorant in the duties of a justice of peace.

28th. I did send for a cup of tee (a China drink) of which I never had drank before, and went away (the King and the Princesse coming up the river this afternoon as we were at our pay). My Lord told me how the ship that brought the Princesse and him (the Tredagh) did knock six times upon the Kentish Knock, which put them in great fear for the ship; but got off well. He told me also how the King had knighted Vice-admiral Lawson and Sir Richard Stayner.

29th. This day or yesterday, I hear, Prince Rupert[159] is come to Court; but welcome to nobody.

October 2nd. At Will's I met with Mr Spicer, and with him to the Abbey to see them at vespers. There I found but a thin congregation.

3rd. To my Lord's, who sent a great iron chest to White Hall; and I saw it carried into the King's closet, where I saw most incomparable pictures. Among the rest a book open upon a desk, which I durst have sworn was a reall book. Back again to my Lord, and dined all alone with him, who did treat me with a great deal of respect; and after dinner did discourse an hour with me, saying that he believed that he might have any thing that he would ask of the King. This day I heard the Duke speak of a great design that he and my Lord of Pembroke have, and a great many others, of sending a venture to some parts of Africa to dig for gold ore there. They intend to admit as many as will venture their money, and so make themselves a company. £250 is the lowest share for every man. But I do not find that my Lord do much like it.

---

159 Son of Frederic, Prince Palatine of the Rhine, afterwards styled King of Bohemia, by Elizabeth, only sister to Charles I. Died 1682.

4th. I and Lieut. Lambert to Westminster Abbey, where we saw Dr Frewen[160] translated to the Archbishoprick of York. Here I saw the Bishops of Winchester,[161] Bangor,[162] Rochester,[163] Bath and Wells,[164] and Salisbury,[165] all in their habits, in King Henry Seventh's chapel. But, Lord! at their going out, how people did most of them look upon them as strange creatures, and few with any kind of love or respect.

6th. Col. Slingsby and I at the office getting a catch ready for the Prince de Ligne to carry his things away today, who is now going home again. I was to give my Lord an account of the stacions and victualls of the fleet, in order to the choosing of a fleet fit for him to take to sea, to bring over the Queen.

7th (Lord's Day). To White Hall on foot calling at my father's to change my long black cloake for a short one (long cloakes being now quite out); but he being gone to church, I could not get one. I heard Dr Spurstow[166] preach before the King a poor dry sermon; but a very good anthem of Captn. Cooke's afterwards. To my Lord's and dined with him; he all dinner-time talking French to me, and telling me the story how the Duke of York hath got my Lord Chancellor's daughter with child, and that she do lay it to him, and that for certain he did promise her marriage, and had signed it with his blood, but that he by stealth had got the paper out of her cabinett. And that the King would have him to marry her, but that he will not. So that the thing is very bad for the Duke, and them all; but my Lord do make light of it, as a thing that he believes is not a new thing for the Duke to do abroad. After dinner to the Abbey, where I heard them read the church-service, but very ridiculously. A poor cold sermon of Dr Lamb's, one of the prebends, in his habitt, come afterwards, and so all ended.

---

160 Dr Accepted Frewen, Bishop of Lichfield and Coventry.
161 Brian Duppa, translated from Salisbury.
162 William Roberts.
163 John Warner, died 1666, aged 86.
164 William Pierce, translated from Peterborough, 1632.
165 Humphrey Henchman, afterwards Bishop of London.
166 William Spurstow, DD, Vicar of Hackney and Master of Katherine Hall, Cambridge, both which pieces of preferment he lost for nonconformity, 1662.

9th. This morning Sir W. Batten with Coll. Birch to Deptford to pay off two ships. Sir W. Pen and I staid to do business, and afterward together to White Hall, where I went to my Lord, and saw in his chamber his picture, very well done; and am with child till I get it copied out, which I hope to do when he is gone to sea.

10th. At night comes Mr Moore and tells me how Sir Hards. Waller[167] (who only pleads guilty),. Scott, Coke,[168] Peters,[169] Harrison, &c. were this day arraigned at the bar of the Sessions House, there being upon the bench the Lord Mayor, General Monk, my Lord of Sandwich, &c.; such a bench of noblemen as had not been ever seen in England! They all seem to be dismayed, and will all be condemned without question. In Sir Orlando Bridgman's charge,[170] he did wholly rip up the unjustnesse of the war against the King from the beginning, and so it much reflects upon all the Long Parliament, though the King had pardoned them, yet they must hereby confess that the King do look upon them as traytors. To-morrow they are to plead what they have to say.

11th. To walk in St James's Park, where we observed the several engines at work to draw up water, with which sight I was very much pleased. Above all the rest, I liked that which Mr Greatorex[171] brought, which do carry up the water with a great deal of ease. Here, in the Park, we met with Mr Salisbury, who took Mr Creed and me to the Cockpit to see *The Moore of Venice*, which was well done. Burt acted the Moore;[172] by the same token, a very pretty lady that sat by me, called out, to see Desdemona smothered.

13th. I went out to Charing Cross, to see Major-general Harrison[173]

167 Sir Hardress Waller, Knt, one of Charles I's judges. His sentence was commuted to imprisonment for life.

168 Coke was solicitor to the people of England.

169 Hugh Peters, the fanatical preacher.

170 Eldest son of John Bridgeman, Bishop of Chester, became, after the Restoration, successively Chief Baron of the Exchequer, Chief Justice of the Common Pleas and Lord Keeper of the Great Seal, and was created Baronet.

171 A mathematical instrument maker.

172 Burt ranked in the list of good actors after the Restoration, though he resigned the part of Othello to Hart. – Davis's *Dramatic Miscellany*.

173 Thomas Harrison, son of a butcher at Newcastle-under-Line, appointed by Cromwell to convey Charles I from Windsor to White Hall, in order to his trial, and afterwards sat as one of his judges.

hanged, drawn, and quartered; which was done there, he looking as cheerful as any man could do in that condition. He was presently cut down, and his head and heart shown to the people, at which there was great shouts of joy. It is said, that he said that he was sure to come shortly at the right hand of Christ to judge them that now had judged him; and that his wife do expect his coming again. Thus it was my chance to see the King beheaded at White Hall, and to see the first blood shed in revenge for the King at Charing Cross.

14th. To White Hall chappell, where one Dr Crofts made an indifferent sermon, and after it an anthem, ill sung, which made the King laugh. Here I first did see the Princesse Royall since she came into England. Here I also observed, how the Duke of York and Mrs Palmer did talk to one another very wantonly through the hangings that parts the King's closet and the closet where the ladies sit.

15th. This morning Mr Carew[174] was hanged and quartered at Charing Cross; but his quarters, by a great favour, are not to be hanged up.

16th. Being come home, Will. told me that my Lord had a mind to speak with me to-night; so I returned by water, and, coming there, it was only to enquire how the ships were provided with victuals that are to go with him to fetch over the Queen, which I gave him a good account of. He seemed to be in a melancholy humour, which, I was told by W. Howe, was for that he had lately lost a great deal of money at cards, which he fears he do too much addict himself to now-a-days.

18th. This morning, it being expected that Colonel Hacker[175] and Axtell[176] should die, I went to Newgate, but found they were reprieved till to-morrow.

19th. This morning my dining-room was finished with greene serge hanging and gilt leather, which is very handsome. This morning Hacker and Axtell were hanged and quartered, as the rest are. This night I sat up late to make up my accounts ready against to-morrow for my Lord.

174 John Carew, one of the regicides.
175 Colonel Francis Hacker commanded the guards at the King's execution.
176 Axtell had guarded the High Court of Justice.

20th. I dined with my Lord and Lady; he was very merry, and did talk very high how he would have a French cooke, and a master of his horse, and his lady and child to wear black patches; which methought was strange, but he is become a perfect courtier; and, among other things, my Lady saying that she could get a good merchant for her daughter Jem., he answered, that he would rather see her with a pedlar's pack at her back, so she married a gentleman, than she should marry a citizen. This afternoon, going through London, and calling at Crowe's the upholsterer's in Saint Bartholomew's, I saw limbs of some of our new traytors set upon Aldersgate, which was a sad sight to see; and a bloody week this and the last have been, there being ten hanged, drawn, and quartered.

21st. George Vines carried me up to the top of his turret, where there is Cooke's head set up for a traytor, and Harrison's set up on the other side of Westminster Hall. Here I could see them plainly, as also a very fair prospect about London.

22nd. All preparing for my Lord's going to sea to fetch the Queen to-morrow. At night my Lord come home, with whom I staid long, and talked of many things. He told me there hath been a meeting before the King and my Lord Chancellor, of some Episcopalian and Presbyterian Divines; but what had passed he could not tell me.

23rd. About eight o'clock my Lord went; and going through the garden, Mr William Montagu told him of an estate of land lately come into the King's hands, that he had a mind my Lord should beg. To which end my Lord writ a letter presently to my Lord Chancellor to do it for him, which (after leave taken of my Lord at White Hall bridge) I did carry to Warwick House to him; and had a fair promise of him, that he would do it this day for my Lord. In my way thither I met the Lord Chancellor and all the Judges riding on horseback and going to Westminster Hall, it being the first day of the terme.

24th. Mr Moore tells me, among other things, that the Duke of York is now sorry for his amour with my Lord Chancellor's daughter, who is now brought to bed of a boy. To Mr Lilly's,[177] where, not finding Mr Spong, I went to Mr Greatorex, where I met him, and where I bought of him a drawing pen; and he did show me

177 William Lilly, the astrologer and almanack-maker.

the manner of the lamp-glasses, which carry the light a great way, good to read in bed by, and I intend to have one of them. So to Mr Lilly's with Mr Spong, where well received, there being a clubb to-night among his friends. Among the rest Esquire Ashmole,[178] who I found was a very ingenious gentleman. With him we two sang afterwards in Mr Lilly's study. That done, we all parted; and I home by coach, taking Mr Rooker with me, who did tell me a great many fooleries, which may be done by nativities, and blaming Mr Lilly for writing to please his friends and to keep in with the times (as he did formerly to his own dishonour,) and not according to the rules of art, by which he could not well erre, as he had done.

26th. By Westminster to White Hall, where I saw the Duke de Soissons go from his audience with a very great deal of state; his own coach all red velvet covered with gold lace, and drawn by six barbes, and attended by twenty pages very rich in clothes. To Westminster Hall, and bought, among other books, one of the Life of our Queen, which I read at home to my wife; but it was so sillily writ, that we did nothing but laugh at it: among other things it is dedicated to that paragon of virtue and beauty the Duchess of Albemarle. Great talk as if the Duke of York do now own the marriage between him and the Chancellor's daughter. To Westminster Abbey, where with much difficulty, going round to the cloysters, I got in; this day being a great day for the consecrating of five Bishopps, which was done after sermon; but I could not get into Henry VII's chappel. After dinner to White Hall chappel; my Lady and my Lady Jemimah and I up to the King's closet, (who is now gone to meet the Queen). So meeting with one Mr Hill, that did know my lady, he did take us into the King's closet, and there we did stay all service-time.

29th. I up early, it being my Lord Mayor's day (Sir Richd. Browne,) and neglecting my office, I went to the Wardrobe, where I met my Lady Sandwich and all the children; and after drinking of some strange and incomparable good clarett of Mr Remball's,[179] he and Mr Townsend[179] did take us, and set the young Lords at one Mr Neville's, a draper in Paul's churchyard; and my Lady and my Lady

178 Elias Ashmole, the antiquarian.
179 Officers of the Wardrobe.

Pickering[180] and I to one Mr Isaacson's, a linen-draper at the Key in Cheapside; where there was a company of fine ladies, and we were very civilly treated, and had a very good place to see the pageants, which were many, and I believe good, for such kind of things, but in themselves but poor and absurd.

30th. I went to the Cockpit all alone, and there saw a very fine play called *The Tamer tamed*:[181] very well acted. I hear nothing yet of my Lord, whether he be gone for the Queen from the Downes or no; but I believe he is, and that he is now upon coming back again.

November 1st. This morning Sir W. Pen and I were mounted early, and had very merry discourse all the way, he being very good company. We come to Sir W. Batten's, where he lives like a prince, and we were made very welcome. Among other things he showed me my Lady's closet, wherein was great store of rarities; as also a chair, which he calls King Harry's chaire, where he that sits down is catched with two irons, that come round about him, which makes good sport. Here dined with us two or three more country gentlemen; among the rest Mr Christmas, my old school-fellow, with whom I had much talk. He did remember that I was a great Roundhead when I was a boy, and I was much afraid that he would have remembered the words that I said the day the King was beheaded (that, were I to preach upon him, my text should be – 'The memory of the wicked shall rot'); but I found afterwards that he did go away from school before that time.

2nd. To White Hall, where I saw the boats coming very thick to Lambeth, and all the stairs to be full of people. I was told the Queen was a-coming; so I got a sculler for sixpence to carry me thither and back again, but I could not get to see the Queen; so come back, and to my Lord's, where he was come; and I supt with him, he being very merry, telling me stories of the country mayors, how they entertained the King all the way as he come along; and how the country gentlewomen did hold up their heads to be kissed by the King, not taking his hand to kiss as they should do. I took leave of my Lord and Lady, and so took coach at White Hall and carried Mr

180 Elizabeth Montagu, sister to the Earl of Sandwich, who had married Sir Gilbert Pickering, Bart. of Nova Scotia, and of Tichmersh, co. Northampton.
181 *The Woman's Prize, or Tamer Tamed*, a comedy by John Fletcher.

Childe as far as the Strand, and myself got as far as Ludgate by all the bonfires, but with a great deal of trouble; and there the coachman desired that I would release him, for he durst not go further for the fires. In Paul's churchyard I called at Kirton's, and there they had got a masse book for me, which I bought and cost me twelve shillings; and, when I come home, sat up late and read in it with great pleasure to my wife, to hear that she was long ago acquainted with it. I observed this night very few bonfires in the City, not above three in all London, for the Queen's coming; whereby I guess that (as I believed before) her coming do please but very few.

3rd. Saturday. In the afternoon to White Hall, where my Lord and Lady were gone to kiss the Queen's hand.

4th (Lord's day). In the morn to our own church, where Mr Mills[182] did begin to nibble at the Common Prayer, by saying 'Glory be to the Father, &c.' after he had read the two psalms: but the people had been so little used to it, that they could not tell what to answer. This declaration of the King's do give the Presbyterians some satisfaction, and a pretence to read the Common Prayer, which they would not do before because of their former preaching against it. After dinner to Westminster, where I went to my Lord's, and, having spoken with him, I went to the Abbey, where the first time that ever I heard the organs in a cathedral. My wife seemed very pretty today, it being the first time I had given her leave to weare a black patch.

5th. At the office at night, to make up an account of what the debts of nineteen of the twenty-five ships that should have been paid off, is increased since the adjournment of the Parliament, they being to sit again to-morrow. This 5th day of November is observed exceeding well in the City; and at night great bonfires and fireworks.

6th. Mr Chetwind told me that he did fear that this late business of the Duke of York's would prove fatal to my Lord Chancellor. To our office, where we met all, for the sale of two ships by an inch of candle (the first time that ever I saw any of this kind), where I observed how they do invite one another, and at last how they all

182 Daniel Milles, DD, thirty-two years rector of St Olave's, Hart Street, and buried there October 1689, aged sixty-three. In 1667 Sir Robert Brooks presented him to the rectory of Wanstead, which he also held till his death.

do cry, and we have much to do to tell who did cry last. The ships were the *Indian*, sold for £1300 and the *Half-moone*, sold for £830.

7th. Went by water to my Lord, where I dined with him, and he in a very merry humour (present Mr Borfett and Childe) at dinner: he, in discourse of the great opinion of the virtue – gratitude, (which he did account the greatest thing in the world to him, and had, therefore, in his mind been often troubled in the late times how to answer his gratitude to the King, who raised his father,) did say it was that did bring him to his obedience to the King; and did also bless himself with his good fortune, in comparison to what it was when I was with him in the Sound, when he durst not own his correspondence with the King; which is a thing that I never did hear of to this day before; and I do from this raise an opinion of him, to be one of the most secret men in the world, which I was not so convinced of before. After dinner he bid all go out of the room, and did tell me how the King had promised him £4000 per annum for ever, and had already given him a bill under his hand (which he showed me) for £4000 that Mr Fox is to pay him. My Lord did advise with me how to get this received, and to put out £3000 into safe hands at use, and the other he will make use for his present occasion. This he did advise with me about with great secresy. After this he called for the fiddles and books, and we two and W. Howe, and Mr Childe, did sing and play some psalmes of Will Lawes's,[183] and some songs; and so I went away. Notwithstanding this was the first day of the King's proclamation against hackney coaches coming into the streets to stand to be hired, yet I got one to carry me home.

10th. The Comtroller[184] and I to the coffee-house, where he showed me the state of his case; how the King did owe him above £6000. But I do not see great likelihood for them to be paid, since they begin already in Parliament to dispute the paying off the just sea-debts, which were already promised to be paid, and will be the undoing of thousands if they be not paid.

183 Brother to Henry Lawes the celebrated composer, and himself a chamber musician to Charles I, in whose service he took up arms, and was killed at the siege of Chester, 1645. The King regretted his loss severely, and used to call him the father of music.
184 Sir R. Slingsby.

15th. My Lord did this day show me the King's picture which was done in Flanders, that the King did promise my Lord before he ever saw him, and that we did expect to have had at sea before the King come to us; but it come but today, and indeed it is the most pleasant and the most like him that ever I saw picture in my life. To Sir W. Batten's to dinner, he having a couple of servants married today; and so there was a great number of merchants, and others of good quality on purpose after dinner to make an offering, which, when dinner was done, we did, and I did give ten shillings and no more, though I believe most of the rest did give more, and did believe that I did so too.

19th. I went with the Treasurer in his coach to White Hall, and in our way, in discourse, do find him a very good-natured man; and, talking of those men who now stand condemned for murdering the King, he says that he believes, that, if the law would give leave, the King is a man of so great compassion that he would wholly acquit them.

20th. Mr Shepley and I to the new play-house near Lincoln's-Inn-Fields (which was formerly Gibbon's tennis-court), where the play of *Beggar's Bush*[185] was newly begun; and so we went in and saw it well acted: and here I saw the first time one Moone,[186] who is said to be the best actor in the world, lately come over with the King, and indeed it is the finest play-house, I believe, that ever was in England. This morning I found my Lord in bed late, he having been with the King, Queen, and Princesse, at the Cockpit all night, where General Monk treated them; and after supper a play, where the King did put a great affront upon Singleton's musique, he bidding them stop and made the French musique play, which, my Lord says, do much outdo all ours.

22nd. This morning come the carpenters to make me a door at the other side of my house, going into the entry. To Mr Fox's, where we found Mrs Fox[187] within, and an alderman of London paying £1000

185 The *Beggar's Bush*, a comedy by Beaumont and Fletcher.
186 Mohun, or Moone, the celebrated actor, who had borne a Major's commission in the King's Army. The period of his death is uncertain.
187 Elizabeth, daughter of William Whittle, Esq., of Lancashire, wife of Stephen Fox, Esq., who was knighted in 1665.

or £1400 in gold upon the table for the King. Mr Fox come in
presently and did receive us with a great deal of respect; and then did
take my wife and I to the Queen's presence-chamber, where he got
my wife placed behind the Queen's chaire, and the two Princesses
come to dinner. The Queen a very little plain old woman, and
nothing more in her presence in any respect nor garbe than any
ordinary woman. The Princesse of Orange I had often seen before.
The Princesse Henrietta is very pretty, but much below my
expectation; and her dressing of herself with her haire frized short up
to her eares, did make her seem so much the less to me. But my wife
standing near her with two or three black patches on, and well
dressed, did seem to me much handsomer than she.

To White Hall at about nine at night, and there, with Laud the
page that went with me, we could not get out of Henry VIII's gallery
into the further part of the boarded gallery, where my Lord was
walking with my Lord Ormond; and we had a key of Sir S.
Morland's, but all would not do; till at last, by knocking, Mr Harrison
the door-keeper did open us the door, and, after some talk with my
Lord about getting a catch to carry my Lord St Albans's[188] goods to
France, I parted and went home on foot.

25th. I had a letter brought me from my Lord to get a ship ready to
carry the Queen's things over to France, she being to go within five
or six days.

27th. To Westminster Hall, and in King Street there being a great
stop of coaches, there was a falling out between a drayman and my
Lord Chesterfield's coachman, and one of his footmen killed. Mr
Moore told me how the House had this day voted the King to have
all the Excise for ever. This day I do also hear that the Queen's going
to France is stopt, which do like me well, because then the King will
be in town the next month, which is my month again at the Privy
Seale.

30th. Sir G. Carteret did give us an account how Mr Holland do
intend to prevail with the Parliament to try his project of discharging
the seamen all at present by ticket, and so promise interest to all men

188 Henry Jermyn, created Lord Jermyn 1614, advanced to the Earldom of St
Albans 1660, KG. Died 1683, without issue. He was supposed to be married to the
Queen Dowager.

that will lend money upon them at eight per cent., for so long as they are unpaid: whereby he do think to take away the growing debt, which do now lie upon the kingdom for lack of present money to discharge the seamen.

December 4th. This day the Parliament voted that the bodies of Oliver, Ireton, Bradshaw, &c., should be taken up out of their graves in the Abbey, and drawn to the gallows, and there hanged and buried under it: which (methinks) do trouble me that a man of so great courage as he was, should have that dishonour, though otherwise he might deserve it enough.

9th. I went to the Duke. And first calling upon Mr Coventry at his chamber, I went to the Duke's bed-side, who had sat up late last night, and lay long this morning. This being done, I went to chapel, and sat in Mr Blagrave's pew, and there did sing my part along with another before the King, and with much ease.

10th. It is expected that the Duke will marry the Lord Chancellor's daughter at last; which is likely to be the ruine of Mr Davis and my Lord Barkley, who have carried themselves so high against the Chancellor; Sir Chas. Barkley swearing that he and others had intrigued with her often, which all believe to be a lie.

16th. In the afternoon I went to White Hall, where I was surprised with the news of a plot against the King's person and my Lord Monk's; and that since last night there were about forty taken up on suspicion; and, amongst others, it was my lot to meet with Simon Beale, the Trumpeter, who took me and Tom Doling into the Guard in Scotland Yard, and showed us Major-General Overton.[189] Here I heard him deny that he is guilty of any such things: but that whereas it is said that he is found to have brought many armes to towne, he says it is only to sell them, as he will prove by oath.

21st. They told me that this is St Thomas's, and that by an old custome, this day the Exchequer men had formerly, and do intend this night to have a supper; which if I could I promised to come to, but did not. To my Lady's, and dined with her; she told me how dangerously ill the Princesse Royal is: and that this morning she was

189 One of Oliver Cromwell's Major-Generals: high Republican.

said to be dead. But she hears that she hath married herself to young Jermyn,[190] which is worse than the Duke of York's marrying the Chancellor's daughter, which is now publicly owned.

26th. To White Hall by water, and dined with my Lady Sandwich, who at table did tell me how much fault was laid upon Dr Frazer and the rest of the Doctors, for the death of the Princesse. My Lord did dine this day with Sir Henry Wright, in order to his going to sea with the Queen.

31st. In Paul's Church-yard I bought the play of Henry IV, and so went to the new Theatre and saw it acted; but my expectation being too great, it did not please me, as otherwise I believe it would: and my having a book, I believe did spoil it a little. That being done I went to my Lord's, where I found him private at cards with my Lord Lauderdale and some persons of honour.

1660/61. At the end of the last and the beginning of this year, I do live in one of the houses belonging to the Navy Office, as one of the principal officers, and have done now about half-a-year: my family being, myself, my wife, Jane, Will. Hewer, and Wayneman, my girl's brother. Myself in constant good health, and in a most handsome and thriving condition. Blessed be Almighty God for it. As to things of State. – The King settled, and loved of all. The Duke of York matched to my Lord Chancellor's daughter, which do not please many. The Queen upon her returne to France with the Princesse Henrietta.[191] The Princesse of Orange lately dead, and we into new mourning for her. We have been lately frighted with a great plot, and many taken up on it, and the fright not quite over. The Parliament, which had done all this great good to the King, beginning to grow factious, the King did dissolve it December 29th last, and another likely to be chosen speedily.

1660/61. January 1st. Mr Moore and I went to Mr Pierce's; in our way seeing the Duke of York bring his Lady today to wait upon the Queen, the first time that ever she did since that business; and the Queen is said to receive her now with much respect and love.

190 Henry Jermyn, Master of the Horse to the Duke of York.
191 Youngest daughter of Charles I, married soon after to Philip Duke of Orleans, only brother of Louis XIV. She died suddenly in 1670, not without suspicion of having been poisoned.

2nd. My Lord did give me many commands in his business. As to write to my uncle that Mr Barnewell's papers should be locked up, in case he should die, he being now suspected to be very ill. Also about consulting with Mr W. Montagu[1] for the settling of the £4000 a-year that the King had promised my Lord. As also about getting Mr George Montagu to be chosen at Huntingdon this next Parliament, &c. That done, he to White Hall stairs with much company, and I with him; where we took water for Lambeth, and there coach for Portsmouth. The Queen's things were all in White Hall Court ready to be sent away, and her Majesty ready to be gone an hour after to Hampton Court to-night, and so to be at Portsmouth on Saturday next. This day I left Sir W. Batten and Captn. Rider my chine of beefe for to serve to-morrow at Trinity House, the Duke of Albemarle being to be there, and all the rest of the Brethren, it being a great day for the reading over of their new Charter, which the King hath newly given them.

3rd. To the Theatre, where was acted Beggars' Bush, it being very well done; and here the first time that ever I saw women come upon the stage.

4th. I had been early this morning at White Hall, at the Jewell Office, to choose a piece of gilt plate for my Lord, in returne of his offering to the King (which it seems is usual at this time of year, and an Earle gives twenty pieces in gold in a purse to the King). I chose a gilt tankard, weighing 31 ounces and a half, and he is allowed 30; so I paid 12s. for the ounce and half over what he is to have: but strange it was for me to see what a company of small fees I was called upon by a great many to pay there, which, I perceive, is the manner that courtiers do get their estates.

7th. This morning, news was brought to me to my bedside, that there had been a great stir in the City this night by the Fanatiques, who had been up and killed six or seven men, but all are fled. My Lord Mayor and the whole City had been in armes, above 40,000. Tom and I and my wife to the Theatre, and there saw The Silent Woman. Among other things here, Kinaston the boy had the good turn to appear in three shapes: first, as a poor woman in ordinary

1 William, third son to Lord Montagu of Boughton; afterwards Attorney-General to the Queen; and made Chief Baron of the Exchequer, 1676.

clothes, to please Morose; then in fine clothes, as a gallant; and in them was clearly the prettiest woman in the whole house: and lastly, as a man; and then likewise did appear the handsomest man in the house. In our way home we were in many places strictly examined, more than in the worst of times, there being great fears of the Fanatiques rising again: for the present I do not hear that any of them are taken.

8th. Some talk today of a head of Fanatiques that do appear about, but I do not believe it. However, my Lord Mayor, Sir Richd. Browne, hath carried himself honourably, and hath caused one of their meeting-houses in London to be pulled down.

9th. Waked in the morning about six o'clock, by people running up and down in Mr Davis's house, talking that the Fanatiques were up in armes in the City. And so I rose and went forth; where in the street I found every body in armes at the doors. So I returned and got my sword and pistol, which, however, I had no powder to charge; and went to the door, where I found Sir R. Ford,[2] and with him I walked up and down as far as the Exchange, and there I left him. In our way, the streets full of train-bands, and great stir. What mischief these rogues have done! and I think near a dozen had been killed this morning on both sides. The shops shut, and all things in trouble.

10th. After dinner Will. comes to tell me that he had presented my piece of plate to Mr Coventry, who takes it very kindly, and sends me a very kind letter, and the plate back again; of which my heart is very glad. Mr Davis told us the particular examinations of these Fanatiques that are taken: and in short it is this, these Fanatiques that have routed all the train-bands that they met with, put the King's life-guards to the run, killed about twenty men, broke through the City gates twice; and all this in the daytime, when all the City was in armes; − are not in all above 31. Whereas we did believe them (because they were seen up and down in every place almost in the City, and had been in Highgate two or three days, and in several other places) to be at least 500. A thing that never was heard of, that so few men should dare and do so much mischief. Their word was, 'The King Jesus, and their heads upon the gates.' Few of them would receive any quarter, but such as were taken by force and kept alive;

2 Lord Mayor of London, 1671.

expecting Jesus to come here and reign in the world presently, and will not believe yet. The King this day come to towne.

11th (Office day). This day comes news, by letters from Portsmouth, that the Princesse Henrietta is fallen sick of the meazles on board the *London*, after the Queen and she was under sail. And so was forced to come back again into Portsmouth harbour; and in their way, by negligence of the pilot, run upon the Horse sand. The Queen and she continue aboard, and do not intend to come on shore till she sees what will become of the young Princesse. This newes do make people think something indeed, that three of the Royal Family should fall sick of the same disease, one after another. This morning likewise, we had order to see guards set in all the King's yards; and so Sir Wm. Batten goes to Chatham, Colonel Slingsby and I to Deptford and Woolwich. Portsmouth being a garrison, needs none.

12th. We fell to choosing four captains to command the guards, and choosing the place where to keep them, and other things in order thereunto. Never till now did I see the great authority of my place, all the captains of the fleete coming cap in hand to us.

13th. After sermon to Deptford again; where, at the Commissioner's and the Globe, we staid long. But no sooner in bed, but we had an alarme, and so we rose; and the Comptroller comes into the Yard to us; and seamen of all the ships present repair to us, and there we armed with every one a handspike, with which they were as fierce as could be. At last we hear that it was five or six men that did ride through the guard in the towne, without stopping to the guard that was there; and, some say, shot at them. But all being quiet there, we caused the seamen to go on board again.

15th. This day I hear the Princesse is recovered again. The King hath been this afternoon at Deptford, to see the yacht that Commissioner Pett is building, which will be very pretty; as also that his brother at Woolwich is making.

19th. To the Comptroller's, and with him by coach to White Hall; in our way meeting Venner[3] and Pritchard upon a sledge, who with

3 Thomas Venner, a cooper, and preacher to a conventicle in Coleman-street. He was a violent enthusiast and leader in the Insurrection on the 7th of January before mentioned. He was much wounded before he could be taken, and fought with courage amounting to desperation.

two more Fifth Monarchy men were hanged today, and the two first drawn and quartered.

21st. It is strange what weather we have had all this winter; no cold at all; but the ways are dusty, and the flyes fly up and down, and the rose-bushes are full of leaves, such a time of the year as was never known in this world before here. This day many more of the Fifth Monarchy men were hanged.

22nd. I met with Dr Thos. Fuller. He tells me of his last and great book that is coming out: that is, the History of all the Families in England; and could tell me more of my owne, than I knew myself. And also to what perfection he hath now brought the art of memory; that he did lately to four eminently great scholars dictate together in Latin, upon different subjects of their proposing, faster than they were able to write, till they were tired; and that the best way of beginning a sentence, if a man should be out and forget his last sentence, (which he never was,) that then his last refuge is to begin with an *Utcunque*.

27th (Lord's day). Before I rose, letters come to me from Ports–mouth, telling me that the Princesse is now well, and my Lord Sandwich set sail with the Queen and her yesterday from thence to France. This day the parson read a proclamation at church, for the keeping of Wednesday next, the 30th of January, a fast for the murther of the late King.

30th (Fast day). The first time that this day hath been yet observed: and Mr Mills made a most excellent sermon, upon 'Lord forgive us our former iniquities', speaking excellently of the justice of God in punishing men for the sins of their ancestors. To my Lady Batten's;[4] where my wife and she are lately come back again from being abroad, and seeing of Cromwell, Ireton,[5] and Bradshaw hanged and buried at Tyburne.

4 Elizabeth Woodcock, married Feb. 3, 1658-59, to Sir W. Batten; and subsequently became, in 1671, the wife of a foreigner called in the register of Battersea parish, Lord Leyenburgh. Lady Leighenburg was buried at Walthamstow, Sept. 16, 1681 – *Lysons' Environs*.

5 Henry Ireton, married Bridget, daughter to Oliver Cromwell, and was afterwards one of Charles I's Judges, and of the Committee who superintended his execution. He died at the siege of Limerick, 1651.

31st. To the Theatre, and there sat in the pitt among the company of
fine ladys, &c.; and the house was exceeding full, to see *Argalus and
Parthenia*,[6] the first time that it hath been acted: and indeed it is good,
though wronged by my over great expectations, as all things else are.

February 2nd. Home; where I found the parson and his wife gone.
And by and by the rest of the company very well pleased, and I too; it
being the last dinner I intend to make a great while.

3rd (Lord's-day). This day I first begun to go forth in my coate and
sword, as the manner now among gentlemen is. To White Hall;
where I staid to hear the trumpets and kettle drums, and then the
other drums, which are much cried up, though I think it dull, vulgar
musick. So to Mr Fox's, unbidd; where I had a good dinner and
special company. Among other discourse, I observed one story, how
my Lord of Northwich,[7] at a public audience before the King of
France, made the Duke of Anjou cry, by making ugly faces as he was
stepping to the King, but undiscovered. And how Sir Phillip
Warwick's[8] lady did wonder to have Mr Daray send for several dozen
bottles of Rhenish wine to her house, not knowing that the wine was
his. Thence to my Lord's; where I am told how Sir Thomas Crew's[9]
Pedro, with two of his countrymen more, did last night kill one
soldier of four that quarrelled with them in the street, about ten
o'clock. The other two are taken; but he is now hid at my Lord's till
night, that he do intend to make his escape away.

5th. Into the Hall; and there saw my Lord Treasurer[10] (who was
sworn today at the Exchequer, with a great company of Lords and
persons of honour to attend him) go up to the Treasury Offices, and
take possession thereof; and also saw the heads of Cromwell,
Bradshaw, and Ireton, set up at the further end of the Hall.

6 *Argalus and Parthenia*, a pastoral, by Henry Glapthorn, taken from Sydney's
Arcadia.
7 George Lord Goring, created Earl of Norwich 1644, died 1662.
8 Sir Philip Warwick, Secretary to Charles I when in the Isle of Wight, and Clerk
of the Signet, to which place he was restored in 1660, knighted, and elected MP for
Westminster. He was also Secretary to the Treasury under Lord Southampton till
1667. Died 1682-83. His second wife here mentioned was Joan, daughter to Sir
Henry Fanshawe, and widow of Sir William Botteler, Bart.
9 Eldest son of Mr afterwards Lord Crewe, whom he succeeded in that title.
10 Earl of Southampton.

7th. To Westminster Hall. And after a walk to my Lord's; where, while I and my Lady were in her chamber in talk, in comes my Lord from sea, to our great wonder. He had dined at Havre de Grace on Monday last, and come to the Downes the next day, and lay at Canterbury that night; and so to Dartford, and thence this morning to White Hall. Among others, Mr Creed and Captn. Ferrers tell me the stories of my Lord Duke of Buckingham's and my Lord's falling out at Havre de Grace, at cards; they two and my Lord St Alban's playing. The Duke did, to my Lord's dishonour, often say that he did in his conscience know the contrary to what he then said, about the difference at cards; and so did take up the money that he should have lost to my Lord. Which my Lord resenting, said nothing then, but that he doubted not but there were ways enough to get his money of him. So they parted that night; and my Lord sent Sir R. Stayner the next morning to the Duke, to know whether he did remember what he said last night, and whether he would owne it with his sword and a second; which he said he would, and so both sides agreed. But my Lord St Alban's, and the Queen, and Ambassador Montagu, did way-lay them at their lodgings till the difference was made up, to my Lord's honour; who hath got great reputation thereby.

8th. Captn. Cuttle, and Curtis, and Mootham, and I, went to the Fleece Taverne to drink; and there we spent till four o'clock, telling stories of Algiers, and the manner of life of slaves there. And truly Captn. Mootham and Mr Dawes (who have been both slaves there) did make me fully acquainted with their condition there: as, how they eat nothing but bread and water. At their redemption they pay so much for the water they drink at the public fountaynes, during their being slaves. How they are beat upon the soles of their feet and bellies at the liberty of their padron. How they are all, at night, called into their master's Bagnard; and there they lie. How the poorest men do love their slaves best. How some rogues do live well, if they do invent to bring their masters in so much a week by their industry or theft; and then they are put to no other work at all. And theft there is counted no great crime at all.

12th. By coach to the Theatre, and there saw *The Scornfull Lady*,[11]

---

11 A comedy, by Beaumont and Fletcher.

now done by a woman, which makes the play appear much better than ever it did to me.

14th. The talk of the towne now is, who the King is like to have for his Queene: and whether Lent shall be kept with the strictnesse of the King's proclamation; which is thought cannot be, because of the poor, who cannot buy fish. And also the great preparation for the King's crowning is now much thought upon and talked of.

18th. It is much talked that the King is already married to the niece of the Prince de Ligne, and that he hath two sons already by her: which I am sorry to hear; but yet am gladder that it should be so, than that the Duke of York and his family should come to the crowne, he being a professed friend to the Catholiques. Met with Sir G. Carteret: who afterwards, with the Duke of York, my Lord Sandwich, and others, went into a private room to consult: and we were a little troubled that we were not called in with the rest. But I do believe it was upon something very private. We staid walking in the gallery; where we met with Mr Slingsby, who showed me the stamps of the King's new coyne; which is strange to see, how good they are in the stamp and bad in the money, for lack of skill to make them. But he says Blondeau will shortly come over, and then we shall have it better, and the best in the world. He tells me, he is sure that the King is not yet married, as it is said; nor that it is known who he will have.

22nd. My wife to Sir W. Batten's, and there sat a while; he having yesterday sent my wife half-a-dozen pair of gloves, and a pair of silk stockings and garters, for her Valentines.

23rd. This my birthday, 28 years. Mr Hartlett told me how my Lord Chancellor had lately got the Duke of York and Duchesse, and her woman, my Lord Ossory,[12] and a Doctor, to make oath before most of the Judges of the kingdom, concerning all the circumstances of their marriage. And in fine, it is confessed that they were not fully married till about a month or two before she was brought to bed; but that they were contracted long before, and time enough for the child to be legitimate. But I do not hear that it was put to the Judges to determine whether it was so or no. To the Play-house, and there saw

12 Thomas, Earl of Ossory, son of the Duke of Ormond. Died 1680, aged 46.

The Changeling,[13] the first time it hath been acted these twenty years, and it takes exceedingly. Besides, I see the gallants do begin to be tyred with the vanity and pride of the theatre actors, who are indeed grown very proud and rich. I also met with the Comptroller, who told me how it was easy for us all, the principall officers, and proper for us, to labour to get into the next Parliament; and would have me to ask the Duke's letter, but I shall not endeavour it. This is now 28 years that I am born. And blessed be God, in a state of full content, and a great hope to be a happy man in all respects, both to myself and friends.

27th. I called for a dish of fish, which we had for dinner, this being the first day of Lent; and I do intend to try whether I can keep it or no.

28th. Notwithstanding my resolution, yet for want of other victualls, I did eat flesh this Lent, but am resolved to eat as little as I can. This month ends with two great secrets under dispute but yet known to very few: first, Who the King will marry; and What the meaning of this fleet is which we are now sheathing to set out for the southward. Most think against Algier against the Turke, or to the East Indys against the Dutch who, we hear, are setting out a great fleet thither.

March 1st. After dinner Mr Shepley and I in private talking about my Lord's intentions to go speedily into the country, but to what end we know not. We fear he is to go to sea with his fleet now preparing. But we wish that he could get his £4000 per annum settled before he do go. To White-fryars, and saw *The Bondman*[14] acted; an excellent play and well done. But above all that ever I saw, Beterton do the Bondman the best.

2nd. After dinner I went to the theatre, where I found so few people (which is strange, and the reason I do not know) that I went out again, and so to Salsbury Court, where the house as full as could be; and it seems it was a new play, *The Queen's Maske*,[15] wherein there are some good humours: among others, a good jeer to the old story of the Siege of Troy, making it to be a common country tale. But

13 *The Changeling,* a tragedy, by Thomas Middleton. The plot is taken from a story in *God's Revenge against Murder.*
14 By Massinger.
15 *Love's Mistress, or The Queen's Masque*, by T. Heywood.

above all it was strange to see so little a boy as that was to act Cupid, which is one of the greatest parts in it.

4th. My Lord went this morning on his journey to Hinchingbroke, Mr Parker with him; the chief business being to look over and determine how, and in what manner, his great work of building shall be done. Before his going he did give me some jewells to keep for him, viz. that that the King of Sweden did give him, with the King's own picture in it, most excellently done; and a brave George, all of diamonds.

8th. All the morning at the office. At noon Sir W. Batten, Col. Slingsby and I by coach to the Tower, to Sir John Robinson's, to dinner; where great good cheer. High company; among others the Duchess of Albemarle,[16] who is ever a plain homely dowdy. After dinner, to drink all the afternoon. Towards night the Duchesse and ladies went away. Then we set to it again till it was very late. And at last come in Sir William Wale, almost fuddled; and because I was set between him and another, only to keep them from talking and spoiling the company (as we did to others,) he fell out with the Lieutenant of the Tower; but with much ado we made him understand his error, and then all quiet.

9th. To my Lord's, where we found him lately come from Hinchingbroke. I staid and dined with him. He took me aside, and asked me what the world spoke of the King's marriage. Which I answering as one that knew nothing, he enquired no further of me. But I do perceive by it that there is something in it that is ready to come out that the world knows not of yet.

11th. After dinner I went to the theatre, and there saw *Love's Mistress* done by them, which I do not like in some things as well as their acting in Salsbury Court.

15th. This day my wife and Pall went to see my Lady Kingston, her brother's[17] lady.

18th. This day an ambassador from Florence was brought into the

---

16 Ann Clarges, daughter of a blacksmith, and bred a milliner; mistress and afterwards wife of General Monk, over whom she possessed the greatest influence.
17 Balthazar St Michel is the only brother of Mrs Pepys, mentioned in the Diary.

towne in state. Yesterday was said to be the day that the Princesse Henrietta was to marry the Duke d'Anjou in France. This day I found in the newes-book that Roger Pepys is chosen at Cambridge for the towne, the first place that we hear of to have made their choice yet.

20th. To White Hall to Mr Coventry, where I did some business with him, and so with Sir W. Pen (who I found with Mr Coventry teaching of him the map to understand Jamaica). The great talk of the towne is the strange election that the City of London made yesterday for Parliament-men; viz. Fowke, Love, Jones, and . . . ,[18] men that, so far from being episcopall, are thought to be Anabaptists; and chosen with a great deal of zeale, in spite of the other party that thought themselves so strong, calling out in the Hall, 'No Bishops! no Lord Bishops!' It do make people to fear it may come to worse, by being an example to the country to do the same. And indeed the Bishops are so high, that very few do love them.

23rd. To the Red Bull (where I had not been since plays come up again) up to the tireing-room, where strange the confusion and disorder that there is among them in fitting themselves, especially here, where the clothes are very poore, and the actors but common fellows. At last into the pitt, where I think there was not above ten more than myself, and not one hundred in the whole house. And the play, which is called *All's lost by Lust*,[19] poorly done; and with so much disorder, among others, in the musique-room the boy that was to sing a song, not singing it right, his master fell about his eares and beat him so, that it put the whole house in an uprore. Met my uncle Wight, and with him Lieut.-Col. Baron, who told us how Crofton, the great Presbyterian minister that had preached so highly against Bishops, is clapped up this day in the Tower. Which do please some, and displease others exceedingly.

April 2nd. To St James's Park, where I saw the Duke of York playing at Pelemele, the first time that ever I saw the sport. Then to the Dolphin to Sir W. Batten, and Pen, and other company; among others Mr Delabar; where strange how these men, who at other times are all wise men, do now, in their drink, betwitt and reproach one

18 Sir W. Thompson was the fourth member.
19 A tragedy, by W. Rowley.

another with their former conditions, and their actions as in public concerns, till I was ashamed to see it.

3rd. I hear that the Dutch have sent the King a great present of money, which we think will stop the match with Portugal; and judge this to be the reason that our so great haste in sending the two ships to the East Indys is also stayed.

7th. To White Hall, and there I met with Dr Fuller[20] of Twickenham, newly come from Ireland; and took him to my Lord's, where he and I dined; and he did give my Lord and me a good account of the condition of Ireland, and how it come to pass, through the joyning of the Fanatiques and the Presbyterians, that the latter and the former are in their declaration put together under the names of Fanatiques.

9th. At the sale of old stores at Chatham; and among other things sold there was all the State's armes, which Sir W. Batten bought; intending to set up some of the images in his garden, and the rest to burn on the Coronacion night.

10th. Then to Rochester, and there saw the Cathedrall, which is now fitting for use, and the organ then a-tuning. Then away thence, observing the great doors of the church, as they say, covered with the skins of the Danes.

13th. Met my Lord with the Duke; and after a little talk with him, I went to the Banquet-house, and there saw the King heale, the first time that ever I saw him do it; which he did with great gravity, and it seemed to me to be an ugly office and a simple one.

20th. Comes my boy to tell me that the Duke of York had sent for all the principall officers, &c., to come to him today. So I went by water to Mr Coventry's, and there staid and talked a good while with him till all the rest come. We went up and saw the Duke dress himself, and in his night habitt he is a very plain man. Then he sent us to his closett, where we saw among other things two very fine chests, covered with gold and Indian varnish, given him by the East Indy Company of Holland. The Duke comes; and after he had told

20 William Fuller of Magdalene Hall, Oxford, was a schoolmaster at Twickenham during the Rebellion; and at the Restoration became Dean of St Patrick's; and in 1663, Bishop of Limerick; and in 1667 was translated to Lincoln. Died 1675.

us that the fleet was designed for Algier (which was kept from us till now,) we did advise about many things as to the fitting of the fleet, and so went away to White Hall; and in the Banqueting-house saw the King create my Lord Chancellor and several others, Earles, and Mr Crewe and several others, Barons: the first being led up by Heralds and five old Earles to the King, and there the patent is read, and the King puts on his vest, and sword, and coronett, and gives him the patent. And then he kisseth the King's hand, and rises and stands covered before the King. And the same for each Baron, only he is led up by three of the old Barons. And they are girt with swords before they go to the King. To the Cockpitt; and there, by the favour of one Mr Bowman, he and I got in, and there saw the King and Duke of York and his Duchesse, (which is a plain woman, and like her mother, my Lady Chancellor). And so saw *The Humersome Lieutenant*[21] acted before the King, but not very well done. But my pleasure was great to see the manner of it, and so many great beauties, but above all Mrs Palmer, with whom the King do discover a great deal of familiarity.

21st. Dined with Doctor Thos. Pepys[22] and Dr Fayrebrother; and all our talk about to-morrow's showe, and our trouble that it is like to be a wet day. All the way is so thronged with people to see the triumphall arches, that I could hardly pass for them.

22nd. The King's going from the Tower to White Hall. Up early and made myself as fine as I could, and put on my velvet coat, the first day that I put it on, though made half a year ago. And being ready, Sir W. Batten, my Lady, and his two daughters and his son and wife, and Sir W. Pen and his son and I, went to Mr Young's, the flagmaker, in Cornehill; and there we had a good room to ourselves, with wine and good cake, and saw the show very well. In which it is impossible to relate the glory of this day, expressed in the clothes of them that rid, and their horses and horses-clothes. Among others, my Lord Sand-wich's embroidery and diamonds were not ordinary among them. The Knights of the Bath was a brave sight of itself; and their Esquires, among which Mr Armiger was an Esquire to one of the Knights. Remarquable were the two men that represent the two Dukes of

21 *The Humorous Lieutenant*, a tragi-comedy, by Beaumont and Fletcher.
22 Doctor in Civil Law.

Normandy and Aquitane. The Bishops come next after Barons, which
is the higher place; which makes me think that the next Parliament
they will be called to the House of Lords. My Lord Monk rode bare
after the King, and led in his hand a spare horse, as being Master of the
Horse. The King, in a most rich embroidered suit and cloak, looked
most noble. Wadlow the vintner, at the Devil, in Fleet-street, did lead
a fine company of soldiers, all young comely men, in white doublets.
There followed the Vice-Chamberlain, Sir G. Carteret, a Company of
men all like Turkes; but I know not yet what they are for. The streets
all gravelled, and the houses hung with carpets before them, made
brave show, and the ladies out of the windows. So glorious was the
show with gold and silver, that we were not able to look at it, our eyes
at last being so much overcome. Both the King and the Duke of York
took notice of us, as they saw us at the window. In the evening, by
water to White Hall to my Lord's, and there I spoke with my Lord.
He talked with me about his suit, which was made in France, and cost
him £200, and very rich it is with embroidery.

CORONACON DAY

23rd. About four I rose and got to the Abbey, where I followed Sir J.
Denham,[23] the Surveyor, with some company that he was leading in.
And with much ado, by the favour of Mr Cooper, his man, did get
up into a great scaffold across the North end of the Abbey, where
with a great deal of patience I sat from past four till eleven before the
King come in. And a great pleasure it was to see the Abbey raised in
the middle, all covered with red, and a throne (that is a chaire) and
footstoole on the top of it; and all the officers of all kinds, so much as
the very fidlers, in red vests. At last comes in the Dean and Prebends
of Westminster, with the Bishops, (many of them in cloth of gold
copes,) and after them the Nobility, all in their Parliament robes,
which was a most magnificent sight. Then the Duke and the King
with a scepter (carried by my Lord Sandwich) and sword and wand
before him, and the crowne too. The King in his robes, bare-headed,
which was very fine. And after all had placed themselves, there was a
sermon and the service; and then in the Quire at the high altar, the
King passed through all the ceremonies of the Coronation, which to

23 Created at the Restoration KB, and Surveyor-General of all the King's buildings;
better known as the author of *Cooper's Hill*. Died 1668.

my great grief I and most in the Abbey could not see. The crowne being put upon his head, a great shout begun, and he come forth to the throne, and there passed through more ceremonies: as taking the oath, and having things read to him by the Bishopp; and his lords (who put on their caps as soon as the King put on his crowne) and bishops come, and kneeled before him. And three times the King at Armes went to the three open places on the scaffold, and proclaimed, that if any one could show any reason why Charles Stewart should not be King of England, that now he should come and speak. And a Generall Pardon also was read by the Lord Chancellor, and meddalls flung up and down by my Lord Cornwallis,[24] of silver, but I could not come by any. But so great a noise that I could make but little of the musique; and indeed, it was lost to every body. I went out a little while before the King had done all his ceremonies, and went round the Abbey to Westminster Hall, all the way within rayles, and 10,000 people with the ground covered with blue cloth; and scaffolds all the way. Into the Hall I got, where it was very fine with hangings and scaffolds one upon another full of brave ladies; and my wife in one little one, on the right hand. Here I staid walking up and down, and at last upon one of the side stalls I stood and saw the King come in with all the persons (but the soldiers) that were yesterday in the cavalcade; and a most pleasant sight it was to see them in their several robes. And the King come in with his crowne on, and his sceptre in his hand, under a canopy borne up by six silver staves, carried by Barons of the Cinque Ports, and little bells at every end. And after a long time, he got up to the farther end, and all set themselves down at their several tables; and that was also a brave sight: and the King's first course carried up by the Knights of the Bath. And many fine ceremonies there was of the Heralds leading up people before him, and bowing; and my Lord of Albemarle's going to the kitchin and eating a bit of the first dish that was to go to the King's table. But, above all, was these three Lords, Northumberland, and Suffolke,[25] and the Duke of Ormond, coming before the courses on horseback, and staying so all dinner-time, and at last bringing up (Dymock) the King's Champion, all in armour on horseback, with his speare and

24 Sir Frederick Cornwallis, Bart., had been created a Baron three days before the Coronation. He was Treasurer of His Majesty's Household, and a Privy Counsellor. Died Jan. 31, 1661/62.
25 James Howard, third Earl of Suffolk.

targett carried before him. And a herald proclaims 'That if any dare
deny Charles Stewart to be lawful King of England, here was a
Champion that would fight with him'; and with these words, the
Champion flings down his gauntlet, and all this he do three times in
his going up towards the King's table. To which when he is come,
the King drinks to him, and then sends him the cup which is of gold,
and he drinks it off, and then rides back again with the cup in his
hand. I went from table to table to see the Bishops and all others at
their dinner, and was infinitely pleased with it. And at the Lords'
table, I met with William Howe, and he spoke to my Lord for me,
and he did give him four rabbits and a pullet, and so Mr Creed and I
got Mr Minshell to give us some bread, and so we at a stall eat it, as
every body else did what they could get. I took a great deal of
pleasure to go up and down, and look upon the ladies, and to hear
the musique of all sorts, but above all, the 24 violins. About six at
night they had dined, and I went up to my wife. And strange it is to
think, that these two days have held up fair till now that all is done,
and the King gone out of the Hall; and then it fell a-raining and
thundering and lightening as I have not seen it do for some years:
which people did take great notice of; God's blessing of the work of
these two days, which is a foolery to take too much notice of such
things. I observed little disorder in all this, only the King's footmen
had got hold of the canopy, and would keep it from the Barons of the
Cinque Ports, which they endeavoured to force from them again, but
could not do it till my Lord Duke of Albemarle caused it to be put
into Sir R. Pye's[26] hand till to-morrow to be decided. At Mr
Bowyer's; a great deal of company, some I knew, others I did not.
Here we staid upon the leads and below till it was late, expecting to
see the fire-works, but they were not performed to-night: only the
City had a light like a glory round about it with bonfires. At last I
went to King-streete, and there sent Crockford to my father's and my
house, to tell them I could not come home tonight, because of the
dirt, and a coach could not be had. And so I took my wife and Mrs
Frankleyn (who I profered the civility of lying with my wife at Mrs
Hunt's to-night) to Axe-yard, in which at the further end there were
three great bonfires, and a great many great gallants, men and

26 Sir Robert Pye, Bart., of Faringdon House, Berks; married Ann, daughter of the
celebrated John Hampden. They lived together 60 years, and died in 1701, within a
few weeks of each other.

women; and they laid hold of us, and would have us drink the King's health upon our knees, kneeling upon a faggot, which we all did, they drinking to us one after another. Which we thought a strange frolique; but these gallants continued there a great while, and I wondered to see how the ladies did tipple. At last I sent my wife and her bedfellow to bed, and Mr Hunt and I went in with Mr Thornbury (who did give the company all their wine, he being yeoman of the wine-cellar to the King); and there, with his wife and two of his sisters, and some gallant sparks that were there, we drank the King's health, and nothing else, till one of the gentlemen fell down stark drunk, and there lay; and I went to my Lord's pretty well. Thus did the day end with joy every where; and blessed be God, I have not heard of any mischance to any body through it all, but only to Serjt. Glynne,[27] whose horse fell upon him yesterday, and is like to kill him, which people do please themselves to see how just God is to punish the rogue at such a time as this: he being now one of the King's Serjeants, and rode in the cavalcade with Maynard,[28] to whom people wish the same fortune. There was also this night in King-streete, a woman had her eye put out by a boy's flinging a firebrand into the coach. Now, after all this, I can say, that, besides the pleasure of the sight of these glorious things, I may now shut my eyes against any other objects, nor for the future trouble myself to see things of state and showe, as being sure never to see the like again in this world.

24th. At night, set myself to write down these three days' diary, and while I am about it, I hear the noise of the chambers,[29] and other things of the fire-works, which are now playing upon the Thames before the King; and I wish myself with them, being sorry not to see them.

27 He had been Recorder of London; and during the Protectorate was made Chief Justice of the Upper Bench: nevertheless he did Charles II great service, and was in consequence knighted and appointed King's Serjeant, and his son created a Baronet. Died 1666.

28 John Maynard, an eminent lawyer; made Serjeant to Cromwell in 1653, and afterwards King's Serjeant by Charles II, who knighted him. In 1661 he was chosen Member for Berealston, and sat in every Parliament till the Revolution. Died 1690, aged 88.

29 Chamber, a species of great gun.

30th. This morning my wife and I and Mr Creed, took coach, and in Fish-street took up Mr Hater and his wife, who through her maske seemed at first to be an old woman, but afterwards I found her to be a very pretty modest black woman. We got a small bait at Leatherhead, and so to Godlyman,[30] where we lay all night. I am sorry that I am not at London, to be at Hide-parke to-morrow, among the great gallants and ladies, which will be very fine.

May 1st. Up early, and bated at Petersfield, in the room which the King lay in lately at his being there. Here very merry, and played with our wives at bowles. Then we set forth again, and so to Portsmouth, seeming to me to be a very pleasant and strong place; and we lay at the Red Lyon, where Haselrigge and Scott and Walton did hold their councill, when they were here, against Lambert and the Committee of Safety.

2nd. To see the room where the Duke of Buckingham was killed by Felton.

6th. I hear to-night that the Duke of York's son is this day dead, which I believe will please everybody; and I hear that the Duke and his Lady themselves are not much troubled at it.

12th. At the Savoy heard Dr Fuller preach upon David's words, 'I will wait with patience all the days of my appointed time until my change comes'; but methought it was a poor dry sermon. And I am afraid my former high esteem of his preaching was more out of opinion than judgment. Met with Mr Creed, with whom I went and walked in Grayes-Inn-walks, and from thence to Islington, and there eate and drank at the house my father and we were wont of old to go to; and after that walked homeward, and parted in Smithfield: and so I home, much wondering to see how things are altered with Mr Creed, who, twelve months ago, might have been got to hang himself almost as soon as go to a drinking-house on a Sunday.

18th. I went to Westminster; where it was very pleasant to see the Hall in the condition it is now, with the Judges on the benches at the further end of it, which I had not seen all this terme till now.

19th (Lord's day). I walked in the morning towards Westminster,

30 Godalming.

and, seeing many people at York House, I went down and found them at masse, it being the Spanish ambassador's; and so I got into one of the gallerys, and there heard two masses done, I think, not in so much state as I have seen them heretofore. After that into the garden, and walked an hour or two, but found it not so fine a place as I always took it for by the outside. Captain Ferrers and Mr Howe and myself to Mr Wilkinson's at the Crowne: then to my Lord's, where we went and sat talking and laughing in the drawing-room a great while. All our talk upon their going to sea this voyage, which Captain Ferrers is in some doubt whether he shall do or no, but swears that he would go, if he were sure never to come back again; and I, giving him some hopes, he grew so mad with joy that he fell a-dancing and leaping like a madman. Now it fell out that the balcone windows were open, and he went to the rayle and make an offer to leap over, and asked what if he should leap over there. I told him I would give him £40 if he did not go to sea. With that thought I shut the doors, and W. Howe hindered him all we could; yet he opened them again, and, with a vault, leaps down into the garden: – the greatest and most desperate frolic that ever I saw in my life. I run to see what was become of him, and we found him crawled upon his knees, but could not rise; so we went down into the garden and dragged him to a bench, where he looked like a dead man, but could not stir; and, though he had broke nothing, yet his pain in his back was such as he could not endure. With this, my Lord (who was in the little new room) come to us in amaze, and bid us carry him up, which, by our strength, we did, and so laid him in East's bedroom, by the doore; where he lay in great pain. We sent for a doctor and chyrurgeon, but none to be found, till by-and-by by chance comes in Dr Clerke, who is afraid of him.[31] So we went for a lodging for him.

21st. Up early, and, with Sir R. Slingsby, (and Major Waters the deafe gentleman, his friend for company's sake) to the Victualling-office (the first time that I ever knew where it was), and there staid while he read a commission for enquiry into some of the King's lands and houses thereabouts, that are given his brother. And then we took boat to Woolwich, where we staid and gave order for the fitting out of some more ships presently. And then to Deptford, where we did the same; and so took barge again, and were overtaken by the King in

31 He recovered.

his barge, he having been down the river with his yacht this day for pleasure to try it; and, as I hear, Commissioner Pett's do prove better than the Dutch one, and that that his brother built. While we were upon the water, one of the greatest showers of rain fell that ever I saw. The Comptroller and I landed with our barge at the Temple, and from thence I went to my father's, and there did give order about some clothes to be made.

23rd. In my black silk suit (the first day I have put it on this year) to my Lord Mayor's by coach, with a great deal of honourable company, and great entertainment. At table I had very good discourse with Mr Ashmole, wherein he did assure me that frogs and many insects do often fall from the sky, ready formed. Dr Bates's singularity in not rising up nor drinking the King's nor other healths at the table was very much observed. From thence we all took coach, and to our office, and there sat till it was late; and so I home and to bed by day-light. This day was kept a holy-day through the towne; and it pleased me to see the little boys walk up and down in procession with their broom-staffs in their hands, as I had myself long ago done.

26th. Sir W. Batten told me how Mr Prin (among the two or three that did refuse today to receive the sacrament upon their knees) was offered by a mistake the drinke afterwards, which he did receive, being denied the drinke by Dr Gunning, unless he would take it on his knees; and after that by another the bread was brought him, and he did take it sitting, which is thought very preposterous.

28th. With Mr Shepley to the Exchange about business, and there, by Mr Rawlinson's favour, got into a balcone over against the Exchange; and there saw the hangman burn, by vote of Parliament, two old acts, the one for constituting us a Commonwealth, and the other[32] I have forgot.

29th (King's birth-day). Rose early, and put six spoons and a porringer of silver in my pocket to give away today. Sir W. Pen and I took coach, and (the weather and way being foule) went to Walthamstow; and being come there heard Mr Radcliffe, my former school fellow at Paul's, (who is yet a merry boy,) preach upon 'Nay, let him take all, since my Lord the King is returned', &c. He read all,

32 It was an Act subscribing the Engagement.

and his sermon very simple. Back to dinner at Sir William Batten's; and then, after a walk in the fine gardens, we went to Mrs Browne's, where Sir W. Pen and I were godfathers, and Mrs Jordan and Shipman godmothers to her boy. And there, before and after the christening, we were with the woman above in her chamber; but whether we carried ourselves well or ill, I know not; but I was directed by young Mrs Batten. One passage of a lady that eate wafers with her dog did a little displease me. I did give the midwife 10s. and the nurse 5s. and the maid of the house 2s. But for as much I expected to give the name to the childe, but did not, (it being called John,) I forbore then to give my plate.

30th. This day, I hear, the Parliament have ordered a bill to be brought in for restoring the Bishops to the House of Lords; which they had not done so soon but to spite Mr Prin, who is every day so bitter against them in his discourse in the House.

31st. Great talk now how the Parliament intend to make a collection of free gifts to the King through the Kingdom; but I think it will not come to much.

June 4th. To my Lord Crewe's to dinner, and had very good discourse about having of young noblemen and gentlemen to think of going to sea, as being as honourable service as the land war. And among other things he told us how, in Queen Elizabeth's time, one young nobleman would wait with a trencher at the back of another till he come to age himself. And witnessed in my young Lord of Kent, that then was, who waited upon my Lord Bedford at table, when a letter come to my Lord Bedford that the Earldome of Kent was fallen to his servant the young Lord; and so he rose from table, and made him sit down in his place, and took a lower for himself, for so he was by place to sit.

9th. To White Hall, and there met with Dean Fuller, and walked a great while with him; among other things discoursed of the liberty the Bishop (by name he of Galloway) takes to admit into orders any body that will; among others Roundtree, a simple mechanique that was a person formerly of the fleet. He told me he would complain of it.

10th. Early to my Lord's, who privately told me how the King had made him Embassador in the bringing over the Queen. That he is to go to Algier, &c., to settle the business, and to put the fleet in order there; and so to come back to Lisbone with three ships, and there to meet the fleet that is to follow him. He sent for me, to tell me that he do intrust me with the seeing of all things done in his absence as to this great preparation, as I shall receive orders from my Lord Chancellor and Mr Edward Montagu. At all which my heart is above measure glad; for my Lord's honour, and some profit to myself, I hope. By and by, out with Mr Shepley, Walden,[33] Parliament-man for Huntingdon, Rolt, Mackworth, and Alderman Backwell, to a house hard by, to drink Lambeth ale. So I back to the Wardrobe, and there found my Lord going to Trinity House, this being the solemn day of choosing Master, and my Lord is chosen.

11th. At the office this morning, Sir G. Carteret with us; and we agreed upon a letter to the Duke of York, to tell him the sad condition of this office for want of money; how men are not able to serve us more without some money; and that now the credit of the office is brought so low, that none will sell us any thing without our personal security given for the same.

12th. Wednesday, a day kept between a fast and a feast, the Bishops not being ready enough to keep the fast for foule weather before fair weather come; and so they were forced to keep it between both. Then to White Hall, where I met my Lord, who told me he must have £300 laid out in cloth, to give in Barbary, as presents among the Turkes.

27th. This day Mr Holden sent me a bever, which cost me £4 5s.

28th. Went to Moorefields, and there walked, and stood and saw the wrestling, which I never saw so much of before, between the north and west countrymen.

29th. Mr Chetwind fell commending of Hooker's *Ecclesiastical Polity* as the best book, and the only one that made him a Christian, which puts me upon the buying of it, which I will do shortly.

30th (Lord's day). To church, where we observe the trade of briefs is

33 Lionel.

come now up to so constant a course every Sunday, that we resolve to give no more to them. This day the Portuguese Embassador come to White Hall to take leave of the King; he being now going to end all with the Queen, and to send her over.

July 2nd. Went to Sir William Davenant's[34] Opera; this being the fourth day that it hath begun, and the first that I have seen it. Today was acted the second part of *The Siege of Rhodes*.[35] We staid a very great while for the King and Queen of Bohemia. And by the breaking of a board over our heads, we had a great deal of dust fell into the ladies' necks and the men's haire, which made good sport. The King being come, the scene opened; which indeed is very fine and magnificent, and well acted, all but the Eunuche, who was so much out that he was hissed off the stage.

3rd. Dined with my Lady, who is in some[36] mourning for her brother, Mr Saml. Crewe, who died yesterday of the spotted fever.

4th. I went to the theatre, and there I saw *Claracilla*[37] (the first time I ever saw it,) well acted. But strange to see this house, that used to be so thronged, now empty since the Opera begun; and so will continue for a while, I believe.

6th. Waked this morning with news, brought me by a messenger on purpose, that my uncle Robert[38] is dead; so I set out on horseback, and got well by nine o'clock to Brampton, where I found my father well. My uncle's corps in a coffin standing upon joynt-stooles in the chimney in the hall; but it begun to smell, and so I caused it to be set forth in the yard all night, and watched by my aunt.

7th (Lord's day). In the morning my father and I read the will; where, though he gives me nothing at present till my father's death, or at least very little, yet I am glad to see that he hath done so well for us all, and well to the rest of his kindred. After that done, we went about getting things, as ribbands and gloves, ready for the burial.

34 Sir William Davenant, the celebrated dramatic writer, and patentee of the Duke's Theatre in Lincoln's Inn Fields. Died 1668, aged 64.
35 Of which Sir W. Davenant was the author.
36 Probably meant for 'handsome' in the manuscript.
37 A tragi-comedy by Thomas Killigrew.
38 Of Brampton, in Huntingdonshire.

Which in the afternoon was done; where, it being Sunday, all people far and near come in; and in the greatest disorder that ever I saw, we made shift to serve them with what we had of wine and other things; and then to carry him to the church, where Mr Taylor buried him, and Mr Turner preached a funerall sermon.

14th. To Hinchingbroke, which is now all in dirt, because of my Lord's building, which will make it very magnificent. Back to Brampton.

15th. Up by three o'clock this morning, and rode to Cambridge to King's College chappel, where I found the scholars in their surplices at the service with the organs, which is a strange sight to what it used in my time to be here. Rode to Impington, where I found my old uncle[39] sitting all alone, like a man out of the world: he can hardly see; but all things else he do pretty livelyly.

22nd. I come to Hatfield before twelve o'clock, and walked all alone to the Vineyard, which is now a very beautiful place again; and coming back I met with Mr Looker, my Lord's gardener, (a friend of Mr Eglin's) who showed me the house, the chappel with brave pictures, and, above all, the gardens, such as I never saw in all my life; nor so good flowers, nor so great gooseburys, as big as nutmegs. To horse again, and with much ado got to London.

26th. Mr Hill of Cambridge tells me, that yesterday put a change to the whole state of England as to the Church; for the King now would be forced to favour Presbytery, or that the City would leave him: but I heed not what he says, though upon enquiry I do find that things in the Parliament are in a great disorder.

27th. To Westminster Hall, where it was expected that the Parliament was to have been adjourned for two or three months, but something hinders it for a day or two. In the lobby I spoke with Mr George Montagu, and advised about a ship to carry my Lord Hinchingbroke and the rest of the young gentlemen to France, and they have resolved of going in a hired vessell from Rye, and not in a man of war. He told me in discourse, that my Lord Chancellor is much envied, and that many great men, such as the Duke of

39 Talbot Pepys.

Buckingham and my Lord of Bristoll,[40] do endeavour to undermine him, and that he believes it will not be done; for that the King (though he loves him not in the way of a companion, as he do these young gallants that can answer him in his pleasures,) yet cannot be without him, for his policy and service.

30th. After my singing-master had done with me this morning, I went to White Hall and Westminster Hall, where I found the King expected to come and adjourne the Parliament. I found the two Houses at a great difference, about the Lords challenging their privileges not to have their houses searched, which makes them deny to pass the House of Commons' Bill for searching for pamphlets and seditious books. Thence by water to the Wardrobe (meeting the King upon the water going in his barge to adjourne the House) where I dined with my Lady.

August 2nd. I made myself ready to get a-horseback for Cambridge.

3rd. At Cambridge Mr Pechell,[41] Sanchy, and others tell me how high the old doctors are in the University over those they found there, though a great deal better scholars than themselves; for which I am very sorry, and, above all, Dr Gunning. At night I took horse, and rode with Roger Pepys and his two brothers to Impington.

4th. To church, and had a good plain sermon. At our coming in the country-people all rose with so much reverence; and when the parson begins, he begins, 'Right worshipfull and dearly beloved' to us. To church again, and, after supper, to talk about publique matters, wherein Roger Pepys told me how basely things had been carried in Parliament by the young men, that did labour to oppose all things that were moved by serious men. That they are the most prophane swearing fellows that ever he heard in his life, which makes him think that they will spoil all, and bring things into a warr again if they can.

6th. Took horse for London, and with much ado, the ways being very bad, got to Baldwick.[42] I find that both here, and every where else that I come, the Quakers do still continue, and rather grow than lessen.

40 George, second Earl of Bristol.
41 John Pechell, made Master of Magdalene College, Cambridge, 1679.
42 Baldock.

9th. I to White Hall, where, after four o'clock, comes my Lord Privy Seale;[43] and so we went up to his chamber over the gate at White Hall, where he asked me what deputacon I had from my Lord. I told him none; but that I am sworn my Lord's deputy by both of the Secretarys, which did satisfye him. So he caused Mr Moore to read over all the bills, and all ended very well.

11th. To Grayes-Inn walks, and there staid a good while; where I met with Ned Pickering, who told me what a great match of hunting of a stagg the King had yesterday; and how the King tired all their horses, and come home with not above two or three able to keep pace with him.

14th. This morning Sir W. Batten, and Sir W. Penn and I, waited upon the Duke of York in his chamber, to give him an account of the condition of the Navy for lack of money, and how our own very bills are offered upon the Exchange, to be sold at 20 in the 100 loss. He is much troubled at it, and will speak to the King and Council of it this morning.

15th. To the Opera, which begins again today with *The Witts*,[44] never acted yet with scenes; and the King and Duke and Duchesse were there (who dined today with Sir H. Finch, reader at the Temple, in great state); and indeed it is a most excellent play, and admirable scenes.

16th. At the office all the morning, though little to do because all our clerkes are gone to the buriall of Tom Whitton, one of the Controller's clerkes, a very ingenious, and a likely young man to live, as any in the Office. But it is such a sickly time both in the City and country every where (of a sort of fever), that never was heard of almost, unless it was in a plague-time. Among others, the famous Tom Fuller[45] is dead of it; and Dr Nichols,[46] Dean of Paul's; and my Lord General Monk is very dangerously ill.

43 William, first Viscount, and second Baron Say and Sele, made Lord Privy Seal at the Restoration. Died April, 1662.
44 A comedy, by Sir W. Davenant.
45 DD, Author of the *Worthies of England*, Chaplain to the King, and Prebendary of Salisbury.
46 Matthew Nicholas, DD, installed Dean of St Paul's, July, 1660. Died August 14, 1661. He was brother to Sir Edward Nicholas, Secretary of State.

17th. At the Privy Seale, where we had a seale this morning. Then met with Ned Pickering, and walked with him into St James's Park (where I had not been a great while), and there found great and very noble alterations. And, in our discourse, he was very forward to complain and to speak loud of the lewdnesse and beggary of the Court, which I am sorry to hear, and which I am afraid will bring all to ruin again. I to the Opera, and saw *The Witts* again, which I like exceedingly. The Queen of Bohemia was here, brought by my Lord Craven.[47]

18th. To White Hall, and there hear that my Lord General Monk continues very ill; and then to walk in St James's Park, and saw a great variety of fowle which I never saw before. At night fell to read in Hooker's *Ecclesiastical Polity*, which Mr Moore did give me last Wednesday very handsomely bound; and which I shall read with great pains and love for his sake.

19th. I am sent for to the Privy Seale, and there I found a thing of my Lord Chancellor's to be sealed this afternoon, and so I am forced to go to Worcester House, where severall Lords are met in Council this afternoon. And while I am waiting there, in comes the King in a plain common riding-suit and velvet cap, in which he seemed a very ordinary man to one that had not known him.

27th. My wife and I to the theatre, and there saw *The Joviall Crew*,[48] where the King, Duke and Duchesse, and Madame Palmer, were; and my wife, to her great content, had a full sight of them all the while.

31st. At Court things are in very ill condition, there being so much emulacion, poverty, and the vices of drinking, swearing, and loose amours, that I know not what will be the end of it, but confusion. And the Clergy so high, that all people that I meet with do protest against their practice. In short, I see no content or satisfaction any where, in any one sort of people. The Benevolence[49] proves so little, and an occasion of so much discontent every where, that it had

47 William, first Earl of Craven, a Privy Councillor, and Colonel of the Coldstream Guards; supposed to be married to the Queen of Bohemia. Died 1697, aged 88.
48 Or the *Merry Beggars*, a comedy, by Richard Brome.
49 A voluntary contribution made by the subjects to their Sovereign.

better it had never been set up. I think to subscribe £20. We are at
our Office quiet, only for lack of money all things go to rack. Our
very bills offered to be sold upon the Exchange at 10 per cent. loss.
We are upon getting Sir R. Ford's house added to our Office. But I
see so many difficulties will follow in pleasing of one another in the
dividing of it, and in becoming bound personally to pay the rent of
£200 per annum, that I do believe it will yet scarce come to pass.
The season very sickly every where of strange and fatal fevers.

September 1st. Captn. Holmes and I by coach to White Hall; in our
way, I found him by discourse, to be a great friend of my Lord's, and
he told me there was a many did seek to remove him; but they were
old seamen, such as Sir J. Minnes,[50] (but he would name no more,
though he do believe Sir W. Batten is one of them that do envy
him,) but he says he knows that the King do so love him, and the
Duke of York too, that there is no fear of him. He seems to be very
well acquainted with the King's mind, and with all the general
factions at Court, and spoke all with so much franknesse, that I do
take him to be my Lord's good friend, and one able to do him great
service, being a cunning fellow, and one (by his own confession to
me) that can put on two several faces, and look his enemies in the
face with as much love as his friends. But, good God! what an age is
this, and what a world is this! that a man cannot live without playing
the knave and dissimulation.

2nd. I find that there are endeavours to get my Lord out of play at
sea, which I believe Mr Coventry and the Duke do think will make
them more absolute; but I hope, for all this, they will not be able to
do it.

3rd. Dined at home, and then with my wife to the Wardrobe, where
my Lady's child was christened, (my Lord Crewe and his Lady, and
my Lady Montagu, my Lord's mother-in-law, were the witnesses),
and named Katherine (the Queen elect's name); but to my and all our
trouble, the Parson of the parish christened her, and did not sign the
child with the sign of the cross. After that was done, we had a very
fine banquet.

7th. Having appointed the young ladies at the Wardrobe to go with

50 A Vice-Admiral, and afterwards Comptroller of the Navy.

them to the play today, my wife and I took them to the theatre, where we seated ourselves close by the King, and Duke of York, and Madame Palmer, which was great content; and, indeed, I can never enough admire her beauty. And here was *Bartholomew Fayre*,[51] with the puppet-showe, acted to-day, which had not been these forty years, (it being so satyricall against puritanism, they durst not till now, which is strange they should already dare to do it, and the King do countenance it,) but I do never a whit like it the better for the puppets, but rather the worse. Thence home with the ladies, it being by reason of our staying a great while for the King's coming, and the length of the play, near nine o'clock before it was done.

11th. To Dr Williams, who did carry me into his garden, where he hath abundance of grapes: and he did show me how a dog that he hath do kill all the cats that come thither to kill his pigeons, and do afterwards bury them; and do it with so much care that they shall be quite covered; that if the tip of the tail hangs out he will take up the cat again, and dig the hole deeper. Which is very strange; and he tells me, that he do believe that he hath killed above a hundred cats.

12th. To my Lady's to dinner at the Wardrobe; and in my way upon the Thames, I saw the King's new pleasure-boat that is come now for the King to take pleasure in above bridge; and also two Gundaloes[52] that are lately brought, which are very rich and fine.

24th. Letters from sea, that speak of my Lord's being well; and his action, though not considerable of any side, at Argier.

25th. Sir W. Pen told me that I need not fear any reflection upon my Lord for their ill successe at Argier, for more could not be done. To my Lord Crewe's, and dined with him, where I was used with all imaginable kindness both from him and her. And I see that he is afraid my Lord's reputacon will a little suffer in common talk by this late successe; but there is no help for it now. The Queen of England (as she is now owned and called) I hear doth keep open Court, and distinct at Lisbone.

27th. At noon, met my wife at the Wardrobe; and there dined,

51 A comedy, by Ben Jonson; first acted in 1614.
52 Gondolas. Davenant uses the expression, 'Step into one of your peascod boats, whose tilts are not so sumptuous as the roofs of Gundaloes.'

where we found Captn. Country, (my little Captain that I loved, who carried me to the Sound,) with some grapes and millons from my Lord at Lisbone. The first that ever I saw; but the grapes are rare things. In the afternoon comes Mr Edwd. Montagu (by appointment this morning) to talk with my Lady and me about the provisions fit to be bought, and sent to my Lord along with him. And told us, that we need not trouble ourselves how to buy them, for the King would pay for all, and that he would take care to get them: which put my Lady and me into a great deal of ease of mind. Here we staid and supped too, and, after my wife had put up some of the grapes in a basket for to be sent to the King, we took coach and home, where we found a hampire of millons sent to me also.

30th. This morning up by moone-shine, at 5 o'clock, to White Hall, to meet Mr Moore at the Privy Seale, and there I heard of a fray between the two Embassadors of Spaine[53] and France;[54] and that, this day, being the day of the entrance of an Embassador from Sweden, they intended to fight for the precedence. Our King, I heard, ordered that no Englishman should meddle in the business, but let them do what they would. And to that end all the soldiers in the town were in arms all the day long, and some of the train-bands in the City; and a great bustle through the City all the day. Then we took coach (which was the business I come for) to Chelsey, to my Lord Privy Seale, and there got him to seal the business. Here I saw by day-light two very fine pictures in the gallery, that a little while ago I saw by night; and did also go all over the house, and found it to be the prettiest contrived house that I ever saw in my life. So back again; and at White Hall light, and saw the soldiers and people running up and down the streets. So I went to the Spanish Embassador's and the French, and there saw great preparations on both sides; but the French made the most noise and ranted most, but the other made no stir almost at all; so that I was afraid the other would have too great a conquest over them. Then to the Wardrobe, and dined there, and then abroad and in Cheapside hear that the Spanish hath got the best of it, and killed three of the French coach-horses and several men,

---

53 The Baron de Vatteville.
54 Godfrey, Count D'Estrades, Marshal of France, and Viceroy of America. He proved himself, upon many occasions, an able diplomatist, and particularly at the conferences of Nimeguen when acting as ambassador in 1673. Died 1686, aged 79.

and is gone through the City next to our King's coach; at which, it is strange to see how all the City did rejoice. And indeed we do naturally all love the Spanish, and hate the French. But I, as I am in all things curious, presently got to the water-side, and there took oares to Westminster Palace, and run after them through all the dirt and the streets full of people: till at last, at the Mewes, I saw the Spanish coach go, with fifty drawn swords at least to guard it, and our soldiers shouting for joy. And so I followed the coach, and then met it at York House,[55] where the Embassador lies; and there it went in with great state. So then I went to the French houses where I observe still, that there is no men in the world of a more insolent spirit where they do well, nor before they begin a matter, and more abject if they do miscarry, than these people are; for they all look like dead men, and not a word among them, but shake their heads. The truth is, the Spaniards were not only observed to fight most desperately, but also they did outwitt them; first in lining their own harnesse with chains of iron that they could not be cut, then in setting their coach in the most advantageous place, and to appoint men to guard every one of their horses, and others for to guard the coach, and others the coachmen. And, above all, in setting upon the French horses and killing them, for by that means the French were not able to stir. There were several men slain of the French, and one or two of the Spaniards and one Englishman, by a bullet. Which is very observable, the French were at least four to one in number, and had near one hundred case of pistols among them, and the Spaniards had not one gun among them; which is for their honour for ever, and the others' disgrace. So, having been very much daubed with dirt, I got a coach, and home; where I vexed my wife in telling of her this story, and pleading for the Spaniards against the French. So ends this month; myself and family in good condition of health, but my head full of my Lord's and my own and the office business; where we are now very busy about sending forces to Tangier, and the fleet of my Lord of Sandwich, who is now at Lisbone to bring over the Queene. The

55 York House belonged to the See of York till James I's time, when Toby Matthews exchanged it with the Crown. Chancellors Egerton and Bacon resided there, after which it was granted to Villiers, Duke of Buckingham. Subsequently to the Restoration his son occupied the house some years, and disposing of the premises, they were converted into the streets still bearing his names, and the general appellation of York Buildings.

business of Argier hath of late troubled me, because my Lord hath not done what he went for, though he did as much as any man in the world could have done. The want of money puts all things, and above all, the Navy, out of order; and yet I do not see that the King takes care to bring in any money, but thinks of new designs to lay out money.

October 4th. By coach to White Hall with Sir W. Pen. So to Mr Montagu, where his man, Mons. Eschar, makes a great complaint against the English, that they did help the Spaniards against the French the other day; and that their Embassador do demand justice of our King, and that he do resolve to be gone for France the next week; which I, and all that I met with, are glad of.

17th. Captn. Cock, a man of great observation and repute, did tell me, that he was confident that the Parliament, when it comes the next month to sit again, would bring trouble with it, and enquire how the King had disposed of offices and money, before they will raise more; which, I fear, will bring all things to ruin again. Dined with Captain Lambert and his father-in-law, and had much talk of Portugall; from whence he is lately come, and he tells me it is a very poor dirty place; I mean the City and Court of Lisbone; that the King is a very rude and simple fellow; and, for reviling of somebody a little while ago, had been killed, had he not told them that he was their king. That there are no glass windows, nor will they have any; which makes sport among our merchants there to talk of an English factor that, being newly come thither, writ into England that glasse would be a good commodity to send thither, &c. That the King has his meat sent up by a dozen of lazy guards and in pipkins, sometimes, to his own table; and sometimes nothing but fruits, and, now-and-then, half a hen. And that now the Infanta is become our Queen, she is come to have a whole hen or goose to her table.

18th. To White Hall, to Mr Montagu's, where I met with Mr Pierce the purser, to advise about the things to be sent to my Lord for the Queene's provision; now there is all haste made, for the fleete's going.

20th. To Sir W. Batten, who is to go to Portsmouth tomorrow to wait upon the Duke of York, who goes to take possession and to set in order the garrison there.

26th. This morning Sir W. Pen and I should have gone out of town with my Lady Batten, to have met Sir William coming back from Portsmouth, at Kingston, but could not, by reason that my Lord of Peterborough[56] (who is to go Governor of Tangier[57]) come this morning, with Sir G. Carteret, to advise with us about completing of the affairs and preparacions for that place. News was brought that Sir R. Slingsby, our Comptroller (who hath this day been sick a week), is dead; which put me into so great a trouble of mind, that all the night I could not sleep, he being a man that loved me, and had many qualitys that made me to love him above all the officers and commissioners in the Navy.

27th (Lord's day). At church in the morning; where in pew both Sir Williams and I had much talk about the death of Sir Robert, which troubles me much; and them in appearance, though I do not believe it; because I know that he was a cheque to their engrossing the whole trade of the Navy-office.

29th. This day I put on my half cloth black stockings and my new coate of the fashion, which pleases me well, and with my beaver I was (after office was done) ready to go to my Lord Mayor's feast, as we are all invited; but the Sir Williams were both loth to go, because of the crowd, and so none of us went. This Lord Mayor, it seems, brings up again the custom of Lord Mayors going the day of their instalment to Paul's, and walking round about the Crosse, and offering something at the altar.

30th. Sir Henry Vane, Lambert, and others, are lately sent suddenly away from the Tower, prisoners to Scilly; but I do not think there is

56 Henry, second Earl of Peterborough, a Privy Councillor, and in 1685 made Groom of the Stole. He was also KG, and died 1697.

57 This place, so often mentioned by Mr Pepys, was first given up to the English Fleet under Lord Sandwich, by the Portuguese, Jan. 30, 1662; and Lord Peterborough left Governor, with a garrison. The greatest pains were afterwards taken to preserve the fortress, and a fine mole was constructed, at a vast expense, to improve the harbour. At length, after immense sums of money had been wasted there, the House of Commons expressed a dislike to the management of the garrison (which they suspected to be a nursery for a Popish army), and seemed disinclined to maintain it any longer. The King consequently, in 1683, sent Lord Dartmouth to bring home the troops, and destroy the works; which he performed most effectually, and Tangier fell into the hands of the Moors, its importance having ceased with the demolition of the mole.

any plot as is said, but only a pretence; as there was once pretended often against the Cavaliers.

November 1st. Sir Wm. sent for his son Mr Wm. Pen[58] lately come from Oxford.

2nd. At the office all the morning; where Sir John Minnes, our new comptroller, was fetched by Sir Wm. Pen and myself from Sir Wm. Batten's, and led to his place in the office. The first time that he had come thither, and he seems in a good fair condition, and one that I am glad hath the office.

4th. With my wife to the Opera, where we saw *The Bondman*, which of old we both did so doate on, and do still; though to both our thinking not so well acted here, (having too great expectations) as formerly at Salisbury-court. But for Beterton,[59] he is called by us both the best actor in the world.

8th. This morning up early, and to my Lord Chancellor's with a letter to him from my Lord, and did speak with him; and he did ask me whether I was son to Mr Talbot Pepys[60] or no, (with whom he was once acquainted in the Court of Requests), and spoke to me with great respect.

10th. At St Gregory's, where I hear our Queene Katherine, the first time by name publickly prayed for.

12th. This day Holmes come to town; and we do expect hourly to hear what usage he hath from the Duke and the King about his late business of letting the Swedish Embassador go by him without striking his flag.

13th. By appointment, we all went this morning to wait upon the Duke of York, which we did in his chamber, as he was dressing

58 The celebrated Quaker, and founder of Pennsylvania.
59 Thomas Betterton, the celebrated actor, born in 1635, was the son of an under cook to Charles I, and first appeared on the stage at the Cockpit in Drury Lane, in 1659. After the Restoration, two distinct theatres were established by Royal Authority; one in Drury Lane, called the King's Company, under a patent granted to Killigrew: the other in Lincoln's Inn Fields, styled the Duke's Troop, the patentee of which was Sir W. Davenant, who engaged Mr Betterton in 1662. Mr B. died in 1710, and was buried in the cloisters of Westminster Abbey.
60 Of Impington, great uncle to our Author.

himself in his riding suit to go this day by sea to the Downes. He is in mourning for his wife's grandmother, which is thought a great piece of fondness. After we had given him our letter relating the bad condition of the Navy for want of money, he referred it to his coming back and so parted. Thence on foot to my Lord Crewe's; here I was well received by my Lord and Sir Thomas; with whom I had great talk: and he tells me in good earnest that he do believe the Parliament, (which comes to sit again the next week,) will be troublesome to the Court and Clergy, which God forbid! But they see things carried so by my Lord Chancellor and some others, that get money themselves, that they will not endure it.

17th. To church; and heard a simple fellow upon the praise of Church musique, and exclaiming against men's wearing their hats on in the church.

20th. To Westminster Hall by water in the morning, where I saw the King going in his barge to the Parliament House; this being the first day of their meeting again. And the Bishops, I hear, do take their places in the Lords' House this day. I walked longe in the Hall, but hear nothing of newes, but what Ned Pickering tells me, which I am troubled at, that Sir J. Minnes should send word to the King, that if he did not remove all my Lord Sandwich's captains out of this fleet, he believed the King would not be master of the fleet at its coming again: and so do endeavour to bring disgrace upon my Lord. But I hope all that will not do, for the King loves him.

21st. At the office all the afternoon; it being the first afternoon that we have sat, which we are now to do always, so long as the Parliament sits, who this day have voted the King £120,000 [61] to be raised to pay his debts.

28th. Letters from my Lord Sandwich, from Tangier; where he continues still, and hath done some execution upon the Turks, and retaken an Englishman from them, one Mr Parker, a merchant in Marke-lane.

29th. I lay long in bed, till Sir Williams both sent me word that we were to wait upon the Duke of York today; and that they would

---

61 According to the Journals £1,200,000.

have me to meet them at Westminster Hall, at noon: so I rose and went thither; and there I understand that they are gone to Mr Coventry's lodgings, in the Old Palace Yard, to dinner (the first time that I knew he had any); and there I met them, and Sir G. Carteret, and had a very fine dinner, and good welcome, and discourse: and so, by water, after dinner to White Hall to the Duke, who met us in his closet; and there did discourse upon the business of Holmes, and did desire of us to know what hath been the common practice about making of forrayne ships to strike sail to us, which they did all do as much as they could; but I could say nothing to it, which I was sorry for. After we were gone from the Duke, I told Mr Coventry that I had heard Mr Selden often say, that he could prove that in Henry the 7th's time, he did give commission to his captains to make the King of Denmark's ships to strike to him in the Baltique.

30th. This is the last day for the old State's coyne to pass in common payments, but they say it is to pass in publique payments to the King three months still.

December 1st. There hath lately been great clapping up of some old statesmen, such as Ireton, Moyer,[62] and others, and they say, upon a great plot, but I believe no such thing; but it is but justice that they should be served as they served the poor Cavaliers; and I believe it will oftentimes be so as long as they live, whether there be cause or no.

6th. To White Hall, where, at Sir G. Carteret's, Sir Williams both and I dined very pleasantly; and after dinner, by appointment, came the Governors of the East India Company, to sign and seal the contract between us (in the King's name) and them. And, that done, we all went to the King's closet, and there spoke with the King and the Duke of York, who promise to be very careful of the India trade to the utmost.

7th. To the Privy Seale, and sealed there; and, among other things that passed, there was a patent for Roger Palmer (Madam Palmer's husband) to be Earle of Castlemaine[63] and Baron of Limbricke in Ireland; but the honor is tied up to the males got of the body of this wife, the Lady Barbary: the reason whereof every body knows. That

62 Samuel Moyer, one of the Council of State, 1653.
63 Died July, 1705.

done, by water to the office, where I found Sir W. Pen, and with him Captn. Holmes, who had wrote his case, and gives me a copy, as he hath many among his friends, and presented the same to the King and Council. Which I have made use of in my attempt of writing something concerning the business of striking sail, which I am now about. But he do cry out against Sir John Minnes, as the veriest knave and rogue and coward in the world.

9th. At noon to dinner at the Wardrobe; where my Lady Wright[64] was, who did talk much upon the worth and the desert of gallantry; and that there was none fit to be courtiers, but such as have been abroad and know fashions. Which I endeavoured to oppose; and was troubled to hear her talk so, though she be a very wise and discreet lady in other things.

15th. I am now full of study about writing something about our making of strangers strike to us at sea; and so am altogether reading Selden and Grotius, and such other authors to that purpose.

16th. After dinner to the Opera, where there was a new play, (*Cutter of Coleman Street*) made in the year 1658, with reflections much upon the late times; and it being the first time the pay was doubled, and so to save money, my wife and I went into the gallery, and there sat and saw very well; and a very good play it is. It seems of Cowly's making.

21st. To White Hall to the Privy Seale, as my Lord Privy Seale did tell me he could seale no more this month, for he goes thirty miles out of towne to keep his Christmas. At which I was glad, but only afraid lest any thing of the King's should force us to go after him to get a seale in the country. I spoke to Mr Falconberge to look whether he could out of Domesday Book, give me any thing concerning the sea, and the dominion thereof; which he says he will look after.

27th. In the morning to my Bookseller's to bespeak a Stephens' Thesaurus, for which I offer £4, to give to Paul's School, and from thence to Paul's Church; and there I did hear Dr Gunning preach a good sermon upon the day, (being St John's day,) and did hear him tell a story, which he did persuade us to believe to be true, that St

John and the Virgin Mary did appear to Gregory, a Bishopp, at his prayer to be confirmed in the faith, which I did wonder to hear from him.

28th. At home all the morning; and in the afternoon all of us at the office, upon a letter from the Duke for the making up of a speedy estimate of all the debts of the Navy, which is put into good forwardness.

31st. To the office; and there late finishing our estimate of the debts of the Navy to this day; and it come to near £374,000. I suppose myself to be worth about £500 clear in the world, and my goods of my house my owne, and what is coming to me from Brampton, when my father dies, which God defer. But, by my uncle's death, the whole care and trouble, and settling of all lies upon me, which is very great, because of law-suits, especially that with T. Frice, about the interest of £200. I am upon writing a little treatise to present to the Duke, about our privilege in the seas, as to other nations striking their flags to us.

1661/62. January 2nd. I went forth, by appointment, to meet with Mr Grant, who promised to bring me acquainted with Cooper,[1] the great limner in little. Sir Richd. Fanshaw is come suddenly from Portugall, and nobody knows what his business is about.

To Faithorne's,[2] and there bought some pictures of him; and while I was there, comes by the King's lifeguard, he being gone to Lincoln's Inne this afternoon to see the Revells there; there being, according to an old custome, a prince and all his nobles, and other matters of sport and charge.

11th. To the Exchange, and there all the news is of the French and Dutch joyning against us; but I do not think it yet true. In the afternoon, to Sir W. Batten's, where in discourse I heard the custome of the election of the Duke of Genoa, who for two years is every day attended in the greatest state, and four or five hundred men always waiting upon him as a king; and when the two years are out, and another is chose, a messenger is sent to him, who stands at the bottom of the stairs, and he at the top, and says, '*Va. Illustrissima Serenita sta*

---

1 Samuel Cooper, the celebrated miniature painter. Died 1672.
2 William Faithorne, the well-known engraver. Died 1691.

finita, et puede andar en casa.' – 'Your serenity is now ended; and now you may be going home;' and so claps on his hat. And the old Duke (having by custom sent his goods home before,) walks away, it may be but with one man at his heels; and the new one brought immediately in his room, in the greatest state in the world. Another account was told us, how in the Dukedom of Ragusa, in the Adriatique, (a State that is little, but more ancient, they say, than Venice, and is called the mother of Venice, and the Turkes lie round about it,) that they change all the officers of their guard, for fear of conspiracy, every twenty-four hours, so that nobody knows who shall be captain of the guard tonight; but two men come to a man, and lay hold of him as a prisoner, and carry him to the place; and there he hath the keys of the garrison given him, and he presently issues his orders for that night's watch: and so always from night to night. Sir Wm. Rider told the first of his own knowledge; and both he and Sir W. Batten confirm the last.

13th. Before twelve o'clock comes, by appointment, Mr Peter and the Dean,[3] and Colonel Honiwood, brothers, to dine with me; but so soon that I was troubled at it. Mr Peter did show us the experiment (which I had heard talke of) of the chymicall glasses, which break all to dust by breaking off a little small end; which is a great mystery to me.

15th. Mr Berkenshaw[4] asked me whether we had not committed a fault in eating today; telling me that it is a fast day ordered by the Parliament, to pray for more seasonable weather; it having hitherto been summer weather, that it is, both as to warmth and every other thing, just as if it were the middle of May or June, which do threaten a plague (as all men think) to follow, for so it was almost the last winter; and the whole year after hath been a very sickly time to this day.

16th. Towards Cheapside; and in Paul's Churchyard saw the funeral of my Lord Cornwallis, late Steward of the King's House, go by. Stoakes told us, that notwithstanding the country of Gambo is so unhealthy, yet the people of the place live very long, so as the present King there is 150 years old, which they count by rains: because every

3 Michael Honywood, installed Dean of Lincoln, 1660. Died 1681, aged 85.
4 Mr Pepys's music master.

year it rains continually four months together. He also told us, that the Kings there have above 100 wives a-piece.

18th. Comes Mr Moore to give me an account how Mr Montagu[5] was gone away of a sudden with the fleet, in such haste that he hath left behind some servants, and many things of consequence; and among others, my Lord's commission for Embassador. Whereupon he and I took coach, and to Whitehall to my Lord's lodgings, to have spoke with Mr Ralph Montagu,[6] his brother; (and here we staid talking with Sarah and the old man,) but by and by hearing that he was in Covent Garden, we went thither: and at my Lady Harvy's, his sister, I spoke with him, and he tells me that the Commission is not left behind.

22nd. After musique-practice, to White Hall, and thence to Westminster, in my way calling at Mr George Montagu's, to condole on the loss of his son, who was a fine gentleman. After this discourse he told me, among other news, the great jealousys that are now in the Parliament House. The Lord Chancellor, it seems, taking occasion from this late plot to raise fears in the people, did project the raising of an army forthwith, besides the constant militia, thinking to make the Duke of York General thereof. But the House did, in very open termes, say, they were grown too wise to be fooled again into another army; and said they had found how that man that hath the command of an army is not beholden to any body to make him King. There are factions (private ones at Court) about Madam Palmer; but what it is about I know not. But it is something about the King's favour to her now that the Queene is coming. He told me, too, what sport the King and Court do make at Mr Edwd. Montagu's leaving his things behind him. But the Chancellor (taking it a little more seriously) did openly say to my Lord Chamberlaine, that had it been such a gallant as my Lord Mandeville[7] his son, it might have been taken as a frolique: but for him that would be thought a grave coxcombe, it was very strange. Thence to the Hall,

5 Edward Montagu.

6 Ralph, eldest son of Edward, second Baron Montagu, of Boughton; created Duke of Montagu, and died 1709. His sister Elizabeth had married Sir D. Harvey, Knt., Ambassador to Constantinople.

7 Lord Mandeville was a Gentleman of the Bedchamber to Charles II. He became Earl of Manchester on his father's death and died at Paris in 1682.

where I heard the House had ordered all the King's murderers, that remain, to be executed, but Fleetwood[8] and Downes.

25th. At home and the office all the morning. Walking in the garden to give the gardener directions what to do this year (for I intend to have the garden handsome), Sir W. Pen come to me, and did break a business to me about removing his son from Oxford to Cambridge to some private college. I proposed Magdalene, but cannot name a tutor at present; but I shall think and write about it. Thence with him to the Trinity-house to dinner; where Sir Richd. Brown, one of the clerkes of the Council, and who is much concerned against Sir N. Crisp's project of making a great sasse[9] in the King's lands about Deptford, to be a wett-dock to hold 200 sail of ships. But the ground, it seems, was long since given by the King to Sir Richard. After the Trinity-house men had done their business, the master, Sir Wm. Rider, come to bid us welcome; and so to dinner. Comes Mr Moore with letters from my Lord Sandwich, speaking of his lying still at Tangier, looking for the fleet; which, we hope, is now in a good way thither.

27th. This morning, both Sir Williams and I by barge to Deptford-yard to give orders in business there; and called on several ships, also to give orders. Going to take water upon Tower-hill, we met with three sleddes standing there to carry my Lord Monson[10] and Sir H. Mildmay[11] and another, to the gallows and back again, with ropes about their necks; which is to be repeated every year, this being the day of their sentencing the King.

8 Charles, son of Sir Wm. Fleetwood, Knt., General and Commander in Chief to the Protector Richard, whose sister, Bridget, widow of Ireton, he had married. After the King's return he lived in contemptible obscurity, and died circa 1689.

9 Sasse, a sluice, or lock, used in water-works. – Bailey's *Dictionary*. This project is mentioned by Evelyn, and Lysons, *Environs*, vol. iv. p. 392.

10 William, second son of Sir Thomas Monson, Bart.; created by Charles I Viscount Castlemaine of the kingdom of Ireland; notwithstanding which, he was instrumental in his Majesty's death: and in 1661, being degraded of his honours, was sentenced, with Sir Henry Mildmay and Mr Robert Wallop, to be drawn on sledges, with ropes round their necks, to Tyburn, and back to the Tower, there to remain prisoners for life. None of their names were subscribed to the King's sentence.

11 Sir H. Mildmay had enjoyed the confidence of Charles I, who made him Master of the Jewels; but he sat a few days as one of the King's Judges. He died in Antwerp.

February 1st. This morning with Commissioner Pett to the office; and he staid there writing, while I and Sir W. Pen walked in the garden talking about his business of putting his son to Cambridge; and to that end I intend to write to-night to Dr Fairebrother, to give me an account of Mr Burton[12] of Magdalene. Thence with Mr Pett to the Paynter's; and he likes our pictures very well, and so do I. Thence he and I to the Countesse of Sandwich, to lead him to her to kiss her hands: and dined with her, and told her the news (which Sir W. Pen told me to do) that expresse is come from my Lord with letters, that by a great storm and tempest the mole of Argier is broken down, and many of their ships sunk into the mole. So that God Almighty hath now ended that unlucky business for us: which is very good news.

4th. To Westminster Hall, where it was full terme. Here all the morning, and at noon to my Lord Crewe's, where one Mr Templer (an ingenious man and a person of honour he seems to be) dined; and, discoursing of the nature of serpents, he told us some in the waste places of Lancashire do grow to a great bigness, and do feed upon larkes, which they take thus: – They observe when the lark is soared to the highest, and do crawl till they come to be just underneath them; and there they place themselves with their mouth uppermost, and there, as is conceived, they do eject poyson upon the bird; for the bird do suddenly come down again in its course of a circle, and falls directly into the mouth of the serpent; which is very strange. He is a great traveller; and, speaking of the tarantula, he says that all the harvest long (about which times they are most busy) there are fidlers go up and down the fields every where, in expectation of being hired by those that are stung. This afternoon, going into the office, one met me and did serve a subpoena upon me for one Field, whom we did commit to prison the other day for some ill words he did give the office. The like he had for others, but we shall scoure him for it.

5th. To the Playhouse, and there saw *Rule a Wife and have a Wife*:[13] very well done. And here also I did look long upon my Lady Castlemaine, who, notwithstanding her sickness, continues a great beauty.

12 Hezekiah Burton, S. T. B. 1661.
13 A comedy, by J. Fletcher.

7th. I hear the prisoners in the Tower that are to die are come to the Parliament-house this morning. To the Wardrobe to dinner with my Lady; where a civitt cat, parrot, apes, and many other things, are come from my Lord by Captain Hill, who dined with my Lady with us today. Thence to the Paynter's, and am well pleased with our pictures.

10th. To Paul's Church-yard, and there I met with Dr Fuller's *England's Worthys*, the first time that I ever saw it; and so I sat down reading in it; being much troubled that (though he had some discourse with me about my family and armes) he says nothing at all, nor mentions us either in Cambridgeshire or Norfolke. But I believe, indeed, our family were never considerable.

13th. Mr Blackburne do tell me plain of the corruption of all our Treasurer's officers, and that they hardly pay any money under ten per cent.; and that the other day for a mere assignation of £200 to some counties, they took £15 which is very strange. Last night died the Queene of Bohemia.

15th. With the two Sir Williams to the Trinity-house; and there in their society had the business debated of Sir Nicholas Crisp's sasse at Deptford. After dinner I was sworn a Younger Brother; Sir W. Rider being Deputy-Master for my Lord of Sandwich; and after I was sworn, all the Elder Brothers shake me by the hand: it is their custom, it seems. No news yet of our fleet gone to Tangier, which we now begin to think long.

17th. This morning, both Sir Williams, myself, and Captn. Cock, and Captn. Tinker of the *Covertine*, which we are going to look upon, (being intended with these ships fitting for the East Indys) down to Deptford; and thence, after being on ship-board, to Woolwich, and there eat something. The Sir Williams being unwilling to eat flesh, Captn. Cock and I had a breast of veale roasted.

18th. Having agreed with Sir Wm. Pen to meet him at the Opera, and finding by my walking in the streets, which were every where full of brick-bates and tyles flung down by the extraordinary winde the last night (such as hath not been in memory before, unless at the death of the late Protector,) that it was dangerous to go out of doors;

and hearing how several persons had been killed today by the fall of things in the streets, and that the pageant in Fleet-streete is most of it blown down, and hath broke down part of several houses, among others Dick Brigden's; and that one Lady Sanderson, a person of quality in Covent Garden, was killed by the fall of the house, in her bed, last night; I sent my boy to forbid him to go forth. But he bringing me word that he is gone, I went thither and saw *The Law against Lovers*,[14] a good play and well performed, especially the little girl's (whom I never saw act before) dancing and singing; and were it not for her, the losse of Roxalana would spoil the house.

20th. Letters from Tangier from my Lord, telling me how, upon a great defete given to the Portuguese there by the Moors, he had put in 300 men into the towne, and so he is in possession, of which we are very glad, because now the Spaniards' designs of hindering our getting the place are frustrated. I went with the letter inclosed to my Lord Chancellor to the House of Lords, and did give it him in the House. Went by promise to Mr Savill's, and there sat the first time for my picture in little, which pleaseth me well.

22nd. This evening I wrote letters to my father; among other things acquainted him with the unhappy accident which hath happened lately to my Lord of Dorset's two oldest sons, who, with two Belasses and one Squire Wentworth, were lately apprehended for killing and robbing of a tanner about Newington on Wednesday last, and are all now in Newgate. I am much troubled for it, and for the grief and disgrace it brings to their familys and friends.[15]

14 A tragi-comedy by Sir William Davenant; taken from *Measure for Measure* and *Much Ado about Nothing*.
15 The following account of this transaction is abridged from the *Mercurius Publicus* of the day: 'Charles Lord Buckhurst, Edward Sackville, Esq., his brother; Sir Henry Belasyse, KB, eldest son of Lord Belasyse; John Belasyse, brother to Lord Faulconberg; and Thomas Wentworth, Esq., only son of Sir G. Wentworth, whilst in pursuit of thieves near Waltham Cross, mortally wounded an innocent tanner named Hoppy, whom they had endeavoured to secure, suspecting him to have been one of the robbers; and as they took away the money found on his person, under the idea that it was stolen property, they were soon after apprehended on the charges of robbery and murder; but the Grand Jury found a bill for manslaughter only.' By a subsequent allusion in the Diary to their trial, it seems probable that a verdict of acquittal was pronounced.

23rd. This day by God's mercy I am twenty-nine years of age, and in very good health, and like to live and get an estate; and if I have a heart to be contented, I think I may reckon myself as happy a man as any in the world, for which God be praised. So to prayers and to bed.

25th. Great talk of the effects of this late great wind; and I heard one say that he had five great trees standing together blown down; and, beginning to lop them, one of them, as soon as the lops were cut off, did, by the weight of the root, rise again and fasten. We have letters from the forest of Deane, that above an thousand oakes and as many beeches are blown down in one walke there. And letters from my father tell me of £20 hurt done to us at Brampton. This day in the news-booke I find that my Lord Buckhurst[16] and his fellows have printed their case as they did give it in upon examination to a Justice of Peace, wherein they make themselves a very good tale that they were in pursuit of thieves, and that they took this man for one of them, and so killed him; and that he himself confessed it was the first time of his robbing; and that he did pay dearly for it, for he was a dead man. But I doubt things will be proved otherwise than they say.

March 1st. To the Opera, and there saw *Romeo and Juliet*, the first time it was ever acted. I am resolved to go no more to see the first time of acting, for they were all of them out more or less.

3rd. I am told that this day the Parliament hath voted 2s. per annum for every chimney in England, as a constant revenue for ever to the Crowne.

7th. Early to White Hall to the chapel, where by Mr Blagrave's means I got into his pew, and heard Dr Creeton, the great Scotchman, and chaplain in ordinary to the King, preach before the King, and Duke and Duchesse, upon the words of Micah: – 'Roule yourselves in dust.' He made a most learned sermon upon the words; but in his application, the most comical man that ever I heard in my life. Just such a man as Hugh Peters; saying that it had been better for the poor Cavalier never to have come with the King into England again; for he that hath the impudence to deny obedience to the lawful magistrate, and to swear to the oath of allegiance, &c., was

16 Charles Lord Buckhurst, eldest son of Richard, fifth Earl of Dorset; created Earl of Middlesex soon after his uncle's death, in 1675, and succeeded his father in 1677. Died 1705/06.

better treated now-a-days in Newgate, than a poor Royalist that hath suffered all his life for the King, is at White Hall among his friends.

8th. By coach with both Sir Williams to Westminster; this being a great day there in the House to pass the business for chimney-money, which was done. In the Hall I met with Surgeon Pierce: and he told me how my Lady Monk hath disposed of all the places which Mr Edwd. Montagu hoped to have had as he was Master of the Horse to the Queene; which I am afraid will undo him, because he depended much upon the profit of what he should make by these places. He told me, also, many more scurvy stories of him and his brother Ralph, which troubles me to hear of persons of honour as they are. Sir W. Pen and I to the office, whither afterward come Sir G. Carteret; and we sent for Sir Thos. Allen, one of the Aldermen of the City,[17] about the business of one Colonel Appesly, whom we had taken counterfeiting of bills with all our hands and the officers of the yards, so well that I should never have mistrusted them. We staid about this business at the office till ten at night, and at last did send him with a constable to the Counter and did give warrants for the seizing of a complice of his, one Blenkinsopp.

12th. This morning we had news from Mr Coventry, that Sir G. Downing[18] (like a perfidious rogue, though the action is good and of service to the King, yet he cannot with a good conscience do it) hath taken Okey,[19] Corbet, and Barkestead at Delfe, in Holland, and sent them home in the Blackmore. Sir W. Pen, talking to me this afternoon of what a strange thing it is for Downing to do this, he told me of a speech he made to the Lords States of Holland, telling them to their faces that he observed that he was not received with the respect and observance now that he was when he came from the traitor and rebell Cromwell: by whom, I am sure, he hath got all he hath in the world, – and they know it too.

14th. Home to dinner. In the afternoon come the German Dr Knuffler, to discourse with us about his engine to blow up ships. We doubted not the matter of fact, it being tried in Cromwell's time, but

---

17 Probably Sheriff of London, 1654.
18 According to Hume, Downing had once been Chaplain to Okey's regiment.
19 John Okey, Miles Corbet, and John Barkstead, three of the regicides; executed April 19th following.

the safety of carrying them in ships; but he do tell us, that when he comes to tell the King his secret, (for none but the Kings, successively, and their heirs must know it,) it will appear to be of no danger at all. We concluded nothing: but shall discourse with the Duke of York tomorrow about it.

16th. Walked to White Hall; and an houre or two in the Parke, which is now very pleasant. Here the King and Duke come to see their fowle play. The Duke took very civil notice of me.

17th. Last night the *Blackmore* pinke brought the three prisoners, Barkestead, Okey, and Corbet, to the Tower, being taken at Delfe in Holland; where, the Captain tells me, the Dutch were a good while before they could be persuaded to let them go, they being taken prisoners in their land. But Sir G. Downing would not be answered so: though all the world takes notice of him for a most ungrateful villaine for his pains.

21st. To Westminster Hall; and there walked up and down and heard the great difference that hath been between my Lord Chancellor and my Lord of Bristol, about a proviso that my Lord Chancellor would have brought into the Bill for Conformity, that it shall be in the power of the King, when he sees fit to dispense with the Act of Conformity; and though it be carried in the House of Lords, yet it is believed it will hardly pass in the Commons.

23rd. To White Hall, and there met with Captn. Isham, this day come from Lisbone, with letters from the Queene to the King. And he did give me letters which speak that our fleet is all at Lisbone; and that the Queene do not intend to embarque sooner than tomorrow come fortnight.

24th. By and by comes La Belle Pierce to see my wife, and to bring her a pair of peruques of hair, as the fashion now is for ladies to wear; which are pretty, and are of my wife's own hair, or else I should not endure them.

April 6th (Lord's day). By water to White Hall, to Sir G. Carteret, to give him an account of the backwardnesse of the ships we have hired to Portugall: at which he is much troubled. Thence to the Chapel, and there, though crowded, heard a very honest sermon before the King by a Canon of Christ Church, upon these words, 'Having a form of godlinesse, but denying,' &c. Among other things he did much insist upon the sin of adultery: which methought might touch the King, and the more because he forced it into his sermon, besides his text. So up and saw the King at dinner; and thence with Sir G. Carteret to his lodgings to dinner, with him and his lady. All their discourse, which was very much, was upon their sufferings and services for the King. Yet not without some trouble, to see that some that had been much bound to them, do now neglect them; and others again most civil that have received least from them: and I do believe that he hath been a good servant to the King. Thence to the Parke, where the King and Duke did walk.

7th. To the Lords' House, and stood within the House, while the Bishops and Lords did stay till the Chancellor's coming, and then we were put out. I sent in a note to my Lord Privy Seale, and he come out to me; and I desired he would make another deputy for me, because of my great business of the Navy this month; but he told me he could not do it without the King's consent, which vexed me. The great talk is, that the Spaniards and the Hollanders do intend to set upon the Portugais by sea, at Lisbone, as soon as our fleet is come away; and by that means our fleet is not likely to come yet these two months or three; which I hope is not true.

9th. Sir George[20] showed me an account in French of the great famine, which is to the greatest extremity in some part of France at this day; which is very strange.

10th. Yesterday come Col. Talbot with letters from Portugall, that the Queene is resolved to embarque for England this week. Thence to the office all the afternoon. My Lord Windsor[21] come to us to discourse of his affairs, and to take his leave of us; he being to go Governor of Jamaica with this fleet that is now going.

11th. With Sir W. Pen by water to Deptford; and among the ships now going to Portugall with men and horse, to see them dispatched. So to Greenwich; and had a fine pleasant walk to Woolwich, having in our company Captn. Minnes, whom I was much pleased to hear

20 Carteret.
21 Thomas Baron Windsor, Lord Lieutenant of Worcestershire; advanced to the Earldom of Plymouth, 1682. Died 1687.

talk. Among other things, he and the Captains that were with us told me that negroes drowned looked white and lose their blackness, which I never heard before. At Woolwich up and down to do the same business; and so back to Greenwich by water. Sir William and I walked into the Parke, where the King hath planted trees and made steps in the hill up to the Castle, which is very magnificent. So up and down the house, which is now repayring in the Queene's lodgings.

13th. To Grayes Inn walkes; and there met Mr Pickering. His discourse most about the pride of the Duchesse of York; and how all the ladies envy my Lady Castlemaine. He intends to go to Portsmouth to meet the Queene this week; which is now the discourse and expectation of the towne.

15th. With my wife, by coach, to the New Exchange, to buy her some things; where we saw some new-fashion pettycoats of sarcenett, with a black broad lace printed round the bottom and before, very handsome, and my wife had a mind to one of them.

19th. This morning, before we sat, I went to Aldgate; and at the corner shop, a draper's, I stood, and did see Barkestead, Okey, and Corbet, drawne towards the gallows at Tiburne; and there they were hanged and quartered. They all looked very cheerful; but I hear they all die defending what they did to the King to be just; which is very strange.

20th (Lord's-day). My intention being to go this morning to White Hall to hear Louth, my Lord Chancellor's chaplain, the famous preacher and oratour of Oxford, (who the last Lord's-day did sink down in the pulpit before the King, and could not proceed,) it did rain, and the wind against me, that I could by no means get a boat or coach to carry me; and so I staid at Paul's, where the Judges did all meet, and heard a sermon, it being the first Sunday of the terme; but they had a very poor sermon.

21st. At noon dined with my Lord Crewe; and after dinner went up to Sir Thos. Crewe's chamber, who is still ill. He tells me how my Lady Duchesse of Richmond[22] and Castlemaine had a falling out the other day; and she calls the latter Jane Shore, and did hope to see her

22 Mary, daughter to George Duke of Buckingham; wife of James, fourth Duke of Lennox, and third Duke of Richmond.

come to the same end. Coming down again to my Lord, he told me that news was come that the Queene is landed; at which I took leave, and by coach hurried to White Hall, the bells ringing in several places; but I found there no such matter, nor anything like it.

22nd. We come to Gilford.

23rd. Up early, and to Petersfield; and thence got a countryman to guide us by Havant, to avoid going through the Forest; but he carried us much out of the way. I lay at Wiard's, the chyrurgeon's, in Portsmouth.

24th. All of us to the Pay-house; but the books not being ready, we went to church to the lecture, where there was my Lord Ormond and Manchester, and much London company, though not so much as I expected. Here we had a very good sermon upon this text: 'In love serving one another'; which pleased me very well. No news of the Queene at all. So to dinner; and then to the Pay all the afternoon. Then W. Pen and I walked to the King's Yard.

26th. Sir George and I, and his clerk Mr Stephens, and Mr Holt our guide, over to Gosport; and so rode to Southampton. In our way, besides my Lord Southampton's[23] parks and lands, which in one viewe we could see £6000 per annum, we observed a little churchyard, where the graves are accustomed to be all sowed with sage. At Southampton. The towne is one most gallant street, and is walled round with stone, &c., and Bevis's picture upon one of the gates; many old walls of religious houses, and the keye, well worth seeing.

27th. I rode to church, and met my Lord Chamberlaine upon the walls of the garrison, who owned and spoke to me. I followed him in the crowde of gallants through the Queene's lodgings to chapel; the rooms being all rarely furnished, and escaped hardly being set on fire yesterday. At chapel we had a most excellent and eloquent sermon.

---

23 Tichfield House, erected by Sir Thomas Wriothesley, on the site of an Abbey of Premonstratenses, granted to him with their estates, 29th Henry VIII. Upon the death of his descendant, Thomas, Earl of Southampton, and Lord Treasurer, without male issue, the house and manor were allotted to his eldest daughter Elizabeth, wife of Edmund, 1st Earl of Gainsborough; and their only son dying without male issue, the property devolved to his sister Elizabeth, married to Henry, Duke of Portland, whose grandson, the 3rd Duke, alienated it to Mr Delme.

By coach to the Yard, and then on board the *Swallow* in the dock, where our navy chaplain preached a sad sermon, full of nonsense and false Latin; but prayed for the Right Honourable the principall officers. Visited the Mayor, Mr Timbrell, our anchorsmith, who showed us the present they have for the Queene; which is a salt-sellar of silver, the walls christall, with four eagles and four greyhounds standing up at the top to bear up a dish; which indeed is one of the neatest pieces of plate that ever I saw, and the case is very pretty also.[24] This evening come a merchantman in the harbour, which we hired at London to carry horses to Portugall; but Lord! what running there was to the seaside to hear what news, thinking it had come from the Queene.

May 1st. Sir G. Carteret, Sir W. Pen, and myself, with our clerks, set out this morning from Portsmouth very early, and got by noon to Petersfield; several officers of the Yard accompanying us so far. At dinner comes my Lord Carlingford[25] from London, going to Portsmouth: tells us that the Duchesse of York is brought to bed of a girle, at which I find nobody pleased; and that Prince Rupert and the Duke of Buckingham are sworne of the Privy Councell.

7th. Walked to Westminster; where I understand the news that Mr Montagu is last night come to the King with news, that he left the Queene and fleete in the Bay of Biscay, coming this wayward; and that he believes she is now at the Isle of Scilly. Thence to Paul's Church Yard; where seeing my Ladys Sandwich and Carteret, and my wife (who this day made a visit the first time to my Lady Carteret), come by coach, and going to Hide Parke, I was resolved to follow them; and so went to Mrs Turner's: and thence at the Theatre, where I saw the last act of the *Knight of the Burning Pestle*,[26] (which pleased me not at all). And so after the play done, she and The. Turner and Mrs Lucin and I, in her coach to the Parke; and there found them out, and spoke to them; and observed many fine ladies, and staid till all were gone almost.

8th. Sir G. Carteret told me, that the Queene and the fleet were in

24 A salt-sellar answering this description is preserved at the Tower.

25 Theobald, second Viscount Taafe, created Earl of Carlingford, co. Louth, 1661/62.

26 A comedy by Beaumont and Fletcher.

Mount's Bay on Monday last; and that the Queene endures her sickness pretty well. He also told me how Sir John Lawson hath done some execution upon the Turkes in the Straight, of which I was glad, and told the news the first on the Exchange, and was much followed by merchants to tell it. Sir G. Carteret, among other discourse, tells me that it is Mr Coventry that is to come to us as a Commissioner of the Navy; at which he is much vexed, and cries out upon Sir W. Pen, and threatens him highly. And looking upon his lodgings, which are now enlarging, he in a passion cried, '*Guarda mi spada*; for, by God, I may chance to keep him in Ireland, when he is there': for Sir W. Pen is going thither with my Lord Lieutenant. But it is my design to keep much in with Sir George; and I think I have begun very well towards it.

9th. The Duke of York went last night to Portsmouth; so that I believe the Queene is near.

10th. At noon to the Wardrobe; there dined. My Lady told me how my Lady Castlemaine do speak of going to lie in at Hampton Court; which she and all our ladies are much troubled at, because of the King's being forced to show her countenance in the sight of the Queene when she comes. In the evening Sir G. Carteret and I did hire a ship for Tangier, and other things together; and I find that he do single me out to join with me apart from the rest, which I am much glad of.

11th. In the afternoon to White Hall; and there walked an houre or two in the Parke, where I saw the King now out of mourning, in a suit laced with gold and silver, which it is said was out of fashion. Thence to the Wardrobe; and there consulted with the ladies about going to Hampton Court tomorrow.

12th. Mr Townsend called us up by four o'clock; and by five the three ladies, my wife and I, and Mr Townsend, his son and daughter, were got to the barge and set out. We walked from Mortlake to Richmond, and so to boat again. And from Teddington to Hampton Court Mr Townsend and I walked again. And then met the ladies, and were showed the whole house by Mr Marriott; which is indeed nobly furnished, particularly the Queene's bed, given her by the States of Holland; a looking-glasse sent by the Queene-mother from France, hanging in the Queene's chamber, and many brave pictures. And so to barge again; and got home about eight at night very well.

14th. Dined at the Wardrobe; and after dinner, sat talking an hour or two alone with my Lady. She is afraid that my Lady Castlemaine will keep still with the King.

15th. To Westminster; and at the Privy Seale I saw Mr Coventry's seal for his being Commissioner with us. At night, all the bells of the towne rung, and bonfires made for the joy of the Queene's arrival, who landed at Portsmouth last night. But I do not see much true joy, but only an indifferent one, in the hearts of the people, who are much discontented at the pride and luxury of the Court, and running in debt.

18th (Whitsunday). By water to White Hall, and there to chapel in my pew belonging to me as Clerke of the Privy Seale; and there I heard a most excellent sermon of Dr Hacket,[27] Bishop of Lichfield and Coventry, upon these words: 'He that drinketh this water shall never thirst.' We had an excellent anthem, sung by Captn. Cooke and another, and brave musique. And then the King come down and offered, and took the sacrament upon his knees; a sight very well worth seeing. After dinner to chapel again; and there had another good anthem of Captn. Cooke's. Thence to the Councell-chamber; where the King and Councell sat till almost eleven o'clock at night, and I forced to walk up and down the gallerys till that time of night. They were reading all the bills over that are to pass to-morrow at the House, before the King's going out of towne and proroguing the House. At last the Councell risen, Sir G. Carteret told me what the Councell hath ordered about the ships designed to carry horse from Ireland to Portugall, which is now altered.

19th. I hear that the House of Commons do think much that they should be forced to huddle over business this morning against afternoon, for the King to pass their Acts, that he may go out of towne. But he, I hear since, was forced to stay till almost nine o'clock at night before he could have done, and then prorogued them; and so to Gilford, and lay there.

27 John Hacket, elected Bishop of that see 1661. Died 1670.

20th. Sir W. Pen and I did a little business at the office, and so home again. Then comes Dean Fuller;[28] and I am most pleased with his company and goodness.

21st. My wife and I to my Lord's lodging; where she and I staid walking in White Hall garden. And in the Privy-garden saw the finest smocks and linnen petticoats of my Lady Castlemaine's, laced with rich lace at the bottom, that ever I saw: and did me good to look at them. Sarah told me how the King dined at my Lady Castlemaine's, and supped, every day and night the last week; and that the night that the bonfires were made for joy of the Queene's arrivall, the King was there; but there was no fire at her door, though at all the rest of the doors almost in the street; which was much observed: and that the King and she did send for a pair of scales and weighed one another; and she, being with child, was said to be heaviest. But she is now a most disconsolate creature, and comes not out of doors, since the King's going.

22nd. This morning comes an order from the Secretary of State, Nicholas, for me to let one Mr Lee, a Councellor, view what papers I have relating to passages of the late times, wherein Sir H. Vane's hand is employed in order to the drawing up his charge; which I did.

23rd. To the Wardrobe, reading of the King's and Chancellor's late speeches at the proroguing of the Houses of Parliament. And while I was reading, news was brought me that my Lord Sandwich is come and gone up to my Lady's chamber; which by and by he did, and looks very well. He very merry, and hath left the King and Queene at Portsmouth, and is come up to stay here till next Wednesday, and then to meet the King and Queene at Hampton Court. So to dinner; and my Lord mighty merry; among other things, saying that the Queene is a very agreeable lady, and paints well. After dinner I showed him my letter from Teddiman about the news from Argier, which pleases him exceedingly; and he writ one to the Duke of York about it, and sent it express.

24th. Abroad with Mr Creed, of whom I informed myself of all I had a mind to know. Among other things, the great difficulty my Lord hath been in all this summer for lack of good and full orders from the

28 Dean of St Patrick's.

King: and I doubt our Lords of the Councell do not mind things as the late powers did, but their pleasure or profit more. That the Bull Feasts are a simple sport, yet the greatest in Spaine. That the Queene hath given no rewards to any of the captains or officers, but only to my Lord Sandwich; and that was a bag of gold, which was no honorable present, of about £1400 sterling. How recluse the Queene hath ever been, and all the voyage never come upon the deck, nor put her head out of her cabin; but did love my Lord's musique, and would send for it down to the state-room, and she sit in her cabin within hearing of it. But my Lord was forced to have some clashing with the Council of Portugall about payment of the portion, before he could get it, which was besides Tangier and free trade in the Indys, two millions of crownes, half now, and the other half in twelve months. But they have brought but little money; but the rest in sugars and other commoditys, and bills of exchange. That the King of Portugall is a very foole almost, and his mother do all, and he is a very poor Prince.

25th. To church and heard a good sermon of Mr Woodcocke's at our church: only in his latter prayer for a woman in childbed, he prayed that God would deliver her from the hereditary curse of childe-bearing, which seemed a pretty strange expression. Out with Captn. Ferrers to Charing Cross; and there at the Triumph taverne he showed me some Portugall ladys, which are come to towne before the Queene. They are not handsome, and their farthingales a strange dress. Many ladies and persons of quality come to see them. I find nothing in them that is pleasing; and I see they have learnt to kiss and look freely up and down already, and I do believe will soon forget the recluse practice of their own country. They complain much for lack of good water to drink. The King's guards and some City companies do walk up and downe the towne these five or six days; which makes me think, and they do say, there are some plots in laying.

26th. To the Trinity House; where the Brethren have been at Deptford choosing a new Master; which is Sir J. Minnes, notwithstanding Sir W. Batten did contend highly for it; at which I am not a little pleased, because of his proud lady.

29th. This day, being the King's birth-day, was very solemnly observed; and the more, for that the Queene this day comes to Hampton Court. In the evening bonfires were made, but nothing to the great number that was heretofore at the burning of the Rump.

31st. The Queene is brought a few days since to Hampton Court: and all people say of her to be a very fine and handsome lady, and very discreet; and that the King is pleased enough with her: which, I fear, will put Madam Castlemaine's nose out of joynt. The Court is wholly now at Hampton. A peace with Argier is lately made; which is also good news. My Lord Sandwich is lately come with the Queene from sea, very well and in good repute. The Act for Uniformity is lately printed, which, it is thought, will make mad work among the Presbyterian ministers. People of all sides are very much discontented; some thinking themselves used, contrary to promise, too hardly; and the other, that they are not rewarded so much as they expected by the King.

June 3rd. At the office, and Mr Coventry brought his patent and took his place with us this morning. To the Wardrobe, where I found my lady come from Hampton Court, where the Queene hath used her very civilly; and my lady tells me is a most pretty woman. Yesterday (Sir R. Ford told me) the Aldermen of the City did attend her in their habits, and did present her with a gold cupp and £1000 in gold therein. But, he told me, that they are so poor in their Chamber, that they were fain to call two or three Aldermen to raise fines to make up this sum.

4th. Povy[29] and Sir W. Batten and I by water to Woolwich; and there saw an experiment made of Sir R. Ford's Holland's yarne, (about which we have lately had so much stir; and I have much concerned myself for our rope-maker, Mr Hughes, who represented it so bad,) and we found it to be very bad, and broke sooner than, upon a fair triall, five threads of that against four of Riga yarne; and also that some of it had old stuffe that had been tarred, covered over with new hempe, which is such a cheat as hath not been heard of.

7th. To the office. I find Mr Coventry is resolved to do much good, and to enquire into all the miscarriages of the office. At noon with him and Sir W. Batten to dinner at Trinity House; where, among

29 Thomas Povy, MP for Bossiney, 1658, and Treasurer for Tangier. Evelyn mentions his house in Lincoln's Inn-fields; and he appears, from an ancient plan of Whitehall Palace, to have had apartments there,

others, Sir J. Robinson, Lieutenant of the Tower, was, who says that yesterday Sir H. Vane had a full hearing at the King's Bench, and is found guilty; and that he did never hear any man argue more simply than he in all his life, and so others say. Sent for to Sir G. Carteret's. I perceive, as he told me, were it not that Mr Coventry had already feathered his nest in selling of places, he do like him very well, and hopes great good from him. But he complains so of lack of money, that my heart is very sad, under the apprehension of the fall of the office.

10th. All the morning much business; and great hopes of bringing things, by Mr Coventry's means, to a good condition in the office.

12th. I tried on my riding cloth suit with close knees, the first that ever I had; and I think they will be very convenient. At the office all the morning. Among other businesses, I did get a vote signed by all, concerning my issuing of warrants, which they did not smell the use I intend to make of it; but it is to plead for my clerks to have their right of giving out all the warrants. A great difference happened between Sir G. Carteret and Mr Coventry, about passing the Victualler's account, and whether Sir George is to pay the Victualler his money, or the Exchequer; Sir George claiming it to be his place to save his three-pences. It ended in anger, and I believe will come to be a question before the King and Council.

13th. Up by 4 o'clock in the morning, and read Cicero's Second Oration against Catiline, which pleased me exceedingly: and more I discern therein than ever I thought was to be found in him; but I perceive it was my ignorance, and that he is as good a writer as ever I read in my life. By and by to Sir G. Carteret's, to talk with him about yesterday's difference at the office; and offered my service to look into my old books or papers that I have, that may make for him. He was well pleased therewith, and did much inveigh against Mr Coventry; telling me how he had done him service in the Parliament, when Prin had drawn up things against him for taking of money for places; that he did at his desire, and upon his letters, keep him off from doing it. And many other things he told me, as how the King was beholden to him, and in what a miserable condition his family would be, if he should die before he hath cleared his accounts. Upon the whole, I do find that he do much esteem of me, and is my friend.

14th. About 11 o'clock, having a room got ready for us, we all went out to the Tower-hill; and there, over against the scaffold, made on purpose this day, saw Sir Henry Vane brought. A very great press of people. He made a long speech, many times interrupted by the Sheriffe and others there; and they would have taken his paper out of his hand, but he would not let it go. But they caused all the books of those that writ after him to be given the Sheriffe; and the trumpets were brought under the scaffold that he might not be heard. Then he prayed, and so fitted himself, and received the blow; but the scaffold was so crowded that we could not see it done. But Boreman, who had been upon the scaffold, told us, that first he began to speak of the irregular proceeding against him; that he was, against Magna Charta, denied to have his exceptions against the indictment allowed; and that there he was stopped by the Sheriffe. Then he drew out his paper of notes, and begun to tell them first his life; that he was born a gentleman; he had been, till he was seventeen years old, a good fellow, but then it pleased God to lay a foundation of grace in his heart, by which he was persuaded, against his worldly interest, to leave all preferment and go abroad, where he might serve God with more freedom. Then he was called home; and made a member of the Long Parliament; where he never did, to this day, any thing against his conscience, but all for the glory of God. Here he would have given them an account of the proceedings of the Long Parliament, but they so often interrupted him, that at last he was forced to give over: and so fell into prayer for England in generall, then for the churches in England, and then for the City of London: and so fitted himself for the block, and received the blow. He had a blister, or issue, upon his neck, which he desired them not to hurt: he changed not his colour or speech to the last, but died justifying himself and the cause he had stood for; and spoke very confidently of his being presently at the right hand of Christ; and in all things appeared the most resolved man that ever died in that manner, and showed more of heate than cowardize, but yet with all humility and gravity. One asked him why he did not pray for the King. He answered, 'You shall see I can pray for the King: I pray God bless him!' The King had given his body to his friends; and, therefore, he told them that he hoped they would be civil to his body when dead; and desired they would let him die like a gentleman and a Christian, and not crowded and pressed as he was. So to the office a little, and to the Trinity-house, and there all of us to dinner; and to the office again all the afternoon till night. This day, I hear, my Lord Peterborough is come unexpected from Tangier, to give the King an account of the place, which, we fear, is in none of the best condition. We had also certain news today that the Spaniard is before Lisbone with thirteen sayle; six Dutch, and the rest his own ships; which will, I fear, be in for Portugall. I writ a letter of all this day's proceedings to my Lord, at Hinchingbroke.

18th. Up early; and after reading a little in Cicero, to my office. To my Lord Crewe's and dined with him; where I hear the courage of Sir H. Vane at his death is talked on every where as a miracle. I walked to Lilly's,[30] the painter's, where I saw among other rare things, the Duchesse of York, her whole body, sitting in state in a chair, in white sattin, and another of the King's, that is not finished; most rare things. I did give the fellow something that showed them us, and promised to come some other time, and he would show me Lady Castlemaine's, which I could not then see, it being locked up! Thence to Wright's,[31] the painter's: but, Lord! the difference that is between their two works.

20th. Drew up the agreement between the King and Sir John Winter[32] about the Forrest of Deane; and having done it, he come himself, (I did not know him to be the Queene's Secretary before, but observed him to be a man of fine parts); and we read it, and both liked it well. That done, I turned to the Forrest of Deane, in Speede's Mapps, and there he showed me how it lies; and the Sea-bayly, with the great charge of carrying it to Lydny, and many other things worth my knowing; and I do perceive that I am very short in my business by not knowing many times the geographical part of my business.

I went to the Exchange, and I hear that the merchants have a great fear of a breach with the Spaniard; for they think he will not brook our having Tangier, Dunkirke, and Jamaica; and our merchants begin to draw home their estates as fast as they can.

30 Peter Lely, the celebrated painter, afterwards knighted. Died 1680.
31 Michael Wright, a native of Scotland, and portrait-painter of some note, settled in London.
32 Secretary and Chancellor to the Queen Dowager.

21st. At noon, Sir W. Pen and I to the Trinity House; where was a feast made by the Wardens. Great good cheer, and much but ordinary company. The Lieutenant of the Tower, upon my demanding how Sir H. Vane died, told me that he died in a passion; but all confess with so much courage as never man did.

22nd. This day I am told of a Portugall lady, at Hampton Court, that hath dropped a child already since the Queene's coming, and the King would not have them searched whose it is; and so it is not commonly known yet. Coming home tonight, I met with Will. Swan, who do talk as high for the Fanatiques as ever he did in his life; and do pity my Lord Sandwich and me that we should be given up to the wickedness of the world; and that a fall is coming upon us all; for he finds that he and his company are the true spirit of the nation, and the greater part of the nation too, who will have liberty of conscience in spite of this 'Act of Uniformity', or they will die; and if they may not preach abroad, they will preach in their own houses. He told me that certainly Sir H. Vane must be gone to Heaven, for he died as much a martyr and saint as ever man did; and that the King hath lost more by that man's death, than he will get again a good while. At all which I know not what to think; but, I confess, I do think that the Bishops will never be able to carry it so high as they do. Meeting with Frank Moore, my Lord Lambeth's man formerly, we, and two or three friends of his did go to a taverne; but one of our company, a talking fellow, did in discourse say much of this Act against Seamen, for their being brought to account; and that it was made on purpose for my Lord Sandwich, who was in debt £100,000 and hath been forced to have pardon oftentimes from Oliver for the same: at which I was vexed.

24th. At night news is brought me that Field the rogue hath this day cast me at Guildhall in £30 for his imprisonment, to which I signed his commitment with the rest of the officers; but they having been parliament-men, he do begin the law with me; but threatens more.

26th. Mr Nicholson,[33] my old fellow-student at Magdalene, come, and we played three or four things upon the violin and basse.

27th. To my Lord, who rose as soon as he heard I was there; and in

33 Thomas Nicholson, AM, 1672.

his night-gowne and shirt stood talking with me alone two hours, I believe, concerning his greatest matters of state and interest. – Among other things, that his greatest design is, first, to get clear of all debts to the King for the Embassy money, and then a pardon. Then, to get his land settled; and then to discourse and advise what is best for him, whether to keep his sea employment longer or no. For he do discern that the Duke would be willing to have him out, and that by Coventry's means. And here he told me, how the terms at Argier were wholly his; and that he did plainly tell Lawson and agree with him, that he would have the honour of them, if they should ever be agreed to; and that accordingly they did come over hither entitled, 'Articles concluded on by Sir J. Lawson, according to instructions received from His Royal Highness James Duke of York, &c. and from His Excellency the Earle of Sandwich'. (Which however was more than needed; but Lawson tells my Lord in his letter, that it was not he, but the Council of Warr that would have 'His Royal Highness' put into the title, though he did not contribute one word to it.) But the Duke of York did yesterday propose them to the Council, to be printed with this title: 'Concluded on by Sir J. Lawson, Knt.' and my Lord quite left out. Here I find my Lord very politique; for he tells me, that he discerns they design to set up Lawson as much as they can: and that he do counterplot them by setting him up higher still; by which they will find themselves spoiled of their design, and at last grow jealous of Lawson. This he told me with much pleasure; and that several of the Duke's servants, by name my Lord Barkeley, Mr Talbot, and others, had complained to my Lord, of Coventry, and would have him out. My Lord do acknowledge that his greatest obstacle is Coventry. He did seem to hint such a question as this: 'Hitherto I have been supported by the King and Chancellor against the Duke; but what if it should come about, that it should be the Duke and Chancellor against the King': which, though he said it in several plain words, yet I could not fully understand it; but may more hereafter. My Lord did also tell me, that the Duke himself at Portsmouth did thank my Lord for all his pains and care; and that he perceived it must be the old Captains that must do the business; and that the new ones would spoil all. And that my Lord did very discreetly tell the Duke, (though quite against his judgement and inclination) that, however, the King's new captaines ought to be borne with a little and encouraged. By which he will oblige that party, and prevent, as much as may be, their envy; but he says certainly things will go to rack if ever the old captains should be wholly out, and the new ones only command.

I met Sir W. Pen; he told me the day now was fixed for his going into Ireland; and that whereas I had mentioned some service he could do a friend of mine there, Saml. Pepys,[34] he told me he would most readily do what I would command him.

28th. Great talk there is of a fear of a war with the Dutch; and we have order to pitch upon twenty ships to be forthwith set out; but I hope it is but a scare-crow to the world, to let them see that we can be ready for them; though, God knows! the King is not able to set out five ships at this present without great difficulty, we neither having money, credit, nor stores.

30th. Told my Lady (Carteret) how my Lady Fanshaw[35] is fallen out with her only for speaking in behalf of the French, which my Lady wonders at, they having been formerly like sisters. Thence to my house, where I took great pride to lead her through the Court by the hand, she being very fine, and her page carrying up her train.

OBSERVATIONS

This I take to be as bad a juncture as ever I observed. The King and his new Queene minding their pleasures at Hampton Court. All people discontented; some that the King do not gratify them enough; and the others, Fanatiques of all sorts, that the King do take away their liberty of conscience; and the height of the Bishops, who I fear will ruin all again. They do much cry up the manner of Sir H. Vane's death, and he deserves it. Much clamour against the chimney-money; and the people say, they will not pay it without force. And in the meantime, like to have war abroad; and Portugall to assist, when we have not money to pay for any ordinary layings-out at home.

July 2nd. Up while the chimes went four, and so put down my journal. So to my office, to read over such instructions as concern the officers of the Yard; for I am much upon seeing into the miscarriages there. By and by, by appointment, comes Commissioner Pett; and

34 Mentioned elsewhere as 'My cousin in Ireland'.
35 Anne, daughter of Sir John Harrison, wife of Sir Richard Fanshawe. She wrote Memoirs of her life – see Seward's *Anecdotes*.

then a messenger from Mr Coventry, who sits in his boat expecting us. So we down to him at the Tower, and there took water all, and to Deptford, (he in our passage taking notice how much difference there is between the old Captains for obedience and order, and the King's new Captains, which I am very glad to hear him confess); and there we went into the Store-house, and viewed first the provisions there, and then his books, (but Mr Davis himself was not there); and I do not perceive that there is one-third of their duties performed; but I perceive, to my great content, Mr Coventry will have things performed. In the evening come Mr Lewis to me, and very ingeniously did enquire whether I ever did look into the business of the Chest at Chatham; and after my readiness to be informed did appear to him, he did produce a paper, wherein he stated the government of the Chest to me; and upon the whole did tell me how it hath ever been abused, and to this day is; and what a meritorious act it would be to look after it; which I am resolved to do, if God bless me: and do thank him very much for it.

3rd. Dined with the Officers of the Ordnance; where Sir W. Compton, Mr O'Neale, and other great persons, were. After dinner, was brought to Sir W. Compton a gun to discharge seven times; the best of all devices that ever I saw, and very serviceable, and not a bawble; for it is much approved of, and many thereof made.

6th. To supper with my Lady (Sandwich); who tells me, with much trouble, that my Lady Castlemaine is still as great with the King, and that the King comes as often to her as ever he did. Jack Cole, my old friend, found me out at the Wardrobe; and, among other things, he told me that certainly most of the chief ministers of London would fling up their livings; and that, soon or late, the issue thereof would be sad to the King and Court.

8th. To the Wardrobe; where, all alone with my Lord above an hour; and he do seem still to have his old confidence in me; and tells me to boot, that Mr Coventry hath spoke of me to him to great advantage; wherein I am much pleased. By and by comes in Mr Coventry to visit my Lord; and so my Lord and he and I walked together in the great chamber a good while; and I found him a most ingenuous man and good company.

16th. This day I was told that my Lady Castlemaine (being quite fallen out with her husband) did yesterday go away from him, with all her plate, jewels, and other best things; and is gone to Richmond to a brother of hers; which, I am apt to think, was a design to get out of town, that the King might come at her the better.

17th. To my office, and by and by to our sitting; where much business. Mr Coventry took his leave, being to go with the Duke over for the Queene-Mother.

19th. In the afternoon I went upon the river: it raining hard upon the water, I put ashore and sheltered myself, while the King come by in his barge, going down towards the Downes to meet the Queene: the Duke being gone yesterday. But methought it lessened my esteem of a king, that he should not be able to command the rain.

21st. To Woolwich to the Rope-yard; and there looked over several sorts of hemp, and did fall upon my great survey of seeing the working and experiments of the strength and the charge in the dressing of every sort; and I do think have brought it to so great a certainty, as I have done the King some service in it; and do purpose to get it ready against the Duke's coming to towne to present to him. I see it is impossible for the King to have things done as cheap as other men.

22nd. I had letters from the Downes from Mr Coventry; who tells me of the foul weather they had last Sunday, that drove them back from near Bologne, whither they were going for the Queene, back again to the Downes, with the loss of their cables, sayles, and masts; but are all safe, only my Lord Sandwich, who went before with the yacht: they know not what is become of him, which do trouble me much; but I hope he got ashore before the storm begun; which God grant!

23rd. Much disturbed, by reason of the talk up and downe the towne, that my Lord Sandwich is lost: but I trust in God the contrary.

24th. I hear, to my great content, that my Lord Sandwich is safe landed in France.

26th. I had a letter from Mr Creed, who hath escaped narrowly in the King's yacht, and got safe to the Downes after the late storm; and he says that there the King do tell him, that he is sure my Lord is landed in

Callis safe. This afternoon I went to Westminster: and there hear that the King and Queene intend to come to White Hall from Hampton Court next week, for all winter. Thence to Mrs Sarah,[36] and there looked over my Lord's lodgings, which are very pretty; and White Hall garden and the Bowling-ally (where lords and ladies are now at bowles), in brave condition. Mrs Sarah told me how the falling out between my Lady Castlemaine and her Lord was about christening of the child lately, which he would have, and had done by a priest: and some days after, she had it again christened by a minister; the King, and Lord of Oxford,[37] and Duchesse of Suffolk[38] being witnesses: and christened with a proviso, that it had not already been christened. Since that she left her Lord, carrying away every thing in the house; so much as every dish, and cloth, and servant but the porter. He is gone discontented into France, they say, to enter a monastery; and now she is coming back again to her house in King-streete. But I hear that the Queene did prick her out of the list presented her by the King; desiring that she might have that favour done her, or that he would send her from whence she come: and that the King was angry and the Queene discontented a whole day and night upon it; but that the King hath promised to have nothing to do with her hereafter. But I cannot believe that the King can fling her off so, he loving her too well: and so I writ this night to my Lady to be my opinion; she calling her my lady, and the lady I admire. Here I find that my Lord hath lost the garden to his lodgings, and that it is turning into a tennis-court.

27th. I to walk in the Parke, which is now every day more and more pleasant, by the new works upon it.

28th. Walked to the water-side, and there took boat for the Tower; hearing that the Queene-Mother is come this morning already as high as Woolwich: and that my Lord Sandwich was with her; at which my heart was glad.

30th. By water to White Hall, and there waited upon my Lord Sandwich; and joyed him, at his lodgings, of his safe coming home after all his danger, which he confesses to be very great. And his

36 Lord Sandwich's housekeeper.
37 Aubrey de Vere, twentieth and last Earl of Oxford. Died 1702/03, without issue.
38 Perhaps a mistake for Countess, as there was no Duchess of Suffolk at that period.

people do tell me how bravely my Lord did carry himself, while my Lord Crofts[39] did cry; and I perceive all the town talk how poorly he carried himself. But the best was one of Mr Rawlins, a courtier, that was with my Lord; and in the greatest danger cried, 'My Lord I won't give you three-pence for your place now.' But all ends in the honour of the pleasure-boats; which, had they not been very good boats, they could never have endured the sea as they did.

31st. At noon Mr Coventry and I by his coach to the Exchange together; and in Lumbard-streete met Captn. Browne of the *Rosebush*: at which he was cruel angry; and did threaten to go today to the Duke at Hampton Court, and get him turned out because he was not sailed.

August 3rd. This day Commissioner Pett told me how despicable a thing it is to be a hangman in Poland, although it be a place of credit. And that, in his time, there was some repairs to be made of the gallows there, which was very fine of stone; but nobody could be got to mend it till the Burgo-master, or Mayor of the towne, with all the companies of those trades which were necessary to be used about those repairs, did go in their habits with flags, in solemn procession to the place, and there the Burgo-master did give the first blow with the hammer upon the wooden work; and the rest of the Masters of the Companys upon the works belonging to their trades; that so workmen might not be ashamed to be employed upon doing of the gallows works.

6th. By water to White Hall; and so to St James's; but there found Mr Coventry gone to Hampton Court. So to my Lord's; and he is also gone: this being a great day at the Council about some business before the King. Here Mr Pierce, the chyrurgeon, told me how Mr Edward Montagu hath lately had a duell with Mr Cholmely, that is first gentleman-usher to the Queene, and was a messenger to her from the King of Portugall, and is a fine gentleman; but had received many affronts from Mr Montagu, and some unkindness from my Lord, upon his score, (for which I am sorry). He proved too hard for Montagu, and drove him so far backward that he fell into a ditch, and dropt his sword, but with honour would take no advantage over

39 William Crofts, created Baron Crofts of Saxham in Suffolk 1658, and died without issue 1677.

him; but did give him his life: and the world says Mr Montagu did carry himself very poorly in the business, and hath lost his honour for ever with all people in it. This afternoon Mr Waith was with me, and did tell me much concerning the Chest, which I am resolved to look into; and I perceive he is sensible of Sir W. Batten's carriage; and is pleased to see any thing work against him.

8th. Dined with Mr Falconer; thence we walked talking all the way to Greenwich, and I do find excellent discourse from him. Among other things, his rule of suspecting every man that proposes any thing to him to be a knave; or, at least, to have some ends of his own in it. Being led thereto by the story of Sir John Millicent, that would have had a patent from King James for every man to have had leave to have given him a shilling; and that he might take it of every man that had a mind to give it; and what he would do to them that would not give him. He answered, he would not force them; but that they should come to the Council of State, to give a reason why they would not. Another rule is a proverb that he hath been taught, which is that a man that cannot sit still in his chamber, (the reason of which I did not understand,) and he that cannot say no, (that is, that is of so good a nature that he cannot deny any thing, or cross another in doing any thing) is not fit for business. The last of which is a very great fault of mine, which I must amend in.

9th. Mr Coventry and I alone sat at the office all the morning upon business. And so to dinner to Trinity House, and thence by his coach towards White Hall; but there being a stop at the Savoy, we light and took water, and my Lord Sandwich being out of towne, we parted there.

10th. I walked to St Dunstan's, the church being now finished; and here I heard Dr Bates,[40] who made a most eloquent sermon; and I am sorry I have hitherto had so low an opinion of the man, for I have not heard a neater sermon a great while, and more to my content. My uncle Fenner told me the new service-booke (which is now lately come forth) was laid upon their deske at St Sepulchre's for Mr George to read; but he laid it aside, and would not meddle with it: and I perceive the Presbyters do all prepare to give over all against

40 Dr Bates, a celebrated Nonconformist divine.

Bartholomewtide. Mr Herring, being lately turned out at St Bride's, did read the psalme to the people while they sung at Dr Bates's, which methought is a strange turn. After dinner to St Bride's, and there heard one Carpenter, an old man, who, they say, hath been a Jesuite priest, and is come over to us; but he preached very well. Mr Calamy hath taken his farewell this day of his people, and others will do so the next Sunday. Mr Turner,[41] the draper, I hear, is knighted, made Alderman, and pricked for Sheriffe, with Sir Thomas Bluddel,[42] for the next year, by the King, and so are called with great honour the King's Sheriffes.

13th. Up early, and to my office. By and by we met on purpose to enquire into the business of flag-makers, where I am the person that do chiefly manage the business against them on the King's part; and I do find it the greatest cheat that I have yet found; they having eightpence per yard allowed them by pretence of a contract, where no such thing appears; and it is threepence more than was formerly paid, and than I now offer the board to have them done. To Lambeth; and there saw the little pleasure-boat in building by the King, my Lord Brunkard,[43] and the virtuosoes of the towne, according to new lines, which Mr Pett cries up mightily, but how it will prove we shall soon see.

14th. Commissioner Pett and I being invited, went by Sir John Winter's coach sent for us, to the Miter, in Fanchurch-street, to a venison-pasty; where I found him a very worthy man; and good discourse. Most of which was concerning the Forest of Deane, and the timber there, and iron-workes with their great antiquity, and the vast heaps of cinders, which they find, and are now of great value, being necessary for the making of iron at this day; and without which they cannot work: with the age of many trees there left at a great fall in Edward III's time, by the name of forbid-trees, which at this day, are called vorbid trees.

15th. I went to Paul's Church Yard to my bookseller's; and there I

41 Sir William Turner, Lord Mayor of London, 1669.
42 A mistake for Bludworth.
43 William, second Lord Brouncker, Viscount of Castle Lyons; created MD, in 1642, at Oxford: Keeper of the Great Seal to the Queen; a Commissioner of the Admiralty; and Master of St Catherine's Hospital. He was a man of considerable talents, and some years President of the Royal Society. Died 1684, aged 64.

hear that next Sunday will be the last of a great many Presbyterian ministers in towne, who, I hear, will give up all. I pray God the issue may be good, for the discontent is great. My mind well pleased with a letter that I found at home from Mr Coventry, expressing his satisfaction in a letter I writ last night, and sent him this morning, to be corrected by him in order to its sending down to all the Yards as a charge to them.

17th. This being the last Sunday that the Presbyterians are to preach, unless they read the new Common Prayer and renounce the Covenant, I had a mind to hear Dr Bates's farewell sermon; and walked to St Dunstan's, where, it not being seven o'clock yet, the doors were not open; and so I walked an hour in the Temple-garden. At eight o'clock I went, and crowded in at a back door among others, the church being half-full almost before any doors were open publicly; and so got into the gallery, beside the pulpit, and heard very well. His text was, 'Now the God of Peace . . . '; the last Hebrews, and the 20th verse: he making a very good sermon, and very little reflections in it to any thing of the times. To Madam Turner's, and dined with her. She had heard Parson Herring take his leave; tho' he, by reading so much of the Common Prayer as he did, hath cast himself out of the good opinion of both sides. After dinner to St Dunstan's again; and the church quite crowded before I come, which was just at one o'clock; but I got into the gallery again, but stood in a crowd. He[44] pursued his text again very well; and only at the conclusion told us, after this manner: 'I do believe that many of you do expect that I should say something to you in reference to the time, this being the last time that possibly I may appear here. You know not it is not my manner to speak anything in the pulpit that is extraneous to my text and business; yet this I shall say, that it is not my opinion, fashion, or humour that keeps me from complying with what is required of us; but something after much prayer, discourse, and study yet remains unsatisfied, and commands me herein. Wherefore, if it is my unhappinesse not to receive such an illuminacion as should direct me to do otherwise, I know no reason why men should not pardon me in this world, as I am confident God will pardon me for it in the next.' And so he concluded. Parson Herring read a psalme and chapters before sermon; and one was the

44 Dr Bates.

chapter in the Acts, where the story of Ananias and Sapphira is. And after he had done, says he, 'This is just the case of England at present. God he bids us to preach, and men bid us not to preach; and if we do, we are to be imprisoned and further punished. All that I can say to it is, that I beg your prayers, and the prayers of all good Christians, for us.' This was all the exposition he made of the chapter in these very words, and no more. I was much pleased with Bates's manner of bringing in the Lord's Prayer after his owne; thus, 'In whose comprehensive words we sum up all our imperfect desires; saying, "Our Father" &c.' I hear most of the Presbyters took their leaves today, and that the City is much dissatisfied with it. I pray God keep peace among men in their rooms, or else all will fly a-pieces; for bad ones will not go down with the City.

18th. Mr Deane[45] of Woolwich and I rid into Waltham Forest, and there we saw many trees of the King's a-hewing; and he showed me the whole mystery of off square, wherein the King is abused in the timber that he buys, which I shall with much pleasure be able to correct. We rode to Illford, and there, while dinner was getting ready, he and I practised measuring of the tables and other things till I did understand measure of timber and board very well.

19th. At the office; and Mr Coventry did tell us of the duell between Mr Jermyn,[46] nephew to my Lord St Alban's, and Colonel Giles Rawlins, the latter of whom is killed, and the first mortally wounded, as it is thought. They fought against Captain Thomas Howard,[47] my Lord Carlisle's brother, and another unknown; who, they say, had armor on that they could not be hurt, so that one of their swords went up to the hilt against it. They had horses ready, and are fled. But what is most strange, Howard sent one challenge before, but they could not meet till yesterday at the old Pall Mall at St James's, and he would not to the last tell Jermyn what the quarrel was; nor do any body know. The Court is much concerned in this fray, and I am glad of it; hoping that it will cause some good laws against it. After sitting, Sir G. Carteret did tell me how he had spoke of me to my Lord

45 Anthony Deane, afterwards knighted and MP for Harwich ; a Commissioner of the Navy, 1672.
46 He became Baron Jermyn on the death of his uncle, the Earl of St Alban's, 1683; and died unmarried, 1703.
47 According to Collins, Lord Carlisle's brother's name was Charles.

Chancellor, and that if my Lord Sandwich would ask my Lord Chancellor, he should know what he had said of me to him to my advantage.

20th. To my Lord Sandwich, whom I found in bed. Among other talk, he do tell me that he hath put me into commission with a great many great persons in the business of Tangier, which is a very great honour to me, and may be of good concernment to me. By and by comes in Mr Coventry to us, whom my Lord tells that he is also put into the commission, and that I am there, of which he said he was glad; and did tell my Lord that I was indeed the life of this office, and much more to my commendation beyond measure. And that, whereas before he did bear me respect for his sake, so he do it now much more for my own; which is a great blessing to me. Sir G. Carteret having told me what he did yesterday concerning his speaking to my Lord Chancellor about me. So that on all hands, by God's blessing, I find myself a very rising man. By and by comes my Lord Peterborough in, with whom we talked a good while, and he is going to-morrow toward Tangier again. I perceive there is yet good hopes of peace with Guyland,[48] which is of great concernment to Tangier.

23rd. Mr Coventry and I did walk together a great while in the Garden, where he did tell me his mind about Sir G. Carteret's having so much the command of the money, which must be removed. And indeed it is the bane of all our business. He observed to me also how Sir W. Batten begins to struggle and to look after his business. I also put him upon getting an order from the Duke for our inquiries into the Chest, which he will see done.

Mr Creed and I walked down to the Tylt Yard, and so all along Thames-street, but could not get a boat: I offered eight shillings for a boat to attend me this afternoon, and they would not, it being the day of the Queene's coming to town from Hampton Court. So we fairly walked it to White Hall, and through my Lord's lodgings we got into White Hall garden, and so to the Bowling-greene, and up to the top of the new Banqueting House there, over the Thames, which was a most pleasant place as any I could have got; and all the show

48 A Moorish usurper, who had put himself at the head of an army for the purpose of attacking Tangier.

consisted chiefly in the number of boats and barges; and two
pageants, one of a King, and another of a Queene, with her Maydes
of Honour sitting at her feet very prettily; and they tell me the
Queene is Sir Richard Ford's daughter. Anon come the King and
Queene in a barge under a canopy with 1000 barges and boats I
know, for we could see no water for them, nor discern the King nor
Queene. And so they landed at White Hall Bridge; and the great
guns on the other side went off. But that which pleased me best was,
that my Lady Castlemaine stood over against us upon a piece of
White Hall. But methought it was strange to see her Lord and her
upon the same place walking up and down without taking notice one
of another, only at first entry he put off his hat, and she made him a
very civil salute, but afterwards took no notice one of another; but
both of them now and then would take their child, which the nurse
held in her armes, and dandle it. One thing more; there happened a
scaffold below to fall, and we feared some hurt, but there was none,
but she of all the great ladies only run down among the common
rabble to see what hurt was done, and did take care of a child that
received some little hurt, which methought was so noble. Anon there
come one there booted and spurred that she talked along with. And
by and by, she being in her haire, she put on his hat, which was but
an ordinary one, to keep the wind off. But it become her mightily, as
every thing else do.

24th. Walked to my uncle Wight's: here I staid supper, and much
company there was; among others, Dr Burnett, Mr Cole the lawyer,
Mr Rawlinson, and Mr Sutton. Among other things they tell me that
there hath been a disturbance in a church in Friday-street; a great
many young people knotting together and crying out 'Porridge'
often and seditiously in the Church, and they took the Common
Prayer Book, they say, away; and, some say, did tear it; but it is a
thing which appears to me very ominous. I pray God avert it.

31st. To Mr Rawlinson's, and there supped with him. Our discourse
of the discontents that are abroad, among, and by reason of the
Presbyters. Some were clapped up today, and strict watch is kept in
the City by the train-bands, and abettors of a plot are taken. God
preserve us, for all these things bode very ill.

September 1st. With Sir W. Batten and Sir W. Pen by coach to St

James's, this being the first day of our meeting there by the Duke's order; but when we come, we found him going out by coach with his Duchesse, and he told us he was to go abroad with the Queene today, (to Durdan's, it seems, to dine with my Lord Barkeley,[49] where I have been very merry when I was a little boy;) so we went and staid a little at Mr Coventry's chamber, and I to my Lord Sandwich's, who is gone to wait upon the King and Queene today.

3rd. Mr Coventry told us how the Fanatiques and Presbyters, that did intend to rise about this time, did choose this day as the most auspicious to them in their endeavours against monarchy: it being fatal twice to the King, and the day of Oliver's death. But, blessed be God! all is likely to be quiet, I hope. Dr Fairbrother tells me, what I heard confirmed since, that it was fully resolved by the King's new Council that an indulgence should be granted the Presbyters; but upon the Bishop of London's[50] speech, (who is now one of the most powerful men in England with the King,) their minds were wholly turned. And it is said that my Lord Albemarle did oppose him most; but that I do believe is only an appearance. He told me also that most of the Presbyters now begin to wish they had complied, now they see that no indulgence will be granted them, which they hoped for; and that the Bishop of London hath taken good care that places are supplied with very good and able men, which is the only thing that will keep all quiet.

4th. At noon to the Trinity House, where we treated, very dearly I believe, the officers of the Ordnance; where was Sir W. Compton and the Lieutenant of the Tower. We had much and good musique. Sir Wm. Compton I heard talk with great pleasure of the difference between the fleet now and in Queene Elizabeth's days; where, in '88, she had but 36 sail great and small, in the world; and ten rounds of powder was their allowance at that time against the Spaniard.

5th. By water to Woolwich: in my way saw the yacht lately built by our virtuosoes (my Lord Brunkard and others, with the help of Commissioner Pett also,) set out from Greenwich with the little Dutch bezan, to try for mastery; and before they got to Woolwich the Dutch beat them half-a-mile; (and I hear this afternoon, that, in

49 Lord Berkeley's seat near Epsom.
50 Gilbert Sheldon.

coming home, it got above three miles;) which all our people are glad of. To Mr Bland's, the merchant, by invitation; where I found all the officers of the Customs, very grave fine gentlemen, and I am very glad to know them; viz. – Sir Job Harvy, Sir John Wolstenholme,[51] Sir John Jacob,[52] Sir Nicholas Crisp, Sir John Harrison, and Sir John Shaw:[53] very good company. And among other discourse, some was of Sir Jerom Bowes, Embassador from Queene Elizabeth to the Emperor of Russia;[54] who, because some of the noblemen there would go up-stairs to the Emperor before him, he would not go up till the Emperor had ordered those two men to be dragged downstairs, with their heads knocking upon every stair till they were killed. And when he was come up, they demanded his sword of him before he entered the room. He told them, if they would have his sword, they should have his boots too. And so caused his boots to be pulled off, and his night-gown and night-cap and slippers to be sent for; and made the Emperor stay till he could go in his nightdress, since he might not go as a soldier. And lastly, when the Emperor in contempt, to show his command of his subjects, did command one to leap from the window down and broke his neck in the sight of our Embassador, he replied that his mistress did set more by, and did make better use of the necks of her subjects: but said, that, to show what her subjects would do for her, he would, and did, fling down his gantlett before the Emperor; and challenged all the nobility there to take it up, in defence of the Emperor against his Queene; for which, at this very day, the name of Sir Jerom Bowes is famous and honoured there. I this day heard that Mr Martin Noell is knighted by the King, which I much wonder at; but yet he is certainly a very useful man.

51 Sir John Wolstenholme; created a Baronet, 1664. An intimate friend of Lord Clarendon's; and collector outward for the Port of London. Died 1679.

52 Sir John Jacob of Bromley, Middlesex; created a Baronet, 1664, for his loyalty and zeal for the Royal Family. Died 1665/66.

53 Sir John Shaw was created a Baronet in 1665, for his services in lending the King large sums of money during his exile. Died 1679/80.

54 In 1583: the object of his mission being to persuade the Muscovite to a peace with John, King of Sweden. He was also employed to confirm the trade of the English with Russia; and having incurred some personal danger, was received with favour on his return by the Queen He died in 1616. There is a portrait of him in Lord Suffolk's collection at Charlton.

7th. Home with Mr Fox and his lady; and there dined with them. Most of our discourse was what ministers are flung out that will not conform: and the care of the Bishop of London that we are here supplied with very good men. Meeting Mr Pierce, the chyrurgeon, he took me into Somersett House; and there carried me into the Queene-Mother's presence-chamber, where she was with our own Queene sitting on her left hand (whom I did never see before); and though she be not very charming, yet she hath a good, modest, and innocent look, which is pleasing. Here I also saw Madam Castlemaine, and, which pleased me most, Mr Crofts,[55] the King's bastard, a most pretty sparke of about fifteen years old, who, I perceive, do hang much upon my Lady Castlemaine, and is always with her; and, I hear, the Queenes both are mighty kind to him. By and by in comes the King, and anon the Duke and his Duchesse; so that, they being all together, was such a sight as I never could almost have happened to see with so much ease and leisure. They staid till it was dark, and then went away; the King and his Queene, and my Lady Castlemaine and young Crofts, in one coach and the rest in other coaches. Here were great stores of great ladies, but very few handsome. The King and Queene were very merry; and he would have made the Queene-Mother believe that his Queene was with child, and said that she said so. And the young Queene answered, 'You lye'; which was the first English word that I ever heard her say: which made the King good sport; and he would have made her say in English, 'Confess and be hanged'.

8th. With Mr Coventry to the Duke; who, after he was out of his bed, did send for us in; and, when he was quite ready, took us into his closet, and there told us that he do intend to renew the old custom for the Admirals to have their principal officers to meet them once a-week, to give them an account what they have done that week; which I am glad of: and so the rest did tell His Royal Highness that I could do it best for the time past. And so I produced my short notes, and did give him an account of all that we have of late done; and proposed to him several things for his commands, which he did give us, and so dismissed us.

55 James, son of Charles II by Mrs Lucy Waters; who bore the name of Crofts till he was created Duke of Monmouth in 1662, previously to his marriage with Lady Anne Scot, daughter to Francis, Earl of Buccleuch.

12th. This day, by letters from my father, I hear that Captn. Ferrers, who is with my Lord in the country, was at Brampton (with Mr Creed) to see him; and that a day or two ago, being provoked to strike one of my Lord's footmen, the footman drew his sword, and hath almost cut the fingers of one of his hands off; which I am very sorry for: but this is the vanity of being apt to command and strike.

14th. To White Hall chapel, where sermon almost done, and I heard Captn. Cooke's new musique. This the first day of having vialls and other instruments to play a symphony between every verse of the anthems; but the musique more full than it was the last Sunday, and very fine it is. But yet I could discern Captn. Cooke to overdo his part at singing, which I never did before. Thence up into the Queene's presence, and there saw the Queene again as I did last Sunday, and some fine ladies with her; but, my troth, not many. Thence to Sir G. Carteret's.

15th. By water with Sir Wm. Pen to White Hall; and, with much ado, was fain to walk over the piles through the bridge, while Sir W. Batten and Sir J. Minnes were aground against the bridge, and could not in a great while get through. At White Hall we hear that the Duke of York is gone a-hunting today; and so we returned: they going to the Duke of Albemarle's, where I left them (after I had observed a very good picture or two there).

18th. At noon Sir G. Carteret, Mr Coventry, and I by invitation to dinner to Sheriff Maynell's, the great money-man; he, Alderman Backewell, and much noble and brave company, with the privilege of their rare discourse, which is great content to me above all other things in the world. And after a great dinner and much discourse, we took leave. Among other discourses, speaking concerning the great charity used in Catholique countrys, Mr Ashburnham did tell us, that this last yeare, there being great want of corne in Paris, and so a collection made for the poor, there was two pearles brought in, nobody knew from whom (till the Queene, seeing them, knew whose they were, but did not discover it), which were sold for 200,000 crownes.

21st (Lord's-day). To the Parke. The Queene coming by in her coach, going to her chapel at St James's (the first time it hath been ready for her), I crowded after her, and I got up to the room where her closet is; and there stood and saw the fine altar, ornaments, and the fryers in their habits, and the priests come in with their fine crosses and many other fine things. I heard their musique too; which may be good, but it did not appear so to me, neither as to their manner of singing, nor was it good concord to my ears, whatever the matter was. The Queene very devout: but what pleased me best was to see my dear Lady Castlemaine, who, tho' a Protestant, did wait upon the Queene to chapel. By and by, after masse was done, a fryer with his cowl did rise up and preach a sermon in Portuguese; which I not understanding, did go away, and to the King's chapel, but that was done; and so up to the Queene's presence-chamber, where she and the King was expected to dine: but she staying at St James's, they were forced to remove the things to the King's presence; and there he dined alone.

23rd. Sir G. Carteret told me how in most cabaretts in France they have writ upon the walls in fair letters to be read *Dieu te regarde*, as a good lesson to be in every man's mind, and have also in Holland their poor's box; in both which places at the making all contracts and bargains they give so much, which they call God's penny.

24th. To my Lord Crewe's, and there dined alone with him, and among other things, he do advise me by all means to keep my Lord Sandwich from proceeding too far in the business of Tangier. First, for that he is confident the King will not be able to find money for the building the Mole; and next, for that it is to be done as we propose it by the reducing of the garrison; and then either my Lord must oppose the Duke of York, who will have the Irish regiment under the command of Fitzgerald continued, or else my Lord Peterborough, who is concerned to have the English continued, but he, it seems, is gone back again merely upon my Lord Sandwich's encouragement.

28th (Lord's-day). To the French Church at the Savoy, and there they have the Common Prayer Book read in French, and, which I never saw before, the minister do preach with his hat off, I suppose in further conformity with our Church.

29th. To Mr Coventry's, and so with him and Sir W. Pen up to the Duke, where the King come also and staid till the Duke was ready. It being Collar-day, we had no time to talk with him about any business. To the King's Theatre, where we saw *Midsummer's Night's dream*, which I had never seen before, nor shall ever again, for it is the most insipid ridiculous play that ever I saw in my life.

30th. My condition at present is this; – I have long been building, and my house to my great content is now almost done. My Lord Sandwich has lately been in the country, and very civil to my wife, and hath himself spent some pains in drawing a plot of some alterations in our house there, which I shall follow as I get money. As for the office, my late industry hath been such, as I am become as high in reputation as any man there, and good hold I have of Mr Coventry and Sir G. Carteret, which I am resolved, and it is necessary for me, to maintain by all fair means. Things are all quiet. The late outing of the Presbyterian clergy by their not renouncing the Covenant as the Act of Parliament commands, is the greatest piece of state now in discourse. But for ought I see they are gone out very peaceably, and the people not so much concerned therein as was expected.

October 2nd. At night hearing that there was a play at the Cockpit, (and my Lord Sandwich, who come to town last night, at it,) I do go thither, and by very great fortune did follow four or five gentlemen who were carried to a little private door in a wall, and so crept through a narrow place and come into one of the boxes next the King's, but so as I could not see the King or Queene, but many of the fine ladies, who yet are not really so handsome generally as I used to take them to be, but that they are finely dressed. Then we saw *The Cardinall*,[56] a tragedy I had never seen before, nor is there any great matter in it. The company that come in with me into the box, were all Frenchmen that could speak no English, but Lord! what sport they made to ask a pretty lady that they got among them that understood both French and English to make her tell them what the actors said.

5th. I to church; and this day the parson has got one to read with a surplice on. I suppose himself will take it up hereafter, for a cunning fellow he is as any of his coate.

6th. To White Hall with Mr Coventry, and so to my Lord

56 A tragi–comedy by James Shirley.

Sandwich's lodgings, but my Lord not within, being at a ball this night with the King at my Lady Castlemaine's at next door.

8th. To my Lord Sandwich's, and among other things to my extraordinary joy, he did tell me how much I was beholding to the Duke of York, who did yesterday of his own accord tell him that he did thank him for one person brought into the Navy, naming myself, and much more to my commendation, which is the greatest comfort and encouragement that ever I had in my life, and do owe it all to Mr Coventry's goodness and ingenuity. At night by coach to my Lord's again, but he is at White Hall with the King, before whom the puppet plays I saw this summer in Covent-garden are acted this night.

9th. To the office; and I bid them adieu for a week, having the Duke's leave got me by Mr Coventry. To whom I did give thanks for my news yesterday of the Duke's words to my Lord Sandwich concerning me, which he took well; and do tell me so freely his love and value of me, that my mind is now in as great a state of quiet as to my interest in the office, as I could ever wish to be. Between one and two o'clock got on horseback at our back gate, with my man Will. with me, both well-mounted on two grey horses. We got to Ware before night; and so I resolved to ride on to Puckeridge, which we did, though the way was bad, and the evening dark before we got thither, by help of company riding before us; among others, a gentleman that took up at the same inn, his name Mr Brian, with whom I supped, and was very good company, and a scholar. He tells me, that it is believed the Queene is with child, for that the coaches are ordered to ride very easily through the streets.

10th. Up, and between eight and nine mounted again, and so rid to Cambridge; the way so good that I got very well thither, and set up at the Beare: and there my cosen Angier come to me, and I must needs to his house; and there found Dr Fairbrother, with a good dinner. But, above all, he telling me that this day there is a Congregation for the choice of some officers in the University, he after dinner gets me a gowne, cap, and hoode, and carries me to the Schooles, where Mr Pepper, my brother's tutor, and this day chosen Proctor, did appoint a M.A. to lead me into the Regent House, where I sat with them, and did vote by subscribing papers thus: '*Ego*

Samuel Pepys eligo Magistrum Bernardum Skelton, (and which was more strange, my old schoolfellow and acquaintance, and who afterwards did take notice of me, and we spoke together,) *alterum e taxatoribus hujus Academiae in annum sequentem.*' The like I did for one Briggs, for the other Taxor, and for other officers, as the Vice-Proctor, (Mr Covell) for Mr Pepper, and which was the gentleman that did carry me into the Regent House.

11th. To Brampton; where I found my father and two brothers, my mother and sister.

12th. To church; where I saw, among others, Mrs Hanbury, a proper lady, and Mr Bernard and his Lady, with her father, my late Lord St John,[57] who looks now like a very plain grave man.

13th. To the Court, and did sue out a recovery, and cut off the entayle; and my brothers there, to join therein. And my father and I admitted to all the lands; he for life, and I for myself and my heirs in reversion. I did with most compleat joy of mind go from the Court with my father home, and away, calling in at Hinchingbroke, and taking leave in three words of my Lady, and the young ladies; and so by moonlight to Cambridge, whither we come at about nine o'clock, and took up at the Beare.

15th. Showed Mr Cooke King's College Chapel, Trinity College, and St John's College Library; and that being done, to our inn again; where I met Dr Fairbrother. He told us how the room we were in, was the room where Cromwell and his associated officers did begin to plot and act their mischiefs in these counties. Took leave of all, and begun our journey about nine o'clock, the roads being every where but bad; but finding our horses in good case, we even made shift to reach London, though both of us very weary. Found all things well, there happening nothing since our going to my discontent in the least degree; which do also please me, that I cannot but bless God for my journey, observing a whole course of successe from the beginning to the end of it.

57 Oliver St John, one of Cromwell's Lords, and Chief Justice; and therefore, after the Restoration, properly called 'My *late* Lord'. His third daughter, Elizabeth, by his second wife, daughter of Henry Cromwell of Upwood, Esq., uncle to the Protector, married Mr John Bernard, who became a Baronet on the death of his father, Sir Robert, in 1666, and was MP for Huntingdon. Died 1689.

16th. I hear Sir H. Bennet[58] is made Secretary of State in Sir Edward Nicholas's stead; not known whether by consent or not.

17th. To Creed's chamber, and there sat a good while and drank chocolate. Here I am told how things go at Court; that the young men get uppermost, and the old serious lords are out of favour; that Sir H. Bennet, being brought into Sir Edward Nicholas's place, Sir Charles Barkeley is made Privy Purse; a most vicious person, and one whom Mr Pierce, the surgeon, did tell me that he offered his wife £300 per annum to be his mistress. He also told me, that none in Court hath more the King's eare now than Sir Charles Barkeley, and Sir H. Bennet, and my Lady Castlemaine, whose interest now is as great as ever: and that Mrs Haslerigge, the great beauty, is now brought to bed, and lays it to the King or the Duke of York. He tells me also, that my Lord St Albans is like to be Lord Treasurer: all which things do trouble me much.

19th (Lord's-day). Put on my first new lace-band; and so neat it is, that I am resolved my great expence shall be lace-bands, and it will set off any thing else the more. I am sorry to hear that the news of the selling of Dunkirke is taken so generally ill, as I find it is among the merchants; and other things, as removal of officers at Court, good for worse; and all things else made much worse in their report among people than they are. And this night, I know not upon what ground, the gates of the City ordered to be all shut, and double guards every where. Indeed I do find every body's spirit very full of trouble: and the things of the Court and Council very ill taken; so as to be apt to appear in bad colours, if there should ever be a beginning of trouble, which God forbid!

20th. In Sir J. Minnes's coach with him and Sir W. Batten to White Hall, where now the Duke is come again to lodge: and to Mr Coventry's little new chamber there. And by and by up to the Duke, who was making himself ready; and there young Killigrew did so commend *The Villaine*, a new play made by Tom Porter, and acted only on Saturday at the Duke's house, as if there never had been any such play come upon the stage. The same yesterday was told me by Captn. Ferrers; and this morning afterwards by Dr Clarke, who saw

58 Created Baron of Arlington 1663, and Viscount Thetford and Earl of Arlington, 1673; he was also KG, and Chamberlain to the King. Died 1685.

it. After I had done with the Duke, with Commissioner Pett to Mr Lilly's, the great painter, who come forth to us; but believing that I come to bespeak a picture, he prevented it by telling us, that he should not be at leisure these three weeks; which methinks is a rare thing. And then to see in what pomp his table was laid for himself to go to dinner; and here, among other pictures, saw the so much desired by me picture of my Lady Castlemaine, which is a most blessed picture; and one that I must have a copy of. From thence I took my wife by coach to the Duke's house, and there was the house full of company: but whether it was in overexpecting or what, I know not, but I was never less pleased with a play in my life. Though there was good singing and dancing, yet no fancy in the play.

21st. By water with Mr Smith, to Mr Lechmore,[59] the Councellor at the Temple, about Field's business; and he tells me plainly that there being a verdict against me, there is no help for it, but it must proceed to judgement. It is £30 damage to me for my joining with others in committing Field to prison, as being not Justices of the Peace in the City, though in Middlesex; which troubled me, and I hope the King will make it good to us.

24th. Mr Pierce, the chyrurgeon, tells me how ill things go at Court: that the King do show no countenance to any that belong to the Queene; nor, above all, to such English as she brought over with her, or hath here since, for fear they should tell her how he carries himself to Mrs Palmer; insomuch that though he has a promise, and is sure of being made her chyrurgeon, he is at a loss what to do in it, whether to take it or no, since the King's mind is so altered and favor to all her dependents, whom she is fain to let go back into Portugall, (though she brought them from their friends against their wills with promise of preferment,) without doing anything for them. That her owne physician did tell him within these three days that the Queene do know how the King orders things, and how he carries himself to my Lady Castlemaine and others, as well as any body; but though she hath spirit enough, yet seeing that she do no good by taking notice of it, for the present she forbears it in policy; of which I am very glad.

59 Nicholas Lechmere, knighted and made a Baron of the Exchequer, 1689. Died 1701.

But I do pray God keep us in peace; for this, with other things, do give great discontent to all people.

26th (Lord's-day). Put on my new Scallop, which is very fine. To church, and there saw the first time Mr Mills in a surplice; but it seemed absurd for him to pull it over his eares in the reading-pew, after he had done, before all the church, to go up to the pulpitt, to preach without it. All this day soldiers going up and down the towne, there being an alarme, and many Quakers and other clapped up; but I believe without any reason: only they say in Dorsetshire there hath been some rising discovered.

27th. To my Lord Sandwich, who now-a-days calls me into his chamber, and alone did discourse with me about the jealousy that the Court have of people's rising wherein he do much dislike my Lord Monk's being so eager against a company of poor wretches, dragging them up and down the street; but would have him rather take some of the greatest ringleaders of them, and punish them; whereas this do but tell the world the king's fears and doubts. For Dunkirke, he wonders any wise people should be so troubled thereat, and scorns all their talk against it, for that he sees it was not Dunkirke, but the other places, that did and would annoy us, though we had that, as much as if we had it not. He also took notice of the new Ministers of State, Sir H. Bennet and Sir Charles Barkeley, their bringing in, and the high game that my Lady Castlemaine plays at Court. Afterwards he told me of poor Mr Spong, that being with other people examined before the King and Council, (they being laid up as suspected persons; and it seems Spong is so far thought guilty as that they intend to pitch upon him to put to the wracke or some other torture,) he do take knowledge of my Lord Sandwich, and said that he was well known to Mr Pepys. But my Lord knows, and I told him, that it was only in matter of musique and pipes, but that I thought him to be a very innocent fellow; and indeed I am very sorry for him. After my Lord and I had done in private, we went out, and with Captain Cuttance and Bunn did look over their draught of a bridge for Tangier, which will be brought by my desire to our office by them to-morrow. To Westminster Hall, and there walked long with Creed. He showed me our commission, wherein the Duke of York, Prince Rupert, Duke of Albemarle, Lord Peterborough, Lord Sandwich, Sir G. Carteret, Sir William Compton,

Mr Coventry, Sir R. Ford, Sir William Rider, Mr Cholmley, Mr Povy, myself, and Captain Cuttance, in this order are joyned for the carrying on the service of Tangier. He told me what great faction there is at Court; and above all, what is whispered, that young Crofts is lawful son to the King, the King being married to his mother. How true this is, God knows; but I believe the Duke of York will not be fooled in this of three crowns. Thence to White Hall, and walked long in the gardens, till (as they are commanded to all strange persons,) one come to tell us, we not being known, and being observed to walk there four or five houres, (which was not true, unless they count my walking there in the morning,) he was commanded to ask who we were; which being told, he excused his question, and was satisfied. These things speake great fear and jealousys.

29th. Sir G. Carteret, who had been at the examining most of the late people that are clapped up, do say that he do not think that there hath been any great plotting among them, though they have a good will to it; and their condition is so poor, and silly, and low, that they do not fear them at all.

30th. To my Lord Sandwich, who was up in his chamber and all alone, and did acquaint me with his business; which was, that our old acquaintance Mr Wade, (in Axe Yard) hath discovered to him £7000 hid in the Tower, of which he was to have two for discovery; my Lord himself two, and the King the other three, when it was found: and that the King's warrant runs for me on my Lord's part, and one Mr Lee for Sir Harry Bennet, to demand leave of the Lieutenant of the Tower for to make search. After he had told me the whole business, I took leave: and at noon, comes Mr Wade with my Lord's letter. So we consulted for me to go first to Sir H. Bennet, who is now with many of the Privy Counsellors at the Tower, examining of their late prisoners, to advise with him when to begin. So I went; and the guard at the Tower Gate, making me leave my sword at the gate, I was forced to stay so long in the ale house close by, till my boy run home for my cloak, that my Lord Mayor that now is, Sir John Robinson, Lieutenant of the Tower, with all his company, was gone with their coaches to his house in Minchen Lane. So my cloak being come, I walked thither: and there, by Sir G. Carteret's means, did presently speak with Sir H. Bennet, who did give me the King's warrant, for the paying of £2000 to my Lord, and other two to the discoverers. After a little discourse, dinner come in; and I dined with them. There was my Lord Mayor, my Lord Lauderdale, Mr Secretary Morris, to whom Sir H. Bennet would give the upper hand; Sir Wm. Compton, Sir G. Carteret, and myself, and some other company, and a brave dinner. After dinner, Sir H. Bennet did call aside the Lord Mayor and me, and did break the business to him, who did not, nor durst appear the least averse to it, but did promise all assistance forthwith to set upon it. So Mr Lee and I to our office, and there walked till Mr Wade and one Evett his guide did come, and W. Griffin, and a porter with his pick-axes, &c.: and so they walked along with us to the Tower, and Sir H. Bennet and my Lord Mayor did give us full power to fall to work. So our guide demands a candle, and down into the cellars he goes, enquiring whether they were the same that Baxter alway had. He went into several little cellars, and then went out a-doors to view, and to the Cole Harbour; but none did answer so well to the marks which was given him to find it by, as one arched vault. Where, after a great deal of council whether to set upon it now, or delay for better and more full advice, to digging we went till almost eight o'clock at night, but could find nothing. But, however, our guides did not at all seem discouraged; for that they being confident that the money is there they look for, but having never been in the cellars, they could not be positive to the place, and therefore will inform themselves more fully now they have been there, of the party that do advise them. So locking the door after us, we left here tonight, and up to the Deputy Governor, (my Lord Mayor, and Sir H. Bennet, with the rest of the company being gone an hour before;) and he do undertake to keep the key of the cellars, that none shall go down without his privity. But, Lord! to see what a young simple fantastick coxcombe is made Deputy Governor, would make me mad; and how he called out for his nightgowne of silk, only to make a show to us: and yet for half an hour I did not think he was the Deputy Governor, and so spoke not to him about the business, but waited for another man; but at last I broke our business to him; and he promising his care, we parted. And Mr Lee and I by coach to White Hall, where I did give my Lord Sandwich a full account of our proceedings, and some encouragement to hope for something here-after. This morning, walking with Mr Coventry in the garden, he did tell me how Sir G. Carteret had carried the business of the Victuallers' money to be paid by himself, contrary to old practice; at which he is angry I perceive, but I believe means no hurt, but that things may be done as they ought. He expects Sir George should not bespatter him privately, in revenge, not openly. Against which he prepares to bedaube him, and swears he will do it from the beginning, from Jersey to this day. And as to his own taking of too large fees or rewards for places that he had sold, he will prove that he was directed to it by Sir George himself among others. And yet he did not deny Sir G. Carteret his due, in saying that he is a man that do take the most pains, and gives himself the most to do business of any about the Court, without any desire of pleasure or divertisements: which is very true. But which pleased me mightily, he said in these words, that he was resolved, whatever it cost him, to make an experiment, and see whether it was possible for a man to keep himself up in Court by dealing plainly and walking uprightly. In the doing whereof, if his ground do slip from under him, he will be contented: but he is resolved to try, and never to baulke taking notice of any thing that is to the King's prejudice, let it fall where it will; which is a most brave resolution. He was very free with me: and by my troth, I do see more reall worth in him than in most men that I do know. I would not forget two passages of Sir J. Minnes's at yesterday's dinner. The one, that to the question how it comes to pass that there are no boars seen in London, but many sowes and pigs; it was answered, that the constable gets them a-nights. The other, Thos. Killigrew's way of getting to see plays when he was a boy. He would go to the Red Bull, and when the man cried to the boys, 'Who will go and be a devil, and he shall see the play for nothing?' then would he go in, and be a devil upon the stage, and so get to see plays.

31st. I thank God I have no crosses, but only much business to trouble my mind with. In all other things as happy a man as any in the world, for the whole world seems to smile upon me, and if my house were done that I could diligently follow my business, I would not doubt to do God, and the King, and myself good service. And all I do impute almost wholly to my late temperance, since my making of my vowes against wine and plays, which keeps me most happily and contentfully to my business; which God continue! Public matters are full of discontent, what with the sale of Dunkirke, and my Lady Castlemaine, and her faction at Court; though I know not what they would have more than to debauch the King, whom God preserve from it! And then great plots are talked to be discovered, and all the prisons in towne full of ordinary people, taken from their meeting-places last Sunday. But for certain some plots there hath been, though not brought to a head.

November 1st. To my office, to meet Mr Lee again, from Sir H. Bennet. And he and I, with Wade, and his intelligencer and labourers, to the Tower cellars, to make one triall more; where we staid two or three hours, and dug a great deal all under the arches, as it was now most confidently directed, and so seriously, and upon pretended good grounds, that I myself did truly expect to speed; but we missed of all: and so we went away the second time like fools. And to our office; and I by appointment to the Dolphin Taverne, to meet Wade and the other, Captain Evett, who now do tell me plainly, that he that do put him upon this is one that had it from Barkestead's own mouth, and was advised with by him, just before the King's coming in, how to get it out, and had all the signs told him how and where it lay, and had always been the great confident of Barkestead even to the trusting him with his life and all he had. So that he did much convince me that there is good ground for what he goes about. But I fear it may be that he did find some conveyance of it away, without the help of this man, before he died. But he is resolved to go to the party once more, and then to determine what we shall do further.

3rd. To White Hall, to the Duke's; but found him gone a-hunting. Thence to my Lord Sandwich, from whom I receive every day more and more signs of his confidence and esteem of me. Here I met with Pierce the chyrurgeon, who tells me that my Lady Castlemaine is with child; but though it be the King's, yet her Lord being still in towne, and sometimes seeing of her, it will be laid to him. He tells me also how the Duke of York is smitten in love with my Lady Chesterfield,[60] (a virtuous lady, daughter to my Lord of Ormond); and so much, that the Duchesse of York hath complained to the King and her father about it, and my Lady Chesterfield is gone into

60 Lady Elizabeth Butler, daughter of James, Duke of Ormond, married Philip, second Earl of Chesterfield. Died 1665. See *Mémoires de Grammont*.

the country for it. At all which I am sorry; but it is the effect of idlenesse, and having nothing else to employ their great spirits upon. At night to my office, and did business; and there come to me Mr Wade and Evett, who have been again with their prime intelligencer, a woman, I perceive: and though we have missed twice, yet they bring such an account of the probability of the truth of the thing, though we are not certain of the place, that we shall set upon it once more; and I am willing and hopefull in it. So we resolved to set upon it again on Wednesday morning; and the woman herself will be there in a disguise, and confirm us in the place.

4th. This morning we had news by letters that Sir Richard Stayner is dead at sea in the *Mary*, which is now come into Portsmouth from Lisbon; which we are sorry for, he being a very stout seaman.

7th. Being by appointment called upon by Mr Lee, he and I to the Tower, to make our third attempt upon the cellar. And now privately the woman, Barkestead's great confident, is brought, who do positively say that this is the place which he did say the money was hid in, and where he and she did put up the £7000 in butter firkins; and the very day that he went out of England did say that neither he nor his would be the better for that money, and therefore wishing that she and hers might. And so left us, and we full of hope did resolve to dig all over the cellar, which by seven o'clock at night we performed. At noon we sent for a dinner, and upon the head of a barrel dined very merrily, and to work again. But at last we saw we were mistaken; and after digging the cellar quite through, and removing the barrels from one side to the other, we were forced to pay our porters, and give over our expectations, though I do believe there must be money hid somewhere by him, or else he did delude this woman in hopes to oblige her to further serving him, which I am apt to believe.

9th (Lord's-day). Walked to my brother's, where my wife is, calling at many churches, and then to the Temple, hearing a bit there too, and observing that in the streets and churches the Sunday is kept in appearance as well as I have known it at any time.

10th. A little to the office, and so with Sir J. Minnes, Sir W. Batten, and myself by coach to White Hall, to the Duke, who, after he was ready, did take us into his closett. Thither come my Lord General

Monk, and did privately talk with the Duke about having the life-guards pass through the City today only for show and to fright people, for I perceive there are great fears abroad; for all which I am troubled and full of doubt that things will not go well. He being gone, we fell to business of the Navy. Among other things, how to pay off this fleet that is now come from Portugall; the King of Portugall sending them home, he having no more use for them, which we wonder at, that his condition should be so soon altered. And our landmen also are coming back, being almost starved in that poor country. To my Lord Crewe's, and dined with him and his brother, I know not his name. Where very good discourse. Among others, of France's intention to make a patriarch of his own, independent from the Pope, by which he will be able to cope with the Spaniard in all councils, which hitherto he has never done. My Lord Crewe told us how he heard my Lord of Holland[61] say, that being Embassador about the match with the Queene-Mother that now is, the King of France insisted upon a dispensation from the Pope, which my Lord Holland making a question of, as he was commanded to yield to nothing to the prejudice of our religion, says the King of France, 'You need not fear that, for if the Pope will not dispense with the match, my Bishop of Paris shall.' By and by come in the great Mr Swinfen,[62] the Parliament-man, who, among other discourse of the rise and fall of familys, told us of Bishop Bridgeman[63] (father of Sir Orlando) who lately hath bought a seat anciently of the Levers, and then the Ashtons; and so he hath in his great hall window (having repaired and beautified the house) caused four great places to be left for coates of armes. In one he hath put the Levers, with this motto, *Olim*. In another the Ashtons, with this, *Heri*. In the next his own, with this, *Hodie*. In the fourth nothing but this motto, *Cras nescio cujus*. The towne I hear is full of discontents, and all know of the King's new bastard by Mrs Haslerigge, and as far as I can hear will never be contented with Episcopacy, they are so cruelly set for Presbytery, and the Bishops carry themselves so high, that they are never likely to gain anything upon them. To the Dolphin Tavern near home, by appointment, and there met with Wade and Evett,

61 Henry Rich, Earl of Holland.
62 John Swinfen, MP for Tamworth.
63 John Bridgeman, Bishop of Chester.

and have resolved to make a new attempt upon another discovery, in which God give us better fortune than in the other, but I have great confidence that there is no cheat in these people, but that they go upon good grounds, though they have been mistaken in the place of the first.

13th. To my office, and there this afternoon we had our first meeting upon our commission of inspecting the Chest. Sir Francis Clerke,[64] Mr Heath, Atturney of the Dutchy, Mr Prinn, Sir W. Rider, Captn. Cooke, and myself. Our first work was to read over the Institution, which is a decree in Chancery in the year 1617, upon an inquisition made at Rochester about that time into the revenues of the Chest, which had then, from the year 1588 or 1590, by the advice of the Lord High Admiral and principal officers then being, by consent of the seamen, been settled, paying sixpence per month, according to their wages then, which was then but 10s. which is now 24s.

17th. To the Duke's today, but he is gone a-hunting. At White Hall by appointment, Mr Creed carried my wife and I to the Cockpitt, and we had excellent places, and saw the King, Queene, Duke of Monmouth, his son, and my Lady Castlemaine, and all the fine ladies; and *The Scornfull Lady*, well performed. They had done by eleven o'clock, and it being fine moonshine, we took coach and home.

18th. Late at my office, drawing up a letter to my Lord Treasurer, which we have been long about.

20th. After dinner to the Temple, to Mr Thurland;[65] and thence to my Lord Chief Baron, Sir Edward Hale's,[66] and take Mr Thurland to his chamber, where he told us that Field will have the better of us; and that we must study to make up the business as well as we can, which do much vex and trouble us: but I am glad the Duke is concerned in it.

21st. This day come the King's pleasure-boats from Calais, with the Dunkirke money, being 400,000 pistolles.

64 MP for Rochester.
65 Edward Thurland, MP for Ryegate, afterwards knighted.
66 Sir Matthew Hale succeeded Sir Orlando Bridgeman as Chief Baron of the Exchequer (according to Beatson) in 1666 ; there is consequently some mistake.

22nd. November This day Mr Moore told me, that for certain the Queene-Mother is married to my Lord St Albans, and he is like to be made Lord Treasurer. News that Sir J. Lawson hath made up a peace now with Tunis and Tripoli, as well as Argiers, by which he will come home very highly honoured.

23rd. I hear today old rich Audley[67] is lately dead, and left a very great estate, and made a great many poor familys rich, not all to one. Among others, one Davis, my old schoolfellow at Paul's, and since a book-seller in Paul's Church Yard: and it seems do forgive one man £6000 which he had wronged him of, but names not his name; but it is well known to be the scrivener in Fleete-streete, at whose house he lodged. There is also this week dead a poulterer, in Gracious-street, which was thought rich, but not so rich, that hath left £800 per annum, taken in other men's names, and 40,000 Jacobs in gold.

24th. Sir J. Minnes, Sir W. Batten, and I, going forth toward White Hall, we hear that the King and Duke are come this morning to the Tower to see the Dunkirke money. So we by coach to them, and there went up and down all the magazines with them; but methought it was but poor discourse and frothy that the King's companions (young Killigrew among the rest,) had with him. We saw none of the money, but Mr Slingsby did show the King, and I did see, the stamps of the new money that is now to be made by Blondeau's fashion, which are very neat, and like the King. Thence the King to Woolwich, though a very cold day; and the Duke to White Hall, commanding us to come after him; and in his closet, my Lord Sandwich being there, did discourse with us about getting some of this money to pay off the Fleets, and other matters.

25th. Great talk among people how some of the Fanatiques do say that the end of the world is at hand, and that next Tuesday is to be the day. Against which, whenever it shall be, good God fit us all.

27th. At my waking, I found the tops of the houses covered with snow, which is a rare sight, which I have not seen these three years. To the office, where we sat till noon; when we all went to the next

---

67 There is an old tract called, "The Way to be Rich, according to the Practice of the great Audley, who began with £200 in 1605, and dyed worth £400,000 November, 1662." London, printed for E. Davis, 1662.

house upon Tower Hill, to see the coming by of the Russian Embassador; for whose reception all the City trained-bands do attend in the streets, and the King's life-guards, and most of the wealthy citizens in their black velvet coats, and gold chains, (which remain of their gallantry at the King's coming in,) but they staid so long that we went down again to dinner. And after I had dined I walked to the Conduit in the Quarrefowr, at the end of Gracious-street and Cornhill; and there (the spouts thereof running very near me upon all the people that were under it) I saw them pretty well go by. I could not see the Embassador in his coach; but his attendants in their habits and fur caps very handsome, comely men, and most of them with hawkes upon their fists to present to the King. But Lord! to see the absurd nature of Englishmen, that cannot forbear laughing and jeering at every thing that looks strange.

28th. A very hard frost; which is news to us after having none almost these three years. By ten o'clock to Ironmongers' Hall, to the funeral of Sir Richard Stayner. Here we were, all the officers of the Navy, and my Lord Sandwich, who did discourse with us about the fishery, telling us of his Majesty's resolution to give £200 to every man that will set out a Brisse;[68] and advising about the effects of this encouragement, which will be a very great matter certainly. Here we had good rings.

29th. To the office; and this morning come Sir G. Carteret to us (being the first time since his coming from France): he tells us, that the silver which is received for Dunkirke did weigh 120,000 weight. To my Lord's, where my Lord and Mr Coventry, Sir Wm. Darcy,[69] one Mr Parham, (a very knowing and well-spoken man in this business), with several others, did meet about starting the business of the fishery, and the manner of the King's giving of this £200 to every man that shall set out a new-made English Brisse by the middle of June next. In which business we had many fine pretty discourses; and I did here see the great pleasure to be had in discoursing of publick matters with men that are particularly acquainted with this or that business. Having come to some issue, wherein a motion of mine was well received, about sending these invitations from the King to

68 A small sea-vessel used by the Hollanders for the herring fishery.
69 Third son of Sir Conyers Darcy, summoned to Parliament as Lord Darcy, 1642.

all the fishing-ports in general, with limiting so many Brisses to this, and that port, before we know the readiness of subscribers, we parted.

30th. Publick matters in an ill condition of discontent against the height and vanity of the Court, and their bad payments: but that which troubles most, is the Clergy, which will never content the City, which is not to be reconciled to Bishopps: but more the pity that differences must still be. Dunkirke newly sold, and the money brought over; of which we hope to get some to pay the Navy: which by Sir J. Lawson's having dispatched the business in the Straights, by making peace with Argier, Tunis, and Tripoli, (and so his fleet will also shortly come home,) will now every day grow less, and so the King's charge be abated; which God send!

December 1st. To my Lord Sandwich's, to Mr Moore; and then over the Parke, (where I first in my life, it being a great frost, did see people sliding with their skeates, which is a very pretty art,) to Mr Coventry's chamber to St James's, where we all met to a venison pasty, Major Norwood being with us, whom they did play upon for his surrendering of Dunkirke. Here we staid till three or four o'clock: and so to the Council Chamber, where there met the Duke of York, Prince Rupert, Duke of Albemarle, my Lord Sandwich, Sir Wm. Compton, Mr Coventry, Sir J. Minnes, Sir R. Ford, Sir W. Rider, myself, and Captain Cuttance, as Commissioners for Tangier. And after our Commission was read by Mr Creed, who I perceive is to be our Secretary, we did fall to discourse of matters: as, first, the supplying them forthwith with victualls; then the reducing it to make way for the money, which upon their reduction is to go to the building of the Molle; and so to other matters, ordered as against next meeting.

3rd. To Deptford; and so by water with Mr Pett home again, all the way reading his Chest accounts, in which I did see things which did not please me, as his allowing himself £300 for one year's looking to the business of the Chest, and £150 per annum for the rest of the years. But I found no fault to him himself, but shall when they come to be read at the Board. We walked to the Temple, in our way seeing one of the Russia Embassador's coaches go along, with his footmen not in liverys, but their country habits; one of one colour and another of another, which was very strange.

5th. I walked towards Guildhall, being summoned by the Commissioners for the Lieutenancy; but they sat not this morning. So meeting in my way W. Swan, I took him to a house thereabouts, he telling me much of his Fanatique stories, as if he were a great zealot, when I know him to be a very rogue. But I do it for discourse, and to see how things stand with him and his party; who I perceive have great expectation that God will not bless the Court nor Church, as it is now settled, but they must be purified. The worst news he tells me, is that Mr Chetwind is dead, my old and most ingenious acquaintance. To the Duke's, where the Committee for Tangier met: and here we sat down all with him at a table, and had much discourse about the business.

13th. We sat, Mr Coventry and I, (Sir G. Carteret being gone,) and among other things, Field and Strip did come, and received the £41 given him by the judgement against me and Harry Kem; and we did also sign bonds in £500 to stand to the award of Mr Porter and Smith for the rest: which, however, I did not sign to till I got Mr Coventry to go up with me to Sir W. Pen; and he did promise me before him to bear his share in what should be awarded, and both concluded that Sir W. Batten would do no less.

15th. To the Duke, and followed him into the Parke, where, though the ice was broken and dangerous, yet he would go slide upon his scates, which I did not like, but he slides very well. So back to his closet, whither my Lord Sandwich comes, and there Mr Coventry, and we three had long discourse together about the matters of the Navy; and, indeed, I find myself more and more obliged to Mr Coventry, who studies to do me all the right he can in every thing to the Duke. Thence walked a good while up and down the gallerys; and among others, met with Dr Clarke, who in discourse tells me, that Sir Charles Barkeley's greatness is only his being pimp to the King, and to my Lady Castlemaine. And yet for all this, that the King is very kind to the Queene; who, he says, is one of the best women in the world. Strange how the King is bewitched to this pretty Castlemaine. I walked up and down the gallerys, spending my time upon the pictures, till the Duke and the Committee for Tangier met, (the Duke not staying with us,) where the only matter was to discourse with my Lord Rutherford,[70] who is this day made Governor of Tangier, for I know not what reasons; and my Lord of Peterborough to be called home: which, though it is said it is done with kindness, I am sorry to see a Catholicke Governor sent to command there, where all the rest of the officers almost are such already. But God knows what the reason is! and all may see how slippery places all courtiers stand in. Thence home, in my way calling upon Sir John Berkenheade,[71] to speak about my assessment of £42 to the Loyal Sufferers; which, I perceive, I cannot help; but he tells me I have been abused by Sir R. Ford. Thence called at the Major-General's, Sir R. Browne, about my being assessed armes to the militia; but he was abroad.

16th. To dinner, thinking to have had Mr Coventry, but he could not go with me; and so I took Captn. Murford. Of whom I do hear what the world says of me; that all do conclude Mr Coventry, and Pett, and me, to be of a knot; and that we do now carry all things before us: and much more in particular of me, and my studiousnesse, &c. to my great content. To White Hall to Secretary Bennet's, and agreed with Mr Lee to set upon our new adventure at the Tower tomorrow.

17th. This morning come Mr Lee, Wade, and Evett, intending to have gone upon our new design to the Tower; but it raining, and the work being to be done in the open garden, we put it off to Friday next.

19th. Up and by appointment with Mr Lee, Wade, Evett, and workmen to the Tower, and with the Lieutenant's leave set them to work in the garden, in the corner against the mayne-guard, a most unlikely place. It being cold, Mr Lee and I did sit all the day till three o'clock by the fire in the Governor's house; I reading a play of Fletcher's, being *A Wife for a Month*, wherein no great wit or language. We went to them at work, and having wrought below the bottom of the foundation of the wall, I bid them give over, and so all our hopes ended.

70 Andrew, created Baron of Rutherford and Earl of Teviot, 1660; successively Governor of Dunkirk and Tangier, where he was killed by the Moors in 1663.
71 Sir John Berkenhead, FRS, a political author, held in some esteem, MP for Wilton, 1661, and knighted the following year. Master of the Faculty Office, and Court of Requests. Died 1679.

20th. To the office, and thence with Mr Coventry in his coach to St James's, with great content and pride to see him treat me so friendly; and dined with him, and so to White Hall together; where we met upon the Tangier Commission, and discoursed many things thereon: but little will be done before my Lord Rutherford comes there, as to the fortification and Mole. That done, my Lord Sandwich and I walked together a good while in the matted gallery, he acquainting me with his late enquiries into the Wardrobe business to his content; and tells me how things stand. And that the first year was worth about £3000 to him, and the next about as much: so that at this day, if he were paid, it will be worth about £7000 to him.

21st. To White Hall, and there to chapel, and from thence up stairs, and up and down the house and gallerys on the King's and Queen's side, and so through the garden to my Lord's lodgings, where there was Mr Gibbons, Madge, Mallard, and Pagett; and by and by comes in my Lord Sandwich, and so we had great store of good musique. By and by comes in my simple Lord Chandois,[72] who (my Lord Sandwich being gone out to Court) began to sing psalms, but so dully that I was weary of it.

22nd. I walked to Mr Coventry's chamber, where I found him gone out into the Parke with the Duke, so I shifted myself into a riding-habitt, and followed him through White Hall, and in the Parke Mr Coventry's people having a horse ready for me (so fine a one that I was almost afraid to get upon him, but I did, and found myself more feared than hurt) and followed the Duke, who, with some of his people (among others Mr Coventry) was riding out. And with them to Hide Parke. Where Mr Coventry asking leave of the Duke, he bids us go to Woolwich. So he and I to the waterside, and our horses coming by the ferry, we by oars over to Lambeth, and from thence, with brave discourse by the way, rode to Woolwich, where we put in practice my new way of the Call-booke, which will be of great use.

23rd. Dr Pierce tells me that my Lady Castlemaine's interest at Court increases, and is more and greater than the Queene's; that she hath brought in Sir H. Bennet, and Sir Charles Barkeley; but that the Queene is a most good lady, and takes all with the greatest meekness

72 William, seventh Lord Chandos. Died 1676.

that may be. He tells me, also, that Mr Edward Montagu is quite broke at Court with his repute and purse; and that he lately was engaged in a quarrell against my Lord Chesterfield: but that the King did cause it to be taken up. He tells me, too, that the King is much concerned in the Chancellor's sickness, and that the Chancellor is as great, he thinks, as ever with the King. He also tells me what the world says of me, 'that Mr Coventry and I do all the business of the office almost': at which I am highly proud.

24th. To my bookseller's, and paid at another shop £4 10s for Stephens's *Thesaurus Graecae Linguae*, given to Paul's Schoole. To my Lord Crewe's, and dined alone with him. I understand there are great factions at Court, and something he said that did imply a difference like to be between the King and the Duke, in case the Queene should not be with child. I understand, about this bastard. He says, also, that some great man will be aimed at when Parliament comes to sit again; I understand, the Chancellor: and that there is a bill will be brought in, that none that have been in armes for the Parliament shall be capable of office. And that the Court are weary of my Lord Albemarle and Chamberlin.[73] He wishes that my Lord Sandwich had some good occasion to be abroad this summer which is coming on, and that my Lord Hinchingbroke were well married, and Sydney[74] had some place at Court. He pities the poor ministers that are put out, to whom, he says, the King is beholden for his coming in, and that if any such thing had been foreseen he had never come in. At my bookseller's in Paul's Church-yard, who takes it ill my letter last night to Mr Povy, wherein I accuse him of the neglect of the Tangier boats, in which I must confess I did not do altogether like a friend; but however it was truth, and I must owne it to be so, though I fall wholly out with him for it.

25th (Christmas-day). Had a pleasant walk to White Hall, where I intended to have received the communion with the family, but I come a little too late. So I walked up into the house and spent my time looking over pictures, particularly the ships in King Henry the VIIIth's Voyage to Bullaen;[75] marking the great difference between

73 Edward, Earl of Manchester.
74 Lord Sandwich's second son.
75 Boulogne.

those built then and now. By and by down to the chapel again, where Bishop Morley[76] preached upon the song of the Angels, 'Glory to God on high, on earth peace, and good will towards men.' Methought he made but a poor sermon, but long, and reprehending the common jollity of the Court for the true joy that shall and ought to be on these days. Particularized concerning their excess in playes and gaming, saying that he whose office it is to keep the gamesters in order and within bounds serves but for a second rather in a duell, meaning the groome-porter. Upon which it was worth observing how far they are come from taking the reprehensions of a bishop seriously, that they all laugh in the chapel when he reflected on their ill actions and courses. He did much press us to joy in these publick days of joy, and to hospitality. But one that stood by whispered in my eare that the Bishop do not spend one groate to the poor himself. The sermon done, a good anthem followed with vialls, and the King come down to receive the Sacrament.

26th. To the Wardrobe. Hither come Mr Battersby; and we falling into discourse of a new book of drollery in use, called *Hudebras*, I would needs go find it out, and met with it at the Temple: cost me 2s. 6d. But when I come to read it, it is so silly an abuse of the Presbyter Knight going to the warrs, that I am ashamed of it; and by and by meeting at Mr Townsend's at dinner, I sold it to him for 18d.

27th. With my wife to the Duke's Theatre, and saw the second part of *Rhodes*,[77] done with the new Roxalana;[78] which do it rather better in all respects for person, voice, and judgment, than the first Roxalana.

29th. To Westminster Hall, where I staid reading at Mrs Mitchell's shop. She told me what I heard not of before, the strange burning of Mr De Laun, a merchant's house in Lothbury, and his lady (Sir Thomas Allen's[79] daughter) and her whole family; not one thing,

---

76 George Morley, Bishop of Winchester, to which see he was translated from Worcester, in 1662. Died 1684.

77 *The Siege of Rhodes,* a tragi-comedy, in two parts, by Sir Wm. Davenant.

78 An actress whose name is unknown, but she had been seduced by the Earl of Oxford, and had recently quitted the stage. For her history, see *Mémoires de Grammont.*

79 Sir Thomas Alleyne, Lord Mayor of London, 1660.

dog nor cat, escaping; nor any of the neighbours almost hearing of it till the house was quite down and burnt. How this should come to passe, God knows, but a most strange thing it is! Hither come Jack Spicer, and talked of Exchequer matters, and how the Lord Treasurer hath now ordered all monies to be brought into the Exchequer, and hath settled the King's revenues, and given to every general expence proper assignments; to the Navy £200,000 and odde. He also told me of the great vast trade of the goldsmiths in supplying the King with money at dear rates. Thence to White Hall, and got up to the top gallerys in the Banquetting House, to see the audience of the Russia Embassador; which took place after our long waiting and fear of the falling of the gallery (it being so full and part of it being parted from the rest, for nobody to come up merely from the weaknesse thereof :) and very handsome it was. After they had come in, I went down and got through the croude almost as high as the King and the Embassadors, where I saw all the presents, being rich furs, hawkes, carpets, cloths of tissue, and sea-horse teeth. The King took two or three hawkes upon his fist, having a glove on wrought with gold, given him for the purpose. The son of one of the Embassadors was in the richest suit for pearl and tissue, that ever I did see, or shall, I believe. After they and all the company had kissed the King's hand, then the three Embassadors and the son, and no more, did kiss the Queene's. One thing more I did observe, that the chief Embassador did carry up his master's letters in state before him on high; and as soon as he had delivered them, he did fall down to the ground and lay there a great while. After all was done, the company broke up; and I spent a little while walking up and down the gallery seeing the ladies, the two Queenes, and the Duke of Monmouth with his little mistress,[80] which is very little, and like my brother-in-law's wife.

30th. Visited Mrs Ferrer, and staid talking with her a good while, there being a little, proud, ugly, talking lady there, that was much crying up the Queene-Mother's Court at Somerset House above our own Queene's; there being before her no allowance of laughing and the mirth that is at the other's; and indeed it is observed that the greatest Court now-a-days is there. Thence to White Hall, where I

80 Lady Anne Scot.

carried my wife to see the Queene in her presence-chamber; and the maydes of honour and the young Duke of Monmouth playing at cards. Some of them, and but a few, were very pretty; though all well dressed in velvet gowns.

31st. Mr Povy and I to White Hall; he taking me thither on purpose to carry me into the ball this night before the King. He brought me first to the Duke's chamber, where I saw him and the Duchesse at supper; and thence into the room where the ball was to be, crammed with fine ladies, the greatest of the Court. By and by comes the King and Queene, the Duke and Duchesse, and all the great ones: and after seating themselves, the King takes out the Duchesse of York; and the Duke, the Duchesse of Buckingham; the Duke of Monmouth, my Lady Castlemaine; and so other lords other ladies: and they danced the Brantle.[81] After that, the King led a lady a single Coranto; and then the rest of the lords, one after another, other ladies: very noble it was, and great pleasure to see. Then to country dances; the King leading the first, which he called for; which was, says he, 'Cuckolds all awry,' the old dance of England. Of the ladies that danced, the Duke of Monmouth's mistress, and my Lady Castlemaine, and a daughter of Sir Harry de Vicke's,[82] were the best. The manner was, when the King dances, all the ladies in the room, and the Queene herself, stand up: and indeed he dances rarely, and much better than the Duke of York. Having staid here as long as I thought fit, to my infinite content, it being the greatest pleasure I could wish now to see at Court, I went home, leaving them dancing.

Thus ends this year with great mirth to me and my wife. Our condition being thus: – we are at present spending a night or two at my Lord's lodgings at White Hall. Our home at the Navy-office, which is and hath a pretty while been in good condition, finished and made very convenient. By my last year's diligence in my office, blessed be God! I am come to a good degree of knowledge therein;

81 Branle. *Espèce de danse de plusieurs personnes, qui se tiennent par la main, et qui se menent tour-a-tour.* – Dictionnaire de l'Académie.
82 Sir Henry de Vic of Guernsey, Bart., had been twenty years Resident for Charles II at Brussels, and was Chancellor of the Order of the Garter. He died 1672, and was buried in Westminster Abbey. His only daughter, Anne Charlotte, married John Lord Fresheville, Baron of Stavely.

and am acknowledged so by all the world, even the Duke himself, to whom I have a good accesse: and by that, and by my being Commissioner for Tangier, he takes much notice of me; and I doubt not but, by the continuance of the same endeavours, I shall in a little time come to be a man much taken notice of in the world, specially being come to so great an esteem with Mr Coventry. Publick matters stand thus: The King is bringing, as is said, his family, and Navy, and all other his charges, to a less expence. In the mean time, himself following his pleasures more than with good advice he would do; at least, to be seen to all the world to do so. His dalliance with my Lady Castlemaine being publick, every day, to his great reproach; and his favouring of none at Court so much as those that are the confidants of his pleasure, as Sir H. Bennet and Sir Charles Barkeley; which, good God! put it into his heart to mend, before he makes himself too much contemned by his people for it! The Duke of Monmouth is in so great splendour at Court, and so dandled by the King, that some doubt, that, if the King should have no child by the Queene (which there is yet no appearance of), whether he would not be acknowledged for a lawful son; and that there will be a difference follow between the Duke of York and him; which God prevent! My Lord Chancellor is threatened by people to be questioned, the next sitting of the Parliament, by some spirits that do not love to see him so great: but certainly he is a good servant to the King. The Queene–Mother is said to keep too great a Court now; and her being married to my Lord St Alban's is commonly talked of; and that they had a daughter between them in France, how true, God knows. The Bishops are high, and go on without any diffidence in pressing uniformity; and the Presbyters seem silent in it, and either conform or lay down, though without doubt they expect a turn, and would be glad these endeavours of the other Fanatiques would take effect; there having been a plot lately found, for which four have been publickly tried at the Old Bayley and hanged. My Lord Sandwich is still in good esteem, and now keeping his Christmas in the country; and I in good esteem, I think, as any man can be, with him. In fine, for the good condition of myself, wife, family, and estate, in the great degree that it is, and for the public state of the nation, so quiet as it is, the Lord God be praised!

1662/63. January 1st. Among other discourse, Mrs Sarah tells us how the King sups at least four times every week with my Lady Castlemaine; and most often stays till the morning with her, and goes home through the garden all alone privately, and that so as the very centrys take notice of it and speak of it. She tells me, that about a month ago she quickened at my Lord Gerard's[1] at dinner, and cried out that she was undone; and all the lords and men were fain to quit the room, and women called to help her.

5th. To the Duke, who himself told me that Sir J. Lawson was come home to Portsmouth from the Streights with great renowne among all men, and, I perceive, mightily esteemed at Court by all. The Duke did not stay long in his chamber; but to the King's chamber, whither by and by the Russia Embassadors come; who, it seems, have a custom that they will not come to have any treaty with our or any King's Commissioners, but they will themselves see at the time the face of the King himself, be it forty days one after another; and so they did to-day only go in and see the King; and so out again to the Council-chamber. To the Duke's closet, where Sir G. Carteret, Sir J. Minnes, Sir W. Batten, Mr Coventry, and myself attended him about the business of the Navy; and after much discourse and pleasant talk he went away. To the Cockpitt, where we saw *Claracilla*,[2] a poor play, done by the King's house; but neither the King nor Queene were there, but only the Duke and Duchesse. Elborough (my old schoolfellow at Paul's) do tell me, and so do others, that Dr Calamy is this day sent to Newgate for preaching, Sunday was se'nnight without leave, though he did it only to supply the place; otherwise the people must have gone away without ever a sermon, they being disappointed of a minister: but the Bishop of London will not take that as an excuse. Dined at home; and there being the famous new play acted the first time to-day, which is called *The Adventures of Five Hours*, at the Duke's house, being they say, made or translated by Colonel Tuke,[3] I did long to see it; and so we went; and though

1 Charles Lord Gerard of Brandon, Gentleman of the Bedchamber to Charles II, and Captain of his Guards; created Earl of Macclesfield 1679, and died about 1693. His wife, mentioned afterwards, was a French lady, whose name has not been preserved.

2 A tragi-comedy by Thomas Killigrew.

3 Sir George Tuke of Cressing Temple in Essex, Mr Evelyn's cousin. The play was taken from the original of the Spanish poet Calderon.

early, were forced to sit, almost out of sight, at the end of one of the lower formes, so full was the house. And the play, in one word, is the best, for the variety and the most excellent continuance of the plot to the very end, that ever I saw, or think ever shall.

12th. I found my Lord within, and he and I went out through the garden towards the Duke's chamber, to sit upon the Tangier matters; but a lady called to my Lord out of my Lady Castlemaine's lodgings, telling him that the King was there and would speak with him. My Lord could not tell me what to say at the Committee to excuse his absence, but that he was with the King; nor would suffer me to go into the Privy Garden, (which is now a through-passage and common,) but bid me to go through some other way, which I did; so that I see he is a servant of the King's pleasures too, as well as business.

19th. Singled out Mr Coventry into the matted gallery, and there I told him the complaints I meet every day about our Treasurer's or his people's paying no money, but at the goldsmith's shops, where they are forced to pay fifteen or twenty sometimes per cent. for their money, which is a most horrid shame, and that which must not be suffered. Nor is it likely that the Treasurer (at least his people) will suffer Maynell the Goldsmith to go away with £100,000 per annum, as he do now get, by making people pay after this manner for their money.

To my Lord Chancellor's, where the King was to meet my Lord Treasurer and many great men, to settle the revenue of Tangier. I staid talking awhile there, but the King not coming I walked to my brother's. This day by Dr Clarke I was told the occasion of my Lord Chesterfield's going and taking his lady (my Lord Ormond's daughter) from Court. It seems he not only hath been long jealous of the Duke of York, but did find them two talking together, though there were others in the room, and the lady by all opinions a most good, virtuous woman. He the next day (of which the Duke was warned by somebody that saw the passion my Lord Chesterfield was in the night before,) went and told the Duke how much he did apprehend himself wronged, in his picking out his lady of the whole Court to be the subject of his dishonor; which the Duke did answer with great calmnesse, not seeming to understand the reason of complaint, and that was all that passed: but my Lord did presently pack his lady into the country in Derbyshire, near the Peake; which is become a proverb at Court, to send a man's wife to the Peake when she vexes him.

23rd. Mr Grant and I to a coffee-house, where Sir J. Cutler[4] was; and he did fully make out that the trade of England is as great as ever it was, only in more hands; and that of all trades there is a greater number than ever there was, by reason of men's taking more 'prentices. His discourse was well worth hearing. I bought *Audley's Way to be Rich*,[5] a serious pamphlett, and some good things worth my minding.

25th. I understand the King of France is upon consulting his divines upon the old question, what the power of the Pope is? and do intend to make war against him, unless he do right him for the wrong his Embassador received; and banish the Cardinall Imperiall, by which I understand is not meant the Cardinall belonging or chosen by the Emperor, but the name of his family is Imperiali. To my Lord, and I staid talking with him an hour alone in his chamber, about sundry publick and private matters. Among others, he wonders what the project should be of the Duke's going down to Portsmouth again now with his Lady, at this time of the year: it being no way, we think, to increase his popularity, which is not great; nor yet safe to do it, for that reason, if it would have any such effect. Captn. Ferrers tells me of my Lady Castlemaine's and Sir Charles Barkeley being the great favourites at Court, and growing every day more and more so; and that upon a late dispute between my Lord Chesterfield, that is the Queene's Lord Chamberlain, and Mr Edward Montagu her Master of the Horse, who should have the precedence in taking the Queene's upper-hand abroad out of the house, which Mr Montagu challenges, it was given to my Lord Chesterfield. So that I perceive he goes down the wind in honor as well as every thing else, every day.

26th. I met with Monsieur Raby, who is lately come from France. I had a great deal of very good discourse with him, concerning the difference between the French and the Pope, and the occasion, which he told me very particularly, and to my great content; and of most of the chief affairs of France, which I did enquire: and that the King is a most excellent Prince, doing all business himself; and that it is true he

4 Citizen and grocer, stigmatised by Pope for his avarice.
5 See note 67, page 178.

hath a mistresse, Mademoiselle La Valiere, one of the Princess Henriette's women, that he courts for his pleasure every other day, but not so as to make him neglect his publick affairs. He tells me how the King do carry himself nobly to the relations of the dead Cardinall,[6] and will not suffer one pasquill to come forth against him; and that he acts by what directions he received from him before his death.

30th. My manuscript is brought home handsomely bound, to my full content; and now I think I have a better collection in reference to the Navy, and shall have by the time I have filled it, than any of my predecessors.

February 1st. This day Creed and I walking in White Hall, did see the King coming privately from my Lady Castlemaine's; which is a poor thing for a Prince to do; and so I expressed my sense of it to Creed in terms which I should not have done, but that I believe he is trusty in that point.

2nd. With Sir J. Minnes and Sir W. Batten to the Duke; and after discourse as usual with him in his closet, I went to my Lord's: the King and the Duke being gone to chapel, it being a collar day, Candlemas-day; where I staid with him until towards noon, there being Jonas Moore[7] talking about some mathematical businesses. With Mr Coventry down to his chamber, where he did tell me how he do make himself an interest by doing business truly and justly, though he thwarts others greater than himself, not striving to make himself friends by addresses; and by this he thinks and observes he do live as contentedly, (now he finds himself secured from fear of want,) and, take one time with another, as void of fear or cares, or more, than they that (as his own termes were) have quicker pleasures and sharper agonies than he.

4th. To Paul's Schoole, it being opposition-day there. I heard some of their speeches, and they were just as schoolboys' used to be, of the seven liberal sciences; but I think not so good as ours were in our time. Thence to Bow Church, to the Court of Arches, where a judge sits, and his proctors about him in their habits, and their pleadings all in Latin. Here I was sworn to give a true answer to my uncle's libells.

6 Cardinal Mazarine.
7 Jonas Moore, a most celebrated mathematician, knighted by Charles II, and made Surveyor of the Ordnance. Died 1679.

And back again to Paul's Schoole, and went up to see the head forms posed in Latin, Greek, and Hebrew. Dr Wilkins[8] and Outram[9] were examiners.

6th. To Lincoln's Inn Fields; and it being too soon to go to dinner, I walked up and down, and looked upon the outside of the new theatre building in Covent Garden, which will be very fine. And so to a bookseller's in the Strand, and there bought *Hudibras* again, it being certainly some ill humour to be so against that which all the world cries up to be the example of wit; for which I am resolved once more to read him, and see whether I can find it or no.

7th. To White Hall to chapel, where there preached little Dr Duport,[10] of Cambridge, upon Josiah's words, – 'But I and my house, we will serve the Lord.' Thence with Mr Creed to the King's Head ordinary. After dinner Sir Thomas Willis[11] and another stranger, and Creed and I fell a-talking; they of the errours and corruption of the Navy, and great expence thereof, not knowing who I was, which at last I did undertake to confute, and disabuse them: and they took it very well, and I hope it was to good purpose, they being Parliament-men. Creed and I and Captn. Ferrers to the Parke, and there walked finely, seeing people slide, we talking all the while; and Captn. Ferrers telling me, among other Court passages, how about a month ago, at a ball at Court, a child was dropped by one of the ladies in dancing, but nobody knew who, it being taken up by somebody in their handkercher. The next morning all the Ladies of Honour appeared early at Court for their vindication, so that nobody could tell whose this mischance should be. But it seems Mrs Wells[12] fell sick that afternoon, and hath disappeared ever since,

8 John Wilkins, DD, afterwards Bishop of Chester.

9 William Outram, DD, Prebendary of Westminster, died 1679; one of the ablest and best of the Conformists, and eminent for his piety and charity, and an excellent preacher.

10 James Duport, DD, Dean of Peterborough 1664, and Master of Magdalene College, Cambridge, 1668. Died 1679.

11 Sir Thomas Willis, Bart, died November 1705, aged 90, and was buried at Ditton, in Cambridgeshire, where he possessed some property. In 1679, he had been put out of the Commission of the Peace for that County, for concurring with the Fanatic party in opposing the Court. Cole's manuscripts.

12 Maid of Honour to the Queen, and one of Charles II's numerous mistresses. See *Memoires de Grammont*.

so that it is concluded it was her. The little Duke of Monmouth, it seems, is ordered to take place of all Dukes, and so do follow Prince Rupert now, before the Duke of Buckingham, or any else.

13th. To my office, where late upon business; Mr Bland sitting with me, talking of my Lord Windsor's being come home from Jamaica, unlooked for; which makes us think that these young Lords are not fit to do any service abroad, though it is said that he could not have his health there, but hath raced a fort of the King of Spain upon Cuba, which is considerable, or said to be so, for his honour.

16th. To Westminster Hall, and there find great expectation what the Parliament will do, when they come two days hence to sit again, in matters of religion. The great question is, whether the Presbyters will be contented to let the Papists have the same liberty of conscience with them, or no, or rather be denied it themselves: and the Papists, I hear, are very busy in designing how to make the Presbyters consent to take their liberty, and to let them have the same with them, which some are apt to think they will. It seems a priest was taken in his vests officiating somewhere in Holborne the other day, and was committed by Secretary Morris, according to law; and they say the Bishop of London did give him thanks for it.

17th. To my Lord Sandwich, whom I found at cards with Pickering; but he made an end soon: and so all alone, he told me he had a great secret to tell me, such as no flesh knew but himself, nor ought; which was this: – that yesterday morning Eschar, Mr Edward Montagu's man, did come to him from his master with some of the Clerkes of the Exchequer, for my Lord to sign to their books for the Embassy money; which my Lord very civilly desired not to do till he had spoke with his master himself. In the afternoon, my Lord and my Lady Wright being at cards in his chamber, in comes Mr Montagu; and desiring to speak with my Lord at the window in his chamber, he began to charge my Lord with the greatest ingratitude in the world: that he that had received his earldom, garter, £4000 per annum, and whatever he has in the world, from him, should now study him all the dishonour that he could: and so fell to tell my Lord, that if he should speak all that he knew of him, he could do so and so. In a word, he did rip up all that could be said they was unworthy, and in the basest terms they could be spoken in. To which my Lord answered with great temper, justifying himself, but endeavouring to lessen his heat, which was a strange temper in him, knowing that he did owe all he hath in the world to my Lord, and that he is now all that he is by his means and favour. But my Lord did forbear to increase the quarrel, knowing that it would be to no good purpose for the world to see a difference in the family; but did allay them so as that he fell to weeping. And after much talk (among other things Mr Montague telling him that there was a fellow in the towne, naming me, that had done ill offices, and that if he knew it to be so, he would have him cudgelled) my Lord did promise him, that, if upon account he saw that there was not many tradesmen unpaid, he would sign the books; but if there was, he could not bear with taking too great a debt upon him. So this day he sent him an account, and a letter assuring him there was not above £200 unpaid; and so my Lord did sign to the Exchequer books. Upon the whole, I understand fully what a rogue he is, and how my Lord do think and will think of him for the future; telling me that thus he has served his father my Lord Manchester, and his whole family, and now himself: and, which is worst, that he hath abused, and in speeches every day do abuse my Lord Chancellor, whose favour he hath lost; and hath no friend but Sir H. Bennet, and that (I knowing the rise of his friendship) only from the likeness of their pleasures, and acquaintance, and concernments, they have in the same matters of lust and baseness; for which, God forgive them! But he do flatter himself, from promises of Sir H. Bennet, that he shall have a pension of £2000 per annum, and be made an Earl. My Lord told me he expected a challenge from him, but told me there was no great fear of him, for there was no man lies under such an imputation as he do in the business of Mr Cholmly, who, though a simple sorry fellow, do brave him and struts before him with the Queene, to the sport and observation of the whole Court. Mr Pickering tells me the story is very true of a child being dropped at the ball at Court; and that the King had it in his closet a week after, and did dissect it; and making great sport of it, said that in his opinion it must have been a month and three houres old; and that, whatever others think, he hath the greatest loss, (it being a boy, as he says,) that hath lost a subject by the business. He tells me too, that Sir H. Bennet is a Catholique, and how all the Court almost is changed to the worse since his coming in, they being afraid of him. And that the Queene-Mother's Court is now the greatest of all; and that our own Queene hath little or no company come to her, which I know also to be very true, and am sorry to see it.

18th. Mr Hater and I alone at the office, finishing our account of the extra charge of the Navy, not properly belonging to the Navy, since the King's coming in to Christmas last; and all extra things being abated, I find that the true charge of the Navy to that time hath been after the rate of £374,743 a year. I made an end by eleven o'clock at night. This day the Parliament met again, after their long prorogation; but I know not any thing what they have done, being within doors all day.

19th. This day I read the King's speech to the Parliament yesterday; which is very short, and not very obliging; but only telling them his desire to have a power of indulging tender consciences, and that he will yield to have any mixture in the uniformity of the Church's discipline; and says the same for the Papists, but declares against their ever being admitted to have any offices or places of trust in the kingdom; but, God knows, too many have.

21st. To the office, where Sir J. Minnes (most of the rest being at the Parliament-house,) all the morning answering petitions and other business. Towards noon there comes a man as if upon ordinary business, and shows me a writ from the Exchequer, called a Commission of Rebellion, and tells me that I am his prisoner in Field's business; which methought did strike me to the heart, to think that we could not sit in the middle of the King's business. I told him how and where we were employed, and bid him have a care; and perceiving that we were busy, he said he would, and did withdraw for an houre: in which time Sir J. Minnes took coach and to Court, to see what he could do from thence; and our solicitor against Field come by chance and told me that he would go and satisfy the fees of the Court, and would end the business. So he went away about that, and I staid in my closet, till by and by the man and four more of his fellows come to know what I would do; and I told them to stay till I heard from the King or my Lord Chief Baron, to both whom I had now sent. With that they consulted, and told me that if I would promise to stay in the house, they would go and refresh themselves, and come again, and know what answer I had: so they away, and I home to dinner. Before I had dined, the bayleys come back again

with the constable, and at the office knock for me, but found me not
there: and I hearing in what manner they were come, did forbear
letting them know where I was; so they stood knocking and
enquiring for me. By and by at my parler-window comes Sir W.
Batten's Mungo, to tell me that his master and lady would have me
come to their house through Sir J. Minnes's lodgings, which I could
not do; but, however, by ladders, did get over the pale between our
yards and their house, where I found them (as they have reason) to be
much concerned for me, my lady, especially. The fellows staid in the
yard swearing with one or two constables, and some time we locked
them into the yard, and by and by let them out again, and so kept
them all the afternoon, not letting them see me, or know where I
was. One time I went up to the top of Sir W. Batten's house, and out
of one of their windows spoke to my wife out of one of ours; which
methought, though I did it in mirth, yet I was sad to think what a sad
thing it would be for me to be really in that condition. By and by
comes Sir J. Minnes, who (like himself and all that he do) tells us that
he can do no good, but that my Lord Chancellor wonders that we
did not cause the seamen to fall about their eares: which we wished
we could have done without our being seen in it; and Captain Grove
being there, he did give them some affront, and would have got some
seamen to have drubbed them, but he had not time, nor did we think
it fit to have done it, they having executed their commission; but
there was occasion given that he did draw upon one of them who did
complain that Grove had pricked him in the breast, but no hurt done;
but I see that Grove would have done our business to them if we had
bid him. By and by comes Mr Clerke, our sollicitor, who brings us a
release from our adverse atturney, we paying the fees of the
commission, which comes to five markes, and the charges of these
fellows, which are called the commissioners, but are the most rake-
shamed rogues that ever I saw in my life; so he showed them this
release, and they seemed satisfied, and went away with him to their
atturney to be paid by him. But before they went, Sir W. Batten and
my lady did begin to taunt them, but the rogues answered them as
high as themselves, and swore they would come again, and called me
rogue and rebel, and they would bring the sheriffe and untile his
house, before he should harbour a rebel in his house, and that they
would be here again shortly. Well, at last they went away, and I by
advice took occasion to go abroad, and walked through the street to

show myself among the neighbours, that they might not think worse than the business is. I home to Sir W. Batten's again, where Sir J. Lawson, Captain Allen, Spragge,[13] and several others, and all our discourse about the disgrace done to our office to be liable to this trouble, which we must get removed. Hither comes Mr Clerke by and by, and tells me that he hath paid the fees of the Court for the commission; but the men are not contented with under £5 for their charges, which he will not give them, and therefore advises me not to stir abroad till Monday that he comes or sends to me again, whereby I shall not be able to go to White Hall to the Duke of York, as I ought. Here I staid vexing, and yet pleased to see every body for me; and so home, where my people are mightily surprized to see this business, but it troubles me not very much, it being nothing touching my particular person or estate. Sir W. Batten tells me that little is done yet in the Parliament-house, but only this day it was moved and ordered that all the members of the House do subscribe to the renouncing of the Covenant, which it is thought will try some of them. There is also a bill brought in for the wearing of nothing but cloth or stuffs of our own manufacture, and is likely to be passed. Among other talk this morning, my lady did speak concerning Commissioner Pett's calling the present King bastard, and other high words heretofore: and Sir W. Batten did tell us, that he did give the Duke and Mr Coventry an account of that and other like matters in writing under oath, of which I was ashamed, and for which I was sorry.

22nd (Lord's-day). Went not out all the morning; but after dinner to Sir W. Batten's and Sir W. Pen's, where discoursing much of yesterday's trouble and scandal; but that which troubled me most was Sir J. Minnes coming from Court at night, and instead of bringing great comfort from thence, (but I expected no better from him,) he tells me that the Duke and Mr Coventry make no great matter of it.

23rd. Up by times; and not daring to go by land, did (Griffin going along with me for fear,) slip to White Hall by water; where to Mr Coventry, and, as we used to do, to the Duke; the other of my fellows

---

13 Afterwards Sir Edward Spragg, a distinguished naval commander, who perished in a boat, which was sunk during an action with Van Tromp, in 1673, whilst he was preparing to hoist his flag on board a third ship, having previously lost two in the engagement.

being come. But we did nothing of our business, the Duke being sent for to the King, that he could not stay to speak with us. This morning come my Lord Windsor[14] to kiss the Duke's hand, being returned from Jamaica. He tells the Duke that from such a degree of latitude going thither he began to be sick, and was never well till his coming so far back again, and then presently begun to be well. He told the Duke of their taking the fort of St Jago, upon Cuba, with his men; but upon the whole, I believe, that he did matters like a young lord, and was weary of being upon service out of his own country, where he might have pleasure. For methought it was a shame to see him this very afternoon, being the first day of his coming to town, to be at a play-house. To my Lord Sandwich: it was a great trouble to me (and I had great apprehensions of it) that my Lord desired me to go to Westminster Hall, to the Parliament house door, about business; and to Sir Wm. Wheeler,[15] which I told him I would, but durst not go for fear of being taken by these rogues; but was forced to go to White Hall and take boat, and so land below the Tower at the Iron-gate, and so the back way over Little Tower Hill; and with my cloak over my face, took one of the watermen along with me, and staid behind our garden-wall, while he went to see whether any body stood within the Merchants' Gate. But there was nobody, and so I got safe into the garden, and coming to open my office door, something behind it fell in the opening, which made me start. So that God knows in what a sad condition I should be if I were truly in debt: and therefore ought to bless God that I have no such reall reason, and to endeavour to keep myself, by my good deportment and good husbandry, out of any such condition. At home I find, by a note that Mr Clerke in my absence hath left here, that I am free; and that he hath stopped all matters in Court; and I was very glad of it. We took coach and to Court, and there saw *The Wilde Gallant*,[16] performed by the King's house, but it was ill acted. The King did not seem pleased at all, the whole play, nor any body else. My Lady Castlemaine was all worth seeing to-night, and little Steward.[17] Mrs Wells do appear at Court again, and looks well; so that, it may be, the late report of laying the

14 Created Earl of Plymouth, 6th December, 1682.
15 MP for Queensborough.
16 A comedy by Dryden.
17 Frances, daughter of Walter Stewart, son of Lord Blantyre, married Charles, fifth Duke of Richmond, and died 1702.

dropped child to her was not true. This day I was told that my Lady
Castlemaine hath all the King's Christmas presents, made him by the
peers, given to her, which is a most abominable thing; and that at the
great ball she was much richer in jewells than the Queene and
Duchesse put both together.

24th. Among other things, my Lord [Sandwich] tells me, that he
hears the Commons will not agree to the King's late declaration, nor
will yield that the Papists have any ground given them to raise
themselves up again in England, which I perceive by my Lord was
expected at Court.

25th. The Commons in Parliament, I hear, are very high to stand to
the Act of Uniformity, and will not indulge the Papists (which is
endeavoured by the Court Party,) nor the Presbyters.

26th. Sir W. Batten and I by water to the Parliament-house: he went
in, and I walked up and down the Hall. All the newes is the great
oddes yesterday in the votes between them that are for the
Indulgence to the Papists and Presbyters, and those that are against it,
which did carry it by 200 against 30. And pretty it is to consider how
the King would appear to be a stiff Protestant and son of the Church;
and yet willing to give a liberty to these people, because of his
promise at Breda. And yet all the world do believe that the King
would not have the liberty given them at all.

27th. About 11 o'clock, Commissioner Pett and I walked to
Chyrurgeon's Hall, (we being all invited thither, and promised to
dine there;) where we were led into the Theatre: and by and by
comes the reader, Dr Tearne,[18] with the Master and Company, in a
very handsome manner: and all being settled, he begun his lecture;
and his discourse being ended, we had a fine dinner and good learned
company, many Doctors of Phisique, and we used with extraordinary
great respect. Among other observables we drunk the King's health
out of a gilt cup given by King Henry VIII to this Company, with
bells hanging at it, which every man is to ring by shaking after he
hath drunk up the whole cup. There is also a very excellent piece of
the King, done by Holbein, stands up in the Hall, with the officers of

18 Christopher Terne, of Leyden, MD, originally of Cambridge, and Fellow of the
College of Physicians. Died 1673.

the Company kneeling to him to receive their Charter. Dr Scarborough took some of his friends, and I went with them, to see the body of a lusty fellow, a seaman, that was hanged for a robbery. It seems one Dillon, of a great family, was, after much endeavours to have saved him, hanged with a silken halter this Sessions, (of his own preparing,) not for honour only, but it being soft and sleek it do slip close and kills, that is, strangles presently: whereas, a stiff one do not come so close together, and so the party may live the longer before killed. But all the Doctors at table conclude, that there is no pain at all in hanging, for that it do stop the circulation of the blood, and so stops all sense and motion in an instant. To Sir W. Batten's to speak upon some business, where I found Sir J. Minnes pretty well fuddled I thought: he took me aside to tell me how being at my Lord Chancellor's to-day, my Lord told him that there was a Great Seal passing for Sir W. Pen, through the impossibility of the Comptroller's duty to be performed by one man; to be as it were joynt-comptroller with him, at which he is stark mad; and swears he will give up his place. For my part, I do hope, when all is done that my following my business will keep me secure against all their envys. But to see how the old man do strut, and swear that he understands all his duty as easily as crack a nut, and easier, he told my Lord Chancellor, for his teeth are gone; and that he understands it as well as any man in England; and that he will never leave to record that he should be said to be unable to do his duty alone; though, God knows, he cannot do it more than a child.

28th. The House have this noon been with the King to give him their reasons for refusing to grant any indulgence to Presbyters or Papists; which he, with great content and seeming pleasure, took, saying, that he doubted not but he and they should agree in all things, though there may seem a difference in judgements, he having writ and declared for an indulgence: and that he did believe never prince was happier in a House of Commons, than he was in them. At the Privy Seale I did see the docquet by which Sir W. Pen is made the Comptroller's assistant, as Sir J. Minnes told me last night.

March 3rd. This afternoon Roger Pepys tells me, that for certain the King is for all this very highly incensed at the Parliament's late opposing the Indulgence; which I am sorry for, and fear it will breed great discontent.

5th. To the Lobby, and spoke with my cousin Roger, who is going to Cambridge to-morrow. In the Hall I do hear that the Catholiques are in great hopes for all this, and do set hard upon the King to get Indulgence. Matters, I hear, are all naught in Ireland, and the people, that is the Papists, do cry out against the Commissioners sent by the King; so that they say the English interest will be lost there.

6th. This day it seems the House of Commons have been very high against the Papists, being incensed by the stir which they make for their having an Indulgence; which, without doubt, is a great folly in them to be so hot upon at this time, when they see how averse already the House have showed themselves from it. This evening Mr Povy tells me that my Lord Sandwich is this day so ill that he is much afraid of him, which puts me to great pain, not more for my own sake than for his poor family's.

7th. Creed told me how for some words of my Lady Gerard's,[19] against my Lady Castlemaine to the Queene, the King did the other day apprehend her in going out to dance with her at a ball, when she desired it as the ladies do, and is since forbid attending the Queene by the King; which is much talked of, my Lord her husband being a great favourite.

8th (Lord's day). To White Hall to-day; I heard Dr King, Bishop of Chichester, make a good and eloquent sermon upon these words, 'They that sow in tears, shall reap in joy.' Whence (the chapel in Lent being hung with black, and no anthem after sermon, as at other times,) to my Lord Sandwich at Sir W. Wheeler's. I found him out of order, thinking himself to be in a fit of ague. After dinner up to my Lord, there being Mr Rumball. My Lord, among other discourse, did tell me of his great difficultys passed in the business of the Sound, and of his receiving letters from the King there, but his sending them by Whetstone was a great folly; and the story how my Lord being at dinner with Sydney,[20] one of his fellow plenipotentiarys and his mortal enemy, did see Whetstone, and put off his hat three times to him, and the fellow would not be known, which my Lord imputed to his coxcombly humour, (of which he was full) and bid Sydney

19 See note 1, page 189.
20 The famous Algernon Sydney, one of the Ambassadors sent to Sweden and Denmark by Richard Cromwell.

take notice of him too, when at the very time he had letters[21] in his pocket from the King as it proved afterwards. And Sydney afterwards did find it out at Copenhagen, the Dutch Commissioners telling him how my Lord Sandwich had desired one of their ships to carry back Whetstone to Lubeck, he being come from Flanders from the King. But I cannot but remember my Lord's aequanimity in all these affairs with admiration.

9th. About noon Sir J. Robinson, Lord Mayor, desiring way through the garden from the Tower, called in at the office and there invited me (and Sir W. Pen, who happened to be in the way) to dinner, and we did go. And there had a great Lent dinner of fish, little flesh. There dined with us to-day Mr Slingsby[22] of the Mint, who showed us all the new pieces both gold and silver (examples of them all) that were made for the King, by Blondeau's way; and compared them with those made for Oliver. The pictures of the latter made by Symons,[23] and of the King by one Rotyr,[24] a German, I think, that dined with us also. He extolls those of Rotyr above the others; and, indeed, I think they are the better, because the sweeter of the two; but, upon my word, those of the Protector are more like in my mind, than the King's, but both very well worth seeing. The crownes of Cromwell are now sold, it seems, for 25s. and 30s. a-piece.

16th. To the Duke where we met of course, and talked of our Navy matters. Then to the Commission of Tangier, and there had my Lord Peterborough's Commission read over; and Mr Secretary Bennet did make his querys upon it, in order to the drawing one for my Lord Rutherford more regularly, that being a very extravagant thing. Here long discoursing upon my Lord Rutherford's despatch, and so broke up. Mr Coventry and I discoursed how the Treasurer doth intend to come to pay in course, which is the thing of the world that will do the King the greatest service in the Navy, and which joys my heart to hear of. He tells me of the business of Sir J. Minnes, and Sir W. Pen; which, he said, was chiefly to make Mr Pett's being joyned with Sir

21 These letters are in Thurloe's State Papers, vol. vii. One was from the King, the other from Chancellor Hyde.
22 Master of the Mint, frequently mentioned by Evelyn.
23 Thomas Simon, an engraver of coins and medals.
24 There were three brothers named Rotier, all medallists; Philip introduced the likeness of Mrs Stewart in the figure of Britannia.

W. Batten to go down the better. And how he well sees that neither one nor the other can do their duties without help.

17th. To St Margaret's Hill in Southwark, where the Judge of the Admiralty come, and the rest of the Doctors of the Civill law, and some other Commissioners, whose Commission of Oyer and Terminer was read, and then the charge, given by Dr Exton,[25] which methought was somewhat dull, though he would seem to intend it to be very rhetoricall, saying that Justice had two wings, one of which spread itself over the land, and the other over the water, which was this Admiralty Court. I perceive that this Court is yet but in its infancy, (as to its rising again) and their design and consultation was, I could overhear them, how to proceed with the most solemnity, and spend time, there being only two businesses to do, which of themselves could not spend much time. Sir W. Batten and I to my Lord Mayor's, where we found my Lord with Colonel Strangways[26] and Sir Richard Floyd,[27] Parliament-men, in the cellar drinking, where we sat with them, and then up; and by and by come in Sir Richard Ford. We had many discourses, but from all of them I do find Sir R. Ford a very able man of his brains and tongue, and a scholler. But my Lord Mayor a talking, bragging, buffle-headed fellow, that would be thought to have led all the City in the great business of bringing in the King, and that nobody understood his plot, and the dark lanthorn he walked by; but led them and plowed with them as oxen and asses (his own words) to do what he had a mind: when in every discourse I observe him to be as very a coxcombe as I could have thought had been in the City. But he is resolved to do great matters in pulling down the shops quite through the City, as he hath done in many places, and will make a thorough passage quite through the City, through Canning Street, which indeed will be very fine. And then his precept, which he, in vain-glory, said he had drawn up himself, and hath printed it, against coachmen and carmen affronting of the gentry in the street; it is drawn so like a fool, and some faults were openly found in it, that I believe he will have so much wit as not to proceed upon it though it be printed. Here we staid talking till eleven at night, Sir R. Ford

25 Sir Thomas Exton, Dean of the Arches and Judge of the Admiralty Court.
26 Giles Strangways, MP for Dorsetshire.
27 Probably Sir Richard Lloyd, MP for Radnorshire.

breaking to my Lord our business of our patent to be Justices of the
Peace in the City, which he stuck at mightily; but, however, Sir R.
Ford knows him to be a fool, and so in his discourse he made him
appear, and cajoled him into a consent to it: but so as I believe when
he comes to his right mind to-morrow he will be of another opinion;
and though Sir R. Ford moved it very weightily and neatly, yet I had
rather it had been spared now. But to see how he rants, and pretends
to sway all the City in the Court of Aldermen, and says plainly that
they cannot do, nor will he suffer them to do, any thing but what he
pleases; nor is there any officer of the City but of his putting in; nor
any man that could have kept the City for the King thus well and
long but him. And if the country can be preserved, he will undertake
that the City shall not dare to stir again. When I am confident there is
no man almost in the City cares for him, nor hath he brains to outwit
any ordinary tradesman.

20th. Meeting with Mr Kirton's kinsman in Paul's Church Yard, he
and I to a coffee-house; where I hear how there had like to have been
a surprizall of Dublin by some discontented protestants, and other
things of like nature; and it seems the Commissioners have carried
themselves so high for the Papists that the others will not endure it.
Hewlett and some others are taken and clapped up; and they say the
King hath sent over to dissolve the Parliament there, who went very
high against the Commissioners. Pray God send all well!

21st. By appointment our full board met, and Sir Philip Warwick
and Sir Robert Long come from my Lord Treasurer to speak with us
about the state of the debts of the Navy; and how to settle it, so as to
begin upon the new foundation of £200,000 per annum, which the
King is now resolved not to exceed.

22nd (Lord's day). Wrote out our bill for the Parliament about our
being made Justices of Peace in the City. So to church, where a dull
formall fellow that prayed for the Right Hon. John Lord Barkeley,
Lord President of Connaught, &c. To my Lord Sandwich, and with
him talking a good while; I find the Court would have this
Indulgence go on, but the Parliament are against it. Matters in Ireland
are full of discontent.

29th. After dinner in comes Mr Moore, and sat and talked with us a
good while; among other things, telling me that neither my Lord nor

he are under apprehensions of the late discourse in the House of Commons, concerning resumption of Crowne lands.

April 1st. I went to the Temple to my Cozen Roger Pepys, to see and talk with him a little; who tells me that, with much ado, the Parliament do agree to throw down Popery: but he says it is with so much spite and passion, and an endeavour of bringing all Non-conformists into the same condition, that he is afraid matters will not yet go so well as he could wish.

2nd. Sir W. Pen told me, that this day the King hath sent to the House his concurrence wholly with them against the Popish priests, Jesuits, &c. which gives great content, and I am glad of it.

3rd. To the Tangier Committee, where we find ourselves at a great stand; the establishment being but £7000 per annum, and the forces to be kept in the town at the least estimate that my Lord Rutherford can be got to bring is £5300. The charge of this year's work of the Mole will be £13,000; besides £1000 a-year to my Lord Peterborough as a pension, and the fortifications and contingencys, which puts us to a great stand. I find at Court that there is some bad news from Ireland of an insurrection of the Catholiques there, which puts them into an alarme. I hear also in the City that for certain there is an embargo upon all our ships in Spayne, upon this action of my Lord Windsor's at Cuba, which signifies little or nothing, but only he hath a mind to say that he hath done something before he comes back again.

4th. After dinner to Hide Parke; at the Parke was the King, and in another coach my Lady Castlemaine, they greeting one another at every turn.

8th. By water to White Hall, to chapel; where preached Dr Pierce, the famous man that preached the sermon so much cried up, before the King against the Papists. His matter was the Devil tempting our Saviour, being carried into the Wilderness by the spirit. And he hath as much of natural eloquence as most men that ever I heard in my life, mixed with so much learning. After sermon I went up and saw the ceremony of the Bishop of Peterborough's paying homage upon the knee to the King, while Sir H. Bennet, Secretary, read the King's grant of the Bishopric of Lincolne, to which he is translated. His name is Dr Lany.[28] Here I also saw the Duke of Monmouth, with his Order of the Garter, the first time I ever saw it. I hear that the University of Cambridge did treat him a little while since with all the honour possible, with a comedy at Trinity College, and banquet; and made him Master of Arts there. All which, they say, the King took very well. Dr Raynbow,[29] Master of Magdalene, being now Vice-Chancellor.

12th (Lord's day). Coming home to-night, a drunken boy was carrying by our constable to our new pair of stocks to handsel them.

14th. Sir G. Carteret tells me to-night that he perceives the Parliament is likely to make a great bustle before they will give the King any money; will call all things in question; and, above all, the expences of the Navy; and do enquire into the King's expences everywhere, and into the truth of the report of people being forced to sell their bills at 15 per cent. losse in the Navy; and, lastly, that they are in a very angry pettish mood at present, and not likely to be better.

17th. It being Good Friday, our dinner was only sugar-sopps and fish; the only time that we have had a Lenten dinner all this Lent. To Paul's Church Yard, to cause the title of my English *Mare Clausum* to be changed, and the new title dedicated to the King, to be put to it, because I am ashamed to have the other seen dedicated to the Commonwealth.

20th. With Sir G. Carteret and Sir John Minnes to my Lord Treasurer's, thinking to have spoken about getting money for paying the Yards; but we found him with some ladies at cards: and so, it being a bad time to speak, we parted. This day the little Duke of Monmouth was marryed at White Hall, in the King's chamber; and to-night is a great supper and dancing at his lodgings, near Charing-Cross. I observed his coate at the tail of his coach: he gives the arms of England, Scotland, and France, quartered upon some other fields, but what it is that speaks his being a bastard I know not.

---

28 Benjamin Lany, STP, made Bishop of Peterborough 1660, translated to Lincoln 1662/63, and to Ely 1667.
29 Edward Rainbow, chaplain to the King, and Dean of Peterborough, and in 1664 Bishop of Carlisle. Died 1684.

25th. I did hear that the Queene is much grieved of late at the King's neglecting her, he having not supped once with her this quarter of a year, and almost every night with my Lady Castlemaine: who hath been with him this St George's feast at Windsor, and come home with him last night; and, which is more, they say is removed as to her bed from her own home to a chamber in White Hall, next to the King's owne; which I am sorry to hear, though I love her much.

27th. By water to White Hall; but found the Duke of York gone to St James's for this summer; and thence with Mr Coventry and Sir W. Pen up to the Duke's closet. And a good while with him about Navy business; and so I to White Hall, and there a long while with my Lord Sandwich discoursing about his debt to the Navy, wherein he hath given me some things to resolve him in.

The Queene (which I did not know,) it seems was at Windsor, at the late St George's feast there: and the Duke of Monmouth dancing with her with his hat in his hand, the King came in and kissed him, and made him put on his hat, which every body took notice of.

28th. To Chelsey, where we found my Lord all alone with one joynt of meat at dinner, and mightily extolling the manner of his retirement, and the goodness of his diet: the mistress of the house hath all things most excellently dressed; among others her cakes admirable, and so good that my Lord's words were, they were fit to present to my Lady Castlemaine. From ordinary discourse my Lord fell to talk of other matters to me, of which chiefly the second part of the fray, which he told me a little while since of, between Mr Edward Montagu and himself; that he hath forborn coming to him almost two months, and do speak not only slightly of my Lord every where, but hath complained to my Lord Chancellor of him, and arrogated all that ever my Lord hath done to be only by his direction and persuasion. Whether he hath done the like to the King or no, my Lord knows not; but my lord hath been with the King since, and finds all things fair; and my Lord Chancellor hath told him of it, but he so much contemns Mr Montagu, as my Lord knows himself very secure against any thing the fool can do; and notwithstanding all this, so noble is his nature, that he professes himself ready to show kindness and pity to Mr Montagu on any occasion. My Lord told me of his presenting Sir H. Bennet with a gold cup of £100, which he refuses, with a compliment; but my Lord would have been glad he had taken it, that he might have had some obligations upon him which he thinks possible the other may refuse to prevent it; not that he hath any reason to doubt his kindness. But I perceive great differences there are at Court: and Sir H. Bennet, and my Lord Bristol, and their faction, are likely to carry all things before them, (which my Lord's judgement is, will not be for the best,) and particularly against the Chancellor, who, he tells me, is irrecoverably lost: but, however, that he do so not actually joyne in any thing against the Chancellor, whom he do own to be a most sure friend, and to have been his greatest; and therefore will not openly act in either, but passively carry himself even. The Queene, my Lord tells me, he thinks he hath incurred some displeasure with, for his kindness to his neighbour my Lady Castlemaine. My Lord tells me he hath no reason to fall for her sake, whose wit, management, nor interest, is not likely to hold up any man, and therefore he thinks it not his obligation to stand for her against his own interest. The Duke and Mr Coventry my Lord sees he is very well with, and fears not but they will show themselves his very good friends, specially at this time, he being able to serve them, and they needing him, which he did not tell me wherein. Talking of the business of Tangier, he tells me that my Lord Teviott is gone away without the least respect paid to him, nor indeed to any man, but without his commission; and (if it be true what he says) having laid out seven or eight thousand pounds in commodities for the place: and besides having not only disobliged all the Commissioners for Tangier, but also Sir Charles Barkeley the other day, who spoke in behalf of Colonel Fitz-Gerald, that having been deputy-governor there already, he ought to have expected and had the governorship upon the death or removal of the former Governor. And whereas it is said that he and his men are Irish, which is indeed the main thing that hath moved the King and Council to put in Teviott to prevent the Irish having too great and the whole command there under Fitz-Gerald; he further said that there was never an Englishman fit to command Tangier; my Lord Teviott answered yes, there were many more fit than himself or Fitz-Gerald either. So that Fitz-Gerald being so great with the Duke of York, and being already made deputy-governor, independent of my Lord Teviott, and he being also left here behind him for a while, my Lord Sandwich do think, that, putting all these things together, the few friends he hath left, and the ill posture of his affairs, my Lord Teviott is not a man of the conduct and management that either people take him to be, or is fit for the command of the place. And here, speaking of the Duke of York and Sir Charles Barkeley, my Lord tells me that he do very much admire the good management, and discretion, and nobleness of the Duke, that however he may be led by him or Mr Coventry singly in private, yet he did not observe that in public matters but he did give as ready hearing, and as good acceptance to any reasons offered by any other man against the opinions of them, as he did to them, and would concur in the prosecution of it. Then we come to discourse upon his own sea-accompts, and come to a resolution how to proceed in them: wherein, though I offered him a way of evading the greatest part of his debt honestly, by making himself debtor to the Parliament before the King's time, which he might justly do, yet he resolved to go openly and nakedly in it, and put himself to the kindness of the King and Duke, which humour, I must confess, and so did tell him (with which he was not a little pleased) had thriven very well with him, being known to be a man of candid and open dealing, without any private tricks or hidden designs as other men commonly have in what they do. From that we had discourse of Sir G. Carteret, and of many others; and upon the whole I do find that it is a troublesome thing for a man of any condition at Court to carry himself even, and without contracting envy or envyers; and that much discretion and dissimulation is necessary to do it.

May 4th. To St James's; where Mr Coventry, Sir W. Pen and I staid for the Duke's coming in, but not coming, we walked to White Hall; and meeting the King, we followed him into the Parke, where Mr Coventry and he talking of building a new yacht out of his private purse, he having some contrivance of his own. The talk being done, we fell off to White Hall, leaving the King in the Park; and going back, met the Duke going towards St James's to meet us. So he turned back again, and to his closet at White Hall; and there, my Lord Sandwich present, we did our weekly errand, and so broke up; and I to the garden with my Lord Sandwich, (after we had sat an hour at the Tangier Committee;) and after talking largely of his own businesses, we began to talk how matters are at Court: and though he did not flatly tell me any such thing, yet I do suspect that all is not kind between the King and the Duke, and that the King's fondness to the little Duke do occasion it; and it may be that there is some fear of his being made heire to the Crown. But this my Lord did not tell me, but is my guess only; and that my Lord Chancellor is without doubt falling past hopes.

5th. With Sir J. Minnes, he telling many old stories of the Navy, and of the state of the Navy at the beginning of the late troubles, and I am troubled at my heart to think, and shall hereafter cease to wonder, at the bad success of the King's cause, when such a knave as he (if it be true what he says) had the whole management of the fleet, and the design of putting out of my Lord Warwicke,[30] and carrying the fleet to the King, wherein he failed most fatally to the King's ruine.

6th. To the Exchange with Creed, where we met Sir J. Minnes, who tells us, in great heat, that the Parliament will make mad work; that they will render all men incapable of any military or civil employment that have borne arms in the late troubles against the King, excepting some persons; which, if it be so, as I hope it is not, will give great cause of discontent, and I doubt will have but bad effects.

Sir Thomas Crewe this day tells me that the Queene, hearing that there was £40,000 per annum brought into her account among the other expences of the Crown before the Committee of Parliament, she took order to let them know that she hath yet for the payment of her whole family received but £4000, which is a notable act of spirit, and I believe is true.

7th. To my Lord Crewe's, and there dined with him. He tells me of the order the House of Commons have made for the drawing an Act for the rendering none capable of preferment or employment in the State, but who have been loyall and constant to the King and Church; which will be fatal to a great many, and makes me doubt lest I myself, with all my innocence during the late times, should be brought in, being employed in the Exchequer; but, I hope, God will provide for me.

10th. Put on a black cloth suit, with white lynings under all, as the fashion is to wear, to appear under the breeches. I walked to St James's, and was there at masse, and was forced in the croud to kneel down: and masse being done, to the King's Head ordinary, where

---

30 Henry Rich, Earl of Warwick and Holland; beheaded for putting himself in arms to aid Charles I.

many Parliament-men; and most of their talk was about the news from Scotland, that the Bishop of Galloway was besieged in his house by some women, and had like to have been outraged, but I know not how he was secured; which is bad news, and looks as it did in the beginning of the late troubles. From thence they talked of rebellion; and I perceive they make it their great maxime to be sure to master the City of London, whatever comes of it or from it.

11th. With Sir W. Pen to St James's, where we attended the Duke of York: and, among other things, Sir G. Carteret and I had a great dispute about the different value of the pieces of eight rated by Mr Creed at 4s. and 5d., and by Pitts at 4s. and 9d., which was the greatest husbandry to the King? he proposing that the greatest sum was; which is as ridiculous a piece of ignorance as could be imagined. However, it is to be argued at the Board, and reported to the Duke next week; which I shall do with advantage, I hope. I went homeward, after a little discourse with Mr Pierce the surgeon, who tells me that my Lady Castlemaine hath now got lodgings near the King's chamber at Court; and that the other day Dr Clarke and he did dissect two bodies, a man and a woman, before the King, with which the King was highly pleased.

14th. Met Mr Moore; and with him to an ale-house in Holborne; where in discourse he told me that he fears the King will be tempted to endeavour the setting the Crown upon the little Duke, which may cause troubles; which God forbid, unless it be his due! He told me my Lord do begin to settle to business again; and that the King did send for him the other day to my Lady Castlemaine's, to play at cards, where he lost £50; for which I am sorry, though he says my Lord was pleased at it, and said he would be glad at any time to lose £50 for the King to send for him to play, which I do not so well like.

15th. I walked in the Parke, discoursing with the keeper of the Pell Mell, who was sweeping of it; who told me of what the earth is mixed that do floor the Mall, and that over all there is cockle-shells powdered, and spread to keep it fast; which, however, in dry weather, turns to dust and deads the ball. Thence to Mr Coventry; and sitting by his bedside, he did tell me that he did send for me to discourse upon my Lord Sandwich's allowances for his several pays, and what his thoughts are concerning his demands; which he could not take the freedom to do face to face, it being not so proper as by me: and did give me a most friendly and ingenuous account of all; telling me how unsafe, at this juncture, while every man's, and his actions particularly, are descanted upon, it is either for him to put the Duke upon doing, or my Lord himself to desire anything extraordinary, 'specially the King having been so bountifull already; which the world takes notice of even to some repinings. All which he did desire me to discourse to my Lord of; which I have undertaken to do. At noon by coach to my Lord Crewe's, hearing that my Lord Sandwich dined there; where I told him what had passed between Mr Coventry and myself; with which he was contented, though I could perceive not very well pleased. And I do believe that my Lord do find some other things go against his mind in the House; for in the motion made the other day in the House by my Lord Bruce, that none be capable of employment but such as have been loyal and constant to the King and Church, that the General and my Lord were mentioned to be excepted; and my Lord Bruce did come since to my Lord, to clear himself that he meant nothing to his prejudice, nor could it have any such effect if he did mean it. After discourse with my Lord, to dinner with him; there dining there my Lord Montagu[31] of Boughton, Mr William Montagu his brother, the Queene's Sollicitor, &c., and a fine dinner. Their talk about a ridiculous falling-out two days ago at my Lord of Oxford's house, at an entertainment of his, there being there my Lord of Albemarle, Lynsey, two of the Porters, my Lord Bellasses, and others, where there were high words and some blows, and pulling off of perriwiggs; till my Lord Monk took away some of their swords, and sent for some soldiers to guard the house till the fray was ended. To such a degree of madness the nobility of this age is come! After dinner, I went up to Sir Thomas Crewe, who lies there not very well in his head, being troubled with vapours and fits of dizzinesse: and there I sat talking with him all the afternoon upon the unhappy posture of things at this time; that the King do mind nothing but pleasures, and hates the very sight or thoughts of business. If any of the sober counsellors give him good advice, and move him in any thing that is to his good and honour, the other part, which are his counsellors of pleasure, take

---

31 Edward, second Lord Montagu of Boughton, in 1664 succeeded his father, who had been created a Baron by James I, and died 1683, leaving a son afterwards Duke of Montagu.

him when he is with my Lady Castlemaine, and in a humour of
delight, and then persuade him that he ought not to hear or listen to
the advice of those old dotards or counsellors that were heretofore his
enemies: when, God knows! it is they that now-a-days do most study
his honour. It seems the present favourites now are my Lord Bristol,
Duke of Buckingham, Sir H. Bennet, my Lord Ashley, and Sir
Charles Barkeley; who, among them, have cast my Lord Chancellor
upon his back, past ever getting up' again: there being now little for
him to do, and he waits at Court attending to speak to the King as
others do: which I pray God may prove of good effects, for it is feared
it will be the same with my Lord Treasurer shortly. But strange to
hear how my Lord Ashley, by my Lord Bristol's means, (he being
brought over to the Catholique party against the Bishops, whom he
hates to the death, and publicly rails against them; not that he is
become a Catholique, but merely opposes the Bishops; and yet, for
aught I hear, the Bishop of London keeps as great with the King as
ever,) is got into favour, so much that, being a man of great business
and yet of pleasure, and drolling too, he, it is thought, will be made
Lord Treasurer upon the death or removal of the good old man.[32] My
Lord Albemarle, I hear, do bear through and bustle among them, and
will not be removed from the King's good opinion and favour,
though none of the Cabinet; but yet he is envied enough. It is made
very doubtful whether the King do not intend the making of the
Duke of Monmouth legitimate; but surely the Commons of England
will never do it, nor the Duke of York suffer it, whose Lady I am told
is very troublesome to him by her jealousy. No care is observed to be
taken of the main chance, either for maintaining of trade or opposing
of factions, which, God knows, are ready to break out, if any of them
(which God forbid!) should dare to begin; the King and every man
about him minding so much their pleasures or profits. My Lord
Hinchingbroke, I am told, hath had a mischance to kill his boy by his
birding-piece going off as he was a fowling. The gun was charged
with small shot, and hit the boy in the face and about the temples, and
he lived four days. In Scotland, it seems, for all the newsbooks tell us
every week that they are all so quiet, and every thing in the Church
settled, the old woman had liked to have killed, the other day, the
Bishop of Galloway, and not half the Churches of the whole kingdom

32 The Earl of Southampton.

conform. Strange were the effects of the late thunder and lightning about a week since at Northampton, coming with great rain, which caused extraordinary floods in a few houres, bearing away bridges, drowning horses, men, and cattle. Two men passing over a bridge on horseback, the arches before and behind them were borne away, and that left which they were upon: but, however, one of the horses fell over, and was drowned. Stacks of faggots carried as high as a steeple, and other dreadful things; which Sir Thomas Crewe showed me letters to him about from Mr Freemantle and others, that it is very true. The Portugalls have choused us, it seems, in the Island of Bombay, in the East Indys; for after a great charge of our fleets being sent thither with full commission from the King of Portugall to receive it, the Governour by some pretence or other will not deliver it to Sir Abraham Shipman, sent from the King, nor to my Lord of Marlborough;[33] which the King takes highly ill, and I fear our Queene will fare the worse for it. The Dutch decay there exceedingly, it being believed that their people will revolt from them there, and they forced to give up their trade. Sir Thomas showed me his picture and Sir Anthony Vandyke's in crayon in little, done exceedingly well.

18th. I walked to White Hall, and into the Parke, seeing the Queene and Maids of Honour passing through the house going to the Parke. But above all, Mrs Stuart is a fine woman, and they say now a common mistress to the King, as my Lady Castlemaine is; which is a great pity.

19th. With Sir John Minnes to the Tower; and by Mr Slingsby, and Mr Howard, Controller of the Mint, we were shown the method of making this new money. That being done, the Controller would have us dine with him and his company, the King giving them a dinner every day. And very merry and good discourse upon the business we have been upon. They now coyne between 16 and 24,000 pounds in a week. At dinner they did discourse very finely to us of the probability that there is a vast deal of money hid in the land, from this: that in King Charles's time there was near ten millions of money coyned, besides what was then in being of King James's and Queene Elizabeth's, of which there is a good deal at this day in being.

33 James Ley, third Earl of Marlborough, killed in the great sea-fight with the Dutch, 1665.

Next, that there was but £750,000 coyned of the Harp and Crosse money, and of this there was £500,000 brought in upon its being called in. And from very good arguments they find that there cannot be less of it in Ireland and Scotland than £100,000; so that there is but £150,000 missing; and of that, suppose that there should be not above £50,000 still remaining, either melted down, hid, or lost, or hoarded up in England, there will then be but £100,000 left to be thought to have been transported. Now, if £750,000 in twelve years' time lost but a £100,000 in danger of being transported, then £10,000,000 in thirty-five years' time will have lost but £3,888,888 and odd pounds; and as there is £650,000 remaining after twelve years' time in England, so after thirty-five years' time, which was within this two years, there ought in proportion to have resting £6,111,120 or thereabouts, besides King James and Queene Elizabeth's money. Now, that most of this must be hid is evident, as they reckon, because of the dearth of money immediately upon the calling-in of the State's money, which was £500,000 that come in; and then there was not any money to be had in this City, which they say to their own observation and knowledge was so. And therefore, though I can say nothing in it myself, I do not dispute it.

23rd. To White Hall; where, in the Matted Gallery, Mr Coventry was, who told us how the Parliament have required of Sir G. Carteret and him an account what money shall be necessary to be settled upon the Navy for the ordinary charge, which they intend to report £200,000 per annum. And how to allott this we met this afternoon, and took their papers for our perusal, and so parted.

24th. Meeting Mr Lewis Phillips of Brampton, he and afterwards others tell me that news come last night to Court, that the King of France is sick of the spotted fever, and that they are struck in again; and this afternoon my Lord Mandeville is gone from the King to make him a visit which will be great news, and of great import through Europe. By and by, in comes my Lord Sandwich: he told me this day a vote hath passed that the King's grants of land to my Lord Monk and him should be made good; which pleases him very much. He also tells me that things do not go right in the House with Mr Coventry; I suppose he means in the business of selling places; but I am sorry for it.

27th. With Pett to my Lord Ashley, Chancellor of the Exchequer; where we met the auditors about settling the business of the accounts of persons to whom money is due before the King's time in the Navy, and the clearing of their imprests for what little of their debts they have received. I find my Lord, as he is reported, a very ready, quiet, and diligent person. Roger Pepys tells me that the King hath sent to the Parliament to hasten to make an end by midsummer, because of his going into the country; so they have set upon four bills to dispatch: the first of which is, he says, too devilish a severe act against conventicles; so beyond all moderation, that he is afraid it will ruin all: telling me that it is matter of the greatest grief to him in the world, that he should be put upon this trust of being a Parliament-man, because he says nothing is done, that he can see, out of any truth and sincerity, but mere envy and design. Then into the Great Garden up to the Banqueting House; and there by my Lord's glass we drew in the species[34] very pretty. Afterwards to nine-pins, Creed and I playing against my Lord and Cooke.

28th. By water to the Royal Theatre; but that was so full they told us we could have no room. And so to the Duke's house; and there saw *Hamlett* done, giving us fresh reason never to think enough of Betterton. Who should we see come upon the stage but Gosnell, my wife's maid? but neither spoke, danced, nor sung; which I was sorry for.

29th. This day is kept strictly as a holy-day, being the King's Coronation. Creed and I abroad, and called at several churches; and it is a wonder to see, and by that to guess the ill temper of the City, at this time, either to religion in general, or to the King, that in some churches there was hardly ten people, and those poor people. To the Duke's house, and there saw *The Slighted Mayde*,[35] wherein Gosnell acted Aeromena, a great part, and did it very well. Then with Creed to see the German Princesse,[36] at the Gate-house, at Westminster.

31st. This month the greatest news is, the height and heat that the

---

34 This word is here used as an optical term, and signifies the image painted on the retina of the eye, and the rays of light reflected from the several points of the surface of objects.

35 A comedy, by Sir Robert Stapylton.

36 Mary Carleton, of whom see more June 7 following, and April 15, 1664.

Parliament is in, in enquiring into the revenue, which displeases the Court, and their backwardness to give the King any money. Their enquiring into the selling of places do trouble a great many; among the chief, my Lord Chancellor (against whom particularly it is carried), and Mr Coventry; for which I am sorry. The King of France was given out to be poisoned and dead; but it proves to be the meazles: and he is well, or likely to be soon well again. I find myself growing in the esteem and credit that I have in the office, and I hope falling to my business again will confirm me in it.

June 1st. The Duke having been a-hunting to-day, and so lately come home and gone to bed, we could not see him, and we walked away. And I with Sir J. Minnes to the Strand Maypole; and there light out of his coach, and walked to the New Theatre, which, since the King's players are gone to the Royal one, is this day begun to be employed by the fencers to play prizes at. And here I come and saw the first prize I ever saw in my life: and it was between one Mathews, who did beat at all weapons, and one Westwicke, who was soundly cut several times both in the head and legs, that he was all over blood: and other deadly blows they did give and take in very good earnest, till Westwicke was in a sad pickle. They fought at eight weapons, three boutes at each weapon. This being upon a private quarrel, they did it in good earnest; and I felt one of the swords, and found it to be very little, if at all blunter on the edge, than the common swords are. Strange to see what a deal of money is flung to them both upon the stage between every boute. This day I hear at Court of the great plot which was lately discovered in Ireland, made among the Presbyters and others, designing to cry up the Covenant, and to secure Dublin Castle and other places; and they have debauched a good part of the army there, promising them ready money. Some of the Parliament there, they say, are guilty, and some withdrawn upon it; several persons taken, and among others a son of Scott's, that was executed here for the King's murder. What reason the King hath, I know not; but it seems he is doubtfull of Scotland: and this afternoon, when I was there, the Council was called extraordinary; and they were opening the letter this last post's coming and going between Scotland and us and other places. The King of France is well again.

2nd. To St James's, to Mr Coventry; where I had an hour's private talk with him concerning his own condition, at present being under the censure of the House, being concerned with others in the Bill for selling of offices. He tells me, that though he thinks himself to suffer much in his fame hereby, yet he values nothing more of evil to hang over him; for that it is against no statute, as is pretended, nor more than what his predecessors time out of mind have taken; and that so soon as he found himself to be in an errour, he did desire to have his fees set, which was done; and since that time he hath not taken a token more. He undertakes to prove, that he did never take a token of any captain to get him employed in his life beforehand, or demanded any thing: and for the other accusation, that the Cavaliers are not employed, he looked over the list of them now in the service, and of the twenty-seven that are employed, thirteen have been heretofore always under the King; two neutralls, and the other twelve men of great courage, and such as had either the King's particular commands, or great recommendation to put them in, and none by himself. Besides that, he sees it is not the King's nor Duke's opinion that the whole party of the late officers should be rendered desperate. And lastly, he confesses that the more of the Cavaliers are put in, the less of discipline hath followed in the fleet; and that, whenever there comes occasion, it must be the old ones that must do any good. He tells me, that he cannot guess whom all this should come from; but he suspects Sir G. Carteret, as I also do, at least that he is pleased with it. But he tells me that he will bring Sir G. Carteret to be the first adviser and instructor of him what is to make his place of benefit to him; telling him that Smith did make his place worth £5000 and he believed £7000 to him the first year; besides something else greater than all this, which he forbore to tell me. It seems one Sir Thomas Tomkins[37] of the House, that makes many mad motions, did bring it into the House, saying that a letter was left at his lodgings, subscribed by one Benson, (which is a feigned name, for there is no such in the Navy,) telling how many places in the Navy have been sold. And by another letter, left in the same manner since, nobody appearing, he writes him that there is one Hughes and another Butler (both rogues, that have for their roguery been turned out of their places,) that will swear that Mr Coventry did sell their places and other things. I offered him my service, and will with all my heart serve him; but he

---

37 MP for Weobly, and one of the proposed Knights of the Royal Oak, for Herefordshire.

tells me he do not think it convenient to meddle, or to any purpose. To Westminster Hall, where I hear more of the plot from Ireland; which it seems hath been hatching, and known to the Lord Lieutenant a great while, and kept close till within three days that it should have taken effect.

4th. In the Hall a good while; where I heard that this day the Archbishop of Canterbury, Juxon,[38] a man well spoken of by all for a good man, is dead; and the Bishop of London[39] is to have his seat. The match between Sir J. Cutts[40] and my Lady Jemimah,[41] he says, is likely to go on; for which I am glad. In the Hall to-day Dr Pierce tells me that the Queene begins to be briske, and play like other ladies, and is quite another woman from what she was. It may be, it may make the King like her the better, and forsake his two mistresses my Lady Castlemaine and Stewart.[42]

6th. To York House, where the Russia Embassador do lie; and there I saw his people go up and down louseing themselves: they are all in a great hurry, being to be gone the beginning of next meek. But that that pleased me best, was the remains of the noble soul of the late Duke of Buckingham appearing in his house, in every place, in the door-cases and the windows. Sir John Hebden, the Russia Resident, did tell me how he is vexed to see things at Court ordered as they are by nobody that attends to business, but every man himself or his pleasures. He cries up my Lord Ashley to be almost the only man that he sees to look after business; and with the ease and mastery, that he wonders at him. He cries out against the King's dealing so much with goldsmiths, and suffering himself to have his purse kept and commanded by them. He tells me also with what exact care and order the States of Holland's stores are kept in their Yards, and every thing managed there by their builders with such husbandry as is not imaginable; which I will endeavour to understand further.

7th. Mrs Turner, who is often at Court, do tell me to-day that for certain the Queene hath much changed her humour, and is become

---

38 William Juxon, made Bishop of London 1633, translated to Canterbury, 1660.
39 Gilbert Sheldon, who did succeed him.
40 Of Childerley near Cambridge.
41 Lady Jemimah Montagu, daughter to the Earl of Sandwich.
42 Spelt indiscriminately in the manuscript – Stuart, Steward and Stewart.

very pleasant and sociable as any; and they say is with child, or believed to be so. After church to Sir W. Batten's; where my Lady Batten enveighed mightily against the German Princesse, and I as high in the defence of her wit and spirit, and glad that she is cleared at the Sessions.

12th. To the Royal Theatre; and there saw *The Committee*,[43] a merry but indifferent play, only Lacey's part, an Irish footman, is beyond imagination. Here I saw my Lord Falconbridge,[44] and his Lady, my Lady Mary Cromwell, who looks as well as I have known her, and well clad: but when the House began to fill she put on her vizard, and so kept it on all the play; which of late is become a great fashion among the ladies, which hides their whole face. So to the Exchange, to buy things with my wife; among others, a vizard for herself.

13th. To the Royal Theatre; and in our way saw my Lady Castlemaine, who, I fear, is not so handsome as I have taken her for, and now she begins to decay something. This is my wife's opinion also. Yesterday, upon conference with the King in the Banqueting House, the Parliament did agree with much ado, it being carried but by forty-two voices, that they would supply him with a sum of money; but what and how is not yet known, but expected to be done with great disputes the next week. But if done at all, it is well.

15th. To the Trinity House; where, among others, I found my Lords Sandwich and Craven, and my cousin Roger Pepys, and Sir Wm. Wheeler. Both at and after dinner we had great discourses of the nature and power of spirits, and whether they can animate dead bodies; in all which, as of the general appearance of spirits, my Lord Sandwich is very scepticall. He says the greatest warrants that ever he had to believe any, is the present appearing of the Devil[45] in Wiltshire, much of late talked of, who beats a drum up and down.

43 *The Committee*, a comedy, by Sir Robert Howard.

44 Thos. Bellasses Viscount Falconberg, frequently called Falconbridge, married Mary, third daughter of Oliver Cromwell. She died 1712.

45 Joseph Glanville published a Relation of the famed disturbance at the house of Mr Mompesson, at Tedworth, Wilts, occasioned by the beating of an invisible drum every night for a year. This story, which was believed at the time, furnished the plot for Addison's play of *The Drummer, or the Haunted House*. In the *Mercurius Publicus*, April 16–23, 1663, there is a curious examination on this subject, by which it appears that one William Drury, of Uscut, Wiltshire, was the invisible drummer.

There are books of it, and, they say, very true; but my Lord observes, that though he do answer to any tune that you will play to him upon another drum, yet one time he tried to play and could not; which makes him suspect the whole; and I think it is a good argument.

16th. Dined with Sir W. Batten; who tells me that the House have voted the supply, intended for the King, shall be by subsidy.

17th. This day I met with Pierce the surgeon; who tells me that the King has made peace between Mr Edward Montagu and his father Lord Montagu, and that all is well again; at which, for the family's sake, I am glad, but do not think it will hold long.

19th. To Lambeth, expecting to have seen the Archbishop lie in state; but it seems he is not laid out yet. At the Privy Seale Office examined the books, and found the grant of increase of salary to the principall officers in the year 1639, £300 among the Controller, Surveyor, and Clerk to the Shippes. Met Captain Ferrers; who tells us that the King of France is well again, and that he saw him train his Guards, all brave men, at Paris; and that when he goes to his mistress, Madame La Valiere, a pretty little woman, now with child by him, he goes publicly, and his trumpets and kettle-drums with him; and yet he says that, for all this, the Queene do not know of it, for that nobody dares to tell her; but that I dare not believe.

22nd. To Westminster, where all along I find the shops evening with the sides of the houses, even in the broadest streets; which will make the City very much better than it was. It seems the House do consent to send to the King to desire that he would be graciously pleased to let them know who it was that did inform him of what words Sir Richard Temple[46] should say, which were to this purpose: 'That if the King would side with him, or be guided by him and his party, that he should not lack money': but without knowing who told it, they do not think fit to call him to any account for it. The Duke being gone a-hunting, by and by come in and shifted himself; he having in his hunting led his horse through a river up to his breast, and came so home: and being ready, we had a long discourse with him.

46 Sir Richard Temple, of Stowe, Bart, MP for Buckingham, and KB. Died 1664.

23rd. To the office; and after an hour or two, by water to the Temple, to my cousen Roger; who, I perceive, is a deadly high man in the Parliament business, and against the Court, showing me how they have computed that the King hath spent, at least hath received, above four millions of money since he come in: and in Sir J. Winter's case, in which I spoke to him, he is so high that he says he deserves to be hanged. To the 'Change; and by and by comes the King and the Queene by in great state, and the streets full of people. I stood in Mr —'s balcone. They dine all at my Lord Mayor's; but what he do for victualls, or room for them, I know not.

24th. To St James's, and there an hour's private discourse with Mr Coventry; he speaking of Sir G. Carteret slightly, and diminishing of his services for the King in Jersey; that he was well rewarded, and had good lands and rents, and other profits from the King, all the time he was there; and that it was always his humour to have things done his way. He brought an example how he would not let the Castle there be victualled for more than a month, that so he might keep it at his beck, though the people of the town did offer to supply it more often themselves. Another thing he told me, how the Duke of York did give Sir G. Carteret and the Island his profit as Admirall, and other things, toward the building of a pier there. But it was never laid out, nor like to be. So it falling out that a lady being brought to bed, the Duke was to be desired to be one of the godfathers; and it being objected that that would not be proper, there being no peer of the land to be joyned with him, the lady replied, 'Why, let him choose; and if he will not be a godfather without a peer, then let him even stay till he hath made a pier of his own.' He tells me, too, that he hath lately been observed to tack about at Court, and to endeavour to strike in with the persons that are against the Chancellor; but this he says of him, that he do not say nor do any thing to the prejudice of the Chancellor. But he told me that the Chancellor was rising again, and that of late Sir G. Carteret's business and employment hath not been so full as it used to be while the Chancellor stood up. From that we discoursed of the evil of putting out men of experience in business as the Chancellor, and of the condition of the King's party at present, who, as the Papists, though otherwise fine persons, yet being by law kept for these fourscore years out of employment, they are now wholly uncapable of business; and so the Cavaliers for twenty years, who, says he, for the most part have either given themselves over to look after country and family business, and those the best of them, and the rest to debauchery, &c.; and that was it that hath made him high against the late Bill brought into the House for the making all men incapable of employment that had served against the King. People, says he, in the sea-service, it is impossible to do any thing without them, there being not more than three men of the whole King's side that are fit to command almost; and these were Captn. Allen, Smith, and Beech;[47] and it may be Holmes, and Utber, and Batts might do something.

25th. Sir G. Carteret did tell us that upon Tuesday last, being with my Lord Treasurer, he showed him a letter from Portugall speaking of the advance of the Spaniards into their country, and yet that the Portuguese were never more courageous than now: for by an old prophecy sent thither some years though not many since from the French King, it is foretold that the Spaniards should come into their country, and in such a valley they should be all killed, and then their country should be wholly delivered from the Spaniards. This was on Tuesday last, and yesterday come the very first news that in this valley they had thus routed and killed the Spaniards.

26th. The House is upon the King's answer to their message about Temple, which is, that my Lord of Bristoll did tell him that Temple did say those words; so the House are resolved upon sending some of their members to him to know the truth, and to demand satisfaction if it be not true. Sir W. Batten, Sir J. Minnes, my Lady Batten, and I by coach to Bednall Green, to Sir W. Rider's to dinner. A fine merry walk with the ladies alone after dinner in the garden: the greatest quantity of strawberrys I ever saw, and good. This very house[48] was built by the blind beggar of Bednall Green, so much talked of and sang in ballads; but they say it was only some of the out-houses of it. At table, discoursing of thunder and lightning, Sir W. Rider did tell a story of his own knowledge, that a Genoese gally in Legorne Roads was struck by thunder, so as the mast was broke a-pieces, and the

---

47 Probably Richard Beach, afterwards knighted, and in 1668 Commissioner at Portsmouth.
48 Called Kirby Castle, the property of Sir William Ryder, Knight, who died herein 1669 – Lysons' *Environs*.

shackle upon one of the slaves was melted clear off his leg without hurting his leg. Sir William went on board the vessel, and would have contributed toward the release of the slave whom Heaven had thus set free, but he could not compass it, and so he was brought to his fetters again.

29th. Up and down the streets is cried mightily the great victory got by the Portugalls against the Spaniards, where 10,000 slain, 3 or 4000 taken prisoners, with all the artillery, baggage, money, &c., and Don John[49] of Austria forced to flee with a man or two with him.

30th. Public matters are in an ill condition: Parliament sitting and raising four subsidys for the King, which is but a little, considering his wants; and yet that parted withal with great hardness. They being offended to see so much money go, and no debts of the public's paid, but all swallowed by a luxurious Court; which the King it is believed and hoped will retrench in a little time, when he comes to see the utmost of the revenue which shall be settled on him; he expecting to have his £1,200,000 made good to him, which is not yet done by above £150,000 as he himself reports to the House. The charge of the Navy intended to be limited to £200,000 per annum, the ordinary charge of it, and that to be settled upon the Customes. The King gets greatly taken up with Madam Castlemaine and Mrs Stewart, which Heaven put an end to!

July 1st. Being in the Parliament lobby, I there saw my Lord of Bristoll come to the Commons House to give his answer to their question, about some words he should tell the King that were spoke by Sir Richard Temple. A chair was set at the bar of the House for him, which he used but little, but made an harangue of half an hour bareheaded, the House covered. His speech being done, he come out into a little room till the House had concluded of an answer to his speech; which they staying long upon, I went away. And by and by out comes Sir W. Batten; and he told me that his Lordship had made a long and a comedian-like speech, and delivered with such action as was not becoming his Lordship. He confesses he did tell the King such a thing of Sir Richard Temple, but that upon his honour the words

49 He was a natural son of Philip IV, King of Spain, who after his father's death in 1665 exerted his whole influence to overthrow the Regency appointed during the young King's minority.

were not spoke by Sir Richard, he having taken a liberty of enlarging to the King upon the discourse which had been between Sir Richard and himself lately; and so took upon himself the whole blame, and desired their pardon, it being not to do any wrong to their fellow-member, but out of zeal to the King. He told them, among many other things, that as to religion he was a Roman Catholick, but such a one as thought no man to have right to the Crown of England but the Prince that hath it; and such a one as, if the King should desire counsel as to his own, he would not advise him to another religion than the old true reformed religion of this kingdom as it now stands; and concluded with a submission to what the House shall do with him, saying, that whatever they shall do, – 'thanks be to God, this head, this heart, and this sword, (pointing to them all) will find me a being in any place in Europe.' The House hath hereupon voted clearly Sir Richard Temple to be free from the imputation of saying those words; but when Sir William Batten come out, had not concluded what to say to my Lord, it being argued that to own any satisfaction as to my Lord from his speech, would be to lay some fault upon the King for the message he should upon no better accounts send to the impeaching of one of their members. Walking out, I hear that the House of Lords are offended that my Lord Digby[50] should come to this House and make a speech there without leave first asked of the House of Lords. I hear also of another difficulty now upon him; that my Lord of Sunderland[51] (whom I do not know) was so near to the marriage of his daughter, as that the wedding-clothes were made, and portion and every thing agreed on and ready; and the other day he goes away nobody yet knows whither, sending her the next morning a release of his right or claim to her, and advice to his friends not to enquire into the reason of this doing, for he hath enough for it; and that he gives them liberty to say and think what they will of him, so they do not demand the reason of his leaving her, being resolved never to have her. To Sir W. Batten, to the Trinity House; and after dinner we fell a-talking, Mr Batten telling us of a late triall of Sir Charles Sedley[52] the other day, before my

50 Digby, Earl of Bristol.

51 Henry, fourth Lord Spence, and second Earl of Sunderland, Ambassador to Spain 1671. Died 1702.

52 Sir Charles Sedley, Bart., celebrated for his wit and profligacy, and author of several plays. He is said to have been fined £500 for this outrage. He was father to James II's mistress, created Countess of Dorchester, and died 1701.

JULY 1663   227

Lord Chief Justice Foster[53] and the whole bench, for his debauchery a
little while since at Oxford Kate's.[54] It seems my Lord and the rest of
the Judges did all of them round give him a most high reproofe; my
Lord Chief Justice saying, that it was for him, and such wicked
wretches as he was, that God's anger and judgments hung over us,
calling him sirrah many times. It seems they have bound him to his
good behaviour (there being no law against him for it) in £5000. It
being told that my Lord Buckhurst was there, my Lord asked whether
it was that Buckhurst that was lately tried for robbery;[55] and when
answered Yes, he asked whether he had so soon forgot his deliverance
at that time, and that it would have more become him to have been at
his prayers begging God's forgiveness, than now running into such
courses again. This day I hear at dinner that Don John of Austria, since
his flight out of Portugall, is dead of his wounds: so there is a great man
gone, and a great dispute like to be indeed for the crown of Spayne, if
the King should have died before him My cousin Roger told us the
whole passage of my Lord Digby to-day, much as I have said here
above; only that he did say that he would draw his sword against the
Pope himself, if he should offer any thing against his Majesty, and the
good of these nations; and that he never was the man that did either
look for a Cardinal's cap for himself, or any body else, meaning Abbot
Montagu:[56] and the House upon the whole did vote Sir Richard
Temple innocent; and that my Lord Digby hath cleared the honour of
His Majesty, and Sir Richard Temple's, and given perfect satisfaction
of his own respects to the House.

2nd. Walking in the garden this evening with Sir G. Carteret and Sir
J. Minnes, Sir G. Carteret told us with great content how like a stage-
player my Lord Digby spoke yesterday, pointing to his head as my
Lord did, and saying, 'First, for his head,' says Sir G. Carteret, 'I know
when a calfe's head would have done better by half: for his heart and
his sword, I have nothing to say to them.' He told us that for certain

53 Sir Robert Foster, Knight, Chief Justice of the King's Bench. Died 1663.
54 The details in the original are too gross to print.
55 See an account of this, February 22nd, 1661/62.
56 Walter, second son to the first Earl of Manchester, embracing the Catholic
religion while on his travels, was made Abbot of Ponthoise through the influence of
Mary de' Medici: he afterwards became Almoner to the Queen-Dowager of
England, and died 1670.

his head cost the late King his, for it was he that broke off the treaty at Uxbridge. He told us also how great a man he was raised from a private gentleman in France by Monsieur Grandmont, and afterwards by the Cardinal, who raised him to be a Lieutenant-generall, and then higher, and entrusted by the Cardinal when he was banished out of France with great matters, and recommended by him to the Queene as a man to be trusted and ruled by: yet when he come to have some power over the Queene, he begun to dissuade her from her opinion of the Cardinal; which she said nothing to till the Cardinal[57] was returned, and then she told him of it; who told my Lord Digby, '*Et bien, Monsieur, vous estes un fort bon amy donc*': but presently put him out of all; and then, from a certainty of coming in two or three years' time to be Mareschall of France, (to which all strangers, even Protestants, and those as often as French themselves, are capable of coming, though it be one of the greatest places in France,) he was driven to go out of France into Flanders; but there was not trusted, nor received any kindness from the Prince of Condé, as one to whom also he had been false, as he had been to the Cardinal and Grandmont. In fine, he told us that he is a man of excellent parts, but of no great faith nor judgment, and one very easy to get up to great height of preferment, but never able to hold it.

3rd. Mr Moore tells me great news that my Lady Castlemaine is fallen from Court, and this morning retired. He gives me no account of the reason, but that it is so: for which I am sorry; and yet if the King do it to leave off not only her but all other mistresses, I should be heartily glad of it, that he may fall to look after business. I hear my Lord Digby is condemned at Court for his speech, and that my Lord Chancellor grows great again. With Mr Creed over the water to Lambeth; but could not see the Archbishop's hearse: so over the fields to Southwarke. I spent half an hour in St Mary Overy's Church, where are fine monuments of great antiquity.

4th. Sir Allen Apsley[58] showed the Duke the Lisbon Gazette in Spanish, where the late victory is set down particularly, and to the

---

57 Cardinal Mazarin.
58 Sir Allen Apsley, a faithful adherent to Charles I, after the Restoration was made Falconer to the King, and Almoner to the Duke of York, in whose regiment he bore a commission. He was in 1661 MP for Thetford, and died 1683.

great honour of the English beyond measure. They have since taken back Evora, which was lost to the Spaniards, the English making the assault, and lost not more than three men. Here I learnt that the English foot are highly esteemed all over the world, but the horse not so much, which yet we count among ourselves the best: but they abroad have had no great knowledge of our horse, it seems. To the King's Head ordinary; and a pretty gentleman in our company, who confirms my Lady Castlemaine's being gone from Court, but knows not the reason; he told us of one wipe the Queene a little while ago did give her, when she come in and found the Queene under the dresser's hands, and had been so long: 'I wonder your Majesty,' says she, 'can have the patience to sit so long a-dressing?' – 'I have so much reason to use patience,' says the Queene, 'that I can very well bear with it.' He thinks it may be the Queene hath commanded her to retire, though that is not likely. Thence with Creed to hire a coach to carry us to Hide Parke, to-day there being a general muster of the King's Guards, horse and foot: but they demand so high, that I, spying Mr Cutler the merchant, did take notice of him, and he going into his coach, and telling me that he was going to the muster, I asked and went along with him; where a goodly sight to see so many fine horses and officers, and the King, Duke, and others come by a-horseback, and the two Queenes in the Queene-Mother's coach, (my Lady Castlemaine not being there). And after long being there, I light, and walked to the place where the King, Duke, &c. did stand to see the horse and foot march by and discharge their guns, to show a French Marquisse (for whom this muster was caused) the goodness of our firemen; which indeed was very good, though not without a slip now and then: and one broadside close to our coach we had going out of the Park, even to the nearnesse as to be ready to burn our hairs. Yet methought all these gay men are not the soldiers that must do the King's business, it being such as these that lost the old King all he had, and were beat by the most ordinary fellows that could be. Thence with much ado out of the Park, and through St James's down the waterside over to Lambeth, to see the Archbishop's corps, (who is to be carried away to Oxford on Monday,) but come too late. This day in the Duke's chamber there being a Roman story in the hangings, and upon the standard written these four letters – S. P. Q. R., Sir G. Carteret came to me to know what the meaning of those four letters were; which ignorance is not to be borne in a Privy Counsellor, methinks, what a schoolboy should be whipt for not knowing.

6th. At my office all the morning, writing out a list of the King's ships in my Navy collections with great pleasure.

7th. In Mr Pett's garden I eat some of the first cherries I have eat this year, off the tree where the King himself had been gathering some this morning. Deane tells me what Mr Pett did to-day, that my Lord Bristoll told the King that he will impeach the Chancellor of High Treason: but I find that my Lord Bristoll hath undone himself already in everybody's opinion, and now he endeavours to raise dust to put out other men's eyes, as well as his own; but I hope it will not take, in consideration merely that it is hard for a Prince to spare an experienced old officer, be he never so corrupt; though I hope this man is not so, as some report him to be. He tells me that Don John is yet alive, and not killed, as was said, in the great victory against the Spaniards in Portugall of late.

9th. Sir W. Pen tells me, my Lady Castlemaine was at Court, for all this talk this week; but it seems the King is stranger than ordinary to her.

10th. I met Pierce the chirurgeon, who tells me that for certain the King is grown colder to my Lady Castlemaine than ordinary, and that he believes he begins to love the Queene, and do make much of her, more than he used to do. Mr Coventry tells me that my Lord Bristoll hath this day impeached my Lord Chancellor in the House of Lords of High Treason. The chief of the articles are these: 1st. That he should be the occasion of the peace made with Holland lately upon such disadvantageous terms, and that he was bribed to it. 2nd. That Dunkirke was also sold by his advice chiefly, so much to the damage of England. 3rd. That he had £6000 given him for the drawing-up or promoting of the Irish declaration lately, concerning the division of the lands there. 4th. He did carry on the design of the Portugall match, so much to the prejudice of the Crown of England, notwithstanding that he knew the Queene is not capable of bearing children. 5th. That the Duke's marrying of his daughter was a practice of his, thereby to raise his family; and that it was done by indiscreet courses. 6th. As to the breaking-off of the match with Parma, in which he was employed at the very time when the match with Portugall was made up here, which he took as a great slur to him, and so it was; and that, indeed, is the chief occasion of all this fewde. 7th. That he hath endeavoured to bring in Popery, and wrote to the Pope for a cap for a subject of the King of England's (my Lord Aubigny[59]); and some say that he lays it to the Chancellor, that a good Protestant Secretary, (Sir Edward Nicholas) was laid aside, and a Papist, Sir H. Bennet, put in his room: which is very strange, when the last of these two is his own creature, and such an enemy accounted to the Chancellor, that they never did nor do agree; and all the world did judge the Chancellor to be falling from the time that Sir H. Bennet was brought in. Besides my Lord Bristoll being a Catholique himself, all this is very strange. These are the main of the Articles. Upon which my Lord Chancellor desired the noble Lord that brought in these Articles, would sign to them with his hand; which my Lord Bristoll did presently. Then the House did order that the Judges should, against Monday next, bring in their opinion, Whether these articles are treason, or no? and next, they would know, Whether they were brought in regularly or no, without leave of the Lords' House?

11th. By barge to St Mary's Creeke; where Commissioner Pett, (doubtful of the growing greatnesse of Portsmouth by the finding of those creekes there,) do design a wett docke at no great charge, and yet no little one; he thinks towards £10,000. And the place, indeed, is likely to be a very fit place, when the King hath money to do it with.

13th. I walked to the Temple; and there, from my cousin Roger, hear that the Judges have this day brought in their answer to the Lords, That the articles against my Lord Chancellor are not Treason; and to-morrow they are to bring in their arguments to the House for the same. This day also the King did send by my Lord Chamberlain to the Lords, to tell them from him, that the most of the articles against my Lord Chancellor he himself knows to be false. I met the Queene-Mother walking in the Pell Mell, led by my Lord St Alban's. And finding many coaches at the Gate, I found upon enquiry that the Duchesse is brought to bed of a boy; and hearing that the King and Queene are rode abroad with the Ladies of Honour to the Parke, and seeing a great crowd of gallants staying here to see their return, I also

59 Brother to the Duke of Lennox, and Almoner to the King.

staid walking up and down. By and by the King and Queene, who looked in this dress (a white laced waistcoate and a crimson short pettycoate, and her hair dressed *à la negligence*) mighty pretty; and the King rode hand in hand with her. Here was also my Lady Castlemaine rode among the rest of the ladies; but the King took, methought, no notice of her; nor when she light, did any body press (as she seemed to expect, and staid for it,) to take her down, but was taken down by her own gentlemen. She looked mighty out of humour, and had a yellow plume in her hat, (which all took notice of,) and yet is very handsome, but very melancholy: nor did any body speak to her, or she so much as smile or speak to any body. I followed them up into White Hall, and into the Queene's presence, where all the ladies walked, talking and fiddling with their hats and feathers, and changing and trying one another's by one another's heads, and laughing. But it was the finest sight to me, considering their great beautys, and dress, that ever I did see in all my life. But, above all, Mrs Stewart in this dresse, with her hat cocked and a red plume, with her sweet eye, little Roman nose, and excellent taille, is now the greatest beauty I ever saw, I think, in my life; and, if ever woman can, do exceed my Lady Castlemaine, at least in this dress: nor do I wonder if the King changes, which I verily believe is the reason of his coldness to my Lady Castlemaine.

14th. This day I hear the Judges, according to order yesterday, did bring into the Lords' House their reasons of their judgments in the business between my Lord Bristoll and the Chancellor; and the Lords do concur with the Judges that the articles are not Treason, nor regularly brought into the House, and so voted that a Committee should be chosen to examine them; but nothing to be done therein till the next sitting of this Parliament, (which is likely to be adjourned in a day or two,) and in the mean time the two Lords to remain without prejudice done to either of them.

15th. Captain Grove come and dined with me. He told me of discourse very much to my honour, both as to my care and ability, happening at the Duke of Albemarle's table the other day, both from the Duke and the Duchesse themselves; and how I paid so much a year to him whose place it was of right, and that Mr Coventry did report this of me.

21st. This day the Parliament kept a fast for the present unseasonable weather.

22nd. To my Lord Crewe's. My Lord not being come home, I met and staid below with Captn. Ferrers, who was come to wait upon my Lady Jemimah to St James's, she being one of the four ladies that hold up the mantle at the christening this afternoon of the Duke's child (a boy). In discourse of the ladies at Court, Captn. Ferrers tells me that my Lady Castlemaine is now as great again as ever she was; and that her going away was only a fit of her own upon some slighting words of the King, so that she called for her coach at a quarter of an hour's warning, and went to Richmond; and the King the next morning, under pretence of going a-hunting, went to see her and make friends, and never was a-hunting at all. After which she came back to Court, and commands the King as much as ever, and hath and doth what she will. No longer ago than last night, there was a private entertainment made for the King and Queene at the Duke of Buckingham's, and she was not invited: but being at my Lady Suffolk's,[60] her aunt's (where my Lady Jemimah and Lord Sandwich dined,) yesterday, she was heard to say, 'Well, much good may it do them, and for all that I will be as merry as they': and so she went home and caused a great supper to be prepared. And after the King had been with the Queene at Wallingford House,[61] he come to my Lady Castlemaine's, and was there all night, and my Lord Sandwich with him. He tells me he believes that, as soon as the King can get a husband for Mrs Stewart, however, my Lady Castlemaine's nose will be out of joynt; for that she comes to be in great esteem, and is more handsome than she. Wotten tells me the reason of Harris's[62] going from Sir Wm. Davenant's house is, that he grew very proud and demanded £20 for himself extraordinary, more than Betterton or any body else, upon every new play, and £10 upon every revive which with other things Sir W. Davenant would not give him, and so he swore he would

60 Barbara, second wife of James Earl of Suffolk, eldest daughter of Sir Edward Villiers, and widow of Sir Richard Wentworth. She died December 1681, leaving one daughter, Elizabeth, who married Sir Thomas Felton, Bart.

61 Wallingford House stood on the site of the present Admiralty: it originally belonged to the Knollys family, and during the Protectorate the office for granting passes to persons going abroad was kept there.

62 Joseph Harris, a celebrated actor, who first appeared at the Theatre in Lincoln's Inn Fields, 1662. He probably died or left the stage about 1676.

never act there more, in expectation of being received in the other House; but the King will not suffer it, upon Sir W. Davenant's desire that he would not, for then he might shut up house, and that is true. He tells me that his going is at present a great loss to the House, and that he fears he hath a stipend from the other House privately. He tells me that the fellow grew very proud of late, the King and every body else crying him up so high, and that above Betterton he being a more ayery man, as he is indeed. But yet Betterton, he says, they all say do act some parts that none but himself can do. I hear that the Moores have made some attaques upon the outworks of Tangier; but my Lord Teviott, with the loss of about 200 men, did beat them off, and killed many of them. To-morrow the King and Queene for certain go down to Tunbridge. But the King comes back again against Monday to raise the Parliament.

25th. Having intended this day to go to Banstead Downes to see a famous race, I sent Will. to get himself ready to go with me: but I hear it is put off; because the Lords do sit in Parliament to-day. After some debate, Creed and I resolved to go to Clapham, to Mr Gauden's.[63] When I come there, the first thing was to show me his house, which is almost built. I find it very regular and finely contrived, and the gardens and offices about it as convenient and as full of good variety as ever I saw in my life. It is true he hath been censured for laying out so much money but he tells me that he built it for his brother, who is since dead, (the Bishop[64]) who when he should come to be Bishop of Winchester, which he was promised, (to which bishopricke at present there is no house), he did intend to dwell here. By and by to dinner, and in comes Mr Creed; I saluted his lady and the young ladies, and his sister, the Bishop's widow; who was, it seems, Sir W. Russel's daughter, the Treasurer of the Navy; who I find to be very well-bred, and a woman of excellent discourse. Towards the evening we bade them adieu! and took horse; being resolved that, instead of the race which fails us, we would go to Epsom. When we come there we could hear of no lodging, the town so full; but which was better, I went towards Ashsted, and there we got a lodging in a little hole we could not stand upright in. While

63 Dennis Gauden, Victualler to the Navy; subsequently knighted when Sheriff of London.
64 Of Exeter.

supper was getting I walked up and down behind my cosen Pepys's house that was, which I find comes little short of what I took it to be when I was a little boy.

26th (Lord's day). Up and to the Wells, where a great store of citizens, which was the greatest part of the company, though there were some others of better quality. Thence I walked to Mr Minnes's house, and thence to Durdan's and walked within the Court Yard and to the Bowling-green, where I have seen so much mirth in my time; but now no family in it, (my Lord Barkeley, whose it is, being with his family at London.) Then rode through Epsom, the whole town over, seeing the various companys that were there walking; which was very pleasant to see how they are there without knowing what to do, but only in the morning to drink waters. But Lord! to see how many I met there of citizens, that I could not have thought to have seen there; that they had ever had it in their heads or purses to go down thither. We went through Nonesuch Parke to the house, and there viewed as much as we could of the outside, and looked through the great gates, and found a noble court, and altogether believe it to have been a very noble house, and a delicate parke about it, where just now there was a doe killed for the King to carry up to Court.

27th. We rode hard home, and set up our horses at Fox Hall, and I by water (observing the King's barge attending his going to the House this day) home, it being about one o'clock. By water to Westminster, and there come most luckily to the Lords' House, as the House of Commons were going into the Lords' House, and there I crowded in along with the Speaker, and got to stand close behind him, where he made his speech to the King (who sat with his crown on and robes, and so all the Lords in their robes, a fine sight); wherein he told his Majesty what they have done this Parliament, and now offered for his royall consent. The greatest matters were a bill for the Lord's day, (which it seems the Lords have lost, and so cannot be passed, at which the Commons are displeased.) The bills against Conventicles and Papists (but it seems the Lords have not passed them), and giving his Majesty four entire subsidys; which last, with about twenty smaller Acts, were passed with this form: the Clerk of the House reads the title of the bill, and then looks at the end and there finds (writ by the King I suppose) '*Le Roy le veult*,' and that he reads. And to others he reads, '*Soit fait comme vous desirez.*' And to the

Subsidys, as well that for the Commons, I mean the layety, as for the Clergy, the King writes, '*Le Roy remerciant les Seigneurs et Prelats et accepte leur benevolences.*' The Speaker's speech was far from any oratory, but was as plain (though good matter) as any thing could be, and void of elocution. After the bills passed, the King, sitting on his throne, with his speech writ in a paper which he held in his lap, and scarce looked off of it all the time he made his speech to them, giving them thanks for their subsidys, of which, had he not need, he would not have asked or received them; and that need, not from any extravagancys of his, he was sure, in any thing, but the disorders of the times compelling him to be at greater charge than he hoped for the future, by their care in their country, he should be: and that for his family expenses and others, he would labour however to retrench in many things convenient, and would have all others to do so too. He desired that nothing of old faults should be remembered, or severity for the same used to any in the country, it being his desire to have all forgot as well as forgiven. But, however, to use all care in suppressing any tumults, &c.; assuring them that the restless spirits of his and their adversaries have great expectations of something to be done this summer. And promised that though the Acts about Conventicles and Papists, were not ripe for passing this Sessions, yet he would take care himself that neither of them should in this intervall be encouraged to the endangering of the peace; and that at their next meeting he would himself prepare two bills for them concerning them. So he concluded, that for the better proceeding of justice he did think fit to make this a Sessions, and to prorogue them to the 16th of March next. His speech was very plain, nothing at all of spirit in it, nor spoke with any; but rather on the contrary imperfectly, repeating many times his words though he read all: which I am sorry to see, it having not been hard for him to have got all the speech without booke. So they all went away, the King out of the House at the upper end, he being by and by to go to Tunbridge to the Queene; and I in the Painted Chamber spoke with my Lord Sandwich while he was putting off his robes, who tells me he will now hasten down into the country. By water to White Hall, and walked over the Parke to St James's, but missed Mr Coventry; and so out again, and there the Duke was coming along the Pell-Mell. It being a little darkish, I staid not to take notice of him, but went directly back again. And in our walk over the Parke, one of the

Duke's footmen come running behind us, and come looking just in our faces to see who we were, and went back again. What his meaning is I know not, but was fearful that I might not go far enough with my hat off.

29th. To Deptford, reading by the way a most ridiculous play, a new one, called *The Politician cheated*.[65]

30th. To Woolwich, and there come Sir G. Carteret, and then by water back to Deptford, where we dined with him at his house. I find his little daughter Betty,[66] that was in hanging sleeves but a month or two ago, and is a very little young child, married, and to whom, but to young Scott,[67] son to Madam Catharine Scott,[68] that was so long in law, and at whose trial I was with her husband; he pleading that it was unlawfully got and would not own it, but it seems a little before his death he did owne the child, and hath left him his estate, not long since. So Sir G. Carteret hath struck up of a sudden a match with him for his little daughter. He hath about £2000 per annum; and it seems Sir G. C. hath by this means over-reached Sir H. Bennet, who did endeavour to get this gentleman for a sister of his. By this means Sir G. Carteret hath married two daughters this year both very well.[69] The towne talk this day is of nothing but the great foot-race run this day on Banstead Downes, between Lee, the Duke of Richmond's footman, and a tyler, a famous runner. And Lee hath beat him though the King and Duke of York and all men almost did bet three or four to one upon the tyler's head.

31st. To the Exchange, where I met Dr Pierce, who tells me of his good luck to get to be groom of the Privy-Chamber to the Queene, and without my Lord Sandwich's help, but only by his good fortune, meeting a man that hath let him have his right for a small matter about £60 for which he can every day have £400. But he tells me my Lord hath lost much honour in standing so long and so much for

65 A comedy by Alexander Green.
66 Her name was Caroline. Elizabeth died unmarried.
67 Thomas, eldest son of Sir Thomas Scott, of Scott's Hall, in the parish of Smeeth, Kent.
68 Prince Rupert was supposed to have intrigued with Mrs Scott, and was probably the father of the child.
69 The other daughter was Anne, wife of Sir Nicholas Slaning, KB.

that coxcomb Pickering, and at last not carrying it for him; but hath his name struck out by the King and Queene themselves after he had been in ever since the Queene's coming. But he tells me he believes that either Sir H. Bennet, my Lady Castlemaine, or Sir Charles Barkeley had received some money for the place, and so the King could not disappoint them, but was forced to put out this fool rather than a better man. And I am sorry to hear what he tells me that Sir Charles Barkeley hath still such power over the King, as to be able to fetch him from the Council-table to my Lady Castlemaine when he pleases. He tells me also, as a friend, the great injury that he thinks I do myself by being so severe in the Yards, and contracting the ill-will of the whole Navy for those offices, singly upon myself. Now I discharge a good conscience therein, and I tell him that no man can (nor do he say any say it,) charge me with doing wrong; but rather do as many good offices as any man. They think, he says, that I have a mind to get a good name with the King and Duke, who he tells me do not consider any such thing; but I shall have as good thanks to let all alone, and do as the rest. But I believe the contrary; and yet I told him I never go to the Duke alone, as others do, to talk of my own services. However, I will make use of his council, and take some course to prevent having the single ill-will of the office. Mr Grant showed me letters of Sir William Petty's, wherein he says, that his vessel which he hath built upon two keeles, (a modell whereof, built for the King, he showed me) hath this month won a wager of £50 in sailing between Dublin and Holyhead with the pacquett-boat, the best ship or vessel the King hath there; and he offers to lay with any vessel in the world. It is about thirty ton in burden, and carries thirty men, with good accommodation, (as much more as any ship of her burden,) and so any vessel of this figure shall carry more men, with better accommodation by half, than any other ship. This carries also ten guns, of about five tons weight. In their coming back from Holyhead they started together, and this vessel come to Dublin by five at night, and the pacquett-boat not before eight the next morning; and when they come they did believe that this vessel had been drowned, or at least behind, not thinking she could have lived in that sea. Strange things are told of this vessel, and he concludes his letter with this position, 'I only affirm that the perfection of sayling lies in my principle, finde it out who can.'

August 8th. I with Mr Coventry down to the waterside, talking, wherein I see so much goodness and endeavours of doing the King service, that I do more and more admire him.

9th. To church, and heard Mr Mills (who is lately returned out of the country, and it seems was fetched in by many of the parishioners, with great state,) preach upon the authority of the ministers, upon these words, 'We are therefore embassadors of Christ.' Wherein, among other high expressions, he said, that such a learned man used to say, that if a minister of the word and an angell should meet him together, he would salute the minister first; which methought was a little too high. This day I begun to make use of the silver pen (Mr Coventry did give me,) in writing of this sermon, taking only the heads of it in Latin, which I shall, I think, continue to do.

10th. To the Committee of Tangier, where my Lord Sandwich, my Lord Peterborough, (whom I have not seen before since his coming back,) Sir W. Compton, and Mr Povy. Our discourse about supplying my Lord Teviott with money, wherein I am sorry to see, though they do not care for him, yet they are willing to let him for civility and compliment only have money also without expecting any account of it; and he being such a cunning fellow as he is, the King is like to pay dear for our courtier's ceremony. Thence by coach with my Lords Peterborough and Sandwich to my Lord Peterborough's house; and there, after an hour's looking over some fine books of the Italian buildings, with fine cuts, and also my Lord Peterborough's bowes and arrows, of which he is a great lover, we sat down to dinner, my Lady[70] coming down to dinner also, and there being Mr Williamson,[71] that belongs to Sir H. Bennet, whom I find a pretty understanding and accomplished man, but a little conceited. Yesterday, I am told, that Sir J. Lenthall,[72] in Southwarke did apprehend about one hundred Quakers, and other such people, and hath sent some of them to the gaole at Kingston, it being now the time of the

70 Penelope, daughter of Barnabas, Earl of Thomond, Countess of Peterborough.

71 Joseph Williamson, Keeper of the Paper Office at White Hall, and in 1665 made Under Secretary of State, and soon afterwards knighted: and in 1674 he became Secretary of State, which situation he retained four years. He represented Thetford and Rochester in several Parliaments, and was in 1678 President of the Royal Society. Died 1701.

72 Son to the Speaker, and Governor of Windsor Castle under Cromwell. Died 1681.

Assizes. Dr Pierce tells me the Queene is grown a very debonnaire lady; but my Lady Castlemaine, who rules the King in matters of state, and do what she list with him, he believes is now falling quite out of favour. After the Queene is come back she goes to the Bath, and so to Oxford, where great entertainments are making for her. This day I am told that my Lord Bristoll hath warrants issued out against him, to have carried him to the Tower, but he is fled away or hid himself. So much the Chancellor hath got the better of him.

13th. Met with Mr Hoole[73] my old acquaintance of Magdalene, and walked with him an hour in the Parke, discoursing chiefly of Sir Samuel Morland, whose lady[74] is gone into France. It seems he buys ground and a farm in that country, and lays out money upon building, and God knows what! so that most of the money he sold his pension of £500 per annum for to Sir Arthur Slingsby,[75] is believed is gone. It seems he hath very great promises from the King, and Hoole hath seen some of the King's letters, under his own hand, to Morland, promising him great things; (and among others, the order of the Garter, as Sir Samuel says,) but his lady thought it below her to ask any thing at the King's first coming, believing the King would do it of himself, when as Hoole do really think if he had asked to be Secretary of State at the King's first coming, he might have had it. And the other day at her going into France, she did speak largely to the King herself, how her husband hath failed of what his Majesty had promised, and she was sure intended him; and the King did promise still, as he is a King and a gentleman, to be as good as his word in a little time, to a tittle: but I never believe it.

21st. Meeting with Mr Creed he told me how my Lord Teviott hath received another attaque from Guyland at Tangier with 10,000 men, and at last, as is said, is come, after a personal treaty with him, to a good understanding and peace with him.

---

73 William, son of Robert Hoole of Walkeringham, admitted of Magdalene College June 1648.

74 Susanne de Milleville, daughter of Daniel de Milleville, Baron of Boessen in France, naturalised 1662. When she died I cannot learn, but Sir Samuel Morland survived a second and a third wife, both buried in Westminster Abbey.

75 A younger son of Sir Guildford Slingsby, Comptroller of the Navy, knighted by Charles II, and afterwards created a Baronet at Brussels 1657; which title has long been extinct.

23rd. To church, and so home to my wife; and with her read *Iter Boreale*,[76] a poem, made first at the King's coming home; but I never read it before, and now like it pretty well, but not so as it was cried up.

24th. At my Lord Sandwich's, where I was a good while alone with my Lord; and I perceive he confides in me and loves me as he uses to do, and tells me his condition, which is now very well; all I fear is that he will not live within compass. There come to him this morning his prints of the river Tagus and the City of Lisbon, which he measured with his own hand, and printed by command of the King. My Lord pleases himself with it, but methinks it ought to have been better done than by Jobing. Besides I put him upon having some took off upon white sattin, which he ordered presently. I offered my Lord my accounts, and did give him up his old bond for £500 and took a new one of him for £700, which I am by lending him more money to make up: and am glad of it.

25th. This noon going to the Exchange, I met a fine fellow with trumpets before him in Leadenhall Street, and upon enquiry I find that he is the clerke of the City Market; and three or four men carried each of them an arrow of a pound weight in their hands. It seems this Lord Mayor[77] begins again an old custome, that upon the three first days of Bartholomew Fayre, the first, there is a match of wrestling, which was done, and the Lord Mayor there and the Aldermen in Moorefields yesterday: second day, shooting: and to-morrow hunting. And this officer of course is to perform this ceremony of riding through the city, I think to proclaim or challenge any to shoot. It seems the people of the faire cry out upon it as a great hindrance to them.

26th. To White Hall, where the Court full of waggons and horses, the King and Court going this day out towards the Bath. Pleased to see Captn. Hickes come to me with a list of all the officers of Deptford Yard, wherein he, being a high old Cavalier, do give me an

---

76 Robert Wild, a Nonconformist Divine, published a poem in 1660, upon Monk's march from Scotland to London, called *Iter Boreale*, and Wood mentions three others of the same name by Eades, Corbett, and Marten, it having been a favourite subject at that time
77 Sir John Frederic.

account of every one of them to their reproach in all respects, and discovers many of their knaverys; and tells me, and so I thank God I hear every where, that my name is up for a good husband to the King, and a good man, for which I bless God; and that he did this by particular direction of Mr Coventry.

28th. Cold all night and this morning, and a very great frost they say abroad, which is much, having had no summer at all almost.

September 2nd. To dinner with my Lord Mayor and the Aldermen, and a very great dinner and most excellent venison, but it almost made me sick by not daring to drink wine. After dinner into a withdrawing-room; and there we talked, among other things, of the Lord Mayor's sword. They tell me this sword is at least a hundred or two hundred years old; and another that he hath, which is called the Black Sword, which the Lord Mayor wears when he mournes, but properly is their Lenten sword to wear upon Good Friday and other Lent days, is older than that. Mr Lewellin, lately come from Ireland, tells me how the English interest falls mightily there, the Irish party being too great, so that most of the old rebells are found innocent, and their lands, which were forfeited and bought or given to the English, are restored to them; which gives great discontent there among the English. Going through the City, my Lord Mayor told me how the piller set up by Exeter House is only to show where the pipes of water run to the City; and observed that this City is as well watered as any city in the world, and that the bringing of water to the City hath cost it first and last above £300,000; but by the new building, and the building of St James's by my Lord St Albans, which is now about (and which the City stomach I perceive highly, but dare not oppose it,) were it now to be done, it would not be done for a million of money.

4th. To Westminster Hall, and there bought the first news books of L'Estrange's[78] writing, he beginning this week; and makes, methinks, but a simple beginning. This day I read a Proclamation for calling in and commanding every body to apprehend my Lord Bristoll.

78 Roger L'Estrange, author of numerous pamphlets and periodical papers. He was Licenser of the Press to Charles II and his successor; and MP for Winchester in James II's Parliament. Died 1704, aged 88.

5th. I did inform myself well in things relating to the East Indys; both of the country, and the disappointment the King met with the last voyage, by the knavery of the Portugall Viceroy, and the inconsiderableness of the place of Bombaim,[79] if we had had it. But, above all things, it seems strange to me that matters should not be understood before they went out; and also that such a thing as this, which was expected to be one of the best parts of the Queene's portion, should not be better understood; it being, if we had it, but a poor place, and not really so as was described to our King in the draught of it, but a poor little island; whereas they made the King and Lord Chancellor, and other learned men about the King believe that that, and other islands which are near it were all one piece; and so the draught was drawn and presented to the King, and believed by the King, and expected to prove so when our men come thither; but it is quite otherwise.

12th. Up betimes, and by water to White Hall: and thence to Sir Philip Warwick, and there had half an hour's private discourse with him: and did give him some good satisfaction in our Navy matters, and he also me, as to the money paid and due to the Navy; so as he makes me assured by particulars, that Sir G. Carteret is paid within £80,000 every farthing that we owe to this day, nay to Michaelmas day next have demanded; and that, I am sure is above £50,000 more than truly our expences have been, whatever is become of the money. Home with great content that I have thus begun an acquaintance with him, who is a great man, and a man of as much business as any man in England; which I will endeavour to deserve and keep.

22nd. This day the King and Queene are to come to Oxford. I hear my Lady Castlemaine is for certain gone to Oxford to meet him, having lain within here at home this week or two, supposed to have miscarried; but for certain is as great in favour as heretofore; at least Mrs Sarah at my Lord's, who hears all from their own family, do say so. Every day brings news of the Turke's advance into Germany, to the awakeing of all the Christian Princes thereabouts, and possessing himself of Hungary.

79 Bombay.

24th. I went forth by water to Sir Philip Warwick's, where I was with him a pretty while; and in discourse he tells me, and made it appear to me that the King cannot be in debt to the Navy at this time £5000; and it is my opinion that Sir G. Carteret do owe the King money, and yet the whole Navy debt paid. Thence I parted, being doubtful of myself that I have not spoke with the gravity and weight that I ought to do in so great a business. But I rather hope it is my doubtfulness of myself, and the haste which he was in, some very great personages waiting for him without, while he was with me, that made him willing to be gone.

28th. To White Hall, where Sir J. Minnes and I did spend an hour in the Gallery, looking upon the pictures, in which he hath some judgement. And by and by the Commissioners for Tangier met: and there my Lord Teviott, together with Captain Cuttance, Captain Evans, and Jonas Moore, sent to that purpose, did bring us a brave draught of the Mole to be built there; and report that it is likely to be the most considerable place the King of England hath in the world; and so I am apt to think it will. After discourse of this, and of supplying the garrison with some more horse, we rose; and Sir J. Minnes and I home again, finding the street about our house full, Sir R. Ford beginning his shrievalty to-day: and, what with his and our houses being new painted, the street begins to look a great deal better than it did, and more gracefull. News that the King comes to town for certain on Thursday next from his great progress.

30th. In the afternoon by water to White Hall, to the Tangier Committee; where my Lord Teviott; which grieves me to see that his accounts being to be examined by us, there are none of the great men at the Board that in compliment will except against any thing in them, and so none of the little persons dare do it: so the King is abused.

October 5th. My Lord Sandwich sent a messenger to know whether the King intends to come to Newmarket, as is talked, that he may be ready to entertain him at Hinchingbroke.

12th. At St James's we attended the Duke all of us. And there, after my discourse, Mr Coventry of his own accord begun to tell the Duke how he found that discourse abroad did run to his prejudice about the fees that he took, and how he sold places and other things wherein he desired to appeal to his Highness, whether he did any thing more than what his predecessors did, and appealed to us all. So Sir G. Carteret did answer that some fees were heretofore taken, but what he knows not; only that selling of places never was nor ought to be countenanced. So Mr Coventry very hotly answered to Sir G. Carteret, and appealed to himself whether he was not one of the first that put him upon looking after this business of fees, and that he told him that Mr Smith should say that he made £5000 the first year, and he believed he made £7000. This Sir G. Carteret denied, and said, that if he did say so he told a lie, for he could not, nor did know, that ever he did make that profit of his place; but that he believes he might say, £2500 the first year. Mr Coventry instanced in another thing particularly wherein Sir G. Carteret did advise with him about the selling of the Auditor's place of the stores, when in the beginning there was an intention of creating such an office. This he confessed, but with some lessening of the tale Mr Coventry told, it being only for a respect to my Lord FitzHarding.[80] In fine, Mr Coventry did put into the Duke's hand a list of above 250 places that he did give without receiving one farthing, so much as his ordinary fees for them, upon his life and oath; and that since the Duke's establishment of fees he had never received one token more of any man; and that in his whole life he never conditioned or discoursed of any consideration from any commanders since he come to the Navy. And afterwards, my Lord Barkeley merrily discoursing that he wished his profit greater than it was, and that he did believe that he had got £50,000 since he come in, Mr Coventry did openly declare that his Lordship, or any of us, should have not only all he had got, but all that he had in the world, (and yet he did not come a beggar into the Navy, nor would yet be thought to speak in any contempt of his Royall Highness's bounty,) and should have a year to consider of it too, for £25,000. The Duke's answer was, that he wished we all had made more profit than we had of our places, and that we had all of us got as much as one man below stayres in the Court, which he presently named, and it was Sir George Lane. [81]

<hr>

80 Sir Charles Berkeley, mentioned before, created Lord Berkeley of Rathdown and Viscount Fitzharding in Ireland, second son to Sir Charles Berkeley of Bruton, co. Somerset; afterwards made an English peer by the titles of Lord Botetourt and Earl of Falmouth, and killed in the great sea-fight, June 1665.
81 One of the Clerks of the Privy Council, and Secretary to the Marquis of Ormond.

13th. I find at Court, that either the King is doubtful of some disturbance, or else would seem so, (and I have reason to hope it is no worse,) by his commanding little commanders of castles, &c. to repair to their charges; and mustering the Guards the other day himself, where he found reason to dislike their condition to my Lord Gerard, finding so many absent men, or dead pays. My Lady Castlemaine, I hear, is in as great favour as ever, and the King supped with her the very first night he come from Bath: and last night and the night before supped with her; when there being a chine of beef to roast, and the tide rising into their kitchen that it could not be roasted there, and the cook telling her of it, she answered 'Zounds! she must set the house on fire but it should be roasted!' So it was carried to Mrs Sarah's husband's, and there it was roasted.

After dinner my wife and I, by Mr Rawlinson's conduct, to the Jewish Synagogue: where the men and boys in their vayles, and the women behind a lettice out of sight; and some things stand up, which I believe is their law, in a press to which all coming in do bow; and at the putting on their vayles do say something, to which others that hear the Priest do cry Amen, and the party do kiss his vayle. Their service all in a singing way, and in Hebrew. And anon their Laws that they take out of the press are carried by several men, four or five several burthens in all, and they do relieve one another; and whether it is that every one desires to have the carrying of it, thus they carried it round about the room while such a service is singing. And in the end they had a prayer for the King, in which they pronounced his name in Portugall; but the prayer, like the rest, in Hebrew. But, Lord! to see the disorder, laughing, sporting, and no attention, but confusion in all their service, more like brutes than people knowing the true God, would make a man forswear ever seeing them more: and indeed I never did see so much, or could have imagined there had been any religion in the whole world so absurdly performed as this.

17th. Some discourse of the Queene's being very sick if not dead, the Duke and Duchesse of York being sent for betimes this morning to come to White Hall to her.

18th. The parson, Mr Mills, I perceive, did not know whether to pray for the Queene or no, and so said nothing about her; which makes me fear she is dead. But enquiring of Sir J. Minnes, he told me that he heard she was better last night.

19th. Waked with a very high wind, and said to my wife, 'I pray God I hear not of the death of any great person, this wind is so high!' fearing that the Queene might be dead. So up; and going by coach with Sir W. Batten and Sir J. Minnes to St James's, they tell me that Sir W. Compton, who it is true had been a little sickly for a week or fortnight, but was very well upon Friday at night last at the Tangier Committee with us, was dead, – died yesterday: at which I was most exceedingly surprised, he being, and so all the world saying that he was, one of the worthyest men and best officers of State now in England; and so in my conscience he was: of the best temper, valour, ability of mind, integrity, worth, fine person, and diligence of any one man he hath left behind him in the three kingdoms, and yet not forty years old, or if so, that is all. I find the sober men of the Court troubled for him; and yet not so as to hinder or lessen their mirth, talking, laughing, and eating, drinking, and doing every thing else, just as if there was no such thing.

Coming to St James's, I hear that the Queene did sleep five hours pretty well to-night, and that she waked and gargled her mouth, and to sleep again; but that her pulse beats fast, beating twenty to the King's or my Lady Suffolk's eleven; but not so strong as it was. It seems she was so ill as to be shaved and pidgeons put to her feet, and to have the extreme unction given her by the priests, who were so long about it that the doctors were angry. The King they all say is most fondly disconsolate for her, and weeps by her, which makes her weep; which one this day told me he reckons a good sign, for that it carries away some rheume from the head. To the Coffee-house in Cornhill; where much talk about the Turke's proceedings, and that the plague is got to Amsterdam, brought by a ship from Argier; and it is also carried to Hambrough. The Duke says the King purposes to forbid any of their ships coming into the river. The Duke also told us of several Christian commanders (French) gone over to the Turkes to serve them; and upon enquiry I find that the King of France do by this aspire to the Empire, and so to get the Crowne of Spayne also upon the death of the King, which is very probable, it seems.

20th. This evening at my Lord's lodgings, Mrs Sarah talking with my wife and I how the Queene do, and how the King tends her being so ill. She tells that the Queene's sickness is the spotted fever; that she was as full of the spots as a leopard: which is very strange that it should be no more known; but perhaps it is not so. And that the King do seem to take it much to heart, for that he hath wept before her; but, for all that, that he hath not missed one night since she was sick, of supping with my Lady Castlemaine; which I believe is true, for she says that her husband hath dressed the suppers every night; and I confess I saw him myself coming through the street dressing up a great supper to-night, which Sarah says is also for the King and her; which is a very strange thing.

22nd. This morning, hearing that the Queene grows worse again, I sent to stop the making of my velvet cloak, till I see whether she lives or dies.

23rd. The Queene slept pretty well last night, but her fever continues upon her still. It seems she hath never a Portuguese doctor here.

24th. The Queene is in a good way of recovery; and Sir Francis Pridgeon[82] hath got great honour by it, it being all imputed to his cordiall, which in her dispaire did give her rest, and brought her to some hopes of recovery. It seems that, after much talk of troubles and a plot, something is found in the North that a party was to rise, and some persons that were to command it, as I find in a letter that Mr Coventry read to-day about it from those parts.

26th. Dr. Pierce tells me that the Queene is in a way to be pretty well again, but that her delirium in her head continues still; that she talks idle not by fits, but always, which in some lasts a week after so high a fever, in some more, and in some for ever; that this morning she talked mightily that she was brought to bed, and that she wondered that she should be delivered without pain and without being sick, and that she was troubled that her boy was but an ugly boy. But the King being by, said 'No, it is a very pretty boy.' – 'Nay,' says she, 'if it be like you it is a fine boy indeed, and I would be very well pleased with it.' They say that the Turkes go on apace, and that my Lord Castlehaven[83] is going

82 Vertue (according to Walpole) had seen a portrait of Dr Prujeon painted by Streater, and a print of 'Opinion sitting on a tree', thus inscribed: '*Viro clariss. Lno Francisco Prujeano Medico, omnium bonarum artium et elegantiarum fautori et admiratori summo; DD. D. H. Peacham.*' He was President of the College of Physicians, 1653.
83 The eldest son of the infamous Earl of Castlehaven, had a new creation to his father's forfeited titles, in 1634, and died, without issue, 1684. He had served with distinction under the Duke of Ormond, and afterwards joined Charles II, at Paris.

to raise 10,000 men here for to go against him; that the King of France do offer to assist the Empire upon condition that he may be their Generalissimo, and the Dolphin chosen King of the Romans: and it is said that the King of France do occasion this difference among the Christian Princes of the Empire, which gives the Turke such advantages. They say also that the King of Spayne is making all imaginable force against Portugall again.

27th. Mr Coventry tells me to-day that the Queene had a very good night last night; but yet it is strange that still she raves and talks of little more than of her having of children, and fancys now that she hath three children, and that the girle is very like the King. And this morning about five o'clock, the physician feeling her pulse, thinking to be better able to judge, she being still and asleep, waked her, and the first word she said was, 'How do the children?'

29th. To Guild Hall; and meeting with Mr Proby, (Sir R. Ford's son,) and Lieutenant-Colonel Baron, a City commander, we went up and down to see the tables; where under every salt there was a bill of fare, and at the end of the table the persons proper for the table. Many were the tables, but none in the Hall but the Mayor's and the Lords of the Privy Council that had napkins or knives, which was very strange. We went into the Buttry, and there stayed and talked, and then into the Hall again: and there wine was offered and they drunk, I only drinking some hypocras, which do not break my vowe, it being, to the best of my present judgement, only a mixed compound drink, and not any wine. If I am mistaken, God forgive me! but I hope and do think I am not. By and by met with Creed; and we, with the others, went within the several Courts, and there saw the tables prepared for the Ladies and Judges and Bishops: all great sign of a great dinner to come. By and by about one o'clock, before the Lord Mayor come, come into the Hall, from the room where they were first led into, the Lord Chancellor (Archbishop before him,) with the Lords of the Council, and other Bishopps, and they to dinner. Anon comes the Lord Mayor, who went up to the lords, and then to the other tables to bid wellcome; and so all to dinner. I set near Proby, Baron, and Creed at the Merchant Strangers' table; where ten good dishes to a messe, with plenty of wine of all sorts, of which I drunk none; but it was very unpleasing that we had no napkins nor change of trenchers, and drunk out of earthen pitchers and wooden dishes. It happened that after the lords had half dined, come the French Embassador up to the lords' table, where he was to have sat; he would not sit down nor dine with the Lord Mayor, who was not yet come, nor have a table to himself, which was offered; but in a discontent went away again. After I had dined, I and Creed rose and went up and down the house, and up to the ladys' room, and there stayed gazing upon them. But though there were many and fine, both young and old, yet I could not discern one handsome face there; which was very strange. I expected musique, but there was none but only trumpets and drums, which displeased me. The dinner, it seems, is made by the Mayor and two Sheriffs for the time being, the Lord Mayor paying one half, and they the other. And the whole, Proby says, is reckoned to come to about 7 or £800 at most. The Queene mends apace, they say; but yet talks idle still.

30th. To my great sorrow find myself £43 worse than I was the last month, which was then £760 and now it is but £717. But it hath chiefly arisen from my layings-out in clothes for myself and wife; viz. for her about £12 and for myself £55, or thereabouts: having made myself a velvet cloak, two new cloth skirts, black, plain both; a new shag gown, trimmed with gold buttons and twist, with a new hat, and silk tops for my legs, and many other things, being resolved, henceforward to go like myself. And also two perriwiggs, one whereof costs me £3 and the other 40s. I have worn neither yet, but will begin next week, God willing. The Queene continues light-headed, but in hopes to recover. The plague is much in Amsterdam, and we in fear of it here, which God defend. The Turke goes on mighty in the Emperor's dominions, and the Princes cannot agree among themselves how to go against him.

November 2nd. Up, and by coach to White Hall, and there in the long matted Gallery I find Sir G. Carteret, Sir J. Minnes, and Sir W. Batten; and by and by comes the King to walk there with three or four with him; and soon as he saw us, says he, 'Here is the Navy Office,' and there walked twenty turns the length of the gallery, talking, methought, but ordinary talk. By and by come the Duke, and he walked, and at last they went into the Duke's lodgings. The King staid so long that we could not discourse with the Duke, and so we parted. I heard the Duke say that he was going to wear a perriwigg; and they say the King also will. I never till this day observed that the King is mighty gray.

6th. Lord Sandwich tells me how Mr Edward Montagu begins to show respect to him again after his endeavouring to bespatter him all was possible; but he is resolved never to admit him into his friendship again. He tells me how he and Sir H. Bennet, the Duke of Buckingham and his Duchesse, was of a committee with somebody else for the getting of Mrs Stewart for the King; but that she proves a cunning slut, and is advised at Somerset House by the Queene-Mother, and by her mother, and so all the plot is spoiled and the whole committee broke, Mr Montagu and the Duke of Buckingham fallen apieces, the Duchesse going to a nunnery; and so Montagu begins to enter friendship with my Lord, and to attend the Chancellor whom he had deserted. My Lord tells me that Mr Montagu, among other things, did endeavour to represent him to the Chancellor's sons as one that did desert their father in the business of my Lord of Bristoll; which is most false, being the only man that hath several times dined with him when no soul hath come to him, and went with him that very day home when the Earl impeached him in the Parliament House, and hath refused ever to pay a visit to my Lord of Bristoll, not so much as in return to a visit of his. So that the Chancellor and my Lord are well known and trusted one by another. But yet my Lord blames the Chancellor for desiring to have it put off to the next Sessions of Parliament, contrary to my Lord Treasurer's advice, to whom he swore he would not do it: and, perhaps, my Lord Chancellor, for ought I see by my Lord's discourse, may suffer by it when the Parliament comes to sit. My Lord tells me that he observes the Duke of York do follow and understand business very well, and is mightily improved thereby.

8th. To church, where I found that my coming in a perriwigg did not prove so strange as I was afraid it would, for I thought that all the church would presently have cast their eyes all upon me.

9th. To the Duke, where, when we come into his closet, he told us that Mr Pepys was so altered with his new perriwigg that he did not know him. So to our discourse, and among and above other things we were taken up in talking upon Sir J. Lawson's coming home, he being come to Portsmouth; and Captain Berkely is come to town with a letter from the Duana of Algier to the King, wherein they do demand again the searching of our ships and taking out of strangers, and their goods; and that what English ships are taken without the Duke's pass they will detain (though it be flat contrary to the words of the peace,) as prizes, till they do hear from our King, which they advise him may be speedy. And this they did the very next day after they had received with great joy the Grand Seignor's confirmation of the Peace from Constantinople by Captain Berkely; so that there is no command nor certainty to be had of these people. The King is resolved to send his will by a fleet of ships; and it is thought best and speediest to send these very ships that are now come home, five sail of good ships, back again after cleaning, victualling, and paying them. But it is a pleasant thing to think how their Basha, Shavan Aga, did tear his hair to see the soldiers order things thus; for (just like his late predecessors,) when they see the evil of war with England, then for certain they complain to the Grand Seignor of him, and cut his head off: this he is sure of, and knows as certain. Thence to Westminster Hall, where I met with Mr Pierce, surgeon: and among other things he asked me seriously whether I knew any thing of my Lord's being out of favour with the King; and told me, that for certain the King do take mighty notice of my Lord's living obscurely in a corner not like himself, and becoming the honour that he is come to. I was sorry to hear, and the truth is, from my Lord's discourse among his people (which I am told) of the uncertainty of princes' favour, and his melancholy keeping from Court, I am doubtful of some such thing; but I seemed wholly strange to him in it, but will make my use of it. He told me also how loose the Court is, nobody looking after business, but every man his lust and gain; and how the King is now become besotted upon Mrs Stewart, that he gets into corners, and will be with her half an hour together kissing her to the observation of all the world; and she now stays by herself and expects it, as my Lady Castlemaine did used to do; to whom the King, he says, is still kind, so as now and then he goes to her as he believes; but with no such fondness as he used to do. But yet it is thought that this new wench is so subtle, that it is verily thought if the Queene had died, he would have married her. Mr Blackburne and I fell to talk of many things, wherein he was very open to me: first, in that of religion, he makes it greater matter of prudence for the King and Council to suffer liberty of conscience; and imputes the loss of Hungary to the Turke from the

Emperor's denying them this liberty of their religion. He says that many pious ministers of the word of God, some thousands of them, do now beg their bread: and told me how highly the present clergy carry themselves every where so as that they are hated and laughed at by every body; among other things, for their excommunications, which they send upon the least occasions almost that can be. And I am convinced in my judgement, not only from his discourse, but my thoughts in general, that the present clergy will never heartily go down with the generality of the commons of England; they have been so used to liberty and freedom, and they are so acquainted with the pride and debauchery of the present clergy. He did give me many stories of the affronts which the clergy receive in all places of England from the gentry and ordinary persons of the parish. He do tell me what the City thinks of General Monk, as of a most perfidious man that hath betrayed every body, and the King also; who, as he thinks, and his party, and so I have heard other good friends of the King say, it might have been better for the King to have had his hands a little bound for the present, than be forced to bring such a crew of poor people about him, and be liable to satisfy the demands of every one of them. He told me that to his knowledge (being present at every meeting at the Treaty at the Isle of Wight,) that the old King did confess himself over-ruled and convinced in his judgement against the Bishopps, and would have suffered and did agree to exclude the service out of the churches, nay his own chapell; and that he did always say, that this he did not by force, for that he would never abate one inch by any vyolence; but what he did was out of his reason and judgement. He tells me that the King by name, with all his dignities, is prayed for by them that they call Fanatiques, as heartily and powerfully as in any of the other churches that are thought better: and that, let the King think what he will, it is them that must help him in the day of warr. For so generally they are the most substantiall sort of people, and the soberest; and did desire me to observe it to my Lord Sandwich, among other things, that of all the old army now you cannot see a man begging about the streets; but what? You shall have this captain turned a shoemaker; the lieutenant, a baker; this a brewer; that a haberdasher; this common soldier, a porter; and every man in his apron and frock, &c., as if they had never done anything else: whereas the other go with their belts and swords, swearing and cursing, and stealing; running into people's houses, by force oftentimes, to carry away something; and this is the difference between the temper of one and the other; and concludes (and I think with some reason,) that the spirits of the old parliament soldiers are so quiet and contented with God's providences, that the King is safer from any evil meant him by them one thousand times more than from his own discontented Cavalier. And then to the publick management of business: it is done, as he observes, so loosely and so carelessly, that the kingdom can never be happy with it, every man looking after himself, and his own lust and luxury; and that half of what money the Parliament gives the King is not so much as gathered. And to the purpose he told me how the Bellamys (who had some of the northern counties assigned them for their debt for the petty warrant victualling) have often complained to him that they cannot get it collected, for that nobody minds, or if they do, they won't pay it in. Whereas (which is a very remarkable thing,) he hath been told by some of the Treasurers at Warr here of late, to whom the most of the £120,000 monthly was paid, that for most months the payments were gathered so duly, that they seldom had so much or more than 40s. or the like, short in the whole collection; whereas now the very Commissioners for Assessments and other publick payments are such persons, and those that they choose in the country so like themselves, that from top to bottom there is not a man carefull of any thing, or if he be, is not solvent; that what between the beggar and the knave, the King is abused the best part of all his revenue. We then talked of the Navy, and of Sir W. Pen's rise to be a general. He told me he was always a conceited man, and one that would put the best side outward, but that it was his pretence of sanctity that brought him into play. Lawson, and Portman, and the fifth-monarchy men, among whom he was a great brother, importuned that he might be general; and it was pleasant to see how Blackburne himself did act it, how when the Commissioners of the Admiralty would enquire of the captains and admirals of such and such men, how they would with a sigh and casting up the eyes say, 'such a man fears the Lord,' or, 'I hope such a man hath the Spirit of God.' But he tells me that there was a cruel articling against Pen after one fight, for cowardice, in putting himself within a coyle of cables, of which he had much ado to acquit himself: and by great friends did it, not without remains of guilt, but that his brethren had a mind to pass it by, and Sir H. Vane did advise him to search his heart, and see whether this fault or a greater sin was not the occasion of this so great tryall. And he tells me, that what Pen gives out about Cromwell's sending and entreating him to go to Jamaica, is very false; he knows the contrary; besides, the Protector never was a man that needed to send for any man, specially such a one as he, twice. He tells me that the business of Jamaica did miscarry absolutely by his pride, and that when he was in the Tower he would cry like a child. And that just upon the turne, when Monk was come from the North to the City, and did begin to think of bringing in the King, Pen was then turned Quaker. That Lawson was never counted any thing but only a seaman, and a stout man, but a false man, and that now he appears the greatest hypocrite in the world. And Pen the same. He tells me that it is much talked of, that the King intends to legitimate the Duke of Monmouth; and that neither he, nor his friends of his persuasion, have any hopes of getting their consciences at liberty but by God Almighty's turning of the King's heart, which they expect, and are resolved to live and die in quiet hopes of it; but never to repine, or act any thing more than by prayers towards it. And that not only himself but all of them have, and are willing at any time to take the oaths of Allegiance and Supremacy. Mr Blackburne observed further to me, some certain notice that he had of the present plot so much talked of; that he was told by Mr Rushworth[84] how one Captain Oates,[85] a great discoverer, did employ several to bring and seduce others into a plot, and that one of his agents met with one that would not listen to him, nor conceal what he had offered him, but so detected the trapan. He also did much insist upon the cowardice and corruption of the King's guards and militia.

11th. At noon to the Coffee-house, where with Dr Allen some good discourse about physick and chymistry. And among other things, I telling him what Dribble the German Doctor do offer of an instrument to sink ships; he tells me that which is more strange, that something made of gold, which they call in chymistry *Aurum Fulminans*, a grain, I think he said, of it put into a silver spoon and fired, will give a blow like a musquett, and strike a hole through the silver spoon downward, without the least force upward; and this he can make a cheaper experiment of, he says, with iron prepared.

84 John Rushworth, Clerk assistant to the House of Commons, and author of the Historical Collections. Died 1690.
85 Titus Oates.

15th. This day being our Queene's birthday, the guns of the Tower went all off; and in the evening the Lord Mayor sent from church to church to order the constables to cause bonfires to be made in every street, which methinks is a poor thing to be forced to be commanded.

19th. With Sir G. Carteret to my Lord Treasurer, to discourse with him about Mr Gauden's having of money, and to offer to him whether it would not be necessary, Mr Gauden's credit being so low as it is, to take security of him if he demands any great sum, such as £20,000 which now ought to be paid him upon his next year's declaration. Which is a sad thing, that being reduced to this by us, we should be the first to doubt his credit; but so it is. However, it will be managed with great tenderness to him. My Lord Treasurer we found in his bed-chamber, being laid up of the goute. I find him a very ready man, and certainly a brave servant to the King: he spoke so quick and sensible of the King's charge. Nothing displeased me in him but his long nails, which he lets grow upon a pretty thick white short hand, that it troubled me to see them. In our way Sir G. Carteret told me there is no such thing likely yet as a Dutch war, neither they nor we being in condition for it, though it will come certainly to that in some time, our interests lying the same way, that is to say, in trade. But not yet.

20th. A great talk there is to-day of a crush between some of the Fanatiques up in arms and the King's men in the North; but whether true I know not yet.

22nd. At chapel I had room in the Privy Seale pew with other gentlemen, and there heard Dr Killigrew[86] preach. The anthem was good after sermon, being the fifty-first psalme, made for five voices by one of Captn. Cooke's boys, a pretty boy. And they say there are four or five of them that can do as much. And here I first perceived that the King is a little musicall, and kept good time with his hand all along the anthem.

23rd. With Alderman Backewell talking of the new money, which he says will never be counterfeited, he believes; but it is so deadly

86 Henry, youngest son of Sir Robert Killigrew, DD, Prebendary of Westminster, and Master of the Savoy, and author of some plays and sermons. His daughter Anne was the celebrated poetess.

inconvenient for telling, it is so thick, and the edges are made to turn up.

26th. The plague, it seems, grows more and more at Amsterdam; and we are going upon making of all ships coming from thence and Hambrough, or any other infected places, to perform their Quarantine (for thirty days as Sir Rd. Browne expressed it in the order of the Council, contrary to the import of the word, though in the general acceptation it signifies now the thing, not the time spent in doing it) in Holehaven, a thing never done by us before.

28th. To Paul's Church Yard, and there looked upon the second part of *Hudibras*, which I buy not, but borrow to read, to see if it be as good as the first, which the world cried so mightily up, though it hath not a good liking in me, though I had tried but twice or three times reading to bring myself to think it witty. Today for certain I am told how in Holland publickly they have pictured our King with reproach. One way is with his pockets turned the wrong side outward, hanging out empty; another with two courtiers picking of his pockets; and a third, leading of two ladies, while other abuse him; which amounts to great contempt.

29th (Lord's day). This morning I put on my best black cloth suit, trimmed with scarlett ribbon, very neat, with my cloak lined with velvett, and a new beaver, which altogether is very noble, with my black silk knit canons I bought a month ago.

30th. At White Hall Sir W. Pen and I met the Duke in the matted Gallery, and there he discoursed with us; and by and by my Lord Sandwich come and stood by, and talked; but it being St Andrew's, and a collar-day, he went to the Chapel, and we parted.

December 1st. After dinner I to Guild Hall to hear a trial at King's Bench, before Lord Chief Justice Hide,[87] about the insurance of a ship; and it was pleasant to see what mad sort of testimonys the seamen did give, and could not be got to speak in order: and then their terms such as the Judge could not understand; and to hear how sillily the Counsel and Judge would speak as to the terms necessary in the matter, would make one laugh: and above all, a Frenchman that was forced to speak in French, and took an English oath he did not

87 Sir Robert Hyde, died 1665.

understand, and had an interpreter sworn to tell us what he said, which was the best testimony of all.

3rd. This day Sir G. Carteret did tell us at the table, that the Navy (excepting what is due to the Yards upon the quarter now going on, and what few bills he hath not heard of,) is quite out of debt; which is extraordinary good news, and upon the 'Change to hear how our credit goes as good as any merchant's upon the 'Change, is a joyfull thing to consider, which God continue! I am sure the King will have the benefit of it, as well as we some peace and creditt.

7th. I hear there was the last night the greatest tide that ever was remembered in England to have been in this river: all White Hall having been drowned. At White Hall; and anon the King and Duke and Duchesse come to dinner in the vane-roome, where I never saw them before; but it seems since the tables are done, he dines there alltogether. The Queene is pretty well, and goes out of her chamber to her little chapel in the house. The King of France, they say, is hiring of sixty sail of ships of the Dutch, but it is not said for what design.

8th. To White Hall, where a great while walked with my Lord Teviott, whom I find a most carefull, thoughtfull, and cunning man, as I also ever took him to be. He is this day bringing in an account where he makes the King debtor to him £10,000 already on the garrison of Tangier account; but yet demands not ready money to pay it, but offers such ways of paying it out of the sale of old decayed provisions as will enrich him finely.

10th. To St Paul's Church Yard, to my bookseller's, and could not tell whether to lay out my money for books of pleasure, as plays, which my nature was most earnest in; but at last, after seeing Chaucer, Dugdale's *History of Paul's*, Stow's *London*, Gesner, *History of Trent*, besides Shakespeare, Jonson, and Beaumont's plays, I at last chose Dr Fuller's *Worthys*, the *Cabbala* or *Collections of Letters of State*, and a little book, *Delices de Hollande*, with another little book or two, all of good use or serious pleasure; and *Hudibras*, both parts, the book now in greatest fashion for drollery, though I cannot, I confess, see enough where the wit lies. My mind being thus settled, I went by link home, and so to my office, and to read in Rushworth; and so home to supper and to-bed. Calling at Wotton's, my shoemaker's, to-day, he tells me that Sir H. Wright is dying; and that Harris is come to the Duke's house again; and of a rare play to be acted this week of Sir William Davenant's. The story of Henry VIII with all his wives.

11th. At the Coffee-house I went and sat by Mr Harrington, and some East country merchants, and talking of the country above Quinsborough,[88] and thereabouts, he told us himself that for fish, none there the poorest body will buy a dead fish, but must be alive, unless it be in the winter; and then they told us the manner of putting their nets into the water. Through holes made in the thick ice, they will spread a net of half a mile long; and he hath known a hundred and thirty and a hundred and seventy barrels of fish taken at one draught. And then the people come with sledges upon the ice, with snow at the bottome, and lay the fish in and cover them with snow, and so carry them to market. And he hath seen when the said fish have been frozen in the sledge, so as he hath taken a fish and broke a-pieces, so hard it hath been; and yet the same fishes taken out of the snow, and brought into a hot room, will be alive and leap up and down. Swallows are often brought up in their nets out of the mudd from under water, hanging together to some twigg or other, dead in ropes, and brought to the fire will come to life. Fowl killed in December (Alderman Barker said) he did buy, and putting into the box under his sledge, did forget to take them out to eate till Aprill next, and they then were found there, and were through the frost as sweet and fresh and eat as well as at first killed. Young beares appear there; their flesh sold in market as ordinarily as beef here, and is excellent sweet meat. They tell us that beares there do never hurt any body, but fly away from you, unless you pursue and set upon them; but wolves do much mischief. Mr Harrington told us how they do to get so much honey as they send abroad. They make hollow a great fir-tree, leaving only a small slitt down straight in one place, and this they close up again, only leave a little hole, and there the bees go in and fill the bodys of those trees as full of wax and honey as they can hold; and the inhabitants at times go and open the slit, and take what they please without killing the bees, and so let them live there still and make more. Fir trees are always planted close together, because of keeping one another from the violence of the windes, and when a

88 Perhaps Mr. Harrington invented the name of this place, and the account of the country.

fellit is made, they leave here and there a grown tree to preserve the young ones coming up. The great entertainment and sport of the Duke of Corland, and the princes thereabouts, is hunting; which is not with dogs as we, but he appoints such a day, and summonses all the country-people as to a campagnia; and by several companies gives every one their circuit, and they agree upon a place where the toyle is to be set; and so making fires every company as they go, they drive all the wild beasts, whether bears, wolves, foxes, swine, and stags, and roes, into the toyle; and there the great men have their stands in such and such places, and shoot at what they have a mind to, and that is their hunting. They are not very populous there, by reason that people marry women seldom till they are towards or above thirty; and men thirty or forty, or more oftentimes, years old. Against a public hunting the Duke sends that no wolves be killed by the people; and whatever harm they do, the Duke makes it good to the person that suffers it; as Mr Harrington instanced in a house where he lodged, where a wolfe broke into a hog-stye, and bit three or four great pieces off of the back of the hog, before the house could come to help it; and the man of the house told him that there were three or four wolves thereabouts that did them great hurt; but it was no matter, for the Duke was to make it good to him, otherwise he would kill them.

12th. We had this morning a great dispute between Mr Gauden, Victualler of the Navy, and Sir J. Lawson, and the rest of the Commanders going against Argier, about their fish and keeping of Lent; which Mr Gauden so much insists upon to have it observed, as being the only thing that makes up the loss of his dear bargain all the rest of the year. This day I heard my Lord Barkeley tell Sir G. Carteret that he hath letters from France that the King hath emduked twelve Dukes, only to show his power, and to crush his nobility, who he said he did see had heretofore laboured to cross him. And this my Lord Barkeley did mightily magnify, as a sign of a brave and vigorous mind, that what he saw fit to be done he dares do.

14th. To the Duke, where I heard a large discourse between one that goes over an agent from the King to Legorne and thereabouts, to remove the inconveniences his ships are put to by denial of pratique; which is a thing that is now-a-days made use of only as a cheat, for a man may buy a bill of health for a piece of eight, and my enemy may agree with the Intendent of the Santè for ten pieces of eight or so, that he shall not give me a bill of health, and so spoil me in my design, whatever it be. This the King will not endure, and so resolves either to have it removed, or to keep all ships from coming in, or going out there, so long as his ships are stayed for want hereof. But among other things, Lord! what an account did Sir J. Minnes and Sir W. Batten make of the pulling down and burning of the head of the *Charles*, where Cromwell was placed with people under his horse, and Peter, as the Duke called him, is praying to him; and Sir J. Minnes would needs infer the temper of the people from their joy at the doing of this and their building a gibbet for the hanging of his head up, when, God knows, it is even the flinging away of £100 out of the King's purse, to the building of another, which it seems must be a Neptune. To the King's Head ordinary, and there dined among a company of fine gentlemen; some of them discoursed of the King of France's greatness, and how he is come to make the Princes of the Blood to take place of all foreign Embassadors, which it seems is granted by them of Venice and other States, and expected from my Lord Hollis,[89] our King's Embassador there; and that either upon that score or something else he hath not had his entry yet in Paris, but hath received several affronts, and among others his harnesse cut, and his gentlemen of his horse killed, which will breed bad blood if true. They say also that the King of France hath hired threescore ships of Holland, and forty of the Swede, but nobody knows what to do: but some great designs he hath on foot against the next year.

21st. To Shoe Lane to see a cocke-fighting at a new pit there, a spot I was never at in my life: but Lord! to see the strange variety of people, from Parliament-man (by name Wildes, that was Deputy Governor of the Tower when Robinson was Lord Mayor) to the poorest 'prentices, bakers, brewers, butchers, draymen, and what not; and all these fellows one with another cursing and betting. I soon had enough of it. It is strange to see how people of this poor rank, that look as if they had not bread to put in their mouths, shall bet three or four pounds at a time, and lose it, and yet bet as much the next battle,

89 Denzil Hollis, second son of John, first Earl of Clare, created in 1661 Baron Hollis of Ifield, afterwards Plenipotentiary for the Treaty of Breda. Died 1679/80, aged 82.

so that one of them will lose 10 or £20 at a meeting. Thence to my Lord Sandwich's, where I find him within with Captain Cooke and his boys, Dr Childe, Mr Madge, and Mallard, playing and singing over my Lord's anthem which he hath made to sing in the King's Chapel: my Lord took me into the withdrawing room to hear it, and indeed it sounds very pretty, and is a good thing, I believe to be made by him, and they all commend it.

22nd. I hear for certain that my Lady Castlemaine is turned Papist, which the Queene for all do not much like, thinking that she do it not for conscience sake.[90] I heard to-day of a great fray lately between Sir H. Finch's coachman, who struck with his whip a coachman of the King's, to the loss of one of his eyes; at which the people of the Exchange seeming to laugh and make sport with some words of contempt to him, my Lord Chamberlin did come from the King to shut up the 'Change, and by the help of a justice, did it; but upon petition to the King it was opened again. At noon I to Sir R. Ford's, where Sir Richard Browne and I met upon the freight of a barge sent to France to the Duchesse of Orleans; and here by discourse I find they greatly cry out against the choice of Sir John Cutler to be treasurer of Paul's, upon condition that he gives £1500 towards it; and it seems he did give it upon condition that he might be Treasurer for the work, which, they say, will be worth three times as much money: and talk as if his being chosen to the office will make people backward to give, but I think him as likely a man as either of them, and better.

28th. Walking through White Hall I heard the King was gone to play at Tennis, so I down to the New Tennis Court, and saw him and Sir Arthur Slingsby play against my Lord of Suffolke and my Lord Chesterfield. The King beat three, and lost two sets, they all, and he particularly playing well, I thought. Thence went and spoke with the Duke of Albemarle about his wound at Newhall, hut I find him a heavy dull man, methinks, by his answers to me.

90 'Le mariage du Chevalier de Grammont,' (says the Count d'Estrades in a letter written to his Royal Master, Louis XIV about this time,) 'et la conversion de Madame de Castlemaine se sont publiez le meme jour: et le Roy d'Angleterre estant tant priè par les parents de la Dame d'aporter quelque obstacle à cette action, repondit galamment que pour l'âme des Dame, il ne s'en mêloit point.'

31st. The Queene after a long and sore sickness is become well again; and the King minds his mistress a little too much, if it pleased God! but I hope all things will go well, and in the Navy particularly, wherein I shall do my duty whatever comes of it. The great talk is the design of the King of France, whether against the Pope or King of Spain nobody knows; but a great and a most promising Prince he is, and all the Princes of Europe have their eye upon him. The Turke very far entered into Germany, and all that part of the world at a loss what to expect from his proceedings. Myself, blessed be God! in a good way, and design and resolution of sticking to my business to get a little money with, doing the best service I can to the King also; which God continue! So ends the old year.

January 1st, 1663/64. At the Coffee-house, where much talking about a very rich widow, young and handsome, of one Sir Nicholas Gold's, a merchant, lately fallen, and of great courtiers that already look after her: her husband not dead a week yet. She is reckoned worth £80,000. Went to the Duke's house, the first play I have been at these six months, according to my last vowe, and here saw the so much cried-up play of *Henry the Eighth*; which, though I went with resolution to like it, is so simple a thing made up of a great many patches, that, besides the shows and processions in it, there is nothing in the world good or well done.

4th. I to my Lord Sandwich's lodgings, but he not being up, I to the Duke's chamber, and there by and by to his closet, where since his lady was ill, a little red bed of velvet is brought for him to lie alone, which is a very pretty one. After doing business here, I to my Lord's again, and there spoke with him, and he seems now almost friends again as he used to be. Here meeting Mr Pierce, the surgeon, he told me among other Court news, how the Queene is very well again; and that she speaks now very pretty English, and makes her sense out now and then with pretty phrazes: as among others this is mightily cried up; that, meaning to say that she did not like such a horse so well as the rest, he being too prancing and full of tricks, she said he did make too much vanity. To the Tennis Court, and there saw the King play at Tennis and others: but to see how the King's play was extolled without any cause at all, was a loathsome sight, though sometimes, indeed, he did play very well and deserved to be commended; but such open flattery is beastly. Afterwards to St

James's Park, seeing people play at Pell Mell; where it pleased me mightily to hear a gallant, lately come from France, swear at one of his companions for suffering his man (a spruce blade) to be so saucy as to strike a ball while his master was playing on the Mall.

6th. This morning I began a practice which I find by the ease I do it with that I shall continue, it saving me money and time; that is, to trimme myself with a razor; which pleases me mightily.

8th. We had great pleasure this afternoon; among other things, to talk of our old passages together in Cromwell's time; and how W. Symons did make me laugh and wonder to-day when he told me how he had made shift to keep in, in good esteem and employment, through eight governments in one year, (the year 1659, which were indeed, and he did name them all) and then failed unhappy in the ninth, viz. that of the King's coming in. He made good to me the story which Luellin did tell me the other day, of his wife upon her death-bed; how she dreamt of her uncle Scobell, and did foretell, from some discourse she had with him, that she should die four days thence, and not sooner, and did all along say so, and did so. Upon the 'Change a great talk there was of one Mr Tryan, an old man, a merchant in Lyme Streete, robbed last night, (his man and maid being gone out after he was a-bed) and gagged and robbed of £1050 in money and about £4000 in jewells, which he had in his house as security for money. It is believed that his man is guilty of confederacy, by their ready going to his secret till in the desk, wherein the key of his cash-chest lay.

9th. By discourse with my wife thought upon inviting my Lord Sandwich to a dinner shortly. It will cost me at least ten or twelve pounds; but, however, some arguments of prudence I have, which I shall think again upon before I proceed to that expence.

10th. All our discourse to-night was about Mr Tryan's late being robbed; and that Colonel Turner, (a mad, swearing, confident fellow, well known by all, and by me,) one much indebted to this man for his very livelihood, was the man that either did or plotted it; and the money and things are found in his hand, and he and his wife now in Newgate for it: of which we are all glad, so very a known rogue he was.

11th. By invitation to St James's; where, at Mr Coventry's chamber, I dined with my Lord Barkeley, Sir G. Carteret, Sir Edward Turner,[1] Sir Ellis Layton,[2] and one Mr Seymour, a fine gentleman: where admirable good discourse of all sorts, pleasant and serious. This morning I stood by the King arguing with a pretty Quaker woman, that delivered to him a desire of hers in writing. The King showed her Sir J. Minnes, as a man the fittest for her quaking religion; she modestly saying nothing till he begun seriously to discourse with her, arguing the truth of his spirit against hers; she replying still with these words, 'O King!' and thou'd all along. The general talk of the towne still is of Colonel Turner, about the robbery; who, it is thought, will be hanged. I heard the Duke of York tell to-night, how letters are come that fifteen are condemned for the late plot by the Judges at York; and, among others, Captain Oates, against whom it was proved that he drew his sword at his going out, and flinging away the scabbard, said that he would either return victor or be hanged.

18th. By coach to the 'Change, after having been at the Coffee-house, where I hear Turner[3] is found guilty of felony and burglary; and strange stories of his confidence at the barr, but yet great indiscretion in his arguing. All desirous of his being hanged.

20th. My Lord Sandwich did seal a lease for the house he is now taking in Lincoln's Inn Fields, which stands him in £250 per annum rent. Sir Richard Ford told me that Turner is to be hanged to-morrow, and with what impudence he hath carried out his trial; but that last night, when he brought him news of his death, he began to be sober and shed some tears, and he hopes will die a penitent; he having already confessed all the thing, but says it was partly done for a joke, and partly to get an occasion of obliging the old man by his care in getting him his things again, he having some hopes of being the better by him in his estate at his death. Mr Pierce tells me that my Lady Castlemaine is not at all set by by the King, but that he do doat upon Mrs Stewart only; and that to the leaving of all business in the world, and to the open slighting of the Queene: that he values not

1 Speaker of the House of Commons, and afterwards Solicitor-general, and Lord Chief Baron. Died 1675.
2 D. C. L., brother to R. Leighton, Bishop of Dumblane, and had been Secretary to the Duke of York.
3 See *State Trials*.

who sees him or stands by him while he dallies with her openly: and then privately in her chamber below, where the very sentrys observe his going in and out; and that so commonly, that the Duke or any of the nobles, when they would ask where the King is, they will ordinarily say, 'Is the King above, or below?' meaning with Mrs Stewart: that the King do not openly disown my Lady Castlemaine, but that she comes to Court; but that my Lord FitzHarding and the Hambletons,[4] and sometimes my Lord Sandwich, they say, intrigue with her. But he says my Lord Sandwich will lead her from her lodgings in the darkest and obscurest manner, and leave her at the entrance into the Queene's lodgings, that he might be the least observed: that the Duke of Monmouth the King do still doat on beyond measure, insomuch that the King only, the Duke of York, and Prince Rupert, and the Duke of Monmouth, do now wear deep mourning, that is, long cloaks, for the Duchesse of Savoy: so that he mourns as a Prince of the Blood, while the Duke of York do no more, and all the nobles of the land not so much; which gives great offence, and he sees the Duke of York do consider. But that the Duke of York do give himself up to business, and is like to prove a noble prince; and so indeed I do from my heart think he will. He says that it is believed, as well as hoped, that care is taken to lay up a hidden treasure of money by the King against a bad day. I pray God it be so!

21st. Up, and after sending my wife to my aunt Wright's to get a place to see Turner hanged, I to the 'Change; and seeing people flock in the City, I enquired, and found that Turner was not yet hanged. And so I went among them to Leadenhall Street, at the end of Lyme Street, near where the robbery was done; and to St Mary Axe, where he lived. And there I got for a shilling to stand upon the wheel of a cart, in great pain, above an hour before the execution was done; he delaying the time by long discourses and prayers one after another, in hopes of a reprieve; but none come, and at last was flung off the ladder in his cloak. A comely-looked man he was, and kept his countenance to the end: I was sorry to see him. It was believed there were at least 12 or 14,000 people in the street.

4 George Hamilton, and the Count Antoine Hamilton, author of the *Mémoires de Grammont*.

22nd. To Deptford, and there viewed Sir W. Petty's vessel; which hath an odd appearance, but not such as people do make of it.

26th. Tom Killigrew told us of a fire last night in my Lady Castlemaine's lodging, where she bid £40 for one to adventure the fetching of a cabinet out, which at last was got to be done; and the fire at last quenched without doing much wrong.

27th. At the Coffee-house, where I sat with Sir G. Ascue[5] and Sir William Petty, who in discourse is, methinks, one of the most rational men that ever I heard speak with a tongue, having all his notions the most distinct and clear. To Covent Garden, to buy a maske at the French House, Madam Charett's, for my wife; in the way observing the street full of coaches at the new play, at *The Indian Queene*;[6] which for show, they say, exceeds *Henry the Eighth*. Called to see my brother Tom, who was not at home, though they say he is in a deep consumption, and will not live two months.

30th. This evening I tore some old papers; among others, a romance which (under the title of *Love a Cheate*) I begun ten years ago at Cambridge: and reading it over to-night, I liked it very well, and wondered a little at myself at my vein at that time when I wrote it, doubting that I cannot do so well now if I would try.

February 1st. I hear how two men last night, justling for the wall about the new Exchange, did kill one another, each thrusting the other through; one of them of the King's Chapel, one Cave, and the other a retayner of my Lord Generall Middleton's. Thence to White Hall; where, in the Duke's chamber, the King come and stayed an hour or two laughing at Sir W. Petty, who was there about his boat; and at Gresham College in general: at which poor Petty was, I perceive, at some loss; but did argue discreetly, and bear the unreasonable follies of the King's objections and other bystanders with great discretion; and offered to take oddes against the King's best boates: but the King would not lay, but cried him down with words only. Gresham College he mightily laughed at, for spending time only

5 A distinguished naval officer before and after the Restoration; but he never went to sea subsequently to the action in 1666, when he was taken prisoner.
6 *The Indian Queen*, a tragedy in heroic verse, by Sir Robert Howard and Mr Dryden.

in weighing of ayre, and doing nothing else since they sat. Mr Pierce tells me how the King, coming the other day to his Theatre to see *The Indian Queene*, (which he commends for a very fine thing,) my Lady Castlemaine was in the next box before he come; and leaning over other ladies awhile to whisper with the King, she rose out of the box and went into the King's, and set herself on the King's right hand, between the King and the Duke of York: which, he swears, put the King himself, as well as every body else, out of countenance; and believes that she did it only to show the world that she is not out of favour yet, as was believed. To the King's Theatre, and there saw *The Indian Queen* acted; which indeed is a most pleasant show, and beyond my expectation; the play good, but spoiled with the ryme, which breaks the sense. But above my expectation most, the eldest Marshall[7] did do her part most excellently well as I ever heard woman in my life; but her voice is not so sweet as Ianthe's:[8] but, however, we come home mightily contented. Here we met Mr Pickering; and he tells me that the business runs high between the Chancellor and my Lord Bristoll against the Parliament; and that my Lord Lauderdale and Cooper open high against the Chancellor; which I am sorry for.

3rd. In Covent Garden to-night, going to fetch my wife, I stopped at the great Coffee-house there, where I never was before: where Dryden the poet (I knew at Cambridge), and all the wits of the town, and Harris the player, and Mr Hoole of our College. And had I had time then, or could at other times, it will be good coming thither, for there, I perceive, is very witty and pleasant discourse. But I could not tarry, and as it was late, they were all ready to go away.

7 Anne Marshall, a celebrated actress, and her youngest sister Becke, so frequently mentioned in the Diary, were, I believe, the daughters of a Presbyterian minister; but very little seems to be known about their history. One of them is erroneously stated, in the notes to the *Mémoires de Grammont*, and Davies' *Dramatic Miscellanies*, to have become Lord Oxford's mistress; for Mr Pepys uniformly calls the Marshalls by their proper name, and only speaks of the other lady as 'the first or old Roxalana, who had quitted the stage' – See February 18, 1661/62, and December 27, in the same year.

8 Malone says, in his *History of the English Stage,* that Mrs Mary Saunderson performed Ianthe in Davenant's play of the Siege of Rhodes, at the first opening of his theatre, April 1662. She married Betterton the following year, and lived till 1712, having filled almost all the female characters in Shakespeare with great success. It is probable, therefore, that she was the person alluded to here, and frequently mentioned afterwards, without any more particular designation.

4th. To St Paul's School, and up to hear the upper form examined; and there was kept by very many of the Mercers, Clutterbucke,[9] Barker, Harrington, and others; and with great respect used by them all, and had a noble dinner. Here they tell me, that in Dr Colett's[10] will he says that he would have a Master found for the School that hath good skill in Latin, and (if it could be) one that had some knowledge of the Greeke; so little was Greeke known here at that time. Dr Wilkins[11] and one Mr Smallwood, Posers.

8th. Mr Pierce told me how the King still do doat upon his women, even beyond all shame: and that the good Queene will of herself stop before she goes sometimes into her dressing-room, till she knows whether the King be there, for fear he should be, as she hath sometimes taken him, with Mrs Stewart; and that some of the best parts of the Queene's joynture are, contrary to faith, and against the opinion of my Lord Treasurer and his Council, bestowed or rented, I know not how, to my Lord Fitzhardinge and Mrs Stewart, and others of that crew; that the King do doat infinitely upon the Duke of Monmouth, apparently as one that he intends to have succeed him. God knows what will be the end of it!

9th. Great talk of the Dutch proclaiming themselves in India, Lords of the Southern Seas, and denying traffick to all ships but their own, upon pain of confiscation: which makes our merchants mad. Great doubt of two ships of ours, the *Greyhound* and another, very rich, coming from the Streights, for fear of the Turkes. Matters are made up between the Pope and the King of France; so that now all the doubt is, what the French will do with their armies.

10th. I did give my wife's brother 10s. and a coat that I had by me, a close-bodied, light-coloured cloth coat, with a gold edgeing in each seam, that was the lace of my wife's best pettycoat that she had when I married her. He is going into Holland to seek his fortune.

9 Probably Alderman Clutterbuck, one of the proposed Knights of the Royal Oak for Middlesex. There was a Sir Thomas Clutterbuck of London, *c.* 1670.

10 Dean of St Paul's, and founder of the School.

11 John Wilkins, Warden of Wadham College, and afterwards Dean of Ripon, consecrated Bishop of Chester 1668; died 1672. He was a learned theologian, and well versed in mathematics and natural philosophy.

15th. To White Hall, to the Duke: where he first put on a periwigg to-day: but methought his hair cut short in order thereto did look very prettily of itself, before he put on his periwigg. Great news of the arrivall of two rich ships, the *Greyhound* and another, which they were mightily afraid of, and great insurance given. This afternoon Sir Thomas Chamberlin[12] come to the office to me, and showed me several letters from the East Indys, showing the height that the Dutch are come to there, showing scorn to all the English, even in our only Factory there at Surat, beating several men, and hanging the English standard St George under the Dutch flag in scorn: saying, that whatever their masters do or say at home, they will do what they list, and be masters of all the world there; and have so proclaimed themselves Soveraigne of all the South Seas; which certainly our King cannot endure, if the Parliament will give him money. But I doubt and yet do hope they will not yet, till we are more ready for it.

17th. Mr Pierce tells me of the King's giving of my Lord FitzHarding two leases which belong indeed to the Queene, worth £20,000 to him; and how people do talk of it.

19th. Mr Cutler come, and walked and talked with me a great while; and then to the 'Change together; and it being early, did tell me several excellent examples of men raised upon the 'Change by their great diligence and saving; as also his own fortune, and how credit grew upon him; that when he was not really worth £1100 he had credit for £100,000; of Sir W. Rider how he rose; and others. By and by joyned with us Sir John Bankes;[13] who told us several passages of the East India Company; and how in every case, when there was due to him and Alderman Mico £64,000 from the Dutch for injury done to them in the East Indys, Oliver presently after the peace, they delaying to pay them the money, sent them word, that if they did not pay them by such a day, he would grant letters of mark to those merchants against them; by which they were so fearful of him, they did presently pay the money every farthing. Took my wife; and taking a coach, went to visit my Ladys Jemimah and Paulina Montagu, and Mrs Elizabeth Pickering,[14] whom we found at their

12 Son of William Chamberlayne, an English Judge, and created a Baronet 1642.
13 An opulent merchant, residing in Lincoln's Inn Fields.
14 Lord Sandwich's niece.

father's new house in Lincolne's Fields; but the house all in dirt. They received us well enough; but I did not endeavour to carry myself over familiarly with them: and so after a little stay, there coming in presently after us my Lady Aberguenny[15] and other ladies, we back again by coach.

22nd. This evening come Mr Alsopp the King's brewer, with whom I spent an hour talking and bewailing the posture of things at present; the King led away by half-a-dozen men, that none of his serious servants and friends can come at him. These are Lauderdale, Buckingham, Hamilton, FitzHarding, (to whom he hath, it seems, given £12,000 per annum in the best part of the King's estate); and that the old Duke of Buckingham could never get of the King. Projers[16] is another, and Sir H. Bennett. He loves not the Queene at all, but is rather sullen to her; and she, by all reports, incapable of children. He is so fond of the Duke of Monmouth, that every body admires it; and he says that the Duke hath said, that he would be the death of any man that says the King was not married to his mother: though Alsopp says, it is well known that she was a common strumpet before the King was acquainted with her. But it seems, he says, that the King is mighty kind to these his bastard children; and at this day will go at midnight to my Lady Castlemaine's nurses, and take the child and dance it in his arms: that he is not likely to have his tables up again in his house, for the crew that are about him will not have him come to common view again, but keep him obscurely among themselves. He hath this night, it seems, ordered that the Hall (which there is a ball to be in to-night before the King) be guarded, as the Queene-Mother's is, by his Horse Guards; whereas heretofore they were by the Lord Chamberlain or Steward, and their people. But it is feared they will reduce all to the soldiery, and all other places be taken away; and what is worst of all, will alter the present militia, and bring all to a flying army. That my Lord Lauderdale, being Middleton's[17] enemy, and one that scorns the Chancellor even to open affronts before the King, hath got the whole power of Scotland

15 Probably Mary, daughter of Thomas Gifford, Esq., of Dunton Walet, Essex, wife to George, ninth Lord Abergavenny.
16 Edward Progers, Esq., the King's Valet-de-Chambre, and the confidant of his amours. Died 1713, aged ninety-six.
17 John Earl of Middleton, General of the Forces in Scotland.

into his hand; whereas the other day he was in a fair way to have had his whole estate, and honour, and life, voted away from him. That the King hath done himself all imaginable wrong in the business of my Lord Antrim,[18] in Ireland; who, though he was the head of rebels, yet he by his letter owns to have acted by his father's and mother's and his commissions: but it seems the truth is, he hath obliged himself, upon the clearing of his estate, to settle it upon a daughter of the Queene-Mother's (by my Lord Germin,[19] I suppose,) in marriage, be it to whom the Queene pleases: which is a sad story. It seems a daughter of the Duke of Lenox's was, by force, going to be married the other day at Somerset House, to Harry Germin; but she got away and run to the King, and he says he will protect her. She is, it seems, very near akin to the King. Such mad doings there are every day among them! There was a French book in verse, the other day, translated and presented to the Duke of Monmouth in such a high stile, that the Duke of York, he tells me, was mightily offended at it. The Duke of Monmouth's mother's brother hath a place at Court; and being a Welchman, (I think he told me,) will talk very broad of the King's being married to his sister. The King did the other day, at the Council, commit my Lord Digby's[20] chaplin, and steward, and another servant, who went upon the process begun there against their lord, to swear that they saw him at church, and receive the Sacrament as a Protestant, (which, the Judges said, was sufficient to prove him such in the eye of the law); the King, I say, did commit them all to the Gate-house, notwithstanding their pleading their dependance upon him, and the faith they owed him as their lord, whose bread they eat. And that the King should say, that he would soon see whether he was King, or Digby. That the Queene-Mother had outrun herself in her expences, and is now come to pay very ill, or run in debt; the money being spent that she received for leases. He believes there is not any money laid up in bank, as I told him some did hope; but he says, from the best informers he can assure me there

---

18 Randall, second Earl and first Marquis of Antrim. Died 1673.

19 The Earl of St Albans.

20 George, Lord Digby, 2nd Earl of Bristol, who had been Secretary of State in 1643; but by changing his religion while abroad, at the instigation of Don John of Austria, incapacitated himself from being restored to that office; and in consequence of the disappointment, which he imputed to the interference of the Lord Chancellor, conspired and effected his ruin. He was installed KG in 1661, and died 1676.

is no such thing, nor any body that should look after such a thing; and that there is not now above £80,000 of the Dunkirke money left in stock. That Oliver the year when he spent £1,400,000 in the Navy did spend in the whole expence of the kingdom £2,600,000. That all the Court are mad for a Dutch war; but both he and I did concur, that it was a thing rather to be dreaded than hoped for; unless by the French King's falling upon Flanders, they and the Dutch should be divided. That our Embassador had, it is true, an audience; but in the most dishonourable way that could be; for the Princes of the Blood (though invited by our Embassador, which was the greatest absurdity that ever Embassador committed these 400 years) were not there; and so were not said to give place to our King's Embassador. And that our King did openly say, the other day in the Privy Chamber, that he would not be hectored out of his right and pre-eminencys by the King of France, as great as he was. That the Pope is glad to yield to a peace with the French (as the news-book says,) upon the basest terms that ever was. That the talk which these people about our King, that I named before, have, is to tell him how neither priviledge of Parliament nor City is any thing; but that his will is all, and ought to be so: and their discourse, it seems, when they are alone, is so base and sordid, that it makes the eares of the very gentlemen of the back-stairs (I think he called them) to tingle to hear it spoke in the King's hearing; and that must be very bad indeed. That my Lord Digby did send to Lisbon a couple of priests, to search out what they could against the Chancellor concerning the match, as to the point of his knowing before-hand that the Queene was not capable of bearing children; and that something was given her to make her so. But as private as they were, when they come thither they were clapped up prisoners. That my Lord Digby endeavours what he can to bring the business into the House of Commons, hoping there to master the Chancellor, there being many enemies of his there: but I hope the contrary. That whereas the late King did mortgage Clarendon[21] to somebody for £20,000, and this to have given it to the Duke of Albemarle, and he sold it to my Lord Chancellor, whose title of Earldome is fetched from thence; the King hath this day sent his order to the Privy Seale for the payment of this £20,000 to my Lord Chancellor, to clear the mortgage. Ireland in a very distracted

21 Clarendon Park, near Salisbury.

condition about the hard usage which the Protestants meet with, and the too good which the Catholiques. And from all together, God knows my heart, I expect nothing but ruin can follow, unless things are better ordered in a little time.

23rd. This day, by the blessing of God, I have lived thirty-one years in the world: and, by the grace of God, I find myself not only in good health in every thing, and particularly as to the stone, but only pain upon taking cold, and also in a fair way of coming to a better esteem and estate in the world, than ever I expected. But I pray God give me a heart to fear a fall, and to prepare for it.

24th (Ash Wednesday). To the Queene's chapel, where I staid and saw their masse, till a man come and bid me go out or kneel down: so I did go out. And thence to Somerset House; and there into the chapel, where Monsieur d'Espagne[22] used to preach. But now it is made very fine, and was ten times more crouded than the Queene's chapel at St James's: which I wonder at. Thence down to the garden of Somerset House, and up and down the new building, which in every respect will be mighty magnificent and costly.

27th. Sir Martin Noell told us the dispute between him, as farmer of the Additional Duty, and the East India Company, whether callico be linnen or no: which he says it is, having been ever esteemed so: they say it is made of cotton woole, and grows upon trees, not like flax or hemp. But it was carried against the Company, though they stand out against the verdict.

28th (Lord's day). Up and walked to Paul's; and by chance it was an extraordinary day for the Readers of the Inns of Court and all the Students to come to church, it being an old ceremony not used these twenty-five years, upon the first Sunday in Lent. Abundance there was of Students, more than there was room to seat but upon forms, and the Church mighty full. One Hawkins preached, an Oxford man. A good sermon upon these words: 'But the wisdom from above is first pure, then peaceable.' Both before and after sermon I was most impatiently troubled at the Quire, the worst that ever I heard. But

22 Probably author of a small volume called *Shibboleth, ou, Reformation de quelques Passages de la Bible*, per Jean d'Espagne ; Ministre du St Evangile, in the Pepysian Collection, printed 1653, and dedicated to Cromwell.

what was extraordinary, the Bishop of London,[23] who sat there in a pew, made a'purpose for him by the pulpitt, do give the last blessing to the congregation; which was, he being a comely old man, a very decent thing, methought. The Lieutenant of the Tower, Sir J. Robinson, would needs have me by coach home with him, where the officers of his regiment dined with him. After dinner to chapel in the Tower with the Lieutenant, with the keyes carried before us, and the Warders and Gentleman-porter going before us. And I sat with the Lieutenant in his pew, in great state. None, it seems, of the prisoners in the Tower that are there now, though they may, will come to prayers there.

29th. To Sir Philip Warwick, who showed me many excellent collections of the state of the Revenue in former Kings' and the late times, and the present. He showed me how the very assessments between 1643 and 1659, which were taxes, (besides Excise, Customes, Sequestrations, Decimations, King and Queene's and Church Lands, or any thing else but just the Assessments,) come to above fifteen millions. He showed me a discourse of his concerning the Revenues of this and foreign States. How that of Spayne was great, but divided with his kingdoms, and so come to little. How that of France did, and do much exceed ours before for quantity; and that it is at the will of the Prince to tax what he will upon his people; which is not here. That the Hollanders have the best manner of tax, which is only upon the expence of provisions, by an excise; and do conclude that no other tax is proper for England but a pound-rate, or excise upon the expence of provisions. He showed me every particular sort of payment away of money, since the King's coming in, to this day; and told me, from one to one, how little he hath received of profit from most of them: and I believe him truly. That the £1,200,000 which the Parliament with so much ado did first vote to give the King, and since hath been re-examined by several committees of the present Parliament, is yet above £300,000 short of making up really to the King the £1,200,000 as by particulars he showed me. And in my Lord Treasurer's excellent letter to the King upon this subject, he tells the King how it was the spending more than the revenue that did give the first occasion of his father's ruine, and did since to the rebels; who,

23 Humphrey Henchman translated from Salisbury, September 1663. Died 1675.

he says, just like Henry the Eighth, had great and sudden increase of wealth, but yet by overspending both died poor: and further tells the King how much of this £1,200,000 depends upon the life of the Prince, and so must be renewed by Parliament again to his successor; which is seldom done without parting with some of the prerogatives of the Crowne; or if denied and he persists to take it of the people, it gives occasion to a civill war, which did in the late business of tonnage and poundage prove fatal to the Crowne. He showed me how many ways the Lord Treasurer did take before he moved the King to farme the Customes in the manner he do, and the reasons that moved him to do it. He showed me a very excellent argument to prove, that our importing lesse than we export, do not impoverish the kingdom, according to the received opinion: which, though it be a paradox, and that I do not remember the argument, yet methought there was a great deal in what he said. And upon the whole I find him a most exact and methodicall man, and of great industry: and very glad that he thought fit to show me all this; though I cannot easily guess the reason why he should do it to me, unless from the plainness that he sees I use to him in telling him how much the King may suffer for our want of understanding the case of our Treasury.

March 2nd. This morning Mr Burgby, one of the writing clerks belonging to the Council, a knowing man, complains to me how most of the Lords of the Council do look after themselves and their own ends, and none the public, unless Sir Edward Nicholas. Sir G. Carteret is diligent, but for all his own ends and profit. My Lord Privy Seale, a destroyer of every body's business, and do no good at all to the public. The Archbishop of Canterbury[24] speaks very little, nor do much, being now come to the highest pitch that he can expect. He tells me, he believes that things will go very high against the Chancellor by Digby, and that bad things will be proved. Talks much of his neglecting the King; and making the King to trot every day to him, when he is well enough to go to visit his cosen Chief-Justice Hide, but not to the Council or King. He commends my Lord of Ormond mightily in Ireland; but cries out cruelly of Sir G. Lane for his corruption; and that he hath done my Lord great dishonour by selling of places here, which are now all taken away, and the poor

24 Gilbert Sheldon.

wretches ready to starve. But nobody almost understands or judges of business better than the King, if he would not be guilty of his father's fault to be doubtfull of himself, and easily be removed from his own opinion. That my Lord Lauderdale is never from the King's care nor council, and that he is a most cunning fellow. Upon the whole, that he finds things go very bad every where; and even in the Council nobody minds the public.

4th. There were several people trying a new-fashion gun brought my Lord Peterborough this morning, to shoot off often, one after another, without trouble or danger. At Greenwich I observed the foundation laying of a very great house for the King, which will cost a great deal of money.

10th. At the Privy Seale I enquired, and found the Bill come for the Corporation of the Royall Fishery: whereof the Duke of York is made present Governor, and severall other very great persons, to the number of thirty-two, made his assistants for their lives: whereof, by my Lord Sandwich's favour, I am one: and take it not only as a matter of honour, but that, that may come to be of profit to me.

14th. To White Hall; and in the Duke's chamber, while he was dressing, two persons of quality that were there did tell his Royal Highness how the other night, in Holborne, about midnight, being at cards, a link-boy come by and run into the house, and told the people the house was a-falling. Upon this the whole family was frighted, concluding that the boy had said that the house was a-fire: so they left their cards above, and one would have got out of the balcony, but it was not open; the other went up to fetch down his children, that were in bed: so all got clear out of the house. And no sooner so, but the house fell down indeed, from top to bottom. It seems my Lord Southampton's canaille did come too near their foundation, and so weakened the house, and down it come: which, in every respect, is a most extraordinary passage. The business between my Lords Chancellor and Bristoll, they say, is hushed up; and the latter gone or going, by the King's licence, to France.

15th. My poor brother Tom died.

16th. To the office, where we sat this afternoon, having changed this day our sittings from morning to afternoon, because of the Parliament

which returned yesterday; but was adjourned till Monday next, upon
pretence that many of the members were said to be upon the road;
and also the King had other affairs, and so desired them to adjourn till
then. But the truth is, the King is offended at my Lord of Bristoll, as
they say, whom he hath found to have been all this while (pretending
a desire of leave to go into France, and to have all the differences
between him and the Chancellor made up,) endeavouring to make
factions in both Houses to the Chancellor. So the King did this to
keep the Houses from meeting; and in the meanwhile sent a guard
and a herald last night to have taken him at Wimbleton, where he
was in the morning, but could not find him: at which the King was
and is still mightily concerned, and runs up and down to and from the
Chancellor's like a boy: and it seems would make Digby's articles
against the Chancellor to be treasonable reflections against his
Majesty. So that the King is very high, as they say; and God knows
what will follow upon it!

18th. To church, and with the grave-maker chose a place for my
brother to lie in, just under my mother's pew. But to see how a man's
tombes[25] are at the mercy of such a fellow, that for sixpence he
would, (as his own words were,) 'I will justle them together but I will
make room for him'; speaking of the fulness of the middle isle, where
he was to lie. I dressed myself, and so did my servant Besse; and so to
my brother's again: whither, though invited, as the custom is, at one
or two o'clock, they come not till four or five. But at last one after
another they come, many more than I bid: and my reckoning that I
bid was one hundred and twenty; but I believe there was nearer one
hundred and fifty. Their service was six biscuits a-piece, and what
they pleased of burnt claret. My cosen Joyce Norton kept the wine
and cakes above; and did give out to them that served, who had
white gloves given them. But above all, I am beholden to Mrs
Holding, who was most kind, and did take mighty pains not only in
getting the house and every thing else ready, but this day in going up
and down to see the house filled and served, in order to mine and
their great content, I think; the men sitting by themselves in some
rooms, and the women by themselves in others, very close, but yet
room enough. Anon to church, walking out into the street to the
Conduit, and so across the street; and had a very good company

25 bones?

along with the corps. And being come to the grave as above, Dr Pierson, the minister of the parish, did read the service for buriall: and so I saw my poor brother laid into the grave.

21st. This day the Houses of Parliament met; and the King met them, with the Queene with him. And he made a speech to them: among other things, discoursing largely of the plots abroad against him and the peace of the kingdom; and that the dissatisfied party had great hopes upon the effect of the Act for a Triennial Parliament granted by his father, which he desired them to peruse, and, I think, repeal. So the Houses did retire to their own House, and did order the Act to be read tomorrow before them; and I suppose it will be repealed, though I believe much against the will of a good many that sit there.

23rd. To the Trinity House, and there dined very well: and good discourse among the old men. Among other things, they observed, that there are but two seamen in the Parliament, viz. Sir W. Batten and Sir W. Pen, and not above twenty or thirty merchants; which is a strange thing in an island.

25th. To White Hall, and there to chapel; where it was most infinite full to hear Dr Critton.[26] The Doctor preached upon the thirty-first of Jeremy, and the twenty-first and twenty-second verses, about a woman compassing a man; meaning the Virgin conceiving and bearing our Saviour. It was the worst sermon I ever heard him make, I must confess; and yet it was good, and in two places very bitter, advising the King to do as the Emperor Severus did, to hang up a Presbyter John (a short coat and a long gowne interchangeably) in all the Courts of England. But the story of Severus was pretty, that he hanged up forty senators before the Senate-house, and then made a speech presently to the Senate in praise of his own lenity; and then decreed that never any senator after that time should suffer in the same manner without consent of the Senate: which he compared to the proceeding of the Long Parliament against my Lord Strafford. He said the greatest part of the lay magistrates in England were Puritans, and would not do justice; and the Bishops' powers were so taken away and lessened, that they could not exercise the power they ought. He told the King and the ladies, plainly speaking of death and of the skulls

26 Creighton.

and bones of dead men and women, how there is no difference; that nobody could tell that of the great Marius or Alexander from a pyoneer; nor, for all the pains the ladies take with their faces, he that should look in a charnel-house could not distinguish which was Cleopatra's, or fair Rosamond's, or Jane Shore's.

26th. Sir W. Batten told me how Sir Richard Temple hath spoke very discontentful words in the house about the Triennial Bill; but it hath been read the second time to-day, and committed; and, he believes, will go on without more ado, though there are many in the house are displeased at it, though they dare not say much. But above all expectation, Mr Prin is the man against it, comparing it to the idoll whose head was of gold, and his body and legs and feet of different metal. So this Bill had several degrees of calling of Parliaments, in case the King, and then the Council, and then the Lord Chancellor, and then the Sheriffes, should fail to do it. He tells me also, how, upon occasion of some 'prentices being put in the pillory to-day for beating of their masters or such like thing, in Cheapside, a company of 'prentices come and rescued them, and pulled down the pillory; and they being set up again, did the like again.

28th. The great matter to-day in the House hath been, that Mr Vaughan,[27] the great speaker, is this day come to town, and hath declared himself in a speech of an hour and a half, with great reason and eloquence, against the repealing of the Bill for Triennial Parliaments, but with no successe: but the House have carried it that there shall be such Parliaments, but without any coercive power upon the King, if he will bring this Act. But, Lord! to see how the best things are not done without some design; for I perceive all these gentlemen that I was with to-day were against it, (though there was reason enough on their side); yet purely I could perceive, because it was the King's mind to have it; and should he demand any thing else, I believe they would give it him.

April 1st. To White Hall; and in the Gallery met the Duke of York; (I also saw the Queene going to the Park, and her Maids of Honour: she herself looks ill, and methinks Mrs Stewart is grown fatter, and

27 John Vaughan, afterwards knighted, and made Chief Justice of the Common Pleas.

not so fair as she was:) and he called me to him, and discoursed a good while with me; and after he was gone, twice or thrice staid and called me again to him, the whole length of the house: and at last talked of the Dutch; and I perceive do much wish that the Parliament will find reason to fall out with them.

3rd. Called up by W. Joyce,[28] he being summonsed to the House of Lords to-morrow, for endeavouring to arrest my Lady Peters[29] for a debt.

4th. Up, and walked to my Lord Sandwich's; and there spoke with him about W. Joyce, who tells me he would do what was fit in so tender a point. I to the Lords' House before they sat; and stood within it, while the Duke of York come to me and spoke to me a good while about the new ship at Woolwich. Afterwards I spoke with my Lord Barkeley and my Lord Peterborough about it. And so staid without a good while, and saw my Lady Peters, an impudent jade, soliciting all the Lords on her behalf. And at last W. Joyce was called in; and by the consequences, and what my Lord Peterborough told me, I find that he did speak all he said to his disadvantage, and so was committed to the Black Rod: which is very hard, he doing what he did by the advice of my Lord Peter's own steward. But the Serjeant of the Black Rod did direct one of his messengers to take him in custody, and peaceably conducted him to the Swan with two Necks, in Tuttle-street, to a handsome dining-room; and there was most civilly used. It was a sad sight, methought, to-day to see my Lord Peters coming out of the House, fall out with his lady (from whom he is parted) about this business, saying that she disgraced him. But she hath been a handsome woman, and is, it seems, not only a lewd woman, but very high-spirited.

5th. Lord Peterborough presented a petition to the House from W. Joyce: and a great dispute, we hear, there was in the House for and against it. At last it was carried that he should be bayled till the House meets again after Easter, he giving bond for his appearance. Anon comes the King and passed the Bill for repealing the Triennial Act,

28 William Joyce had married Mr Pepys's first cousin, Kate Fenner.
29 Elizabeth, daughter of John Earl Rivers, and first wife to William fourth Lord Petre, who was, in 1678, impeached by the Commons of High Treason, and died under confinement in the Tower, January 5th, 1683, without issue.

and another about Writs of Errour. I crowded in and heard the King's speech to them; but he speaks the worst that ever I heard man in my life: worse than if he read it all, and he had it in writing in his hand. I went to W. Joyce, where I found the order come, and bayle (his father and brother) given; and he paying his fees, which come to above £12, besides £5 he is to give one man, and his charges of eating and drinking here, and 10s. a-day as many days as he stands under bayle: which, I hope, will teach him hereafter to hold his tongue better than he used to do.

8th. Home to the only Lenten supper I have had of wiggs[30] and ale.

15th. To the Duke's house, and there saw *The German Princesse* [31] acted, by the woman herself; but never was any thing so well done in earnest, worse performed in jest upon the stage.

18th. Up and by coach to Westminster, and there solicited W. Joyce's business again; and did speak to the Duke of York about it, who did understand it very well. I afterwards did without the House fall in company with my Lady Peters, and endeavoured to mollify her: but she told me she would not, to redeem her from hell, do any thing to release him; but would be revenged while she lived, if she lived the age of Methusalem. I made many friends, and so did others. At last it was ordered by the Lords that it should be referred to the Committee of Priviledges to consider. So I away by coach to the 'Change; and there do hear that a Jew hath put in a policy of four per cent. to any man, to insure him against a Dutch warr for four months: I could find in my heart to take him at this offer. To Hide Park, where I have not been since last year: where I saw the King with his periwigg, but not altered at all; and my Lady Castlemaine in a coach by herself, in yellow satin and a pinner on; and many brave persons. And myself being in a hackney and full of people, was ashamed to be seen by the world, many of them knowing me.

---

30 Buns, still called wiggs in the West of England.
31 Mary Moders, alias Stedman, alias Carleton, a celebrated impostor, who had induced the son of a London citizen to marry her under the pretence that she was a German Princess. She next became an actress, after having been tried for bigamy and acquitted. The rest of her life was one continued course of robbery and fraud; and in 1678 she suffered at Tyburn, for stealing a piece of plate from a tavern in Chancery-lane.

19th. To the Physique Garden in St James's Parke; where I first saw orange-trees, and other fine trees.

20th. Mr Coventry told me how the Committee for Trade have received now all the complaints of the merchants against the Dutch, and were resolved to report very highly the wrongs they have done us, (when God knows! it is only our own negligence and laziness that hath done us the wrong): and this to be made to the House to-morrow.

21st. At the Lords' House heard that it is ordered, that, upon submission upon the knee both to the House and my Lady Peters, W. Joyce shall be released. I forthwith made him submit, and ask pardon upon his knees; which he did before several Lords. But my Lady would not hear it; but swore she would post the Lords, that the world might know what pitifull Lords the King hath: and that revenge was sweeter to her than milk; and that she would never be satisfied unless he stood in a pillory, and demand pardon there. But I perceive the Lords are ashamed of her. I find that the House this day have voted that the King be desired to demand right for the wrong done us by the Dutch, and that they will stand by him with their lives and fortunes: which is a very high vote, and more than I expected. What the issue will be, God knows!

23rd. I met with Mr Coventry, who himself is now full of talk of a Dutch war: for it seems the Lords have concurred in the Commons' vote about it; and so the next week it will be presented to the King.

26th. Saw W. Joyce: and the late business hath cost the poor man above £40, besides, he is likely to lose his debt. Lady Peters, Creed says, is a drunken jade, he himself having seen her drunk in the lobby of their House. My wife gone this afternoon to the buriall of my she-cosen Scott, a good woman: and it is a sad consideration how the Pepys's decay, and nobody almost that I know in a present way of encreasing them.

27th. This day the Houses attended the King, and delivered their votes to him upon the business of the Dutch; and he thanks them, and promises an answer in writing.

May 3rd. To Westminster Hall; and there, in the Lords' house, did in a great crowd, from ten o'clock till almost three, hear the cause of

Mr Roberts,[32] my Lord Privy Seale's son, against Win, who by false ways did get the father of Mr Roberts's wife (Mr Bodvill) to give him the estate and disinherit his daughter. The cause was managed for my Lord Privy Seale by Finch the solicitor; but I do really think that he is a man of as great eloquence as ever I heard, or ever hope to hear in all my life. Mr Cutler told me how for certain Lawson hath proclaimed war again with Argier, though they had at his first coming given back the ships which they had taken, and all their men; though they refused afterwards to make him restitution for the goods which they had taken out of them.

5th. My eyes beginning every day to grow less and less able to bear with long reading or writing, though it be by daylight; which I never observed till now.

13th. In the Painted Chamber I heard a fine conference between some of the two Houses upon the Bill for Conventicles. The Lords would be freed from having their houses searched by any but the Lord Lieutenant of the County: and upon being found guilty, to be tried only by their peers; and thirdly, would have it added, that whereas the Bill says, 'That that, among other things, shall be a conventicle wherein any such meeting is found doing any thing contrary to the Liturgy of the Church of England,' they would have it added, 'or practice.' The Commons to the Lords said, that they knew not what might hereafter be found out which might be called the practice of the Church of England: for there are many things may be said to be the practice of the Church, which were never established by any law, either common, statute, or canon; as singing of psalms, binding up prayers at the end of the Bible, and praying extempore before and after sermon: and though these are things indifferent, yet things for aught they at present know may be started, which may be said to be the practice of the Church which would not be fit to allow. For the Lords' priviledges, Mr Waller told them how tender their predecessors had been of the priviledges of the Lords; but, however, where the peace of the kingdom stands in competition with them, they apprehend those priviledges must give place. He told them that he thought, if they should own all to be the priviledges of the Lords which might be demanded, they should be led like the man (who granted leave to his neighbour to pull off his horse's tail, meaning that he could not do it at once,) that hair by hair had his horse's tail pulled off indeed: so the Commons, by granting one thing after another, might be served by the Lords. Mr Vaughan, whom I could not to my grief perfectly hear, did say, if that they should be obliged in this manner to exempt the Lords from every thing, it would in time come to pass that whatèver (be it ever so great) should be voted by the Commons as a thing penall for a commoner, the contrary should be thought a priviledge to the Lords: that also in this business, the work of a conventicle being but the work of an hour, the cause of a search would be over before a Lord Lieutenant, who may be many miles off, can be sent for; and that all this dispute is but about £100: for it is said in the Act, that it shall be banishment or payment of £100. I thereupon heard the Duke of Lennox say, that there might be Lords who could not always be ready to lose £100, or some such thing. They broke up without coming to any end in it. There was also in the Commons' House a great quarrel about Mr Prin, and it was believed that he should have been sent to the Tower, for adding something to a Bill (after it was ordered to be engrossed) of his own head – a Bill for measures for wine and other things of that sort, and a Bill of his own bringing in; but it appeared he could not mean any hurt in it. But, however, the King was fain to write in his behalf, and all was passed over. But it is worth my remembrance, that I saw old Ryly the Herald, and his son; and spoke to his son, who told me in very bad words concerning Mr Prin, that the King had given him an office of keeping the Records; but that he never comes thither, nor had been there these six months: so that I perceive they expect to get his employment from him.

19th. To a Committee of Tangier; where God forgive how our Report of my Lord Peterborough's accounts was read over and agreed to by the Lords, without one of them understanding it! And had it been what it would, it had gone: and, besides, not one thing touching the King's profit in it minded or hit upon.

20th. Mr Edward Montagu is turned out of the Court, not to return again. His fault, I perceive, was his pride, and most of all his affecting to be great with the Queene: and it seems indeed he had more of her eare than every body else, and would be with her talking alone two or three hours together; insomuch that the Lords about the King, when he would be jesting with them about their wives, would tell the King that he must have a care of his wife too, for she hath now the gallant: and they say the King himself did once ask Montagu how his mistress (meaning the Queene) did. He grew so proud and despised every body, besides suffering nobody he or she to get or do any thing about the Queene, that they all laboured to do him a good turn. They all say that he did give some affront to the Duke of Monmouth, which the King himself did speak to him of. So he is gone, nobody pitying, but laughing at him: and he pretends only that he is gone to his father that is sick in the country.

23rd. The King is gone down with the Duke and a great crew this morning by break of day to Chatham.

29th. Mr Coventry and I did long discourse together of the business of the office, and the war with the Dutch; and he seemed to argue mightily with the little reason that there is for all this. For first, as to the wrong we pretend they have done us; that of the East Indys, for their not delivering of Poleron, it is not yet known whether they have failed or no; that of their hindering the *Leopard* cannot amount to above £3000 if true; that of the Guinny Company, all they had done us did not amount to above 2 or £300 he told me truly; and that now, from what Holmes, without any commission, hath done in taking an island and two forts, hath set us much in debt to them: and he believes that Holmes will have been so puffed up with this, that he by this time hath been enforced with more strength than he had then, hath, I say, done a great deal more wrong to them. He do, as to the effect of the war, tell me clearly that it is not any skill of the Dutch that can hinder our trade if we will, we having so many advantages over them, of winds, good ports, and men; but it is our pride, and the laziness of the merchant. The main thing he desired to speak with me about was, to understand my Lord Sandwich's intentions as to going to sea with this fleet; saying, that the Duke, if he desires it, is most willing to do it; but thinking that twelve ships is not a fleet fit for my Lord to be troubled to go out with, he is not willing to offer it to him till he hath some intimations of his mind to go, or not. To the King's closet; whither by and by the King come, my Lord Sandwich carrying the sword. A Bishop preached, but he speaking too low for me to hear. By and by my Lord Sandwich come forth, and called me to him: and we fell into discourse a great while about his business, wherein he seems to be very open with me, and to receive my opinion as he used to do: and I hope I shall become necessary to him again. He desired me to think of the fitness, or not, for him to offer himself to go to sea; and to give him my thoughts in a day or two. Thence after sermon among the ladies in the Queene's side; where I saw Mrs Stewart, very fine and pretty, but far beneath my Lady Castlemaine. Thence with Mr Povy[33] home to dinner; where extraordinary cheer. And after dinner up and down to see his house. And in a word, methinks, for his perspective in the little closet; his room floored above with woods of several colours, like but above the best cabinet-work I ever saw; his grotto and vault, with his bottles of wine, and a well therein to keep them cool; his furniture of all sorts; his bath at the top of the house, good pictures, and his manner of eating and drinking; do surpass all that ever I did see of one man in all my life.

31st. I was told to-day, that upon Sunday night last, being the King's birth-day, the King was at my Lady Castlemaine's lodgings (over the hither-gate at Lambert's lodgings) dancing with fiddlers all night almost; and all the world coming by taking notice of it.

June 1st. Southwell (Sir W. Pen's friend) tells me the very sad newes of my Lord Teviott's and nineteen more commission officers being killed at Tangier by the Moores, by an ambush of the enemy upon them, while they were surveying their lines: which is very sad, and he says, afflicts the King much. To the King's house, and saw *The Silent Woman*; but methought not so well done or so good a play as I formerly thought it to be. Before the play was done, it fell such a storm of hayle, that we in the middle of the pit were fain to rise; and all the house in a disorder.

2nd. It seems my Lord Teviott's design was to go a mile and half out of the town, to cut down a wood in which the enemy did use to lie in ambush. He had sent several spyes: but all brought word that the way was clear, and so might be for any body's discovery of an enemy before you are upon them. There they were all snapt, he and all his officers, and about two hundred men, as they say; there being left now in the garrison but four captains. This happened the 3rd of May last, being not before that day twelvemonth of his entering into his

33 Evelyn mentions Mr Povy's house in Lincoln's Inn.

government there: but at his going out in the morning he said to
some of his officers, 'Gentlemen, let us look to ourselves, for it was
this day three years that so many brave Englishmen were knocked on
the head by the Moores, when Fines made his sally out.'

4th. Mr Coventry discoursing this noon about Sir W. Batten, (what
a sad fellow he is!) told me how the King told him the other day how
Sir W. Batten, being in the ship with him and Prince Rupert when
they expected to fight with Warwicke, did walk up and down
sweating with a napkin under his throat to dry up his sweat: and that
Prince Rupert being a most jealous man, and particularly of Batten,
do walk up and down swearing bloodily to the King, that Batten had
a mind to betray them to-day, and that the napkin was a signal; 'but,
by God,' says he, 'if things go ill, the first thing I will do is to shoot
him.' He discoursed largely and bravely to me concerning the
different sorts of valours, the active and passive valour. For the latter,
he brought as an instance General Blake, who, in the defending of
Taunton and Lime for the Parliament, did through his sober sort of
valour defend it the most opiniâstrement that ever any man did any
thing; and yet never was the man that ever made an attaque by land
or sea, but rather avoyded it on all, even fair occasions. On the other
side, Prince Rupert, the boldest attaquer in the world for personal
courage; and yet in the defending of Bristol no man did any thing
worse, he wanting the patience and seasoned head to consult and
advise for defence, and to bear with the evils of a siege. The like he
says of my Lord Teviott, who was the boldest adventurer of his
person in the world, and from a mean man in few years was come to
this greatness of command and repute only by the death of all his
officers, he many times having the luck of being the only survivor of
them all, by venturing upon services for the King of France that
nobody else would; and yet no man upon a defence, he being all fury
and no judgment in a fight. He tells me above all of the Duke of
York, that he is more himself and more of judgment is at hand in him
in the middle of a desperate service, than at other times, as appeared
in the business of Dunkirke, wherein no man ever did braver things,
or was in hotter service in the close of that day, being surrounded
with enemies; and then, contrary to the advice of all about him, his
counsel carried himself and the rest through them safe, by advising
that he might make his passage with but a dozen with him; 'For,' says

he, 'the enemy cannot move after me so fast with a great body, and with a small one we shall be enough to deal with them': and though he is a man naturally martiall to the hottest degree, yet a man that never in his life talks one word of himself or service of his own, but only that he saw such or such a thing, and lays it down for a maxime that a Hector can have no courage. He told me also, as a great instance of some men, that the Prince of Condé's excellence is, that there not being a more furious man in the world, danger in fight never disturbs him more than just to make him civill, and to command in words of great obligation to his officers and men; but without any the least disturbance in his judgment or spirit.

6th. By barge with Sir W. Batten to Trinity House. Here were my Lord Sandwich, Mr Coventry, my Lord Craven, and others. A great dinner, and good company. Mr Prin also, who would not drink any health, no, not the King's, but sat down with his hat on all the while; but nobody took notice of it to him at all.

11th. With my wife only to take the ayre, it being very warm and pleasant, to Bowe and Old Ford: and thence to Hackney. There light, and played at shuffleboard, eat cream and good cherries: and so with good refreshment home.

13th. Spent the whole morning reading of some old Navy books; wherein the order that was observed in the Navy then, above what it is now, is very observable.

15th. At home, to look after things for dinner. And anon at noon comes Mr Creed by chance, and by and by the three young ladies:[34] and very merry we were with our pasty, very well baked; and a good dish of roasted chickens; pease, lobsters, strawberries. And after dinner to cards: and about five o'clock, by water down to Greenwich; and up to the top of the hill, and there played upon the ground at cards. And so to the Cherry Garden, and then by water singing finely to the Bridge, and there landed; and so took boat again, and to Somerset House. And by this time, the tide being against us, it was past ten of the clock; and such a troublesome passage, in regard of my Lady Paulina's fearfullness, that in all my life I never did see any poor wretch in that condition. Being come

34 Lord Sandwich's daughters.

hither, there waited for them their coach; but it being so late, I doubted what to do how to get them home. After half an hour's stay in the street, I sent my wife home by coach with Mr Creed's boy; and myself and Creed in the coach home with them. But, Lord! the fear that my Lady Paulina was in every step of the way: and indeed at this time of the night it was no safe thing to go that road; so that I was even afraid myself, though I appeared otherwise. We come safe, however, to their house; where we knocked them up, my Lady and all the family being in bed. So put them into doors; and leaving them with the maids, bade them good night.

16th. The talk upon the 'Change is, that De Ruyter is dead, with fifty men of his own ship, of the plague, at Cales:* that the Holland Embassador here do endeavour to sweeten us with fair words; and things like to be peaceable.

20th. I to the Duke, where we did our usual business. And among other discourse of the Dutch, he was merrily saying how they print that Prince Rupert, Duke of Albemarle, and my Lord Sandwich, are to be Generalls; and soon after is to follow them 'Vieux Pen': and so the Duke called him in mirth Old Pen. They have, it seems, lately wrote to the King, to assure him that their setting-out ships was only to defend their fishing-trade, and to stay near home, not to annoy the King's subjects; and to desire that he would do the like with his ships: which the King laughs at, but yet is troubled they should think him such a child, to suffer them to bring home their fish and East India Company's ships, and then they will not care for us. To my Lord's lodgings; and were merry with the young ladies, who made a great story of their appearing before their mother the morning after we carried them, the last week, home so late; and that their mother took it very well, at least without any anger. Here I heard how the rich widow, my Lady Gold, is married to one Neale, after he had received a box on the eare by her brother (who was there a sentinel, in behalf of some courtier,) at the door; but made him draw, and wounded him. She called Neale up to her, and sent for a priest, married presently, and went to bed. The brother sent to the Court, and had a serjeant sent for Neale; but Neale sent for him up to be seen in bed, and she owned him for her husband: and so all is past.

* Cales: Cadiz.

23rd. W. How was with me this afternoon, to desire some things to be got ready for my Lord against his going down to his ship, which will be soon; for it seems the King and both the Queenes intend to visit him. The Lord knows how my Lord will get out of this charge; for Mr Moore tells me to-day that he is £10,000 in debt: and this will, with many other things that daily will grow upon him, (while he minds his pleasure as he do,) set him further backward.

24th. To White Hall; and Mr Pierce showed me the Queene's bed-chamber, and her closet, where she had nothing but some pretty pious pictures, and books of devotion; and her holy water at her head as she sleeps, with a clock by her bed-side, wherein a lamp burns that tells her the time of the night at any time. Thence with him to the Park, and there met the Queene coming from Chapell, with her Maids of Honour, all in silver-lace gowns again; which is new to me, and that which I did not think would have been brought up again. Thence he carried me to the King's closet: where such variety of pictures, and other things of value and rarity, that I was properly confounded and enjoyed no pleasure in the sight of them; which is the only time in my life that ever I was so at a loss for pleasure, in the greatest plenty of objects to give it me.

26th. At my Lord Sandwich's; where his little daughter, my Lady Katharine was brought, who is lately come from my father's at Brampton, to have her cheeke looked after, which is and hath long been sore. But my Lord will rather have it be as it is, with a scarr in her face, than endanger it being worse with tampering.[35]

July 4th. This day the King and the Queenes went to visit my Lord Sandwich and the fleet, going forth in the Hope.

7th. The King is pretty well to-day, though let blood the night before yesterday.

10th. My Lady Sandwich showed us my Lady Castlemaine's[36] picture, finely done: given my Lord; and a most beautiful picture it is.

35 She married, first, Nicholas, son and heir of Sir N. Bacon, KB; and secondly, the Revd Mr Gardeman; and lived to be 96, dying 1757.
36 There is a beautiful portrait of Lady Castlemaine in the dining-room at Hinchingbroke.

14th. To my Lord's. He did begin with a most solemn profession of the same confidence in and love for me that he ever had, and then told me what a misfortune was fallen upon me and him: in me, by a displeasure which my Lord Chancellor did show to him last night against me, in the highest and most passionate manner that ever any man did speak, even to the not hearing of anything to be said to him: but he told me, that he did say all that could be said for a man as to my faithfullnesse and duty to his Lordship, and did me the greatest right imaginable. And what should the business be, but that I should be forward to have the trees in Clarendon Park[37] marked and cut down, which he, it seems, hath bought of my Lord Albemarle; when, God knows! I am the most innocent man in the world in it, and did nothing of myself, nor knew of his concernment therein, but barely obeyed my Lord Treasurer's warrant for the doing thereof. And said that I did most ungentlemanly-like with him, and had justified the rogues in cutting down a tree of his; and that I had sent the veriest Fanatique that is in England to mark them, on purpose to nose him. All which I did assure my Lord, was most properly false, and nothing like it true; and told my Lord the whole passage. My Lord do seem most nearly affected with him; partly, I believe, for me, and partly for himself. So he advised me to wait presently upon my Lord, and clear myself in the most perfect manner I could, with all submission and assurance that I am his creature both in this and all other things: and that I do own that all I have, is derived through my Lord Sandwich from his Lordship. So, full of horror, I went, and found him busy in trials of law in his great room; and it being Sitting-day, durst not stay, but went to my Lord and told him so: whereupon he directed me to take him after dinner: and so away I home, leaving my Lord mightily concerned for me. So I to my Lord Chancellor's; and there coming out after dinner I accosted him, telling him that I was the unhappy Pepys that had fallen into his high displeasure, and come to desire him to give me leave to make myself better understood to his Lordship, assuring him of my duty and service. He

37 Near Salisbury, granted by Edward VI to Sir W. Herbert, Earl of Pembroke, for two lives, which term ended in 1601, when it reverted to the Crown, and was conferred on the Duke of Albemarle, whose family, as I imagine, got back the estate after Lord Clarendon's fall; for, according to Britton, Clarendon Park was alienated by Christopher, second Duke of Albemarle, to the Earl of Bath, from whom it passed, by purchase, to Mr Bathurst, the ancestor of the present possessor.

answered me very pleasingly, that he was confident upon the score of my Lord Sandwich's character of me, but that he had reason to think what he did, and desired me to call upon him some evening: I named to-night, and he accepted of it. To my Lord Chancellor's, and there heard several trials, wherein I perceive my Lord is a most able and ready man. After all done, he himself called, 'Come, Mr Pepys, you and I will take a turn in the garden.' So he was led down stairs, having the goute, and there walked with me, I think, above an hour, talking most friendly, yet cunningly. I told him clearly how things were; how ignorant I was of his Lordship's concernment in it; how I did not do nor say one word singly, but what was done was the act of the whole Board. He told me by name that he was more angry with Sir G. Carteret than with me, and also with the whole body of the Board. But thinking who it was of the Board that did know him least, he did place his fear upon me: but he finds that he is indebted to none of his friends there. I think I did thoroughly appease him, till he thanked me for my desire and pains to satisfy him; and upon my desiring to be directed who I should of his servants advise with about this business, he told me nobody, but would be glad to hear from me himself. He told me he would not direct me in anything, that it might not be said that the Lord Chancellor did labour to abuse the King; or (as I offered) direct the suspending the Report of the Purveyors: but I see what he means, and will make it my work to do him service in it. But, Lord! to see how he is incensed against poor Deane, as a fanatick rogue, and I know not what: and what he did was done in spite to his Lordship, among all his friends and tenants. He did plainly say that he would not direct me in any thing, for he would not put himself into the power of any man to say that he did so and so; but plainly told me as if he would be glad I did something. Lord! to see how we poor wretches dare not do the King good service for fear of the greatness of these men. He named Sir G. Carteret, and Sir J. Minnes, and the rest; and that he was as angry with them all as me. But it was pleasant to think that, while he was talking to me, comes into the garden Sir G. Carteret; and my Lord avoided speaking with him, and made him and many others stay expecting him, while I walked up and down above an hour, I think; and would have me walk with my hat on. And yet, after all, there has been so little ground for his jealousy of me, that I am sometimes afraid that he do this only in policy to bring me to his side by scaring me; or else, which is worse, to try how faithfull I would be to the King; but I rather think the former of the two. I parted with great assurance how I acknowledged all I had to come from his Lordship; which he did not seem to refuse, but with great kindness and respect parted.

15th. Up, and to my Lord Sandwich's; where he sent for me up, and I did give my Lord an account of what had passed with my Lord Chancellor yesterday; with which he was pleased, and advised me by all means to study in the best manner I could to serve him in this business. After this discourse ended, he began to tell me that he had now pitched upon his day of going to sea upon Monday next, and that he would now give me an account how matters are with him. He told me that his work now in the world is only to keep up his interest at Court, having little hopes to get more considerably, he saying that he hath now about £8000 per annum. It is true, he says, he oweth about £10,000; but he hath been at great charges in getting things to this pass in his estate; besides his building and good goods that he hath bought. He says that he hath now evened his reckonings at the Wardrobe till Michaelmas last, and hopes to finish it to Lady-day before he goes. He says now there is due, too, £7000 to him there, if he knew how to get it paid, besides £2000 that Mr Montagu do owe him. As to his interest, he says that he hath had all the injury done him that ever man could have by another bosom friend that knows all his secrets, by Mr Montagu: but he says that the worst of it all is past, and he gone out and hated, his very person by the King, and he believes the more upon the score of his carriage to him; nay, that the Duke of York did say a little while since in his closet, that he did hate him because of his ungrateful carriage to my Lord of Sandwich. He says that he is as great with the Chancellor, or greater, than ever in his life. That with the King he is the like; and told me an instance, that whereas he formerly was of the private council to the King before he was last sick, and that by the sickness an interruption was made in his attendance upon him; the King did not constantly call him as he used to do to his private council, only in businesses of the sea and the like; but of late the King did send a message to him by Sir Harry Bennet, to excuse the King to my Lord that he had not of late sent for him as he used to do to his private council, for it was not out of any distaste, but to avoid giving offence to some others whom he did not name; but my Lord supposes it might be Prince Rupert, or it may be only that the King would rather pass it by an excuse, than be thought unkind; but that now he did desire him to attend him constantly, which of late he hath done, and the King never more kind to him in his life than now. The Duke of York, as much as is possible; and in the business of late, when I was to speak to my Lord about his going to sea, he says that he finds the Duke did it with the greatest ingenuity and love in the world: 'and whereas,' says my Lord, 'here is a wise man hard by that thinks himself so, and it may be is in a degree so, (naming by and by my Lord Crewe,) would have had me condition with him that neither Prince Rupert nor any body should come over his head, and I know not what,' the Duke himself hath caused in his commission, that he be made Admirall of this and what other ships or fleets shall hereafter be put out after these; which is very noble. He tells me in these cases, and that of Mr Montagu's, and all others, he finds that bearing of them patiently is the best way, without noise or trouble, and things wear out of themselves and come fair again. But says he takes it from me, never to trust too much to any man in the world, for you put yourself into his power; and the best seeming friend and real friend as to the present may have or take occasion to fall out with you, and then out comes all. Then he told me of Sir Harry Bennet, though they were always kind, yet now it is become to an acquaintance and familiarity above ordinary, that for these months he hath done no business but with my Lord's advice in his chamber, and promises all faithfull love to him and service upon all occasions. My Lord says, that he hath the advantage of being able by his experience to help out and advise him; and he believes that that chiefly do invite Sir Harry to this manner of treating him. 'Now,' says my Lord, 'the only and the greatest embarras that I have in the world is, how to behave myself to Sir H. Bennet and my Lord Chancellor, in case that there do lie any thing under the embers about my Lord Bristoll, which nobody can tell; for then,' says he, 'I must appear for one or other, and I will lose all I have in the world rather than desert my Lord Chancellor: so that,' says he, 'I know not for my life what to do in that case.' For Sir H. Bennet's love is come to the height, and his confidence, that he hath given my lord a character,[38] and will oblige my Lord to correspond with him. 'This,' says he, 'is the whole condition of my estate and interest; which I tell

38 A cypher.

you, because I know not whether I shall see you again or no.' Then as to the voyage, he thinks it will be of charge to him, and no profit; but that he must not now look after nor think to encrease, but study to make good what he hath, that what is due to him from the Wardrobe or elsewhere may be paid, which otherwise would fail, and all a man hath be but small content to him. So we seemed to take leave one of another; my Lord of me, desiring me that I would write to him and give him information upon all occasions in matters that concern him; which, put together with what he preambled with yesterday, makes me think that my Lord do truly esteem me still, and desires to preserve my service to him; which I do bless God for. In the middle of our discourse my Lady Crewe come in to bring my Lord word that he hath another son, my Lady being brought to bed just now, for which God be praised! and send my Lord to study the laying up of something the more! Thence with Creed to St James's, and missing Mr Coventry, to White Hall; where, staying for him in one of the galleries, there comes out of the chayre-roome Mrs Stewart in a most lovely form, with her hair all about her eares, having her picture taken there. There was the King and twenty more I think, standing by all the while, and a lovely creature she in the dress seemed to be.

18th. Sir G. Carteret and I did talk together in the Parke about my Lord Chancellor's business of the timber; he telling me freely that my Lord Chancellor was never so angry with him in all his life, as he was for this business, and in a great passion; and that when he saw me there, he knew what it was about. And plots now with me how we may serve my Lord, which I am mightily glad of; and I hope together we may do it. Thence I to my Lord Chancellor, and discoursed his business with him. I perceive, and he says plainly, that he will not have any man to have it in his power to say that my Lord Chancellor did contrive the wronging the King of his timber; but yet I perceive, he would be glad to have service done him therein; and told me Sir G. Carteret hath told him that he and I would look after his business to see it done in the best manner for him.

20th. With Mr Deane, discoursing upon the business of my Lord Chancellor's timber, in Clarendon Park, and how to make a report therein without offending him; which at last I drew up, and hope it will please him. But I would to God neither I nor he ever had any thing to have done with it! To White Hall, to the Committee for Fishing; but nothing done, it being a great day to-day there upon drawing at the Lottery[39] of Sir Arthur Slingsby. I got in and stood by the two Queenes and the Duchesse of York, and just behind my Lady Castlemaine, whom I do heartily admire; and good sport to see how most that did give their ten pounds did go away with a pair of globes only for their lot, and one gentlewoman, one Mrs Fish, with the only blanke. And one I staid to see draw a suit of hangings valued at £430 and they say are well worth the money, or near it. One other suit there is better than that; but very many lots of three and four-score pounds. I observed the King and Queene did get but as poor lots as any else. But the wisest man I met with was Mr Cholmley, who insured as many as would, from drawing of the one blank for 12d.; in which case there was the whole number of persons to one, which I think was three or four hundred. And so he insured about 200 for 200 shillings, so that he could not have lost if one of them had drawn it; for there was enough to pay the £10 but it happened another drew it, and so he got all the money he took.

25th. Met with a printed copy of the King's commission for the repairs of Paul's, which is very large, and large power for collecting money, and recovering of all people that had bought or sold formerly any thing belonging to the Church. No news, only the plague is very hot still, and encreases among the Dutch.

26th. Great discourse of the fray yesterday in Moorefields, how the butchers at first did beat the weavers, (between whom there hath been ever an old competition for mastery,) but at last the weavers rallied and beat them. At first the butchers knocked down all for weavers that had green or blue aprons, till they were fain to pull them off and put them in their breeches. At last the butchers were fain to pull off their sleeves, that they might not be known, and were soundly beaten out of the field, and some deeply wounded and bruised; till at last the weavers went out tryumphing, calling £100 for a butcher.

28th. I am overjoyed in hopes that upon this month's account I shall find myself worth £1000 besides the rich present of two silver and

39 Evelyn says this Lottery was a shameful imposition.

gilt flaggons, which Mr Gauden did give me the other day. My Lord Sandwich newly gone to sea, and he did before his going, and by his letter since, show me all manner of respect and confidence.

30th. To the 'Change, where great talk of a rich present brought by an East India ship from some of the Princes of India, worth to the King £70,000 in two precious stones.

August 1st. To the Coffee-house, and there all the house full of the victory Generall Soushe (who is a Frenchman, a soldier of fortune, commanding part of the German army) hath had against the Turke; killing 4000 men, and taking most extraordinary spoil.

2nd. To the King's play-house, and there saw *Bartholomew Fayre*; which do still please me; and is, as it is acted, the best comedy in the world, I believe. I chanced to sit by Tom Killigrew, who tells me that he is setting up a nursery; that is, is going to build a house in Moorefields, wherein he will have common plays acted. But four operas it shall have in the year, to act six weeks at a time: where we shall have the best scenes and machines, the best musique, and everything as magnificent as is in Christendome; and to that end hath sent for voices and painters and other persons from Italy. Thence homeward called upon my Lord Marlborough.

4th. To a play at the King's house, *The Rivall Ladys*,[40] a very innocent and most pretty witty play. I was much pleased with it, and it being given me,[41] I look upon it as no breach of my oath. Here we hear that Clun, one of their best actors, was, the last night, going out of towne (after he had acted the Alchymist, wherein was one of his best parts that he acts) to his country-house, set upon and murdered; one of the rogues taken, an Irish fellow. It seems most cruelly butchered and bound. The house will have a great miss of him. Thence visited my Lady Sandwich, who tells me my Lord FitzHarding is to be made a Marquis.

5th. About ten o'clock I dressed myself, and so mounted upon a very pretty mare, sent me by Sir W. Warren, according to his promise yesterday. And so through the City, not a little proud, God knows, to be seen upon so pretty a beast, and to my cosen W. Joyce's, who

40 A tragedy by Dryden.
41 His companion paid for him.

presently mounted too, and he and I out of towne toward Highgate; in the way, at Kentish-towne, he showing me the place and manner of Clun's being killed and laid in a ditch, and yet was not killed by any wounds, having only one in his arm, but bled to death through his struggling. He told me, also, the manner of it, of his going home so late drinking with his mistress, and manner of having it found out.

7th. I saw several poor creatures carried by, by constables, for being at a conventicle. They go like lambs, without any resistance. I would to God they would either conform, or be more wise, and not be catched!

9th. This day come the news that the Emperour hath beat the Turke: killed the Grand Vizier and several great Bassas, with an army of 80,000 men killed and routed; with some considerable loss of his own side, having lost three generals, and the French forces all cut off almost. Which is thought as good a service to the Emperour as beating the Turke almost.

10th. Abroad to find out one to engrave my tables upon my new sliding rule with silver plates, it being so small that Browne that made it cannot get one to do it. So I got Cocker,[42] the famous writing-master, to do it, and I set an hour by him to see him design it all: and strange it is to see him with his natural eyes to cut so small at his first designing it, and read it all over, without any missing, when for my life I could not, with my best skill, read one word, or letter of it; but it is use. He says that the best light for his life to do a very small thing by, (contrary to Chaucer's words to the Sun, 'that he should lend his light to them that small seals grave,') it should be by an artificial light of a candle, set to advantage, as he could do it. I find the fellow, by his discourse, very ingenious: and among other things, a great admirer and well read in the English poets, and undertakes to judge of them all, and that not impertinently.

11th. Comes Cocker with my rule, which he hath engraved to admiration, for goodness and smallness of work: it cost me 14s. the doing. This day, for a wager before the King, my Lords of Castlehaven and Arran, (a son of my Lord of Ormond's) they two alone did run down and kill a stoute bucke in St James's parke.

---

42 Edward Cocker, the well known writing-master and arithmetician. Died c. 1679.

13th. To the new play, at the Duke's house, of *Henry the Fifth*: a most noble play, writ by my Lord Orrery; wherein Betterton, Harris, and Ianthe's parts most incomparably wrote and done, and the whole play the most full of height and raptures of wit and sense, that ever I heard; having but one incongruity, that King Harry promises to plead for Tudor to their Mistress, Princesse Katherine of France, more than when it comes to it he seems to do; and Tudor refused by her with some kind of indignity, not with a difficulty and honour that it ought to have been done in to him.

15th. With Sir J. Minnes, he talking of his cures abroad, while he was with the King as a doctor. And among others, Sir J. Denham he told me he had cured to a miracle. At Charing Cross, and there saw the great Dutchman that is come over, under whose arm I went with my hat on, and could not reach higher than his eyebrowes with the tip of my fingers. He is a comely and well-made man, and his wife a very little but pretty comely Dutch woman.

16th. Wakened about two o'clock this morning with a noise of thunder, which lasted for an hour, with such continued lightnings, not flashes, but flames, that all the sky and ayre was light; and that for a great while, not a minute's space between new flames all the time: such a thing as I never did see, nor could have believed had even been in nature. And being put into a great sweat with it, could not sleep till all was over. And that accompanied with such a storm of rain as I never heard in my life. I expected to find my house in the morning overflowed; but I find not one drop of rain in my house, nor any news of hurt done. Mr Pierce tells me the King do still sup every night with my Lady Castlemaine.

19th. The news of the Emperour's victory over the Turkes is by some doubted, but by most confessed to be very small (though great,) of what was talked, which was 80,000 men to be killed and taken of the Turke's side.

20th. I walked to Cheapside to see the effect of a fire there this morning, since four o'clock: which I find in the house of Mr Bois, that married Doctor Fuller's niece, who are both out of town, leaving only a maid and man in town. It begun in their house, and hath burned much and many houses backward, though none forward; and that in the great uniform pile of buildings in the middle of Cheapside.

I am very sorry for them, for the Doctor's sake. Thence to the 'Change, and so home to dinner. And thence to Sir W. Batten's, whither Sir Richard Ford come, the Sheriffe, who hath been at this fire all the while; and he tells me, upon my question, that he and the Mayor[43] were there, as it is their dutys to be, not only to keep the peace, but they have power of commanding the pulling down of any house or houses, to defend the City. By and by comes in the Common Cryer of the City to speak with him; and when he was gone, says he, 'You may see by this man the constitution of the Magistracy of this City; that this fellow's place, I dare give him (if he will be true to me,) £1000 for his profits every year, and expect to get £500 more to myself thereby. When,' says he, 'I in myself am forced to spend many times as much.'

26th. To see some pictures at one Hiseman's,[44] a picture-drawer, a Dutchman, which is said to exceed Lilly, and indeed there is both of the Queenes and Maids of Honour (particularly Mrs Stewart's[45] in a buff doublet like a soldier) as good pictures I think as ever I saw. The Queene is drawn in one like a shepherdess, in the other like St Katharin, most like and most admirably. I was mightily pleased with this sight indeed. Mr Pen, Sir William's son, is come back from France, and come to visit my wife. A most modish person grown, she says a fine gentleman.

27th. All the news this day is, that the Dutch are, with twenty-two sail of ships of warr, crewsing up and down about Ostend: at which we are alarmed. My Lord Sandwich is come back into the Downes with only eight sail, which is or may be a prey to the Dutch, if they knew our weakness and inability to set out any more speedily.

31st. Prince Rupert I hear this day is to go to command this fleet going to Guinny against the Dutch. I doubt few will be pleased with his going, being accounted an unhappy man.

September 5th. With the Duke; where all our discourse of war in the highest measure. Prince Rupert was with us; who is fitting himself to go to sea in the *Heneretta*. And afterwards I met him and Mr Gray, and says he, 'I can answer but for one ship, and in that I will do my part;

43 Sir John Robinson.   44 Huysman.
45 Still to be seen at Kensington Palace.

for it is not in that as in the army, where a man can command every thing.'

6th. This day Mr Coventry did tell us how the Duke did receive the Dutch Embassador the other day: by telling him that, whereas they think us in jest, he believes that the Prince (Rupert) which goes in this fleet to Guinny will soon tell them that we are in earnest, and that he himself will do the like here, in the head of the fleet here at home; and that he did not doubt to live to see the Dutch as fearfull of provoking the English, under the government of a King, as he remembers them to have been under that of a Coquin.

11th. With Mr Blagrave walking in the Abbey, he telling me the whole government and discipline of White Hall Chapel, and the caution now used against admitting any debauched persons.

12th. Up, and to my cosen Anthony Joyce's, and there took leave of my aunt James, and both cosens, their wives, who are this day going down to my father's by coach. I did give my Aunt 20s., to carry as a token to my mother, and 10s. to Poll.[46] With the Duke; and saw him with great pleasure play with his little girle, like an ordinary private father of a child.

19th. Dr Pierce tells me (when I was wondering that Fraizer should order things with the Prince in that confident manner,) that Fraizer is so great with my Lady Castlemaine, and Stewart, and all the ladies at Court, in helping to slip their calfes when there is occasion, and with the great men in curing of them, that he can do what he please with the King in spite of any man, and upon the same score with the Prince; they all having more or less occasion to make use of him.

22nd. Home to-bed; having got a strange cold in my head, by flinging off my hat[47] at dinner, and sitting with the wind in my neck.

23rd. We were told to-day of a Dutch ship of 3 or 400 tons, where all the men were dead of the plague, and the ship cast ashore at Gottenburgh.

46 His sister Paulina.
47 In Lord Clarendon's Essay on the decay of respect paid to Age, he says, that in his younger days he never kept his hat on before those older than himself, except at dinner.

29th. Fresh newes come of our beating the Dutch at Guinny quite out of all their castles almost, which will make them quite mad here at home sure. And Sir G. Carteret did tell me, that the King do joy mightily at it; but asked him laughing, 'But,' says he, 'how shall I do to answer this to the Embassador when he comes?' Nay they say that we have beat them out of the New Netherlands too; so that we have been doing them mischief for a great while in several parts of the world, without publick knowledge or reason. Their fleete for Guinny is now, they say, ready, and abroad, and will be going this week.

October 1st. We go now on with vigour in preparing against the Dutch; who, they say, will now fall upon us without doubt upon this high news come of our beating them so wholly in Guinny.

2nd. After church I walked to my Lady Sandwich's, through my Lord Southampton's new buildings in the fields behind Gray's Inn: and, indeed, they are a very great and a noble work.

3rd. With Sir J. Minnes, by coach, to St James's; and there all the news now of very hot preparations for the Dutch: and being with the Duke, he told us he was resolved to take a tripp himself, and that Sir W. Pen should go in the same ship with him. Which honour, God forgive me! I could grudge him, for his knavery and dissimulation, though I do not envy much the having the same place myself. Talk also of great haste in the getting out another fleet, and building some ships; and now it is likely we have put one another's dalliance past a retreate.

4th. After dinner to a play, to see *The Generall*; which is so dull and so ill-acted, that I think it is the worst I ever saw or heard in all my days. I happened to sit near to Sir Charles Sedley: who I find a very witty man, and he did at every line take notice of the dullness of the poet and badness of the action, that most pertinently; which I was mightily taken with.

5th. To the Musique-meeting at the Post-office, where I was once before. And thither anon come all the Gresham College, and a great deal of noble company: and the new instrument was brought called the Arched Viall, where being tuned with lute-strings, and played on with kees like an organ, a piece of parchment is always kept moving;

and the strings, which by the kees are pressed down upon it, are grated in imitation of a bow, by the parchment; and so it is intended to resemble several vyalls played on with one bow, but so basely and so harshly, that it will never do. But after three hours' stay it could not be fixed in tune: and so they were fain to go to some other musique of instruments. This morning, by three o'clock, the Prince[48] and King, and Duke with him, went down the River, and the Prince under sail the next tide after, and so is gone from the Hope. God give him better success than he used to have!

10th. This day, by the blessing of God, my wife and I have been married nine years: but my head being full of business, I did not think of it to keep it in any extraordinary manner. But bless God for our long lives and loves and health together, which the same God long continue, I wish, from my very heart!

11th. Luellin tells me what an obscene loose play this *Parson's Wedding*[49] is, that is acted by nothing but women at the King's house. My wife tells me the sad news of my Lady Castlemaine's being now become so decayed, that one would not know her; at least far from a beauty, which I am sorry for. This day with great joy Captain Titus told us the particulars of the French's expedition against Gigery upon the Barbary Coast, in the Straights, with 6000 chosen men. They have taken the Fort of Gigery, wherein were five men and three guns, which makes the whole story of the King of France's policy and power to be laughed at.

12th. For news, all say De Ruyter is gone to Guinny before us. Sir J. Lawson is come to Portsmouth; and our fleet is hastening all speed: I mean this new fleet. Prince Rupert with his is got into the Downes.

13th. In my way to Brampton in this day's journey I met with Mr White, Cromwell's chaplin that was, and had a great deal of discourse with him. Among others, he tells me that Richard is, and hath long been, in France, and is now going into Italy. He owns publickly that he do correspond, and return him all his money. That Richard hath been in some straits in the beginning but relieved by his friends. That he goes by another name, but do not disguise himself, nor deny

48 Rupert.
49 A comedy by Thomas Killigrew.

himself to any man that challenges him. He tells me, for certain, that offers had been made to the old man, of marriage between the King and his daughter, to have obliged him, but he would not. He thinks (with me) that it never was in his power to bring in the King with the consent of any of his officers about him; and that he scorned to bring him in as Monk did, to secure himself and deliver every body else. When I told him of what I found writ in a French book of one Monsieur Sorbiere,[50] that gives an account of his observations here in England; among other things he says, that it is reported that Cromwell did, in his lifetime, transpose many of the bodies of the Kings of England from one grave to another, and that by that means it is not known certainly whether the head that is now set up upon a post be that of Cromwell, or of one of the Kings; Mr White tells me that he believes he never had so poor a low thought in him to trouble himself about it. He says the hand of God is much to be seen; that all his children are in good condition enough as to estate, and that their relations that betrayed their family are all now either hanged or very miserable.

15th. My father and I up and walked alone to Hinchingbroke; and among the late chargeable works that my Lord hath done there, we saw his water-works, which are very fine; and so is the house all over, but I am sorry to think of the money at this time spent therein.

16th (Lord's day). It raining, we set out betimes, and about nine o'clock got to Hatfield in church-time; and I light and saw my simple Lord Salsbury sit there in the gallery.

18th. At Somerset-House I saw the Queene's new rooms, which are most stately and nobly furnished; and there I saw her and the Duke of York and Duchesse. The Duke espied me, and come to me, and talked with me a very great while.

24th. Into the galleries at White Hall to talk with my Lord Sandwich; among other things, about the Prince's writing up to tell us of the danger he and his fleet lie in at Portsmouth, of receiving affronts from

50 Samuel Sorbiere, who, after studying divinity and medicine at Paris, travelled in different parts of Europe, and published his Voyage into England, described by Voltaire as a dull, scurrilous satire upon a nation of which the author knew nothing. Died 1670.

the Dutch; which, my Lord said, he would never have done, had he lain there with one ship alone: nor is there any great reason for it, because of the sands. However, the fleet will be ordered to go and lay themselves up at the Cowes. Much beneath the prowesse of the Prince, I think, and the honour of the nation, at the first to be found to secure themselves. My Lord is well pleased to think, that, if the Duke and the Prince go, all the blame of any miscarriage will not light on him: and that if any thing goes well, he hopes he shall have the share of the glory, for the Prince is by no means well esteemed of by any body. This day the great O'Neale died; I believe, to the content of all the Protestant pretenders in Ireland.

26th. At Woolwich; I there up to the King and Duke. Here I staid above with them while the ship was launched, which was done with great success, and the King did very much like the ship, saying, she had the best bow that ever he saw. But Lord! the sorry talk and discourse among the great courtiers round about him, without any reverence in the world, but with so much disorder. By and by the Queene comes and her Maids of Honour; one whereof, Mrs Boynton,[51] and the Duchesse of Buckingham had been very sick coming by water in the barge, (the water being very rough); but what silly sport they made with them in very common terms, methought was very poor, and below what people think these great people say and do. The launching being done, the King and company went down to take barge; and I sent for Mr Pett,[52] and put the flaggon into the Duke's hand, and he, in the presence of the King, did give it Mr Pett, taking it upon his knee. The City did last night very freely lend the King £100,000 without any security but the King's word, which was very noble.

29th. All the talk is that De Ruyter is come over-land home with six or eight of his captaines to command here at home, and their ships kept abroad in the Straights: which sounds as if they had a mind to do something with us.

51 Daughter of Matthew, second son to Sir Matthew Boynton, Bart., of Barnston, Yorkshire. She became the first wife of Richard Talbot, afterwards Duke of Tyrconnel.
52 He had built the ship.

31st. This day I hear young Mr Stanly, a brave young gentleman, that went out with young Jermin, with Prince Rupert, is already dead of the small-pox, at Portsmouth. All preparations against the Dutch; and the Duke of York fitting himself with all speed to go to the fleet which is hastening for him; being now resolved to go in the Charles.

November 5th. To the Duke's house to see *Macbeth*, a pretty good play, but admirably acted. Thence home; the coach being forced to go round by London Wall home, because of the bonfires; the day being mightily observed in the City.

8th. At noon, I and Sir J. Minnes and Lord Barkeley (who with Sir J. Duncum,[53] and Mr Chichly, are made Masters of the Ordnance), to the office of the Ordnance, to discourse about wadding for guns. Thence to dinner, all of us to the Lieutenant's of the Tower; where a good dinner, but disturbed in the middle of it by the King's coming into the Tower: and so we broke up, and to him, and went up and down the store-houses and magazines; which are, with the addition of the new great storehouse, a noble sight.

9th. To White Hall, and there the King being in his Cabinet Council, (I desiring to speak with Sir G. Carteret,) I was called in, and demanded by the King himself many questions, to which I did give him full answers. There were at this Council my Lord Chancellor, Archbishop of Canterbury, Lord Treasurer, the two Secretarys, and Sir G. Carteret. Not a little contented at this chance of being made known to these persons, and called often by my name by the King. The Duke of York is this day gone away to Portsmouth.

11th. A gentleman told us he saw the other day, (and did bring the draught of it to Sir Francis Prigeon,) a monster born of an hostler's wife at Salsbury, two women children perfectly made, joyned at the lower part of their bellies, and every part perfect as two bodies, and only one payre of legs coming forth on one side from the middle where they were joined. It was alive 24 hours, and cried and did as all hopefull children do; but, being showed too much to people, was killed. To the Council at White Hall, where a great many lords: Annesly in the chair. But, Lord! to see what work they will make us, and what trouble we shall have to inform men in a business they are

53 MP for Bury St Edmunds.

to begin to know, when the greatest of our hurry is, is a thing to be lamented; and I fear the consequence will be bad to us. Put on my new shaggy, purple gown with gold buttons and loop lace.

14th. Up, and with Sir W. Batten to White Hall, to the Lords of the Admiralty, and there did our business betimes. Thence to Sir Philip Warwick about Navy business: and my Lord Ashly; and afterwards to my Lord Chancellor, who is very well pleased with me, and my carrying of his business. And so to the 'Change, where mighty busy; and so home to dinner, where Mr Creed and Moore: and after dinner I to my Lord Treasurer's, to Sir Philip Warwick there, and then to White Hall, to the Duke of Albemarle, about Tangier; and then homeward to the Coffee-house to hear news. And it seems the Dutch, as I afterwards found by Mr Coventry's letters, have stopped a ship of masts of Sir W. Warren's, coming for us in a Swede's ship, which they will not release upon Sir G. Downing's claiming her: which appears as the first act of hostility; and is looked upon as so by Mr Coventry. The *Elias*, coming from New England (Captain Hill, commander,) is sunk; only the captain and a few men saved. She foundered in the sea.

21st. This day for certain news is come that Teddiman hath brought in eighteen or twenty Dutchmen, merchants, their Bourdeaux fleet, and two men of warr to Portsmouth. And I had letters this afternoon, that three are brought into the Downes and Dover; so that the warr is begun: God give a good end to it!

22nd. To my Lord Treasurer's; where with Sir Philip Warwick, studying all we could to make the last year swell as high as we could. And it is much to see how he do study for the King, to do it to get all the money from the Parliament he can: and I shall be serviceable to him therein, to help him to heads upon which to enlarge the report of the expence. He did observe to me how obedient this Parliament was for awhile, and the last Session how they began to differ, and to carp at the King's officers; and what they will do now, he says, is to make agreement for the money, for there is no guess to be made of it. He told me he was prepared to convince the Parliament that the Subsidys are a most ridiculous tax, (the four last not rising to £40,000) and unequall. He talks of a tax of Assessment of £70,000 for five years; the people to be secured that it shall continue no longer than there is really a warr; and the charges thereof to be paid. He told me, that one year of the late Dutch war, cost £1,623,000. Thence to my Lord Chancellor's and there staid long with Sir W. Batten, and Sir J. Minnes, to speak with my lord about our Prize Office business; but, being sick and full of visitants, we could not speak with him, and so away home. Where Sir Richard Ford did meet us with letters from Holland this day, that it is likely the Dutch fleet will not come out this year; they have not victuals to keep them out, and it is likely they will be frozen before they can get back. Captain Cocke is made Steward for sick and wounded seamen.

23rd. Sir G. Carteret was here this afternoon; and strange to see how we plot to make the charge of this war to appear greater than it is, because of getting money.

25th. At my office all the morning, to prepare an account of the charge we have been put to extraordinary by the Dutch already; and I have brought it to appear £852,700: but God knows this is only a scare to the Parliament, to make them give the more money. Thence to the Parliament House, and there did give it to Sir Philip Warwick; the House being hot upon giving the King a supply of money. Mr Jenings tells me the mean manner that Sir Samuel Morland lives near him, in a house he hath bought and laid out money upon, in all to the value of £1200; but is believed to be a beggar. At Sir W. Batten's I hear that the House have given the King £2,500,000 to be paid for this war, only for the Navy, in three years' time: which is a joyful thing to all the King's party I see, but was much opposed by Mr Vaughan and others, that it should be so much.

28th. Certain news of our peace made by Captain Allen with Argier; and that the Dutch have sent part of their fleet round by Scotland; and resolve to pay off the rest half-pay, promising the rest in the Spring, hereby keeping their men. But how true this, I know not.

December 3rd. The Duke of York is expected to-night with great joy from Portsmouth, after his having been abroad at sea three or four days with the fleet; and the Dutch are all drawn into their harbours. But it seems like a victory: and a matter of some reputation to us it is, and blemish to them; but in no degree like what it is esteemed at, the weather requiring them to do so.

5th. Up, and to White Hall with Sir J. Minnes; and there, among an infinite crowd of great persons, did kiss the Duke's hand; but had no time to discourse.

6th. To the Old Exchange, and there hear that the Dutch are fitting their ships out again, which puts us to new discourse, and to alter our thoughts of the Dutch, as to their want of courage or force.

15th. It seems, of all mankind there is no man so led by another as the Duke is by Lord Muskerry[54] and this FitzHarding. Insomuch, as when the King would have him to be Privy-Purse, the Duke wept, and said, 'But, Sir, I must have your promise, if you will have my dear Charles from me, that i' ever you have an occasion for an army again, I may have him with me; believing him to be the best commander of an army in the world.' But Mr Cholmly thinks, as all other men I meet with do, that he is a very ordinary fellow. It is strange how the Duke also do love naturally, and affect the Irish above the English. He, of the company he carried with him to sea, took above two thirds Irish and French. He tells me the King do hate my Lord Chancellor; and that they, that is the King and Lord FitzHarding, do laugh at him for a dull fellow; and in all this business of the Dutch war do nothing by his advice, hardly consulting him. Only he is a good minister in other respects, and the King cannot be without him; but, above all, being the Duke's father-in-law, he is kept in; otherwise FitzHarding were able to fling down two of him. This, all the wise and grave lords see, and cannot help it; but yield to it. But he bemoans what the end of it may be, the King being ruled by these men, as he hath been all along since his coming; to the rasing all the strongholds in Scotland, and giving liberty to the Irish in Ireland, whom Cromwell had settled all in one corner; who are now able, and it is feared every day a massacre beginning among them.

17th. Mighty talk there is of this Comet that is seen a'nights; and the King and Queene did sit up last night to see it, and did, it seems. And to-night I thought to have done so too; but it is cloudy, and so no stars appear. But I will endeavour it. Mr Gray did tell me tonight, for certain, that the Dutch, as high as they seem, do begin to buckle; and

54 Eldest son of the Earl of Clancarty. He had served with distinction in Flanders, as colonel of an infantry regiment, and was killed on board the Duke of York's ship, in the sea fight, 1665.

that one man in this kingdom did tell the King that he is offered
£40,000 to make a peace, and others have been offered money also.
It seems the taking of their Bourdeaux fleet thus, arose from a printed
Gazette of the Dutch's boasting of fighting, and having beaten the
English: in confidence whereof, (it coming to Bourdeaux,) all the
fleet comes out, and so falls into our hands.

19th. With Sir J. Minnes to White Hall, and there we waited on the
Duke. And among other things Mr Coventry took occasion to
vindicate himself before the Duke and us, being all there, about the
choosing of Taylor[55] for Harwich. Upon which the Duke did clear
him, and did tell us that he did expect, that, after he had named a
man, none of us shall then oppose or find fault with the man; but if
we had any thing to say, we ought to say it before he had chose him.
Sir G. Carteret thought himself concerned, and endeavoured to clear
himself: and by and by Sir W. Batten did speak, knowing himself
guilty, and did confess, that being pressed by the Council he did say
what he did, that he was accounted a fanatique; but did not know
that at that time he had been appointed by his Royal Highness. To
which the Duke: that it was impossible but he must know that he had
appointed him; and so it did appear that the Duke did mean all this
while Sir W. Batten.

21st. My Lord Sandwich this day writes me word that he hath seen
(at Portsmouth) the Comet, and says it is the most extraordinary thing
he ever saw.

22nd. Met with a copy of verses, mightily commended by some
gentlemen there, of my Lord Mordaunt's,[56] in excuse of his going to
sea this late expedition, with the Duke of York. But Lord! they are
sorry things; only a Lord made them. Thence to the 'Change; and
there, among the merchants, I hear fully the news of our being beaten
to dirt at Guinny, by De Ruyter with his fleet. The particulars, as
much as by Sir G. Carteret afterwards I heard, I have said in a letter to
my Lord Sandwich this day at Portsmouth; it being most wholly to
the utter ruine of our Royall Company, and reproach and shame to
the whole nation, as well as justification to them in their doing wrong
to no man as to his private property, only taking whatever is found to

55 Silas Taylor, Storekeeper at Harwich.
56 See note, November 26, 1666.

belong to the Company, and nothing else. To Redriffe; and just in time within two minutes, and saw the new vessel of Sir William Petty's launched, the King and Duke being there. It swims and looks finely, and I believe will do well.

24th. At noon to the 'Change, to the Coffee-house; and there heard Sir Richard Ford tell the whole story of our defeat at Guinny. Wherein our men are guilty of the most horrid cowardice and perfidiousness, as he says and tells it, that ever Englishmen were. Captain Raynolds, that was the only commander of any of the King's ships there, was shot at by De Ruyter, with a bloody flag flying. He, instead of opposing (which, indeed, had been to no purpose, but only to maintain honour) did poorly go on board himself, to ask what De Ruyter would have; and so yield to whatever Ruyter would desire. The King and Duke are highly vexed at it, it seems, and the business deserves it. I saw the Comet, which is now, whether worn away or no I know not, but appears not with a tail, but only is larger and duller than any other star, and is come to rise betimes, and to make a great arch, and is gone quite to a new place in the heavens than it was before: but I hope in a clearer night something more will be seen.

28th. To Sir W. Pen's to his Lady,[57] who is a well-looked, fat, short, old Dutch woman; but one that hath been heretofore pretty handsome, and is I believe very discreet, and hath more wit than her husband.

31st. Public matters are all in a hurry about a Dutch warr. Our preparations great; our provocations against them great; and after all our presumption, we are now afraid as much of them, as we lately contemned them. Every thing else in the State quiet, blessed be God! My Lord Sandwich at sea with the fleet at Portsmouth; sending some about to cruise for taking of ships, which we have done to a great number. This Christmas I judged it fit to look over all my papers and books; and to tear all that I found either boyish or not to be worth keeping, or fit to be seen, if it should please God to take me away suddenly. Among others, I found these two or three notes, which I thought fit to keep.

57 Margaret, daughter of John Jasper, a merchant at Rotterdam.

AGE OF MY GRANDFATHER'S CHILDREN.

Thomas,   1595
Mary, March 16, 1597
Edith, October 11, 1599
John, (my Father,) January 14, 1601
My father and mother marryed at Newington,
            in Surry, Oct. 15, 1626

THEYR CHILDREN'S AGES.

Mary, July 24, 1627   *mort.*[58]
Paulina, September 18, 1628 *mort.*
Esther, March 27, 1630   *mort.*
John, January 10, 1631   *mort.*
Samuel,[59] February 23, 1632
Thomas, June 18, 1634   *mort.*
Sarah, August 25, 1635   *mort.*
Jacob, May 1, 1637   *mort.*
Robert, November 18, 1638   *mort.*
Paulina, October 18, 1640
John, November 26, 1641   *mort.*

December 31, 1664

Charmes

I. FOR STENCHING BLOOD.

Sanguis mane in te,
Sicut Christus fuit in se;
Sanguis mane in tua vena
Sicut Christus in sua poena
Sanguis mane fixus,
Sicut Christus quando fuit crucifixus.

---

58 The word *mort* must have been in some instances added long after the entry was first made.
59 To this name is affixed the following note: – Went to reside in Magd. Coll., Camb. and did put on my gown first, March 5, 1650-1.

2. A THORNE.

Jesus, that was of a Virgin born,
Was pricked both with nail and thorn;
It neither wealed, nor belled, rankled nor boned;
In the name of Jesus no more shall this.

Or, thus: —

Christ was of a Virgin born,
And he was pricked with a thorn
And it did neither bell, nor swell,
And I trust in Jesus this never will.

3. A CRAMP.

Cramp be thou faintless,
As our Lady was sinless,
When she bare Jesus.

4. A BURNING.

There came three Angells out of the East;
The one brought fire, the other brought frost —
Out fire; in frost.
In the name of the Father, and Son, and Holy Ghost.

AMEN.

1664/65. January 2nd. To my Lord Brouncker's, by appointment, in the Piazza, in Covent-Garden; where I occasioned much mirth with a ballet[1] I brought with me, made from the seamen at sea to their ladies in town; saying Sir W. Pen, Sir G. Ascue, and Sir J. Lawson made them. Here a most noble French dinner and banquet. The street full of footballs, it being a great frost.

4th. To my Lord of Oxford's, but his Lordship was in bed at past ten o'clock: and, Lord help us! so rude a dirty family I never saw in my life.

9th. I saw the Royal Society bring their new book, wherein is nobly writ their charter and laws, and comes to be signed by the Duke as a

1 The Earl of Dorset's song, 'To all ye ladies now at land,' &c.

Fellow; and all the Fellows' hands are to be entered there, and lie as a monument; and the King hath put his with the word Founder. Holmes was this day sent to the Tower, but I perceive it is made matter of jest only; but if the Dutch should be our masters, it may come to be of earnest to him, to be given over to them for a sacrifice, as Sir W. Rawly was. To a Tangier committee, where I was accosted and most highly complimented by my Lord Bellasses, our new governor, beyond my expectation; and I may make good use of it. Our patent is renewed, and he and my Lord Barkeley, and Sir Thomas Ingram[2] put in as commissioners.

11th. This evening, by a letter from Plymouth, I hear that two of our ships, the *Leopard* and another, in the Straights, are lost by running aground; and that three more had like to have been so, but got off, whereof Captain Allen one: and that a Dutch fleet are gone thither; and if they should meet with our lame ships, God knows what would become of them. This I reckon most sad news; God make us sensible of it!

12th. Spoke with a Frenchman who was taken, but released, by a Dutch man-of-war of thirty-six guns, (with seven more of the King's or greater ships), off the North Foreland, by Margett. Which is a strange attempt, that they should come to our teeth; but the wind being easterly, the wind that should bring our force from Portsmouth, will carry them away home.

13th. Yesterday's news confirmed, though a little different; but a couple of ships in the Straights we have lost, and the Dutch have been in Margaret Road.[3]

14th. To the King's house, there to see *Vulpone*,[4] a most excellent play: the best I think I ever saw, and well acted.

15th. With Sir W. Pen in his coach to my Lord Chancellor's, where by and by Mr Coventry, Sir W. Pen, Sir J. Lawson, Sir G. Ascue, and myself were called in to the King, there being several of the Privy Council, and my Lord Chancellor lying at length upon a couch (of the goute I suppose); and there Sir W. Pen spoke pretty well to

2 Chancellor of the Duchy of Lancaster, and a Privy Counsellor. Died 1671.
3 Margate?
4 A comedy by Ben Johnson.

dissuade the King from letting the Turkey ships go out: saying (in short) the King having resolved to have 130 ships out by the spring, he must have above 20 of them merchantmen. Towards which, he in the whole River could find but 12 or 14 and of them the five ships taken up by these merchants were a part, and so could not be spared. That we should need 30,000 sailors to man these 130 ships, and of them in service we have not above 16,000: so that we shall need 14,000 more. That these ships will with their convoys carry about 2000 men, and those the best men that could be got; it being the men used to the Southward that are the best men of warr, though those bred in the North among the colliers are good for labour. That it will not be safe for the merchants, nor honourable for the King, to expose these rich ships with his convoy of six ships to go, it not being enough to secure them against the Dutch, who, without doubt, will have a great fleet in the Straights. This, Sir J. Lawson enlarged upon. Sir G. Ascue chiefly spoke that the warr and trade could not be supported together. Mr Coventry showed how the medium of the men the King hath one year with another employed in his Navy since his coming, hath not been above 3000 men, or at most 4000 men; and now having occasion of 30,000, the remaining 26,000 must be found out of the trade of the nation. He showed how the cloaths, sending by these merchants to Turkey, are already bought and paid for to the workmen, and are as many as they would send these twelve months or more; so the poor do not suffer by their not going, but only the merchant, upon whose hands they lie dead; and so the inconvenience is the less. And yet for them he propounded, either the King should, if his Treasurer would suffer it, buy them, and showed the loss would not be so great to him: or, dispense with the Act of Navigation, and let them be carried out by strangers; and ending that he doubted not but when the merchants saw there was no remedy, they would and could find ways of sending them abroad to their profit. All ended with a conviction (unless future discourse with the merchants should alter it,) that it was not fit for them to go out, though the ships be loaded. So we withdrew, and the merchants were called in. Staying without, my Lord FitzHarding come thither, and fell to discourse of Prince Rupert's disease,[5] telling the horrible degree of its breaking out on his head. He observed also from the

5 Morbus, *scil.* Gallicus.

Prince, that courage is not what men take it to be, a contempt of death; for, says he, how chagrined the Prince was the other day when he thought he should die.

16th. To a Tangier committee, where my Lord Ashly, I observe, is a most clear man in matters of accounts, and most ingeniously did discourse and explain all matters.

19th. This day was buried (but I could not be there) my cosen Percivall Angier: and yesterday I received the news that Dr Tom Pepys is dead, at Impington.

21st. Mr Povy carried me to Somerset House, and there showed me the Queene-Mother's chamber and closet, most beautiful places for furniture and pictures; and so down the great stone stairs to the garden, and tried the brave echo upon the stairs; which continues a voice so long as the singing three notes, concords, one after another, they all three shall sound in consort together a good while most pleasantly.

23rd. Up, and with Sir W. Batten and Sir W. Pen to White Hall; but there finding the Duke gone to his lodgings in St James's for alltogether, his Duchesse being ready to lie in, we to him, and there did our usual business. And here I met the great news confirmed by the Duke's own relation, by a letter from Captain Allen. First, of our own loss of two ships, the *Phoenix* and *Nonsuch*, in the Bay of Gibraltar: then of his and his seven ships with him, in the Bay of Cales, or thereabouts, fighting with the 34 Dutch Smyrna fleet; sinking the *King Salamon*, a ship worth a £150,000 or more, some say £200,000 and another; and taking of three merchant-ships. Two of our ships were disabled, by the Dutch unfortunately falling against their will against them; the *Advice*, Captain W. Poole, and *Antelope*, Captain Clerke. The Dutch then of war did little service. Captain Allen, before he would fire one gun, come within pistol-shot of the enemy. The Spaniards, at Cales, did stand laughing at the Dutch, to see them run away and flee to the shore, 34 or thereabouts, against eight Englishmen at most. I do purpose to get the whole relation, if I live, of Captain Allen himself. In our loss of the two ships in the Bay of Gibraltar, the world do comment upon the misfortune of Captain Moone of the *Nonsuch*, (who did lose, in the same manner, the *Satisfaction*,) as a person that hath ill-luck attending him; without considering that the whole fleet was ashore. Captain Allen led the way, and himself writes that all the masters of the fleet, old and young, were mistaken, and did carry their ships aground. But I think I heard the Duke say that Moone, being put into *Oxford*, had in this conflict regained his credit, by sinking one and taking another. Captain Seale of the *Milford* hath done his part very well, in boarding the *King Salamon*, which held out half an hour after she was boarded; and his men kept her an hour after they did master her, and then she sunk, and drowned about 17 of her men.

24th. The Dutch have, by consent of all the Provinces, voted no trade to be suffered for eighteen months, but that they apply themselves wholly to the war.[6]

27th. Mr Slingsby, a very ingenious person about the Mint, tells me that the money passing up and down in business is £700,000. He also made me fully understand that the old law of prohibiting bullion to be exported, is, and ever was a folly and an injury, rather than good.

February 3rd. To visit my Lady Sandwich, and she discoursed largely to me her opinion of a match, if it could be thought fit by my Lord, for my Lady Jemimah, with Sir G. Carteret's eldest son; but I doubt he hath yet no settled estate in land. But I will inform myself, and give her my opinion. Then Mrs Pickering (after private discourse ended, we going into the other room) did, at my Lady's command, tell me the manner of a masquerade before the King and the Court the other day. Where six women (my Lady Castlemaine and Duchesse of Monmouth being two of them,) and six men, (the Duke of Monmouth and Lord Avon and Monsieur Blanfort,[7] being three of them) in vizards, but

6 This statement of a total prohibition of all trade, and for so long a period as eighteen months, by a government so essentially commercial as that of the United Provinces seems extraordinary. The fact, as I am informed, was, that when in the beginning of the year 1665 the States General saw that the war with England was become inevitable, they took several vigorous measures, and determined to equip a formidable fleet, and with a view to obtain a sufficient number of men to man it, prohibited all navigation, especially in the great and small fisheries as they were then called, and in the whale fishery. This measure appears to have resembled the embargoes so commonly resorted to in this country on similar occasions, rather than a total prohibition of trade.

7 Lewis Duras, Marquis de Blanquefort, naturalised in 1665 by Charles II, and created Baron Duras 1672, and KG by James II, whom he had attended in the sea-fight, 1665, as Captain of the guard.

most rich and antique dresses, did dance admirably and most glori-
ously. God give us cause to continue the mirth!

4th. I to the Sun behind the 'Change, to dinner to my Lord Belasses.
He told us a very handsome passage of the King's sending him his
message about holding out the town of Newarke, of which he was
then governor for the King. This message he sent in a slugg-bullet,
being writ in cipher, and wrapped up in lead and sealed. So the
messenger come to my Lord and told him he had a message from the
King, but it was yet in his belly; so they did give him some physick,
and out it come. This was a month before the King's flying to the
Scots; and therein he told him that at such a day, the 3rd or 6th. of
May, he should hear of his being come to the Scots, being assured by
the King of France that in coming to them he should be used with all
the liberty, honour, and safety, that could be desired. And at the just
day he did come to the Scots. He told us another odd passage: how
the King having newly put out Prince Rupert of his generalship,
upon some miscarriage at Bristol, and Sir Richard Willis of his
governorship of Newarke, at the entreaty of the gentry of the
County, and put in my Lord Bellasses; the great officers of the King's
army mutinyed, and come in that manner with swords drawn, into
the market-place of the town where the King was; which the King
hearing says, 'I must horse.' And there himself personally, when
everybody expected they should have been opposed, the King come,
and cried to the head of the mutineers, which was Prince Rupert,
'Nephew, I command you to be gone.' So the Prince, in all his fury
and discontent, withdrew, and his company scattered.

6th. One of the coldest days, all say, they ever felt in England.

9th. Sir William Petty tells me that Mr Barlow[8] is dead; for which,
God knows my heart, I could be as sorry as is possible for one to be
for a stranger, by whose death he gets £100 per annum.

12th. To Church to St Lawrence to hear Dr Wilkins, the great
scholar, for curiosity, I having never heard him: but was not satisfied
with him at all.

15th. At noon, with Creed to the Trinity-house, where a very good
dinner among the old jokers, and an extraordinary discourse of the

8 Mr Pepys's predecessor as Clerk of the Acts, to whom he paid part of the salary.

manner of the loss of the *Royall Oake* coming home from Bantam, upon the rocks of Scilly. Thence with Creed to Gresham College, where I had been by Mr Povy the last week proposed to be admitted a member; and was this day admitted, by signing a book and being taken by the hand by the President, my Lord Brouncker, and some words of admittance said to me. But it is a most acceptable thing to hear their discourse, and see their experiments, which were this day on fire, and how it goes out in a place where the ayre is not free, and sooner out where the ayre is exhausted, which they showed by an engine on purpose. After this being done, they to the Crown Tavern, behind the 'Change, and there my Lord and most of the company to a club supper; Sir P. Neale,[9] Sir R. Murrey,[10] Dr Clerke, Dr Whistler,[11] Dr Goddard,[12] and others, of the most eminent worth. Above all, Mr Boyle was at the meeting, and above him Mr Hooke, who is the most, and promises the least, of any man in the world that ever I saw. Here excellent discourse till ten at night, and then home.

17th. Povy tells me how my Lord Barkeley will say openly, that he hath fought more set fields than any man in England hath done.

18th. At noon, to the Royall Oak taverne in Lombard Street; where Sir William Petty and the owners of the double-bottomed boat (the Experiment) did entertain my Lord Brouncker, Sir R. Murrey, myself, and others, with marrow bones, and a chine of beef of the victuals they have made for this ship; and excellent company and good discourse: but, above all, I do value Sir William Petty. Thence home; and took my Lord Sandwich's draught of the harbour of Portsmouth down to Ratcliffe, to one Burston, to make a plate for the King, and another for the Duke, and another for himself; which will be very neat.

9 Sir Paul Neile, of White Waltham, Berkshire, eldest son to Neile, Archbishop of York.

10 One of the Founders of the Royal Society, made a Privy Counsellor for Scotland after the Restoration.

11 Daniel Whistler, Fellow of Merton College, took the degree of MD at Leyden, 1645; and after practising in London, went as Physician to the Embassy, with Bulstrode Whitlock, into Sweden. On his return he became Fellow, and at length President, of the College of Physicians. Died 1684.

12 Jonathan Goddard, MD, FRS. He had been Physician to Cromwell.

20th. Rode into the beginning of my Lord Chancellor's new house, near St James's; which common people have already called Dunkirke-house, from their opinion of his having a good bribe for the selling of that towne. And very noble I believe it will be. Near that is my Lord Barkeley beginning another one side, and Sir J. Denham on the other.

21st. My Lady Sandwich tells me how my Lord Castlemaine is coming over from France, and is believed will soon be made friends with his Lady again. What mad freaks the Mayds of Honour at Court have: that Mrs Jenings,[13] one of the Dutchesse's maids, the other day dressed herself like an orange wench, and went up and down and cried oranges; till falling down, or by some accident her fine shoes were discerned, and she put to a great deal of shame; that such as these tricks being ordinary, and worse among them, thereby few will venture upon them for wives: my Lady Castlemaine will in merriment say, that her daughter (not above a year old or two) will be the first mayd in the Court that will be married. This day my Lord Sandwich writ me word from the Downes, that he is like to be in town this week.

22nd. At noon to the 'Change, busy; where great talk of a Dutch ship in the North put on shore, and taken by a troop of horse.

25th. At noon to the 'Change; where just before I come, the Swede that had told the King and the Duke so boldly a great lie of the Dutch flinging our men back to back into the sea at Guinny, so particularly, and readily, and confidently, was whipt round the 'Change: he confessing it a lie, and that he did it in hopes to get something.

27th. We to a Committee of the Council to discourse concerning pressing of men; but Lord! how they meet; never sit down: one comes, now another goes, then comes another; one complaining that nothing is done, another swearing that he hath been there these two hours and nobody come. At last my Lord Annesly[14] says, 'I think we must be forced to get the King to come to every committee; for I do not see that we do any thing at any time but

13 Frances, daughter of Richard Jennings, Esq., of Sandridge, near St Alban's, and eldest sister of Sarah, Duchess of Marlborough, married 1st, George Hamilton, afterwards knighted, and in the French service; and 2nd, Richard Talbot, created Duke of Tyrconnel. She died in Ireland, 1730. The anecdote here related will be found in the *Mémoires de Grammont*.
14 Created Earl of Anglesea.

when he is here.' And I believe he said the truth: and very constant he is on council-days; which his predecessors, it seems, very rarely were. To Sir Philip Warwick's; and there he did contract with me a kind of friendship and freedom of communication, wherein he assures me to make me understand the whole business of the Treasurer of the Navy, that I shall know as well as Sir G. Carteret what money he hath; and will needs have me come to him sometimes, or he meet me, to discourse of things tending to the serving the King: and I am mighty proud and happy in becoming so known to such a man. And I hope shall pursue it.

March 1st. To Gresham College, where Mr Hooke read a second very curious lecture about the late Comet; among other things proving very probably that this is the very same Comet that appeared before in the year 1618, and that in such a time probably it will appear again, which is a very new opinion; but all will be in print. Then to the meeting, where Sir G. Carteret's two sons, his own, and Sir N. Slaning,[15] were admitted of the society: and this day I did pay my admission money, 40s. to the society.

4th. William Howe come to see me, being come up with my Lord from sea: he is grown a discreet, but very conceited fellow. He tells me how little respectfully Sir W. Pen did carry it to my Lord on board the Duke's ship at sea; and that Captain Minnes, a favourite of Prince Rupert's, do show my Lord little respect; but that every body else esteems my Lord as they ought. This day was proclaimed at the 'Change the war with Holland.

5th. To my Lord Sandwich's and dined with my Lord; it being the first time he hath dined at home since his coming from sea: and a pretty odd demand it was of my Lord to my Lady before me: 'How do you, sweetheart? How have you done all this week?' himself taking notice of it to me, that he had hardly seen her the week before. At dinner he did use me with the greatest solemnity in the world, in carving for me, and nobody else, and calling often to my Lady to cut for me; and all the respect possible.

6th. With Sir J. Minnes to St James's, and there did our business with the Duke. Great preparations for his speedy return to sea. I saw him

15 Sir Nicholas Slaning, KB, married a daughter of Sir George Carteret.

try on his buff coat and hat-piece covered with black velvet. It troubles me more to think of his venture, than of any thing else in the whole warr.

8th. This morning is brought me to the office the sad news of the *London*, in which Sir J. Lawson's men were all bringing her from Chatham to the Hope, and thence he was to go to sea in her; but a little on this side the buoy of the Nower, she suddenly blew up. About 24 men and a woman that were in the round-house and coach saved; the rest, being about 300, drowned: the ship breaking all in pieces, with 80 pieces of brass ordnance. She lies sunk, with her round-house above water. Sir J. Lawson hath a great loss in this of so many good chosen men, and many relations among them. I went to the 'Change, where the news taken very much to heart.

10th. At noon to the 'Change, where very hot, people's proposal of the City giving the King another ship for the *London*, that is lately blown up. It would be very handsome, and if well managed, might be done; but I fear if it be put into ill hands, or that the courtiers do solicit it, it will never be done.

13th. This day my wife begun to wear light-coloured locks, quite white almost, which, though it makes her look very pretty, yet not being natural, vexes me, that I will not have her wear them. This day I saw my Lord Castlemaine at St James's, lately come from France.

17th. The Duke did give us some commands, and so broke up, not taking leave of him. But the best piece of newes is, that instead of a great many troublesome Lords, the whole business is to be left with the Duke of Albemarle to act as Admirall in his stead; which is a thing that do cheer my heart. For the other would have vexed us with attendance, and never done the business.

19th. Mr Povy and I in his coach to Hyde Parke, being the first day of the tour there. Where many brave ladies; among others, Castlemaine lay impudently upon her back in her coach asleep, with her mouth open. There was also my Lady Kerneguy,[16] once my Lady Anne Hambleton.

16 Daughter of William Duke of Hamilton, wife of Lord Carnegy, who became Earl of Southesk on his father's death. She is frequently mentioned in the *Mémoires de Grammont.*

20th. Creed and I had Mr Povy's coach sent for us, and we to his house; where we did some business in order to the work of this day. Povy and I to my Lord Sandwich, who tells me that the Duke is not only a friend to the business, but to me, in terms of the greatest love and respect. The Duke did direct Secretary Bennet to declare his mind to the Tangier committee, that he approves of me for treasurer; and with a character of me to be a man whose industry and discretion he would trust soon as any man's in England: and did the like to my Lord Sandwich. So to White Hall to the Committee of Tangier, where there were present, my Lord of Albemarle, my Lord Peterborough, Sandwich, Barkeley, FitzHarding, Secretary Bennet, Sir Thomas Ingram, Sir John Lawson, Povy and I. Where, after other business, Povy did declare his business very handsomely; that he was sorry he had been so unhappy in his accounts, as not to give their Lordships the satisfaction he intended, and that he was sure his accounts were right, and continues to submit them to examination, and is ready to lay down in ready money the fault of his account; and that for the future, that the work might be better done and with more quiet to him, he desired, by approbation of the Duke, he might resign his place to Mr Pepys. Whereupon, Secretary Bennet did deliver the Duke's command, which was received with great content and allowance beyond expectation; the Secretary repeating also the Duke's character of me. And I could discern my Lord FitzHarding was well pleased with me, and signified full satisfaction, and whispered something seriously of me to the Secretary. And there I received their constitution under all their hands presently; so that I am already confirmed their treasurer, and put into a condition of striking of tallys; and all without one harsh word of dislike, but quite the contrary; which is a good fortune beyond all imagination.

22nd. Sir William Petty did tell me that in good earnest he hath in his will left some parts of his estate to him that could invent such and such things. As among others, that could discover truly the way of milk coming into the breasts of a woman; and he that could invent proper characters to express to another the mixture of relishes and tastes. And says, that to him that invents gold, he gives nothing for the philosopher's stone; for (says he) they that find out that, will be able to pay themselves. But, says he, by this means it is better than to go to a lecture; for here my executors, that must part with this, will be sure to be well convinced of the invention before they do part with their money. I saw the Duke, kissed his hand, and had his most kind expressions of his value and opinion of me, which comforted me above all things in the world: the like from Mr Coventry most heartily and affectionately. Saw, among other fine ladies, Mrs Middleton,[17] a very great beauty; and I saw Waller[18] the poet, whom I never saw before.

23rd. To my Lord Sandwich, who follows the Duke this day by water down to the Hope, where the Prince lies. He received me, busy as he was, with mighty kindness and joy at my promotions; telling me most largely how the Duke hath expressed on all occasions his good opinion of my service and love for me. I paid my thanks and acknowledgement to him; and so back home, where at the office all the morning.

27th. Up betimes to Mr Povy's, and there did sign and seal my agreement with him about my place of being treasurer for Tangier. Thence to the Duke of Albemarle, the first time that we officers of the Navy have waited upon him since the Duke of York's going, who hath deputed him to be Admirall in his absence. And I find him a quiet heavy man, that will help business when he can, and hinder nothing. I did afterwards alone give him thanks for his favour to me about my Tangier business, which he received kindly, and did speak much of his esteem of me. Thence, and did the same to Sir H. Bennet, who did the like to me very fully.

April 1st. With Sir G. Carteret, Sir W. Batten, and Sir J. Minnes to my Lord Treasurer, and there did lay open the expence for the six months past, and an estimate of the seven months to come, to November next: the first arising to above £500,000, and the latter will, as we judge, come to above £1,000,000. But to see how my Lord Treasurer did bless himself, crying he would do no more than he could, nor give more money than he had, if the occasion and expence were never so great, which is but a bad story.

17 Jane, daughter to Sir Robert Needham, frequently mentioned in the *Mémoires de Grammont*. Her portrait is at Windsor Castle amongst the beauties of Charles II's Court.
18 Edmund Waller.

3rd. To a play at the Duke's, of my Lord Orrery's, called *Mustapha*,[19] which being not good, made Beterton's part and Ianthe's but ordinary too. All the pleasure of the play was, the King and my Lady Castlemaine were there; and pretty witty Nell,[20] at the King's house, and the younger Marshall sat next us; which pleased me mightily.

6th. Great talk of a new Comet; and it is certain do appear as bright as the late one at the best; but I have not seen it myself.

7th. Sir Philip Warwick did show me nakedly the King's condition for money for the Navy; and he do assure me, unless the King can get some noblemen or rich money-gentlemen to lend him money, or to get the City to do it, it is impossible to find money: we having already, as he says, spent one year's share of the three-years tax, which comes to £2,500,000.

10th. My Lord Brouncker took me and Sir Thomas Harvy in his coach to the Park, which is very troublesome with the dust; and ne'er a great beauty there to-day but Mrs Middleton.

12th. Sir G. Carteret, my Lord Brouncker, Sir Thomas Harvy, and myself, down to my Lord Treasurer's chamber to him and the Chancellor, and the Duke of Albemarle; and there I did give them a large account of the charge of the Navy, and want of money. But strange to see how they hold up their hands, crying, 'What shall we do?' says my Lord Treasurer, 'Why what means all this, Mr Pepys? This is true, you say; but what would you have me to do? I have given all I can for my life. Why will not people lend their money? Why will they not trust the King as well as Oliver? Why do our prizes come to nothing, that yielded so much heretofore?' And this was all we could get, and went away without other answer.

16th. Captain Taylor can, as he says, show the very originall Charter to Worcester, of King Edgar's, wherein he stiles himself, *Rex Marium Britanniae*, &c.; which is the great text that Mr Selden and others do quote, but imperfectly and upon trust. But he hath the very originall, which he says he will show me.

---

19 There was another tragedy of this name, by Fulk, Lord Brook.
20 Nell Gwynne.

17th. To the Duke of Albemarle's, where he showed me Mr Coventry's letters, how three Dutch privateers are taken, in one whereof Everson's son is captaine. But they have killed poor Captaine Golding in the *Diamond*. Two of them, one of 32 and the other of 20 odd guns, did stand stoutly up against her, which hath 46, and the *Yarmouth* that hath 52 guns, and as many more men as they. So that they did more than we could expect, not yielding till many of their men were killed. And Everson, when he was brought before the Duke of York, and was observed to be shot through the hat, answered, that he wished it had gone through his head, rather than been taken. One thing more is written; that two of our ships the other day appearing upon the coast of Holland, they presently fired their beacons round the country to give them notice. And news is brought the King, that the Dutch Smyrna fleet is seen upon the back of Scotland; and thereupon the King hath wrote to the Duke, that he do appoint a fleet to go to the Northward to try to meet them coming home round: which God send! Thence to White Hall; where the King seeing me, did come to me, and calling me by name, did discourse with me about the ships in the River: and this is the first time that ever I knew the King did know me personally; so that hereafter I must not go thither, but with expectation to be questioned, and to be ready to give good answers.

19th. Up by five o'clock, and by water to White Hall; and there took coach, and with Mr Moore to Chelsy; where, after all my fears what doubts and difficulties my Lord Privy Seale[21] would make at my Tangier Privy Seale, he did pass it at first reading, without my speaking with him. And then called me in, and was very civil to me. I passed my time in contemplating (before I was called in) the picture of my Lord's son's lady, a most beautiful woman, and most like to Mrs Butler. Thence very much joyed to London back again, and found out Mr Povy; told him this; and then went and left my Privy Seale at my Lord Treasurer's; and so to the 'Change, and thence to Trinity-house; where a great dinner of Captain Crisp, who is made an Elder Brother. And so, being very pleasant at dinner, away home, Creed with me; and there met Povy; and we to Gresham College.

21 John Lord Roberts.

20th. This night I am told the first play is played in White Hall noon-hall, which is now turned to a house of playing.

23rd. To White Hall chapel, and heard the famous young Stillingfleete,[22] whom I knew at Cambridge, and he is now newly admitted one of the King's chaplains. And was presented, they say, to my Lord Treasurer for St Andrew's Holborn, where he is now minister, with these words: that they (the Bishops of Canterbury, London, and another) believed he is the ablest young man to preach the Gospel of any since the Apostles. He did make a most plain, honest, good, grave sermon, in the most unconcerned and easy yet substantial manner, that ever I heard in my life, upon the words of Samuel to the people, 'Fear the Lord in truth with all your heart, and remember the great things that he hath done for you.' It being proper to this day, the day of the King's Coronation. Thence to the Cocke-pitt, and there walked an hour with my Lord Duke of Albemarle alone in his garden, where he expressed in great words his opinion of me; that I was the right hand of the Navy here, nobody but I taking any care of any thing therein; so that he should not know what could be done without me. At which I was (from him) not a little proud.

28th. Down the River to visit the victualling-ships, where I find all out of order. And come home to dinner, and then to write a letter to the Duke of Albemarle about them, and carried it myself to the Council-chamber; and when they rose, my Lord Chancellor passing by stroked me on the head, and told me that the Board had read my letter, and taken order for the punishing of the watermen for not appearing on board the ships. And so did the King afterwards, who do now know me so well, that he never sees me but he speaks to me about our Navy business.

30th. Thus I end this month in great content as to my estate and gettings: in much trouble as to the pains I have taken, and the rubs I expect to meet with, about the business of Tangier. The fleet, with about 100 ships upon the coast of Holland, in sight of the Dutch, within the Texel. Great fears of the sicknesse here in the City, it being said that two or three houses are already shut up. God preserve us all!

22 Edward Stillingfleet, a most learned Divine, consecrated Bishop of Worcester, 1689. Died 1699.

May 1st. I met my Lord Brouncker, Sir Robert Murrey, Dean Wilkins, and Mr Hooke, going by coach to Colonel Blunt's[23] to dinner. So they stopped and took me with them. Landed at the Tower-wharf, and thence by water to Greenwich; and there coaches met us; and to his house, a very stately sight for situation and brave plantations; and among others, a vine-yard, the first that ever I did see. No extraordinary dinner, nor any other entertainment good; but afterwards to the tryal of some experiments about making of coaches easy. And several we tried; but one did prove mighty easy, (not here for me to describe, but the whole body of the coach lies upon one long spring,) and we all, one after another, rid in it; and it is very fine and likely to take. Thence to Deptford, and in to Mr Evelyn's,[24] which is a most beautiful place; but it being dark and late, I staid not; but Dean Wilkins and Mr Hooke and I, walked to Redriffe; and noble discourse all day long did please me.

3rd. My Lord Chief-Justice Hide did die suddenly this week, a day or two ago, of an apoplexy.

5th. After dinner, to Mr Evelyn's; he being abroad, we walked in his garden, and a lovely noble ground he hath indeed. And among other rarities, a hive of bees, so as being hived in glass, you may see the bees making their honey and combs mighty pleasantly.

10th. To the Cocke-pitt, where the Duke did give Sir W. Batten and me an account of the late taking of eight ships, and of his intent to come back to the Gunfleete with the fleet presently; which creates us much work and haste therein, against the fleet comes. And thence to the Guard in Southwarke, there to get some soldiers, by the Duke's order, to go keep pressmen on board our ships.

14th. To church, it being Whit-sunday; my wife very fine in a new yellow bird's-eye hood, as the fashion is now. I took a coach, and to Wemstead, the house where Sir H. Mildmay died, and now Sir

23 Wricklesmarsh, in the parish of Charlton, which belonged, in 1617, to Edward Blount, Esq., whose family alienated it towards the end of the seventeenth century. The old mansion was pulled down by Sir Gregory Page, Bart., who erected a magnificent stone structure on the site; which, devolving to his great nephew, Sir Gregory Page Turner, shared the same fate as the former house, having been sold in lots in 1784.
24 Says-Court, the well-known residence of John Evelyn, Esq.

Robert Brookes[25] lives, having bought it of the Duke of York, it being forfeited to him. A fine seat, but an old-fashioned house; and being not full of people looks flatly.

17th. The Duchesse of York went down yesterday to meet the Duke.

18th. To the Duke of Albemarle, where we did examine Nixon and Stanesby, about their late running from two Dutchmen; for which they were committed to a vessel to carry them to the fleet to be tried. A most fowle unhandsome thing as ever was heard, for plain cowardice on Nixon's part.

23rd. Late comes Sir Arthur Ingram[26] to my office, to tell me, that, by letters from Amsterdam of the 18th. of this month, the Dutch fleet, being about 100 men-of-war, besides fire-ships, &c., did set out upon the 13th. and 14th. inst. Being divided into seven squadrons, viz. – 1. General Opdam. 2. Cottenar,[27] of Rotterdam. 3. Trump. 4. Schram, of Horne. 5. Stillingworth, of Freezland. 6. Everson. 7. One other, not named, of Zealand.

24th. To the Coffee-house, where all the news is of the Dutch being gone out, and of the plague growing upon us in this town; and of remedies against it: some saying one thing, and some another.

26th. In the evening by water to the Duke of Albemarle, whom I found mightily off the hooks, that the ships are not gone out of the River; which vexed me to see.

28th. I hear that Nixon is condemned to be shot to death, for his cowardice, by a Council of War. To my Lady Sandwich's, where, to my shame, I had not been a great while. Here, upon my telling her a story of my Lord Rochester's[28] running away on Friday night last with Mrs Mallett,[29] the great beauty and fortune of the North,

---

25 Sir Robert Brookes, Lord of the Manor of Wanstead, from 1662 to 1667. MP for Aldborough in Suffolk. He afterwards retired to France, and died there in bad circumstances. From a letter among the Pepys manuscripts, Sir Robert Brookes appears to have been drowned in the river at Lyon.

26 Sir Arthur Ingram, Knight, of Knottingley, Surveyor of the Customs at Hull.

27 Died of his wounds after the sea-fight in 1665.

28 John second Earl of Rochester, celebrated for his wit and profligacy. Died 1680.

29 Elizabeth, daughter of John Mallett, Esq., of Enmere, co. Somerset; married soon afterwards to the Earl of Rochester.

who had supped at White Hall with Mrs Stewart, and was going home to her lodgings with her grand-father, my Lord Haly,[30] by coach: and was at Charing Cross seized on by both horse and foot-men, and forcibly taken from him, and put into a coach with six horses, and two women provided to receive her, and carried away. Upon immediate pursuit, my Lord of Rochester (for whom the King had spoke to the lady often, but with no success,) was taken at Uxbridge: but the lady is not yet heard of, and the King mighty angry, and the Lord sent to the Tower. Hereupon my Lady did confess to me, as a great secret, her being concerned in this story. For if this match breaks between my Lord Rochester and her, then, by the consent of all her friends, my Lord Hinchingbroke stands fair, and is invited for her. She is worth, and will be at her mother's death, (who keeps but a little from her,) £2500 per annum. Pray God give a good success to it! But my poor Lady who is afraid of the sickness, and resolved to be gone into the country, is forced to stay in town a day or two, or three about it, to see the event of it. Thence to see my Lady Pen, where my wife and I were shown a fine rarity: of fishes kept in a glass of water, that will live so for ever; and finely marked they are, being foreign.

29th. We have every where taken some prizes. Our merchants had good luck to come home safe; Colliers from the North, and some Streights men, just now. And our Hambrough ships, of whom we were so much afraid, are safe in Hambrough. Our fleete resolve to sail out again from Harwich in a day or two.

31st. To the 'Change, where great the noise and trouble of having our Hambrough ships lost; and that very much placed upon Mr Coventry's forgetting to give notice to them of the going away of our fleet from the coast of Holland. But all without reason, for he did; but the merchants not being ready, staid longer than the time ordered for the convoy to stay, which was ten days.

June 1st. After dinner I put on my new camelott suit; the best that ever I wore in my life, the suit costing me above £24. In this I went

30 Sir Francis Hawley of Buckland House, co. Somerset, created a Baronet 1642, and in 1646 an Irish Peer, by the title of Baron Hawley of Donamore; in 1671 he was chosen MP for St Michael's, and in 1673 became a Gentleman of the Bedchamber to the Duke of York. Died 1684, aged 76.

with Creed to Goldsmiths' Hall, to the burial of Sir Thomas Viner;[31] which Hall, and Haberdashers' also, was so full of people, that we were fain for ease and coolness to go forth to Pater Noster Row, to choose a silk to make me a plain ordinary suit. That done, we walked to Cornehill, and there at Mr Cade's stood in the balcon and saw all the funeral, which was with the blue-coat boys and old men, all the Aldermen, and Lord Mayor, &c. and the number of the company very great: the greatest I ever did see for a taverne.

3rd. All this day by all people upon the River, and almost every where else hereabout were heard the guns, our two fleets for certain being engaged; which was confirmed by letters from Harwich, but nothing particular: and all our hearts full of concernment for the Duke, and I particularly for my Lord Sandwich and Mr Coventry after his Royall Highness.

6th. To my Lady Sandwich's; who, poor lady, expects every hour to hear of my Lord; but in the best temper, neither confident nor troubled with fear, that I ever did see in my life. She tells me my Lord Rochester is now declaredly out of hopes of Mrs Mallett, and now she is to receive notice in a day or two how the King stands inclined to the giving leave for my Lord Hinchingbroke to look after her, and that being done, to bring it to an end shortly.

7th. The hottest day that ever I felt in my life. This day, much against my will, I did in Drury Lane see two or three houses marked with a red cross upon the doors, and 'Lord have mercy upon us', writ there; which was a sad sight to me, being the first of the kind that to my remembrance I ever saw.

8th. I to my Lord Treasurer's by appointment of Sir Thomas Ingram's, to meet the Goldsmiths; where I met with the great news at last newly come, brought by Bab. May[32] from the Duke of York, that we have totally routed the Dutch; that the Duke himself, the Prince, my Lord Sandwich, and Mr Coventry are all well: which did put me into such joy, that I forgot almost all other thoughts. With great joy to the Cocke-pitt: where the Duke of Albemarle, like a man

31 Sheriff of London 1648, Lord Mayor 1654.
32 Baptist May, keeper of the Privy Purse to Charles II; there is an original portrait of him by Lely, at Audley End.

out of himself, with content new-told me all: and by and by comes a letter from Mr Coventry's own hand to him, which he never opened, (which was a strange thing,) but did give it me to open and read, and consider what was fit for our office to do in it, and leave the letter with Sir W. Clerke; which upon such a time and occasion was a strange piece of indifference, hardly possible. I copied out the letter, and did also take minutes out of Sir W. Clerke's other letters; and the sum of the news is:

Victory over the Dutch, June 3, 1665.

This day they engaged: the Dutch neglecting greatly the opportunity of the wind they had of us; by which they lost the benefit of their fire-ships. The Earl of Falmouth, Muskerry, and Mr Richard Boyle[33] killed on board the Duke's ship, the *Royall Charles*, with one shot: their blood and brains flying in the Duke's face; and the head of Mr Boyle striking down the Duke, as some say. Earle of Marlborough, Portland, Rear-Admirall Sansum (to Prince Rupert) killed, and Captain Kerby and Ableson. Sir John Lawson wounded on the knee: hath had some bones taken out, and is likely to be well again. Upon receiving the hurt, he sent to the Duke for another to command the *Royal Oake*. The Duke sent Jordan out of the *St George,* who did brave things in her. Captain Jer. Smith of the *Mary* was second to the Duke, and stepped between him and Captain Seaton of the *Urania,* (76 guns and 400 men) who had sworn to board the Duke; killed him 200 men, and took the ship; himself losing 99 men, and never an officer saved but himself and lieutenant. His master indeed is saved, with his leg cut off. Admirall Opdam blown up, Trump killed, and said by Holmes; all the rest of their admiralls, as they say, but Everson, (whom they dare not trust for his affection to the Prince of Orange,) are killed; we having taken and sunk, as is believed, about 24 of their best ships; killed and taken near 8 or 10,000 men, and lost, we think, not above 700. A greater victory never known in the world. They are all fled, some 43 got into the Texell, and others elsewhere, and we in pursuit of the rest.

9th. To White Hall, and in my way met Mr Moore, who eases me in one point wherein I was troubled; which was, that I heard of nothing said or done by my Lord Sandwich: but he tells me that Mr

---

33 Second son to the Earl of Burlington.

Cowling, my Lord Chamberlain's secretary, did hear the King say that my Lord Sandwich had done nobly and worthily. The King, it seems, is much troubled at the fall of my Lord Falmouth; but I do not meet with any man else that so much as wishes him alive again, the world conceiving him a man of too much pleasure to do the King any good, or offer any good office to him. But I hear of all hands he is confessed to have been a man of great honour, that did show it in this his going with the Duke, the most that ever any man did.

10th. In the evening home to supper; and there, to my great trouble, hear that the plague is come into the City (though it hath these three or four weeks since its beginning been wholly out of the City); but where should it begin but in my good friend and neighbour's, Dr Burnett,[34] in Fanchurch Street: which in both points troubles me mightily.

11th. I saw poor Dr Burnett's door shut; but he hath, I hear, gained great good-will among his neighbours; for he discovered it himself first, and caused himself to be shut up of his own accord: which was very handsome.

13th. At noon with Sir G. Carteret to my Lord Mayor's to dinner, where much company in a little room. His name, Sir John Lawrence. Here were at table three Sir Richard Brownes, viz.: he of the Councill, a clerk, and the Alderman, and his son; and there was a little grandson also Richard, who will hereafter be Sir Richard Browne. My Lord Mayor very respectfull to me.

14th. I met with Mr Cowling, who observed to me how he finds every body silent in the praise of my Lord Sandwich, to set up the Duke and the Prince; but that the Duke did both to the King and my Lord Chancellor write abundantly of my Lord's courage and service. And I this day met with a letter of Captain Ferrers, wherein he tells how my Lord was with his ship in all the heat of the day, and did most worthily. To Westminster; and there saw my Lord Marlborough brought to be buried, several Lords of the Council carrying him, and with the herald in some state. This day the Newsbook (upon Mr Moore's showing L'Estrange Captain Ferrers letter) did do my Lord Sandwich great right as to the late victory. The Duke of York not yet

34 He was a physician.

come to town. The town grows very sickly, and people to be afraid of it; there dying this last week of the plague 112, from 43 the week before, whereof but one in Fanchurch-streete, and one in Broad Streete, by the Treasurer's office.

16th. After dinner, and doing some business at the office, I to White Hall, where the Court is full of the Duke and his courtiers returned from sea. All fat and lusty, and ruddy by being in the sun. I kissed his hands, and we waited all the afternoon. By and by saw Mr Coventry, which rejoiced my very heart. Anon he and I, from all the rest of the company, walked into the Matted Gallery; where after many expressions of love, we fell to talk of business. Among other things, how my Lord Sandwich, both in his councils and personal service, hath done most honourably and serviceably. Sir J. Lawson is come to Greenwich; but his wound in his knee yet very bad. Jonas Poole, in the *Vantguard*, did basely, so as to be, or will be, turned out of his ship. Captain Holmes expecting upon Sansum's death to be made Rear-admirall to the Prince, (but Harman is put in) hath delivered up to the Duke his commission, which the Duke took and tore. He, it seems, had bid the Prince, who first told him of Holmes's intention, that he should dissuade him from it; for that he was resolved to take it if he offered it. Yet Holmes would do it, like a rash, proud coxcombe. But he is rich, and hath, it seems, sought an occasion of leaving the service. Several of our Captains have done ill. The great ships are the ships do the business, they quite deadening the enemy. They run away upon sight of the Prince. It is strange to see how people do already slight Sir William Barkeley,[35] my Lord FitzHarding's brother, who, three months since, was the delight of the Court. Captain Smith of the *Mary* the Duke talks mightily of; and some great thing will be done for him. Strange to hear how the Dutch do relate, as the Duke says, that they are the conquerors; and bonfires are made in Dunkirke in their behalf; though a clearer victory can never be expected. Mr Coventry thinks they cannot have lost less than 6000 men, and we not dead above 200, and wounded about 400; in all about 600. Captain Grove, the Duke told us this day, hath done the basest thing at Lowestoffe, in hearing of the guns, and could not (as others) be got out, but staid there; for which he will be tried; and is reckoned a prating coxcombe, and of no courage.

35 Killed in the sea-fight the following year. See June 16, 1666.

17th. It struck me very deep this afternoon going with a hackney coach from Lord Treasurer's down Holborne, the coachman I found to drive easily and easily, at last stood still, and come down hardly able to stand, and told me that he was suddenly struck very sick, and almost blind, he could not see; so I light and went into another coach, with a sad heart for the poor man and for myself also, lest he should have been struck with the plague. Sir John Lawson, I hear, is worse than yesterday: the King went to see him to-day most kindly. It seems his wound is not very bad; but he hath a fever, a thrush, and a hick-up, all three together, which are, it seems, very bad symptoms.

20th. Thankes-giving-day for victory over the Dutch. To the Dolphin Taverne, where all we officers of the Navy met with the Commissioners of the Ordnance by agreement, and dined: where good musique at my direction. Our club come to 34s. a man, nine of us. By water to Fox-hall, and there walked an hour alone, observing the several humours of the citizens that were there this holyday, pulling off cherries, and God knows what. This day I informed myself that there died four of five at Westminster of the plague, in several houses upon Sunday last, in Bell-Alley, over against the Palace-gate: yet people do think that the number will be fewer in the town than it was the last week. The Dutch are come out again with 20 sail under Banker: supposed gone to the Northward to meet their East India fleet.

21st. I find our tallys will not be money in less than sixteen months, which is a sad thing for the King to pay all that interest for every penny he spends; and, which is strange, the goldsmiths with whom I spoke, do declare that they will not be moved to part with money upon the increase of their consideration of ten per cent. which they have. I find all the town almost going out of town, the coaches and waggons being all full of people going into the country.

23rd. To a Committee for Tangier, where unknown to me comes my Lord of Sandwich, who, it seems, come to town last night. After the Committee was up, my Lord Sandwich did take me aside in the robe-chamber, telling me how much the Duke and Mr Coventry did, both in the fleet and here, make of him, and that in some opposition to the Prince; and as a more private message, he told me that he hath been with them both when they have made sport of the

Prince and laughed at him: yet that all the discourse of the town, and the printed relation, should not give him one word of honour my Lord thinks very strange; he assuring me, that though by accident the Prince was in the van in the beginning of the fight for the first pass, yet all the rest of the day my Lord was in the van, and continued so. That notwithstanding all this noise of the Prince, he had hardly a shot in his side or a man killed, whereas he above 30 in her hull, and not one mast whole nor yard: but the most battered ship of the fleet, and lost most men, saving Captain Smith of the *Mary*. That the most the Duke did was almost out of gun-shot: but that, indeed, the Duke did come up to my Lord's rescue after he had a great while fought with four of them. How poorly Sir John Lawson performed, notwith-standing all that was said of him; and how his ship turned out of the way while Sir J. Lawson himself was upon the deck, to the endangering of the whole fleet. From that discourse my Lord did begin to tell me how much he was concerned to dispose of his children, and would have my advice and help; and propounded to match my Lady Jemimah to Sir G. Carteret's[36] eldest son, which I approved of, and did undertake the speaking with him about it as from myself, which my Lord liked. Home by hackney-coach, which is become a very dangerous passage now-a-days, the sickness encreasing mightily.

24th. To Dr Clerke's, and there I in the best manner I could, broke my errand about a match between Sir G. Carteret's eldest son and my Lord Sandwich's eldest daughter, which he (as I knew he would) took with great content: and he did undertake to find out Sir George this morning, and put the business in execution. So I to White Hall, where I with Creed and Povy attended my Lord Treasurer, and did prevail with him to let us have an assignment for 15 or £20,000 which, I hope, will do our business for Tangier. To Sir G. Carteret, and in the best manner I could, moved the business: he received it with great respect and content, and thanks to me, and promised that he would do what he possibly could for his son, to render him fit for my Lord's daughter, and showed great kindness to me, and sense of my kindness to him herein. Sir William Pen told me this day that Mr Coventry is to be sworn a Privy Counsellor, at which my soul is glad.

36 Philip Carteret, afterwards knighted. He perished on board Lord Sandwich's flag-ship at the battle of Solebay.

25th. To White Hall, where, after I again visited Sir G. Carteret, and received his (and now his Lady's) full content in my proposal, my Lord Sandwich did direct me to return to Sir G. Carteret, and give him thanks for his kind acceptation of this offer, and that he would the next day be willing to enter discourse with him about the business. My Lord, I perceive, intends to give £5000 with her, and expects about £800 per annum joynture. To Greenwich by water, thinking to have visited Sir J. Lawson, where, when I come, I find that he died this morning; and indeed the nation hath a great loss. Mr Coventry, among other talk, entered about the great question now in the House about the Duke's going to sea again; about which the whole House is divided. The plague encreases mightily, I this day seeing a house, at a bitt-maker's over against St Clement's Church, in the open street shut up; which is a sad sight.

28th. I did take my leave of Sir William Coventry, who it seems was knighted, and sworn a Privy-Counsellor two days since; who with his old kindness treated me, and I believe I shall ever find a noble friend. In my way to Westminster Hall, I observed several plague houses in King's street and the Palace.

29th. To White Hall, where the Court full of waggons and people ready to go out of town. This end of the town every day grows very bad of the plague. The Mortality Bill is come to 267: which is about ninety more than the last: and of these but four in the City, which is a great blessing to us. Took leave again of Mr Coventry; though I hope the Duke is not gone to stay, and so do others too. Home; calling at Somerset House, where all were packing up too: the Queene-Mother setting out for France this day to drink Bourbon waters this year, she being in a consumption; and intends not to come till winter come twelve-months.

30th. Thus this book of two years ends. Myself and family in good health, consisting of myself and wife, Mercer, her woman, Mary, Alce, and Susan our maids, and Tom my boy. In a sickly time of the plague growing on. Having upon my hands the troublesome care of the Treasury of Tangier, with great sums drawn upon me, and nothing to pay them with: also the business of the office great. Considering of removing my wife to Woolwich; she lately busy in learning to paint, with great pleasure and successe. All other things well; especially a new interest I am making, by a match in hand between the eldest son of Sir G. Carteret, and my Lady Jemimah Montagu. The Duke of York gone down to the fleet; but all suppose not with intent to stay there, as it is not fit, all men conceive, he should.

July 1st. Sad at the news that seven or eight houses in Burying Hall[37] street, are shut up of the plague.

2nd. Sir G. Carteret did send me word that the business between my Lord and him is fully agreed on, and is mightily liked of by the King and the Duke of York. Sir J. Lawson was buried late last night at St Dunstan's by us, without any company at all.

4th. I hear this day the Duke and Prince Rupert are both come back from sea, and neither of them go back again. Mr Coventry tells me how matters are ordered in the fleet: my Lord Sandwich goes Admiral; under him Sir G. Ascue, and Sir T. Teddiman: Vice-Admiral, Sir W. Pen; and under him Sir W. Barkeley, and Sir Jos. Jordan: RearAdmiral, Sir Thomas Allen; and under him Sir Christopher Mings, and Captain Harman. Walked round to White Hall, the Park being quite locked up; and I observed a house shut up this day in the Pell Mell, where heretofore in Cromwell's time we young men used to keep our weekly clubs.

6th. Alderman Backewell is ordered abroad upon some private score with a great sum of money; wherein I was instrumental the other day in shipping him away. It seems some of his creditors have taken notice of it, and he was like to be broke yesterday in his absence: Sir G. Carteret telling me that the King and the kingdom must as good as fall with that man at this time; and that he was forced to get £4000 himself to answer Backewell's people's occasions, or he must have broke; but committed this to me as a great secret. I could not see Lord Brouncker, nor had much mind, one of the great houses within two doors of him being shut up: and Lord! the number of houses visited, which this day I observed through the town quite round in my way by Long Lane and London Wall. Sir W. Pen, it seems, sailed last night from Solebay with about sixty sail of ship, and my Lord Sandwich in the *Prince* and some others, it seems, going after them to overtake them.

37 Probably Basinghall.

7th. At this time I have two tierces of Claret, two quarter casks of Canary, and a smaller vessel of Sack; a vessel of Tent, another of Malaga, and another of white wine, all in my wine cellar together.

9th. I took occasion to have much discourse with Mr. Ph. Carteret, and find him a very modest man; and I think verily of mighty good nature, and pretty understanding. He did give me a good account of the fight with the Dutch. Having promised Harman yesterday, I to his house: the most observable thing I found there to my content, was to hear him and his clerk tell me that in this parish of Michell's Cornhill, one of the middle-most parishes and a great one of the town, there hath, notwithstanding this sickliness, been buried of any disease, man, woman, or child, not one for thirteen months last past; which is very strange. And the like in a good degree in most other parishes, I hear, saving only of the plague in them.

12th. A solemn fast-day for the plague growing upon us.

13th. Above 700 died of the plague this week.

14th. I by water to Sir G. Carteret's, and there find my Lady Sandwich buying things for my Lady Jem's wedding: and my Lady Jem is beyond expectation come to Dagenham's,[38] where Mr Carteret is to go to visit her to-morrow; and my proposal of waiting on him, he being to go alone to all persons strangers to him, was well accepted, and so I go with him. But Lord! to see how kind my Lady Carteret is to her! Sends her most rich jewells, and provides bedding and things of all sorts most richly for her.

15th. Mr Carteret and I to the ferry-place at Greenwich, and there staid an hour crossing the water to and again to get our coach and horses over; and by and by set out, and so toward Dagenhams. But Lord! what silly discourse we had as to love-matters, he being the most awkerd man ever I met with in my life as to that business. Thither we come, and by that time it begun to be dark, and were

38 Dagenhams near Romford, now belonging to Sir Thomas Neave, Bart. This estate was devised by Mrs Anne Rider, only surviving child of Sir Henry Wright, to her relative and friend Edward Carteret, Esq., Postmaster-General; whose daughters in 1749 sold it to Henry Muilman, Esq.; in 1772 it was again disposed of to Mr Neave, father of the present proprietor, who pulled down the old house built by Sir H. W., and erected the present mansion on a different site. See Lysons's *Environs*.

kindly received by Lady Wright and my Lord Crewe. And to discourse they went, my Lord discoursing with him, asking of him questions of travell, which he answered well enough in a few words; but nothing to the lady from him at all. To supper, and after supper to talk again, he yet taking no notice of the lady. My Lord would have had me have consented to leaving the young people together to-night, to begin their amours, his staying being but to be little. But I advised against it, lest the lady might be too much surprised. So they led him up to his chamber, where I staid a little, to know how he liked the lady, which he told me he did mightily: but Lord! in the dullest insipid manner that ever lover did. So I bid him good night, and down to prayers with my Lord Crewe's family, and after prayers, my Lord and Lady Wright, and I, to consult what to do; and it was agreed at last to have them go to church together, as the family used to do, though his lameness was a great objection against it.

16th (Lord's day). I up, having lain with Mr Moore in the chaplin's chamber. And having trimmed myself, down to Mr Carteret; and we walked in the gallery an hour or two, it being a most noble and pretty house that ever, for the bigness, I saw. Here I taught him what to do: to take the lady always by the hand to lead her, and telling him that I would find opportunity to leave them together, he should make these and these compliments, and also take a time to do the like to Lord Crewe and Lady Wright. After I had instructed him, which he thanked me for, owning that he needed my teaching him, my Lord Crewe come down and family, the young lady among the rest; and so by coaches to church four miles off: where a pretty good sermon, and a declaration of penitence of a man that had undergone the Churche's censure for his wicked life. Thence back again by coach, Mr Carteret having not had the confidence to take his lady once by the hand, coming or going, which I told him of when we come home, and he will hereafter do it. So to dinner. My Lord excellent discourse. Then to walk in the gallery, and to sit down. By and by my Lady Wright and I go out, (and then my Lord Crewe, he not by design,) and lastly my Lady Crewe come out, and left the young people together. And a little pretty daughter of my Lady Wright's most innocently come out afterwards, and shut the door to, as if she had done it, poor child, by inspiration: which made us without have good sport to laugh at. They together an hour, and by and by church-time, whither he led her into the coach and into the church, where several handsome ladies. But it was most extraordinary hot that ever I knew it. Anon to supper, and excellent discourse and dispute between my Lord Crewe and the chaplin, who is a good scholler, but a nonconformist. Here this evening I spoke with Mrs Carter, my old acquaintance, that hath lived with my lady these twelve or thirteen years, the sum of all whose discourse and others for her, is, that I would get her a good husband; which I have promised, but know not when I shall perform. After Mr Carteret was carried to his chamber, we to prayers and then to bed.

17th. Up all of us, and to billiards; my Lady Wright, Mr Carteret, myself, and every body. By and by the young couple left together. Anon to dinner; and after dinner Mr Carteret took my advice about giving to the servants £10 among them. Before we went, I took my Lady Jem apart, and would know how she liked this gentleman, and whether she was under any difficulty concerning him. She blushed, and hid her face awhile; but at last I forced her to tell me. She answered that she could readily obey what her father and mother had done; which was all she could say, or I expect. So anon took leave, and for London. In our way Mr Carteret did give me mighty thanks for my care and pains for him, and is mightily pleased.

18th. I was much troubled this day to hear at Westminster, how the officers do bury the dead in the open Tuttle-fields, pretending want of room elsewhere: whereas the new chapel church-yard was walled-in at the publick charge in the last plague-time, merely for want of room and now none, but such as are able to pay dear for it, can be buried there.

20th. Walked to Redriffe, where I hear the sickness is, and indeed is scattered almost every where. There dying 1089 of the plague this week. My Lady Carteret did this day give me a bottle of plague-water home with me. I received yesterday a letter from my Lord Sandwich, giving me thanks for my care about their marriage business, and desiring it to be dispatched, that no disappointment may happen therein.

21st. Late in my chamber, setting some papers in order; the plague growing very raging, and my apprehensions of it great.

22nd. The Duke of Albemarle being gone to dinner to my Lord of Canterbury's, I thither, and there walked and viewed the new hall, a new old-fashion hall as possible. Begun, and means left for the ending of it, by Bishop Juxon. To Fox-hall, where to the Spring garden; but I do not see one guest there, the town being so empty of any body to come thither. I by coach home, not meeting with but two coaches, and but two carts from White Hall to my own house, that I could observe; and the streets mighty thin of people. All the news is great: that we must of necessity fall out with France, for He will side with the Dutch against us. That Alderman Backewell is gone over (which indeed he is,) with money, and that Ostend is in our present possession. But it is strange to see how poor Alderman Backewell is like to be put to it in his absence, Mr Shaw his right hand being ill. And the Alderman's absence gives doubts to people, and I perceive they are in great straits for money, besides what Sir G. Carteret told me about fourteen days ago. Our fleet under my Lord Sandwich being about the latitude 55½ (which is a great secret) to the Northward of the Texell.

23rd. To Hampton Court, where I followed the King to chapel, and there heard a good sermon; and after sermon with my Lord Arlington, Sir Thomas Ingram and others, spoke to the Duke about Tangier, but not to much purpose. I was not invited any whither to dinner, though a stranger, which did also trouble me; but yet I must remember it is a Court, and indeed where most are strangers: but, however, Cutler carried me to Mr Marriott's the house-keeper, and there we had a very good dinner and good company, among others Lilly, the painter.

24th. I find Mr Carteret yet as backward almost in his caresses, as he was the first day.

25th. Sad the story of the plague in the City, it growing mightily. This day my Lord Brouncker did give me Mr Grant's book upon the Bills of Mortality, new printed and enlarged. This day come a letter to me from Paris, from my Lord Hinchingbroke, about his coming over; and I have sent this night an order from the Duke of Albemarle for a ship of 36 guns to go to Calais to fetch him.

26th. To Greenwich to the Park, where I heard the King and Duke are come by water this morn from Hampton Court. They asked me several questions. The King mightily pleased with his new buildings there. I followed them to Castle's ship in building, and there met Sir W. Batten, and thence to Sir G. Carteret's, where all the morning with them; they not having any but the Duke of Monmouth, and Sir W. Killigrew,[39] and one gentleman, and a page more. Great variety of talk, and was often led to speak to the King and Duke. By and by they to dinner, and all to dinner and sat down to the King saving myself. The King having dined, he came down, and I went in the barge with him, I sitting at the door. Down to Woolwich (and there I just saw and kissed my wife, and saw some of her painting, which is very curious; and away again to the King,) and back again with him in the barge, hearing him and the Duke talk, and seeing and observing their manner of discourse And God forgive me! though I admire them with all the duty possible, yet the more a man considers and observes them, the less he finds of difference between them and other men, though (blessed be God!) they are both princes of great nobleness and spirits. The Duke of Monmouth is the most skittish leaping gallant that ever I saw, always in action, vaulting or leaping, or clambering. Sad news of the death of so many in the parish of the plague, forty last night. The bell always going. This day poor Robin Shaw at Backewell's died, and Backewell himself in Flanders. The King himself asked about Shaw, and being told he was dead, said he was very sorry for it. The sickness is got into our parish this week, and is got, indeed, every where: so that I begin to think of setting things in order, which I pray God enable me to put both as to soul and body.

27th. To Hampton Court, where I saw the King and Queene set out towards Salisbury, and after them the Duke and Duchesse, whose hands I did kiss. And it was the first time I did ever, or did see any body else, kiss her hand, and it was a most fine white and fat hand. But it was pretty to see the young pretty ladies dressed like men, in velvet coats, caps with ribbands, and with laced bands, just like men. Only the Duchesse herself it did not become. At home met the weekly Bill, where above 100 encreased in the Bill, and of them, in all about 1700 of the plague, which hath made the officers this day resolve of sitting at Deptford, which puts me to some consideration what to do.

39 Vice-Chamberlain to the Queen.

28th. Set out with my Lady Sandwich all alone with her with six horses to Dagenhams; going by water to the Ferry. And a pleasant going, and a good discourse; and when there very merry, and the young couple now well acquainted. But Lord! to see in what fear all the people here do live. How they are afraid of us that come to them, insomuch that I am troubled at it, and wish myself away. But some cause they have; for the chaplin, with whom but a week or two ago we were here mighty high disputing, is since fallen into a fever and dead, being gone hence to a friend's a good way off. A sober and a healthful man. These considerations make us all hasten the marriage, and resolve it upon Monday next.

30th. It was a sad noise to hear our bell to toll and ring so often to-day, either for death or burials: I think five or six times.

31st. Up; and very betimes by six o'clock at Deptford, and there find Sir G. Carteret, and my Lady ready to go: I being in my new coloured silk suit, and coat trimmed with gold buttons and gold broad lace round my hands, very rich and fine. By water to the Ferry, where, when we come, no coach there; and tide of ebb so far spent as the horse-boat could not get off on the other side the river to bring away the coach. So we were fain to stay there in the unlucky Isle of Doggs, in a chill place, the morning cool, and wind fresh, above two if not three hours to our great discontent. Yet being upon a pleasant errand, and seeing that it could not be helped, we did bear it very patiently; and it was worth my observing, to see how upon these two scores, Sir G. Carteret, the most passionate man in the world, and that was in greatest haste to be gone, did bear with it, and very pleasant all the while, at least not troubled much so as to fret and storm at it. Anon the coach comes: in the mean time there coming a news thither with his horse to go over, that told us he did come from Islington this morning; and that Proctor the vintner of the Miter in Wood Street, and his son, are dead this morning there, of the plague; he having laid out abundance of money there, and was the greatest vintner for some time in London for great entertainments. We, fearing the canonicall hour would be past before we got thither, did with a great deal of unwillingness send away the licence and wedding-ring. So that when we come, though we drove hard with six horses, yet we found them gone from home; and going towards the church, met them coming from church, which troubled us. But, however, that trouble was soon over; hearing it was well done: they being both in their old clothes; my Lord Crewe giving her, there being three coach fulls of them. The young lady mighty sad, which troubled me; but yet I think it was only her gravity in a little greater degree than usual. All saluted her, but I did not till my Lady Sandwich did ask me whether I had saluted her or no. So to dinner, and very merry we were; but in such a sober way as never almost any thing was in so great families: but it was much better. After dinner company divided, some to cards, others to talk. My Lady Sandwich and I up to settle accounts, and pay her some money. And mighty kind she is to me, and would fain have had me gone down for company with her to Hinchingbroke; but for my life I cannot. At night to supper, and so to talk; and which, methought, was the most extraordinary thing, all of us to prayers as usual, and the young bride and bridegroom too: and so after prayers soberly to bed; only I got into the bridegroom's chamber while he undressed himself, and there was very merry, till he was called to the bride's chamber, and into bed they went. I kissed the bride in bed, and so the curtaines drawne with the greatest gravity that could be, and so good night. But the modesty and gravity of this business was so decent, that it was to me indeed ten times more delightful than if it had been twenty times more merry and jovial. Thus I ended this month with the greatest joy that ever I did any in my life, because I have spent the greatest part of it with abundance of joy, and honour, and pleasant journeys, and brave entertainments, and without cost of money; and at last live to see the business ended with great content on all sides. Thus we end this month, as I said, after the greatest glut of content that ever I had; only under some difficulty because of the plague, which grows mightily upon us, the last week being about 1700 or 1800 of the plague. My Lord Sandwich at sea with a fleet of about 100 sail, to the Northward, expecting De Ruyter, or the Dutch East India fleet. My Lord Hinchingbroke coming over from France, and will meet his sister at Scott's-hall. Myself having obliged both these families in this business very much; as both my Lady and Sir G. Carteret and his Lady do confess exceedingly, and the latter do also now call me cozen, which I am glad of. So God preserve us all friends long, and continue health among us.

August 3rd. To Dagenhams. All the way people, citizens, walking to and fro, enquire how the plague is in the City this week by the Bill; which by chance, at Greenwich, I had heard was 2020 of the plague, and 3000 and odd of all diseases. By and by met my Lord Crewe returning; Mr Marr telling me by the way how a maidservant of Mr John Wright's (who lives thereabouts) falling sick of the plague, she was removed to an outhouse, and a nurse appointed to look to her; who, being once absent, the maid got out of the house at the window, and run away. The nurse coming and knocking, and having no answer, believed she was dead, and went and told Mr Wright so; who and his lady were in great strait what to do to get her buried. At last resolved to go to Burntwood hard by, being in the parish, and there get people to do it. But they would not; so he went home full of trouble, and in the way met the wench walking over the common, which frighted him worse than before; and was forced to send people to take her, which he did; and they got one of the pest coaches and put her into it to carry her to a pest house. And passing in a narrow lane, Sir Anthony Browne,[40] with his brother and some friends in the coach, met this coach with the curtains drawn close. The brother being a young man, and believing there might be some lady in it that would not be seen, and the way being narrow, he thrust his head out of his own into her coach, and to look, and there saw somebody look very ill, and in a sick dress, and stunk mightily; which the coachman also cried out upon. And presently they come up to some people that stood looking after it, and told our gallants that it was a maid of Mr Wright's carried away sick of the plague; which put the young gentleman into a fright had almost cost him his life, but is now well again.

5th. I am told of a great ryott upon Thursday last in Cheapside; Colonel Danvers, a delinquent, having been taken, and in his way to the Tower was rescued from the captain of the guard, and carried away; one only of the rescuers being taken.

8th. To my office a little, and then to the Duke of Albemarle's about some business. The streets empty all the way, now even in London, which is a sad sight. And to Westminster Hall, where talking, hearing very sad stories from Mrs Mumford; among others, of Mr Michell's

40 He commanded a troop of horse in the Train-bands, 1662.

son's family. And poor Will. that used to sell us ale at the Hall-door, his wife and three children died, all, I think, in a day. So home through the City again, wishing I may have taken no ill in going; but I will go, I think, no more thither. The news of De Ruyter's coming home is certain; and told to the great disadvantage of our fleet, and the praise of De Ruyter; but it cannot be helped.

10th. By and by to the office, where we sat all the morning; in great trouble to see the Bill this week rise so high, to above 4000 in all, and of them above 3000 of the plague. Home, to draw over anew my will, which I had bound myself by oath to dispatch by to-morrow night; the town growing so unhealthy, that a man cannot depend upon living two days.

12th. The people die so, that now it seems they are fain to carry the dead to be buried by day-light, the nights not sufficing to do it in. And my Lord Mayor commands people to be within at nine at night all, as they say, that the sick may have liberty to go abroad for ayre. There is one also dead out of one of our ships at Deptford, which troubles us mightily; the *Providence*, fire-ship, which was just fitted to go to sea. But they tell me to-day no more sick on board. And this day W. Bodham tells me that one is dead at Woolwich, not far from the Rope-yard. I am told, too, that a wife of one of the groomes at Court is dead at Salisbury; so that the King and Queene are speedily to be all gone to Milton. So God preserve us!

15th. It was dark before I could get home, and so land at Churchyard stairs, where, to my great trouble, I met a dead corps of the plague, in the narrow ally just bringing down a little pair of stairs. But I thank God I was not much disturbed at it. However, I shall beware of being late abroad again.

16th. To the Exchange, where I have not been a great while. But, Lord! how sad a sight it is to see the streets empty of people, and very few upon the 'Change. Jealous of every door that one sees shut up, lest it should be the plague; and about us two shops in three, if not more, generally shut up. This day I had the ill news from Dagenhams, that my poor Lord of Hinchingbroke his indisposition is turned to the small-pox. Poor gentleman that he should be come from France so soon to fall sick, and of that disease too, when he should be gone to see a fine lady, his mistress. I am most heartily sorry for it.

18th. To Sheernesse, where we walked up and down, laying out the ground to be taken in for a yard to lay provisions for cleaning and repairing of ships, and a most proper place it is for the purpose.

19th. Come letters from the King and Lord Arlington, for the removal of our office to Greenwich. I also wrote letters, and made myself ready to go to Sir G. Carteret, at Windsor; and having borrowed a horse of Mr Blackbrough, sent him to wait for me at the Duke of Albemarle's door: when, on a sudden, a letter comes to us from the Duke of Albemarle, to tell us that the fleet is all come back to Solebay, and are presently to be dispatched back again. Whereupon I presently by water to the Duke of Albemarle to know what news; and there I saw a letter from my Lord Sandwich to the Duke of Albemarle, and also from Sir W. Coventry and Captain Teddiman; how my Lord having commanded Teddiman with twenty-two ships (of which but fifteen could get thither, and of those fifteen but eight or nine could come up to play) to go to Bergen; where, after several messages to and fro from the Governor of the Castle, urging that Teddiman ought not to come thither with more than five ships, and desiring time to think of it, all the while he suffering the Dutch ships to land their guns to the best advantage; Teddiman on the second presence, began to play at the Dutch ships, (whereof ten East India-men,) and in three hours' time (the town and castle, without any provocation, playing on our ships,) they did cut all our cables, so as the wind being off the land, did force us to go out, and rendered our fire-ships useless; without doing any thing, but what hurt of course our guns must have done them: we having lost five commanders, besides Mr Edward Montagu, and Mr Windham. Our fleet is come home to our great grief with not above five weeks' dry, and six days' wet provisions: however, must go out again; and the Duke hath ordered the *Soveraigne*, and all other ships ready, to go out to the fleet and strengthen them. This news troubles us all, but cannot be helped. Having read all this news, and received commands of the Duke with great content, he giving me the words which to my great joy he hath several times said to me, that his greatest reliance is upon me. And my Lord Craven also did come out to talk with me, and told me that I am in mighty esteem with the Duke, for which I bless God. Home; and having given my fellow-officers an account hereof, to Chatham, and wrote other letters. I by water to Charing-Cross, to the post-house, and there the people tell me they are shut up; and so I went to the new post-house, and there got a guide and horses to Hounslow. So to Stanes, and there by this time it was dark night, and got a guide who lost his way in the forest, till by help of the moone (which recompences me for all the pains I ever took about studying of her motions,) I led my guide into the way back again; and so we made a man rise that kept a gate, and so he carried us to Cranborne.[41] Where in the dark I perceive an old house new building with a great deal of rubbish, and was fain to go up a ladder to Sir G. Carteret's chamber. And there in his bed I sat down, and told him all my bad news, which troubled him mightily; but yet we were very merry, and made the best of it; and being myself weary did take leave, and after having spoken with Mr Fenn[42] in bed, I to bed in my Lady's chamber that she uses to lie in, and where the Duchesse of York, that now is, was born. So to sleep; being very well, but weary, and the better by having carried with me a bottle of strong water; whereof now and then a sip did me good.

20th. I up and to walk forth to see the place; and I find it to be a very noble seat in a noble forest, with the noblest prospect towards Windsor, and round about over many countys, that can be desired; but otherwise a very melancholy place, and little variety save only trees. To Brainford; and there at the inn that goes down to the waterside, I light and paid off my post-horses, and so slipped on my shoes, and laid my things by, the tide not serving, and to church, where a dull sermon, and many Londoners. After church to my inn, and eat and drank, and so about seven o'clock by water, and got between nine and ten to Queenhive,[43] very dark. And I could not get my waterman to go elsewhere for fear of the plague. Thence with a lanthorn, in great fear of meeting of dead corpses, carrying to be buried; but, blessed be God, met none, but did see now and then a linke (which is the mark of them) at a distance.

22nd. I went away and walked to Greenwich, in my way seeing a coffin with a dead body therein, dead of the plague, lying in an open close belonging to Coome farme, which was carried out last night, and

41 One of the Lodges belonging to the Crown in Windsor Forest.
42 Nicholas Fenne is mentioned as a Commissioner of the Victualling Office, 1683. – Pepys's manuscript letters.
43 Queenhithe.

the parish have not appointed any body to bury it; but only set a watch there all day and night, that nobody should go thither or come thence: this disease making us more cruel to one another than we are to dogs.

25th. This day I am told that Dr Burnett, my physician, is this morning dead of the plague; which is strange, his man dying so long ago, and his house this month open again. Now himself dead. Poor unfortunate man!

28th. I think to take adieu to-day of the London streets. In much the best posture I ever was in in my life, both as to the quantity and the certainty I have of the money I am worth; having most of it in my hand. But then this is a trouble to me what to do with it, being myself this day going to be wholly at Woolwich; but for the present I am resolved to venture it in an iron chest, at least for a while.

30th. Abroad, and met with Hadley, our clerke, who, upon my asking how the plague goes, told me it encreases much, and much in our parish; for, says he, there died nine this week, though I have returned but six: which is a very ill practice, and makes me think it is so in other places; and therefore the plague much greater than people take it to be. I went forth and walked towards Moorefields to see (God forgive my presumption) whether I could see any dead corpse going to the grave; but, as God would have it, did not. But, Lord! how every body looks, and discourse in the street is of death, and nothing else, and few people going up and down, that the town is like a place distressed and forsaken.

31st. Up; and after putting several things in order to my removal to Woolwich; the plague having a great encrease this week beyond all expectation of almost 2000, making the general Bill 7000, odd 100; and the plague above 6000. Thus this month ends with great sadness upon the publick, through the greatness of the plague every where through the kingdom almost. Every day sadder and sadder news of its encrease. In the City died this week 7496, and of them 6102 of the plague. But it is feared that the true number of the dead this week is near 10,000; partly from the poor that cannot be taken notice of, through the greatness of the number, and partly from the Quakers and others that will not have any bell ring for them. Our fleet gone out to find the Dutch, we having about 100 sail in our fleet, and in them the *Soveraigne* one; so that it is a better fleet than the former with which the Duke was. All our fear is that the Dutch should be got in before them; which would be a very great sorrow to the publick, and to me particularly, for my Lord Sandwich's sake. A great deal of money being spent, and the kingdom not in a condition to spare, nor a parliament without much difficulty to meet to give more. And to that; to have it said, what hath been done by our late fleets? As to myself I am very well, only in fear of the plague, and as much of an ague by being forced to go early and late to Woolwich, and my family to lie there continually. My late gettings have been very great to my great content, and am likely to have yet a few more profitable jobbs in a little while; for which Tangier and Sir W. Warren I am wholly obliged to.

September 3rd (Lord's day). Up; and put on my coloured silk suit very fine, and my new periwigg, bought a good while since, but durst not wear, because the plague was in Westminster when I bought it; and it is a wonder what will be the fashion after the plague is done, as to periwiggs, for nobody will dare to buy any haire, for fear of the infection, that it had been cut off the heads of people dead of the plague. My Lord Brouncker, Sir J. Minnes, and I up to the Vestry at the desire of the Justices of the Peace, in order to the doing something for the keeping of the plague from growing; but Lord! to consider the madness of people of the town, who will (because they are forbid) come in crowds along with the dead corpses to see them buried; but we agreed on some orders for the prevention thereof. Among other stories, one was very passionate, methought, of a complaint brought against a man in the town for taking a child from London from an infected house. Alderman Hooker told us it was the child of a very able citizen in Gracious Street, a saddler, who had buried all the rest of his children of the plague, and himself and wife now being shut up and in despair of escaping, did desire only to save the life of this little child; and so prevailed to have it received stark-naked into the arms of a friend, who brought it (having put it into new fresh clothes) to Greenwich; where upon hearing the story, we did agree it should be permitted to be received and kept in the town.

4th. Walked home, my Lord Brouncker giving me a very neat cane to walk with; but it troubled me to pass by Coome farme where about twenty-one people have died of the plague.

5th. After dinner comes Colonel Blunt in his new chariot made with springs; as that was of wicker, wherein a while since we rode at his house. And he hath rode, he says, now his journey, many miles in it with one horse, and out-drives any coach, and out-goes any horse, and so easy, he says. So for curiosity I went into it to try it, and up the hill to the heath, and over the cart-ruts and found it pretty well, but not so easy as he pretends.

6th. To London, to pack up more things; and there I saw fires burning in the streets, as it is through the whole City, by the Lord Mayor's order. Thence by water to the Duke of Albemarle's: all the way fires on each side of the Thames, and strange to see in broad daylight two or three burials upon the Bankside, one at the very heels of another: doubtless all of the plague; and yet at least forty or fifty people going along with every one of them. The Duke mighty pleasant with me; telling me that he is certainly informed that the Dutch were not come home upon the 1st instant, and so he hopes our fleet may meet with them.

7th. To the Tower, and there sent for the Weekly Bill, and find 8252 dead in all, and of them 6978 of the plague; which is a most dreadful number, and shows reason to fear that the plague hath got that hold that it will yet continue among us. To Swakely[44] to Sir R. Viner's. A very pleasant place, bought by him of Sir James Harrington's lady. He took us up and down with great respect, and showed us all his house and grounds; and it is a place not very moderne in the garden nor house, but the most uniforme in all that ever I saw; and some things to excess. Pretty to see over the screene of the hall (put up by Sir J. Harrington, a Long Parliament-man) the King's head, and my Lord of Essex[45] on one side, and Fairfax on the other; and upon the other side of the screene, the parson of the parish, and the lord of the manor and his sisters. The window-cases, door-cases, and

---

44 Swakeley House, in the parish of Ickenham, Middlesex, was built in 1638 by Sir Edmund Wright, whose daughter marrying Sir James Harrington, one of Charles I's judges, he became possessed of it, *jure uxoris*. Sir Robert Vyner, Bart., to whom the property was sold in 1665, entertained Charles II at Guildhall, when Lord Mayor. The house is now the residence of Thomas Clarke, Esq., whose father in 1750 bought the estate of Mr Lethieullier, to whom it had been alienated by the Vyner family — Lysons's *Environs*.
45 The Parliament General.

chimnys of all the house are marble. He showed me a black boy that he had, that died of a consumption, and being dead, he caused him to be dried in an oven, and lies there entire in a box. By and by to dinner, where his lady I find yet handsome, but hath been a very handsome woman: now is old. Hath brought him near £100,000 and now lives, no man in England in greater plenty, and commands both King and Council with his credit he gives them. After dinner Sir Robert led us up to his long gallery, very fine, above stairs, (and better, or such furniture I never did see). A most pleasant journey we had back. Povy tells me by a letter he showed me, that the King is not, nor hath been of late, very well, but quite out of humour; and, as some think, in a consumption, and weary of every thing. He showed me my Lord Arlington's house that he was born in, in a towne called Harlington: and so carried me through a most pleasant country to Brainford, and there put me into my boat, and good night. So I wrapped myself warm, and by water got to Woolwich about one in the morning.

9th. I was forced to get a bed at Captain Cocke's, where I find Sir W. Doyly,[46] and he and Evelyn at supper: and I with them full of discourse of the neglect of our masters, the great officers of State, about all business, and especially that of money: having now some thousands prisoners kept to no purpose at a great charge, and no money provided almost for the doing of it. We fell to talk largely of the want of some persons understanding to look after businesses, but all goes to rack. 'For,' says Captain Cocke, 'my Lord Treasurer, he minds his ease, and lets things go how they will: if he can have his £8000 per annum, and a game at l'ombre, he is well. My Lord Chancellor he minds getting of money and nothing else; and my Lord Ashly will rob the Devil and the Alter, but he will get money if it be to be got.' But that which put us into this great melancholy, was news brought to-day, which Captain Cocke reports as a certain truth, that all the Dutch fleet, men-of-war and merchant East India ships, are got every one in from Bergen the 3rd of this month, Sunday last; which will make us all ridiculous.

46 Sir William Doyly, of Shottisham, Norfolk, knighted 1642, created Baronet 1663. MP for Yarmouth. Died 1677. He and Mr Evelyn were at this time appointed Commissioners for the care of the sick and wounded seamen and prisoners of war.

10th (Lord's day). Walked home; being forced thereto by one of my watermen falling sick yesterday, and it was God's great mercy I did not go by water with them yesterday, for he fell sick on Saturday night, and it is to be feared of the plague. So I sent him away to London with his family; but another boat come to me this morning. My wife before I come out telling me the ill news that she hears that her father is very ill, and then I told her I feared of the plague, for that the house is shut up. And so she much troubled, and did desire me to send them something; and I said I would, and will do so. But before I come out there happened news to come to me by an expresse from Mr Coventry, telling the most happy news of my Lord Sandwich's meeting with part of the Dutch; his taking two of their East India ships, and six or seven others, and very good prizes: and that he is in search of the rest of the fleet, which he hopes to find upon the *Well-bancke*, with the loss only of the *Hector*, poor Captn. Cuttle. To Greenwich, and there sending away Mr Andrews, I to Captn. Cocke's, where I find my Lord Brouncker and his mistress,[47] and Sir J. Minnes. Where we supped; (there was also Sir W. Doyly and Mr Evelyn,) but the receipt of this news did put us all into such an extasy of joy, that it inspired into Sir J. Minnes and Mr Evelyn such a spirit of mirth, that in all my life I never met with so merry a two hours as our company this night was. Among other humours, Mr Evelyn's repeating of some verses made up of nothing but the various acceptations of *may* and *can*, and doing it so aptly upon occasion of something of that nature, and so fast, did make us all die almost with laughing, and did so stop the mouth of Sir J. Minnes in the middle of all his mirth, (and in a thing agreeing with his own manner of genius) that I never saw any man so out-done in all my life; and Sir J. Minnes's mirth too to see himself outdone, was the crown of all our mirth. In this humour we sat till about ten at night, and so my Lord and his mistress home, and we to bed.

13th. My Lord Brouncker, Sir J. Minnes, and I took boat, and in my Lord's coach to Sir W. Hickes's,[48] whither by and by my Lady Batten and Sir William comes. It is a good seat, with a fair grove of trees by

47 Mrs Williams.
48 Sir William Hickes, created a baronet 1619. Died 1680, aged 84. His country-seat was called Ruckholts, or Rookwood, at Layton, in Essex, where he entertained King Charles II after hunting.

it, and the remains of a good garden; but so let to run to ruine, both house and every thing in and about it, so ill furnished and miserably looked after, I never did see in all my life. Not so much as a latch to his dining-room door; which saved him nothing, for the wind blowing into the room for want thereof, flung down a great bow pott, that stood upon the side-table, and that fell upon some Venice glasses, and did him a crown's worth of hurt. He did give us the meanest dinner, (of beef, shoulder and umbles of venison which he takes away from the keeper of the Forest,[49] and a few pigeons, and all in the meanest manner,) that ever I did see, to the basest degree. I was only pleased at a very fine picture of the Queene-Mother, when she was young, by Vandike; a very good picture, and a lovely face.

14th. To the Duke of Albemarle, where I find a letter of the 12th from Solebay, from my Lord Sandwich, of the fleet's meeting with about eighteen more of the Dutch fleet, and his taking of most of them; and the messenger says, they had taken three after the letter was wrote and sealed; which being twenty-one, and the fourteen took the other day, is forty-five sail; some of which are good, and others rich ships. And having taken a copy of my Lord's letter, I away toward the Change, the plague being all thereabouts. Here my news was highly welcome, and I did wonder to see the 'Change so full, I believe 200 people; but not a man or merchant of any fashion, but plain men all. And Lord! to see how I did endeavour all I could to talk with as few as I could, there being now no observation of shutting up of houses infected, that to be sure we do converse and meet with people that have the plague upon them. I spent some thoughts upon the occurrences of this day, giving matter for as much content on one hand and melancholy on another, as any day in all my life. For the first; the finding of my money and plate, and all safe at London, and speeding in my business of money this day. The hearing of this good news to such excess, after so great a despair of my Lord's doing any thing this year; adding to that, the decrease of 500 and more, which is the first decrease we have yet had in the sickness since it begun: and great hopes that the next week it will be greater. Then, on the other side, my finding that though the Bill in general is abated, yet the City within the walls is encreased, and likely to continue so, and is close to our house there. My meeting dead corpses of the plague, carried to be

49 Of which he was Ranger.

buried close to me at noon-day through the City in Fanchurch Street. To see a person sick of the sores, carried close by me by Grace-church in a hackney-coach. My finding the Angel tavern, at the lower end of Tower-hill, shut up, and more than that, the alehouse at the Tower-stairs, and more than that, that the person was then dying of the plague when I was last there, a little while ago, at night. To hear that poor Payne, my waiter, had buried a child, and is dying himself. To hear that a labourer I sent but the other day to Dagenhams, to know how they did there, is dead of the plague; and that one of my own watermen, that carried me daily, fell sick as soon as he had landed me on Friday morning last, when I had been all night upon the water, (and I believe he did get his infection that day at Brainford) and is now dead of the plague. To hear that Captain Lambert and Cuttle are killed in the taking these ships; and that Mr Sidney Montague is sick of a desperate fever at my Lady Carteret's, at Scott's-hall. To hear that Mr Lewes hath another daughter sick. And, lastly, that both my servants, W. Hewer, and Tom Edwards, have lost their fathers, both in St Sepulchre's parish of the plague this week, do put me into great apprehension of melancholy, and with good reason.

17th. To Gravesend in the *Bezan* Yacht, and there come to anchor for all night.

18th. By break of day we come to within sight of the fleet, which was a very fine thing to behold, being above 100 ships, great and small; with the flag ships of each squadron, distinguished by their several flags on their main, fore, or mizen masts. Among others, the *Soveraigne*, *Charles*, and *Prince*; in the last of which my Lord Sandwich was. And so we come on board, and we find my Lord Sandwich newly up in his night-gown very well. He received us kindly; telling us the state of the fleet, lacking provisions, having no beer at all, nor have had most of them these three weeks or month, and but few days' dry provisions. And indeed he tells us that he believes no fleet was ever set to sea in so ill condition of provision, as this was when it went out last. He did inform us in the business of Bergen, so as to let us see how the judgment of the world is not to be depended on in things they know not; it being a place just wide enough, and not so much hardly, for ships to go through to it, the yard-armes sticking in the very rocks. He do not, upon his best enquiry, find reason to except against any part of the management of the business by Teddiman; he having staid treating no longer than during the night, whiles he was fitting himself to fight, bringing his ship abreast, and not a quarter of an hour longer, (as it is said); nor could more ships have been brought to play, as is thought. Nor could men be landed, there being 10,000 men effectively always in armes of the Danes; nor, says he, could we expect more from the Dane than he did, it being impossible to set fire on the ships but it must burn the towne. But that wherein the Dane did amisse, is that he did assist them, the Dutch, all the time, while he was treating with us, when he should have been newtrall to us both. But, however, he did demand but the treaty of us; which is, that we should not come with more than five ships. A flag of truce is said, and confessed by my Lord, that he believes it was hung out; but while they did hang it out, they did shoot at us; so that it was not seen, or perhaps they would not cease upon sight of it, while they continued actually in action against us. But the main thing my Lord wonders at, and condemns the Dane for, is, that the blockhead, who is so much in debt to the Hollander, having now a treasure more by much than all his Crowne was worth, and that which would for ever have beggared the Hollander, should not take this time to break with the Hollander, and thereby pay his debt which must have been forgiven him, and have got the greatest treasure into his hands that ever was together in the world. By and by my Lord took me aside to discourse of his private matters, who was very free with me touching the ill condition of the fleet that it hath been in, and the good fortune that he hath had, and nothing else that these prizes are to be imputed to. He also talked with me about Mr Coventry's dealing with him in sending Sir W. Pen away before him, which was not fair nor kind; but that he hath mastered and cajoled Sir W. Pen, that he hath been able to do nothing in the fleet, but been obedient to him; but withal tells me he is a man that is but of very mean parts, and a fellow not to be lived with, so false and base he is; which I know well enough to be true, and did, as I had formerly done, give my Lord my knowledge of him. By and by was called a Council of Warr on board, when comes Sir W. Pen there, and Sir Christopher Mings,[50] Sir Edward Spragg, Sir Jos. Jordan,[51] Sir Thomas Teddiman, and Sir Roger Cuttance. So to our

50 The son of a shoemaker, bred to the sea service, and rose to the rank of an Admiral. He was killed in the naval action with the Dutch, June 1666.
51 Distinguished himself as an Admiral in the battle of Soleby, and on other occasions.

Yacht again, having seen many of my friends there, and continued till we come into Chatham river.

20th. To Lambeth. But, Lord! what a sad time it is to see no boats upon the River; and grass grows all up and down White Hall court, and nobody but poor wretches in the streets! And, which is worst of all, the Duke showed us the number of the plague this week, brought in the last night from the Lord Mayor; that it is encreased about 600 more than the last, which is quite contrary to our hopes and expectations, from the coldness of the late season. For the whole general number is 8297, and of them the plague 7165; which is more in the whole by above 50, than the biggest Bill yet: which is very grievous to us all.

21st. To Nonsuch, to the Exchequer, by appointment, and walked up and down the house and park; and a fine place it hath heretofore been, and a fine prospect about the house. A great walk of an elme and a walnutt set one after another in order. And all the house on the outside filled with figures of stories, and good painting of Rubens' or Holben's doing. And one great thing is, that most of the house is covered, I mean the post, and quarters in the walls, with lead, and gilded. I walked also into the ruined garden.

22nd. At Blackwall. Here is observable what Johnson tells us, that in digging the late Docke, they did 12 feet under ground find perfect trees over-covered with earth. Nut trees, with the branches and the very nuts upon them; some of whose nuts he showed us. Their shells black with age, and their kernell, upon opening, decayed, but their shell perfectly hard as ever. And a yew tree, (upon which the very ivy was taken up whole about it,) which upon cutting with an addes, we found to be rather harder than the living tree usually is. Among other discourse concerning long life, Sir J. Minnes saying that his great-grandfather was alive in Edward the Vth's time; my Lord Sandwich did tell us how few there have been of his family since King Harry the VIIIth that is to say, the then Chiefe Justice,[52] and his son and the Lord Montagu, who was father[53] to Sir Sidney,[54] who was his father.

52 Sir Edward Montagu, died 1556.
53 I think this should be brother, as Edward first Lord Montagu and Sir Sidney Montagu were both sons of the second Sir Edward Montagu.
54 Master of the Requests to Charles I.

And yet, what is more wonderfull, he did assure us from the mouth of my Lord Montagu himself, that in King James's time, (when he had a mind to get the King to cut off the entayle of some land which was given in Harry the VIIIth's time to the family, with the remainder in the Crowne;) he did answer the King in showing how unlikely it was that ever it could revert to the Crown, but that it would be a present convenience to him; and did show that at that time there were 4000 persons derived from the very body of the Chiefe Justice. It seems the number of daughters in the family had been very great, and they too had most of them many children, and grandchildren, and great-grand-children. This he tells as a most known and certain truth.

25th. Found ourselves come to the fleet, and so aboard the *Prince*; and there, after a good while in discourse, we did agree a bargain of £5000 for my Lord Sandwich for silk, cinnamon, nutmegs, and indigo. And I was near signing to an undertaking for the payment of the whole sum: but I did by chance escape it, having since, upon second thoughts, great cause to be glad of it, reflecting upon the craft and not good condition, it may be, of Captain Cocke.

27th. To Captain Cocke's, and (he not yet come from town) to Mr Evelyn, where much company; and thence in his coach with him to the Duke of Albemarle by Lambeth, who was in a mighty pleasant humour; and tells us that the Dutch do stay abroad, and our fleet must go out again, or be ready to do so. Here we got several things ordered as we desired for the relief of the prisoners, and sick and wounded men. Here I saw this week's Bill of Mortality, wherein, blessed be God! there is above 1800 decrease, being the first considerable decrease we have had. Most excellent discourse with Mr Evelyn touching all manner of learning; wherein I find him a very fine gentleman, and particularly of paynting, in which he tells me the beautifull Mrs Middleton is rare, and his own wife do brave things.

29th. Sir Martin Noell[55] is this day dead of the plague in London.

---

55 He had been a Farmer of the Excise and Customs before the Restoration. The Messenger described in *Hudibras*, Part III, Canto II, 1407 as disturbing the Cabal with the account of the mobs burning Rumps, is said to have been intended for Sir Martin Noell.

October 1st. Embarked on board the *Bezan*, and come to the fleet about two of the clock. My Lord received us mighty kindly, and did discourse to us of the Dutch fleet being abroad, eighty-five of them still.

2nd. Having sailed all night, (and I do wonder how they in the dark could find the way) we got by morning to Gillingham, and thence all walked to Chatham; and there with Commissioner Pett viewed the Yard; and among other things, a team of four horses come close by us, he being with me, drawing a piece of timber that I am confident one man could easily have carried upon his back. I made the horses be taken away, and a man or two to take the timber away with their hands.

3rd. Sir W. Batten is gone this day to meet to adjourne the Parliament to Oxford. This night I hear that of our two watermen that used to carry our letters, and were well on Saturday last, one is dead, and the other dying sick of the plague; the plague, though decreasing elsewhere, yet being greater about the Tower and thereabouts.

4th. This night comes Sir George Smith to see me at the office, and tells me how the plague is decreased this week 740, for which God be praised! but that it encreases at our end of the town still.

5th. Read a book of Mr Evelyn's translating and sending me as a present, about directions for gathering a Library; but the book is above my reach, but his epistle to my Lord Chancellor is a very fine piece. Then to Mr Evelyn's to discourse of our confounded business of prisoners, and sick and wounded seamen, wherein he and we are so much put out of order. And here he showed me his gardens, which are for variety of evergreens, and hedge of holly, the finest things I ever saw in my life. Thence in his coach to Greenwich, and there to my office, all the way having fine discourse of trees and the nature of vegetables.

7th. Did business, though not much, at the office; because of the horrible crowd and lamentable moan of the poor seamen that lie starving in the streets for lack of money. Which do trouble and perplex me to the heart; and more at noon when we were to go through them, for then above a whole hundred of them followed us; some cursing, some swearing, and some praying to us. At night come two waggons from Rochester with more goods from Captain Cocke; and in housing them come two of the Custom-house, and did seize them: but I showed them my *Transire*. However, after some angry words, we locked them up, and sealed up the key, and did give it to the constable to keep till Monday, and so parted. But, Lord! to think how the poor constable come to me in the dark going home; 'Sir,' says he, 'I have the key, and if you would have me do any service for you, send for me betimes to-morrow morning, and I will do what you would have me.' Whether the fellow do this out of kindness or knavery, I cannot tell; but it is pretty to observe. Talking with him in the high way, come close by the bearers with a dead corpse of the plague; but, Lord! to see what custom is, that I am come almost to think nothing of it.

8th. To the office, where ended my business with the Captains; and I think of twenty-two ships we shall make shift to get out seven. (God help us! men being sick, or provisions lacking.)

9th. Called upon by Sir John Shaw, to whom I did give a civil answer about our prize goods, that all his dues as one of the Farmers of the Customes are paid, and showed him our *Transire,* with which he was satisfied, and parted.

11th. We met Mr Seamour, one of the Commissioners for Prizes, and a Parliament-man, and he was mighty high, and had now seized our goods on their behalf; and he mighty imperiously would have all forfeited. But I could not but think it odd that a Parliament-man, in a serious discourse before such persons as we and my Lord Brouncker, and Sir John Minnes, should quote *Hudibras*, as being the book I doubt he hath read most.

12th. Good news this week that there are about 600 less dead of the plague than the last.

13th. Sir Jer. Smith[56] to see me in his way to Court, and a good man he is, and one that I must keep fair with.

14th. My heart and head to-night is full of the Victualling business, being overjoyed and proud at my success in my proposal about it, it

56 A distinguished Naval Officer, made a Commissioner of the Navy, vice Sir W. Pen, 1669.

being read before the King, Duke, and the Caball with complete applause and satisfaction. This Sir G. Carteret and Sir W. Coventry both writ me. My own proper accounts are in great disorder, having been neglected about a month. This, and the fear of the sickness, and providing for my family, do fill my head very full, besides the infinite business of the office, and nobody here to look after it but myself.

15th. The Parliament, it seems, have voted the King £1,250,000 at £50,000 per month, tax for the war; and voted to assist the King against the Dutch, and all that shall adhere to them; and thanks to be given him for his care of the Duke of York, which last is a very popular vote on the Duke's behalf. The taxes of the last assessment, which should have been in good part gathered, are not yet laid, and that even in part of the City of London; and the Chimny-money comes almost to nothing, nor any thing else looked after.

16th. I walked to the Tower; but, Lord! how empty the streets are and melancholy, so many poor sick people in the streets full of sores; and so many sad stories overheard as I walk, every body talking of this dead, and that man sick, and so many in this place, and so many in that. And they tell me that, in Westminster, there is never a physician and but one apothecary left, all being dead; but that there are great hopes of a great decrease this week: God send it! At the Tower found my Lord Duke and Duchesse at dinner; so I sat down. And much good cheer, the Lieutenant and his lady, and several officers with the Duke. But, Lord! to hear the silly talk was there, would make one mad; the Duke having none almost but fools about him. I have received letters from my Lord Sandwich to-day, speaking very high about the prize goods, that he would have us to fear nobody, but be very confident in what we have done, and not to confess any fault or doubt of what he hath done; for the King hath allowed it, and do now confirm it, and send orders, as he says, for nothing to be disturbed that his Lordshipp hath ordered therein as to the division of the goods to the fleet; which do comfort us. Much talk there is of the Chancellor's speech and the King's at the Parliament's meeting, which are very well liked; and that we shall certainly, by their speeches, fall out with France at this time, together with the Dutch, which will find us work.

26th. Sir Christopher Mings and I together by water to the Tower; and I find him a very witty well-spoken fellow, and mighty free to tell his parentage, being a shoemaker's son. I to the 'Change, where I hear how the French have taken two and sunk one of our merchantmen in the Straights, and carried the ships to Toulon: so that there is no expectation but we must fall out with them. The 'Change pretty full, and the town begins to be lively again, though the streets very empty, and most shops shut.

27th. The Duke of Albemarle proposed to me from Mr Coventry, that I should be Surveyor-Generall of the Victualling business, which I accepted. But, indeed, the terms in which Mr Coventry proposes it for me are the most obliging that ever I could expect from any man, and more; he saying that I am the fittest man in England, and that he is sure, if I will undertake, I will perform it: and that it will be also a very desirable thing that I might have this encouragement, my encouragement in the Navy alone being in no wise proportionable to my pains or deserts. This, added to the letter I had three days since from Mr Southerne,[57] signifying that the Duke of York had in his master's absence opened my letters, and commanded him to tell me that he did approve of my being the Surveyor-General, do make me joyful beyond myself that I cannot express it, to see that as I do take pains, so God blesses me, and hath sent me masters that do observe that I take pains.

28th. The Parliament hath given the Duke of York £120,000, to be paid him after £1,250,000 is gathered upon the tax which they have now given the King. He tells me that the Dutch have lately launched sixteen new ships; all which is great news. The King and Court, they say, have now finally resolved to spend nothing upon clothes, but what is of the growth of England; which, if observed, will be very pleasing to the people, and very good for them.

29th. In the street did overtake and almost run upon two women crying and carrying a man's coffin between them. I suppose the husband of one of them, which, methinks, is a sad thing.

31st. Meeting yesterday the Searchers with their rods in their hands coming from Captain Cocke's house, I did overhear them say that his

57 Secretary to Sir W. Coventry.

Black did not die of the plague. About nine at night I come home, and anon comes Mrs Coleman[58] and her husband, and she sung very finely, though her voice is decayed as to strength but mighty sweet though soft, and a pleasant jolly woman, and in mighty good humour. She sung part of the Opera, though she would not own she did get any of it without book in order to the stage. Thus we end the month. The whole number of deaths being 1388, and of them of the plague, 1031. Want of money in the Navy puts every thing out of order. Men grow mutinous; and nobody here to mind the business of the Navy but myself. I in great hopes of my place of Surveyor-General of the Victualling, which will bring me £300 per annum.

November 1st. My Lord Brouncker with us to Mrs Williams's lodgings, and Sir W. Batten, Sir Edmund Pooly,[59] and others; and there, it being my Lord's birthday, had every one a green riband tied in our hats very foolishly; and methinks mighty disgracefully for my Lord to have his folly so open to all the world with this woman.

5th. By water to Deptford, and there made a visit to Mr Evelyn, who, among other things, showed me most excellent painting in little; in distemper, Indian incke, water colours: graveing; and, above all, the whole secret of mezzo-tinto, and the manner of it, which is very pretty, and good things done with it. He read to me very much also of his discourse, he hath been many years and now is about, about Gardenage; which will be a most noble and pleasant piece. He read me part of a play or two of his making, very good, but not as he conceits them, I think, to be. He showed me his *Hortus Hyemalis*; leaves laid up in a book of several plants kept dry, which preserve colour, however, and look very finely, better than an herball. In fine, a most excellent person he is, and must be allowed a little for a little conceitedness; but he may well be so, being a man so much above others. He read me, though with too much gusto, some little poems of his own that were not transcendant, yet one or two very pretty

58 Probably the person mentioned in the following extract from Malone's *Account of the English Stage*. 'In 1659 or 60, in imitation of foreign theatres, women were first introduced on the scene. In 1656, indeed, Mrs Coleman, wife to Mr Edward Coleman, represented Ianthe in the first part of the *Siege of Rhodes*: but the little she had to say was spoken in recitative.'
59 MP for Bury St Edmunds, and in the list of proposed Knights of the Royal Oak for Suffolk.

epigrams; among others, of a lady looking in at a grate, and being pecked at by an eagle that was there.

6th. Sir G. Carteret and I did walk an hour in the garden before the house, talking of my Lord Sandwich's business; what enemies he hath, and how they have endeavoured to bespatter him: and particularly about his leaving of 30 ships of the enemy, when Pen would have gone, and my Lord called him back again: which is most false. However, he says, it was purposed by some hotheads in the House of Commons, at the same time when they voted a present to the Duke of York, to have voted £10,000 to the Prince, and half-a-crowne to my Lord of Sandwich; but nothing come of it. But, for all this, the King is most firme to my Lord, and so is my Lord Chancellor, and my Lord Arlington. The Prince, in appearance, kind; the Duke of York silent, says no hurt; but admits others to say it in his hearing. Sir W. Pen, the falsest rascal that ever was in the world; and that this afternoon the Duke of Albemarle did tell him that Pen was a very cowardly rogue, and one that hath brought all these rogueish fanatick Captains into the fleet, and swears he should never go out with the fleet again. That Sir W. Coventry is most kind to Pen still; and says nothing nor do any thing openly to the prejudice of my Lord. He agrees with me, that it is impossible for the King to set out a fleet again the next year; and that he fears all will come to ruine, there being no money in prospect but these prizes, which will bring, it may be £20,000, but that will signify nothing in the world for it.

9th. The Bill of Mortality, to all our griefs, is encreased 399 this week, and the encrease generally through the whole City and suburbs, which makes us all sad.

14th. Captain Cocke and I in his coach through Kent-streete, (a sad place through the plague, people sitting sick and with plaisters about them in the street begging).

15th. The plague, blessed be God! is decreased 400; making the whole this week but 1300 and odd: for which the Lord be praised!

16th. To Eriffe; where after making a little visit to Madam Williams, she did give me information of W. How's having bought eight bags of precious stones taken from about the Dutch Vice-admirall's neck, of which there were eight dyamonds which cost him £4000 sterling, in India, and hoped to have made £12,000 here for them. And that this is told by one that sold him one of the bags, which hath nothing but rubys in it, which he had for 35s.; and that it will be proved he hath made £125 of one stone that he bought. This she desired, and I resolved I would give my Lord Sandwich notice of. So I on board my Lord Brouncker; and there he and Sir Edmund Pooly carried me down into the hold of the India shipp, and there did show me the greatest wealth lie in confusion that a man can see in the world. Pepper scattered through every chink, you trod upon it; and in cloves and nutmegs, I walked above the knees: whole rooms full. And silk in bales, and boxes of copper-plate, one of which I saw opened. Having seen this, which was as noble a sight as ever I saw in my life, I away on board the other ship in despair to get the pleasure-boat of the gentlemen there to carry me to the fleet. They were Mr Ashburnham[60] and Colonell Wyndham; but pleading the King's business, they did presently agree I should have it. So I presently on board, and got under sail, and had a good bedd by the shift, of Wyndham's; and so sailed all night, and got down to Quinbrough water, where all the great ships are now come, and there on board my Lord, and was soon received with great content. And after some little discourse, he and I on board Sir W. Pen; and there held a council of Warr about many wants of the fleet; and so followed my Lord Sandwich, who was gone a little before me on board the *Royall James*. And there spent an hour, my Lord playing upon the gittarr, which he now commends above all musique in the world. As an infinite secret, my Lord tells me, the factions are high between the King and the Duke, and all the Court are in an uproar with their loose amours; the Duke of York being in love desperately with Mrs Stewart. Nay, that the Duchesse herself is fallen in love with her new Master of the Horse, one Harry Sidney,[61] and another, Harry Savill.[62] So that God knows what will be the end of it. And that the Duke is not so obsequious as he used to be, but

60 John Ashburnham, a Groom of the Bedchamber to Charles I whom he attended during the whole of the Rebellion, and afterwards filled the same post under Charles II. He was in 1661 MP for Sussex; and died 1671.

61 Younger son of Robert Earl of Leicester, created Earl of Romney, 1694. He was Lord Lieutenant of Ireland, Master of the Ordnance, and Warden of the Cinque Ports in the reign of King William. Died 1704, unmarried.

62 Henry Saville, some time one of the grooms of the Bedchamber to the Duke of York.

very high of late; and would be glad to be in the head of an army as Generall; and that it is said that he do propose to go and command under the King of Spayne, in Flanders. That his amours to Mrs Stewart are told the King. So that all is like to be nought among them.

22nd. I was very glad to hear that the plague is come very low; that is, the whole under 1000, and the plague 600 and odd: and great hopes of a further decrease, because of this day's being a very exceeding hard frost, and continues freezing. This day the first of the Oxford Gazettes come out, which is very pretty, full of news, and no folly in it. Wrote by Williamson. It pleased me to have it demonstrated, that a purser without professed cheating is a professed loser, twice as much as he gets.

23rd. Captn. Cuttance tells me how W. How is laid by the heels, and confined to the *Royall Katharin*, and his things all seized.

24th. To the 'Change, where very busy with several people, and mightily glad to see the 'Change so full, and hopes of another abatement still the next week. Visited Mr Evelyn, where most excellent discourse with him; among other things he showed me a lieger of a Treasurer of the Navy, his great grandfather, just 100 years old; which I seemed mighty fond of, and he did present me with it, which I take as a great rarity; and he hopes to find me more, older than it. He also showed us several letters of the old Lord of Leicester's,[63] in Queen Elizabeth's time, under the very hand-writing of Queen Elizabeth, and Queen Mary, Queen of Scotts; and others, very venerable names. But, Lord! how poorly, methinks, they wrote in those days, and in what plain uncut paper.

27th. With Sir G. Carteret, who tells me that my Lord hath received still worse and worse usage from some base people about the Court. But the King, is very kind, and the Duke do not appear the contrary; and my Lord Chancellor swore to him 'by — I will not forsake my Lord of Sandwich.' I into London, it being dark night, by a hackny coach; the first I have durst to go in many a day, and with great pain

63 There are some letters and papers answering to this description in the Pepysian Library, and amongst them an account of the Coroner's Inquest held upon the Countess of Leicester at Cumnor.

now for fear. But it being unsafe to go by water in the dark and frosty cold, and unable being weary with my morning walk to go on foot, this was my only way. Few people yet in the streets, nor shops open, here and there twenty in a place almost; though not above five or six o'clock at night.

30th. Great joy we have this week in the weekly Bill, it being come to 544 in all, and but 333 of the plague; so that we are encouraged to get to London soon as we can. And my father writes as great news of joy to them, that he saw York's waggon go again this week to London, and full of passengers; and tells me that my aunt Bell hath been dead of the plague these seven weeks.

December 3rd. To Captn. Cocke's, and there dined with him, and Colonell Wyndham, a worthy gentleman, whose wife was nurse to the present King, and one that while she lived governed him and every thing else, as Cocke says, as a minister of state; the old King putting mighty weight and trust upon her. They talked much of matters of State and persons, and particularly how my Lord Barkeley hath all along been a fortunate, though a passionate and but weak man as to policy; but as a kinsman brought in and promoted by my Lord of St Alban's, and one that is the greatest vapourer in the world, this Colonell Wyndham says; and to whom only, with Jacke Ashburne[64] and Colonel Legg,[65] the King's removal to the Isle of Wight from Hampton Court was communicated; and (though betrayed by their knavery, or at best by their ignorance, insomuch that they have all solemnly charged one another with their failures therein, and have been at daggers-drawing publickly about it,) yet now none greater friends in the world.

4th. Upon the 'Change to-day Colvill tells me, from Oxford, that the King in person hath justified my Lord Sandwich to the highest degree; and is right in his favour to the uttermost.

6th. Up betimes, it being fast-day; and by water to the Duke of Albemarle, who come to town from Oxford last night. He is mighty brisk, and very kind to me, and asks my advice principally in every

64 This should be Ashburnham.
65 William Legge, Groom of the Bedchamber to Charles I., and father to the first Lord Dartmouth. He was MP for Southampton. Died 1672.

thing. He surprises me with the news that my Lord Sandwich goes Embassador to Spayne speedily; though I know not whence this arises, yet I am heartily glad of it. The King hath done my Lord Sandwich all the right imaginable, by showing him his countenance before all the world on every occasion, to remove thoughts of discontent; and he is to go Embassador, and the Duke of York is made generall of all forces by land and sea, and the Duke of Albemarle, lieutenant-generall.

8th. To White Hall, where we found Sir G. Carteret with the Duke, and also Sir G. Downing, whom I had not seen in many years before. He greeted me very kindly, and I him; though methinks I am touched that it should be said that he was my master heretofore, as doubtless he will.

9th. My Lord Brouncker and I dined with the Duke of Albemarle. At table the Duchesse, a very ill-looked woman, complaining of her Lord's going to sea the next year, said these cursed words: 'If my Lord had been a coward he had gone to sea no more: it may be then he might have been excused, and made an embassador,' (meaning my Lord Sandwich). This made me mad, and I believed she perceived my countenance change, and blushed herself very much. I was in hopes others had not minded it, but my Lord Brouncker, after we were come away, took notice of the words to me with displeasure.

11th. That I may remember it the more particularly, I thought fit to insert this memorandum of Temple's discourse this night with me, which I took in writing from his mouth. Before the Harp and Crosse money was cried down, he and his fellow goldsmiths did make some particular trials what proportion that money bore to the old King's money, and they found that generally it come to, one with another, about £25 in every £100. Of this money there was upon the calling of it in, £650,000 at least brought into the Tower; and from thence he computes that the whole money of England must be full £16,250,000. But for all this believes that there is about £30,000,000; he supposing that about the King's coming in (when he begun to observe the quantity of the new money) people begun to be fearful of this money's being cried down, and so picked it out and set it a-going as fast as they could, to be rid of it; and he thinks £30,000,000 the rather, because if there were but £16,250,000 the King having £2,000,000 every year, would have the whole money of the kingdom in his hands in eight years. He tells me about £350,000 sterling was coined out of the French money, the proceeds of Dunkirke; so that, with what was coined of the Cross money, there is new coined about £1,000,000 besides the gold, which is guessed at £500,000. He tells me, that, though the King did deposit the French money in pawn all the while for the £350,000 he was forced to borrow thereupon till the tools could be made for the new Minting in the present form. Yet the interest he paid for that time come to £35,000. Viner having to his knowledge £10,000 for the use of £100,000 of it.

13th. Away to the 'Change, and there hear the ill news, to my great and all our great trouble, that the plague is encreased again this week, notwithstanding there hath been a long day or two great frosts; but we hope it is only the effects of the late close warm weather, and if the frost continue the next week, may fall again; but the towne do thicken so much with people, that it is much if the plague do not grow again upon us.

15th. Met with Sir James Bunch;[66] 'This is the time for you,' says he, 'that were for Oliver heretofore; you are full of employment, and we poor Cavaliers sit still and can get nothing;' which was a pretty reproach I thought, but answered nothing to it, for fear of making it worse.

22nd. I to my Lord Brouncker's, and there spent the evening by my desire in seeing his Lordship open to pieces and make up again his watch, thereby being taught what I never knew before; and it is a thing very well worth my having seen, and am mightily pleased and satisfied with it.

25th (Christmas day). To church in the morning, and there saw a wedding in the church, which I have not seen many a day; and the young people so merry one with another, and strange to see what delight we married people have to see these poor fools decoyed into our condition, every man and woman gazing and smiling at them.

26th. Saw some fine writing work and flourishing of Mr Hore, with one that I knew long ago, an acquaintance of Mr Tomson's, at

66 Probably James Bunce, an Alderman of London, 1660.

Westminster, that is this man's clerk. It is the story of the several Archbishops of Canterbury engrossed in vellum, to hang up in Canterbury Cathedrall in tables, in lieu of the old ones, which are almost worn out.

30th. All the afternoon to my accounts; and there find myself, to my great joy, a great deal worth above £4000 for which the Lord be praised! and is principally occasioned by my getting £500 of Cocke, for my profit in his bargains of prize goods, and from Mr Gauden's making me a present of £500 more, when I paid him £800 for Tangier.

31st. Thus ends this year, to my great joy, in this manner. I have raised my estate from £1300 in this year to £4400. I have got myself greater interest I think by my diligence, and my imployments encreased by that of Treasurer for Tangier, and Surveyor of the Victualls. It is true we have gone through great melancholy because of the great plague, and I put to great charges by it, by keeping my family long at Woolwich, and myself and another part of my family, my clerks, at my charge at Greenwich, and a maid at London; but I hope the King will give us some satisfaction for that. But now the plague is abated almost to nothing, and I intending to get to London as fast as I can. The Dutch war goes on very ill, by reason of lack of money; having none to hope for, all being put into disorder by a new Act that is made as an experiment to bring credit to the Exchequer, for goods and money to be advanced upon the credit of that Act. The great evil of this year, and the only one indeed, is the fall of my Lord of Sandwich, whose mistake about the prizes hath undone him, I believe, as to interest at Court; though sent (for a little palliating it) Embassador into Spayne, which he is now fitting himself for. But the Duke of Albemarle goes with the Prince to sea this next year, and my Lord is very meanly spoken of; and, indeed, his miscarriage about the prize goods is not to be excused, to suffer a company of rogues to go away with ten times as much as himself, and the blame of all to be deservedly laid upon him. My whole family hath been well all this while, and all my friends I know of, saving my aunt Bell, who is dead, and some children of my cosen Sarah's, of the plague. But many of such as I know very well, dead; yet, to our great joy, the town fills apace, and shops begin to be open again. Pray God continue the plague's decrease! for that keeps the Court away from the place of business, and so all goes to rack as to publick matters, they at this distance not thinking of it.

1665/66. January 3rd. I to the Duke of Albemarle and back again: and at the Duke's with great joy I received the good news of the decrease of the plague this week to 70, and but 253 in all; which is the least Bill hath been known these twenty years in the City. Through the want of people in London, is it that must make it so low below the ordinary number for Bills.

5th. I with my Lord Brouncker and Mrs Williams by coach with four horses to London, to my Lord's house in Covent-Garden. But, Lord! what staring to see a nobleman's coach come to town. And porters every where bow to us; and such begging of beggars! And delightful it is to see the town full of people again; and shops begin to open, though in many places seven or eight together, and more, all shut; but yet the town is full, compared with what it used to be. I mean the City end: for Covent-Garden and Westminster are yet very empty of people, no Court nor gentry being there. Reading a discourse about the River of Thames, the reason of its being choked up in several places with shelfes: which is plain is by the encroachments made upon the River, and running out of causeways into the River at every wood-wharfe; which was not heretofore when Westminster Hall and White Hall were built, and Redriffe Church, which now are sometimes overflown with water.

7th. The town talks of my Lord Craven being to come into Sir G. Carteret's place; but sure it cannot be true. But I do fear those two families, his and my Lord Sandwich's, are quite broken. And I must now stand upon my own legs.

9th. Pierce tells me how great a difference hath been between the Duke and Duchesse, he suspecting her to be naught with Mr Sidney. But some way or other the matter is made up; but he was banished the Court, and the Duke for many days did not speak to the Duchesse at all. He tells me that my Lord Sandwich is lost there at Court, though the King is particularly his friend. But people do speak every where slightly of him; which is a sad story to me, but I hope it may be better again. And that Sir G. Carteret is neglected, and hath great enemies at work against him. That matters must needs go bad, while all the town, and every boy in the street, openly cries, 'The King cannot go away till my Lady Castlemaine be ready to come along with him;' she being lately put to bed. And that he visits her and Mrs Stewart every morning before he eats his breakfast.

10th. The plague is encreased this week from seventy to eighty-nine. We have also great fear of our Hambrough fleet, of their meeting with the Dutch; as also have certain news, that by storms Sir Jer. Smith's fleet is scattered, and three of them come without masts back to Plymouth.

13th. Home with his Lordship to Mrs Williams's, in Covent-Garden, to dinner, (the first time I ever was there,) and there met Captain Cocke; and pretty merry, though not perfectly so, because of the fear that there is of a great encrease again of the plague this week. And again my Lord Brouncker do tell us, that he hath it from Sir John Baber,[1] who is related to my Lord Craven, that my Lord Craven do look after Sir G. Carteret's place, and do reckon himself sure of it.

16th. Mightily troubled at the news of the plague's being encreased, and was much the saddest news that the plague hath brought me from the beginning of it; because of the lateness of the year, and the fear, we may with reason have, of its continuing with us the next summer. The total being now 375, and the plague 158.

17th. I rode to Dagenhams in the dark. It was my Lord Crewe's desire that I should come, and chiefly to discourse with me of my Lord Sandwich's matters; and therein to persuade, what I had done already, that my Lord should sue out a pardon for his business of the prizes, as also for Bergen, and all he hath done this year past, before he begins his Embassy to Spain. For it is to be feared that the Parliament will fly out against him and particular men, the next Session. He is glad also that my Lord is clear of his sea-imployment, though sorry as I am, only in the manner of its bringing about.

18th. My wife and I anon and Mercer, by coach, to Pierce; where mighty merry, and sing and dance with great pleasure; and I danced, who never did in company in my life.

1 Physician in Ordinary to the King.

19th. It is a remarkable thing how infinitely naked all that end of the town, Covent-Garden, is at this day of people; while the City is almost as full again of people as ever it was.

22nd. At noon my Lord Brouncker did come, but left the keys of the chests we should open, at Sir G. Carteret's lodgings, of my Lord Sandwich's, wherein How's supposed jewells are; so we could not, according to my Lord Arlington's order, see them to-day; but we parted, resolving to meet here at night: my Lord Brouncker being going with Dr Wilkins, Mr Hooke,[2] and others, to Colonel Blunt's, to consider again of the business of chariots, and to try their new invention. Which I saw here my Lord Brouncker ride in; where the coachman sits astride upon a pole over the horse, but do not touch the horse, which is a pretty odde thing; but it seems it is most easy for the horse, and, as they say, for the man also. The first meeting of Gresham College, since the plague. Dr Goddard did fill us with talk, in defence of his and his fellow physicians going out of town in the plague-time; saying that their particular patients were most gone out of town, and they left at liberty; and a great deal more, &c. But what, among other fine discourse pleased me most, was Sir G. Ent[3] about Respiration; that it is not to this day known, or concluded on among physicians, nor to be done either, how the action is managed by nature, or for what use it is.

23rd. Good news beyond all expectation of the decrease of the plague, being now but 79, and the whole but 272. So home with comfort to bed. A most furious storme all night and morning.

24th. My Lord and I, the weather being a little fairer, by water to Deptford to Sir G. Carteret's house, where W. How met us, and there we opened the chests, and saw the poor sorry rubys which have caused all this ado to the undoing of W. How; though I am not much sorry for it, because of his pride and ill nature. About 200 of these very small stones, and a cod of muske (which it is strange I was not able to smell) is all we could find; so locked them up again, and my Lord and I, the wind being again very furious, so as we durst not

2 Dr Robert Hooke, before mentioned, Professor of Geometry at Gresham College, and Curator of the Experiments to the Royal Society, of which he was one of the earliest and most distinguished members. Died 1678.
3 Sir George Ent, FRS, President of the College of Physicians.

go by water, walked to London quite round the bridge, no boat being able to stirre; and, Lord! what a dirty walk we had, and so strong the wind, that in the fields we many times could not carry our bodies against it, but were driven backwards. We went through Horslydowne, where I never was since a boy, that I went to enquire after my father, whom we did give over for lost coming from Holland. It was dangerous to walk the streets, the bricks and tiles falling from the houses that the whole streets were covered with them; and whole chimneys, nay, whole houses in two or three places, blowed down. But, above all, the pales of London-bridge on both sides were blown away, so that we were fain to stoop very low for fear of blowing off of the bridge. We could see no boats in the Thames afloat, but what were broke loose, and carried through the bridge, it being ebbing water. And the greatest sight of all was, among other parcels of ships driven here and there in clusters together, one was quite overset and lay with her masts all along in the water, and keel above water.

25th. It is now certain that the King of France hath publickly declared war against us, and God knows how little fit we are for it.

28th. Took coach, and to Hampton Court, where we find the King, and Duke, and Lords, all in council; so we walked up and down: there being none of the ladies come, and so much the more business I hope will be done. The Council being up, out comes the King, and I kissed his hand, and he grasped me very kindly by the hand. The Duke also, I kissed his, and he mighty kind, and Sir W. Coventry. I found my Lord Sandwich there, poor man! I see with a melancholy face, and suffers his beard to grow on his upper lip more than usual. I took him a little aside to know when I should wait on him, and where he told me, and that it would be best to meet at his lodgings, without being seen to walk together. Which I liked very well; and, Lord! to see in what difficulty I stand, that I dare not walk with Sir W. Coventry, for fear my Lord or Sir G. Carteret should see me: nor with either of them, for fear Sir W. Coventry should. I went down into one of the Courts, and there met the King and Duke; and the Duke called me to him. And the King come to me of himself, and told me, 'Mr Pepys,' says he, 'I do give you thanks for your good service all this year, and I assure you I am very sensible of it.'

29th. Mr Evelyn and I into my Lord Brouncker's coach, and rode together with excellent discourse till we come to Clapham. Talking of the vanity and vices of the Court, which makes it a most contemptible thing; and indeed in all his discourse I find him a most worthy person. Particularly he entertained me with discourse of an Infirmary, which he hath projected for the sick and wounded seamen against the next year; which I mightily approve of; and will endeavour to promote it, being a worthy thing, and of use, and will save money.

30th. This is the first time I have been in the church[4] since I left London for the plague, and it frighted me indeed to go through the church more than I thought it could have done, to see so many graves lie so high upon the churchyards where people have been buried of the plague. I was much troubled at it, and do not think to go through it again a good while.

31st. I find many about the City that live near the churchyards solicitous to have the churchyards covered with lime, and I think it is needfull, and ours I hope will be done. To my Lord Chancellor's new house which he is building, only to view it, hearing so much from Mr Evelyn of it; and, indeed, it is the finest pile I ever did see in my life, and will be a glorious house. To White Hall, and to my great joy people begin to bustle up and down there, the King holding his resolution to be in town to-morrow, and hath good encouragement, blessed be God! to do so, the plague being decreased this week to 56, and the total to 227.

February 2nd. My Lord Sandwich is come to town with the King and Duke.

4th (Lord's day;) and my wife and I the first time together at church since the plague, and now only because of Mr Mills his coming home to preach his first sermon; expecting a great excuse for his leaving the parish before any body went, and now staying till all are come home; but he made but a very poor and short excuse, and a bad sermon. It was a frost, and had snowed last night, which covered the graves in the churchyard, so as I was the less afraid for going through.

8th. Lord Brouncker with the King and Duke upon the water to-day, to see Greenwich house, and the yacht Castle is building of.

4 Probably St Olave's, Hart Street.

9th. Thence to Westminster, to the Exchequer, about my Tangier business, and so to Westminster Hall, where the first day of the Terme and the hall very full of people, and much more than was expected, considering the plague that hath been.

11th (Lord's day). Up; and put on a new black cloth suit to an old coat that I make to be in mourning at Court, where they are all, for the King of Spain. I to the Park, and walked two or three times of the Pell Mell with the company about the King and Duke: the Duke speaking to me a good deal. There met Lord Brouncker and Mr Coventry, and discoursed about the Navy business; and all of us much at a loss that we yet can hear nothing of Sir Jeremy Smith's fleet, that went away to the Straights the middle of December, through all the storms that we have had since that have driven back three or four of them with their masts by the board. Yesterday come out the King's Declaration of War against the French, but with such mild invitations of both them and the Dutch to come over here with promise of their protection, that every body wonders at it.

12th. Comes Mr Caesar, my boy's lute-master, whom I have not seen since the plague before, but he hath been in Westminster Hall all this while very well; and tells me in the height of it, how bold people there were, to go in sport to one another's burials: and in spite too, ill people would breathe in the faces (out of their windows) of well people going by.

13th. Ill news this night that the plague is encreased this week, and in many places else about the town, and at Chatham and elsewhere.

14th. I took Mr Hill to my Lord Chancellor's new house that is building, and went with trouble up to the top of it, and there is the noblest prospect that ever I saw in my life, Greenwich being nothing to it; and in everything is a beautiful house, and most strongly built in every respect; and as if, as it hath, it had the Chancellor for its master. I staid a meeting of the Duke of York's, and the officers of the Navy and Ordnance. My Lord Treasurer lying in bed of the gowte.

15th. Mr Hales[5] begun my wife's portrait in the posture we saw one of my Lady Peters, like a St Katharine. While he painted,

5 John Hayls, or Hales, a portrait-painter remarkable for copying Vandyke well, and being a rival of Lely.

Knipp,[6] and Mercer, and I, sang. We hear this night of Sir Jeremy Smith, that he and his fleet have been seen at Malaga; which is good news.

16th. To the Coffee-House, the first time I have been there, where very full, and company it seems hath been there all the plague time. The Queene comes to Hampton Court to-night.

18th. It being a brave day, I walked to White Hall, where the Queene and ladies are all come: I saw some few of them, but not the Queene, nor any of the great beauties.

19th. I am told for certain, what I have heard once or twice already, of a Jew in town, that in the name of the rest do offer to give any man £10 to be paid £100, if a certain person now at Smyrna be within these two years owned by all the Princes of the East, and particularly the grand Segnor as the King of the world, in the same manner we do the King of England here, and that this man is the true Messiah. One named a friend of his that had received ten pieces in gold upon this score, and says that the Jew hath disposed of £1100 in this manner, which is very strange; and certainly this year of 1666 will be a year of great action; but what the consequences of it will be, God knows! To White Hall, and there saw the Queene at cards with many ladies, but none of our beauties were there. But glad I was to see the Queene so well, who looks prettily; and methinks hath more life than before, since it is confessed of all that she miscarried lately; Dr Clerke telling me yesterday of it at White Hall.[7]

20th. Up, and to the office; where among other businesses, Mr Evelyn's proposition about publick Infirmarys was read and agreed on, he being there: and at noon I took him home to dinner, being desirous of keeping my acquaintance with him; and a most excellent humoured man I still find him, and mighty knowing.

21st. The Duke did bring out a book of great antiquity of some of the customs of the Navy, about 100 years since, which he did lend us

6 Of Mrs Knipp's history, nothing seems known; except that she was a married actress belonging to the King's house, and as late as 1677 her name occurs among the performers in the *Wily False One*.

7 The details in the original leave no doubt of the fact, and exculpate the Chancellor from the charge of having selected the Queen as incapable of bearing children.

to read and deliver him back again. To Trinity-house, being invited to an Elder Brother's feast; and there met and sat by Mr Prin, and had good discourse about the privileges of Parliament, which, he says, are few to the Commons' House, and those not examinable by them, but only by the House of Lords. Thence with my Lord Brouncker to Gresham College, the first time after the sickness that I was there, and the second time any met. And here a good lecture of Mr Hooke's about the trade of felt-making, very pretty. And anon alone with me about the art of drawing pictures by Prince Rupert's rule and machine, and another of Dr. Wren's;[8] but he says nothing do like squares, or, which is the best in the world, like a darke roome.

22nd. We are much troubled that the sickness in general (the town being so full of people) should be but three, and yet of the particular disease of the plague there should be ten encrease.

23rd. To my Lord Sandwich's, who did lie the last night at his house in Lincoln's Inne Fields. It being fine walking in the morning, and the streets full of people again. There I staid, and the house full of people come to take leave of my Lord, who this day goes out of towne upon his embassy towards Spayne. And I was glad to find Sir W. Coventry to come, though I know it is only a piece of courtshipp. Comes Mrs Knipp to see my wife and I spent all the night talking with this baggage, and teaching her my song of 'Beauty retire', which she sings and makes go most rarely, and a very fine song it seems to be. She also entertained me with repeating many of her own and others' parts of the play-house, which she do most excellently; and tells me the whole practices of the playhouse and players, and is in every respect most excellent company.

25th. With our coach of four horses to Windsor, and so to Cranborne, about eleven o'clock, and found my Lord[9] and the ladies at a sermon in the house; which being ended we to them, and all the company glad to see us, and mighty merry to dinner. Here was my Lord, and Lord Hinchingbroke, and Mr Sidney,[10] Sir Charles Herbert, and Mr Carteret, my Lady Carteret, my Lady Jemimah, and

8 Sir Christopher Wren.
9 Sandwich.
10 Sidney Montagu, Lord Sandwich's second son.

Lady Slaning.[11] After dinner to walk in the Park, my Lord and I alone; and he tells me my Lord of Suffolk, Lord Arlington, Archbishop of Canterbury, Lord Treasurer, Mr Atturny Montagu, Sir Thomas Clifford in the House of Commons, Sir G. Carteret, and some others I cannot presently remember, are friends that I may rely on for him. He dreads the issue of this year, and fear there will be some very great revolutions before his coming back again. He doubts it is needful for him to have a pardon for his last year's actions, all which he did without commission, and at most but the King's private single word for that of Bergen; but he dares not ask it at this time, lest it should make them think that there is something more in it than yet they know; and if it should be denied, it would be of very ill consequence. He says also, if it should in Parliament be enquired into the selling of Dunkirke, (though the Chancellor was the man that would have sold it to France, saying the King of Spain had no money to give for it;) yet he will be found to have been the greatest adviser of it; which he is a little apprehensive may be called upon by this Parliament. Then I with the young ladies and gentlemen, who played on the guittar, and mighty merry, and anon to supper; and then my Lord going away to write, the young gentlemen to flinging of cushions, and other mad sports till towards twelve at night, and then being sleepy, I and my wife in a passage-room to bed, and slept not very well because of noise.

26th. Called up about five in the morning, and my Lord up, and took leave, a little after six, very kindly of me and the whole company. So took coach and to Windsor, to the Garter, and thither sent for Dr Childe:[12] who come to us, and carried us to St George's Chapel, and there placed us among the Knights' stalls; (and pretty the observation, that no man, but a woman may sit in a Knight's place, where any brass-plates are set,) and hither come cushions to us, and a young singing-boy to bring us a copy of the anthem to be sung. And here, for our sakes, had this anthem and the great service sung extraordinary, only to entertain us. It is a noble place indeed, and a good Quire of voices. Great bowing by all the people, the poor Knights in particularly, to the Alter. After prayers, we to see

11 Sir G. Carteret's daughter Caroline.
12 William Child, Doctor of Music, Organist of St George's Chapel, at Windsor. Died 1696, aged 91.

the plate of the chapel, and the robes of Knights, and a man to show us the banners of the several Knights in being, which hang up over the stalls. And so to other discourse very pretty, about the Order. Was shown where the late King is buried, and King Henry the Eighth, and my Lady Seymour. This being done, to the King's house, and to observe the neatness and contrivance of the house and gates: it is the most romantique castle that is in the world. But, Lord! the prospect that is in the balcone in the Queene's lodgings, and the terrace and walk, are strange things to consider, being the best in the world, sure; and so giving a great deal of money to this and that man and woman, we to our tavern, and there dined, the Doctor with us; and so took coach and away to Eton, the Doctor with me. At Eton I left my wife in the coach, and he and I to the College, and there find all mighty fine. The school good, and the custom pretty of boys cutting their names in the shuts of the windows when they go to Cambridge, by which many a one hath lived to see himself a Provost and Fellow, that hath his name in the window standing. To the Hall, and there find the boys' verses, 'De Peste'; it being their custom to make verses at Shrove-tide. I read several, and very good they were; better, I think, than ever I made when I was a boy, and in rolls as long and longer than the whole Hall, by much. Here is a picture of Venice hung up, and a monument made of Sir H. Wotton's giving it to the College. Thence to the porter's, in the absence of the butler, and did drink of the College beer, which is very good; and went into the back fields to see the scholars play. And so to the chapel, and there saw, among other things, Sir H. Wotton's stone with this Epitaph:

> Hic jacet primus hujus sententiae Author: –
> Disputandi pruritus fit ecclesiae scabies.

But unfortunately the word 'Author' was wrong writ, and now so basely altered that it disgraces the stone.

March 1st. Blessed be God! a good Bill this week we have; being but 237 in all, and 42 of the plague, and of them but six in the City: though my Lord Brouncker says, that these six are most of them in new parishes where they were not the last week.

3rd. To Hales's, and there saw my wife sit; and I do like her picture mightily, and very like it will be, and a brave piece of work. But he do complain that her nose hath cost him as much work as another's face, and he hath done it finely indeed.

5th. News for certain of the King of Denmark's declaring for the Dutch, and resolution to assist them. I find my Lord Brouncker and Mrs Williams, and they would of their own accord, though I had never obliged them (nor my wife neither) with one visit for many of theirs, go see my house and my wife; which I showed them, and made them welcome with wine and China oranges, (now a great rarity since the war, none to be had). My house happened to be mighty clean, and did me great honour, and they mightily pleased with it.

7th. Up betimes, and to St James's, thinking Mr Coventry had lain there; but he do not, but at White Hall; so thither I went to him. We walked an hour in the Matted Gallery: he of himself begun to discourse of the unhappy differences between him and my Lord of Sandwich, and from the beginning to the end did run through all passages wherein my Lord hath, at any time, gathered any dissatisfaction, and cleared himself to me most honourably; and in truth, I do believe he do as he says. I did afterwards purge myself of all partiality in the business of Sir G. Carteret, (whose story Sir W. Coventry did also run over,) that I do mind the King's interest, notwithstanding my relation to him; all which he declares he firmly believes, and assures me he hath the same kindness and opinion of me as ever. And when I said I was jealous of myself, that having now come to such an income as I am, by his favour, I should not be found to do as much service as might deserve it; he did assure me, he thinks it not too much for me, but thinks I deserve it as much as any man in England. All this discourse did cheer my heart, and sets me right again, after a good deal of melancholy, out of fears of his disinclination to me, upon the difference with my Lord Sandwich and Sir G. Carteret; but I am satisfied thoroughly, and so went away quite another man, and by the grace of God will never lose it again by my folly in not visiting and writing to him, as I used heretofore to do. The King and Duke are to go to-morrow to Audly End, in order to the seeing and buying of it of my Lord Suffolke.

9th. Made a visit to the Duke of Albemarle, and to my great joy find him the same man to me that heretofore, which I was in great doubt of, through my negligence in not visiting of him a great while; and having now set all to rights there, I shall never suffer matters to run so far backwards again as I have done of late, with reference to my neglecting him and Sir W. Coventry. The truth is, I do indulge myself a little the more in pleasure, knowing that this is the proper age of my life to do it; and out of my observation that most men that do thrive in the world, do forget to take pleasure during the time that they are getting their estate, but reserve that till they have got one, and then it is too late for them to enjoy it.

12th. My Uncle Talbot Pepys died the last week. All the news now is, that Sir Jeremy Smith is at Cales[13] with his fleet; and Mings in the Elve. The King is come this noon to town from Audly End, with the Duke of York and a fine train of gentlemen.

13th. The plague encreased this week 29 from 28, though the total fallen from 238 to 207.

14th. With my Lord Brouncker towards London, and in our way called in Covent Garden, and took in Sir John (formerly Dr) Baber; who hath this humour that he will not enter into discourse while any stranger is in company, till he be told who he is that seems a stranger to him. This he did declare openly to me, and asked my Lord who I was. Thence to Guildhall, (in our way taking in Dr Wilkins,) and there my Lord and I had full and large discourse with Sir Thomas Player,[14] the Chamberlain of the City, (a man I have much heard of) about the credit of our tallies, which are lodged there for security to such as should lend money thereon to the use of the Navy. I had great satisfaction therein: and the truth is, I find all our matters of credit to be in an ill condition. To walk all alone in the fields behind Grayes Inne, making an end of reading over my dear *Faber fortunae*, of my Lord Bacon's.

15th. To Hales, where I met my wife and people; and do find the picture, above all things, a most pretty picture, and mighty like my wife; and I asked him his price: he says £14 and the truth is, I think he do deserve it.

13 Cadiz.
14 One of the City Members in the Oxford and Westminster Parliaments. See more of him in the Notes, by Scott, to Absalom and Achitophel; in which poem he is introduced under the designation of 'railing Rabsheka'.

17th. To Hales's, and paid him £14 for the picture, and £1 5s. for the frame. This day I began to sit, and he will make me, I think, a very fine picture. He promises it shall be as good as my wife's, and I sit to have it full of shadows, and do almost break my neck looking over my shoulder to make the posture for him to work by. Home, having a great cold: so to bed, drinking butter-ale.

19th. After dinner we walked to the King's play-house, all in dirt, they being altering of the stage to make it wider. But God knows when they will begin to act again; but my business here was to see the inside of the stage and all the tiring-rooms and machines: and, indeed, it was a sight worthy seeing. But to see their clothes, and the various sorts, and what a mixture of things there was; here a wooden-leg, there a ruff, here a hobby-horse, there a crown, would make a man split himself with laughing; and particularly Lacy's[15] wardrobe, and Shotrell's.[16] But then again, to think how fine they show on the stage by candle-light, and how poor things they are to look at too near hand, is not pleasant at all. The machines are fine, and the paintings very pretty. With Sir W. Warren, talking of many things belonging to us particularly, and I hope to get something considerably by him before the year be over. He gives me good advice of circumspection in my place, which I am now in great mind to improve; for I think our office stands on very ticklish terms, the Parliament likely to sit shortly and likely to be asked more money, and we able to give a very bad account of the expence of what we have done with what they did give before. Besides, the turning out the prize officers may be an example for the King's giving us up to Parliament's pleasure as easily, for we deserve it as much. Besides, Sir G. Carteret did tell me to-night how my Lord Brouncker, whose good-will I could have depended as much on as any, did himself to him take notice of the many places I have; and though I was a painful man, yet the Navy was enough for any man to go through with in his own single place there, which much troubles me, and shall yet provoke me to more and more care and diligence than ever.

15 John Lacy, the celebrated comedian, author of four plays. Died 1681.
16 Robert and William Shotterel both belonged to the King's company at the opening of their new Theatre in 1663. One of them had been Quartermaster to the troop of horse in which Hart was serving as Lieutenant under Charles I's standard. He is called by Downs a good actor, but nothing further is recorded of his merits or career. Note to Cibber's *Apology*.

21st. Sir Robert Long[17] told us of the plenty of partridges in France, where he says the King of France and his company killed with their guns, in the plain de Versailles, 300 and odd partridges at one bout. With Sir W. Warren, who tells me that at the Committee of the Lords for the prizes to-day, there passed very high words between my Lord Ashly and Sir W. Coventry, about our business of the prize ships. And that my Lord Ashly did snuff and talk as high as him, as he used to do to any ordinary man. And that Sir W. Coventry did take it very quietly, but yet for all did speak his mind soberly and with reason, and went away, saying that he had done his duty therein.

24th. After the Committee up, I had occasion to follow the Duke into his lodgings, into a chamber where the Duchesse was sitting to have her picture drawn by Lilly, who was then at work. But I was well pleased to see that there was nothing near so much resemblance of her face in his work, which is now the second, if not the third time, as there was of my wife's at the very first time. Nor do I think at last it can be like, the lines not being in proportion to those of her face.

26th. My Lord Brouncker and I to the Tower, to see the famous engraver, to get him to grave a seal for the office. And did see some of the finest pieces of work in embossed work, that ever I did see in my life, for fineness and smallness of the images thereon.

28th. To the Cockpitt, and dined with a great deal of company at the Duke of Albemarle's, and a bad and dirty, nasty dinner. This night, I am told, the Queene of Portugall, the mother to our Queene, is lately dead, and news brought of it hither this day.

30th. I out to Lombard Streete, and there received £2200 and brought it home; and, contrary to expectation, received £35 for the use of £2000 of it for a quarter of a year, where it hath produced me this profit, and hath been a convenience to me as to care and security at my house, and demandable at two days' warning, as this hath been. To Hales's, and there sat till almost quite dark upon working my gowne, which I hired to be drawn in; an Indian gowne.

---

17 Sir Robert Long, Secretary to Charles II during his exile, and subsequently made Auditor of the Exchequer, and a Privy Counsellor, and created a Baronet, 1662. Died, unmarried, 1673.

April 1st. To Charing Cross, to wait on Sir Philip Howard; whom I found in bed: and he do receive me very civilly. My request was about suffering my wife's brother to go to sea, and to save his pay in the Duke's guards; which after a little difficulty he did with great respect agree to. I find him a very fine-spoken gentleman, and one of great parts, and very courteous. Meeting Dr Allen,[18] the Physician, he and I and another walked in the Park, a most pleasant warm day and to the Queene's chapel; where I do not so dislike the musick. Here I saw on a post an invitation to all good Catholics to pray for the soul of such a one departed this life. The Queene, I hear, do not yet hear of the death of her mother, she being in a course of physick, that they dare not tell it her. Up and down my Lord St Albans his new building and market-house, looking to and again into every place building. I this afternoon made a visit to my Lady Carteret, whom I understood newly come to towne; and she took it mighty kindly, but I see her face and heart are dejected from the condition her husband's matters stand in. But I hope they will do all well enough. And I do comfort her as much as I can, for she is a noble lady.

5th. The plague is, to our great grief, encreased nine this week, though decreased a few in the total. And this encrease runs through many parishes, which makes us much fear the next year.

6th. Met by agreement with Sir Stephen Fox and Mr Ashburnham, and discoursed the business of our Excise tallies; the former being Treasurer of the guards, and the other Cofferer of the King's household. This day great news of the Swedes declaring for us against the Dutch, and so far as that I believe it.

8th. To the Duke of York, where we all met to hear the debate between Sir Thomas Allen and Mr Wayth; the former complaining of the latter's ill usage of him at the late pay of his ship. But a very sorry poor occasion he had for it. The Duke did determine it with great judgement, chiding both, but encouraging Wayth to continue to be a check to all captains in any thing to the King's right. And, indeed, I never did see the Duke do any thing more in order, nor with more judgement than he did pass the verdict in this business.

18 Probably Thomas Allen, MD of Caius College, Cambridge, and Member of the College of Physicians. Died 1685.

The Court full this morning of the news of Tom Cheffins's[19] death, the King's closet-keeper. He was well last night as ever, playing at tables in the house, and not very ill this morning at six o'clock, yet dead before seven they think, of an imposthume in his breast. But it looks fearfully among people now-a-days, the plague, as we hear encreasing every where again. To the Chapel, but could not get in to hear well. But I had the pleasure once in my life to see an Archbishop[20] (this was of York) in a pulpit. Then at a loss how to get home to dinner, having promised to carry Mrs Hunt thither. At last got my Lord Hinchingbroke's coach, he staying at Court; and so took her up in Axe-yard, and home and dined. And good discourse of the old matters of the Protector and his family, she having a relation to them. The Protector lives in France: spends about £500 per annum.

9th. By coach to Mrs Pierce's, and with her and Knipp and Mrs Pierce's boy and girl abroad, thinking to have been merry at Chelsey; but being come almost to the house by coach near the waterside, a house alone, I think the Swan, a gentleman walking by called to us to tell us that the house was shut up of the sickness. So we with great affright turned back, being holden to the gentleman: and went away (I for my part in great disorder) for Kensington.

11th. To Hales's, where there was nothing to be done more to my picture,[21] but the musique, which now pleases me mightily, it being painted true. To Gresham College, where a great deal of do and formality in choosing of the Council and Officers. I had three votes to be of the Council, who am but a stranger, nor expected any.

15th. Walked into the Park to the Queen's chapel, and there heard a good deal of their mass, and some of their musique, which is not so contemptible, I think, as our people would make it, it pleasing me

19 Sir E. Walker, Garter King at Arms, in 1644 gave a grant of arms *gratis* to Thomas Chiffinch, Esq., one of the Pages of His Majesty's Bedchamber, Keeper of his private Closet, and Comptroller of the Excise. His brother William appears to have succeeded to the two first-named appointments, and became a great favourite with the King, whom he survived. There is a portrait of William Chiffinch at Gorhambury.

20 Richard Sterne, Bishop of Carlisle, elected Archbishop of York, 1664. Died 1683.

21 This portrait is now in the possession of Samuel Pepys Cockerel, Esq.

very well; and, indeed, better than the anthem I heard afterwards at White Hall, at my coming back. I staid till the King went down to receive the Sacrament, and stood in his closet with a great many others, and there saw him receive it, which I did never see the manner of before. Thence walked to Mr Pierce's, and there dined: very good company and good discourse, they being able to tell me all the businesses of the Court: the amours and the mad doings that are there: how for certain Mrs Stewart is become the King's mistress; and that the King hath many bastard children that are known and owned, besides the Duke of Monmouth.

18th. To Mr Lilly's, the painter's; and there saw the heads, some finished, and all begun, of the flaggmen in the late great fight with the Duke of York against the Dutch. The Duke of York hath them done to hang in his chamber, and very finely they are done indeed. Here are the Prince's, Sir G. Askue's, Sir Thomas Teddiman's, Sir Christopher Mings, Sir Joseph Jordan, Sir William Barkeley, Sir Thomas Allen, and Captain Harman's,[22] as also the Duke of Albemarle's; and will be my Lord Sandwich's, Sir W. Pen's, and Sir Jeremy Smith's. I was very well satisfied with this sight, and other good pictures hanging in the house.

21st. I down to walk in the garden at White Hall, it being a mighty hot and pleasant day; and there was the King, who, among others, talked to us a little; and among other pretty things, he swore merrily that he believed the ketch that Sir W. Batten bought the last year at Colchester, was of his own getting, it was so thick to its length. Another pleasant thing he said of Christopher Pett, commanding him that he will not alter his moulds of ships upon any man's advice; 'as,' says he, 'Commissioner Taylor I fear do of his New *London*, that he makes it differ, in hopes of mending the Old *London*, built by him.' 'For,' says he, 'he finds that God hath put him into the right, and so will keep in it while he is in.' 'And,' says the King, 'I am sure it must be God put him in, for no art of his own ever could have done it'; for it seems he cannot give a good account of what he do as an artist. Thence with my Lord Brouncker in his coach to Hide Parke, the first time I have been there this year. There the King was; but I was sorry to see my Lady Castlemaine, for the mourning forceing all the ladies

22 Afterwards Sir John Harman.

to go in black, with their hair plain and without spots. I find her to be a much more ordinary woman than ever I durst have thought she was; and, indeed, is not so pretty as Mrs Stewart.

22nd. To the Cockpitt, and there took my leave of the Duke of Albemarle, who is going to-morrow to sea. He seems mightily pleased with me, which I am glad of; but I do find infinitely my concernment in being careful to appear to the King and Duke to continue my care of his business, and to be found diligent as I used to be.

23rd. To White Hall, where I had the opportunity to take leave of the Prince, and again of the Duke of Albemarle; and saw them kiss the King's hands and the Duke's; and much content indeed, there seems to be in all people at their going to sea, and they promise themselves much good from them. This morning the House of Parliament do meet, only to adjourne again till winter. The plague, I hear, encreases in the town much, and exceedingly in the country every where. Bonfires in the street, for being St George's day, and the King's Coronation, and the day of the Prince and Duke's going to sea.

25th. I to the office, where Mr Prin come to meet about the Chest-business; and till company come, did discourse with me a good while in the garden about the laws of England, telling me the main faults in them; and among others, their obscurity through multitude of long statutes, which he is about to abstract out of all of a sort; and as he lives, and Parliaments come, get them put into laws, and the other statutes repealed, and then it will be a short work to know the law. Having supped upon the leads, to bed. The plague, blessed be God! is decreased sixteen this week.

29th. To Mr Evelyn's, where I walked in his garden till he come from Church, with great pleasure reading Ridly's discourse, all my way going and coming, upon the Civill and Ecclesiastical Law. He being come home, he and I walked together in the garden with mighty pleasure, he being a very ingenious man; and the more I know him, the more I love him.

30th. I after dinner to even all my accounts of this month; and, bless God, I find myself, notwithstanding great expences of late; viz. £80 now to pay for a necklace; near £40 for a set of chairs and couch; near £40 for my three pictures: yet I do gather, and am worth

£5200. My wife comes home by and by, and hath pitched upon a necklace with three rows, which is a very good one, and £80 is the price. So ends this month with great layings-out. Good health and gettings, and advanced well in the whole of my estate, for which God make me thankful!

May 1st. At noon, my cosen Thomas Pepys did come to me, to consult about the business of his being a Justice of the Peace, which he is much against; and among other reasons, tells me, as a confidant, that he is not free to exercise punishment according to the Act against Quakers and other people, for religion. Nor do he understand Latin, and so is not capable of the place as formerly, now all warrants do run in Latin. Nor he in Kent, though he be of Deptford parish, his house standing in Surry. However, I did bring him to incline towards it, if he be pressed to take it. I do think it may be some repute to me to have my kinsman in Commission there, specially, if he behave himself to content in the country.

12th. Met Sir G. Downing on White Hall bridge, and there walked half an hour, talking of the success of the late new Act; and indeed it is very much, that that hath stood really in the room of £800,000[23] now since Christmas, being itself but £1,250,000. And so I do really take it to be a very considerable thing done by him; for the beginning, end, and every part of it, is to be imputed to him. The fleet is not yet gone from the Nore. The plague encreases in many places, and is 53 this week with us.

13th. Into St Margett's[24] Church, where I heard a young man play the fool upon the doctrine of Purgatory.

15th. I to my Lord Crowe's, who is very lately come to town, and he talked for half an hour of the business of the warr, wherein he is very doubtful, from our want of money, that we shall fail. And I do concur with him therein. After some little discourse of ordinary matters, I away to Sir Philip Warwick's again, and he was come in, and gone out to my Lord Treasurer's; whither I followed him, and there my business was, to be told that my Lord Treasurer hath got £10,000 for us in the Navy, to answer our great necessities, which I

23 There appears to be some error in these figures.
24 St Margaret's.

did thank him for; but the sum is not considerable. The five brothers Houblons[25] came, and Mr Hill, to my house; and a very good supper we had, and good discourse with great pleasure. My new plate sets off my cupboard very nobly. Here they were till about eleven at night: and a fine sight it is to see these five brothers thus loving one to another, and all industrious merchants.

19th. Mr Deane and I did discourse about his ship *Rupert*, built by him there, which succeeds so well as he hath got great honour by it, and I some by recommending him; the King, Duke, and every body, saying it is the best ship that was ever built. And then he fell to explain to me his manner of casting the draught of water which a ship will draw beforehand: which is a secret the King and all admire in him; and he is the first that hath come to any certainty beforehand of foretelling the draught of water of a ship before she be launched.

20th. I discoursed awhile with Mr Yeabsly, whom I met and took up in my coach with me, and who hath this day presented my Lord Ashly with £100 to bespeak his friendship to him in his accounts now before us; and my Lord hath received, and so I believe is as bad, as to bribes, as what the world says of him.

21st. I away in some haste to my Lord Ashly, where it is stupendous to see how favourably, and yet closely, my Lord Ashly carries himself to Mr Yeabsly, in his business, so as I think we shall do his business for him in very good manner. But it is a most extraordinary thing to observe, and that which I would not but have had the observation of for a great deal of money.

25 Two of these brothers, Sir James and Sir John Houblon, Knts. and Aldermen, rose to great wealth: the former represented the City of London, and the latter became Lord Mayor in 1695.

The following epitaph, in memory of their father, who was interred in the church of St Mary Woolnoth, is here inserted, as having been written by Mr Pepys:

> Jacobus Houblon,
> Londin. Petri filius,
> Ob fidem Flandria exulantis:
> Ex c. Nepotibus habuit LXX superstites:
> Filios v videns mercatores florentissimos;
> Ipse Londinensis Bursæ Pater.
> Piissime obiit Nonagenarius,
> AD MDCLXXXII.

23rd. Towards White Hall, calling in my way on my Lord Bellasses,[26] where I come to his bedside, and he did give me a full and long account of his matters, how he kept them at Tangier. Declares himself fully satisfied with my care: seems cunningly to argue for encreasing the number of men there. Told me the whole story of his gains by the Turky prizes, which he owns he hath got about £5000 by. Promised me the same profits Povy was to have had; and in fine, I find him a pretty subtle man; and so I left him. Staid at Sir G. Carteret's chamber till the Council rose, and then he and I, by agreement this morning, went forth in his coach by Tiburne, to the park; discoursing of the state of the Navy as to money, and the state of the Kingdom too, how ill able to raise more: and of our office, as to the condition of the officers; he giving me caution as to myself, that there are those that are my enemies as well as his, and by name my Lord Brouncker who hath said some odd speeches against me. So that he advises me to stand on my guard; which I shall do, and unless my too-much addiction to pleasure undo me, will be acute enough for any of them.

25th. A gentleman arrived here this day, Mr Brown of St Maloes, among other things tells me the meaning of the setting out of dogs every night out of the town walls, which are said to secure the city: but it is not so, but only to secure the anchors, cables, and ships that lie dry, which might otherwise in the night be liable to be robbed. And these dogs are set out every night, and called together in, every morning by a man with a horne, and they go in very orderly.

29th. Home this evening, but with great trouble in the streets by bonfires, it being the King's birth-day and day of Restoration; but Lord! to see the difference how many there were on the other side, and so few ours, the City side of the Temple, would make one wonder the difference between the temper of one sort of people and the other: and the difference among all between what they do now, and what it was the night when Monk came into the City. Such a night as that I never think to see again, nor think it can be.

26 John Lord Bellassis, second son of Thomas Viscount Falconberg, an officer of distinction on the King's side, during the Civil War. He was afterwards Governor of Tangier, and Captain of the Band of Gentlemen Pensioners. Being a Catholic, the Test Act deprived him of all his appointments in 1672; but James II, in 1684, made him first Commissioner of the Treasury. Died 1689.

30th. I find the Duke gone out with the King to-day on hunting.

31st. A public Fast-day appointed to pray for the good success of the fleet. But it is a pretty thing to consider how little a matter they make of this keeping of a Fast, that it was not so much as declared time enough to be read in the churches, the last Sunday; but ordered by proclamation since: I suppose upon some sudden news of the Dutch being come out. As to public business; by late tidings of the French fleet being come to Rochell, (how true, though, I know not) our fleet is divided; Prince Rupert being gone with about thirty ships to the Westward as is conceived to meet the French, to hinder their coming to join with the Dutch. My Lord Duke of Albemarle lies in the Downes with the rest, and intends presently to sail to the Gunfleete.

June 2nd. Up, and to the office, where certain news is brought us of a letter come to the King this morning from the Duke of Albemarle, dated yesterday at eleven o'clock, as they were sailing to the Gunfleete, that they were in sight of the Dutch fleet, and were fitting themselves to fight them; so that they are ere this certainly engaged: besides, several do averr they heard the guns yesterday in the afternoon. This put us at the Board into a tosse. Presently come orders for our sending away to the fleet a recruite of 200 soldiers. So I rose from the table, and to the Victualling-office, and thence upon the River among several vessels, to consider of the sending them away; and lastly, down to Greenwich, and there appointed two yachts to be ready for them; and did order the soldiers to march to Blackewall. Having set all things in order against the next flood, I went on shore with Captain Erwin at Greenwich, and into the parke, and there we could hear the guns from the fleete most plainly. We walked to the water-side, and there seeing the King and Duke come down in their barge to Greenwich-house, I to them, and did give them an account what I was doing. They went up to the park to hear the guns of the fleet go off. All our hopes now are that Prince Rupert with his fleet is coming back and will be with the fleet this even: a message being sent to him for that purpose on Wednesday last; and a return is come from him this morning, that he did intend to sail from St Ellen's point about four in the afternoon yesterday; which gives us great hopes, the wind being very fair, that he is with them this even, and the fresh going off of the guns makes us believe the same. Down to Blackewall, and there saw the soldiers (who were by this time gotten most of them drunk) shipped off. But, Lord! to see how the poor fellows kissed their wives and sweethearts in that simple manner at their going off, and shouted, and let off their guns, was strange sport. In the evening come up the River the *Katharine* yacht, Captain Fazeby, who hath brought over my Lord of Alesbury[27] and Sir Thomas Liddall[28] (with a very pretty daughter, and in a pretty travelling-dress) from Flanders, who saw the Dutch fleet on Thursday, and ran from them; but from that hour to this hath not heard one gun, nor any news of any fight. Having put the soldiers on board, I home.

3rd (Lord's-day; Whit-sunday). Up; and by water to White Hall, and there met with Mr Coventry, who tells me the only news from the fleet is brought by Captain Elliott, of the *Portland*, which, by being run on board by the *Guernsey*, was disabled from staying abroad: so is come in to Albrough. That he saw one of the Dutch great ships blown up, and three on fire. That they begun to fight on Friday; and at his coming into port, could make another ship of the King's coming in, which he judged to be the *Rupert*; that he knows of no other hurt to our ships. With this good news I home by water again. The Exchange as full of people, and hath been all this noon as of any other day, only for news. To White Hall, and there met with this bad news farther, that the Prince come to Dover but at ten o'clock last night, and there heard nothing of a fight; so that we are defeated of all our hopes of his help to the fleet. It is also reported by some Victuallers that the Duke of Albemarle and Holmes[29] their flags were shot down, and both fain to come to anchor to renew their rigging and sails. A letter is also come this afternoon, from Harman in the *Henery*; which states, that she was taken by Elliott for the *Rupert*; that being fallen into the body of the Dutch fleet, he made his way through them, was set on by three fire-ships one after another, got two of them off, and disabled the third; was set on fire himself; upon which many of his men leapt into the sea and perished; among others, the parson first. Have lost above 100 men, and a good many women, (God knows what is become of Balty[30]) and at last quenched

27 Robert Bruce, created Earl of Aylesbury, 1663. Died 1685.
28 Of Ravensworth Castle, Durham, succeeded his grandfather, the first Baronet, 1650. He had three daughters. Died 1697.
29 Sir Robert Holmes.
30 Balthazar St Michel, Mrs Pepys's brother, employed in the office for sick and hurt at Deal afterwards, and in 1686 Commissioner at Woolwich and Deptford.

his own fire and got to Albrough; being, as all say, the greatest hazard that ever any ship escaped, and so bravely managed by him. The mast of the third fire-ship fell into their ship on fire, and hurt Harman's leg, which makes him lame now, but not dangerous. I to Sir G. Carteret, who told me there hath been great bad management in all this; that the King's orders that went on Friday for calling back the Prince, were sent but by the ordinary post on Wednesday; and come to the Prince his hands but on Friday; and then, instead of sailing presently, he stays till four in the evening. And that which is worst of all, the *Hampshire*, laden with merchants' money, come from the Straights, set out with or but just before the fleet, and was in the Downes by five in the clock yesterday morning; and the Prince with his fleet come to Dover but at ten of the clock at night. This is hard to answer, if it be true. This puts great astonishment into the King, and Duke, and Court, every body being out of countenance. Home by the 'Change, which is full of people still, and all talk highly of the failure of the Prince in not making more haste after his instructions did come, and of our managements here in not giving it sooner and with more care and oftener.

4th. To White Hall, where, when we come, we find the Duke at St James's, whither he is lately gone to lodge. So walking through the Park we saw hundreds of people listening at the Gravell-pits, and to and again in the Park to hear the guns. I saw a letter, dated last night, from Strowd, Governor of Dover Castle, which says that the Prince come thither the night before with his fleet; but that for the guns which we writ that we heard, it is only a mistake for thunder; and so far as to yesterday it is a miraculous thing that we all Friday, and Saturday and yesterday, did hear every where most plainly the guns go off, and yet at Deal and Dover to last night they did not hear one word of a fight, nor think they heard one gun. This, added to what I have set down before the other day about the *Katharine*, makes room for a great dispute in philosophy, how we should hear it and they not, the same wind that brought it to us being the same that should bring it to them: but so it is. Major Halsey, however, (he was sent down on purpose to hear news) did bring news this morning that he did see the Prince and his fleet at nine of the clock yesterday morning, four or five leagues to sea behind the Goodwin, so that by the hearing of the guns this morning, we conclude he is come to the fleet. After wayting upon the Duke with Sir W. Pen, (who was commanded to go to-night by water down to Harwich, to dispatch away all the ships he can,) I home: where no sooner come, but news is brought me of a couple of men come to speak with me from the fleet; so I down, and who should it be but Mr Daniel, all muffled up, and his face as black as the chimney, and covered with dirt, pitch, and tar, and powder, and muffled with dirty clouts, and his right eye stopped with okum. He is come last night at five o'clock from the fleet, with a comrade of his that hath endangered another eye. They were set on shore at Harwich this morning, and at two o'clock, in a catch with about twenty more wounded men from the *Royall Charles*. They being able to ride, took post about three this morning, and were here between eleven and twelve. I went presently into the coach with them, and carried them to Somerset House-stairs, and there took water (all the world gazing upon us, and concluding it to be news from the fleet, and every body's face appeared expecting of news,) to the Privy-stairs, and left them at Mr Coventry's lodgings (he, though, not being there); and so I into the Park to the King, and told him my Lord Generall was well the last night at five o'clock, and the Prince come with his fleet and joyned with his about seven. The King was mightily pleased with this news, and so took me by the hand and talked a little of it, giving him the best account I could; and then he bid me to fetch the two seamen to him, he walking into the house. So I went and fetched the seamen into the vane room to him, and there he heard the whole account.

THE FIGHT

How we found the Dutch fleet at anchor on Friday half seas over, between Dunkirke and Ostend, and made them let slip their anchors. They about ninety, and we less than sixty. We fought them, and put them to the run, till they met with about sixteen sail of fresh ships, and so bore up again. The fight continued till night, and then again the next morning from five till seven at night. And so, too, yesterday morning they begun again, and continued till about four o'clock, they chasing us for the most part of Saturday, and yesterday we flying from them. The Duke himself, and then those people who were put into the catch, by and by spied the Prince's fleet coming, upon which De Ruyter called a little council, (being in chase at this time of us,) and thereupon their fleet divided into two squadrons; forty in one, and about thirty in the other (the fleet being at first about ninety, but by one accident or other, supposed to be lessened to about seventy); the bigger to follow the Duke, the less to meet the Prince. But the Prince come up with the Generall's fleet, and the Dutch come together again and bore towards their own coast, and we with them; and now what the consequence of this day will be, we know not. The Duke was forced to come to anchor on Friday, having lost his sails and rigging. No particular person spoken of to be hurt but Sir W. Clerke, who hath lost his leg, and bore it bravely. The Duke himself had a little hurt in his thigh, but signified little. The King did pull out of his pocket about twenty pieces in gold, and did give it Daniel for himself and his companion; and so parted, mightily pleased with the account he did give him of the fight, and the success it ended with, of the Prince's coming, though it seems the Duke did give way again and again. The King did give order for care to be had of Mr Daniel and his companion; and so we parted from him, and then met the Duke of York, and gave him the same account: and so broke up, and I left them going to the surgeon's. To the Crown, behind the 'Change, and there supped at the club with my Lord Brouncker, Sir G. Ent, and others of Gresham College; and all our discourse is of this fight at sea, and all are doubtful of the success, and conclude all had been lost if the Prince had not come in, they having chased us the greatest part of Saturday and Sunday. Thence with my Lord Brouncker and Creed by coach to White Hall, where fresh letters are come from Harwich, where the *Gloucester*, Captain Clerke, is come in, and says that on Sunday night upon coming in of the Prince, the Duke did fly; but all this day they have been fighting; therefore they did face again to be sure. Captain Bacon of the *Bristoll* is killed. They cry up Jenings of the *Ruby*, and Saunders of the *Sweepstakes*. They condemn mightily Sir Thomas Teddiman for a coward, but with what reason time must show.

5th. At noon, though I should have dined with my Lord Mayor and Aldermen at an entertainment of Commissioner Taylor's, yet it being a time of expectation of the success of the fleet, I did not go. No manner of news this day, but of the *Rainbow*'s being put in from the fleet, maimed as the other ships are.

6th. By and by walking a little further, Sir Philip Frowde[31] did meet the Duke with an express to Sir W. Coventry (who was by) from Captain Taylor, the Store-keeper at Harwich, being the narration of Captain Hayward of the *Dunkirke*; who gives a very serious account, how upon Monday the two fleets fought all day till seven at night, and then the whole fleet of Dutch did betake themselves to a very plain flight, and never looked back again. That Sir Christopher Mings is wounded in the leg; that the Generall is well. That it is conceived reasonably, that of all the Dutch fleet, which, with what recruits they had, come to one hundred sail, there is not above fifty got home; and of them, few if any of their flags. And that little Captain Bell, in one of the fireships, did at the end of the day fire a ship of 70 guns. We were also so overtaken with this good news, that the Duke ran with it to the King, who was gone to chapel, and there all the Court was in a hubbub, being rejoiced over head and ears in this good news. Away go I by coach to the new Exchange, and there did spread this good news a little, though I find it had broke out before. And so home to our own church, it being the common Fast-day, and it was just before sermon; but, Lord! how all the people in the church stared upon me to see me whisper to Sir John Minnes and my Lady Pen. Anon I saw people stirring and whispering below, and by and by comes up the sexton from my Lady Ford to tell me the news, (which I had brought) being now sent into the church by Sir W. Batten in writing, and passed from pew to pew. But that which pleased me as much as the news, was, to have the fair Mrs Middleton at our church, who indeed is a very beautiful lady. Idled away the whole night till twelve at night at the bonfire in the streets. Some of the people thereabouts going about with musquets, and did give me two or three vollies of their musquets, I giving them a crown to drink; and so home. Mightily pleased with this happy day's news, and the more, because confirmed by Sir Daniel Harvy,[32] who was in the whole fight with the Generall, and tells me that there appear but thirty-six in all of the Dutch fleet left at the end of the voyage when they run home. The joy of the City was this night exceeding great.

7th. Up betimes, and to my office about business, (Sir W. Coventry having sent me word that he is gone down to the fleet to see how

31 Secretary to the Duchess of York.
32 Ranger of Richmond Park.

matters stand, and to be back again speedily); and with the same expectation of congratulating ourselves with the victory that I had yesterday. But my Lord Brouncker and Sir T. H.[33] that come from Court, tell me the contrary news, which astonishes me: that is to say, that we are beaten, lost many ships and good commanders; have not taken one ship of the enemy's; and so can only report ourselves a victory: nor is it certain that we were left masters of the field. But, above all, that the Prince run on shore upon the Galloper, and there stuck; was endeavoured to be fetched off by the Dutch, but could not; and so they burned her; and Sir G. Ascue is taken prisoner, and carried into Holland. This news do much trouble me, and the thoughts of the ill consequences of it, and the pride and presumption that brought us to it. At noon to the 'Change, and there find the discourse of town, and their countenances much changed; but yet not very plain. By and by comes Mr Wayth to me; and discoursing of our ill success, he tells me plainly from Captain Page's own mouth, (who hath lost his arm in the fight,) that the Dutch did pursue us two hours before they left us, and then they suffered us to go on homewards, and they retreated towards their coast; which is very sad news. The Duke much damped in his discourse, touching the late fight, and all the Court talk sadly of it. The Duke did give me several letters he had received from the fleet, and Sir W. Coventry and Sir W. Pen, who are gone down thither, for me to pick out some works to be done for the setting out the fleet again; and so I took them home with me, and was drawing out an abstract of them till midnight. And as to news, I do find great reason to think that we are beaten in every respect, and that we are the losers. The Prince upon the Galloper, where both the *Royall Charles* and *Royall Katharine* had come twice aground, but got off. The *Essex* carried into Holland; the *Swiftsure* missing (Sir W. Barkeley) ever since the beginning of the fight. Captains Bacon, Tearne, Wood, Mootham, Whitty, and Coppin, slayne. The Duke of Albemarle writes, that he never fought with worse officers in his life, not above twenty of them behaving themselves like men. Sir William Clerke lost his leg; and in two days died. The *Loyall George*, *Seven Oakes*, and *Swiftsure*, are still missing, having never, as the Generall writes himself, engaged with them. It was as great an alteration to find myself required to write a sad letter

33 Probably Sir Thomas Harvey.

instead of a triumphant one, to my Lady Sandwich this night, as ever on any occasion I had in my life.

8th. To my very great joy I find Balty come home without any hurt, after the utmost imaginable danger he hath gone through in the *Henery*, being upon the quarterdeck with Harman all the time; and for which service, Harman I heard this day commended most seriously and most eminently by the Duke of York. As also the Duke did do most utmost right to Sir Thomas Teddiman, of whom a scandal was raised, but without cause, he having behaved himself most eminently brave all the whole fight, and to extraordinary great service and purpose, having given Trump himself such a broadside as was hardly ever given to any ship. Mings is shot through the face, and into the shoulder, where the bullet is lodged. Young Holmes is also ill-wounded, and Atber in the *Rupert*. Balty tells me the case of the *Henery*; and it was, indeed, most extraordinary sad and desperate. After dinner Balty and I to my office, and there talked a great deal of this fight; and I am mightily pleased in him, and have great content in, and hopes of his doing well. Thence out to White Hall to a Committee for Tangier, but it met not. But, Lord! to see how melancholy the Court is, under the thoughts of this last overthrow, (for so it is,) instead of a victory, so much and so unreasonably expected. We hear the *Swiftsure*, Sir W. Barkeley, is come in safe to the Nowre, after her being absent ever since the beginning of the fight, wherein she did not appear at all from beginning to end.

9th. The Court is divided about the *Swiftsure* and the *Essex*'s being safe. And wagers and odds laid on both sides. Sir W. Coventry is come to town; so I to his chamber. But I do not hear that he is at all pleased or satisfied with the late fight; but he tells me more news of our suffering, by the death of one or two captains more than I knew before. But he do give over the thoughts of the safety of the *Swiftsure* or *Essex*.

10th. I met with Pierce the surgeon, who is lately come from the fleet, and tells me that all the commanders, officers, and even the common seamen do condemn every part of the late conduct of the Duke of Albemarle: both in his fighting at all, running among them in his retreat, and running the ships on ground; so as nothing can be worse spoken of. That Holmes, Spragg, and Smith do all the business, and the old and wiser commanders nothing. So as Sir Thomas Teddiman (whom the King and all the world speak well of) is mightily discontented, as being wholly slighted. He says we lost more after the Prince came, than before too. The Prince was so maimed, as to be forced to be towed home. He says all the fleet confess their being chased home by the Dutch; and yet the body of the Dutch that did it, was not above forty sail at most. And yet this put us into the fright, as to bring all our ships on ground. He says, however, that the Duke of Albemarle is as high almost as ever, and pleases himself to think that he hath given the Dutch their bellies full, without sense of what he hath lost us; and talks how he knows how the way to beat them. But he says, that even Smith himself, one of his creatures, did himself condemn the late conduct from the beginning to the end. He tells me further, how the Duke of York is wholly given up to his new mistress, my Lady Denham,[34] going at noonday with all his gentlemen with him to visit her in Scotland Yard; she declaring, she will not be his mistress, as Mrs Price, to go up and down the Privy-stairs, but will be owned publicly; and so she is. Mr Brouncker,[35] it seems, was the pimp to bring it about, and my Lady Castlemaine, who designs thereby to fortify herself by the Duke; there being a falling-out the other day between the King and her: on this occasion, the Queene, in ordinary talk before the ladies in her drawing-room, did say to my Lady Castlemaine that she feared the King did take cold, by staying so late abroad at her house. She answered before them all, that he did not stay so late abroad with her, for he went betimes thence, (though he do not before one, two, or three in the morning,) but must stay somewhere else. The King then coming in and overhearing, did whisper in the eare aside, and told her she was a bold impertinent woman, and bid her to be gone out of the Court, and not to come again till he sent for her; which she did presently, and went to a lodging in the Pell Mell, and kept there two or three days, and then sent to the King to know whether she might send for her things away out of her house. The King sent to her, she must first come and view them: and so she come, and the King went to her,

34 Miss Brookes, a relative of the Earl of Bristol, married to Sir J. Denham, frequently mentioned in the *Mémoires de Grammont*.

35 Henry Brouncker, younger brother to Lord Brouncker, whom he succeeded in his title. He was Groom of the Bed-chamber to the Duke of York, and a famous chess-player.

and all friends again. He tells me she did, in her anger, say she would be even with the King, and print his letters to her. So putting all together, we are and are like to be in a sad condition. We are endeavouring to raise money by borrowing it of the City; but I do not think the City will lend a farthing. Sir G. Carteret and I walked an hour in the church-yard, under Henry VII's Chapel, he being lately come from the fleet; and tells me, as I hear from every body else, that the management in the late fight was bad from top to bottom. That several said that this would not have been if my Lord Sandwich had had the ordering of it. Nay, he tells me that certainly had my Lord Sandwich had the misfortune to have done as they have done, the King could not have saved him. There is, too, nothing but discontent among the officers; and all the old experienced men are slighted. He tells me to my question, (but as a great secret,) that the dividing of the fleet did proceed first from a proposition from the fleet, though agreed to hence. But he confesses it arose from want of due intelligence. He do, however, call the fleet's retreat on Sunday a very honourable one, and that the Duke of Albemarle did do well in it, and would have been well if he had done it sooner, rather than venture the loss of the fleet and crown, as he must have done if the Prince had not come. He was surprised when I told him I heard that the King did intend to borrow some money of the City, and would know who had spoke of it to me; I told him Sir Ellis Layton this afternoon. He says it is a dangerous discourse, for that the City certainly will not be invited to do it, and then for the King to ask it and be denied, will be the beginning of our sorrow. He seems to fear we shall all fall to pieces among ourselves. This evening we hear that Sir Christopher Mings is dead of his late wounds; and Sir W. Coventry did commend him to me in a most extraordinary manner. But this day, after three days' trial in vain, and the hazard of the spoiling of the ship in lying till next spring, besides the disgrace of it, news is brought that the *Loyall London* is launched at Deptford.

11th. I with my Lady Pen and her daughter to see Harman; whom we find lame in bed. His bones of his ancle are broke, but he hopes to do well soon; and a fine person by his discourse he seems to be: and he did plainly tell me that at the Council of War before the fight, it was against his reason to begin the fight then, and the reasons of most sober men there, the wind being such, and we to windward, that they could not use their lower tier of guns. Late comes Sir Jo. Bankes to see me, who tells me that coming up from Rochester he overtook three or four hundred seamen, and he believes every day they come flocking from the fleet in like numbers: which is a sad neglect there, when it will be impossible to get others, and we have little reason to think these will return presently again. Walking in the galleries at White Hall, I find the Ladies of Honour dressed in their riding garbs, with coats and doublets with deep skirts, just for all the world like mine, and buttoned their doublets up the breast, with perriwigs and with hats; so that, only for a long petticoat dragging under their men's coats, nobody could take them for women in any point whatever; which was an odde sight, and a sight did not please me. It was Mrs Wells and another fine lady that I saw thus.

13th. Sir H. C. Cholmly[36] tells me there are great jarrs between the Duke of York and the Duke of Albemarle, about the latter's turning out one or two of the commanders put in by the Duke of York. Among others, Captain Du Tell, a Frenchman, put in by the Duke of York, and mightily defended by him; and is therein led by Monsieur Blancford, that it seems hath the same command over the Duke of York as Sir W. Coventry hath; which raises ill blood between them. And I do in several little things observe that Sir W. Coventry hath of late, by the by, reflected on the Duke of Albemarle and his captains, particularly in that of old Teddiman, who did deserve to be turned out this fight, and was so; but I heard Sir W. Coventry say that the Duke of Albemarle put in one as bad as he in his room, and one that did as little. Invited to Sir Christopher Mings's funeral, but find them gone to church. However I into the church (which is a fair large church, and a great chapel) and there heard the service, and staid till they buried him, and then out. And there met with Sir W. Coventry (who was there out of great generosity, and no person of quality there but he) and went with him into his coach, and being in it with him there happened this extraordinary case, – one of the most romantique that ever I heard in my life, and could not have believed, but that I did see it; which was this: – About a dozen able, lusty, proper men come to the coach-side with tears in their eyes, and one of them that

36 Sir Hugh Cholmely of Whitby, Yorkshire, Bart., was employed in constructing the Mole at Tangier, and resided there some years. Died 1688.

spoke for the rest begun and said to Sir W. Coventry, 'We are here a dozen of us, that have long known and loved, and served our dead commander, Sir Christopher Mings, and have now done the last office of laying him in the ground. We would be glad we had any other to offer after him, and in revenge of him. All we have is our lives; if you will please to get His Royal Highness to give us a fireship among us all, here are a dozen of us, out of all which choose you one to be commander, and the rest of us, whoever he is, will serve him; and, if possible, do that which shall show our memory of our dead commander, and our revenge.' Sir W. Coventry was herewith much moved, (as well as I, who could hardly abstain from weeping,) and took their names, and so parted; telling me that he would move his Royal Highness as in a thing very extraordinary. The truth is, Sir Christopher Mings was a very stout man, and a man of great parts, and most excellent tongue among ordinary men: and as Sir W. Coventry says, could have been the most useful man at such a pinch of time as this. He was come into great renowne here at home, and more abroad in the West Indys. He had brought his family into a way of being great; but dying at this time, his memory and name (his father being always and at this day a shoemaker, and his mother a hoyman's daughter; of which he was used frequently to boast) will be quite forgot in a few months as if he had never been, nor any of his name be the better by it; he having not had time to will any estate, but is dead poor rather than rich. So we left the church and crowd.

14th. With my wife and father to Hales's, and there looked only on my father's picture, (which is mighty like); and so away to White Hall to a committee for Tangier. Where the Duke of York was, and Sir W. Coventry, and a very full committee: and instead of having a very prejudiced meeting, they did, though inclined against Yeabsly, yield to the greatest part of his account, so as to allow of his demands to the value of £7000 and more, and only give time for him to make good his pretence to the rest; which was mighty joy to me: and so we rose up. But I must observe the force of money, which did make my Lord Ashly to argue and behave himself in the business with the greatest friendship, and yet with all the discretion imaginable; and it will be a business of admonition and instruction to me concerning him (and other men, too, for aught I know) as long as I live.

16th. The King, Duke of York, and Sir W. Coventry are gone down to the fleet. It seems the Dutch do mightily insult of their victory, and they have great reason. Sir William Barkeley was killed before his ship taken; and there he lies dead in a sugar-chest, for every body to see, with his flag standing up by him. And Sir George Ascue is carried up and down the Hague for people to see.

18th. Sir W. Coventry is returned this night from the fleet; he being the activest man in the world, and we all (myself particularly) more afraid of him than of the King or his service, for aught I see; God forgive us! This day the great news is come of the French, their taking the island of St Christopher from us; and it is to be feared they have done the like of all those islands thereabouts: this makes me mad.

19th. I to Sir G. Carteret's by appointment: where I perceive by him the King is going to borrow some money of the City; but I fear it will do no good, but hurt. He tells me how the Generall is displeased, and there have been some high words between the Generall and Sir W. Coventry. And it may be so; for I do not find Sir W. Coventry so highly commending the Duke as he used to be, but letting fall now and then some little jerkes: as this day, speaking of news from Holland, he says, 'I find their victory begins to shrinke there as well as ours here.' Here I met with Captain Cocke, and he tells me that the first thing the Prince said to the King upon his coming was, complaining of the Commissioners of the Navy: that they could have been abroad in three or four days but for us; that we do not take care of them: which I am troubled at, and do fear may in violence break out upon this office some time or other; for we shall not be able to carry on the business.

21st. Up, and at the office all the morning; where by several circumstances I find Sir W. Coventry and the Duke of Albemarle do not agree as they used to do; Sir W. Coventry commending Aylett, (in some reproach to the Duke), whom the Duke hath put out for want of courage; and found fault with Steward, whom the Duke keeps in, though as much in fault as any commander in the fleet. Sir George Smith tells me that this day my Lord Chancellor and some of the Court have been with the City, and that the City have voted to lend the King £100,000; which, if soon paid, (as he says he believes it will,) will be a greater service than I did ever expect at this time from the City.

23rd. Reading *Pompey the Great*, (a play translated from the French by several noble persons; among others, my Lord Buckhurst,) that to me is but a mean play, and the words and sense not very extraordinary. From Deptford I walked to Redriffe, and in my way was overtaken by Bagwell, lately come from sea in the *Providence*, who did give me an account of several particulars in the late fight, and how his ship was deserted basely by the *York*, Captain Swanly, commander.

24th. In the gallery among others met with Major Halsey, a great creature of the Duke of Albemarle's: who tells me that the Duke by name hath said that he expected to have the work here up in the River done, having left Sir W. Batten and Mr Phipps there. He says that the Duke of Albemarle do say that this is a victory we have had, having, as he was sure, killed them 8000 men, and sunk about fourteen of their ships; but nothing like this appears true. He lays much of the little success we have had, however, upon the fleet's being divided by order from above, and the want of spirit in the commanders; and that he was commanded by order to go out of the Downes to the Gunfleete, and in the way meeting the Dutch fleet, what should he do? should he not fight them? especially having beat them heretofore at as great disadvantage. He tells me further, that having been downe with the Duke of Albemarle, he finds that Holmes and Spragge do govern most business of the Navy; and by others I understand that Sir Thomas Allen is offended thereat: that he is not so much advised with as he ought to be. He tells me also, as he says of his own knowledge, that several people before the Duke went out did offer to supply the King with £100,000 provided he would be treasurer of it, to see it laid out for the Navy; which he refused, and so it died. But I believe none of this. This day I saw my Lady Falmouth,[37] with whom I remember now I have dined at my Lord Barkeley's heretofore, a pretty woman: she was now in her second or third mourning, and pretty pleasant in her looks. By and by the Council rises, and Sir W. Coventry come out; and he and I went aside, and discoursed of much business of the Navy; and afterwards took his coach, and to Hide-Parke, he and I alone: there

37 Elizabeth, daughter of Hervey Bagot, Esq., and widow of Charles Berkeley, Earl of Falmouth, married secondly, Charles first Duke of Dorset. She had been Maid of Honour to the Duchess of York.

we had much talk. First, he stated a discourse of a talk he hears about the town, which, says he, is a very bad one, and fit to be suppressed, if we knew how: which is, the comparing of the success of the last year with that of this; saying that that was good, and that bad. I was as sparing in speaking as I could, being jealous of him and myself also, but wished it could be stopped; but said I doubted it could not otherwise than by the fleet's being abroad again, and so finding other work for men's minds and discourse. Then to discourse of himself, saying, that he heard that he was under the lash of people's discourse about the Prince's not having notice of the Dutch being out, and for him to come back again, nor the Duke of Albemarle notice that the Prince was sent for back again: to which he told me very particularly how careful he was the very same night that it was resolved to send for the Prince back, to cause orders to be writ, and waked the Duke, who was then in bed, to sign them; and that they went by express that very night, being the Wednesday night before the fight, which begun on the Friday; and that for sending them by the post express, and not by gentlemen on purpose, he made a sport of it, and said, I knew of none to send it with but would at least have lost more time in fitting themselves out, than any diligence of theirs beyond that of the ordinary post would have recovered. I told him that this was not so much the towne talk as the reason of dividing the fleete. To this he told me he ought not to say much; but did assure me in general that the proposition did first come from the fleet, and the resolution not being prosecuted with orders so soon as the Generall thought fit, the Generall did send Sir Edward Spragge up on purpose for them; and that there was nothing in the whole business which was not done with the full consent and advice of the Duke of Albemarle. But he did adde, (as the Catholiques call *le secret de la Masse*) that Sir Edward Spragge – who had even in Sir Christopher Mings's time, put in to be the great favourite of the Prince, but much more now had a mind to be the great man with him, and to that end had a mind to have the Prince at a distance from the Duke of Albemarle, that they might be doing something alone – did, as he believed, put on this business of dividing the fleet, and that thence it came. He tells me as to the business of intelligence, the want whereof the world did complain much of, that for that it was not his business, and as he was therefore to have no share in the blame, so he would not meddle to lay it any where else. That De Ruyter was ordered by the States not to make it his business to come into much danger, but to preserve himself as much as was fit out of harm's way, to be able to direct the fleet. He do, I perceive, with some violence, forbear saying any thing to the reproach of the Duke of Albemarle; but, contrarily, speaks much of his courage; but I do as plainly see that he do not like the Duke of Albemarle's proceedings, but, contrarily, is displeased therewith. And he do plainly diminish the commanders put in by the Duke, and do lessen the miscarriages of any that have been removed by him. He concurs with me, that the next bout will be a fatal one to one side or other, because, if we be beaten, we shall not be able to set out our fleet again. He do confess with me that the hearts of our seamen are much saddened; and for that reason, among others, wishes Sir Christopher Mings was alive, who might inspire courage and spirit into them. Speaking of Holmes, how great a man he is, and that he do for the present, and hath done all the voyage, kept himself in good order and within bounds: but, says he, a cat will be a cat still, and some time or other out his humours must break again. He do not disowne but that the dividing of the fleet upon the presumptions that were then had, (which, I suppose, was the French fleet being come this way,) was a good resolution.

25th. News from Sir W. Coventry that the Dutch are certainly come out. Mrs Pen carried us to two gardens at Hackny, (which I every day grow more and more in love with,) Mr Drake's one, where the garden is good, and house and the prospect admirable; the other my Lord Brooke's,[38] where the gardens are much better, but the house not so good, nor the prospect good at all. But the gardens are excellent; and here I first saw oranges grow: some green, some half, some a quarter, and some full ripe, on the same tree, and one fruit of the same tree do come a year or two after the other. I pulled off a little one by stealth (the man being mightily curious of them) and eat it, and it was just as other little green small oranges are: as big as half the end of my little finger. Here were also great variety of other exotique plants, and several labarinths, and a pretty aviary.

38 Robert Lord Brooke, died 1676. Evelyn mentions this garden as Lady Brooke's. Brook House at Clapton, was lately occupied as a private madhouse.

26th. In the morning come Mr Chichly[39] to Sir W. Coventry, to tell him the ill success of the guns made for the *Loyall London*; which is, that in the trial every one of the great guns, the whole cannon of seven (as I take it), broke in pieces.

27th. To Sir W. Coventry's chamber (where I saw his father my Lord Coventry's picture hung up, done by Stone, who then brought it home. It is a good picture, drawn in his judge's robes, and the great seal by him. And while it was hanging up, 'This,' says Sir W. Coventry, merrily, 'is the use we make of our fathers.') But what I observed most from the discourse was this of Sir W. Coventry, that he do look upon ourselves in a desperate condition. The issue of all standing upon this one point, that by the next fight, if we beat, the Dutch will certainly be content to take eggs for their money, (that was his expression); or if we be beaten, we must be contented to make peace, and glad if we can have it without paying too dear for it. And withall we do rely wholly upon the Parliament's giving us more money the next sitting, or else we are undone. I did this afternoon visit my Lord Bellasses, who professes all imaginable satisfaction in me. My Lord is going down to his garrison to Hull, by the King's command, to put it in order for fear of an invasion: which course I perceive is taken upon the sea-coasts round; for we have a real apprehension of the King of France's invading us.

28th. The Dutch are now known to be out, and we may expect them every hour upon our coast. But our fleet is in pretty good readiness for them.

29th. To the office; where I met with a letter from Dover, which tells me (and it did come by express) that news is brought over by a gentleman from Callice that the Dutch fleet, 130 sail, are come upon the French coast; and that the country is bringing in picke-axes, and shovells, and wheel-barrows into Callice; that there are 6000 men armed with head, back, and breast, (Frenchmen) ready to go on board the Dutch fleet, and will be followed by 1200 more. That they pretend they are to come to Dover; and that thereupon the Governor of Dover Castle is getting the victuallers' provision out of the town into the Castle to secure it. But I do think this is a ridiculous conceit; but a little time will show.

39 Mr, afterwards Sir Thomas Chicheley, a Privy Counsellor and Commissioner of the Ordnance.

30th. Mightily troubled all this morning with going to my Lord Mayor, (Sir Thomas Bludworth, a silly[40] man I think,) and other places, about getting shipped some men that they have these two last nights pressed in the City out of houses: the persons wholly unfit for sea, and many of them people of very good fashion, which is a shame to think of, and carried to Bridewell they are, yet without being impressed with money legally as they ought to be. But to see how the King's business is done; my Lord Mayor himself did scruple at this time of extremity to do this thing, because he had not money to pay the pressed-money to the men. I did out of my own purse disburse £15 to pay for their pressing and diet last night and this morning; which is a thing worth record of my Lord Mayor. Busy about this all the morning, and about the getting off men pressed by our officers of the fleet into the service; even our own men that are at the office, and the boats that carry us. So that it is now become impossible to have so much as a letter carried from place to place, or any message done for us: nay, out of Victualling ships full loaden to go down to the fleet, and out of the vessels of the officers of the Ordnance, they press men, so that for want of discipline in this respect I do fear all will be undone.

July 1st. Comes Sir W. Pen to town, which I little expected, having invited my Lady and her daughter Pegg to dine with me to-day; which at noon they did, and Sir W. Pen with them: and pretty merry we were. And though I do not love him, yet I find it necessary to keep in with him: his good service at Shearnesse in getting out the fleet being much taken notice of, and reported to the King and Duke, even from the Prince and Duke of Albemarle themselves, and made the most of to me and them by Sir W. Coventry: therefore I think it discretion, great and necessary discretion, to keep in with him. To the Tower several times, about the business of the pressed men, and late at it till twelve at night shipping of them. But, Lord! how some poor women did cry; and in my life I never did see such natural expression of passion as I did here in some women's bewailing themselves, and running to every parcel of men that were brought, one after another, to look for their husbands, and wept over every vessel that went off, thinking they might be there, and looking after the ship as far as ever they could by moone-light, that it grieved me to the heart to hear them. Besides, to see poor patient labouring men

40 As his conduct during the Great Fire fully proved.

and housekeepers leaving poor wives and families, taken up on a sudden by strangers, was very hard, and that without press-money, but forced against all law to be gone. It is a great tyranny.

2nd. Up betimes, and forced to go to my Lord Mayor's, about the business of the pressed men; and indeed I find him a mean man of understanding and dispatch of any publick business. Thence out of curiosity to Bridewell to see the pressed men, where there are about 300; but so unruly that I durst not go among them: and they have reason to be so, having been kept these three days prisoners, with little or no victuals, and pressed out and contrary to all course of law, without press-money, and men that are not liable to it. Here I met with prating Colonel Cox, one of the City collonells, heretofore a great presbyter: but to hear how the fellow did commend himself and the service he do the King; and, like an asse, at Paul's did take me out of my way on purpose to show me the gate, (the little north gate) where he had two men shot close by him on each time, and his own hair burnt by a bullet-shot in the insurrection of Venner, and himself escaped. I found one of the vessels loaden with the Bridewell birds in a great mutiny, and they would not sail, not they; but with good words, and cajoling the ringleader into the Tower, (where, when he was come, he was clapped up in the Hole) they were got very quietly: but I think it is much if they do not run the vessel on ground.

3rd. Mr Finch, one of the Commissioners of Excise, and I fell to discourse of the Parliament, and the great men there; and among others, Mr Vaughan, whom he reports as a man of excellent judgement and learning, but most passionate and opiniastre. He had done himself the most wrong (though he values it not), that is, the displeasure of the King in his standing so long against the breaking of the Act for a triennial parliament; but yet do believe him to be a most loyall gentleman. He told me Mr Prin's character; that he is a man of mighty labour and reading, and memory, but the worst judge of matters, or layer together of what he hath read, in the world, (which I do not, however, believe him in;) that he believes him very true to the King in his heart, but can never be reconciled to episcopacy; that the House do not lay much weight upon him, or any thing he says. News come yesterday from Harwich, that the Dutch had appeared upon our coast with their fleet, and we believe did go to the Gunfleete, and they are supposed to be there now; but I have heard nothing of them to-day. Yesterday Dr Whistler, at Sir W. Pen's, told me that Alexander Broome,[41] the great song-maker, is lately dead.

4th. Thanks be to God, the plague is, as I hear, encreased but two this week; but in the country in several places it rages mightily, and particularly in Colchester, where it hath long been, and is believed will quite depopulate the place. With the Duke, all of us discoursing about the places where to build ten great ships: the King and Council have resolved on none to be under third-rates; but it is impossible to do it, unless we have more money towards the doing it than yet we have in any view. But, however, the show must be made to the world. In the evening Sir W. Pen came to me, and we walked together, and talked of the late fight. I find him very plain, that the whole conduct of the late fight was ill; that two-thirds of the commanders of the whole fleet have told him so: they all saying, that they durst not oppose it at the Council of War, for fear of being called cowards, though it was wholly against their judgement to fight that day with the disproportion of force, and then we not being able to use one gun of our lower tier, which was a greater disproportion than the other. Besides, we might very well have staid in the Downs without fighting or any where else, till the Prince could have come up to them; or at least, till the weather was fair, that we might have the benefit of our whole force in the ships that we had. He says three things must be remedied, or else we shall be undone by this fleet. 1. That we must fight in a line, whereas we fight promiscuously, to our utter and demonstrable ruine: the Dutch fighting otherwise; and we, whenever we beat them. – 2. We must not desert ships of our own in distress, as we did, for that makes a captain desperate, and he will fling away his ship, when there are no hopes left him of succour. – 3. That ships when they are a little shattered, must not take the liberty to come in of themselves, but refit themselves the best they can, and stay out – many of our ships coming in with very small disableness. He told me that our very commanders, nay, our very flag-officers, do stand in need of exercising among themselves, and discoursing the business of commanding a fleet: he telling me that

41 Alexander Broome, an attorney in the Lord Mayor's Court, author of *Loyal Songs and Madrigals*, much sung by the Cavaliers, and of a translation of Horace. He was regretted as an agreeable companion.

even one of our flag-men in the fleet, did not know which tacke lost the wind, or kept it, in the last engagement. He says it was pure dismaying and fear that made them all run upon the Galloper, not having their wits about them: and that it was a miracle they were not all lost. He much inveighs upon my discoursing of Sir John Lawson's saying heretofore, that sixty sail would do as much as one hundred; and says that he was a man of no counsel at all, but had got the confidence to say as the gallants did, and did propose to himself to make himself great by them, and saying as they did: but was no man of judgement in his business, but hath been out in the greatest points that have come before them. And then in the business of fore-castles, which he did oppose, all the world sees now the use of them for shelter of men. He did talk very rationally to me, insomuch that I took more pleasure this night in hearing him discourse, than I ever did in my life in any thing that he said.

6th. I believe not less than one thousand people in the streets. But it is a pretty thing to observe that both there and every where else, a man shall see many women now-a-days of mean sort in the streets, but no men; men being so afraid of the press. I dined with Sir G. Carteret, and after dinner had much discourse about our public business; and he do seem to fear every day more and more what I do; which is a general confusion in the State; plainly answering me to the question, who is it that the weight of the warr depends upon? that it is only Sir W. Coventry. He tells me, too, the Duke of Albemarle is dissatisfied, and that the Duchesse do curse Coventry as the man that betrayed her husband to the sea: though I believe that it is not so. Thence to Lumburd Streete, and received £2000, and carried it home: whereof £1000 in gold. This I do for security sake, and convenience of carriage; though it costs me above £70 the change of it, at 18½d. per peece. Creed tells me he finds all things mighty dull at Court; and that they now begin to lie long in bed; it being, as we suppose, not seemly for them to be found playing and gaming as they used to be; nor that their minds are at ease enough to follow those sports, and yet not knowing how to employ themselves, (though there be work enough for their thoughts and councils and pains,) they keep long in bed. But he thinks with me, that there is nothing in the world can help us but the King's personal looking after his business and his officers, and that with that we may yet do well; but otherwise must be undone: nobody at this day taking care of anything, nor hath any body to call him to account for it.

10th. To the office; the yard being very full of women, (I believe above three hundred) coming to get money for their husbands and friends that are prisoners in Holland; and they lay clamouring and swearing and cursing us, that my wife and I were afraid to send a venison-pasty that we have for supper tonight, to the cook's to be baked, for fear of their offering violence to it: but it went, and no hurt done. To the Tower to speak with Sir John Robinson about the bad condition of the pressed men for want of clothes.

11th. I away by coach to St James's, and there hear that the Duchesse is lately brought to bed of a boy. By and by called to wait on the Duke, the King being present; and there agreed, among other things, of the places to build the ten new great ships ordered to be built; and as to the relief of prisoners in Holland. And then about several stories of the basenesse of the King of Spain's being served with officers: they in Flanders having as good common men as any Prince in the world, but the veriest cowards for the officers, nay for the general officers, as the Generall and Lieutenant-generall, in the whole world. But, above all things, the King did speak most in contempt of the ceremoniousnesse of the King of Spain, that he do nothing but under some ridiculous form or other. I shall get in near £2000 into my own hands, which is in the King's, upon tallies; which will be a pleasure to me, and satisfaction to have a good sum in my own hands, whatever evil disturbances should be in the State; though it troubles me to lose so great a profit as the King's interest of ten per cent. for that money.

12th. With Sir W. Coventry into London, to the office. And all the way I observed him mightily to make mirth of the Duke of Albemarle and his people about him, saying, that he was the happiest man in the world for doing of great things by sorry instruments. And so particularized in Sir W. Clerke, and Riggs, and Halsey, and others. And then again said that the only quality eminent in him was, that he did persevere; and indeed he is a very drudge, and stands by the King's business.

14th. Up betimes to the office, to write fair a laborious letter I wrote as from the Board to the Duke of York, laying out our want of money again; and particularly the business of Captain Cocke's tender

of hemp, which my Lord Brouncker brought in under an unknown
hand without name. Wherein his Lordship will have no great success,
I doubt. That being done, I down to Thames-streete, and there
agreed for four or five tons of corke, to send this day to the fleet, being
a new device to make barricados with, instead of junke. After a song
in the garden, which is now the greatest pleasure I take, and indeed do
please me mightily, to bed. This evening I had Davila brought home
to me, and find it a most excellent history as ever I read.

16th. A wonderful dark sky, and shower of rain this morning. At
Harwich a shower of hail as big as walnuts.

18th. To St James's after my fellows; and here, among other things,
before us all, the Duke of York did say, that now at length is come to
a sure knowledge that the Dutch did lose in the late engagements
twenty-nine captains and thirteen ships. Upon which Sir W. Coventry did publickly move, that if his Royal Highness had this of a
certainty, it would be of use to send this down to the fleet, and to
cause it to be spread about the fleet, for the recovering of the spirits of
the officers and seamen; who are under great dejectedness, for want of
knowing that they did do any thing against the enemy, notwithstanding all that they did to us. Which, though it be true, yet methought
was one of the most dishonourable motions to our countrymen that
ever was made; and is worth remembering. Thence with Sir W. Pen
home, calling at Lilly's, to have a time appointed when to be drawn
among the other Commanders of Flags the last year's fight. And so full
of work Lilly is, that he was fain to take his table-book out to see how
his time is appointed, and appointed six days hence for him to come
between seven and eight in the morning. Thence with him home;
and there by appointment I find Dr Fuller, now Bishop of Limericke,
in Ireland; whom I knew in his low condition at Twittenham, and
find the Bishop the same good man that ever; and in a word, kind to
us, and, methinks, one of the comeliest and most becoming prelates in
all respects that ever I saw in my life. During dinner comes an
acquaintance of his, Sir Thomas Littleton;[42] whom I knew not while
he was in my house, but liked his discourse: and afterwards, by Sir W.
Pen, do come to know that he is one of the greatest speakers in the

42 Afterwards made Treasurer of the Navy in conjunction with Sir Thomas
Osborn.

House of Commons, and the usual second to the great Vaughan. So was sorry I did observe him no more, and gain more of his acquaintance. Walked to Woolwich, reading the *Rivall Ladys* [43] all the way, and find it a most pleasant and fine writ play.

19th. Full of wants of money, and much stores to buy, for to replenish the stores, and no money to do it with. The fleet is sailed this morning; God send us good news of them!

21st. At noon walked in the garden with Commissioner Pett, (newly come to town) who tells me how infinite the disorders are among the commanders and all officers of the fleet. No discipline: nothing but swearing and cursing, and every body doing what they please; and the Generalls, understanding no better, suffer it, to the reproaching of this Board, or whoever it will be. He himself hath been challenged twice to the field, or something as good, by Sir Edward Spragge and Captain Seamons.[44] He tells me that captains carry, for all the late orders, what men they please. So that he fears, and I do no less, that God Almighty can bless us while we keep in this disorder that we are in: he observing to me too, that there is no man of counsel or advice in the fleet; and the truth is, that the gentlemen captains will undo us, for they are not to be kept in order, their friends about the King and Duke, and their own houses are so free, that it is not for any person but the Duke himself to have any command over them.

22nd. Walked to White Hall, where saw nobody almost, but walked up and down with Hugh May,[45] who is a very ingenious man. Among other things, discoursing of the present fashion of gardens to make them plain, that we have the best walks of gravell in the world, France having none, nor Italy: and our green of our bowling allies is better than any they have. So our business here being ayre, this is the best way; only with a little mixture of statues, or pots, which may be handsome, and so filled with another pot of such or such a flower or greene as the season of the year will bear. And then for flowers, they are best seen in a little plat by themselves; besides, their borders spoil the walks of another garden; and then for fruit, the best way is to have walls built circularly one within another, to the South, on purpose for

43 A tragi-comedy by Dryden.
44 Seymour?
45 An architect, and Comptroller of the works at Windsor Castle. Died 1684.

fruit, and leave the walking garden only for that use. Sir Richard Fanshaw is lately dead at Madrid. The fleet cannot get clear of the River, but expect the first wind to be out, and then to be sure to fight. The Queene and Maids of Honour are at Tonbridge.

23rd. All full of expectation of the fleet's engagement, but it is not yet. Sir W. Coventry says they are eighty-nine men-of-war, but one fifth-rate; and that the *Sweepstakes*, which carries forty guns. They are most infinitely manned. He tells me the *Loyall London*, Sir J. Smith, (which, by the way, he commends to be the best ship in the world, large and small) hath above eight hundred men; and moreover takes notice, which is worth notice, that the fleet hath lain now near fourteen days without any demand for a farthing-worth of any thing of any kind, but only to get men. He also observes, that with this excess of men, nevertheless, they have thought fit to leave behind them sixteen ships, which they have robbed of their men, which certainly might have been manned, and they have been serviceable in the fight, and yet the fleet well-manned, according to the excess of supernumeraries, which we hear they have. At least two or three of them might have been left manned, and sent away with the Gottenburgh ships. They conclude this to be much the best fleet, for force of guns, greatness and number of ships and men, that ever England did see; being as Sir W. Coventry reckons, besides those left behind, eighty-nine men-of-war, and twenty-five ships, though we cannot hear that they have with them above eighteen. The French are not yet joined with the Dutch, which do dissatisfy the Hollanders, and if they should have a defeat, will undo De Witt; the people generally of Holland do hate this league with France.

25th. At White Hall; we find the Court gone to Chapel, it being St James's-day. And by and by, while they are at chapel, and we waiting chapel being done, come people out of the Park, telling us that the guns are heard plainly. And so every body to the Park, and by and by the chapel done, and the King and Duke into the bowling-green, and upon the leads, whither I went, and there the guns were plain to be heard; though it was pretty to hear how confident some would be in the lowdnesse of the guns, which it was as much as ever I could do to hear them. By and by the King to dinner, and I waited there his dining; but, Lord! how little I should be pleased, I think, to have so many people crowding about me; and among other things it astonished me to see my Lord Barkeshire[46] waiting at table, and serving the King drink, in that dirty pickle as I never saw man in my life. Here I met Mr Williams, who would have me to dine where he was invited to dine, at the Backe-stayres. So after the King's meat was taken away, we thither; but he could not stay, but left me there among two or three of the King's servants, where we dined with the meat that come from his table; which was most excellent, with most brave drink cooled in ice, (which at this hot time was welcome,) and I drinking no wine, had metheglin for the King's own drinking, which did please me mightily.

27th. To Sir W. Coventry's lodging, and there he showed me Captain Talbot's letter, wherein he says that the fight begun on the 25th: that our White squadron begun with one of the Dutch squadrons, and then the Red with another, so hot that we put them both to giving way, and so they continued in pursuit all the day, and as long as he stayed with them: that the blow fell to the Zealand squadron; and after a long dispute, he against two or three great ships, received eight or nine dangerous shots, and so come away; and says, he saw the *Resolution* burned by one of their fire-ships, and four or five of the enemy's. But says that two or three of our great ships were in danger of being fired by our fire-ships, which Sir W. Coventry nor I cannot understand. But upon the whole, he and I walked two or three turns in the Park under the great trees, and no doubt that this gallant is come away a little too soon, having lost never a mast nor sail. And then we did begin to discourse of the young genteel captains, which he was very free with me in speaking his mind of the unruliness of them; and what a loss the King hath of his old men, and now of this Hannam, of the *Resolution*, if he be dead. He told me how he is disturbed to hear the commanders at sea called cowards here on shore.

28th. To my Lord Lauderdale's, where we find some Scotch people at supper. Pretty odd company; though my Lord Brouncker tells me, my Lord Lauderdale is a man of mighty good reason and judgement. But at supper there played one of their servants upon the viallin some Scotch tunes only; several, and the best of their country, as they seemed to esteem them, by their praising and admiring them: but,

46 Thomas Howard, second son of Thomas first Earl of Suffolk, created Earl of Berkshire 1625/26, KG. Died 1669, aged nearly 90.

Lord! the strangest ayre that ever I heard in my life, and all of one cast. But strange to hear my Lord Lauderdale say himself that he had rather hear a cat mew than the best musique in the world; and the better the musique, the more sick it makes him; and that of all instruments, he hates the lute most, and next to that, the baggpipe.

29th. All the town is full of a victory. By and by a letter from Sir W. Coventry tells me that we have the victory. Beat them into the Weelings: had taken two of their great ships; but by the orders of the Generalls they are burned. This being, methought, but a poor result after the fighting of two so great fleets, and four days having no tidings of them: I was still impatient; but could know no more. I to Sir W. Batten, where the Lieutenant of the Tower was, and Sir John Minnes, and the news I find is what I had heard before; only that our Blue squadron, it seems, was pursued the most of the time, having more ships, a great many, than its number allotted to its share. Young Seamour is killed, the only captain slain. The *Resolution* burned; but, as they say, most of her crew and commander saved. This is all, only we keep the sea, which denotes a victory, or at least that we are not beaten; but no great matters to brag of, God knows.

30th. To Sir W. Coventry, at St James's, where I find him in his new closet, which is very fine, and well supplied with handsome books. I find him speak very slightly of the late victory: dislikes their staying with the fleet up their coast, believing that the Dutch will come out in fourteen days, and then we with our unready fleet, by reason of some of the ships being maymed, shall be in bad condition to fight them upon their own coast: is much dissatisfied with the great number of men, and their fresh demands of twenty-four victualling ships, they going out the other day as full as they could stow. He spoke slightly of the Duke of Albemarle, saying, when De Ruyter come to give him a broadside – 'Now,' says he, (chewing of tobacco the while) 'will this fellow come and give me two broadsides, and then he shall run'; but it seems he held him to it two hours, till the Duke himself was forced to retreat to refit, and was towed off, and De Ruyter staid for him till he come back again to fight. One in the ship saying to the Duke, 'Sir, methinks De Ruyter hath given us more than two broadsides'; – 'Well,' says the Duke, 'but you shall find him run by and by,' and so he did, says Sir W. Coventry; but after the Duke himself had been first made to fall off. The *Resolution* had all brass guns, being the same that Sir J. Lawson had in her in the Straights. It is observed, that the fleets were even in number to one ship. Thence home; and to sing with my wife and Mercer[47] in the garden; and coming in I find my wife plainly dissatisfied with me, that I can spend so much time with Mercer, teaching her to sing, and could never take the pains with her. Which I acknowledge; but it is because that the girl do take musick mighty readily, and she do not, and musick is the thing of the world that I love most, and all the pleasure almost that I can now take. So to bed in some little discontent, but no words from me.

31st. The Court empty, the King being gone to Tunbridge, and the Duke of York a-hunting. I had some discourse with Povy, who is mightily discontented, I find, about his disappointments at Court; and says, of all places, if there be hell, it is here. No faith, no truth, no love, nor any agreement between man and wife, nor friends. He would have spoke broader, but I put it off to another time; and so parted. Povy discoursed with me about my Lord Peterborough's £50 which his man did give me from him, the last year's salary I paid him, which he would have Povy pay him again; but I have not taken it to myself yet, and therefore will most heartily return him, and mark him out for a coxcomb. Povy went down to Mr Williamson's, and brought me up this extract out of the Flanders' letters to-day come: That Admiral Everson, and the Admiral and Vice-Admiral of Freezeland, with many captains and men, are slain; that De Ruyter is safe, but lost 250 men out of his own ship; but that he is in great disgrace, and Trump in better favour; that Bankert's ship is burned, himself hardly escaping with a few men on board De Haes; that fifteen captains are to be tried the seventh of August; and that the hangman was sent from Flushing to assist the Council of Warr. How much of this is true, time will show.

August 1st. Walked over the Park with Sir W. Coventry, who I clearly see is not thoroughly pleased with the late management of the fight, nor with any thing that the Generalls do; only is glad to hear that De Ruyter is out of favour, and that this fight hath cost them 5000 men, as they themselves do report. And it is a strange thing, as he observes, how now and then the slaughter runs on one hand;

47 Mrs Pepys's maid.

there being 5000 killed on theirs, and not above 400 or 500 killed and wounded on ours, and as many flag-officers on theirs as ordinary captains in ours.

3rd. The death of Everson, and the report of our success, beyond expectation, in the killing of so great a number of men, hath raised the estimation of the late victory considerably; but it is only among fools: for all that was but accidental. But this morning, getting Sir W. Pen to read over the Narrative with me, he did sparingly, yet plainly, say that we might have intercepted their Zealand squadron coming home, if we had done our parts; and more, that we might have run before the wind as well as they, and have overtaken their ships in the pursuite, in all the while.

4th. This evening, Sir W. Pen come into the garden, and walked with me, and told me that he had certain notice that at Flushing they are in great distraction. De Ruyter dares not come on shore for fear of the people: nor any body open their houses or shops for fear of the tumult: which is a very good hearing.

6th. In Fenchurch Street met with Mr Battersby; says he, 'Do you see Dan Rawlinson's door shut up?' (which I did, and wondered.) 'Why,' says he, 'after all this sickness, and himself spending all the last year in the country, one of his men is now dead of the plague, and his wife and one of his maids sick, and himself shut up'; which troubles me mightily. So home; and there do hear also from Mrs Sarah Daniel, that Greenwich is at this time much worse than ever it was, and Deptford too: and she told us that they believed all the town would leave the town, and come to London; which is now the receptacle of all the people from all infected places. God preserve us!

7th. I receive fresh intelligence that Deptford and Greenwich are now afresh exceedingly afflicted with the sickness more than ever.

8th. Discoursed with Mr Hooke about the nature of sounds, and he did make me understand the nature of musicall sounds made by strings, mighty prettily, and told me that having come to a certain number of vibrations proper to make any tone, he is able to tell how many strokes a fly makes with her wings, (those flies that hum in their flying) by the note that it answers to in musique, during their flying. That, I suppose, is a little too much refined; but his discourse in general of sound was mighty fine. To St James's, where we attended with the rest of my fellows on the Duke, whom I found with two or three patches upon his nose and about his right eye, which came from his being struck with the bough of a tree the other day in his hunting; and it is a wonder it did not strike out his eye. To Bow, to my Lady Pooly's,[48] where my wife was with Mr Batelier and his sisters; and there I found a noble supper. About ten o'clock we rose from table, and sang a song; and so home in two coaches, (Mr Batelier and his sister Mary and my wife and I in one, and Mercer alone in the other); and after being examined at Allgate whether we were husbands and wives, home. So to bed mighty sleepy, but with much pleasure. Reeves lying at my house; and mighty proud I am (and ought to be thankful to God Almighty) that I am able to have a spare bed for my friends.

9th. In the evening to Lumbard-street, about money, to enable me to pay Sir G. Carteret's £3000 which he hath lodged in my hands, in behalf of his son and my Lady Jemimah, towards their portion. Mrs Rawlinson is dead of the sickness, and her maid continues mighty ill. He himself is got out of the house. I met with Mr Evelyn in the street, who tells me the sad condition at this very day at Deptford, for the plague, and more at Deale, (within his precinct as one of the Commissioners for sick and wounded seamen,) that the towne is almost quite depopulated.

10th. Homeward, and hear in Fenchurch-street, that now the maid also is dead at Mr Rawlinson's; so that there are three dead in all, the wife, a man-servant, and maid-servant.

14th. Povy tells me how mad my letter makes my Lord Peterborough, and what a furious letter he hath writ to me in answer, though it is not come yet. This did trouble me; for though there be no reason, yet to have a nobleman's mouth open against a man, may do a man hurt; so I endeavoured to have found him out and spoke with him, but could not. After dinner with my wife and Mercer to the Beare-garden; where I have not been, I think, of many years, and saw some good sport of the bull's tossing of the dogs: one into the very boxes. But it is a very rude and nasty pleasure. We had a great many

48 Wife of Sir Edmund Pooly, mentioned before.

hectors in the same box with us, (and one very fine went into the pit, and played his dog for a wager, which was a strange sport for a gentleman,) where they drank wine, and drank Mercer's health first; which I pledged with my hat off. We supped at home, and very merry. And then about nine o'clock to Mrs Mercer's gate, where the fire and boys expected us, and her son had provided abundance of serpents and rockets; and there mighty merry (my Lady Pen and Pegg going thither with us, and Nan Wright,) till about twelve at night, flinging our fireworks, and burning one another and the people over the way. And at last our businesses being most spent, we into Mrs Mercer's, and there mighty merry, smutting one another with candle grease and soot, till most of us were like devils. And that being done, then we broke up, and to my house; and there I made them drink, and upstairs we went, and then fell into dancing, (W. Batelier dancing well,) and dressing him and I and one Mr Banister (who with my wife come over also with us) like women; and Mercer put on a suit of Tom's, like a boy, and mighty mirth we had, and Mercer danced a jigg; and Nan Wright and my wife and Pegg Pen put on perriwigs. Thus we spent till three or four in the morning, mighty merry; and then parted, and to bed.

15th. Mighty sleepy; slept till past eight of the clock, and was called up by a letter from Sir W. Coventry; which among other things, tells me how we have burned one hundred and sixty ships of the enemy within the Fly. I up, and with all possible haste, and in pain for fear of coming late, it being our day of attending the Duke of York, to St James's, where they are full of the particulars; how they are generally good merchant-ships, some of them laden and supposed rich ships. We spent five fire-ships upon them. We landed on the Schelling, (Sir Philip Howard, with some men, and Holmes, I think, with others, about 1000 in all,) and burned a town; and so come away. By and by the Duke of York with his books showed us the very place and manner; and that it was not our design and expectation to have done this, but only to have landed on the Fly and burned some of their stores; but being come in, we spied those ships, and with our long boats, one by one, fired them, our ships running all a-ground, it being so shoal water. We were led to this by, it seems, a renegado captain of the Hollanders, who found himself ill used by De Ruyter for his good service, and so come over to us, and hath done us good service; so that now we trust him, and he himself did go on this expedition. The service is very great, and our joys as great for it. All this will make the Duke of Albemarle in repute again, I doubt. The guns of the Tower going off, and bonfires also in the street for this late good successe.

16th. This day Sir W. Batten did show us at the table a letter from Sir T. Allen, which says, that we have taken ten or twelve ships, (since the late great expedition of burning their ships and town) laden with hemp, flax, tar, deals, &c. This was good news; but by and by comes in Sir G. Carteret, and he asked us with full mouth what we would give for good news. Says Sir W. Batten 'I have better than you for a wager.' They laid sixpence, and we that were by were to give sixpence to him that told the best news. So Sir W. Batten told his of the ten or twelve ships. Sir G. Carteret did then tell us that upon the news of the burning of the ships and town, the common people of Amsterdam did besiege De Witt's house, and he was forced to flee to the Prince of Orange, who is gone to Cleve, to the marriage of his sister. This we concluded all the best news, and my Lord Brouncker and myself did give Sir G. Carteret our sixpence a-piece, which he did give Mr Smith to give the poor. Thus we made ourselves mighty merry.

17th. With Captain Erwin, discoursing about the East Indys, where he hath often been. And among other things, he tells me how the King of Syam seldom goes out without thirty or forty thousand people with him, and not a word spoke, nor a hum or cough in the whole company to be heard. He tells me the punishment frequently there for malefactors, is cutting off the crowne of their head, which they do very dexterously, leaving their brains bare, which kills them presently. He told me what I remember he hath once done heretofore; that every body is to lie flat down at the coming by of the King, and nobody to look upon him upon pain of death. And that he and his fellows being strangers, were invited to see the sport of taking of a wild elephant; and they did only kneel, and look towards the King. Their druggerman[49] did desire them to fall down, for otherwise he should suffer for their contempt of the King. The sport being ended, a messenger comes from the King, which the druggerman thought had been to have taken away his life. But it was to enquire how the strangers liked the sport. The druggerman answered, that

49 Dragoman.

they did cry it up to be the best that ever they saw, and that they never heard of any Prince so great in every thing as this King. The messenger being gone back, Erwila and his company asked their druggerman what he had said, which he told them. 'But why,' say they, 'would you say that without our leave, it being not true?' – 'It makes no matter for that,' says he, 'I must have said it, or have been hanged, for our King do not live by meat, nor drink, but by having great lyes told him.' In our way back we come by a little vessel that come into the river this morning, and says she left the fleet in Sole Bay, and that she hath not heard (she belonging to Sir W. Jenings in the fleet) of any such prizes taken as the ten or twelve I enquired about, and said by Sir W. Batten yesterday to be taken, so I fear it is not true. I had the good fortune to see Mrs Stewart, who is grown a little too tall, but is a woman of most excellent features. Sir Richard Ford did, very understandingly methought, give us an account of the originall of the Hollands Bank, and the nature of it, and how they do never give any interest at all to any person that brings in their money, though what is brought in upon the public faith interest is given by the State for. The unsafe condition of a Bank under a Monarch, and the little safety to a Monarch to have any; or Corporation alone (as London in answer to Amsterdam,) to have so great a wealth or credit, it is that makes it hard to have a Bank here. And as to the former, he did tell us how it sticks in the memory of most merchants how the late King (when by the war between Holland and France and Spain all the bullion of Spain was brought hither, one third of it to be coyned; and indeed it was found advantageous to the merchant to coyne most of it,) was persuaded in a strait by my Lord Cottington[50] to seize upon the money in the Tower: which, though in a few days the merchants concerned did prevail to get it released, yet the thing will never be forgot.

20th. To Deptford by water, reading *Othello, Moore of Venice*, which I ever heretofore esteemed a mighty good play, but having so lately read *The Adventures of Five Houres*, it seems a mean thing. All the afternoon upon my Tangier accounts, getting Tom Wilson to help me in writing as I read; and I find myself right to a farthing in an account of £127,000.

50 Francis, created Lord Cottington, Baron of Hanworth, by Charles I. Died at Valladolid 1653, without issue.

21st. Mr Batelier told me how, being with some others at Bourdeaux, making a bargain with another man at a taverne for some clarets, they did hire a fellow to thunder (which he had the art of doing upon a deale board) and to rain and hail, that is, make the noise of, so as did give them a pretence of undervaluing their merchants' wines, by saying this thunder would spoil and turn them. Which was so reasonable to the merchant, that he did abate two pistolls per ton for the wine in belief of that.

22nd. I to St James's, and there with the Duke of York. I had opportunity of much talk with Sir W. Pen to-day (he being newly come from the fleet); and he do much undervalue the honour that is given to the conduct of the late business of Holmes in burning the ships and town, saying it was a great thing indeed, and of great profit to us in being of great loss to the enemy, but that it was wholly a business of chance. Mrs Knipp tells me my song of 'Beauty Retire' is mightily cried up, which I am not a little proud of; and do think I have done 'It is Decreed' better, but I have not finished it.

23rd. Sir W. Coventry sent me word that the Dutch fleet is certainly abroad; and so we are to hasten all we have to send to our fleet with all speed. But, Lord! to see how my Lord Brouncker undertakes the despatch of the fire-ships, when he is no more fit for it than a porter; and all the while Sir W. Pen, who is the most fit, is unwilling to displease him, and do not look after it; and so the King's work is like to be well done.

26th. I was a little disturbed with news my Lord Brouncker brought me, that we are to attend the King at White Hall this afternoon, and that it is about a complaint from the Generalls against us. Sir W. Pen and I by coach to White Hall, and there staid till the King and Cabinet met in the Green Chamber, and then we were called in; and there the King begun with me, to hear how the victualls of the fleet stood. I did in a long discourse tell him and the rest (the Duke of York, Lord Chancellor, Lord Treasurer, both the Secretarys, Sir G. Carteret, and Sir W. Coventry,) how it stood, wherein they seemed satisfied, but press mightily for more supplies: and the letter of the Generalls, which was read, did lay their not going or too soon returning from the Dutch coast, this next bout, to the want of victuals. They then proceeded to the enquiry after the fire-ships; and did all very superficially, and without any severity at all. But, however, I was in pain, after we come out, to know how I had done; and here, well enough. But, however, it shall be a caution to me to prepare myself against a day of inquisition. Being come out, I met with Mr Moore, and he and I an hour together in the Gallery, telling me how far they are gone in getting my Lord Sandwich's pardon, so as the Chancellor is prepared in it; and Sir H. Bennet do promote it, and the warrant for the King's signing is drawn. The business between my Lord Hinchingbroke and Mrs Mallet is quite broke off; he attended her at Tunbridge, and she declaring her affections to be settled; and he not being fully pleased with the vanity and liberty of her carriage. Thence to discourse of the times; and he tells me he believes both my Lord Arlington and Sir W. Coventry, as well as my Lord Sandwich and Sir G. Carteret, have reason to fear, and are afraid, of this Parliament now coming on. He tells me that Bristoll's faction is getting ground apace against my Lord Chancellor. He told me that my old Lord Coventry[51] was a cunning, crafty man, and did make as many bad decrees in Chancery as any man; and that in one case, that occasioned many years' dispute, at last when the King come in, it was hoped by the party grieved, to get my Lord Chancellor to reverse a decree of his. Sir W. Coventry took the opportunity of the business between the Duke of York and the Duchess, and said to my Lord Chancellor, that he had rather be drawn up Holborne to be hanged, than live to see any decree of his father's reversed. And so the Chancellor did not think fit to do it, but it still stands, to the undoing of one Norton, a printer, about his right to the printing of the Bible, and Grammar, &c. Sir J. Minnes had a very bad fit this day.

27th. Sir G. Carteret tells me what is done about my Lord's pardon, and is not for letting the Duke of York know any thing of it beforehand, but to carry it as speedily and quietly as we can. He seems to be very apprehensive that the Parliament will be troublesome and inquisitive into faults; but seems not to value them as to himself.

28th. To the wedding of Mr Longracke, our purveyor, a civil man, and hath married a sober, serious mayde; but the whole company was

51 The Lord Keeper. Died 1639/40.

very simple and innocent. Sir W. Coventry did read me a letter from the Generalls to the King, a most scurvy letter, reflecting most upon him, and then upon me for my accounts, (not that they are not true, but that we do not consider the expence of the fleet,) and then upon the whole office, in neglecting them and the King's service, and this in very plain and sharp and menacing terms. But a great supply must be made, and shall be, in grace of God.

29th. To St James's, and there Sir W. Coventry took Sir W. Pen and me apart, and read to us his answer to the Generalls' letter to the King, that he read last night; wherein he is very plain, and states the matter in full defence of himself, and of me with him, which he could not avoid; which is a good comfort to me, that I happened to be involved with him in the same cause. And then speaking of the supplies which have been made to this fleet, more than ever in all kinds to any, even that wherein the Duke of York himself was, 'Well,' says he, 'if this will not do, I will say, as Sir J. Falstaffe did to the Prince, "Tell your father that if he do not like this, let him kill the next Piercy himself." '

September 1st. My wife and I to Polichinelly,[52] but were there horribly frighted to see Young Killigrew come in with a great many more young sparks; but we hid ourselves, so as we think they did not see us.

2nd (Lord's day). Some of our maids sitting up late last night to get things ready against our feast to-day, Jane called us up about three in the morning, to tell us of a great fire they saw in the City. So I rose, and slipped on my night-gown, and went to her window; and thought it to be on the back-side of Marke-lane at the farthest, but being unused to such fires as followed, I thought it far enough off; and so went to bed again, and to sleep. About seven rose again to dress myself, and there looked out at the window, and saw the fire not so much as it was, and further off. So to my closet to set things to rights, after yesterday's cleaning. By and by Jane comes and tells me that she hears that above 300 houses have been burned down to-night by the fire we saw, and that it is now burning down all Fish-street, by London Bridge. So I made myself ready presently, and

52 Polichinello in Moorfields.

walked to the Tower, and there got up upon one of the high places, Sir J. Robinson's little son going up with me; and there I did see the houses at that end of the bridge all on fire, and an infinite great fire on this and the other side the end of the bridge; which, among other people, did trouble me for poor little Michell and our Sarah on the bridge. So down with my heart full of trouble to the Lieutenant of the Tower, who tells me that it begun this morning in the King's baker's[53] house in Pudding-lane, and that it hath burned down St Magnes Church and most part of Fish-street already. So I down to the water-side, and there got a boat, and through bridge, and there saw a lamentable fire. Poor Michell's house, as far as the Old Swan, already burned that way, and the fire running further, that in a very little time it got as far as the Steele-yard, while I was there. Every body endeavouring to remove their goods, and flinging into the river, or bringing them into lighters that lay off; poor people staying in their houses as long as till the very fire touched them, and then running into boats, or clambering from one pair of stairs by the water-side to another. And among other things, the poor pigeons, I perceive, were loth to leave their houses, but hovered about the windows and balconys, till they burned their wings, and fell down. Having staid, and in an hour's time seen the fire rage every way, and nobody, to my sight, endeavouring to quench it, but to remove their goods, and leave all to the fire, and having seen it get as far as the Steele-yard, and the wind mighty high, and driving it into the City: and every thing after so long a drought proving combustible, even the very stones of churches, and among other things, the poor steeple[54] by which pretty Mrs — lives, and whereof my old schoolfellow Elborough is parson, taken fire in the very top, and there burned till it fell down; I to White Hall (with a gentleman with me, who desired to go off from the Tower, to see the fire, in my boat): and there up to the King's closet in the Chapel, where people come about me, and I did give them an account dismayed them all, and word was carried in to the King. So I was called for, and did tell the King and Duke of York what I saw, and that unless his Majesty did command houses to be pulled down, nothing could stop the fire. They seemed much troubled, and the King commanded me to go to

53 His name was Faryner.
54 St Lawrence Poultney, of which Thomas Elborough was Curate.

my Lord Mayor[55] from him, and command him to spare no houses, but to pull down before the fire every way. The Duke of York bid me tell him, that if he would have any more soldiers, he shall: and so did my Lord Arlington afterwards, as a great secret. Here meeting with Captain Cocke, I in his coach, which he lent me, and Creed with me to Paul's, and there walked along Watling-street, as well as I could, every creature coming away loaded with goods to save, and here and there sick people carried away in beds. Extraordinary good goods carried in carts and on backs. At last met my Lord Mayor in Canning-street, like a man spent, with a handkercher about his neck. To the King's message, he cried, like a fainting woman, 'Lord! what can I do? I am spent: people will not obey me. I have been pulling down houses; but the fire overtakes us faster than we can do it.' That he needed no more soldiers; and that, for himself, he must go and refresh himself, having been up all night. So he left me, and I him, and walked home; seeing people all almost distracted, and no manner of means used to quench the fire. The houses too so very thick thereabouts, and full of matter for burning, as pitch and tar, in Thames-street; and warehouses of oyle, and wines, and brandy, and other things. Here I saw Mr Isaac Houblon, the handsome man, prettily dressed and dirty at his door at Dowgate, receiving some of his brother's things, whose houses were on fire; and, as he says, have been removed twice already; and he doubts (as it soon proved) that they must be in a little time removed from his house also, which was a sad consideration. And to see the churches all filling with goods by people, who themselves should have been quietly there at this time. By this time it was about twelve o'clock; and so home, and there find my guests, who were Mr Wood and his wife Barbary Shelden, and also Mr Moone; she mighty fine, and her husband for aught I see, a likely man. But Mr Moone's design and mine, which was to look over my closet, and please him with the sight thereof, which he hath long desired, was wholly disappointed; for we were in great trouble and disturbance at this fire, not knowing what to think of it. However, we had an extraordinary good dinner, and as merry as at this time we could be. While at dinner Mrs Batelier come to enquire after Mr Woolfe and Stanes, (who it seems are related to them,) whose houses in Fish-street are all burned, and they in a sad

55 Sir Thomas Bludworth.

condition. She would not stay in the fright. Soon as dined, I and Moone away, and walked through the City, the streets full of nothing but people, and horses and carts loaden with goods, ready to run over one another, and removing goods from one burned house to another. They now removing out of Canning-street (which received goods in the morning) into Lumbard-street, and further: and among others I now saw my little goldsmith Stokes receiving some friend's goods, whose house itself was burned the day after. We parted at Paul's; he home, and I to Paul's Wharf, where I had appointed a boat to attend me, and took in Mr Carcasse and his brother, whom I met in the street, and carried them below and above bridge too. And again to see the fire, which was now got further, both below and above, and no likelihood of stopping it. Met with the King and Duke of York in their barge, and with them to Queenhith, and there called Sir Richard Browne to them. Their order was only to pull down houses apace, and so below bridge at the water-side; but little was or could be done, the fire coming upon them so fast. Good hopes there was of stopping it at the Three Cranes above, and at Buttolph's Wharf below bridge, if care be used; but the wind carries it into the City, so as we know not by the water-side what it do there. River full of lighters and boats taking in goods, and good goods swimming in the water, and only I observed that hardly one lighter or boat in three that had the goods of a house in, but there was a pair of Virginalls[56] in it. Having seen as much as I could now, I away to White Hall by appointment, and there walked to St James's Park, and there met my wife and Creed and Wood and his wife, and walked to my boat; and there upon the water again, and to the fire up and down, it still encreasing, and the wind great. So near the fire as we could for smoke; and all over the Thames, with one's faces in the wind, you were almost burned with a shower of fire-drops. This is very true: so as houses were burned by these drops and flakes of fire, three or four, nay, five or six houses, one from another. When we could endure no more upon the water, we to a little alehouse on the Bankside, over against the Three Cranes, and there staid till it was dark almost, and saw the fire grow, and as it grew darker, appeared more and more, and in corners and upon steeples, and between

56 A sort of spinet.

churches and houses, as far as we could see up the hill of the City, in a most horrid malicious bloody flame, not like the fine flame of an ordinary fire. Barbary and her husband away before us. We staid till, it being darkish, we saw the fire as only one entire arch of fire from this to the other side the bridge, and in a bow up the hill for an arch of above a mile long: it made me weep to see it. The churches, houses, and all on fire, and flaming at once; and a horrid noise the flames made, and the cracking of houses at their ruine. So home with a sad heart, and there find every body discoursing and lamenting the fire; and poor Tom Hater come with some few of his goods saved out of his house, which was burned upon Fish-street Hill. I invited him to lie at my house, and did receive his goods, but was deceived in his lying there, the news coming every moment of the growth of the fire; so as we were forced to begin to pack up our own goods, and prepare for their removal; and did by moonshine (it being brave dry and moonshine and warm weather) carry much of my goods into the garden, and Mr Hater and I did remove my money and iron chests into my cellar, as thinking that the safest place. And got my bags of gold into my office, ready to carry away, and my chief papers of accounts also there, and my tallies into a box by themselves. So great was our fear, as Sir W. Batten hath carts come out of the country to fetch away his goods this night. We did put Mr Hater, poor man, to bed a little; but he got but very little rest, so much noise being in my house, taking down of goods.

3rd. About four o'clock in the morning, my Lady Batten sent me a cart to carry away all my money, and plate, and best things, to Sir W. Rider's at Bednall-greene. Which I did, riding myself in my night-gown, in the cart; and, Lord! to see how the streets and the highways are crowded with people running and riding, and getting of carts at any rate to fetch away things. I find Sir W. Rider tired with being called up all night, and receiving things from several friends. His house full of goods, and much of Sir W. Batten's and Sir W. Pen's. I am eased at my heart to have my treasure so well secured. Then home, and with much ado to find a way, nor any sleep all this night to me nor my poor wife. But then all this day she and I, and all my people labouring to get away the rest of our things, and did get Mr Tooker to get me a lighter to take them in, and we did carry them (myself some) over Tower Hill, which was by this time full of people's goods, bringing their goods thither; and down to the lighter, which lay at the next quay, above the Tower Dock. And here was my neighbour's wife, Mrs —, with her pretty child, and some few of her things, which I did willingly give way to be saved with mine; but there was no passing with any thing through the postern, the crowd was so great. The Duke of York come this day by the office, and spoke to us, and did ride with his guard up and down the City to keep all quiet, (he being now General, and having the care of all). This day, Mercer being not at home, but against her mistress's order gone to her mother's, and my wife going thither to speak with W. Hewer, beat her there, and was angry; and her mother saying that she was not a 'prentice girl, to ask leave every time she goes abroad, my wife with good reason was angry, and when she come home bid her be gone again. And so she went away, which troubled me, but yet less than it would, because of the condition we are in, in fear of coming in a little time to being less able to keep one in her quality. At night lay down a little upon a quilt of W. Hewer's, in the office, all my own things being packed up or gone; and after me my poor wife did the like, we having fed upon the remains of yesterday's dinner, having no fire nor dishes, nor any opportunity of dressing any thing.

4th. Up by break of day, to get away the remainder of my things; which I did by a lighter at the Iron gate: and my hands so full, that it was the afternoon before we could get them all away. Sir W. Pen and I to the Tower-street, and there met the fire burning three or four doors beyond Mr Howell's, whose goods, poor man, his trayes, and dishes, shovells, &c., were flung all along Tower-street in the kennels, and people working therewith from one end to the other; the fire coming on in that narrow street, on both sides, with infinite fury. Sir W. Batten not knowing how to remove his wine, did dig a pit in the garden, and laid it in there; and I took the opportunity of laying all the papers of my office that I could not otherwise dispose of. And in the evening Sir W. Pen and I did dig another, and put our wine in it; and I my parmazan cheese, as well as my wine and some other things. The Duke of York was at the office this day, at Sir W. Pen's, but I happened not to be within. This afternoon, sitting melancholy with Sir W. Pen in our garden, and thinking of the certain burning of this office, without extraordinary means, I did propose for the sending up of all our workmen from the Woolwich and Deptford yards, (none whereof yet appeared,) and to write to Sir W. Coventry to have the Duke of York's permission to pull down houses, rather than lose this office, which would much hinder the King's business. So Sir W. Pen went down this night, in order to the sending them up to-morrow morning; and I wrote to Sir W. Coventry about the business,[57] but received no answer. This night Mrs Turner (who, poor woman, was removing her goods all this day, good goods into the garden, and knows not how to dispose of them), and her husband supped with my wife and me at night, in the office, upon a shoulder of mutton from the cook's, without any napkin, or any thing, in a sad manner, but were merry. Only now and then, walking into the garden, saw how horribly the sky looks, all on a fire in the night, was enough to put us out of our wits; and, indeed, it was extremely dreadful, for it looks just as if it was at us, and the whole heaven on fire. I after supper walked in the dark down to Tower-street, and there saw it all on fire, at the Trinity House on that side, and the Dolphin Tavern on this side, which was very near us; and the fire with extraordinary vehemence. Now begins the practice of blowing up of houses in Tower-street, those next the Tower, which at first did frighten people more than any thing; but it stopped the fire where it was done, it bringing down the houses to the ground in the same places they stood, and then it was easy to quench what little fire was in it, though it kindled nothing almost. W. Hewer this day went to see how his mother did, and comes late home, telling us how he hath been forced to remove her to Islington, her house in Pye-corner being burned; so that the fire is got so far that way, and to the Old

57 A copy of this letter, preserved among the Pepys manuscripts in the author's own hand-writing, is subjoined:

Sir – The fire is now very neere us as well on Tower Street as Fanchurch Street side, and we little hope of our escape but by that remedy, to ye want whereof we doe certainly owe ye loss of ye City, namely, ye pulling down of houses, in ye way of ye fire. This way Sir W. Pen and myself have so far concluded upon ye practising, that he is gone to Woolwich and Deptford to supply himself with men and necessarys in order to the doeing thereof, in case at his returne our condition be not bettered and that he meets with his R. H.s approbation, which I have thus undertaken to learn of you. Pray please to let me have this night (at whatever hour it is) what his R. H.s directions are in this particular. Sir J. Minnes and Sir W. Batten having left us, we cannot add, though we are well assured of their, as well as all ye neighbourhood's concurrence.

Sir W. Coventry,   Yr obedient servant,
Septr 4, 1666.   S. P.

Bayly, and was running down to Fleet-street; and Paul's is burned, and all Cheapside. I wrote to my father this night, but the post-house being burned, the letter could not go.

5th. I lay down in the office again upon W. Hewer's quilt, being mighty weary, and sore in my feet with going till I was hardly able to stand. About two in the morning my wife calls me up, and tells me of new cryes of fire, it being come to Barking Church, which is the bottom of our lane.[58] I up; and finding it so, resolved presently to take her away, and did, and took my gold, which was about £2350. W. Hewer, and Jane, down by Proundy's boat to Woolwich; but Lord! what a sad sight it was by moone-light to see the whole City almost on fire, that you might see it plain at Woolwich, as if you were by it. There, when I come, I find the gates shut, but no guard kept at all; which troubled me, because of discourses now begun, that there is a plot in it, and that the French had done it. I got the gates open, and to Mr Shelden's, where I locked up my gold, and charged my wife and W. Hewer never to leave the room without one of them in it, night or day. So back again, by the way seeing my goods well in the lighters at Deptford, and watched well by people. Home, and whereas I expected to have seen our house on fire, it being now about seven o'clock, it was not. But to the fire, and there find greater hopes than I expected; for my confidence of finding our office on fire was such, that I durst not ask any body how it was with us, till I come and saw it was not burned. But going to the fire, I find by the blowing up of houses, and the great help given by the workmen out of the King's yards, sent up by Sir W. Pen, there is a good stop given to it, as well at Marke-lane end, as ours; it having only burned the dyall of Barking Church, and part of the porch, and was there quenched. I up to the top of Barking steeple, and there saw the saddest sight of desolation that I ever saw; every where great fires, oyle-cellars, and brimstone, and other things burning. I became afraid to stay there long, and therefore down again as fast as I could, the fire being spread as far as I could see it; and to Sir W. Pen's, and there eat a piece of cold meat, having eaten[59] nothing since Sunday, but the remains of Sunday's dinner. Here I met with Mr Young and Whistler; and having removed all my things, and received good hopes that the fire at our

58 Sethinge Lane.
59 He forgot the shoulder of mutton from the cook's the day before.

end is stopped, they and I walked into the town, and find Fanchurch-street, Gracious-street, and Lumbard-street all in dust. The Exchange a sad sight, nothing standing there, of all the statues or pillars, but Sir Thomas Gresham's picture in the corner. Into Moorefields, (our feet ready to burn, walking through the town among the hot coles,) and find that full of people, and poor wretches carrying their goods there, and every body keeping his goods together by themselves; (and a great blessing it is to them that it is fair weather for them to keep abroad night and day;) drunk there, and paid twopence for a plain penny loaf. Thence homeward, having passed through Cheapside, and Newgate market, all burned; and seen Anthony Joyce's house in fire. And took up (which I keep by me) a piece of glass of Mercer's chapel in the street, where much more was, so melted and buckled with the heat of the fire like parchment. I also did see a poor cat taken out of a hole in a chimney, joyning to the wall of the Exchange, with the hair all burned off the body, and yet alive. So home at night, and find there good hopes of saving our office; but great endeavours of watching all night, and having men ready; and so we lodged them in the office, and had drink and bread and cheese for them. And I lay down and slept a good night about midnight: though when I rose, I heard that there had been a great alarme of French and Dutch being risen, which proved nothing. But it is a strange thing to see how long this time did look since Sunday, having been always full of variety of actions, and little sleep, that it looked like a week or more, and I had forgot almost the day of the week.

6th. Up about five o'clock; and met Mr Gauden at the gate of the office, (I intending to go out, as I used, every now and then to-day, to see how the fire is,) to call our men to Bishop's-gate, where no fire had yet been near, and there is now one broke out: which did give great grounds to people, and to me too, to think that there is some kind of plot in this, (on which many by this time have been taken, and it hath been dangerous for any stranger to walk in the streets,) but I went with the men, and we did put it out in a little time; so that that was well again. It was pretty to see how hard the women did work in the cannells, sweeping of water; but then they would scold for drink, and be as drunk as devils. I saw good butts of sugar broke open in the street, and people give and take handsfull out, and put into beer, and drink it. And now all being pretty well, I took boat, and over to

Southwarke, and took boat on the other side the bridge, and so to Westminster, thinking to shift myself, being all in dirt from top to bottom; but could not there find any place to buy a shirt or a pair of gloves, Westminster Hall being full of people's goods, those in Westminster having removed all their goods, and the Exchequer money put into vessels to carry to Nonsuch;[60] but to the Swan, and there was trimmed: and then to White Hall, but saw nobody; and so home. A sad sight to see how the River looks: no houses nor church near it, to the Temple, where it stopped. At home, did go with Sir W. Batten, and our neighbour, Knightly, (who, with one more, was the only man of any fashion left in all the neighbourhood thereabouts, they all removing their goods, and leaving their houses to the mercy of the fire,) to Sir R. Ford's, and there dined in an earthen platter – a fried breast of mutton; a great many of us, but very merry, and indeed as good a meal, though as ugly a one, as ever I had in my life. Thence down to Deptford, and there with great satisfaction landed all my goods at Sir G. Carteret's safe, and nothing missed I could see or hear. This being done to my great content, I home, and to Sir W. Batten's, and there with Sir R. Ford, Mr Knightly, and one Withers, a professed lying rogue, supped well, and mighty merry, and our fears over. From them to the office, and there slept with the office full of labourers, who talked, and slept, and walked all night long there. But strange it is to see Clothworkers' Hall on fire these three days and nights in one body of flame, it being the cellar full of oyle.

7th. Up by five o'clock; and, blessed be God! find all well; and by water to Pane's Wharfe. Walked thence, and saw all the towne burned, and a miserable sight of Paul's church, with all the roofs fallen, and the body of the quire fallen into St Fayth's; Paul's school also, Ludgate, and Fleet-street. My father's house, and the church, and a good part of the Temple the like. So to Creed's lodging, near the New Exchange, and there find him laid down upon a bed; the house all unfurnished, there being fears of the fire's coming to them. There borrowed a shirt of him, and washed. To Sir W. Coventry, at St James's, who lay without curtains, having removed all his goods; as the King at White Hall, and every body had done, and was doing. He hopes we shall have no public distractions upon this fire, which is

60 Nonsuch House near Epsom, where the Exchequer had formerly been kept.

what every body fears, because of the talk of the French having a hand in it. And it is a proper time for discontents; but all men's minds are full of care to protect themselves, and save their goods: the militia is in arms every where. Our fleetes, he tells me, have been in sight one of another, and most unhappily by fowle weather were parted, to our great loss, as in reason they do conclude; the Dutch being come out only to make a shew, and please their people; but in very bad condition as to stores, victuals, and men. They are at Boulogne, and our fleet come to St Ellen's. We have got nothing, but have lost one ship, but he knows not what. Thence to the Swan, and there drank; and so home, and find all well. My Lord Brouncker, at Sir W. Batten's, tells us the Generall is sent for up, to come to advise with the King about business at this juncture, and to keep all quiet; which is great honour to him, but I am sure is but a piece of dissimulation. So home, and did give orders for my house to be made clean; and then down to Woolwich, and there find all well. Dined, and Mrs Markham come to see my wife. This day our Merchants first met at Gresham College, which, by proclamation, is to be their Exchange. Strange to hear what is bid for houses all up and down here; a friend of Sir W. Rider's having £150 for what he used to let for £40 per annum. Much dispute where the Custome-house shall be; thereby the growth of the City again to be foreseen. My Lord Treasurer, they say, and others, would have it at the other end of the town. I home late to Sir W. Pen's, who did give me a bed; but without curtains or hangings, all being down. So here I went the first time into a naked bed, only my drawers on; and did sleep pretty well: but still both sleeping and waking had a fear of fire in my heart, that I took little rest. People do all the world over cry out of the simplicity of my Lord Mayor in generall; and more particularly in this business of the fire, laying it all upon him. A proclamation is come out for markets to be kept at Leadenhall and Mile-end-greene, and several other places about the town; and Tower-hill, and all churches to be set open to receive poor people.

8th. I stopped with Sir G. Carteret to desire him to go with us, and to enquire after money. But the first he cannot do, and the other as little, or says, 'when we can get any, or what shall we do for it?' He, it seems, is employed in the correspondence between the City and the King every day, in settling of things. I find him full of trouble, to think how things will go. I left him, and to St James's, where we met first at Sir W. Coventry's chamber, and there did what business we could, without any books. Our discourse, as every thing else, was confused. The fleet is at Portsmouth, there staying a wind to carry them to the Downes, or towards Boulogne, where they say the Dutch fleet is gone, and stays. We concluded upon private meetings for a while, not having any money to satisfy any people that may come to us. I bought two eeles upon the Thames, cost me six shillings. Thence with Sir W. Batten to the Cock-pit, whither the Duke of Albemarle is come. It seems the King holds him so necessary at this time, that he hath sent for him, and will keep him here. Indeed his interest in the City, being acquainted, and his care in keeping things quiet, is reckoned that wherein he will be very serviceable. We to him: he is courted in appearance by every body. He very kind to us; and I perceive he lays by all business of the fleet at present, and minds the City, and is now hastening to Gresham College, to discourse with the Aldermen. Sir W. Batten and I home, (where met by my brother John, come to town to see how things are done with us,) and then presently he with me to Gresham College; where infinity of people, partly through novelty to see the new place, and partly to find out and hear what has become one man of another. I met with many people undone, and more that have extraordinary great losses. People speaking their thoughts variously about the beginning of the fire, and the rebuilding of the City. Then to Sir W. Batten's and took my brother with me, and there dined with a great company of neighbours, and much good discourse; among others, of the low spirits of some rich men in the City, in sparing any encouragement to the poor people that wrought for the saving their houses. Among others, Alderman Starling, a very rich man, without children, the fire at next door to him in our lane, after our men had saved his house, did give 2s. 6d. among thirty of them, and did quarrel with some that would remove the rubbish out of the way of the fire, saying that they come to steal. Sir W. Coventry told me of another this morning in Holborne, which he showed the King; that when it was offered to stop the fire near his house for such a reward that come but to 2s. 6d. a man among the neighbours he would give but 18d. Thence to Bednall Green by coach, my brother with me, and saw all well there, and fetched away my journall-book to enter for five days past. I was much frighted and kept awake in my bed, by some noise I heard a great while below stairs; and the boys not coming up to me when I knocked. It was by their discovery of some people stealing of some neighbours' wine that lay in vessels in the streets. So to sleep; and all well all night.

9th. Sunday. Up; and was trimmed, and sent my brother to Woolwich to my wife, to dine with her. I to church, where our parson made a melancholy but good sermon; and many and most in the church cried, specially the women. The church mighty full; but few of fashion, and most strangers. To church again, and there preached Dean Harding;[61] but, methinks, a bad, poor sermon, though proper for the time; nor eloquent, in saying at this time that the City is reduced from a large folio to a decimo-tertio. So to my office, there to write down my journall, and take leave of my brother, whom I send back this afternoon, though rainy: which it hath not done a good while before. To Sir W. Pen's to bed, and made my boy Tom to read me asleep.

10th. All the morning clearing our cellars, and breaking in pieces all my old lumber, to make room, and to prevent fire. And then to Sir W. Batten's, and dined; and there hear that Sir W. Rider says that the town is full of the report of the wealth that is in his house, and would be glad that his friends would provide for the safety of their goods there. This made me get a cart; and thither, and there brought my money all away. Took a hackney-coach myself, (the hackney-coaches now standing at Allgate). Much wealth indeed there is at his house. Blessed be God, I got all mine well thence, and lodged it in my office; but vexed to have all the world see it. And with Sir W. Batten, who would have taken away my hands before they were stowed. But by and by comes brother Balty from sea, which I was glad of; and so got him, and Mr Tooker, and the boy, to watch with them all in the office all night, while I went down to my wife.

11th. In the evening at Sir W. Pen's at supper: he in a mad, ridiculous, drunken humour; and it seems there have been some late distances between his lady and him, as my wife tells me. After supper, I home, and with Mr Hater, Gibson,[62] and Tom alone, got all my chests and money into the further cellar with much pains, but great content to me when done. So very late and weary to bed.

61 Probably Nathaniel Hardy, Dean of Rochester.
62 Probably Clerk of the Cheque at Deptford in 1688.

12th. Up, and with Sir W. Batten and Sir W. Pen to St James's by water, and there did our usual business with the Duke of York.

13th. Up, and down to Tower Wharfe; and there, with Balty and labourers from Deptford, did get my goods housed well at home. So down to Deptford again to fetch the rest, and there eat a bit of dinner at the Globe, with the master of the *Bezan* with me, while the labourers went to dinner. Here I hear that this poor town do bury still of the plague seven or eight in a day. So to Sir G. Carteret's to work, and there did to my content ship off in the *Bezan* all the rest of my goods, saving my pictures and fine things, that I will bring home in wherrys when the house is fit to receive them; and so home, and unload them by carts and hands before night, to my exceeding satisfaction; and so after supper to bed in my house, the first time I have lain there.

14th. Up, and to work, having carpenters come to help in setting up bedsteads and hangings; and at that trade my people and I all the morning, till pressed by publick business to leave them against my will in the afternoon: and yet I was troubled in being at home, to see all my goods lie up and down the house in a bad condition, and strange workmen going to and fro might take what they would almost. All the afternoon busy; and Sir W. Coventry come to me, and found me, as God would have it, in my office, and people about me setting my papers to rights; and there discoursed about getting an account ready against the Parliament, and thereby did create me infinity of business, and to be done on a sudden; which troubled me; but, however, he being gone, I about it late, and to good purpose. And so home, having this day also got my wine out of the ground again, and set it in my cellar; but with great pain to keep the porters that carried it in from observing the money-chests there.

15th. Captain Cocke says he hath computed that the rents of the houses lost this fire in the City comes to £600,000 per annum; that this will make the Parliament more quiet than otherwise they would have been, and give the King a more ready supply; that the supply must be by excise, as it is in Holland; that the Parliament will see it necessary to carry on the war; that the late storm hindered our beating the Dutch fleet, who were gone out only to satisfy the people, having no business to do but to avoid us; that the French, as late in the year as it is, are coming; that the Dutch are really in bad condition, but that this unhappiness of ours do give them heart: that there was a late difference between my Lord Arlington and Sir W. Coventry about neglect in the latter to send away an express of the other's in time; that it come before the King, and the Duke of York concerned himself in it; but this fire hath stopped it. The Dutch fleet is not gone home, but rather to the North, and so dangerous to our Gottenburgh fleet. That the Parliament is likely to fall foul upon some persons; and, among others, on the Vice-chamberlaine,[63] though we both believe with little ground. That certainly never so great a loss as this was borne so well by citizens in the world; he believing that not one merchant upon the 'Change will break upon it. That he do not apprehend there will be any disturbances in State upon it; for that all men are busy in looking after their own business to save themselves. He gone, I to finish my letters, and home to bed; and find to my infinite joy many rooms clean; and myself and wife lie in our own chamber again. But much terrified in the nights now-a-days with dreams of fire, and falling down of houses.

17th. Up betimes, and shaved myself after a week's growth: but, Lord! how ugly I was yesterday and how fine to-day! By water, seeing the City all the way, a sad sight indeed, much fire being still in. Sir W. Coventry was in great pain lest the French fleet should be passed by our fleet, who had notice of them on Saturday, and were preparing to go meet them; but their minds altered, and judged them merchant-men, when the same day the *Success*, Captain Ball, made their whole fleet, and come to Brighthelmstone, and thence at five o'clock afternoon, Saturday, wrote Sir W. Coventry news thereof; so that we do much fear our missing them. Here come in and talked with him Sir Thomas Clifford,[64] who appears a very fine gentleman, and much set by at Court for his activity in going to sea, and stoutness every where, and stirring up and down.

18th. This day the Parliament met, and adjourned till Friday, when the King will be with them.

---

63 Sir G. Carteret.
64 Eldest son of Hugh Clifford, Esq., of Ugbrooke, MP for Totnes, 1661, and knighted for his conduct in the sea-fight 1665. After filling several high offices, he was in 1672 created Baron Clifford of Chudleigh, and constituted High Treasurer; which place he resigned the following year, a few months before his death.

19th. To St James's, and did our usual business before the Duke of York; which signified little, our business being only complaints of lack of money. Here I saw a bastard of the late King of Sweden's come to kiss his hands; a mighty modish French-like gentleman. Thence to White Hall, with Sir W. Batten and W. Pen, to Wilkes's; and there did hear many stories of Sir Henry Wood.[65] About Lord Norwich drawing a tooth at a health. Another time, he and Pinchbacke and Dr Goffe,[66] now a religious man: – Pinchbacke did begin a frolick to drink out of a glass with a toad in it: he did it without harm. Goffe, who knew sacke would kill the toad, called for sack; and when he saw it dead, says he, 'I will have a quick toad, and will not drink from a dead toad.' By that means, no other being to be found, he escaped the health.

20th. The fleet is come into the Downes. Nothing done, nor French fleet seen: we drove all from our anchors. But Sir G. Carteret says news is come that De Ruyter is dead, or very near it, of a hurt in his mouth, upon the discharge of one of his own guns: which put him into a fever, and he likely to die, if not already dead.

21st. The Parliament meet to-day, and the King to be with them. At the office, about our accounts, which now draw near the time they should be ready, the House having ordered Sir G. Carteret, upon his offering them, to bring them in on Saturday next.

23rd. Mr Wayth and I by water to White Hall, and there at Sir G. Carteret's lodgings Sir W. Coventry met, and we did debate the whole business of our accounts to the Parliament; where it appears to us that the charge of the war from September 1, 1664, to this Michaelmas, will have been but £3,200,000, and we have paid in that time somewhat about £2,200,000; so that we owe above £900,000: but our method of accounting, though it cannot, I believe, be far wide from the mark, yet will not abide a strict examination if the Parliament should be troublesome. Here happened a pretty question of Sir W. Coventry, whether this account of ours will not put my Lord Treasurer to a difficulty to tell what is become of all the money the Parliament have given in this time for the war, which hath

---

65 Clerk of the Spicery to Charles I; and, after the Restoration, Clerk to the Board of Green Cloth.
66 Dr Gough, Clerk of the Queen's Closet, and her Assistant Confessor.

amounted to about £4,000,000, which nobody there could answer; but I perceive they did doubt what his answer could be.

24th. Up, and down to look for Sir W. Coventry; and at last found him and Sir G. Carteret with the Lord Treasurer at White Hall, consulting how to make up my Lord Treasurer's general account, as well as that of the Navy particularly.

25th. With all my people to get the letter writ over about the Navy Accounts; and by coach to Lord Brouncker's, and got his hand to it; and then to the Parliament House and got it signed by the rest, and then delivered it at the House-door to Sir Philip Warwicke; Sir G. Carteret being gone into the House with his book of accounts under his arme, to present to the House. All night still mightily troubled in my sleep with fire and houses pulling down.

26th. By coach home, calling at Bennet's, our late mercer, who is come into Covent Garden to a fine house looking down upon the Exchange. And I perceive many Londoners every day come. And Mr Pierce hath let his wife's closet, and the little blind bedchamber, and a garret, to a silk-man for £50 fine, and £30 per annum, and £40 per annum more for dieting the master and two prentices. By Mr Dugdale I hear the great loss of books in St Paul's Church-yard, and at their Hall also, which they value at about £150,000; some booksellers being wholly undone, and among others they say my poor Kirton. And Mr Crumlum,[67] all his books and household was burned; they trusting to St Fayth's, and the roof of the church falling, broke the arch down into the lower church, and so all the goods burned. A very great loss. His father hath lost above £1000 in books; one book newly printed, a Discourse, it seems, of Courts. Here I had the hap to see my Lady Denham: and at night went into the dining-room and saw several fine ladies; among others, Castlemaine, but chiefly Denham again; and the Duke of York taking her aside and talking to her in the sight of all the world, all alone; which was strange, and what also I did not like. Here I met with good Mr Evelyn, who cries out against it, and calls it bickering; for the Duke of York talks a little to her, and then she goes away, and then he follows her again like a dog. He observes that none of the nobility come out of the country at all, to help the King, or comfort him, or prevent

67 Samuel Cromleholme, or Crumlum, Master of St Paul's School.

commotions at this fire; but do as if the King were nobody; nor ne'er a priest comes to give the King and Court good council, or to comfort the poor people that suffer; but all is dead, nothing of good in any of their minds: he bemoans it, and says he fears more ruin hangs over our heads. My wife tells me she hath bought a gown of 15s. per yard; the same, before her face, my Lady Castlemaine this day bought also. Sir W. Pen proposes his and my looking out into Scotland about timber, and to use Pett there; for timber will be a good commodity this time of building the City. Our fleet abroad, and the Dutch too, for all we know. The weather very bad: and under the command of an unlucky man, I fear. God bless him and the fleet under him!

27th. A very furious blowing night all the night; and my mind still mightily perplexed with dreams, and burning the rest of the town; and waking in much pain for the fleet. I to look out Penny, my tailor, to speak for a cloak and cassock for my brother, who is coming to town; and I will have him in a canonical dress, that he may be the fitter to go abroad with me. No news of the fleet yet, but that they went by Dover on the 25th towards the Gun-fleet; but whether the Dutch be yet abroad, or no, we hear not. De Ruyter is not dead, but like to do well. Most think that the gross of the French fleet are gone home again.

28th. Comes the bookbinder to gild the backs of my books. Sir W. Pen broke to me a proposition of his and my joining in a design of fetching timber and deals from Scotland, by the help of Mr Pett upon the place; which, while London is building, will yield good money. I approve it.

29th. Sir W. Coventry and I find to our great joy, that the wages, victuals, wear and tear, cast by the medium of the men, will come to above £3,000,000; and that the extraordinaries, which all the world will allow us, will arise to more than will justify the expence we have declared to have been at since the war; viz. £320,000.

30th (Lord's day). Up, and to church, where I have not been a good while; and there the church infinitely thronged with strangers since the fire come into our parish; but not one handsome face in all of them, as if, indeed, there was a curse, as Bishop Fuller heretofore said, upon our parish. This month ends with my mind full of business and concernment how this office will speed with the Parliament, which begins to be mighty severe in the examining our accounts, and the expence of the Navy this war.

October 1st. All the morning at the office, getting the list of all the ships and vessels employed since the war, for the Committee of Parliament.

2nd. Sir G. Carteret tells me how our lists are referred to a Sub-committee to consider and examine, and that I am ordered to be there. By and by the Committee met, and appointed me to attend them to-morrow at the office to examine our lists.

3rd. The Committee met, and I did make shift to answer them better than I expected. Sir W. Batten, Lord Brouncker, W. Pen, come in, but presently went out; and J. Minnes come in, and said two or three words from the purpose but to do hurt; so away he went also, and left me all the morning with them alone to stand or fall. And it ended with good peace, and much seeming satisfaction; but I find them wise and reserved, and instructed to hit all our blots.

4th. To Sir G. Carteret, and there discoursed much of the want of money, and our being designed for destruction. How the King hath lost his power, by submitting himself to this way of examining his accounts, and is become but as a private man. He says the King is troubled at it, but they talk an entry[68] shall be made; that it is not to be brought into example; that the King must, if they do not agree presently, make them a courageous speech, which he says he may do (the City of London being now burned, and himself master of an army) better than any prince before him.

5th. The Sub-committee have made their report to the Grand Committee, and in pretty kind terms. Captain Cocke told me of a wild motion made in the House of Lords by the Duke of Buckingham, for all men that have cheated the King to be declared traitors and felons; and that my Lord Sandwich was named. Mr Kirton's kinsman, my bookseller, come in my way; and so I am told by him that Mr Kirton is utterly undone, and made 2 or £3000 worse than nothing, from being worth 7 or £8000. That the goods laid in the Churchyard fired through the windows those in St Fayth's

68 In the Journals of the House of Commons.

church; and those coming to the warehouses' doors fired them, and burned all the books and the pillars of the church, so as the roof falling down, broke quite down; which it did not do in the other places of the church, which is alike pillared, (which I knew not before;) but being not burned, they stood still. He do believe there is above £150,000 of books burned; all the great booksellers almost undone: not only these, but their warehouses at their Hall and under Christ-church, and elsewhere, being all burned. A great want thereof there will be of books, specially Latin books and foreign books; and, among others, the Polyglottes and new Bible, which he believes will be presently worth £40 a-piece.

6th. Sir W. Coventry and I discoursed of, among others, our sad condition by want of a Controller; and it was his words, that he believes, besides all the shame and trouble he[69] hath brought on the office, the King had better have given £100,000 than ever have had him there. He did discourse about some of these discontented Parliament-men, and says that Birch is a false rogue, but that Garraway is a man that hath not been well used by the Court, though very stout to death, and hath suffered all that is possible for the King from the beginning. But discontented as he is, yet he never knew a Session of Parliament but that he hath done some good deed for the King before it rose. I told him the passage Cocke told me of – his having begged a brace of bucks of the Lord Arlington for him, and when it come to him, he sent it back again. Sir W. Coventry told me, it is much to be pitied that the King should lose the service of a man so able and faithful; and that he ought to be brought over, but that it is always observed, that by bringing over one discontented man, you raise up three in his room; which is a state lesson I never knew before. But when others discover your fear, and that discontent procures fear, they will be discontented too, and impose on you.

7th. To White Hall, where met by Sir W. Batten and Lord Brouncker, to attend the King and Duke of York at the Cabinet; but nobody had determined what to speak of, but only in general to ask for money. So I was forced immediately to prepare in my mind a method of discoursing. And anon we were called in to the Green

69 Sir John Minnes, who performed the duties inefficiently.

Room, where the King, Duke of York, Prince Rupert, Lord Chancellor, Lord Treasurer, Duke of Albemarle, Sirs G. Carteret, W. Coventry, Morrice. Nobody beginning, I did, and made a current, and I thought a good speech, laying open the ill state of the Navy: by the greatness of the debt; greatness of the work to do against next year; the time and materials it would take; and our incapacity, through a total want of money. I had no sooner done, but Prince Rupert rose up and told the King in a heat, that whatever the gentleman had said, he had brought home his fleet in as good a condition as ever any fleet was brought home; that twenty boats would be as many as the fleet would want: and all the anchors and cables left in the storm, might be taken up again. This arose from my saying, among other things we had to do, that the fleet was come in, – the greatest fleet that ever his Majesty had yet together, and that in as bad condition as the enemy or weather could put it. And to use Sir W. Pen's words, who is upon the place taking a survey, he dreads the reports he is to receive from the Surveyors of its defects. I therefore did only answer, that I was sorry for his Highness's offence, but that what I said was but the report we received from those entrusted in the fleet to inform us. He muttered and repeated what he had said; and so, after a long silence on all hands, nobody, not so much as the Duke of Albemarle, seconding the Prince, nor taking notice of what he said, we withdrew. I was not a little troubled at this passage, and the more when speaking with Jacke Fenn about it, he told me that the Prince will be asking who this Pepys is, and find him to be a creature of my Lord Sandwich's, and therefore this was done only to disparage him. After all this pains, the King hath found out how to supply us with 5 or £6000, when £100,000 were at this time but absolutely necessary, and we mentioned £50,000. I made my brother in his cassocke to say grace this day, but I like his voice so ill, that I begin to be sorry he hath taken orders.

8th. Towards noon, by water to Westminster Hall, and there by several hear that the Parliament do resolve to do something to retrench Sir G. Carteret's great salary; but cannot hear of any thing bad they can lay to his charge. The House did this day order to be engrossed the Bill against importing Irish cattle: a thing, it seems carried on by the Western Parliament-men, wholly against the sense of most of the rest of the House; who think if you do this, you give the Irish again cause to rebel. Mr Pierce says, the Duke of York and Duke of Albemarle do not agree. The Duke of York is wholly given up to this Lady Denham. The Duke of Albemarle and Prince Rupert do less agree. The King hath yesterday in Council declared his resolution of setting a fashion for clothes, which he will never alter. It will be a vest, I know not well how; but it is to teach the nobility thrift, and will do good. By and by comes down from the Committee Sir W. Coventry, and I find him troubled at several things happened this afternoon. Which vexes me also; our business looking worse and worse, and our work growing on our hands. Time spending, and no money to set any thing in hand with; the end thereof must be speedy ruin. The Dutch insult and have taken off Bruant's head, which they had not dared to do (though found guilty of the fault he did die for, of something of the Prince of Orange's faction) till just now, which speaks more confidence in our being worse than before. Alderman Maynell, I hear, is dead. Thence returned in the dark by coach all alone, full of thoughts of the consequences of this ill complexion of affairs, and how to save the little I have, which if I can do, I have cause to bless God that I am so well, and shall be well contented to retreat to Brampton, and spend the rest of my days there. So to my office, and finished my Journal with resolutions, if God bless me, to apply myself soberly to settle all matters for myself, and expect the event of all with comfort.

9th. To the office, where we sat the first day since the fire.

10th. Fast-day for the fire. With Sir W. Batten by water to White Hall, and anon had a meeting before the Duke of York, where pretty to see how Sir W. Batten, that carried the surveys of all the fleet with him to show their ill condition to the Duke of York, when he found the Prince there, did not speak one word, though the meeting was of his asking; for nothing else. And when I asked him, he told me he knew the Prince too well to anger him, so that he was afraid to do it. Thence with him to Westminster, to the parish church, where the Parliament-men; and Stillingfleete in the pulpit. So full, no standing there; so he and I to eat herrings at the Dog Tavern. And then to church again, and there was Mr Frampton in the pulpit, whom they cry up so much, a young man, and of a mighty ready tongue. I heard a little of his sermon. Captain Cocke, who is mighty conversant with Garraway and those people, tells me what they object as to the mal-administration of things as to money. But that they mean well, and will do well; but their reckonings are very good, and show great faults, as I will insert here. They say the King hath had towards this war expressly thus much: –

Royal Ayde	£2,450,000
More	£1,250,000
Three months tax given the King by a power of raising a month's tax of £70,000 every year for three years	£210,000
Customes, out of which the King did promise to pay £240,000 which for two years come to	£480,000
Prizes, which they moderately reckon at	£300,000
A debt declared by the Navy, by us	£900,000
	£5,590,000
The whole charge of the Navy, as we state it for two years and a month, hath been but	£3,200,000
So what is become of all this sum?[70]	£2,390,000

He and I did bemoan our public condition. He tells me the Duke of Albemarle is under a cloud, and they have a mind at Court to lay him aside. This I know not; but all things are not right with him: and I am glad of it, but sorry for the time.

11th. *Memorandum.* I had taken my Journall during the fire and the disorders following in loose papers until this very day, and could not get time to enter them in my book till January 18, in the morning, having made my eyes sore by frequent attempts this winter to do it. But now it is done; for which I thank God, and pray never the like occasion may happen.

12th. The House have cut us off £150,000 of our wear and tear, for

70 The remainder of the receipts.

that which was saved by the King while the fleet lay in harbour in winter. However, he seems pleased, and so am I, that they have abated no more: and do intend to allow of 28,000 men for the next year; and this day have appointed to declare the sum they will give the King, and to propose the way of raising it; so that this is likely to be the great day.

13th. To White Hall, and there the Duke of York (who is gone over to all his pleasures again, and leaves off care of business, what with his woman, my Lady Denham, and his hunting three times a week) was just come in from hunting. So I stood and saw him dress himself, and try on his vest, which is the King's new fashion, and he will be in it for good and all on Monday next, and the whole Court: it is a fashion, the King says, he will never change. He being ready, he and my Lord Chancellor, and Duke of Albemarle, and Prince Rupert, Lord Bellasses, Sir H. Cholmly, Povy, and myself, met at a Committee for Tangier. My Lord Bellasses's propositions were read and discoursed of, about reducing the garrison to less charge; and indeed I am mad in love with my Lord Chancellor, for he do comprehend and speak out well, and with the greatest easiness and authority that ever I saw man in my life. I did never observe how much easier a man do speak when he knows all the company to be below him, than in him; for though he spoke indeed excellent well, yet his manner and freedom of doing it, as if he played with it, and was informing only all the rest of the company, was mighty pretty. He did call again and again upon Mr Povy for his accounts. I did think fit to make the solemn tender of my accounts that I intended. I said something that was liked, touching the want of money, and the bad credit of our tallies. My Lord Chancellor moved that without any trouble to any of the rest of the Lords, I might alone attend the King, when he was with his private Council, and open the state of the garrison's want of credit: and all that could be done, should. Most things moved were referred to Committees, and so we broke up. And at the end Sir W. Coventry come; so I away with him, and he discoursed with me something of the Parliament's business. They have voted giving the King for the next year £1,800,000; which, were it not for his debts, were a great sum.

14th. I met with Sir Stephen Fox, who told me much right I have done myself, and how well it is represented by the Committee to the

House my readiness to give them satisfaction in every thing when they were at the office. I was glad of this. He did further discourse of Sir W. Coventry's great abilities, and how necessary it were that I were of the House to assist him. I did not own it, but do myself think it were not unnecessary, if either he should die, or be removed to the Lords, or any thing happen to hinder his doing the like service the next trial; which makes me think that it were not a thing very unfit; but I will not move in it.

15th. Colvill tells me of the viciousness of the Court; the contempt the King brings himself into thereby; his minding nothing, but doing all things just as his people about him will have it! The Duke of York becoming a slave to this Lady Denham, and wholly minds her. That there really were amours between the Duchesse and Sidny; that there is reason to fear that, as soon as the Parliament have raised this money, the King will see that he hath got all that he can get, and then make up a peace; that Sir W. Coventry is of the caball with the Duke of York, and Brouncker with this Lady Denham: which is a shame, and I am sorry for it, and that Sir W. Coventry do make her visits: but yet I hope it is not so. Pierce tells me, that Lady Castlemaine is concluded to be with child again; and that all the people about the King do make no scruple of saying that the King do intrigue with Mrs Stewart, who, he says, is a most excellent-natured lady. This day the King begins to put on his vest, and I did see several persons of the House of Lords and Commons too, great courtiers, who are in it; being a long cassocke close to the body, of black cloth, and pinked with white silk under it, and a coat over it, and the legs ruffled with black riband like a pigeon's leg: and upon the whole I wish the King may keep it, for it is a very fine and handsome garment. Lady Carteret tells me ladies are to go into a new fashion shortly, and that is, to wear short coats, above their ancles; which she and I do not like; but conclude this long trayne to be mighty graceful. But she cries out of the vices of the Court, and how they are going to set up plays already; and how, the next day after the late great fast, the Duchesse of York did give the King and Queene a play. Nay, she told me that they have heretofore had plays at Court, the very nights before the fast for the death of the late King. She do much cry out upon these things, and that which she believes will undo the whole nation: and I fear so too. This day the great debate was in Parliament, the manner of raising the £1,800,000 they voted the King on Friday: and at last, after many proposals, one moved that the Chimney-money might be taken from the King, and an equal revenue of something else might be found for the King; and people be enjoyned to buy off this tax of Chimney-money for ever at eight years' purchase, which will raise present money, as they think, £1,600,000, and the State be eased of an ill burthen, and the King be supplied of something as good or better for his use. The House seems to like this, and put off the debate to to-morrow.

17th. The Court is all full of vests, only my Lord St Albans not pinked, but plain black; and they say the King says the pinking upon whites makes them look too much like magpyes, and therefore hath bespoke one of plain velvet.

18th. To Lovett's house, where I stood godfather. But it was pretty, that, being a Protestant, a man stood by and was my proxy to answer for me. A priest christened it, and the boy's name is Samuel. The ceremonies many, and some foolish. The priest in a gentleman's dress, more than my own: but is a Capuchin, one of the Queen-mother's priests. He did give my proxy and the woman proxy, (my Lady Bills,[71] absent, had a proxy also,) good advice to bring up the child, and at the end that he ought never to marry the child nor the godmother, nor the godmother the child or the godfather: but, which is strange, they say the mother of the child and the godfather may marry. By and by the Lady Bills come in, a well-bred but crooked woman. The poor people of the house had good wine, and a good cake; and she a pretty woman in her lying-in dress. It cost me near 40s. the whole christening: to midwife 20s., nurse 10s., maid 2s. 6d., and the coach 5s. The business of buying off the Chimney-money is passed in the House; and so the King to be satisfied some other way, and the King supplied with the money raised by this purchasing off of the chimnies.

19th. Nothing but distraction and confusion in the affairs of the Navy; which makes me wish with all my heart, that I were well and quietly settled with what little I have got at Brampton, where I might live peaceably, and study, and pray for the good of the King and my country.

71 Probably the widow of Sir Thomas Pelham, who re-married John Bills, Esq., of Caen Wood, and retained the title derived from her first husband with the name of her second.

20th. Commissioner Middleton[72] says, that the fleet was in such a condition, as to discipline, as if the Devil had commanded it; so much wickedness of all sorts. Enquiring how it came to pass that so many ships had miscarried this year, he tells me that he enquired; and the pilots do say, that they dare not do nor go but as the Captains will have them; and if they offer to do otherwise, the Captains swear they will run them through. He says that he heard Captain Digby (my Lord of Bristoll's son, a young fellow that never was but one year, if that, in the fleet,) say that he did hope he should not see a tarpawlin[73] have the command of a ship within this twelve months. He observed while he was on board the Admirall, when the fleet was at Portsmouth, that there was a faction there. Holmes commanded all on the Prince's side, and Sir Jeremy Smith on the Duke's, and every body that come did apply themselves to one side or other; and when the Duke of Albemarle was gone away to come hither, then Sir Jeremy Smith did hang his head, and walked in the General's ship but like a private commander. He says he was on board the Prince, when the news come of the burning of London; and all the Prince said was, that now Shipton's prophecy was out; and he heard a young commander presently swear, that a citizen's wife that would not take under half a piece before, would be contented with half-a-crowne: and made mighty sport of it. My Lord Chancellor the other day did ask Sir G. Carteret how it come to pass that his friend Pepys do so much magnify the bad condition of the fleet. Sir G. Carteret tells me that he answered him, that I was but the mouth of the rest, and spoke what they have dictated to me; which did, as he says, presently take off his displeasure. They talk that the Queene hath a great mind to alter her fashion, and to have the feet seen; which she loves mightily.

21st. Sir H. Cholmly tells me how Mr Williamson stood in a little place to have come into the House of Commons, and they would not choose him; they said, 'No courtier.' And which is worse, Bab May went down in great state to Winchelsea with the Duke of York's letters, not doubting to be chosen; and there the people chose a private gentleman in spite of him, and cried out they would have no Court pimp to be their burgesse; which are things that bode very ill.

72 Thomas Middleton, made a Commissioner of the Navy, 1664.
73 Tarpawlin, a sailor.

24th. Holmes did last Sunday deliver in his articles to the King and Cabinet against Smith, and Smith hath given in his answer, and lays his not accompanying the fleet to his pilot, who would not undertake to carry the ship further; which the pilot acknowledges. The thing is not accommodated, but only taken up, and both sides commanded to be quiet, but no peace like to be. The Duke of Albemarle is Smith's friend, and hath publickly sworn that he would never go to sea again, unless Holmes's commission were taken from him. I find by Hayes[74] that they did expect great glory in coming home in so good condition as they did with the fleet; and therefore I the less wonder that the Prince was distasted with my discourse the other day about the sad state of the fleet. But it pleases me to hear that he did expect great thanks, and lays the fault of the want of it upon the fire, which deadened every thing, and the glory of his services.

25th. To Mrs Pierce's, where she was making herself mighty fine to go to a great ball to-night at Court, being the Queene's birth-day; so the ladies for this one day wear laces, but are to put them off again to-morrow. To Mrs Williams's, where we met Knipp. I was glad to see the jade. Made her sing; and she told us they begin at both houses to act on Monday next. But I fear after all this sorrow, their gains will be but little. Mrs Williams says, the Duke's house will now be much the better of the two, because of their women; which I was glad to hear.

27th. The two Houses begin to be troublesome: the Lords to have quarrels one with another. My Lord Duke of Buckingham having said to the Lord Chancellor (who is against the passing of the Bill for prohibiting the bringing over of Irish cattle,) that whoever was against the Bill, was there led to it by an Irish interest, or an Irish understanding, which is as much as to say he is a fool; this bred heat from my Lord Chancellor, and something he said did offend my Lord of Ossory (my Lord Duke of Ormond's son,) and they two had hard words, upon which the latter sends a challenge to the former; of which the former complains to the House, and so the business is to be heard on Monday next. Then as to the Commons; some ugly knives, like poignards, to stab people with, about two or three hundred of them were brought in yesterday to the House, found in one of the house's rubbish that was burned, and said to be the house of a

74 Prince Rupert's secretary.

Catholique. This and several letters out of the country, saying how high the Catholiques are every where and bold in the owning their religion, hath made the Commons mad, and they presently voted that the King be desired to put all Catholiques out of employment, and other high things; while the business of money hangs in the hedge.

28th. Captain Guy to dine with me, and he and I much talk together. He cries out of the discipline of the fleet, and confesses really that the true English valour we talk of, is almost spent and worn out; few of the commanders doing what they should do, and he much fears we shall therefore be beaten the next year. He assures me we were beaten home the last June fight, and that the whole fleet was ashamed to hear of our bonfires. He commends Smith and cries out of Holmes for an idle, proud, conceited, though stout fellow. He tells me we are to owe the loss of so many ships on the sands, not to any fault of the pilots, but to the weather; but in this I have good authority to fear there was something more. He says the Dutch do fight in very good order, and we in none at all. He says that in the July fight, both the Prince and Holmes had their belly-fulls, and were fain to go aside; though, if the wind had continued, we had utterly beaten them. He do confess the whole to be governed by a company of fools, and fears our ruine. The *Revenge* having her forecastle blown up with powder to the killing of some men in the River, and the *Dyamond*'s being overset in the careening at Sheernese, are further marks of the method all the King's work is now done in. The *Foresight* also and another come to disasters in the same place this week in the cleaning; which is strange.

29th. Up, and to the office to do business, and thither comes to me Sir Thomas Teddiman, and he and I walked a good while in the garden together, discoursing of the disorder and discipline of the fleet, wherein he told me how bad every thing is; but was very wary in speaking any to the dishonour of the Prince or Duke of Albemarle, but do magnify my Lord Sandwich much before them both, from ability to serve the King, and do heartily wish for him here. For he fears that we shall be undone the next year, but that he will, however, see an end of it. To Westminster; and I find the new Lord Mayor Bolton a-swearing at the Exchequer, with some of the Aldermen and Livery; but Lord! to see how meanely they now look, who upon this day used to be all little lords, is a sad sight and worthy consideration.

And every body did reflect with pity upon the poor City, to which they are now coming to choose and swear their Lord Mayor, compared with what it heretofore was. To my goldsmith to bid him look out for some gold for me; and he tells me that ginnys, which I bought 2000 of not long ago, and cost me but 18½d. change, will now cost me 22d.; and but very few to be had at any price. However, some more I will have, for they are very convenient, and of easy disposal. To White Hall, and into the new playhouse there, the first time I ever was there, and the first play I have seen since before the great plague. By and by Mr Pierce comes, bringing my wife and his, and Knipp. By and by the King and Queen, Duke and Duchesse, and all the great ladies of the Court; which, indeed, was a fine sight. But the play, being Love in a Tub,[75] a silly play, and though done by the Duke's people, yet having neither Beterton nor his wife,[76] and the whole thing done ill, and being ill also, I had no manner of pleasure in the play. Besides, the House, though very fine, yet bad for the voice, for hearing. The sight of the ladies, indeed, was exceeding noble; and above all, my Lady Castlemaine. The play done by ten o'clock.

November 2nd. On board the Ruby, French prize, the only ship of war we have taken from any of our enemies this year. It seems a very good ship, but with galleries quite round the sterne to walk in as a balcone, which will be taken down.

4th. My taylor's man brings my vest home, and coat to wear with it and belt, and silver-hilted sword. I waited in the gallery till the Council was up, and did speak with Mr Cooling, my Lord Chamberlain's secretary, who tells me my Lord Generall is become mighty low in all people's opinion, and that he hath received several slurs from the King and Duke of York. The people at Court do see the difference between his and the Prince's management, and my Lord Sandwich's. That this business which he is put upon of crying out against the Catholiques and turning them out of all employment, will undo him, when he comes to turn the officers out of the Army, and this is a thing of his own seeking. That he is grown a drunken sot, and drinks with nobody but Troutbecke, whom nobody else will keep company with. Of whom he told me this story; that once the

75 A comedy, by Sir George Etheridge.
76 See note to February 1, 1663/64.

Duke of Albemarle in his drink taking notice as of a wonder that Nan Hide should ever come to be Duchesse of York: 'Nay,' says Troutbecke, 'ne'er wonder at that; for if you will give me another bottle of wine, I will tell you as great, if not greater, a miracle.' And what was that, but that our dirty Besse (meaning his Duchesse) should come to be Duchesse of Albemarle?

5th. To my Lady Peterborough, who had sent to speak with me. She makes mighty mourn of the badness of the times, and her family as to money. My Lord's passionateness for want thereof, and his want of coming in of rents, and no wages from the Duke of York. No money to be had there for wages or disbursements, and therefore prays my assistance about his pension. To my Lord Crewe's, and there dined, and mightily made of. Here my Lord, and Sir Thomas Crewe, Mr John, and Dr Crewe,[77] and two strangers. The best family in the world for goodness and sobriety. Here beyond my expectation I met my Lord Hinchingbroke, who is come to town two days since from Hinchingbroke, and brought his sister and brother Carteret with him, who are at Sir G. Carteret's. After dinner I and Sir Thomas Crewe went aside to discourse of public matters, and do find by him that all the country gentlemen are publickly jealous of the courtiers in the Parliament, and that they do doubt every thing that they propose; and that the true reason why the country-gentlemen are for a land-tax and against a general excise, is, because they are fearful that if the latter be granted, they shall never get it down again; whereas the land-tax will be but for so much, and when the war ceases, there will be no ground got by the Court to keep it up. He says the House would be very glad to get something against Sir G. Carteret, and will not let their inquiries die till they have got something. He do, from what he hath heard at the Committee for examining the burning of the City, conclude it as a thing certain, that it was done by plots; it being proved by many witnesses that endeavours were made in several places to encrease the fire, and that both in City and country it was bragged by several Papists, that upon such a day or in such a time we should find the hottest weather that ever was in England; and words of plainer sense. But my Lord Crewe was discoursing at table how the Judges have determined in the case whether the landlords or

77 Nathaniel, afterwards Bishop of Durham and Baron Crewe.

the tenants (who are, in their leases, all of them generally tied to maintain and uphold their houses,) shall bear the loss of the fire; and they say, that tenants should against all casualties of fire beginning either in their own, or in their neighbour's; but, where it is done by an enemy, they are not to do it. And this was by an enemy, there having been one convicted and hanged upon this very score. This is an excellent salvo for the tenants, and for which I am glad, because of my father's house. After dinner and this discourse, I took coach, and at the same time find my Lord Hinchingbroke and Mr John Crewe and the Doctor going out to see the ruins of the City; so I took the Doctor into my hackney-coach, (and he is a very fine sober gentleman,) and so through the City. But Lord! what pretty and sober observations he made of the City and its desolation; till anon we come to my house, and there I took them upon Tower-Hill to show them what houses were pulled down there since the fire; and then to my house, where I treated them with good wine of several sorts, and they took it mighty respectfully, and a fine company of gentlemen they are; but above all I was glad to see my Lord Hinchingbroke drink no wine at all. I home by coach, but met not one bonfire through the whole town in going round by the wall, which is strange, and speaks the melancholy disposition of the City at present, while never more was said of, and feared of, and done against the Papists, than just at this time.

7th. Called at Faythorne's to buy some prints for my wife to draw by this winter, and here did see my Lady Castlemaine's picture, done by him from Lilly's, in red chalke, and other colours, by which he hath cut it in copper to be printed. The picture in chalke is the finest thing I ever saw in my life, I think; and I did desire to buy it; but he says he must keep it awhile to correct his copper-plate by, and when that is done he will sell it me. By the Duke of York his discourse to-day in his chamber, they have it at Court, as well as we here, that a fatal day is to be expected shortly, of some great mischief; whether by the Papists, or what, they are not certain. But the day is disputed; some say next Friday, others a day sooner, others later, and I hope all will prove a foolery. But it is observable how every body's fears are busy at this time.

8th. I to Westminster Hall, and there met Mr Grey, who tells me the House is sitting still, (and now it was six o'clock,) and likely to sit till midnight; and have proceeded fair to give the King his supply presently. And herein have done more to-day than was hoped for. Sir W. Coventry did this night tell me how the business is about Sir J. Minnes; that he is to be a commissioner, and my Lord Brouncker and Sir W. Pen are to be Controller jointly, which I am very glad of, and better than if they were either of them alone; and do hope truly that the King's business will be better done thereby, and infinitely better than now it is. Mr Grey did assure me this night, that he was told this day, by one of the greater Ministers of State in England, and one of the King's Cabinet, that we had little left to agree on between the Dutch and us towards a peace, but only the place of treaty; which do astonish me to hear, but I am glad of it, for I fear the consequence of the war. But he says that the King, having all the money he is like to have, we shall be sure of a peace in a little time.

9th. To Mrs Pierce's by appointment, where we find good company: a fair lady, my Lady Prettyman, Mrs Corbet, Knipp; and for men, Captain Downing, Mr Lloyd, Sir W. Coventry's clerk, and one Mr Tripp, who dances well. After our first bout of dancing, Knipp and I to sing, and Mercer and Captain Downing (who loves and understands musick) would by all means have my song of 'Beauty retire': which Knipp had spread abroad, and he extols it above any thing he ever heard. Going to dance again, and then comes news that White Hall was on fire. And presently more particulars, that the Horse-guard was on fire. And so we run up to the garret, and find it so; a horrid great fire. And by and by we saw and heard part of it blown up with powder. The ladies begun presently to be afraid: one fell into fits. The whole town in an alarm. Drums beat and trumpets, and the Horse-guards every where spread, running up and down in the street. And I begun to have mighty apprehensions how things might be, for we are in expectation (from common fame) this night or to-morrow to have a massacre, by the having so many fires one after another, as that in the City, and at same time begun in Westminster, by the Palace, but put out; and since in Southwarke, to the burning down some houses. And now this do make all people conclude there is something extraordinary in it; but nobody knows what. By and by comes news that the fire is slackened; so then we were a little cheered up again, and to supper, and pretty merry. But above all there comes in the dumb boy that I knew in Oliver's time, who is mightily acquainted here, and with Downing. And he made strange signs of the fire, and how the King was abroad, and many things they understood, but I could not. Which I wondered at, and discoursing with Downing about it, 'Why,' says he, 'it is only a little use, and you will understand him, and make him understand you with as much ease as may be.' So I prayed him to tell him that I was afraid that my coach would be gone, and that he should go down and steal one of the seats out of the coach and keep it, and that would make the coachman to stay. He did this, so that the dumb boy did go down, and like a cunning rogue went into the coach, pretending to sleep, and by and by fell to his work, but finds the seats nailed to the coach. So he could not do it; however, stayed there, and stayed the coach, till the coachman's patience was quite spent, and beat the dumb boy by force, and so went away. So the dumb boy came up and told him all the story, which they below did see all that passed, and knew it to be true. After supper another dance or two, and then news that the fire is as great as ever, which put us all to our wits'-end; and I mightily anxious to go home, but the coach being gone, and it being about ten at night, and rainy dirty weather, I knew not what to do; but to walk out with Mr Batelier, myself resolving to go home on foot, and leave the women there. And so did; but at the Savoy got a coach, and come back and took up the women, and so (having, by people come from the fire, understood that the fire was overcome, and all well,) we merrily parted, and home. Stopped by several guards and constables quite through the town, (round the wall as we went,) all being in arms.

10th. The Parliament did fall foul of our accounts again yesterday; and we must arme to have them examined, which I am sorry for: it will bring great trouble to me, and shame upon the office. This is the fatal day that every body hath discoursed for a long time to be the day that the Papists, or I know not who, have designed to commit a massacre upon; but, however, I trust in God we shall rise to-morrow morning as well as ever. I hear that my Lady Denham is exceeding sick, even to death, and that she says, and every body else discourses, that she is poisoned; and Creed tells me, that it is said that there hath been a design to poison the King. What the meaning of all these sad signs is the Lord only knows, but every day things look worse and worse. God fit us for the worst!

12th. Creed tells me of my Lady Denham, whom every body says is poisoned, and she hath said it to the Duke of York; but is upon the mending hand, though the town says she is dead this morning. This day I received 450 pieces of gold more of Mr Stokes, but cost me 22½d. change. But I am well contented with it, I having now nearly £2800 in gold, and will not rest till I get full £3000. Creed and I did stop (the Duke of York being just going away from seeing of it) at Paul's, and in the Convocation-House-Yard did there see the body of Robert Braybrooke, Bishop of London, that died 1404. He fell down in the tomb out of the great church into St Fayth's this late fire, and is here seen his skeleton with the flesh on; but all tough and dry like a spongy dry leather, or touchwood all upon his bones. His head turned aside. A great man in his time, and Lord Chancellor. And now exposed to be handled and derided by some, though admired for its duration by others. Many flocking to see it.

14th. Knipp tells me how Smith, of the Duke's house, hath killed a man upon a quarrel in play; which makes every body sorry, he being a good actor, and they say a good man, however this happens. The ladies of the Court do much bemoan him. Sir G. Carteret tells me that just now my Lord Hollis had been with him, and wept to think in what a condition we are fallen. Dr Croone[78] told me, that at the meeting at Gresham College to-night (which it seems, they now have every Wednesday again,) there was a pretty experiment of the blood of one dog let out (till he died) into the body of another on one side, while all his own run out on the other side. The first died upon the place, and the other very well, and likely to do well. This did give occasion to many pretty wishes, as of the blood of a Quaker to be let into an Archbishop, and such like; but, as Dr Croone says, may, if it takes, be of mighty use to man's health, for the amending of bad blood by borrowing from a better body.

15th. To Mrs Pierce's, where I find her as fine as possible, and Mr Pierce going to the ball at night at Court, it being the Queene's birth-day. I also to the ball, and with much ado got up to the loft, where with much trouble I could see very well. Anon the house grew full, and the candles light, and the King and Queene and all the

78 William Croune, of Emmanuel College, Cambridge, chosen Rhetoric Professor at Gresham College 1659, FRS and MD. Died 1684.

ladies sat: and it was, indeed, a glorious sight to see Mrs Stewart in black and white lace, and her head and shoulders dressed with diamonds, and the like many great ladies more (only the Queene none;) and the King in his rich vest of some rich silk and silver trimming, as the Duke of York and all the dancers were, some of cloth of silver, and others of other sorts, exceeding rich. Presently after the King was come in, he took the Queene, and about fourteen more couple there was, and begun the Bransles. As many of the men as I can remember presently, were, the King, Duke of York, Prince Rupert, Duke of Monmouth, Duke of Buckingham, Lord Douglas, Mr Hamilton, Colonell Russell, Mr Griffith, Lord Ossory, Lord Rochester; and of the ladies, the Queene, Duchesse of York, Mrs Stewart, Duchesse of Monmouth, Lady Essex Howard,[79] Mrs Temple, Swedes Embassadresse, Lady Arlington,[80] Lord George Barkeley's daughter, and many others I remember not; but all most excellently dressed in rich petticoats and gowns, and dyamonds and pearls. After the Bransles, then to a Corant, and now and then a French dance; but that so rare that the Corants grew tiresome, that I wished it done. Only Mrs Stewart danced mighty finely, and many French dances, specially one the King called the New Dance, which was very pretty. But upon the whole matter, the business of the dancing of itself was not extraordinary pleasing. But the clothes and sight of the persons were indeed very pleasing, and worth my coming, being never likely to see more gallantry while I live, if I should come twenty times. Above twelve at night it broke up. My Lady Castlemaine (without whom all is nothing) being there very rich, though not dancing.

16th. This noon I met with Mr Hooke, and he tells me the dog which was filled with another dog's blood, at the College the other day, is very well, and like to be so as ever, and doubts not its being found of great use to men; and so do Dr Whistler, who dined with us at the tavern.

---

79 Only daughter of James third Earl of Suffolk, by his first wife Susan, daughter of Henry Rich Earl of Holland; afterwards married to Edward Lord Griffin of Braybrooke. There is a portrait of her at Audley End, by Lely.

80 Isabella of Nassau, daughter of Lord Beverweert, natural son of Prince Maurice. She was sister to the Countess of Ossory, and mother of the first Duchess of Grafton.

19th. To Barkeshire-house,[81] where my Lord Chancellor hath been ever since the fire. Sir Thomas Crewe told me how hot words grew again to-day in the House of Lords between my Lord Ossory and Ashly, the former saying that something said by the other was said like one of Oliver's Council. Ashly said he must give him reparation, or he would take it his own way. The House therefore did bring my Lord Ossory to confess his fault, and ask pardon for it, as he did also to my Lord Buckingham, for saying that something was not truth that my Lord Buckingham had said.

20th. To church, it being thanksgiving-day for the cessation of the plague; but, Lord! how the town do say that it is hastened before the plague is quite over, there being some people still ill of it, but only to get ground of plays to be publickly acted, which the Bishops would not suffer till the plague was over; and one would think so, by the suddenness of the notice given of the day, which was last Sunday, and the little ceremony. By coach to Barkeshire-house, and there did get a very great meeting; the Duke of York being there, and much business done, through not in proportion to the greatness of the business, and my Lord Chancellor sleeping and snoring the greater part of the time.

21st. I to wait on Sir Philip Howard, whom I find dressing himself in his night-gown and turban like a Turke, but one of the finest persons that ever I saw in my life. He had several gentlemen of his own waiting on him, and one playing finely on the gittar. He discourses as well as ever I heard a man, in few words and handsome. He expressed all kindness to Balty, when I told him how sicke he is. He says that before he comes to be mustered again, he must bring a certificate of his swearing the oaths of Allegiance and Supremacy, and having taken the Sacrament according to the rites of the Church of England. This, I perceive, is imposed on all.

22nd. My Lord Brouncker did show me Hollar's new print of the City, with a pretty representation of that part which is burnt, very fine indeed; and tells me, that he was yesterday sworn the King's servant, and that the King hath commanded him to go on with his

81 Belonging to the Earl of Berkshire: afterwards purchased by Charles II, and presented to the Duchess of Cleveland. It was then of great extent, and stood on or near the site of Lord Stafford's present residence.

great map of the City, which he was upon before the City was burned, like Gombout of Paris, which I am glad of. Mr Batelier tells me the news how the King of France hath in defiance to the King of England caused all his footmen to be put into vests, and that the noblemen of France will do the like; which, if true, is the greatest indignity ever done by one Prince to another, and would excite a stone to be revenged; and I hope our King will, if it be so, as he tells me it is: being told by one that come over from Paris with my Lady Fanshaw, (who is come over with the dead body of her husband,) and that saw it before he come away. This makes me mighty merry, it being an ingenious kind of affront; but yet makes me angry, to see that the King of England is become so little as to have the affront offered him.

23rd. I spoke with Sir G. Downing about our prisoners in Holland, and their being released; which he is concerned in, and most of them are. Then discoursing of matters of the House of Parliament, he tells me that it is not the fault of the House, but the King's own party that have hindered the passing of the Bill for money, by their popping in of new projects for raising it: which is a strange thing; and mighty confident he is, that what money is raised, will be raised and put into the same form that the last was, to come into the Exchequer. And for aught I see, I must confess I think it is the best way.

24th. With Sir J. Minnes by coach to Stepney to the Trinity House, where it is kept again now since the burning of their other house in London. And here a great many met at Sir Thomas Allen's feast, of his being made an Elder Brother; but he is sick, and so could not be there. Here was much good company, and very merry; but the discourse of Scotland it seems is confirmed, and that they are 4000 of them in armes, and do declare for King and Covenant, which is very ill news. I pray God deliver us from the ill consequences we may justly fear from it. Sir Philip Warwick I find is full of trouble in his mind to see how things go, and what our wants are; and so I have no delight to trouble him with discourse, though I honour the man with all my heart, and I think him to be a very able right-honest man.

25th. To Sir G. Carteret's to dinner; where much company. Among others, Mr Carteret and my Lady Jemimah, and Mr

Ashburnham, the great man; who is a pleasant man, and that hath seen much of the world, and more of the Court. Into the Court, and attended there till the Council met, and then was called in, and I read my letter. My Lord Treasurer declared that the King had nothing to give, till the Parliament did give him some money. So the King did of himself bid me to declare to all that would take our tallies for payment, that he should, soon as the Parliament's money do come in, take back their tallies, and give them money: which I giving him occasion to repeat to me (it coming from him against the gré, I perceive, of my Lord Treasurer,) I was content therewith, and went out. All the talk of Scotland, where the highest report I perceive, runs but upon three or four hundred in armes. Here I saw Mrs Stewart this afternoon, methought the beautifullest creature that ever I saw in my life, more than ever I thought her, so often as I have seen her; and I do begin to think do exceed my Lady Castlemaine, at least now. This being St Katherine's day, the Queene was at masse by seven o'clock this morning; and Mr Ashburnham do say that he never saw any one have so much zeale in his life as she hath: and (the question being asked by my Lady Carteret,) much beyond the bigotry that ever the old Queene-mother had. I spoke with Mr May,[82] who tells me that the design of building the City do go on apace, and by his description it will be mighty handsome, and to the satisfaction of the people; but I pray God it come not out too late. Mr Ashburnham to-day at dinner told how the rich fortune Mrs Mallett reports of her servants; that my Lord Herbert[83] would have her; my Lord Hinchingbroke was indifferent to have her: my Lord John Butler[84] might not have her; my Lord of Rochester would have forced her, and Sir — Popham[85] (who nevertheless is likely to have her) would do anything to have her.

26th. Into the House of Parliament, where at a great committee I did hear as long as I would the great case against my Lord

82 Hugh May.
83 William Lord Herbert succeeded his father as (sixth) Earl of Pembroke, 1669. Died unmarried 1674.
84 Seventh son of the Duke of Ormond, created 1676 Baron of Aghrim, Viscount of Clonmore, and Earl of Gowran. Died 1677, without issue.
85 Probably Sir Francis Popham, KB.

Mordaunt,[86] for some arbitrary proceedings of his against one Taylor, whom he imprisoned and did all the violence to imaginable, only to get him to give way to his abusing his daughter. Here was Mr Sawyer,[87] my old chamber-fellow,[88] a counsel against my Lord; and I was glad to see him in so good play. No news from the North at all to-day; and the news-book makes the business nothing but that they are all dispersed.

27th. To my Lord Crewe, and had some good discourse with him, he doubting that all will break in pieces in the kingdom; and that the taxes now coming out, which will tax the same man in three or four several capacities, as for land, office, profession, and money at interest, will be the hardest that ever came out; and do think that we owe it, and the lateness of its being given, wholly to the unpreparedness of the King's own party, to make their demand and choice; for they have obstructed the giving it by land-tax, which had been done long since.

86 John Mordaunt, younger son to the first, and brother to the second Earl of Peterborough, having incurred considerable personal risk in endeavouring to promote the King's Restoration, was, in 1659, created Baron Mordaunt of Reigate, and Viscount Mordaunt of Avalon. He was soon afterwards made KG, and constituted Lord Lieutenant of Surrey, and Constable of Windsor Castle; which offices he held till his death, in 1675. In January 1666/67 Lord Mordaunt was impeached by the House of Commons for forcibly ejecting William Tayleur and his family from the apartments which they occupied in Windsor Castle, where Tayleur held some appointment, and imprisoning him because he had presumed to offer himself as a candidate for the borough of Windsor. Lord M. was also accused of improper conduct towards Tayleur's daughter. He, however, denied all these charges in his place in the House of Lords, and put in an answer to the articles of impeachment, for hearing which a day was absolutely fixed; but the Parliament being shortly afterwards prorogued, the enquiry seems to have been entirely abandoned, notwithstanding the vehemence with which the House of Commons had taken the matter up. Perhaps the King interfered in Lord Mordaunt's behalf; because Andrew Marvel in his 'Instructions to a Painter', after saying, in allusion to this business,

> Now Mordaunt may within his castle tower
> Imprison parents and the child deflower,

proceeds to observe,

> Each does the other blame, and all distrust,
> But Mordaunt *new obliged* would sure be just.

87 Afterwards Sir Robert Sawyer, Attorney General from 1681 to 1687. Died 1692.
88 At Magdalene College, where he was admitted a Pensioner, June 1648.

28th. To White Hall; where, though it blows hard and rains hard, yet the Duke of York is gone a-hunting. We therefore lost our labour, and so to get things ready against dinner at home, and at noon comes my Lord Hinchingbroke, Sir Thomas Crewe, Mr John Crewe, Mr Carteret, and Brisband. I had six noble dishes for them, dressed by a man-cook, and commended, as indeed they deserved, for exceeding well done. We eat with great pleasure, and I enjoyed myself in it; eating in silver plates, and all things mighty rich and handsome about me. Till dark at dinner, and then broke up with great pleasure, especially to myself; and they away, only Mr Carteret and I to Gresham College. Here was Mr Henry Howard,[89] that will hereafter be Duke of Norfolke, who is admitted this day into the Society, and being a very proud man, and one that values himself upon his family, writes his name, as he do every where, Henry Howard of Norfolke.

29th. I late at the office, and all the news I hear I put into a letter this night to my Lord Brouncker at Chatham, thus:

I doubt not of your Lordship's hearing of Sir Thomas Clifford's succeeding Sir H. Pollard[90] in the Controllership of the King's house; but perhaps our ill (but confirmed) tidings from the Barbadoes may not have reached you yet, it coming but yesterday; viz. that about eleven ships (whereof two of the King's, the *Hope* and *Coventry*) going thence with men to attack St Christopher were seized by a violent hurricana, and all sunk. Two only of thirteen escaping, and those with loss of masts, &c. My Lord Willoughby[91] himself is involved in the disaster, and I think two ships thrown upon an island of the French, and so all the men (to 500) become their prisoners. 'Tis said, too, that eighteen Dutch men-of-war are passed the Channell, in order to meet with our Smyrna ships; and some I hear do fright us with the King of Sweden's seizing our mast-ships at Gottenburgh. But we

89 Henry Howard, second son of Henry Earl of Arundel, became, on the death of his brother Thomas in 1677, sixth Duke of Norfolk, having been previously created Baron Howard of Castle Rising, in 1669, and advanced to the Earldom of Norwich, 1672. He was a great benefactor to the Royal Society, and presented the Arundel Marbles to the University of Oxford. Died 1683/84.

90 MP for Devonshire. Died November 27, 1666.

91 Francis fifth Lord Willoughby of Parnham, drowned at Barbados, 1666.

have too much ill news true, to afflict ourselves with what is uncertain. That which I hear from Scotland is, the Duke of York's saying yesterday, that he is confident the Lieutenant Generall there hath driven them into a pound somewhere towards the mountains.

To show how mad we are at home here, and unfit for any troubles: my Lord St John did a day or two since openly pull a gentleman in Westminster Hall by the nose, (one Sir Andrew Henly,) while the Judges were upon their benches, and the other gentleman did give him a rap over the pate with his cane. Of which fray the Judges, they say, will make a great matter: men are only sorry the gentleman did proceed to return a blow; for otherwise my Lord would have been soundly fined for the affront and may be yet for his affront to the Judges.

30th. To White Hall; and pretty to see (it being St Andrew's day,) how some few did wear St Andrew's crosse; but most did make a mockery at it, and the House of Parliament, contrary to practice, did sit also: people having no mind to observe the Scotch saint's days till they hear better news from Scotland.

December 1st. Walking to the Old Swan I did see a cellar in Tower-streete in a very fresh fire, the late great winds having blown it up. It seemed to be only of log-wood that hath kept the fire all this while in it. Going further I met my late Lord Mayor Bludworth, under whom the City was burned; but a very weak man he seems to be. By coach home in the evening, calling at Faythorne's, buying three of my Lady Castlemaine's heads, printed this day, which indeed is, as to the head, I think a very fine picture, and like her. I did this afternoon get Mrs Michell to let me only have a sight of a pamphlet lately printed, but suppressed and much called after, called *The Catholique's Apology*; lamenting the severity of the Parliament against them, and comparing it with the lenity of other princes to Protestants. Giving old and late instances of their loyalty to their princes, whatever is objected against them; and excusing their disquiets in Queene Elizabeth's time, for that it was impossible for them to think her a lawfull Queene, if Queene Mary, who had been owned as such, were so; one being the daughter of the true, and the other of a false wife: and that of the Gunpowder Treason, by saying that it was only the practice of some of us, if not the King, to trepan some of their religion into it, it never being defended by the generality of their Church, nor indeed known by them; and ends with a large Catalogue, in red letters, of the Catholiques which have lost their lives in the quarrel of the late King and this. The thing is very well writ indeed.

2nd. Took coach, and no sooner in the coach but something broke, that we were fain there to stay till a smith could be fetched, which was above an hour, and then it costing me 6s. to mend. Away round by the wall and Cow-lane, for fear it should break again, and in pain about the coach all the way. I went to Sir W. Batten's, and there I hear more ill news still: that all our New-England fleet, which went out lately, are put back a third time by foul weather, and dispersed, some to one port and some to another; and their convoys also to Plymouth; and whether any of them be lost or no, we do not know. This, added to all the rest, do lay us flat in our hopes and courages, every body prophesying destruction to the nation.

3rd. More cheerful than I have been a good while, to hear that for certain the Scott rebels are all routed; they having been so bold as to come within three miles of Edinburgh, and there given two or three repulses to the King's forces, but at last were mastered. Three or four hundred killed or taken, among which their leader, Wallis, and seven ministers (they having all taken the Covenant a few days before, and sworn to live and die in it, as they did;) and so all is likely to be there quiet again. There is also the very good news come of four New-England ships come home safe to Falmouth with masts for the King; which is a blessing mighty unexpected, and without which (if for nothing else) we must have failed the next year. But God be praised for thus much good fortune, and send us the continuance of his favour in other things!

6th. After dinner my wife and brother[92] (in another habit) go out to see a play; but I am not to take notice that I know of my brother's going. This day, in the Gazette, is the whole story of defeating of Scotch rebels, and of the creation of the Duke of Cambridge, Knight of the Garter.

92 John Pepys, who, being in holy orders, had lately assumed the canonical habit. He died in 1677, at which period he held some office in the Trinity-house – Pepys's manuscript letters.

7th. To the King's playhouse, where two acts were almost done when I come in; and there I sat with my cloak about my face, and saw the remainder of The Mayd's Tragedy;[93] a good play, and well acted, especially by the younger Marshall, who is become a pretty good actor; and is the first play I have seen in either of the houses, since before the great plague, they having acted now about fourteen days publickly. But I was in mighty pain, lest I should be seen by any body to be at a play.

8th. The great Proviso passed the House of Parliament yesterday: which makes the King and Court mad, the King having given order to my Lord Chamberlain to send to the playhouses and brothels, to bid all the Parliament-men that were there to go to the Parliament presently. This is true, it seems; but it was carried against the Court by thirty or forty voices. It is a Proviso to the Poll Bill, that there shall be a Committee of nine persons that shall have the inspection upon oath, and power of giving others, of all the accounts of the money given and spent for this warr. This hath a most sad face, and will breed very ill blood. He tells me, brought in by Sir Robert Howard,[94] who is one of the King's servants, at least hath a great office, and hath got, they say, £20,000 since the King come in. Mr Pierce did also tell me as a great truth, as being told it by Mr Cowly,[95] who was by and heard it, that Tom Killigrew should publickly tell the King that his matters were coming into a very ill state; but that yet there was a way to help all. Says he, 'There is a good, honest, able man that I could name, that if your Majesty would employ, and command to see all things well executed, all things would soon be mended; and this is one Charles Stuart, who now spends his time in employing his lips about the Court, and hath no other employment; but if you would give him this employment, he were the fittest man in the world to perform it.' This, he says, is most true; but the King do not profit by any of this, but lays all aside, and remembers nothing,

---

93 By Beaumont and Fletcher.
94 A younger son of Thomas Earl of Berkshire; educated at Magdalene College, Cambridge; knighted at the Restoration, and chosen MP for Stockbridge, and afterwards for Castle Rising. He was Auditor of the Exchequer, and a creature of Charles II, who employed him in cajoling the Parliament for money. He published some poems, plays, and political tracts. Died 1698.
95 Abraham Cowley, the poet.

but to his pleasures again: which is a sorrowful consideration. To the King's playhouse, and there did see a good part of *The English Monsieur*,[96] which is a mighty pretty play, very witty and pleasant. And the women do very well; but above all, little Nelly. I hear that this Proviso in Parliament is mightily ill taken by all the Court party as a mortal blow, and that that strikes deep into the King's prerogative; which troubles me mightily. In much fear of ill news of our colliers. A fleet of 200 sail, and 14 Dutch men-of-war between them and us: and they coming home with small convoy; and the City in great want, coals being at £3 3s. per chaldron, as I am told. I saw smoke in the ruines this very day.

10th. Captain Cocke, with whom I walked in the garden, tells me how angry the Court is at the late Proviso brought in by the House. How still my Lord Chancellor is, not daring to do or say any thing to displease the Parliament; that the Parliament is in a very ill humour, and grows every day more and more so; and that the unskilfulness of the Court, and their difference among one another, is the occasion of all not agreeing in what they would have, and so they give leisure and occasion to the other part to run away with what the Court would not have.

11th. This day the Poll Bill was to be passed, and great endeavours used to take away the Proviso.

12th. Sir H. Cholmly did with grief tell me how the Parliament hath been told plainly that the King hath been heard to say, that he would dissolve them rather than pass this Bill with the Proviso. But tells me, that the Proviso is removed, and now carried that it shall be done by a Bill by itself. He tells me how the King hath lately paid above £30,000 to clear the debts of my Lady Castlemaine's; and that she and her husband are parted for ever, upon good terms, never to trouble one another more. He says that he hears that above £400,000 hath gone into the Privy-purse since this warr; and that that hath consumed so much of our money, and makes the King and Court so mad to be brought to discover it. The very good newes is just come of our four ships from Smyrna, come safe without convoy even into the Downes, without seeing any enemy; which is the best, and indeed only considerable good news to our Exchange, since the

96 A comedy, by James Howard.

burning of the City; and it is strange to see how it do cheer up men's hearts. Here I saw shops now come to be in this Exchange; and met little Batelier who sits here but at £3 per annum, whereas he sat at the other at £100; which he says he believes will prove as good account to him now as the other did at that rent. They talk for certain, that now the King do follow Mrs Stewart wholly, and my Lady Castlemaine not above once a-week; that the Duke of York do not haunt my Lady Denham so much; that she troubles him with matters of State, being of my Lord Bristoll's faction, and that he avoids; that she is ill still. News this day from Brampton, of Mr Ensum, my sister's sweetheart, being dead: a clowne.

13th. W. Hewer dined with me, and showed me a Gazette,[97] in April last, (which I wonder should never be remembered by any body,) which tells how several persons were then tried for their lives, and were found guilty of a design of killing the King, and destroying the Government; and as a means to it, to burn the City; and that the day intended for the plot was the 3rd of last September. And the fire did indeed break out on the 2nd of September: which is very strange, methinks.

---

97 This circumstance was so remarkable that it has been thought worth while extracting the whole passage from the Gazette of April 23-26, 1666:

At the Sessions in the Old Bailey, John Rathbone, an old Army Colonel, William Saunders, Henry Tucker, Thomas Flint, Thomas Evans, John Myles, Will. Westcot, and John Cole, officers or soldiers in the late Rebellion, were indicted for conspiring the death of his Majesty, and the overthrow of the Government. Having laid their plot and contrivance for the surprisal of the Tower, the killing his Grace the Lord General, Sir John Robinson, Lieutenant of the Tower, and Sir Richard Brown; and then to have declared for an equal division of lands, &c. *The better to effect this hellish design the City was to have been fired,* and the portcullis let down to keep out all assistance; and the Horse Guard to have been surprised in the Inns where they were quartered, several ostlers having been gained for that purpose. The Tower was accordingly viewed, and its surprise ordered by boats over the moat, and from thence to scale the wall. One Alexander, not yet taken, had likewise distributed money to these conspirators, and for the carrying on the design more effectually, they were told of a Council of the great ones that sat frequently in London, from whom issued all orders; which Council received their directions from another in Holland, who sat with the States; and that *the third of September* was pitched on for the attempt, as being found by Lilly's Almanack, and a scheme erected for that purpose, to be a lucky day, a planet then ruling which prognosticated the downfall of Monarchy. The evidence against these persons was very full and clear, and they were accordingly found guilty of High Treason.

14th. Met my good friend Mr Evelyn, and walked with him a good while, lamenting our condition for want of good council, and the King's minding of his business and servants. The House sat till three o'clock, and then up: and I home with Sir Stephen Fox to his house to dinner, and the Cofferer[98] with us. There I found his Lady, a fine woman, and seven the prettiest children of theirs that ever I knew almost. A very genteel dinner, and in great state and fashion, and excellent discourse: and nothing like an old experienced man and a courtier, and such is the Cofferer Ashburnham. The House have been mighty hot to-day against the Paper Bill, showing all manner of averseness to give the King money; which these courtiers do take mighty notice of, and look upon the others as bad rebells as ever the last were. But the courtiers did carry it against those men upon a division of the House, a great many, that it should be committed; and so it was: which they reckon good news.

15th. To the office, where my Lord Brouncker (newly come to town from his being at Chatham and Harwich to spy enormities): and at noon I with him and his lady, Williams, to Captain Cocke's; where a good dinner, and very merry. Good news to-day upon the Exchange, that our Hamburgh fleet is got in; and good hopes that we may soon have the like of our Gottenburgh, and then we shall be well for this winter. And by and by comes in Matt Wren[99] from the Parliament-house; and tells us that he and all his party of the House, which is the Court party, are fools, and have been made so this day by the wise men of the other side; for after the Court party had carried it yesterday so powerfully for the Paper Bill, yet now it is laid aside wholly, and to be supplied by a land-tax; which it is true will do well and will be the sooner finished, which was the great argument for the doing of it. But then it shows them fools, that they would not permit this to have been done six weeks ago, which they might have

98 William Ashburnham, an officer of distinction in the King's Army during the Civil War, and after the Restoration made Cofferer to Charles II. Died without issue, 1671.

99 Matthew Wren, eldest son of the Bishop of Ely of both his names, MP for St Michael's 1661, and made Secretary to Lord Clarendon; after whose fall he filled the same office under the Duke of York till his death in 1672. He was one of the earliest Members of the Royal Society, and published two tracts in answer to Harrington's *Oceana*.

had. And next they have parted with the Paper Bill, which when once begun might have proved a very good flower in the Crowne, as any there. So they are truly outwitted by the other side.

16th. To White Hall, and there walked up and down to the Queene's side, and there saw my dear Lady Castlemaine, who continues admirable, methinks, and I do not hear that but the King is the same to her still as ever. Anon to chapel by the King's closet, and heard a very good anthem. Then with Lord Brouncker to Sir W. Coventry's chamber; and there we sat with him and talked. He is weary of any thing to do, he says, in the Navy. He tells us this Committee of Accounts will enquire sharply into our office. To Sir P. Neale's chamber; Sir Edward Walker being there, and telling us how he hath lost many fine rowles of antiquity in heraldry by the late fire, but hath saved the most of his papers. Here was also Dr Wallis,[100] the famous scholar and mathematician; but he promises little. The Duke of Monmouth, Lord Brouncker says, spends his time the most viciously and idle of any man, nor will be fit for any thing; yet he speaks as if it were not impossible but the King would own him for his son, and that there was marriage between his mother and him.

17th. My wife well home in the evening from the play; which I was glad of, it being cold and dark, and she having her necklace of pearl on, and none but Mercer with her.

19th. Talked of the King's family with Mr Hingston, the organist. He says many of the musique are ready to starve, they being five years behind hand for their wages: nay, Evens, the famous man upon the Harp, having not his equal in the world, did the other day die for mere want, and was fain to be buried at the almes of the parish, and carried to his grave in the dark at night without one linke, but that Mr Hingston met it by chance, and did give 12d. to buy two or three links. Thence I up to the Lords' House to enquire for my Lord Bellasses; and there hear how at a conference this morning between the two Houses about the business of the Canary Company, my Lord Buckingham leaning rudely over my Lord Marquis Dorchester,[101] my Lord Dorchester removed his elbow. Duke of Buckingham asked

100 John Wallis, STP, FRS, Savilian Professor of Geometry. Died 1703, aged 87.
101 Henry second Earl of Kingston, created Marquis of Dorchester 1645. Died 1680. See an account of this quarrel in Lord Clarendon's Life.

whether he was uneasy; Dorchester replied, yes, and that he durst not do this were he any where else: Buckingham replied, yes he would, and that he was a better man than himself; Dorchester said that he lyed. With this Buckingham struck off his hat, and took him by his periwigg, and pulled it aside, and held him. My Lord Chamberlain and others interposed, and upon coming into the House the Lords did order them both to the Tower, whither they are to go this afternoon. I down into the Hall, and there the Lieutenant of the Tower took me with him, and would have me to the Tower to dinner; where I dined at the head of his table next his lady, who is comely and seeming sober and stately, but very proud and very cunning, or I am mistaken, and wanton too. This day's work will bring the Lieutenant of the Tower £350. Thence home, and upon Tower Hill saw about 3 or 400 seamen get together; and one standing upon a pile of bricks made his sign with his handkercher upon his stick, and called all the rest to him, and several shouts they gave. This made me afraid; so I got hence as fast as I could. But by and by Sir W. Batten and Sir R. Ford do tell me that the seamen have been at some prisons to release some seamen, and the Duke of Albemarle is in armes, and all the Guards at the other end of the town; and the Duke of Albemarle is gone with some forces to Wapping to quell the seamen; which is a thing of infinite disgrace to us. I sat long talking with them. And, among other things, Sir R. Ford did make me understand how the House of Commons is a beast not to be understood, it being impossible to know beforehand the success almost of any small plain thing, there being so many to think and speak to any business, and they of so uncertain minds and interests and passions. He did tell me, and so did Sir W. Batten, how Sir Allen Brodericke[102] and Sir Allen Apsly did come drunk the other day into the House, and did both speak for half an hour, together, and could not be either laughed, or pulled, or bid to sit down and hold their peace, to the great contempt of the King's servants and cause; which I am grieved at with all my heart.

23rd (Lord's day).   To church, where a vain fellow with a periwigg preached, Chaplain (as by his prayer appeared) to the Earle of Carlisle.

102 Son of Sir Thomas Broderick of Richmond, Yorkshire, and Wandsworth, Surrey; knighted by Charles II, and Surveyor General in Ireland to his Majesty.

24th. It being frost and dry, as far as Paul's, and so back again through the City by Guildhall, observing the ruins thereabouts till I did truly lose myself. No news yet of our Gottenburgh fleet; which makes us have some fears, it being of mighty concernment to have our supply of masts safe. I met with Mr Cade to-night, my stationer; and he tells me that he hears for certain, that the Queene-Mother is about and hath near finished a peace with France, which as a Presbyterian he do not like, but seems to fear it will be a means to introduce Popery.

26th. To the Duke's house to a play. It was indifferently done, Gosnell not singing, but a new wench that sings naughtily.

27th. Up; and called up by the King's trumpets, which cost me 10s. By coach to the King's playhouse, and there saw *The Scornful Lady* well acted; Doll Common doing Abigail most excellently, and Knipp the widow very well, (and will be an excellent actor, I think). In other parts the play not so well done as need be by the old actors. This day a house or two was blown up with powder in the Minorys, and several people spoiled, and manye dug out from under the rubbish.

28th. I to my Lord Crewe's, where I find and hear the news how my Lord's brother, Mr Nathaniel Crewe, hath an estate of 6 or £700 per annum left him by the death of an old acquaintance of his, but not akin to him at all. And this man is dead without will, but had above ten years since made over his estate to this Mr Crewe, to him and his heirs for ever, and given Mr Crewe the keeping of the deeds in his own hand all this time; by which, if he would, he might have taken present possession of the estate, for he knew what they were. This is as great an action of confident friendship as this latter age, I believe, can show. From hence to the Duke's house, and there saw *Macbeth* most excellently acted, and a most excellent play for variety. I had sent for my wife to meet me there, who did come: so I did not go to White Hall, and got my Lord Bellasses to get me into the playhouse and there, after all staying above an hour for the players (the King and all waiting, which was absurd,) saw *Henry the Fifth* well done by the Duke's people, and in most excellent habit, all new vests, being put on but this night. But I sat so high and far off that I missed most of the words, and sat with a wind coming into my back and neck, which did much trouble me. The play continued till twelve at night; and then up, and a most horrid cold night it was, and frosty, and moonshine.

29th. Called up with news from Sir W. Batten that Hogg hath brought in two prizes more: and so I thither, and hear the particulars, which are good; one of them, if prize, being worth £4000: for which God be thanked! Then to the office, and have the news brought us of Captain Robinson's coming with his fleet from Gottenburgh: dispersed, though, by foul weather. But he hath light of five Dutch men-of-war, and taken three, whereof one is sunk; which is very good news to close up the year with, and most of our merchant-men already heard of to be safely come home, though after long lookings for, and now to several ports as they could make them.

30th (Lord's day). To church. Here was a collection for the sexton. But it come into my head why we should be more bold in making the collection while the psalm is singing, than in the sermon or prayer.

31st. To my accounts, wherein at last I find them clear and right; but to my great discontent do find that my gettings this year have been £573 less than my last: it being this year in all but £2986; whereas, the last, I got £3560. And then again my spendings this year have exceeded my spendings the last, by £644: my whole spendings last year being but £509; whereas this year it appears I have spent £1154 which is a sum not fit to be said that ever I should spend in one year, before I am master of a better estate than I am. Yet, blessed be God! and I pray God make me thankful for it, I do find myself worth in money, all good, above £6200: which is above £1800 more than I was the last year. Thus ends this year of publick wonder and mischief to this nation. Publick matters in a most sad condition; seamen discouraged for want of pay, and are become not to be governed: nor, as matters are now, can any fleet go out next year. Our enemies, French and Dutch, great, and grow more by our poverty. The Parliament backward in raising, because jealous of the spending of the money; the City less and less likely to be built again, every body settling elsewhere, and nobody encouraged to trade. A sad, vicious, negligent Court, and all sober men there fearful of the ruin of the whole kingdom this next year; from which, good God deliver us! One thing I reckon remarkable in my own condition is, that I am come to abound in good plate, so as at all entertainments to be served wholly with silver plates, having two dozen and a half.

1666/67. January 2nd. My wife up, and with Mrs Pen to walk in the fields to frost-bite themselves. I find the Court full of great apprehensions of the French, who have certainly shipped landsmen, great numbers at Brest; and most of our people here guess his design for Ireland. We have orders to send all the ships we can possible to the Downes, every day bringing us news of new mutinies among the seamen; so that our condition is like to be very miserable. Mr George Montagu tells me of the King displeasing the House of Commons by evading their Bill for examining Accounts, and putting it into a Commission, though therein he hath left out Coventry and . . . [1], and named all the rest the Parliament named, and all country Lords, not one Courtier: this do not please them. He finds the enmity almost over for my Lord Sandwich. Up to the Painted Chamber, and there heard a conference between the House of Lords and Commons about the Wine Patent; which I was exceeding glad to be at, because of my hearing exceeding good discourses, but especially from the Commons; among others Mr Swinfen, and a young man, one Sir Thomas Meres:[2] and do outdo the Lords infinitely. Alone to the King's house, and there saw *The Custome of the Country*,[3] the second time of its being acted, wherein Knipp does the Widow well; but of all the plays that ever I did see, the worst, having neither plot, language, nor any thing in the earth that is acceptable; only Knipp sings a song admirably.

3rd. This day, I hear, hath been a conference between the two Houses about the Bill for examining Accounts, wherein the House of Lords their proceedings in petitioning the King for doing it by Commission, are in great heat voted by the Commons, after the conference, unparliamentary.

4th. Comes our company to dinner; my Lord Brouncker, Sir W. Pen, his lady, and Peg,[4] and her servant, Mr Lowther.[5] At night to sup, and then to cards, and last of all to have a flaggon of ale and apples, drunk out of a wood cup, as a Christmas draught, which made all merry; and they full of admiration at my plate. Mr Lowther a

1 A blank in the manuscript.
2 Knight, MP for Lincoln, made a Commissioner of the Admiralty 1679.
3 A tragi-comedy, by Beaumont and Fletcher.
4 Their daughter.
5 Anthony Lowther, Esq., of Marske, co. York. Died 1692.

pretty gentleman, too good for Peg. Sir W. Pen was much troubled to hear the song I sung, 'The New Droll', it touching him home.

5th. With my wife to the Duke's house, and there saw *Mustapha*,[6] a most excellent play.

6th. Young Michell and I, it being an excellent frosty day, did walk out. He showed me the baker's house in Pudding-lane, where the late great fire begun: and thence all along Thames-street, where I did view several places, and so up by London Wall by Blackfriars to Ludgate; and thence to Bridewell, which I find to have been heretofore an extraordinary good house, and a fine coming to it before the house by the bridge was built.

7th. Lord Brouncker tells me that my Lady Denham is at last dead. Some suspect her poisoned, but it will be best known when her body is opened to-day, she dying yesterday morning. The Duke of York is troubled for her; but hath declared he will never have another public mistress again; which I shall be glad of, and would the King would do the like. He tells me how the Parliament is grown so jealous of the King's being unfayre to them in the business of the Bill for examining Accounts, Irish Bill, and the business of the Papists, that they will not pass the business for money till they see themselves secure that those Bills will pass; which they do observe the Court to keep off till all the Bills come together, that the King may accept what he pleases, and what he pleases to object to. He tells me how Mr Henry Howard of Norfolke hath given our Royal Society all his grandfather's library: which noble gift they value at £1000; and gives them accommodation to meet in at his house (Arundell House), they being now disturbed at Gresham College. To the Duke's house, and saw *Macbeth*, which though I saw it lately, yet appears a most excellent play in all respects, but especially in divertisement, though it be a deep tragedy; which is a strange perfection in a tragedy, it being most proper here, and suitable.

9th. In a hackney-coach to White Hall, the way being most horribly bad upon the breaking up of the frost, so as not to be passed almost. I do hear by my Lord Brouncker, that for certain Sir W. Coventry hath resigned his place of Commissioner up; which I believe he hath

6 A tragedy, by Roger Earl of Orrery.

done upon good grounds of security to himself from all the blame which must attend our office this next year; but I fear the King will suffer by it. Thence to Westminster Hall, and there to the conference of the Houses about the word 'Nusance,' which the Commons would have, and the Lords will not, in the Irish Bill. The Commons do it professedly to prevent the King's dispensing with it; which Sir Robert Howard and others did expressly repeat often: viz., 'that no King ever could do any thing which was hurtful to his people.' Now the Lords did argue that it was an ill precedent, and that which will ever hereafter be used as a way of preventing the King's dispensation with acts; and therefore rather advise to pass the Bill without that word, and let it go accompanied with a petition to the King that he will not dispense with it; this being a more civil way to the King. They answered well, that this do imply that the King should pass their Bill, and yet with design to dispense with it; which is to suppose the King guilty of abusing them. And more, they produce precedents for it; namely, that against new buildings, and about leather, where the word 'Nusance' is used to the purpose: and further, that they do not rob the King of any right he ever had, for he never had a power to do hurt to his people, nor would exercise it; and therefore there is no danger in the passing this Bill of imposing on his prerogative; and concluded that they think they ought to do this, so as the people may really have the benefit of it when it is passed, for never any people could expect so reasonably to be indulged something from a King, they having already given him so much money, and are likely to give more. Thus they broke up, both adhering to their opinions; but the Commons seemed much more full of judgment and reason than the Lords. Then the Commons made their Report to the Lords of their vote that their Lordships' proceedings in the Bill for examining Accounts were unparliamentary, they having, while a Bill was sent up to them from the Commons about the business, petitioned his Majesty that he would do the same thing by his Commission. They did give their reasons: viz. that it had no precedent; that the King ought not to be informed of any thing passing in the Houses till it comes to a Bill; that it will wholly break off all correspondence between the two Houses, and in the issue wholly infringe the very use and being of Parliaments. Thence to Faythorne, and bought a head or two; one of them my Lord of Ormond's, the best I ever saw. To Arundell House, where first the Royal Society meet by the favour of Mr Harry Howard, who was there. And here was a great meeting of worthy noble persons; but my Lord Brouncker, who pretended to make a congratulatory speech upon their coming hither, and great thanks to Mr Howard, did do it in the worst manner in the world.

14th. Sir W. Batten tells me the Lords do agree at last with the Commons about the word 'Nusance' in the Irish Bill, and do desire a good correspondence between the two Houses; and that the King do intend to prorogue them the last of this month.

16th. Sir W. Coventry came to me aside in the Duke's chamber to tell that he had not answered part of a late letter of mine, because *littera scripta manet*. About his leaving the office, he tells me, it is because he finds that his business at Court will not permit him to attend it; and then he confesses that he seldom of late could come from it with satisfaction, and therefore would not take the King's money for nothing. I professed my sorrow for it, and prayed the continuance of his favour; which he promised. I do believe he hath acted like a very wise man in reference to himself; but I doubt it will prove ill for the King, and for the office. Prince Rupert, I hear, is very ill; yesterday given over, but better to-day. Sir Stephen Fox, among other things, told me his whole mystery in the business of the interest he pays as Treasurer for the Army. They give him 12d. per pound quite through the Army, with condition to be paid weekly. This he undertakes for his own private credit, and to be paid by the King at the end of every four months. If the King pay him not at the end of every four months, then, for all the time he stays longer, my Lord Treasurer by agreement allows him eight per cent. per annum for the forbearance. So that, in fine, he hath about twelve per cent. from the King, and the Army, for fifteen or sixteen months' interest; out of which he gains soundly, his expense being about £130,000 per annum; and hath no trouble in it, compared (as I told him) to the trouble I must have to bring in an account of interest. Talk there is of a letter to come from Holland, desiring a place of treaty; but I do doubt it. This day I observe still in many places the smoking remains of the late fire: the ways mighty bad and dirty. This night Sir R. Ford told me how this day, at Christ church Hospital, they have given a living of £200 per annum to Mr Sanchy, my old acquaintance, which I wonder at, he commending him mightily; but am glad of it. He tells me too how the famous Stillingfleete was a Blue-coat boy.

18th. This morning come Captain Cocke to me, and tells me that the King comes to the House this day to pass the Poll Bill and the Irish Bill; and that, though the Faction is very froward in the House, yet all will end well there. But he says that one had got a Bill ready to present in the House against Sir W. Coventry for selling of places, and says he is certain of it, and how he was withheld from doing it. He says that the Vice-chamberlaine is now one of the greatest men in England again, and was he that did prevail with the King to let the Irish Bill go with the word 'Nusance.' He told me that Sir G. Carteret's declaration of giving double to any man that will prove that any of his people have demanded or taken any thing for forwarding the payment of the wages of any man, (of which he sent us a copy yesterday, which we approved of,) is set up, among other places, upon the House of Lords' door. I do not know how wisely this is done. Sir W. Pen told me this night how the King did make them a very sharp speech in the House of Lords to-day, saying that he did expect to have had more Bills; that he purposes to prorogue them on Monday come se'nnight; that whereas they have unjustly conceived some jealousys of his making a peace, he declares he knows of no such thing or treaty: and so left them. But with so little effect, that as soon as he came into the House, Sir G. Coventry moved, that now the King hath declared his intention of proroguing them, it would be loss of time to go on with the thing they were upon when they were called to the King, which was the calling over the defaults of Members appearing in the House; for that before any person could now come or be brought to town, the House would be up. Yet the Faction did desire to delay time, and contend so as to come to a division of the House; where, however, it was carried by a few voices that the debate should be laid by. But this shows that they are not pleased, or that they have not any awe over them from the King's displeasure.

20th. I was sorry to hear of the heat the House was in yesterday about the ill management of the Navy; though I think they were well answered both by Sir G. Carteret and Sir W. Coventry, as he informs me the substance of their speeches. I to church, and there beyond expectation find our seat and all the church crammed by twice as many people as used to be: and to my great joy find Mr Frampton in the pulpit; and I think the best sermon, for goodness and oratory, without affectation or study, that ever I heard in my life. The truth is, he preaches the most like an apostle that ever I heard man; and it was much the best time that ever I spent in my life at church.

21st. To the Swede's-Resident's in the Piazza, to discourse with him about two of our prizes. A cunning fellow. He lives in one of the great houses there, but ill-furnished; and come to us out of bed in his furred mittins and furred cap. Up to the Lords' House, and there come mighty seasonably to hear the Solicitor about my Lord Buckingham's pretence to the title of Lord Rosse. Mr Atturny Montagu is also a good man, and so is old Sir P. Ball;[7] but the Solicitor, and Scroggs[8] after him, are excellent men. This night at supper comes from Sir W. Coventry the Order of Councill for my Lord Brouncker to do all the Controller's part relating to the Treasurer's accounts, and Sir W. Pen all relating to the Victualler's, and Sir J. Minnes to do the rest. This, I hope, will do much better for the King, and I think will give neither of them ground to over-top me, as I feared they would; which pleases me mightily. This evening Mr Wren and Captain Cocke called upon me at the office, and there told me how the House was in better temper to-day, and hath passed the Bill for the remainder of the money, but not to be passed finally till they have done some other things which they will have passed with it; wherein they are very open, what their meaning is, which was but doubted before, for they do in all respects doubt the King's pleasing them.

23rd. My Lord Brouncker and I walking into the Park, I did observe the new buildings: and my Lord seeing I had a desire to see them, they being the place for the priests and friers, he took me back to my Lord Almoner;[9] and he took us quite through the whole house and chapel, and the new monastery, showing me most excellent pieces in wax-worke: a crucifix given by a Pope to Mary Queene of Scotts, where a piece of the Cross is; two bits set in the manner of a cross in the foot of the crucifix: several fine pictures, but especially very good prints of holy pictures. I saw the dortoire[10] and the cells of the priests,

7 Sir Peter Bell, the Queen's Attorney.
8 Sir William Scroggs, King's Serjeant 1669, and made a Judge 1676.
9 Cardinal Howard of Norfolk, the Queen's Almoner.
10 Dormitory.

and we went into one; a very pretty little room, very clean, hung with pictures, set with books. The Priest was in his cell, with his hair clothes to his skin, bare-legged with a sandall only on, and his little bed without sheets, and no feather-bed; but yet, I thought, soft enough. His cord about his middle; but in so good company, living with ease, I thought it a very good life. A pretty library they have. And I was in the refectoire, where every man his napkin, knife, cup of earth, and basin of the same; and a place for one to sit and read while the rest are at meals. And into the kitchen I went, where a good neck of mutton at the fire, and other victuals boiling. I do not think they fared very hard. Their windows all looking into a fine garden and the Park; and mighty pretty rooms all. I wished myself one of the Capuchins. To the King's house, and there saw *The Humerous Lieutenant*:[11] a silly play, I think; only the Spirit in it that grows very tall and then sinks again to nothing, having two heads breeding upon one, and then Knipp's singing, did please us. Here in a box above we spied Mrs Pierce; and going out they called us, and so we staid for them; and Knipp took us all in, and brought to us Nelly,[12] a most pretty woman, who acted the great part Coelia to-day very fine, and did it pretty well: I kissed her, and so did my wife; and a mighty pretty soul she is. We also saw Mrs Ball, which is my little Roman-nose black girl, that is mighty pretty: she is usually called Betty. Knipp made us stay in a box and see the dancing preparatory to to-morrow for *The Goblins*, a play of Suckling's,[13] not acted these twenty-five years; which was pretty. In our way home we find the Guards of horse in the street, and hear the occasion to be news that the seamen are in a mutiny; which put me into a great fright.

24th. Company at home: amongst others, Captain Rolt. And anon at about seven or eight o'clock comes Mr Harris of the Duke's play-house, and brings Mrs Pierce with him, and also one dressed like a country-maid with a straw-hat on, and at first I could not tell who it was, though I expected Knipp: but it was she coming off the stage just as she acted this day in *The Goblins*; a merry jade. Now my house is full, and four fiddlers that play well. Harris I first took to my closet: and I find him a very curious and understanding person in all pictures

11 A tragi-comedy, by Beaumont and Fletcher.
12 Nell Gwynne.
13 Sir John Suckling, the poet.

and other things, and a man of fine conversation; and so is Rolt. Among other things, Harris sung his Irish song, the strangest in itself and the prettiest sung by him that ever I heard.

25th. This afternoon I saw the Poll Bill, now printed; wherein I do fear I shall be very deeply concerned, being to be taxed for all my offices, and then for my money that I have, and my title as well as my head. It is a very great tax; but yet I do think it is so perplexed, it will hardly ever be collected duly. The late invention of Sir G. Downing's is continued of bringing all the money into the Exchequer. This day the House hath passed the Bill for the Assessment; which I am glad of. And also our little Bill, for giving any of us in the office the power of justice of peace, is done as I would have it.

27th. Roger Pepys and I to walk in the Pell Mell. I find by him that the House of Parliament continues full of ill humours; and do say how in their late Poll Bill, which cost so much time, the yeomanry, and indeed two-thirds of the nation, are left out to be taxed. Walked to White Hall, and there I showed my cosen Roger the Duchesse of York sitting in state, while her own mother stands by her: and my Lady Castlemaine, whom he approves to be very handsome, and wonders that she cannot be as good within as she is fair without. Her little black boy come by him, and a dog being in his way, the little boy swore at the dog: 'How,' says he, blessing himself, 'would I whip this child till the blood come, if it were my child!'

28th. To Westminster, where I spent the morning at the Lords' House door to hear the conference between the two Houses about my Lord Mordaunt, of which there was great expectation. Many hundreds of people coming to hear it. But when they come, the Lords did insist upon my Lord Mordaunt's having leave to sit upon a stool uncovered within their barr, and that he should have counsel, which the Commons would not suffer, but desired leave to report their Lordships' resolution to the House of Commons; and so parted for this day, which troubled me, I having by this means lost the whole day. Here I hear from Mr Hayes that Prince Rupert is very bad still, and so bad that he do now yield to be trepanned. After supper and reading a little, and my wife's cutting off my hair short, which is grown too long upon my crown of my head, I to bed.

February 2nd. I am very well pleased this night with reading a poem I brought home with me last night from Westminster Hall, of Dryden's, upon the present war; a very good poem.

3rd. To White Hall, and there to Sir W. Coventry's chamber, and there staid till he was ready. Talking, and among other things of the Prince's being trepanned, which was in doing just as we passed through the Stone Gallery, we asking at the door of his lodgings, and were told so. We are full of wishes for the good success; though I dare say but few do really concern ourselves for him in our hearts. With others into the House, and there hear that the work is done to the Prince in a few minutes without any pain at all to him, he not knowing when it was done. It was performed by Moulins. Having cut the outward table, as they call it, they find the inner all corrupted, so as it come out without any force; and their fear is, that the whole inside of his head is corrupted like that, which do yet make them afraid of him; but no ill accident appeared in the doing of the thing, but all with all imaginable success, as Sir Alexander Frazier did tell me himself, I asking him, who is very kind to me. To Sir G. Carteret's to dinner; and before dinner he tells me that he believes the Duke of York will go to sea with the fleet, which I am sorry for in respect to his person, but yet there is no person in condition to command the fleet, now the Captains are grown so great, but him. By and by to dinner, where very good company. Among other discourse, we talked much of Nostradamus[14] his prophecy of these times, and the burning of the City of London, some of whose verses are put into Booker's[15] Almanack this year: and Sir G. Carteret did tell a story, how at his death he did make the town swear that he should never be dug up, or his tomb opened, after he was buried; but they did after sixty years do it, and upon his breast they found a plate of brasse, saying what a wicked and unfaithful people the people of that place were, who after so many vows should disturb and open him such a day and year and hour; which, if true, is very strange. Then we fell to talk of the burning

14 Michael Nostradamus, a physician and astrologer, born in the diocese of Avignon, 1503. Amongst other predictions he prophesied the death of Henry II of France, by which the celebrity he had before acquired was not a little increased. He succeeded also in rendering assistance to the inhabitants of Aix, during the plague, by a powder of his own invention. He died at Salon, July 1566.
15 John Booker, an eminent astrologer and writing-master at Hadley.

of the City. And my Lady Carteret herself did tell us how abundance of pieces of burnt papers were cast by the wind as far as Cranborne; and among others she took up one, or had one brought her to see, which was a little bit of paper that had been printed, whereon there remained no more nor less than these words: 'Time is, it is done.' Away home, and received some letters from Sir W. Coventry, touching the want of victuals to Kempthorne's[16] fleet going to the Streights and now in the Downes: which did trouble me, he saying that this disappointment might prove fatal; and the more, because Sir W. Coventry do intend to come to the office upon business to-morrow morning, and I shall not know what answer to give him.

4th. When Sir W. Coventry did come, and the rest met, I did appear unconcerned, and did give him answer pretty satisfactory what he asked me; so that I did get off this meeting without any ground lost. Soon as dined, my wife and I out to the Duke's playhouse, and there saw *Heraclius*,[17] an excellent play, to my extraordinary content; and the more from the house being very full, and great company; among others Mrs Stewart, very fine, with her locks done up with puffes, as my wife calls them: and several other great ladies had their hair so, though I do not like it; but my wife do mightily; but it is only because she sees it is the fashion. Here I saw my Lord Rochester and his lady, Mrs Mallett, who hath after all this ado married him; and, as I hear some say in the pit, it is a great act of charity, for he hath no estate. But it was so pleasant to see how every body rose up when my Lord John Butler, the Duke of Ormond's son, come into the pit towards the end of the play, who was a servant to Mrs Mallett, and now smiled upon her, and she on him. Home, and to my chamber, and there finished my Catalogue of my books with my own hand.

5th. Heard this morning that the Prince is much better, and hath good rest. All the talk is that my Lord Sandwich hath perfected the peace with Spain; which is very good, if true. Sir H. Cholmly was with me this morning, and told me of my Lord Bellasses' base dealings with him by getting him to give him great gratuities to near

16 John Kempthorne, a distinguished naval officer, afterwards knighted and made Commissioner at Portsmouth, which place he represented in Parliament. Died 1679. See some curious letters about his election in the Correspondence.
17 A tragedy, by Lodowick Carlell, taken from Corneille.

£2000 for his friendship in the business of the Molle, and hath been lately underhand endeavouring to bring another man into his place as Governor, so as to receive his money of Sir H. Cholmly for nothing. To the King's house to see *The Chances*.[18] A good play I find it, and the actors most good in it. And pretty to hear Knipp sing in the play very properly, 'All night I weepe'; and sung it admirably. The whole play pleases me well: and most of all, the sight of many fine ladies; among others my Lady Castlemaine and Mrs Middleton: the latter of the two hath also a very excellent face and body, I think. And so home in the dark over the ruins with a link.

6th. To Westminster Hall, and walked up and down, and hear that the Prince do still rest well by day and night, and out of pain; so as great hopes are conceived of him; though I did meet Dr Clerke and Mr Pierce, and they do say they believe he will not recover it, they supposing that his whole head within is eaten by this corruption, which appeared in this piece of the inner table. To White Hall to attend the Council; but they sat not to-day. So to Sir W. Coventry's chamber, and find him within, and with a letter from the Downes in his hands, telling the loss of the *St Patricke* coming from Harwich in her way to Portsmouth; and would needs chase two ships (she having the Malago fire-ship in company) which from English colours put up Dutch, and he would clap on board the Vice-Admirall; and after long dispute the Admirall comes on the other side of him, and both together took her. Our fire-ship (Seely) not coming in to fire all three, but come away, leaving her in their possession, and carried away by them: a ship built at Bristoll the last year, of fifty guns and upwards, and a most excellent good ship.

8th. Sir W. Batten come this morning from the House, where the King hath prorogued this Parliament to October next. I am glad they are up. The Bill for Accounts was not offered, the party being willing to let it fall; but the King did tell them he expected it. They are parted with great heart-burnings, one party against the other. Pray God bring them hereafter together in better temper! It is said that the King do intend himself in this interval to take away Lord Mordaunt's government,[19] so as to do something to appease the House against

18 A comedy, by the Duke of Buckingham.
19 Windsor Castle.

they come together, and let them see he will do that of his own
accord which is fit, without their forcing him; and that he will have
his Commission for Accounts go on: which will be good things. At
dinner we talked much of Cromwell; all saying he was a brave fellow,
and did owe his crowne he got to himself as much as any man that
ever got one.

9th. Read a piece of a play, *Every Man in his Humour*, wherein is the
greatest propriety of speech that ever I read in my life; and so to bed.
This noon come my wife's watch-maker, and received £12 of me
for her watch; but Captain Rolt coming to speak with me about a
little business, he did judge of the work to be very good, and so I am
well contented.

10th (Lord's day). To church, where Mr Mills made an unnecessary
sermon upon Original Sin, neither understood by himself nor the
people. Home, where come Mr Carter,[20] my old acquaintance of
Magdalene College, who hath not been here of many years. He hath
spent his time in the country with the Bishop of Carlisle much. He is
grown a very comely person, and of good discourse, and one that I
like very much. We had much talk of all our old acquaintance of the
College, concerning their various fortunes; wherein, to my joy, I met
not with any that have sped better than myself. Mrs Turner do tell
me very odde stories how Mrs Williams do receive the applications of
people, and hath presents, and she is the hand that receives all, while
my Lord do the business.

12th. With my Lord Brouncker by coach to his house, there to hear
some Italian musique: and here we met Tom Killigrew, Sir Robert
Murray, and the Italian Signor Baptista,[21] who hath proposed a play
in Italian for the Opera, which T. Killigrew do intend to have up;
and here he did sing one of the acts. He himself is the poet as well as
the musician; which is very much, and did sing the whole from the
words without any musique prickt, and played all along upon a
harpsicon most admirably and the composition most excellent. The
words I did not understand, and so know not how they are fitted,
but believe very well, and all in the recitativo very fine. But I

20 Thomas Carter, STP. 1669.
21 Giovanni Baptista Draghi, an Italian musician in the service of Queen Catherine,
and a composer of merit. Burney, *History of Music.*

perceive there is a proper accent in every country's discourse, and that do reach in their setting of notes to words, which, therefore, cannot be natural to any body else but them; so that I am not so much smitten with it as it may be I should be if I were acquainted with their accent. But the whole composition is certainly most excellent; and the poetry, T. Killigrew and Sir R. Murray, who understood the words, did say most excellent. I confess I was mightily pleased with the musique. He pretends not to voice, though it be good, but not excellent. This done, T. Killigrew and I to talk: and he tells me how the audience at his house is not above half so much as it used to be before the late fire. That Knipp is like to make the best actor that ever come upon the stage, she understanding so well: that they are going to give her £30 a-year more. That the stage is now by his pains a thousand times better and more glorious than ever heretofore. Now wax-candles, and many of them; then not above 3lb. of tallow: now all things civil, no rudeness any where; then, as in a bear-garden: then two or three fiddlers, now nine or ten of the best: then nothing but rushes upon the ground, and every thing else mean; now all otherwise: then the Queene seldom and the King never would come; now, not the King only for state, but all civil people do think they may come as well as any. He tells me that he hath gone several times (eight or ten times, he tells me,) hence to Rome, to hear good musique; so much he loves it, though he never did sing or play a note. That he hath ever endeavoured in the late King's time and in this to introduce good musique, but he never could do it, there never having been any musique here better than ballads. And says 'Hermitt poore' and 'Chiny Chese' was all the musique we had; and yet no ordinary fiddlers get so much money as ours do here, which speaks our rudeness still. That he hath gathered our Italians from several Courts in Christendome, to come to make a concert for the King, which he do give £200 a-year a-piece to; but badly paid, and do come in the room of keeping four ridiculous Gundilows, he having got the King to put them away, and lay out money this way. And indeed I do commend him for it; for I think it is a very noble undertaking. He do intend to have some times of the year these operas to be performed at the two present theatres, since he is defeated in what he intended in Moorefields on purpose for it. And he tells me plainly that the City audience was as good as the Court; but now they are most gone. Baptista tells me that Giacomo Charissimi[22] is still alive at Rome, who was master to Vinnecotio, who is one of the Italians that the King hath here, and the chief composer of them. My great wonder is, how this man do to keep in memory so perfectly the musique of the whole act, both for the voice and the instrument too. I confess I do admire it: but in recitativo the sense much helps him, for there is but one proper way of discoursing and giving the accents. Having done our discourse, we all took coaches (my Lord's and T. Killigrew's) and to Mrs Knipp's chamber, where this Italian is to teach her to sing her part. And so we all thither, and there she did sing an Italian song or two very fine, while he played the bass upon a harpsicon there; and exceedingly taken I am with her singing, and believe she will do miracles at that and acting.

13th. To the Duke of York, and there did our usual business; but troubled to see that at this time, after our declaring a debt to the Parliament of £900,000 and nothing paid since, but the debt encreased, and now the fleet to set out, to hear that the King hath ordered but £35,000 for the setting out of the fleet, out of the Poll Bill to buy all provisions, when five times as much had been little enough to have done any thing to purpose. They have, indeed, ordered more for paying off of seamen and the Yards to some time, but not enough for that neither. A foul evening this was to-night, and I mightily troubled to get a coach home; and, which is now my common practice, going over the ruins in the night, I rid with my sword drawn in the coach.

14th. By coach to my Lord Chancellor's, and there a meeting: the Duke of York, Duke of Albemarle, and several other Lords of the Commission of Tangier. And there I did present a state of my accounts, and managed them well; and my Lord Chancellor did say, though he was in other things in an ill humour, that no man in England was of more method, nor made himself better understood, than myself. But going, after the business of money was over, to other businesses, of settling the garrison, he did fling out, and so did the Duke of York, two or three severe words touching my Lord Bellasses: that he would have no Governor come away from thence

22 Giacomo Chiarissimi, Maestro di Cappella of the Church of St Apollinare in the German College at Rome, an excellent Italian musician. He lived to be 90. – Burney

in less than three years: no, though his lady were with child. 'And,' says the Duke of York, 'there should be no Governor continue so, longer than three years.' – 'And,' says Lord Arlington, 'when our rules are once set, and upon good judgment declared, no Governor should offer to alter them.' 'We must correct the many things that are amiss there; for (says the Lord Chancellor) you must think we do hear of more things amiss than we are willing to speak before our friends' faces.' My Lord Bellasses would not take notice of their reflecting on him, and did wisely. H. Cholmly and I to the Temple, and there walked in the dark in the walks talking of news; and he surprises me with the certain news that the King did last night in Council declare his being in treaty with the Dutch: that they had sent him a very civil letter, declaring that if nobody but themselves were concerned, they would not dispute the place of treaty, but leave it to his choice; but that being obliged to satisfy therein a prince of equal quality with himself, they must except any place in England or Spain. Also the King hath chosen the Hague, and thither hath chose my Lord Hollis and Harry Coventry to go Embassadors to treat; which is so mean a thing as all the world will believe that we do go to beg a peace of them, whatever we pretend. And it seems all our Court are mightily for a peace, taking this to be the time to make one while the King hath money, that he may save something of what the Parliament hath given him to put him out of debt, so as he may need the help of no more Parliaments, as to the point of money: but our debt is so great, and expence daily so encreased, that I believe little of the money will be saved between this and the making of the peace up. But that which troubles me most is, that we have chosen a son of Secretary Morris, a boy never used to any business, to go Secretary to the Embassy.

This morning come up to my wife's bedside, I being up dressing myself, little Will Mercer to be her Valentine; and brought her name writ upon blue paper in gold letters, done by himself, very pretty; and we were both well pleased with it. But I am also this year my wife's Valentine, and it will cost me £5; but that I must have laid out if we had not been Valentines.

15th. Pegg Pen is married this day privately: no friends but two or three relations of his and hers. Borrowed many things of my kitchen for dressing their dinner. This wedding, being private, is imputed to its being just before Lent, and so in vain to make new clothes till Easter, that they might see the fashions as they are like to be this summer; which is reason good enough.

16th. To my Lord Brouncker's, and there was Sir Robert Murray, a most excellent man of reason and learning, and understands the doctrine of musique, and every thing else I could discourse of, very finely. Here come Mr Hooke, Sir George Ent, Dr Wren, and many others; and by and by the musique, that is to say, Signior Vincentio, who is the master composer, and six more, whereof two eunuches (so tall that Sir T. Harvy said well that he believes they do grow large as our oxen do), and one woman very well dressed and handsome enough, but would not be kissed, as Mr Killigrew, who brought the company in, did acquaint us. They sent two harpsicons before, and by and by after tuning them they begun; and, I confess, very good musique they made; that is, the composition exceeding good, but yet not at all more pleasing to me than what I have heard in English by Mrs Knipp, Captain Cocke, and others. Their justness in keeping time by practice much before any that we have, unless it be a good band of practiced fiddlers. I find that Mrs Pierce's little girl is my Valentine, she having drawn me; which I was not sorry for, it easing me of something more that I must have given to others. But here I do first observe the fashion of drawing of mottos as well as names; so that Pierce, who drew my wife, did draw also a motto, and this girl drew another for me. What mine was I have forgot; but my wife's was, 'Most courteous and most fair': which as it may be used, or an anagram made upon each name, might be very pretty. One wonder I observed to-day, that there was no musique in the morning to call up our new-married people; which is very mean methinks.

17th. Staid till the council was up, and attended the King and Duke of York round the Park, and was asked several questions by both; but I was in pain lest they should ask me what I could not answer; as the Duke of York did the value of the hull of the St Patricke lately lost, which I told him I could not presently answer: though I might have easily furnished myself to answer all those questions. They stood a good while to see the ganders and geese in the water. At home by appointment comes Captain Cocke to me, to talk of State matters and about the peace; who told me that the whole business is managed between Kevet, Burgomaster, of Amsterdam, and my Lord Arlington, who hath through his wife[23] there some interest. We have proposed the Hague, but know not yet whether the Dutch will like it; or if they do, whether the French will. We think we shall have the help of the information of their affairs and state, and the helps of the Prince of Orange his faction: but above all, that De Witt, who hath all this while said he cannot get peace, his mouth will now be stopped, so that he will be forced to offer fit terms for fear of the people; and lastly, if France or Spain do not please us, we are in a way presently to clap up a peace with the Dutch, and secure them. But we are also in treaty with France, as he says; but it must be to the excluding our alliance with the King of Spain or House of Austria: which we do not know presently what will be determined in. He tells me the Vice-chamberlaine is so great with the King, that let the Duke of York, and Sir W. Coventry, and this office do or say what they will, while the King lives Sir G. Carteret will do what he will; and advises me to be often with him, and eat and drink with him; and tells me that he doubts he is jealous of me, and was mighty mad to-day at our discourse to him before the Duke of York. But I did give him my reasons, that the office is concerned to declare that without money the King's work cannot go on. He assures me that Henry Brouncker is one of the shrewdest fellows for parts in England, and a dangerous man: that while we want money so much in the Navy, the officers of the Ordnance have at this day £300,000 good in tallies, which they can command money upon: that Harry Coventry, who is to go upon this treaty with Lord Hollis (who he confesses to be a very wise man) into Holland, is a mighty, quick, ready man, but not so weighty as he should be, he knowing him so well in his drink as he do: that unless the King do something against my Lord Mordaunt and the Patents for the Canary Company before the Parliament next meets, he do believe there will be a civil war before there will be any more money given, unless it may be at their perfect disposal; and that all things are now ordered to the provoking of the Parliament against they come next, and the spending the King's money, so as to put him into a necessity of having it at the time it is prorogued for, or sooner. This evening going to the Queene's side to see the ladies, I did find the Queene, the Duchesse of York, and another or two, at cards, with the room full of great ladies and men; which I was amazed at to see

23 See note, November 15, 1666.

on a Sunday, having not believed it, but contrarily, flatly denied the same a little while since to my cosen Roger Pepys.

18th. To the King's house to *The Mayd's Tragedy*; but vexed all the while with two talking ladies and Sir Charles Sedley; yet pleased to hear their discourse, he being a stranger. And one of the ladies would and did sit with her mask on all the play; and being exceedingly witty as ever I heard woman, did talk most pleasantly with him; but was, I believe, a virtuous woman, and of quality. He would fain know who she was, but she would not tell; yet did give him many pleasant hints of her knowledge of him, by that means setting his brains at work to find out who she was, and did give him leave to use all means to find out who she was, but pulling off her mask. He was mighty witty, and she also making sport with him very inoffensively, that a more pleasant rencontre I never heard. But by that means lost the pleasure of the play wholly, to which now and then Sir Charles Sedley's exceptions against both words and pronouncing were very pretty.

20th. They talked how the King's viallin, Bannister, is mad; that the King hath a Frenchman come to be chief of some part of the King's musique. I with Lord Bellasses, to Lord Chancellor's. Lord Bellasses tells me how the King of France hath caused the stop to be made to our proposition of treating in the Hague; that he being greater than they, we may better come and treat at Paris: so that God knows what will become of the peace! He tells me, too, as a grand secret, that he do believe the offensive and defensive between Spain and us is quite finished, but must not be known, to prevent the king of France's present falling upon Flanders. He do believe the Duke of York will be made General of the Spanish Armies there, and Governor of Flanders, if the French should come against it, and we assist the Spaniard: that we have done the Spaniard abundance of mischief in the West Indys by our privateers at Jamaica, which they lament mightily, and I am sorry for it to have it done at this time. By and by come to my Lord Chancellor, who heard mighty quietly my complaints for lack of money, and spoke mighty kind to me, but little hopes of help therein.

24th. To White Hall, and there meeting my Lord Arlington, he by I know not what kindness offered to carry me along with him to my Lord Treasurer's, whither I told him I was going. I believe he had a mind to discourse of some Navy businesses, but Sir Thomas Clifford coming into the coach to us, we were prevented; which I was sorry for, for I had a mind to begin an acquaintance with him. He speaks well, and hath pretty slight superficial parts, I believe. He, in our going, talked much of the plain habit of the Spaniards; how the King and Lords themselves wear but a cloak of Colchester bayze, and the ladies mantles in cold weather of white flannell: and that the endeavours frequently of setting up the manufactory of making these stuffs there, have only been prevented by the Inquisition. Captain Cocke did tell me what I must not forget: that the answer of the Dutch, refusing the Hague for a place of treaty, and proposing Boysse, Bredah, Bergen-op-Soome, or Mastricht, was seemingly stopped by the Swedes Embassador (though he did show it the King, but the King would take no notice of it, nor does not,) from being delivered to the King; and he hath wrote to desire them to consider better of it. So that, though we know their refusal of the place, yet they know not that we know it, nor the King obliged to show his sense of the affront. That the Dutch are in very great straits, so as to be said to be not able to set out their fleet this year. By and by comes Sir Robert Viner and Lord Mayor[24] to ask the King's direction about measuring out the streets according to the new Act for building of the City, wherein the King is to be pleased. But he says that the way proposed in Parliament by Colonel Birch would have been the best, to have chosen some persons in trust, and sold the whole ground, and let it be sold again by them with preference to the old owner, which would have certainly caused the City to be built where these Trustees pleased; whereas now great differences will be, and the streets built by fits, and not entire till all differences be decided. This, as he tells it, I think would have been the best way. I enquired about the Frenchman that was said to fire the City, and was hanged for it by his own confession, that he was hired for it by a Frenchman of Roane, and that he did with a stick reach in a fire-ball in at a window of the house: whereas the master of the house, who is the King's baker, and his son, and daughter, do all swear there was no such window, and that the fire did not begin thereabouts. Yet the fellow, who, though a mopish besotted fellow, did not speak like a madman, did swear that he did fire it: and did not this like a madman; for being tried on purpose, and landed with his keeper at the Town-

24 Sir William Bolton.

Wharf, he could carry the keeper to the very house. Asking Sir R. Viner what he thought was the cause of the fire, he tells me, that the baker, son, and his daughter, did all swear again and again, that their oven was drawn by ten o'clock at night: that having occasion to light a candle about twelve, there was not so much fire in the bakehouse as to light a match for a candle, so that they were fain to go into another place to light it: that about two in the morning they felt themselves almost choked with smoke, and rising did find the fire coming upstairs; so they rose to save themselves; but that at that time the bavins were not on fire in the yard. So that they are, as they swear, in absolute ignorance how this fire should come; which is a strange thing, that so horrid an effect should have so mean and uncertain a beginning.

25th. Lay long in bed, talking with pleasure with my poor wife, how she used to make coal fires, and wash my foul clothes with her own hand for me, poor wretch! in our little room at my Lord Sandwich's; for which I ought for ever to love and admire her, and do: and persuade myself she would do the same thing again, if God should reduce us to it. At my goldsmith's did observe the King's new medall, where in little there is Mrs Stewart's face as well done as ever I saw any thing in my whole life, I think: and a pretty thing it is, that he should choose her face to represent Brittannia by.

27th. This day at a leisure, the King and Duke of York being gone down to Sheerenesse this morning to lay out the design for a fortification there to the river Medway; and so we do not attend the Duke of York as we should otherwise have done. To the Dock Yard, and went into Mr Pett's; and there beyond expectation he did present me with a Japan cane with a silver head; and his wife sent me by him a ring with a Woolwich stone, now much in request; which I accepted, the values not being great: and then at my asking did give me an old draught of an ancient-built ship, given him by his father, of the Beare in Queene Elizabeth's time. Mr Hunt, newly come out of the country, tells me the country is much impoverished by the greatness of taxes: the farmers do break every day almost, and £1000 a year become not worth £500. He told me some ridiculous pieces of thrift of Sir G. Downing's, who is his countryman, in inviting some poor people at Christmas last, to charm the country people's mouths; but did give them nothing but beef, porridge, pudding, and pork, and nothing said all dinner, but only his mother would say, 'It's good broth, son.' He would answer, 'Yes, it is good broth.' Then says his lady, 'Confirm all, and say, Yes, very good broth.' By and by she would begin and say, 'Good pork': 'Yes,' says the mother, 'good pork.' Then he cries, 'Yes, very good pork.' And so they said of all things; to which nobody made any answer, they going there not out of love or esteem of them, but to eat his victuals, knowing him to be a niggardly fellow; and with this he is jeered now all over the country. Met Mr Cooling, who tells me of my Lord Duke of Buckingham's being sent for last night by a Sergeant at Armes to the Tower for treasonable practices, and that the King is infinitely angry with him, and declared him no longer one of his Council. I know not the reason of it, or occasion.

28th. Mr Holland gives it me as his opinion, that the City will never be built again together, as is expected, while any restraint is laid upon them. I did within these six days see smoke still remaining of the late fire in the City. Sir J. Minnes this night tells me that he hears for certain that ballads are made of us in Holland for begging of a peace; which I expected, but am vexed at. So ends this month with nothing of weight upon my mind but for my father and mother, who are both very ill, and have been so for some weeks: whom God help! but I do fear my poor father will hardly be ever naturally well again.

March 1st. In Mark-lane I do observe (it being St David's day) the picture of a man, dressed like a Welchman, hanging by the neck upon one of the poles that stand out at the top of one of the merchant's houses, in full proportion, and very handsomely done; which is one of the oddest sights I have seen a good while. Tom Woodall, the known chyrurgeon, is killed at Somerset House by a Frenchman in a drunken quarrel.

2nd. After dinner with my wife to the King's house to see *The Mayden Queene*, a new play of Dryden's, mightily commended for the regularity of it, and the strain and wit: and the truth is, there is a comical part done by Nell, which is Florimell, that I never can hope ever to see the like done again by man or woman. The King and Duke of York were at the play. But so great performance of a comical part was never, I believe, in the world before as Nell do this, both as a mad girle, then most and best of all when she comes in like a young gallant; and hath the motions and carriage of a spark the most that ever I saw any man have. It makes me, I confess, admire her.

3rd. It is believed that the Dutch will yield to have the treaty at London or Dover, neither of which will get our King any credit, we having already consented to have it at the Hague; which, it seems, De Witt opposed, as a thing wherein the King of England must needs have some profound design, which in my conscience he hath not. They do also tell me that news is this day come to the King, that the King of France is come with his army to the frontiers of Flanders, demanding leave to pass through their country towards Poland, but is denied, and thereupon that he is gone into the country. How true this is I dare not believe till I hear more. I walked into the Park, it being a fine but very cold day; and there took two or three turns the length of the Pell Mell: and there I met Serjeant Bearcroft, who was sent for the Duke of Buckingham, to have brought him prisoner to the Tower. He come to town this day, and brings word that being overtaken and outrid by the Duchesse of Buckingham within a few miles of the Duke's house of Westhorp, he believes she got thither about a quarter of an hour before him, and so had time to consider; so that when he come the doors were kept shut against him. The next day coming with officers of the neighbour market-town to force open the doors, they were open for him, but the Duke gone: so he took horse presently, and heard upon the road that the Duke of Buckingham was gone before him for London: so that he believes he is this day also come to town before him; but no news is yet heard of him. This is all he brings. Thence to my Lord Chancellor's, and there meeting Sir H. Cholmly, he and I walked in my Lord's garden, and talked among other things, of the treaty; and he says there will certainly be a peace, but I cannot believe it. He tells me that the Duke of Buckingham his crimes, as far as he knows, are his being of a caball with some discontented persons of the late House of Commons, and opposing the desires of the King in all his matters in that House: and endeavouring to become popular, and advising how the Commons' House should proceed, and how he would order the House of Lords. And that he hath been endeavouring to have the King's nativity calculated: which was done, and the fellow now in the Tower about it: which itself hath heretofore, as he says, been held treason, and people died for it: but by the Statute of Treason in Queen Mary's time and since, it hath been left out. He tells me that this silly Lord hath provoked by his ill carriage the Duke of York, my Lord Chancellor, and all the great persons; and therefore most likely will die. He tells me too many practices of treachery against this King; as betraying him in Scotland, and giving Oliver an account of the King's private councils: which the King knows very well, and yet hath pardoned him.

6th. To White Hall; and here the Duke of York did acquaint us (and the King did the like also afterwards coming in) with his resolution of altering the manner of the war this year: that is, we shall keep what fleet we have abroad in several squadrons: so that now all is come out; but we are to keep it as close as we can, without hindering the work that is to be done in preparation to this. Great preparations there are to fortify Sheerenesse and the yard at Portsmouth, and forces are drawing down to both those places, and elsewhere by the sea-side; so that we have some fear of invasion: and the Duke of York himself did declare his expectation of the enemy's blocking us up here in the River, and therefore directed that we should send away all the ships that we have to fit out hence. Sir W. Pen told me, going with me this morning to White Hall, that for certain the Duke of Buckingham is brought into the Tower, and that he hath had an hour's private conference with the King before he was sent thither. Every body complains of the dearness of coals, being at £4 per chaldron, the weather too being become most bitter cold, the King saying to-day that it was the coldest day he ever knew in England. Thence by coach to my Lord Crewe's, where very welcome. Here I find they are in doubt where the Duke of Buckingham is; which makes me mightily reflect on the uncertainty of all history, when in a business of this moment, and of this day's growth, we cannot tell the truth.

7th. To Devonshire House, to a burial of a kinsman of Sir R. Viner's; and there I received a ring. To the Duke's playhouse, and saw *The English Princesse, or Richard the Third*:[25] a most sad, melancholy play, and pretty good, but nothing eminent in it, as some tragedys are; only little Miss Davis[26] did dance a jigg after the end of

25 A tragedy, by J. Caryl.
26 Mary Davis, some time a comedian in the Duke of York's troop, was, according to Pepys, natural daughter of the Earl of Berkshire: she afterwards became the King's mistress, and had by him a child named Mary Tudor, married to Francis Ratcliffe, 2nd Earl of Derwentwater; whose Son James, the 3rd Earl, was attainted, and beheaded for High Treason. There is a fine whole-length portrait of Miss Davis, by Kneller, lately removed to Audley End, from the collection at Billingbear, in which she is represented as a tall handsome woman, and her general appearance ill accords with the description given of her in the Diary.

the play, and there telling the next day's play, so that it come in by force only to please the company to see her dance in boy's clothes; and the truth is, there is no comparison between Nell's dancing the other day at the King's house in boy's clothes and this, this being infinitely beyond the other. This day was reckoned by all people the coldest day that ever was remembered in England; and, God knows, coals at a very great price.

8th. Sir H. Cholmly and I to the Temple, and there parted, he telling me of my Lord Bellasses's want of generosity, and that he will certainly be turned out of his government, and he thinks himself stands fair for it.

9th. Captain Cocke, who was here to-night, did tell us that he is certain that yesterday a proclamation was voted at the council touching the proclaiming of my Lord Duke of Buckingham a traytor, and that it will be out on Monday.

11th. Yesterday the King did publicly talk of the King of France's dealing with all the Princes of Christendome. As to the States of Holland he hath advised them, on good grounds, to refuse to treat with us at the Hague, because of having opportunity of spies by reason of our interest in the House of Orange; and then, it being a town in one particular province, it would not be fit to have it but in a town wherein the provinces have equal interest, as at Mastricht and other places named. That he advises them to offer no terms, nor accept of any, without his privity and consent, according to agreement; and tells them, if not so, he hath in his power to be even with them, the King of England being come to offer any terms he pleases: and that my Lord St Albans is now at Paris, Plenipotentiary, to make what peace he pleases; and so he can make it and exclude them (the Dutch) if he sees fit. A copy of this letter of the King of France's the Spanish Ambassador here gets, and comes and tells all to our King; which our King denies, and says the King of France only uses his power of saying anything. At the same time the King of France writes to the Emperor, that he is resolved to do all things to express affection to the Emperor, having it now in his power to make what peace he pleases between the King of England and him, and the States of the United Provinces; and therefore, that he would not have him to concern himself in a friendship with us; and assures him that on that regard he will not offer any thing to his disturbance in his interest in Flanders or elsewhere. He writes at the same time to Spain, to tell him that he wonders to hear of a league almost ended between the Crown of Spain and England, by my Lord Sandwich, and all without his privity, while he was making a peace upon what terms he pleased with England. That he is a great lover of the Crown of Spain, and would take the King and his affairs during his minority into his protection, nor would offer to set his foot in Flanders or any where else to disturb him; and therefore would not have him to trouble himself to make peace with any body; only he hath a desire to offer an exchange, which he thinks may be of moment to both sides: that is, that he will enstate the King of Spain in the kingdom of Portugall, and he and the Dutch will put him into possession of Lisbon; and that being done, he may have Flanders: and this, they say, do mightily take in Spain, which is sensible of the fruitless expence Flanders, so far off, gives them; and how much better it would be for them to be master of Portugall: and the King of France offers for security herein that the King of England shall be bond for him, and that he will counter-secure the King of England with Amsterdam: and it seems hath assured our King, that if he will make a league with him, he will make a peace exclusive to the Hollander. These things are almost romantique, but yet true, as Sir H. Cholmly tells me the King himself did relate it all yesterday; and it seems as if the King of France did think other princes fit for nothing but to make sport for him: but simple princes they are that are forced to suffer this from him. The proclamation has this day come out against the Duke of Buckingham, commanding him to come in to one of the Secretaries, or to the Lieutenant of the Tower. A silly, vain man to bring himself to this: and there be many hard circumstances in the proclamation of the causes of this proceeding of the King's, which speak great displeasure of the King's, and crimes of his.

13th. The Duke of Buckingham is concluded gone over sea, and, it is thought, to France.

14th. To my Lord Treasurer's. By and by comes the King and Duke of York, and presently the officers of the Ordnance were called; my Lord Barkeley, Sir John Duncomb, and Mr Chichly; then my Lord Brouncker, W. Batten, W. Pen, and myself; where we find only the King and Duke of York, and my Lord Treasurer, and Sir G. Carteret; when I only did speak, laying down the state of our wants, which the

King and Duke of York seemed very well pleased with, and we did get what we asked, £500,000, signed upon the eleven months' tax: but that is not so much ready-money, or what will raise £40,000 per week, which we desired, and the business will want. The King did prevent my offering any thing by and by as Treasurer for Tangier, telling me that he had ordered us £30,000 on the same tax; but that is not what we would have to bring our payments to come within a year. So we gone out, in went others; viz. one after another, Sir Stephen Fox for the Army, Captain Cocke for sick and wounded, Mr Ashburnham for the household. Thence W. Batten, W. Pen, and I back again; I mightily pleased with what I had said and done, and the success thereof.

15th. Letters this day come to Court do tell us that we are likely not to agree, the Dutch demanding high terms, and the King of France the like in a most braveing manner. This morning I was called up by Sir John Winter, poor man! come in a sedan from the other end of the town, about helping the King in the business of bringing down his timber to the sea-side in the forest of Deane.

16th. The weather is now grown warm again after much cold; and it is observable that within these eight days I did see smoke remaining, coming out of some cellars from the late great fire, now above six months since.

17th. I to the Duke of York's lodging, where in his dressing-chamber, he talking of his journey to-morrow or next day to Harwich, to prepare some fortifications there; so that we are wholly upon the defensive part this year. I to walke in the Parke; where to the Queene's chapel, and there heard a fryer preach with his cord about his middle in Portuguese, something I could understand, showing that God did respect the meek and humble as well as the high and rich. He was full of action, but very decent and good, I thought, and his manner of delivery very good. Then I went back to White Hall, and there up to the closet, and spoke with several people till sermon was ended, which was preached by the Bishop of Hereford,[27] an old good man, that they say made an excellent sermon. He was by birth a

27 Dr Herbert Croft was made Bishop of Hereford 1661, but he could not then be very old, as he lived till 1691. The Bishop's father was a knight, and his son a baronet.

Catholique, and a great gallant, having £1500 per annum patrimony, and is a Knight Barronet: was turned from his persuasion by the late Archbishop Laud. He and the Bishop of Exeter, Dr Ward, are the two Bishops that the King do say he cannot have bad sermons from. Here I met with Sir H. Cholmly, who tells me, that undoubtedly my Lord Bellasses do go no more to Tangier, and that he do believe he do stand in a likely way to go Governor; though he sees and showed me a young silly lord (one Lord Allington[28]) who hath offered a great sum of money to go, and will put hard for it, he having a fine lady, and a great man would be glad to have him out of the way. The King is very kind to my Lord Sandwich, and did himself observe to him (Sir G. Carteret) how those very people (meaning the Prince, and Duke of Albemarle) are punished in the same kind as they did seek to abuse my Lord Sandwich.

18th. Comes my old good friend Mr Richard Cumberland[29] to see me, being newly come to town, whom I have not seen almost, if not quite these seven years. In a plain country-parson's dress. I could not spend much time with him, but prayed him to come with his brother, who was with him, to dine with me to-day; which he did do: and I had a great deal of his good company; and a most excellent person he is as any I know, and one that I am sorry should be lost and buried in a little country town, and would be glad to remove him thence; and the truth is, if he would accept of my sister's fortune, I should give £100 more with him than to a man able to settle her four times as much as I fear he is able to do. Comes Captain Jenifer to me, a great servant of my Lord Sandwich's, who tells me that he do hear for certain, though I do not yet believe it, that Sir W. Coventry is to be Secretary of State, and my Lord Arlington Lord Treasurer. I only wish that the latter were as fit for the latter office as the former is for the former, and more fit than my Lord Arlington. Anon Sir W. Pen come and talked with me in the garden; and tells me that for certain the Duke of Richmond is to marry Mrs Stewart, he having this day brought in an account of his estate and debts to the King on that account. This day Mr Caesar told me a pretty experiment of his, of

28 William 2nd Baron Allington of Killard, Ireland, created an English Peer 1682; which title was extinct 1692. He was thrice married.
29 Richard Cumberland, educated at St Paul's School, and Magdalene College, Cambridge, made Bishop of Peterborough 1691. Died 1718, aged 86.

angling with a minikin, a gut-string varnished over, which keeps it from swelling, and is beyond any hair for strength and smallness. The secret I like mightily.

19th. It comes in my mind this night to set down how a house was the other day in Bishopsgate-street blowed up with powder; a house that was untenanted; but, thanks be to God, it did no more hurt; and all do conclude it a plot. This afternoon I am told again that the town do talk of my Lord Arlington's being to be Lord Treasurer, and Sir W. Coventry to be Secretary of State; and that for certain the match is concluded between the Duke of Richmond and Mrs Stewart; which I am well enough pleased with: and it is pretty to consider how his quality will allay people's talk; whereas had a meaner person married her, he would for certain have been derided at first dash.

20th. To our church to the vestry, to be assessed by the late Poll Bill, where I am rated as an Esquire, and for my office all will come to about £50. But not more than I expected, nor so much by a great deal as I ought to be for all my offices. The Duke of Richmond and Mrs Stewart were betrothed last night. It is strange how Rycaut's *Discourse of Turky*, which before the fire I was asked but 8s. for, there being all but twenty-two or thereabouts burned, I did now offer 20s., and he demands 50s., and I think I shall give it him, though it be only as a monument of the fire.

21st. To the Duke of York's playhouse, where unexpectedly I come to see only the young men and women of the house act; they having liberty to act for their own profit on Wednesdays and Fridays this Lent: and the play they did yesterday, being Wednesday, was so well taken, that they thought fit to venture it publickly to-day; a play of my Lord Falkland's,[30] called *The Wedding Night*, a kind of a tragedy, and some things very good in it, but the whole together, I thought, not so. I confess I was well enough pleased with my seeing it; and the people did do better (without the great actors) than I did expect, but yet far short of what they do when they are there. Our trial for a good prize came on to-day, 'The Phoenix, worth 2 or £3000' when by and by Sir W. Batten told me we had got the day, which was mighty welcome news to me and us all. But it is pretty to see what

30 Henry Carey, third Viscount Falkland, MP for Arundell 1661. Died 1664.

money will do. Yesterday Walker[31] was mighty cold on our behalf, till Sir W. Batten promised him, if we sped in this business of the goods, a coach; and if at the next trial we sped for the ship, we would give him a pair of horses. And he hath strove for us to-day like a prince. Though the Swedes' Agent was there with all the vehemence he could to save the goods, but yet we carried it against him.

23rd. At the office, where Sir W. Pen come, being returned from Chatham, from considering the means of fortifying the river Medway, by a chain at the stakes, and ships laid there with guns to keep the enemy from coming up to burn our ships; all our care being now to fortify ourselves against their invading us.

24th. With Sir G. Carteret and Sir J. Minnes; and they did talk of my Lord Brouncker, whose father it seems did give Mr Ashburnham and the present Lord Digby[32] £1200 to be made an Irish lord, and swore the same day that he had not 12d. left to pay for his dinner: they made great mirth at this, my Lord Brouncker having lately given great matter of offence both to them and us all, that we are at present mightily displeased with him. By and by to the Duke of York, where we all met, and there was the King also; and all our discourse was about fortifying of the Medway and Harwich, which is to be entrenched quite round, and Portsmouth: and here they advised with Sir Godfrey Lloyd and Sir Bernard de Gunn,[33] the two great engineers, and had the plates drawn before them; and indeed all their care they now take is to fortify themselves, and are not ashamed of it; for when by and by my Lord Arlington come in with letters, and seeing the King and Duke of York give us and the officers of the Ordnance directions in this matter, he did move that we might do it as privately as we could, that it might not come into the Dutch Gazette presently, as the King's and Duke of York's going down the other day to Sheerenesse was the week after in the Harlem Gazette. The King and Duke of York both laughed at it, and made no matter, but said, 'Let us be safe, and let them talk, for there is nothing will trouble them more, nor will prevent their coming more, than to hear

31 Sir W. Walker.

32 The Earl of Bristol, frequently called in the Diary Lord Digby, long after he had succeeded to the Earldom.

33 Engineer-general, who had been employed in 1661 to construct the works at Dunkirk.

that we are fortifying ourselves.' And the Duke of York said further, 'What said Marshal Turenne, when some in vanity said that the enemies were afraid, for they entrenched themselves? "Well," says he, "I would they were not afraid, for then they would not entrench themselves, and so we could deal with them the better." ' Away thence, and met with Sir H. Cholmly, who tells me that he do believe the government of Tangier is bought by my Lord Allington for a sum of money to my Lord Arlington, and something to Lord Bellasses. I did this night give the waterman who uses to carry me 10s. at his request, for the painting of his new boat, on which shall be my arms.

25th. Called at Mr Lilly's, who was working; and indeed his pictures are without doubt much beyond Mr Hales's, I think I may say I am convinced: but a mighty proud man he is, and full of state. To the King's playhouse; and by and by comes Mr Lowther and his wife and mine, and into a box forsooth, neither of them being dressed, which I was almost ashamed of. Sir W. Pen and I in the pit, and here saw *The Mayden Queene* again; which indeed the more I see the more I like, and is an excellent play, and so done by Nell her merry part, as cannot be better done in nature.

26th. To Exeter House, where the Judge was sitting, and there heard our cause pleaded; Sir — Turner, Sir W. Walker, and Sir Ellis Layton being our counsel against only Sir Robert Wiseman[34] on the other. The second of our three counsel was the best, and indeed did speak admirably, and is a very shrewd man. Nevertheless as good as he did make our case, and the rest, yet when Wiseman come to argue (nay, and though he did begin so sillily that we laughed in scorn in our sleeves at him,) he did so state the case, that the Judge[35] did not think fit to decide the cause to-night, but took to to-morrow, and did stagger us in our hopes, so as to make us despair of the success. I am mightily pleased with the Judge, who seems a very rational, learned, and uncorrupt man, though our success do shake me.

34 D.C.L. King's Advocate 1669.
35 Sir Leoline Jenkins, Principal of Jesus College, Oxford, and afterwards made Judge of the Admiralty and the Prerogative Court. He was subsequently employed on several Embassies, and in 1680 succeeded Henry Coventry as Secretary of State. Died 1685, aged 62.

27th. To the Castle Taverne by Exeter House; and there Sir Ellis Layton, whom I find a wonderful witty, ready man for sudden answers and little tales, and sayings very extraordinary witty. He did give me a full account, upon my demand, of this Judge of the Admiralty, Judge Jenkins; who, he says, is a man never practised in this Court, but taken merely for his merit and ability's sake from Trinity Hall, where he had always lived; only by accident the business of the want of a Judge being proposed, the present Archbishop of Canterbury sent for him up: and here he is against the gré and content of the old Doctors made Judge, but is a very excellent man both for judgment and temper (yet majesty enough), and by all men's report not to be corrupted. After dinner to the Court, where Sir Ellis Layton did make a very silly motion in our behalf, but did neither hurt nor good. After him Walker and Wiseman. And then the Judge did pronounce his sentence; for some a part of the goods and ship, and the freight of the whole to be free and returned and paid by us, and the remaining (which was the greater part) to be ours. The loss of so much troubles us; but we have got a pretty good part, thanks be to God! Received from my brother the news of my mother's dying on Monday about five or six o'clock in the afternoon, and that the last time she spoke of her children was on Friday last, and her last words were, 'God bless my poor Sam!' The reading hereof did set me a-weeping heartily.

29th. The great streets in the City are marked out with piles drove into the ground; and if ever it be built in that form with so fair streets, it will be a noble sight. To a periwigg-maker's and there bought two periwiggs, mighty fine indeed; too fine, I thought, for me; but he persuaded me, and I did buy them for £4 10s. the two. To the Bull-Head Taverne, whither was brought my French gun; and one Truelocke, the famous gunsmith, that is a mighty ingenious man, did take my gun in pieces, and made me understand the secrets thereof: and upon the whole I do find it a very good piece of work, and truly wrought; but for certain not a thing to be used much with safety: and he do find that this very gun was never yet shot off.

30th. To see the silly play of my Lady Newcastle's,[36] called *The Humourous Lovers*; the most silly thing that ever came upon a stage. I

36 Margaret, daughter of Thomas Lucas of Colchester, and sister to John Lord Lucas, married William Marquis of Newcastle, created a Duke 1664.

was sick to see it, but yet would not but have seen it, that I might the better understand her.

31st. To church; and with my mourning, very handsome, and new periwigg, make a great show. Walked to my Lord Treasurer's, where the King, Duke of York, and the Caball, and much company without; and a fine day. Anon come out from the Caball my Lord Hollis and Mr H. Coventry,[37] who, it is conceived, have received their instructions from the King this day; they being to begin their journey towards their treaty at Bredagh speedily, their passes being come. Here I saw the Lady Northumberland[38] and her daughter-in-law (my Lord Treasurer's daughter) my Lady Piercy,[39] a beautiful lady indeed. The month shuts up only with great desires of peace in all of us, and a belief that we shall have a peace, in most people if it can be had on any terms, for there is a necessity of it; for we cannot go on with the war, and our masters are afraid to come to depend upon the good will of the Parliament any more, as I do hear.

April 1st. To White Hall, and there had the good fortune to walk with Sir W. Coventry into the garden, and there read our melancholy letter to the Duke of York, which he likes. And so to talk: and he flatly owns that we must have a peace, for we cannot set out a fleet; and (to use his own words) he fears that we shall soon have enough of fighting in this new way that we have thought on for this year. He bemoans the want of money, and discovers himself jealous that Sir G. Carteret do not look after or concern himself for getting money; and did further say, that he and my Lord Chancellor do at this very day labour all they can to vilify this new way of raising money, and making it payable as it now is into the Exchequer; and that in pursuance hereof my Lord Chancellor hath prevailed with the

37 Third son of Thomas first Lord Coventry; after the Restoration made a Groom of the Bedchamber, and elected MP for Droitwich. In 1664 he was sent Envoy Extraordinary to Sweden, where he remained two years, and was again employed on an Embassy to the same Court in 1671. He also succeeded in negotiating the peace at Breda here alluded to, and in 1672 became Secretary of State; which office he resigned in 1679, on account of ill health. He died unmarried, December 7, 1686.
38 Lady Elizabeth Howard, daughter of Theophilus Earl of Suffolk wife of Algernon tenth Earl of Northumberland.
39 Lady Elizabeth Wriothesly, daughter to the Earl of Southampton, married Joscelin Lord Percy.

King in the close of his speech to the House to say, that he did hope to see them come to give money as it used to be given, without so many provisos, meaning this new method of the Act. Mrs Rebecca Allen, poor heart! come to desire favour for her husband, who is clapt up, being a Lieutenant, for sending a challenge to his Captain in the most saucy, base language that could be writ. I perceive Sir W. Coventry is wholly resolved to bring him to punishment; for 'bear with this,' says he, 'and no discipline shall ever be expected.' Sir J. Minnes did tell of the discovery of his own great-grandfather's murder, fifteen years after he was murdered.

3rd. To the Duke of York, where Sir G. Carteret did say that he had no funds to raise money on; and being asked by Sir W. Coventry whether the eleven months' tax was not a fund, he answered 'No,' that the banquers would not lend money upon it. Then Sir W. Coventry burst out and said he did supplicate His Royal Highness, and would do the same to the King, that he would remember who they were that did persuade the King from parting with the Chimney-money to the Parliament, and taking that in lieu which they would certainly have given, and which would have raised infallibly ready-money; meaning the bankers and the farmers of the Chimney-money, (whereof Sir G. Carteret, I think, is one;) saying plainly, that whoever did advise the King to that, did as much as in them lay cut the King's throat, and did wholly betray him. To which the Duke of York did assent; and remembered that the King did say again and again at the time, that he was assured, and did fully believe, the money would be raised presently upon a land-tax. This put us all into a stound. And Sir W. Coventry went on to declare that he was glad he was come to have so lately concern in the Navy as he hath, for he cannot now give any good account of the Navy business; and that all his work now was to be able to provide such orders as would justify His Royal Highness in business when it shall be called to account: and that he do do, not concerning himself whether they are or can be performed, or no: and that when it comes to be examined and falls on my Lord Treasurer, he cannot help it, whatever the issue of it shall be. One thing more Sir W. Coventry did say to the Duke of York, when I moved again, that of about £9000 debt to Lanyon at Plymouth, he might pay £3700 worth of prize-goods that he bought lately at the candle out of this debt due to him from the King; and the

Duke of York, and Sir G. Carteret, and Lord Barkeley, saying all of
them that my Lord Ashly would not be got to yield it, who is
Treasurer of the Prizes: Sir W. Coventry did plainly desire that it
might be declared whether the proceeds of the prizes were to go to
the helping on of the war, or no; and if it were, how then this could
be denied? Which put them all into another stound; and it is true,
God forgive us! Thence to the chapel, and there by chance hear that
Dr Crewe is to preach; and so into the organ loft, where I met Mr
Carteret, and my Lady Jemimah, and Sir Thomas Crewe's two
daughters, and Dr Childe playing: and Dr Crewe did make a very
pretty, neat, sober, honest sermon; and delivered it very readily,
decently, and gravely, beyond his years: so as I was exceedingly taken
with it, and I believe the whole chapel, he being but young; but his
manner of his delivery I do like exceedingly. His text was, 'But first
seek the kingdom of God, and all things shall be added unto you.'
The Dutch letters are come, and say that the Dutch have ordered a
passe to be sent for our Commissioners, and that it is now upon the
way coming with a trumpeter blinded, as is usual. But I perceive
every body begins to doubt the success of the treaty, all their hopes
being only that if it can be had on any terms, the Chancellor will have
it; for he dare not come before a Parliament, nor a great many more
of the courtiers, and the King himself do declare he do not desire it,
nor intend but on a strait; which God defend him from! Here I hear
how the King is not so well pleased of this marriage between the
Duke of Richmond and Mrs Stewart, as is talked; and that he by a
wile did fetch her to the Beare, at the Bridge-foot, where a coach was
ready, and they are stole away into Kent without the King's leave;
and that the King hath said he will never see her more: but people do
think that it is only a trick. This day I saw Prince Rupert abroad in
the vane-room, pretty well as he used to be, and looks as well, only
something appears to be under his periwigg on the crown of his head.

4th. I find the Duke of Albemarle at dinner with sorry company,
some of his officers of the Army: dirty dishes and a nasty wife at table,
and bad meat, of which I made but an ill dinner. Pretty to hear how
she talked against Captain Du Tel, the Frenchman, that the Prince and
her husband put out the last year; and how, says she, the Duke of
York hath made him for his good services his cupbearer, yet he fired
more shot into the Prince's ship, and others of the King's ships, than

of the enemy. And the Duke of Albemarle did confirm it, and that somebody in the fight did cry out that a little Dutchman by his ship did plague him more than any other; upon which they were going to order him to be sunk, when they looked and found it was Du Tell, who, as the Duke of Albemarle says, had killed several men in several of our ships. He said, but for his interest, which he knew he had at Court, he had hanged him at the yard's-arm without staying for a Court-martiall. One Colonell Howard, at the table, magnified the Duke of Albemarle's fight in June last, as being a greater action than ever was done by Caesar. The Duke of Albemarle did say it had been no great action, had all his number fought, as they should have done, to have beat the Dutch: but of his 55 ships, not above 25 fought. He did give an account that it was a fight he was forced to: the Dutch being come in his way, and he being ordered to the buoy of the Nore, he could not pass by them without fighting, nor avoid them without great disadvantage and dishonour, (and this Sir G. Carteret, I afterwards giving him an account of what he said, says that it is true that he was ordered up to the Nore). But I remember he said, had all his captains fought, he would no more have doubted to have beat the Dutch with all their number, than to eat the apple that lay on his trencher. My Lady Duchesse, among other things, discoursed of the wisdom of dividing the fleet; which the Generall said nothing to, though he knew well that it come from themselves in the fleet, and was brought up hither by Sir Edward Spragge. Colonell Howard, asking how the Prince did, the Duke of Albemarle answering 'Pretty well,' the other replied, 'But not so well as to go to sea again.' – 'How!' says the Duchesse, 'what should he go for, if he were well, for there are no ships for him to command? And so you have brought your hogs to a fair market,' said she. It was pretty to hear the Duke of Albemarle himself to wish that they would come on our ground (meaning the French), for that he would pay them so as to make them glad to go back to France again; which was like a general, but not like an admiral. One at the table told an odd passage in this late plague: that at Petersfield (I think he said) one side of the street had every house almost infected through the town, and the other, not one shut up. I made Sir G. Carteret merry with telling him how many land-admirals we are to have this year: Allen at Plymouth, Holmes at Portsmouth, Spragge for Medway, Teddiman at Dover, Smith to the Northward, and Harman to the Southward. With Sir Stephen Fox, talking of the sad condition of the King's purse, and affairs thereby; and how sad the King's life must be, to pass by his officers every hour, that are four years behind hand unpaid. Sir W. Coventry tells me plainly, that to all future complaints of lack of money he will answer but with the shrug of the shoulder; which methought did come to my heart, to see him to begin to abandon the King's affairs, and let them sink or swim. My wife had been to-day at White Hall to the Maunday, it being Maunday Thursday; but the King did not wash the poor people's feet himself, but the Bishop of London did it for him.

5th. Mr Young was talking about the building of the City again: and he told me that those few churches that are to be new built are plainly not chosen with regard to the convenience of the City; they stand a great many in a cluster about Cornhill: but that all of them are either in the gift of the Lord Archbishop, or Bishop of London, or Lord Chancellor, or gift of the City. Thus all things, even to the building of churches, are done in this world! This morning come to me the collectors for my Poll-money; for which I paid for my title as Esquire and place of Clerk of Acts, and my head and wife's servants', and their wages, £40 17s. And though this be a great deal, yet it is a shame I should pay no more: that is, that I should not be assessed for my pay, as in the victualling business and Tangier; and for my money, which of my own accord I had determined to charge myself with £1000 money, till coming to the Vestry, and seeing nobody of our ablest merchants, as Sir Andrew Rickard,[40] to do it, I thought it not decent for me to do it.

7th. To White Hall, and there saw the King come out of chapel after prayers in the afternoon, which he is never at but after having received the Sacrament: and the Court, I perceive, is quite out of mourning; and some very fine; among others, my Lord Gerard, in a very rich vest and coate. Here I met with my Lord Bellasses: and it is pretty to see what a formal story he tells me of his leaving his place upon the death of my Lord Cleveland,[41] by which he is become

40 A leading man in the East India Company, who was committed in 1668 by the House of Lords, during their proceedings on the petition of Skinner; See *Journals*. He purchased the advowson of his parish, St Olave, Hart Street, and left it to trustees *in perpetuum*, who still present the rector. He was knighted by Charles II, July 10, 1662.

41 Thomas Wentworth Earl of Cleveland.

Captain of the Pensioners; and that the King did leave it to him to keep the other or take this; whereas I know the contrary, that they had a mind to have him away from Tangier. Into Moorfields, and did find houses built two stories high, and like to stand; and must become a place of great trade till the City be built; and the street is already paved as London streets used to be.

8th. Away to the Temple, to my new bookseller's; and there I did agree for Rycaut's[42] late *History of the Turkish Policy*, which cost me 55s.: whereas it was sold plain before the late fire for 8s., and bound and coloured as this is for 20s.; for I have bought it finely bound and truly coloured all the figures, of which there was but six books done so, whereof the King and Duke of York and Duke of Monmouth, and Lord Arlington, had four. The fifth was sold, and I have bought the sixth.

9th. Towards noon I to the Exchange, and there do hear mighty cries for peace, and that otherwise we shall be undone; and yet do suspect the badness of the peace we shall make. Several do complain of abundance of land flung up by tenants out of their hands for want of ability to pay their rents; and by name, that the Duke of Buckingham hath £6000 so flung up. And my father writes that Jasper Trice, upon this pretence of his tenants' dealing with him, is broke up house-keeping, and gone to board with his brother, Naylor, at Offord; which is very sad. To the King's house, and there saw *The Tameing of a Shrew*, which hath some very good pieces in it, but generally is but a mean play; and the best part, Sawny, done by Lacy; and hath not half its life, by reason of the words, I suppose, not being understood, at least by me.

10th. I begun to discourse with Sir W. Coventry the business of Tangier, which by the removal of my Lord Bellasses is now to have a new Governor; and did move him, that at this season all the business of reforming the garrison might be considered, while nobody was to be offended. And I told him it is plain that we do overspend our revenue: that it is of no more profit to the King than it was the first day, nor in itself of better credit; no more people of condition willing to live there, nor any thing like a place likely to turn his Majesty to

42 This book is in the Pepysian Library.

account: that it hath been hitherto, and for aught I see likely only to be used as a jobb to do a kindness to some lord, or he that can get to be Governor. Sir W. Coventry agreed with me so as to say, that unless the King hath the wealth of the Mogull, he would be a beggar to have his businesses ordered in the manner they now are: that his garrisons must be made places only of convenience to particular persons: that he hath moved the Duke of York in it: and that it was resolved to send no Governor thither till there had been Commissioners sent to put the garrison in order, so as that he that goes may go with limitations and rules to follow, and not to do as he please, as the rest have hitherto done. That he is not afraid to speak his mind, though to the displeasure of any man; and that I know well enough. But that when it is come (as it is now), that to speak the truth in behalf of the King plainly do no good, but all things bore down by other measures than by what is best for the King, he hath no temptation to be perpetually fighting of battles, it being more easy to him on those terms to suffer things to go on without giving any man offence, than to have the same thing done, and he contract the displeasure of all the world, as he must do, that will be for the King. To the King's little chapel; and afterwards to see the King heal the King's Evil (wherein no pleasure, I having seen it before): and then to see him and the Queene, and Duke of York and his wife, at dinner in the Queene's lodgings. And so with Sir G. Carteret to his lodgings to dinner; where very good company. And after dinner he and I to talk alone how things are managed, and to what ruin we must come if we have not a peace. He did tell me one occasion, how Sir Thomas Allen (whom I took for a man of known courage and service on the King's side) was tried for his life in Prince Rupert's fleet, in the late times for cowardice, and condemned to be hanged, and fled to Jerzy; where Sir G. Carteret received him, not knowing the reason of his coming thither; and that thereupon Prince Rupert wrote to the Queene-Mother his dislike of Sir G. Carteret's receiving a person that stood condemned; and so Sir G. Carteret was forced to bid him betake himself to some other place. This was strange to me. Our Commissioners are preparing to go to Bredah to the treaty, and do design to be going the next week.

11th. To White Hall, thinking there to have seen the Duchesse of Newcastle's coming this night to Court to make a visit to the

Queene, the King having been with her yesterday to make her a visit since her coming to town. The whole story of this lady is a romance, and all she does is romantic. Her footmen in velvet coats, and herself in an antique dress, as they say; and was the other day at her own play, *The Humourous Lovers*; the most ridiculous thing that ever was wrote, but yet she and her Lord mightily pleased with it; and she at the end made her respects to the players from her box, and did give them thanks. There is as much expectation of her coming to Court, that so people may come to see her, as if it were the Queene of Sweden: but I lost my labour, for she did not come this night. There have been two fires in the City within this week.

12th. By water to White Hall, and there did our usual business before the Duke of York: but it fell out that, discoursing of matters of money, it rose to a mighty heat, very high words arising between Sir G. Carteret and Sir W. Coventry, the former in his passion saying that the other should have helped things if they were so bad; and the other answered, So he would, and things should have been better had he been Treasurer of the Navy. I was mightily troubled at this heat, and it will breed ill blood between them, I fear; but things are in that bad condition, that I do daily expect we shall all fly in one another's faces, when we shall be reduced every one to answer for himself. We broke up; and I soon after to Sir G. Carteret's chamber, where I find the poor man telling his lady privately, and she weeping. I went in to them, and did seem, as indeed I was, troubled for this; and did give the best advice I could, which I think did please them: and they do apprehend me their friend, as indeed I am, for I do take the Vice-chamberlain for a most honest man. He did assure me that he was not, all expences and things paid, clear in estate £15,000 better than he was when the King come in; and that the King and Lord Chancellor did know that he was worth, with the debt the King owed him, £50,000 (I think he said) when the King come into England.

15th. Called up by Sir H. Cholmly, who tells me that my Lord Middleton[43] is for certain chosen Governor of Tangier; a man of moderate understanding, not covetous, but a soldier of fortune, and poor. To the King's house by chance, where a new play: so full as I

43 John first Earl of Middleton, in Scotland.

never saw it; I forced to stand all the while close to the very door till I took cold, and many people went away for want of room. The King and Queene and Duke of York and Duchesse there, and all the Court, and Sir W. Coventry. The play called, *The Change of Crownes*: a play of Ned Howard's,[44] the best that I ever saw at that house, being a great play and serious; only Lacy did act the country-gentleman come up to Court, who do abuse the Court with all the imaginable wit and plainness about selling of places, and doing every thing for money. The play took very much. Thence I to my new bookseller's, and there bought Hooker's *Polity*, the new edition, and Dugdale's *History of the Inns of Court*, of which there was but a few saved out of the fire. Carried my wife to see the new play I saw yesterday: but there, contrary to expectation, I find *The Silent Woman*.

16th. Knipp tells me the King was so angry at the liberty taken by Lacy's part to abuse him to his face, that he commanded they should act no more, till Moone[45] went and got leave for them to act again, but not this play. The King mighty angry; and it was bitter indeed, but very fine and witty. I never was more taken with a play than I am with this *Silent Woman*, as old as it is, and as often as I have seen it. There is more wit in it than goes to ten new plays. Pierce told us the story how in good earnest the King is offended with the Duke of Richmond's marrying, and Mrs Stewart's sending the King his jewels again. As she tells it, it is the noblest romance and example of a brave lady that ever I read in my life.

17th. In our way in Tower-street we saw Desbrough[46] walking on foot; who is now no more a prisoner, and looks well, and just as he used to do heretofore.

19th. Some talk about Sir W. Pen's being to buy Wanstead-House of Sir Robert Brookes.

20th. Met Mr Rolt, who tells me the reason of no play to-day at the King's house. That Lacy had been committed to the porter's lodge

44 A younger son of the Earl of Berkshire, and brother to Sir Robert Howard.
45 Michael Mohun, a celebrated actor belonging to the King's Company; he had served as a Major in the Royal Army.
46 Major-general John Desborough, Cromwell's brother-in-law, and one of his Council of State; afterwards promoted to the Chancellorship of Ireland by his nephew Richard.

for his acting his part in the late new play, and being thence released to come to the King's house, he there met with Ned Howard, the poet of the play, who congratulated his release; upon which Lacy cursed him as that it was the fault of his nonsensical play that was the cause of his ill usage. Mr Howard did give him some reply: to which Lacy answered him, that he was more a fool than a poet; upon which Howard did give him a blow on the face with his glove; on which Lacy, having a cane in his hand, did give him a blow over the pate. Here Rolt and others that discoursed of it in the pit this afternoon, did wonder that Howard did not run him through, he being too mean a fellow to fight with. But Howard did not do any thing but complain to the King of it; so the whole house is silenced: and the gentry seem to rejoice much at it, the house being become too insolent. I have a mind to buy enough ground to build a coach-house and stable; for I have had it much in my thoughts lately that it is not too much for me now in degree or cost to keep a coach, but contrarily, that I am almost ashamed to be seen in a hackney. To Hackney church. A knight and his lady very civil to me when they came, being Sir George Viner, and his lady in rich jewells, but most in beauty: almost the finest woman that ever I saw. That which I went chiefly to see was the young ladies of the schools, whereof there is great store, very pretty; and also the organ, which is handsome, and tunes the psalm and plays with the people; which is mighty pretty, and makes me mighty earnest to have a pair at our church, I having almost a mind to give them a pair if they would settle a maintenance on them for it.

22nd. To the Lord Chancellor's house, the first time I have been therein; and it is very noble, and brave pictures of the ancient and present nobility. The King was vexed the other day for having no paper laid for him at the Council table, as was usual; and Sir Richard Broune did tell his Majesty he would call the person whose work it was to provide it: who being come, did tell his Majesty that he was but a poor man, and was out 4 or £500 for it, which was as much as he is worth; and that he cannot provide it any longer without money, having not received a penny since the King's coming in. So the King spoke to my Lord Chamberlain. And many such mementos the King do now-a-days meet withall, enough to make an ingenuous man mad.

23rd. St George's-day; the feast being kept at White Hall, out of design, as it is thought, to make the best countenance we can to the Swede's Embassadors before their leaving us to go to the treaty abroad, to show some jollity.

24th. To Sir John Duncomb's lodging in the Pell Mell, in order to the money spoken of in the morning; and there awhile sat and discoursed: and I find that he is a very proper man for business, being very resolute and proud, and industrious. He told me what reformation they had made in the office of the Ordnance, taking away Legg's fees: have got an order that no Treasurer after him shall ever sit at the Board; and it is a good one: that no Master of the Ordnance here shall ever sell a place. He tells me they have not paid any increase of price for any thing during this war, but in most have paid less; and at this day have greater stores than they know where to lay if there should be peace, and than ever was any time this war. Then to talk of news: that he thinks the want of money hath undone the King, for the Parliament will never give the King more money without calling all people to account, nor, as he believes, will ever make war again, but they will manage it themselves: unless, which I proposed, he would visibly become a severer inspector into his own business and accounts, and that would gain upon the Parliament yet: which he confesses and confirms as the only lift to set him upon his legs, but says that it is not in his nature ever to do. He thinks that much of our misfortune hath been for want of an active Lord Treasurer, and that such a man as Sir W. Coventry would do the business thoroughly.

26th. To White Hall, and there saw the Duke of Albemarle, who is not well, and do grow crazy. While I was waiting in the Matted Gallery, a young man was working in Indian inke, the great picture of the King and Queene sitting by Van Dike; and did it very finely. Then I took a turn with Mr Evelyn; with whom I walked two hours, till almost one of the clock: talking of the badness of the Government, where nothing but wickedness, and wicked men and women command the King: that it is not in his nature to gainsay any thing that relates to his pleasures; that much of it arises from the sickliness of our Ministers of State, who cannot be about him as the idle companions are, and therefore he gives way to the young rogues; and then from the negligence of the clergy, that a Bishop shall never be seen about him, as the King of France hath always: that the King would fain have some of the same gang to be Lord Treasurer, which would be yet worse, for now some delays are put to the getting gifts of the King, as Lady Byron,[47] who had been, as he called it, the King's seventeenth mistress abroad, did not leave him till she had got him to give her an order for £4000 worth of plate to be made for her; but by delays, thanks be to God! she died before she had it. He confirmed to me the business of the want of paper at the Council table the other day, which I have observed; Wooly being to have found it, and did, being called, tell the King to his face the reason of it. And Mr Evelyn tells me of several of the menial servants of the Court lacking bread, that have not received a farthing wages since the King's coming in. He tells me the King of France hath his mistresses, but laughs at the foolery of our King, that makes his bastards princes, and loses his revenue upon them, and makes his mistresses his masters. And the King of France did never grant Lavaliere any thing to bestow on others, and gives a little subsistence, but no more, to his bastards. He told me the whole story of Mrs Stewart's going away from Court, he knowing her well; and believes her, up to her leaving the Court, to be as virtuous as any woman in the world: and told me, from a Lord that she told it to but yesterday with her own mouth, and a sober man, that when the Duke of Richmond did make love to her, she did ask the King, and he did the like also; and that the King did not deny it, and told this Lord that she was come to that pass as to resolve to have married any gentleman of £1500 a-year that would have had her in honour: for it was come to that pass, that she could not longer continue at Court without prostituting herself to the King, whom she had so long kept off, though he had liberty more than any other had, or he ought to have, as to dalliance. She told this Lord that she had reflected upon the occasion she had given the world to think her a bad woman, and that she had no way but to marry and leave the Court, rather in this way of discontent than otherwise, that the world might see that she sought not any thing but her humour; and that she will never come to live at Court more than when she comes to town to kiss the Queene her mistress's hand: and hopes, though she hath little reason

47 Eleanor, daughter of Robert Needham, Viscount Kilmurrey, and widow of Peter Warburton, became in 1644 the second wife of Richard first Lord Byron. Died 1663.

to hope, she can please her Lord so as to reclaim him, that they may yet live comfortably in the country on his estate. She told this Lord that all the jewells she ever had given her at Court, or any other presents (more than the King's Allowance of £700 per annum out of the Privy-purse for her clothes), were at her first coming, the King did give her a necklace of pearl of about £1100; and afterwards, about seven months since, when the King had hopes to have obtained some courtesy of her, the King did give her some jewells, I have forgot what, and I think a pair of pendants. The Duke of York, being once her Valentine, did give her a jewell of about £800; and my Lord Mandeville, her Valentine this year, a ring of about £300; and the King of France would have had her mother (who, he says, is one of the most cunning women in the world,) to have let her stay in France, saying that he loved her not as a mistress, but as one that he could marry as well as any lady in France; and that, if she might stay, for the honour of his Court he would take care she should not repent. But her mother, by command of the Queene-mother, thought rather to bring her into England; and the King of France did give her a jewell: so that Evelyn believes she may be worth in jewells about £6000 and that is all she hath in the world: and a worthy woman; and in this hath done as great an act of honour as ever was done by woman. That now the Countesse Castlemaine do carry all before her: and among other arguments to prove Mrs Stewart to have been honest to the last, he says that the King's keeping in still with my Lady Castlemaine do show it; for he never was known to keep two mistresses in his life, and would never have kept to her had he prevailed any thing with Mrs Stewart. She is gone yesterday with her Lord to Cobham. He did tell me of the ridiculous humour of our King and Knights of the Garter the other day, who, whereas heretofore their robes were only to be worn during their ceremonies and service, these, as proud of their coats, did wear them all day till night, and then rode into the Park with them on. Nay, and he tells me he did see my Lord Oxford and Duke of Monmouth in a hackney-coach with two footmen in the Park, with their robes on; which is a most scandalous thing, so as all gravity may be said to be lost among us. By and by we discoursed of Sir Thomas Clifford, whom I took for a very rich and learned man, and of the great family of that name. He tells me he is only a man of about seven-score pounds a-year, of little learning more than the law of a justice of peace; which he knows well; a parson's[48] son, got to be burgess in a little borough in the West, and here fell into the acquaintance of my Lord Arlington, whose creature he is, and never from him; a man of virtue, and comely, and good parts enough; and hath come into his place with a great grace, though with a great skip over the heads of a great many, as Chichly and Denham, and some Lords that did expect it. By the way, he tells me that of all the great men of England there is none that endeavours more to raise those that he takes into favour than my Lord Arlington; and that on that score he is much more to be made one's patron than my Lord Chancellor, who never did, nor never will do any thing, but for money. Certain news of the Dutch being abroad on our coast with twenty-four great ships. Met my Lady Newcastle going with her coaches and footmen all in velvet: herself (whom I never saw before), as I have heard her often described (for all the town-talk is now-a-days of her extravagancies), with her velvet-cap, her hair about her ears; many black patches, because of pimples about her mouth; naked-necked, without any thing about it, and a black just-au-corps. She seemed to me a very comely woman: but I hope to see more of her on May-day.

28th. To Deptford, and there I walked down the Yard, Shish and Cox with me; and discoursed about cleaning of the wet docke, and heard (which I had before) how, when the docke was made, a ship of near 500 tons was there found; a ship supposed of Queene Elizabeth's time, and well wrought, with a great deal of stone shot in her of eighteen inches diameter, which was shot then in use: and afterwards meeting with Captain Perriman and Mr Castle at Half-way Tree, they tell me of stone-shot of thirty-six inches diameter, which they shot out of mortar-pieces.

29th. I hear that the Duke of Cambridge,[49] the Duke of York's son, is very sick; and my Lord Treasurer very bad of the stone, and hath been so some days. Sir G. Carteret tells me my Lord Arlington hath done like a gentleman by him in all things. He says, if my Lord were

48 Collins states, that Sir Thomas Clifford's father was a Colonel in the King's Army during the Scotch Rebellion 1639, and died the same year on his return from the Northern March.
49 James, second son to the Duke of York, born 1663, and created Duke of Cambridge that year. Died 1667.

here, he were the fittest man to be Lord Treasurer of any man in England; and he thinks it might be compassed; for he confesses that the King's matters do suffer through the inability of this man, who is likely to die, and he will propound him to the King. It will remove him from his place at sea, and the King will have a good place to bestow. He says to me, that he could wish when my Lord comes that he would think fit to forbear playing as a thing below him, and which will lessen him, as it do my Lord St Albans, in the King's esteem: and as a great secret tells me that he hath made a match for my Lord Hinchingbroke to a daughter of my Lord Burlington's,[50] where there is great alliance, £10,000 portion; a civil family, and relation to my Lord Chancellor, whose son hath married one of the daughters: and that my Lord Chancellor do take it with very great kindness, so that he do hold himself obliged by it. My Lord Sandwich hath referred it to my Lord Crewe, Sir G. Carteret, and Mr Montagu, to end it. My Lord Hinchingbroke and the ladies know nothing yet of it. It will, I think, be very happy.

30th. I met with Mr Pierce, and he tells me the Duke of Cambridge is very ill and full of spots about his body, that Dr Frazier knows not what to think of it.

May 1st. To Westminster; in the way meeting many milkmaids with their garlands upon their pails, dancing with a fiddler before them; and saw pretty Nelly[51] standing at her lodgings' door in Drury-lane in her smock sleeves and bodice, looking upon one: she seemed a mighty pretty creature. My Lord Crewe walked with me, giving me an account of the meeting of the Commissioners for Accounts, whereof he is one. How some of the gentlemen, Garraway, Littleton, and others, did scruple at their first coming there, being called thither to act, as Members of Parliament, which they could not do by any authority but that of the Parliament, and therefore desired the King's direction in it, which was sent for by my Lord Bridgewater, who brought answer, very short, that the King expected they should obey his Commission. Then they went on and observed upon a power to be given them of administering and framing an oath, which they thought they could not do by any power but Act of Parliament; and

50 Richard Boyle, second Earl of Cork, created Earl of Burlington 1663.
51 Nell Gwynne.

the whole Commission did think fit to have the Judges' opinion in it, and so drawing up their scruples in writing they all attended the King, who told them he would send to the Judges to be answered, and did so; who have, my Lord tells me, met three times about it, not knowing what answer to give it: and they have met this week, doing nothing but expecting the solution of the Judges in this point. My Lord tells me he do believe this Commission will do more hurt than good: it may undo some accounts, if these men shall think fit; but it can never clear an account, for he must come into the Exchequer for all this. Besides, it is a kind of inquisition that hath seldom ever been granted in England: and he believes it will never, besides, give any satisfaction to the People or Parliament, but be looked upon as a forced, packed business of the King, especially if these Parliament-men that are of it shall not concur with them; which he doubts they will not, and therefore wishes much that the King would lay hold of this fit occasion and let the Commission fall. Then to talk of my Lord Sandwich, whom my Lord Crewe hath a great desire might get to be Lord Treasurer if the present Lord should die, as it is believed he will in a little time; and thinks he can have no competitor but my Lord Arlington, who, it is given out, desires it: but my Lord thinks not, for that the being Secretary do keep him a greater interest with the King than the other would do; at least do believe that if my Lord would surrender him his Wardrobe place, it would be a temptation to Arlington to assist my Lord in getting the Treasurer's. I did object to my Lord that it would be no place of content, nor safety, nor honour for my Lord, the State being so indigent as it is, and the King so irregular, and those about him, that my Lord must be forced to part with any thing to answer his warrants; and that, therefore, I do believe the King had rather have a man that may be one of his vicious caball, than a sober man that will mind the publick, that so they may sit at cards and dispose of the revenue of the kingdom. This my Lord was moved at, and said he did not indeed know how to answer it, and bid me think of it; and so said he himself would also do. He do mightily cry out of the bad management of our monies, the King having had so much given him; and yet when the Parliament do find that the King should have £900,000 in his purse by the best account of issues they have yet seen, yet we should report in the Navy a debt due from the King of £900,000: which I did confess I doubted was true in the first, and knew to be true in the last, and did believe that there was some great miscarriages in it: which he owned to believe also, saying, that at this rate it is not in the power of the kingdom to make a war, nor answer the King's wants. Thence away to the King's playhouse, and saw *Love in a Maze*:[52] but a sorry play; only Lacy's clowne's part, which he did most admirably indeed; and I am glad to find the rogue at liberty again. Here was but little, and that ordinary company. We sat at the upper bench next the boxes; and I find it do pretty well, and have the advantage of seeing and hearing the great people, which may be pleasant when there is good store. Now was only Prince Rupert and my Lord Lauderdale, and my Lord —,[53] the naming of whom puts me in mind of my seeing at Sir Robert Viner's two or three great silver flagons, made with inscriptions as gifts of the King to such and such persons of quality as did stay in town the late great plague, for the keeping things in order in the town. Thence Sir W. Pen and I in his coach Tiburne way into the Park, where a horrid dust, and number of coaches, without pleasure or order. That which we and almost all went for was to see my Lady Newcastle; which we could not, she being followed and crowded upon by coaches all the way she went, that nobody could come near her; only I could see she was in a large black coach adorned with silver instead of gold, and so white curtains, and every thing black and white, and herself in her cap. Sir W. Pen did give me an account this afternoon of his design of buying Sir Robert Brookes's fine house at Wansted: which I so wondered at, and did give him reasons against it, which he allowed of: and told me that he did intend to pull down the house and build a less, and that he should get £1500 by the old house, and I know not what fooleries. But I will never believe he ever intended to buy it, for my part, though he troubled Mr Gauden to go and look upon it, and advise him in it.

3rd. To the Duke of York's chamber, which, as it is now fretted at the top, and the chimney-piece made handsome, is one of the noblest and best-proportioned rooms that ever, I think, I saw. To Westminster by coach: the Cofferer[54] telling us odd stories how he was dealt with by the men of the Church at Westminster in taking a lease of them at the King's coming in, and particularly the devilish covetousness of Dr

52 Downes mentions this play, which was never printed, nor is the author known.
53 Probably Craven.
54 Mr Ashburnham.

Busby.[55] Took a turn with my old acquaintance Mr Pechell, whose red nose makes me ashamed to be seen with him, though otherwise a good-natured man. This day the news is come that the fleet of the Dutch, of about 20 ships, which come upon our coasts upon design to have intercepted our colliers (but by good luck failed), is gone to the Frith, and there lies, perhaps to trouble the Scotch privateers, which have galled them of late very much, it may be more than all our last year's fleet.

5th. Sir John Robinson tells me he hath now got a street ordered to be continued, forty feet broad, from Paul's through Cannon-street to the Tower, which will be very fine. He and others this day, where I was in the afternoon, do tell me of at least six or eight fires within these few days; and continually stirs of fire, and real fires there have been, in one place or other, almost ever since the late great fire, as if there was a fate sent people for fire. I walked over the Park to Sir W. Coventry's. We talked of Tangier, of which he is ashamed; also that it should put the King to this charge for no good in the world: and now a man going over that is a good soldier, but a debauched man, which the place need not to have. And so used these words: 'That this place was to the King as my Lord Carnarvon[56] says of wood, that it is an excrescence of the earth provided by God for the payment of debts.' This day Sir W. Coventry tells me the Dutch fleet shot some shot, four or five hundred, into Burnt Island in the Frith, but without any hurt; and so are gone.

7th. To St James's; but there find Sir W. Coventry gone out betimes this morning on horseback with the King and Duke of York to Putny-heath, to run some horses.

9th. In our street, at the Three Tuns Tavern, I find a great hubbub: and what was it but two brothers had fallen out, and one killed the other? And who should they be but the two Fieldings? one whereof, Bazill, was page to my Lady Sandwich; and he hath killed the other, himself being very drunk, and so is sent to Newgate.

55 Richard Busby, DD, Master of Westminster School, and in 1660 made a Prebendary of Westminster. Notwithstanding the character given of him here, he was a liberal benefactor to Christ Church, Oxford, and Lichfield Cathedral. Died 1695, aged 89.
56 Charles Dormer succeeded his father, who fell at the battle of Newbury, as Earl of Carnarvon. Died, without issue, 1709.

10th. At noon to Kent's, at the Three Tuns Tavern: and there the constable of the parish did show us the picklocks and dice that were found in the dead man's pocket, and but 18d. in money; and a table-book, wherein were entered the names of several places where he was to go; and among others his house, where he was to dine, and did dine yesterday. And after dinner went into the church, and there saw his corpse with the wound in his left breast; a sad spectacle, and a broad wound, which makes my hand now shake to write of it. His brother intending, it seems, to kill the coachman, who did not please him, this fellow stepped in and took away his sword; who thereupon took out his knife, which was of the fashion, with a falchion blade, and a little cross at the hilt like a dagger; and with that stabbed him. Drove hard towards Clerkenwell, thinking to have overtaken my Lady Newcastle, whom I saw before us in her coach, with 100 boys and girls running looking upon her; but I could not: and so she got home before I could come up to her. But I will get a time to see her.

12th. Walked over the fields to Kingsland, and back again; a walk, I think, I have not taken these twenty years; but puts me in mind of my boy's time when I boarded at Kingsland, and used to shoot with my bow and arrows in these fields.

13th. This morning come Sir H. Cholmly to me for a tally or two; and tells me that he hears that we are by agreement to give the King of France Nova Scotia; which he do not like: but I do not know the importance of it. Sir Philip Warwick do please himself like a good man to tell some of the good ejaculations of my Lord Treasurer concerning the little worth of this world, to buy it with so much pain, and other things fit for a dying man.

14th. To my Lord Chancellor's, where I met Mr Povy expecting the coming of the rest of the Commissioners for Tangier. Here I understand how the two Dukes, both the only sons of the Duke of York, are sick even to danger; and that on Sunday last they were both so ill, as that the poor Duchesse was in doubt which would die; the Duke of Cambridge, of some general disease, the other little Duke, whose title I know not, of the convulsion fits, of which he had four this morning. Fear that either of them might be dead, did make us think that it was the occasion that the Duke of York and others were not come to the meeting of the Commission which was designed, and my Lord Chancellor did expect. And it was pretty to observe how, when my Lord sent down to St James's to see why the Duke of York come not, and Mr Povy, who went, returned, my Lord did ask (not how the Princes or the Dukes do, as other people do, but) 'How do the Children?' which methought was mighty great, and like a great man and grandfather. I find every body mightily concerned for these children, as a matter wherein the State is much concerned that they should live.

15th. I away with Sir G. Carteret to London, talking all the way: and he do tell me that the business of my Lord Hinchingbroke his marriage with my Lord Burlington's daughter, is concluded on by all friends; and that my Lady is now told of it, and do mightily please herself with it: which I am mightily glad of. News still that my Lord Treasurer is so ill as not to be any man of this world; and it is said that the Treasury shall be managed by Commission. I would to God Sir G. Carteret, or my Lord Sandwich, be in it! But the latter is the more fit for it.

16th. This being Holy Thursday, when the boys go our procession round the parish, we were to go to the Three Tuns Tavern to dine with the rest of the parish; where all the parish almost was, Sir Andrew Rickard and others; and of our house, J. Minnes, W. Batten, W. Pen, and myself: and Mr Mills did sit uppermost at the table. Sir John Fredricke[57] and Sir R. Ford did talk of Paul's School, which, they tell me, must be taken away; and then I fear it will be long before another place, such as they say is promised, is found: but they do say that the honour of their Company[58] is concerned in the doing of it, and that it is a thing that they are obliged to do. To my Lord Treasurer's, where I find the porter crying, and suspected it was that my Lord is dead; and, poor Lord! we did find that he was dead just now. There is a good man gone: and I pray God that the Treasury may not be worse managed by the hand or hands it shall now be put into; though, for certain, the slowness (though he was of great integrity) of this man and remissness have gone as far to undo the nation, as any thing else that

---

57 Lord Mayor of London 1662, and President of Christ's Hospital. His eldest son, John, was created a Baronet 1723.
58 The Mercers' Company, under whose superintendence St Paul's School was placed by the Founder.

hath happened; and yet, if I knew all the difficulties that he hath lain under, and his instrument Sir Philip Warwick, I might be true to another mind. It is remarkable that this afternoon Mr Moore come to me, and there among other things did tell me how Mr Moyer the merchant, having procured an order from the King and Duke of York and Council, with the consent of my Lord Chancellor, and by assistance of Lord Arlington, for the releasing out of prison his brother Samuel Moyer, who was a great man in the late times in Haberdashers'-hall, and was engaged under hand and seal to give the man that obtained it so much in behalf of my Lord Chancellor: but it seems my Lady Duchesse of Albemarle had before undertaken it for so much money, but hath not done it. The Duke of Albemarle did the next day send for this Moyer, to tell him that notwithstanding this order of the King and Council's being passed for release of his brother, yet, if he did not consider the pains of some friends of his, he would stop that order. This Moyer being an honest, bold man, told him that he was engaged to the hand that had done the thing to give him a reward; and more, he could not give, nor could own any kindness done by his Grace's interest: and so parted. The next day Sir Edward Savage did take the said Moyer in tax about it, giving ill words of this Moyer and his brother; which he not being able to bear, told him he would give to the person that had engaged him what he promised, and not any thing to any body else; and that both he and his brother were as honest men as himself or any man else: and so sent him going, and bid him do his worst. It is one of the most extraordinary cases that ever I saw or understood; but it is true.

17th. To Sir R. Viner's with 600 pieces of gold to turn into silver, for the enabling me to answer Sir G. Carteret's £3000; which he now draws all out of my hand towards the paying for a purchase he hath made for his son and my Lady Jemimah, in Northamptonshire, of Sir Samuel Luke,[59] in a good place: a good house, and near all her friends; which is a very happy thing.

19th. Great talk of the good end that my Lord Treasurer made; closing his own eyes, and wetting his mouth, and bidding adieu with the greatest content and freedom in the world: and is said to die with the cleanest hands that ever any Lord Treasurer did. Mr How come

59 Sir Samuel Luke was (according to Granger) the original Hudibras of Butler.

to see us; and, among other things, told us how the Barristers and Students of Gray's Inne rose in rebellion against the Benchers the other day; who outlawed them, and a great deal of do: but now they are at peace again.

20th. Among other news I hear that the Commissioners for the Treasury were named by the King yesterday; but who they are nobody could tell: but the persons are the Lord Chancellor, the two Secretaries, Lord Ashly, and others say Sir W. Coventry and Sir John Duncomb, but all conclude the Duke of Albemarle: but reports do differ.

22nd. Up, and by water to White Hall to Sir G. Carteret, who tells me now for certain how the Commission for the Treasury is disposed of; viz. to Duke of Albemarle, Lord Ashly, Sir W. Coventry, Sir John Duncomb, and Sir Thomas Clifford: at which, he says, all the whole Court is disturbed; it having been once concluded otherwise into the other hands formerly mentioned in yesterday's notes, but all of a sudden the King's choice was changed, and these are to be the men: the first of which is only for a puppet to give honour to the rest. He do presage that these men will make it their business to find faults in the management of the late Lord Treasurer, and in discouraging the bankers: but I am (whatever I in compliance do say to him) of another mind, and my heart is very glad of it, for I do expect they will do much good, and that it is the happiest thing that hath appeared to me for the good of the nation since the King come in. Thence to St James's, and up to the Duke of York; and there in his chamber Sir W. Coventry did of himself take notice of this business of the Treasury, wherein he is in the Commission, and desired that I would be thinking of any thing fit for him to be acquainted with for the lessening of charge and bettering of our credit, and what our expence hath been since the King's coming home, which he believes will be one of the first things they shall enquire into: which I promised him, and from time to time, which he desires, give him an account of what I can think of worthy his knowledge. I am mighty glad of this opportunity of professing my joy to him in what choice the King hath made, and the hopes I have that it will save the kingdom from perishing: and how it do encourage me to take pains again, after my having through despair neglected it! which he told me of himself that it was so with him, that he had given himself up to more ease than ever he expected, and that his opinion of matters was so bad that there was no public employment in the kingdom should have been accepted by him but this which the King hath now given him; and therein he is glad, in hopes of the service he may do therein; and in my conscience he will. So into the Duke of York's closet, and there, among other things, Sir W. Coventry did take notice of what he told me the other day, about a report of Commissioner Pett's dealing for timber in the Navy, and selling it to us in other names; and besides his own proof, did produce a paper I had given him this morning about it, in the case of Widow Murford and Morecocke, which was so handled, that the Duke of York grew very angry, and commanded us presently to fall into the examination of it, saying that he would not trust a man for his sake that lifts up the whites of his eyes. And it was declared that if he be found to have done so, he should be reckoned unfit to serve the Navy; and I do believe he will be turned out: and it was, methought, a worthy saying of Sir W. Coventry to the Duke of York, 'Sir,' says he, 'I do not make this complaint out of any disrespect to Commissioner Pett, but because I do love to do these things fairly and openly.' This day coming from Westminster with W. Batten, we saw at White Hall stairs a fisher-boat with a sturgeon that he had newly catched in the River; which I saw, but it was but a little one; but big enough to prevent my mistake of that for a colt, if ever I become Mayor of Huntingdon.

23rd. Sir John Duncomb is sworn yesterday a Privy-councillor. This day I hear also that last night the Duke of Kendall,[60] second son of the Duke of York, did die; and that the other, Duke of Cambridge, continues very ill still.

26th. All our discourse about Brampton, and my intentions to build there if I could be free of my engagement to my uncle Thomas and his son, that they may not have what I have built against my will in case of me and my brother's being without heirs male; which is the true reason why I am against laying out money upon that place, together with my fear of some inconvenience by being so near Hinchingbroke; being obliged to be a servant to that family, and subject to what expence they shall call me; and to have all that I shall buy or do esteemed as got by the death of my Uncle, when indeed what I have from him is not worth naming.

60 Henry Stuart, created Duke of Kendall, 1664.

27th. The new Commissioners of the Treasury have chosen Sir G. Downing for their Secretary: and I think in my conscience they have done a great thing in it; for he is active and a man of business, and values himself upon having of things do well under his hand; so that I am mightily pleased in their choice. Abroad, and stopped at Beargarden stairs, there to see a prize fought. But the house so full there was no getting in there, so forced to go through an alehouse into the pit, where the bears are baited; and upon a stool did see them fight, which they did very furiously, a butcher and a waterman. The former had the better all along till by and by the latter dropped his sword out of his hand, and the butcher, whether not seeing his sword dropped I know not, but did give him a cut over the wrist, so as he was disabled to fight any longer. But Lord! to see how in a minute the whole stage was full of watermen to revenge the foul play, and the butchers to defend their fellow, though most blamed him; and there they all fell to it to knocking down and cutting many on each side. It was pleasant to see, but that I stood in the pit, and feared that in the tumult I might get some hurt. At last the battle broke up, and so I away. The Duke of Cambridge very ill still.

28th. Up, and by coach to St James's, where I find Sir W. Coventry desirous to have spoke with me. It was to read over a draught of a letter which he hath made for his brother Commissioners and him to sign to us, demanding an account of the whole business of the Navy accounts; and I perceive, by the way he goes about it, that they will do admirable things. He tells me that they have chosen Sir G. Downing their Secretary, who will be as fit a man as any in the world: and he said, by the by, speaking of the banquers being fearful of Sir G. Downing's being Secretary, he being their enemy, that they did not intend to be ruled by their Secretary but do the business themselves. My heart is glad to see so great hopes of good to the nation as will be by these men; and it do me good to see Sir W. Coventry so cheerfull as he now is on the same score. My wife away down with Jane and W. Hewer to Woolwich, in order to a little ayre and to lie there to night, and so to gather May-dew to-morrow morning, which Mrs Turner hath taught her is the only thing in the world to wash her face with; and I am contented with it. I by water to Fox-hall, and there walked in Spring-garden. A great deal of company, and the weather and garden pleasant: and it is very pleasant and cheap going thither, for a man may go to spend what he will, or nothing, all as one. But to hear the nightingale and other birds, and hear fiddles and there a harp, and here a Jew's trump, and here laughing, and there fine people walking, is mighty divertising.

29th. Our parson Mills having the offer of another benefice[61] by Sir Robert Brookes, who was his tutor, he by my Lord Barkeley is made one of the Duke's Chaplains, which qualifies him for two livings. But to see how slightly such things are done, the Duke of York only taking my Lord Barkeley's word upon saying, that we the officers of the Navy do say that he is a good man and minister of our parish, and the Duke of York admits him to kiss his hand, but speaks not one word to him; but so a warrant will be drawn from the Duke of York to qualify him, and there's an end of it.

30th. After dinner I walked to Arundell House, the way very dusty, (the day of meeting of the Society being changed from Wednesday to Thursday, which I knew not before, because the Wednesday is a Council-day, and several of the Council are of the Society, and would come but for their attending the King at Council;) where I find very much company, in expectation of the Duchesse of Newcastle, who had desired to be invited to the Society; and was; after much debate *pro* and *con*, it seems many being against it; and we do believe the town will be full of ballads of it. Anon comes the Duchesse with her women attending her; among others the Ferabosco, of whom so much talk is that her lady would bid her show her face and kill the gallants. She is indeed black, and hath good black little eyes, but otherwise a very ordinary woman I do think, but they say sings well. The Duchesse hath been a good, comely woman; but her dress so antick, and her deportment so ordinary, that I do not like her at all, nor did I hear her say any thing that was worth hearing, but that she was full of admiration, all admiration. Several fine experiments were shown her of colours, loadstones, microscopes, and of liquors: among others, of one that did while she was there turn a piece of roasted mutton into pure blood, which was very rare. Here was Mrs Moore of Cambridge, whom I had not seen before, and I was glad to see her; as also a very black boy that ran up and down the room, somebody's child in Arundell House. After they had shown her many

61 The Rectory of Wanstead in Essex, to which he was presented.

experiments, and she cried still she was full of admiration, she departed, being led out and in by several Lords that were there; among others, Lord George Barkeley and Earl of Carlisle,[62] and a very pretty young man, the Duke of Somerset.[63]

31st. At the Treasury chamber. Here I saw Duncomb look as big, and take as much state on him, as if he had been born a lord. Here I met with Sir H. Cholmly, who tells me that he is told this day by Secretary Morris that he believes we are, and shall be only fooled by the French; and that the Dutch are very high and insolent, and do look upon us as come over only to beg a peace; which troubles me very much, and I do fear it is true. Thence to Sir G. Carteret at his lodgings; who, I perceive, is mightily displeased with this new Treasury; and he hath reason, for it will eclipse him. And he tells me that my Lord Ashly says they understand nothing; and he says he believes the King do not intend they shall sit long. But I believe no such thing, but that the King will find such benefit by them as he will desire to have them continue, as we see he hath done in the late new Act that was so much decried about the King; but yet the King hath since permitted it, and found good by it. He says, and I believe, that a great many persons at Court are angry at the rise of this Duncomb, whose father, he tells me, was a long-Parliament man, and a great Committee-man; and this fellow used to carry his papers to Committees after him: he was a kind of an atturny: but for all this, I believe will be a great man, in spite of all. In the evening home, and there to my unexpected satisfaction did get my intricate accounts of interest (which have been of late much perplexed by mixing of some moneys of Sir G. Carteret's with mine) evened and set right: and so late to supper, and with great quiet to bed; finding by the balance of my account that I am creditor £6900 for which the Lord of Heaven be praised!

June 1st. Up; and there comes to me Mr Commander, whom I employ about hiring of some ground behind the office, for the building of me a stable and coach-house: for I do find it necessary for me, both in respect of honour and the profit of it also, (my expense in hackney-coaches being now so great), to keep a coach, and therefore

---

62 Charles Howard, created Earl of Carlisle 1661, employed on several Embassies, and Governor of Jamaica. Died 1684.
63 Francis fifth Duke of Somerset, murdered in Italy 1678.

will do it. Having given him some instructions about it, I to the office; where we have news that our peace with Spain as to trade is wholly concluded, and we are to furnish him with some men for Flanders against the French. How that will agree with the French I know not; but they say that he also hath liberty to get what men he pleases out of England. But for the Spaniard, I hear that my Lord Castlehaven is raising a regiment of 4000 men which he is to command there; and several young gentlemen are going over in commands with him: and they say the Duke of Monmouth is going over only as a traveller, not to engage on either side, but only to see the campagne, which will be becoming him much more than to live as he now do.

3rd. Met Mr Mills, our parson, whom I went back with to bring him to Sir W. Coventry to give him the form of a qualification for the Duke of York to sign to, to enable him to have two livings; which was a service I did, but much against my will, for a lazy, fat priest. Sir William Doyly did lay a wager with me, the Treasurership would be in one hand (notwithstanding this present Commission) before Christmas; on which we did lay a poll of ling, a brace of carps, and a bottle of wine; and Sir W. Pen and Mr Scowen to be at the eating of them. Thence down by water to Deptford, it being Trinity Monday, when the Master is chosen. And so I down with them; and we had a good dinner of plain meat, and good company at our table: among others my good Mr Evelyn, with whom after dinner I stepped aside and talked upon the present posture of our affairs; which is, that the Dutch are known to be abroad with eighty sail of ships of war, and twenty fire-ships, and the French come into the Channell with twenty sail of men-of-war, and five fire-ships, while we have not a ship at sea to do them any hurt with, but are calling in all we can, while our Embassadors are treating at Bredah, and the Dutch look upon them as come to beg peace, and use them accordingly: and all this through the negligence of our Prince, who had power, if he would, to master all these with the money and men that he hath had the command of, and may now have, if he would mind his business. In the Treasury-chamber an hour or two, where we saw the Country Receivers and Accountants come to attend; and one of them a brisk young fellow (with his hat cocked like a fool behind, as the present fashion among the blades is) committed to the Serjeant. By and by I upon desire was called in, and delivered in my Report of my Accounts. Present, Lord Ashly, Clifford, and Duncomb. But I do like the way of these lords, that they admit nobody to use many words, nor do they spend many words themselves, but in great state do hear what they see necessary, and say little themselves, but bid withdraw.

5th. Captain Perriman brings us word how the *Happy Returne*'s crew below in the Hope, ordered to carry the Portugal Embassador to Holland, (and the Embassador, I think, on board,) refuse to go till paid; and by their example two or three more ships are in a mutiny: which is a sad consideration, while so many of the enemy's ships are at this day triumphing in the sea. Sir G. Carteret showed me a gentleman coming by in his coach who hath been sent for up out of Lincolnshire, (I think he says he is a justice of peace there,) that the Council have laid by the heels here, and here lies in a messenger's hands, for saying that a man and his wife are but one person, and so ought to pay but 12d. for both to the Poll Bill; by which others were led to do the like: and so here he lies prisoner.

7th. With Mr Townsend, whom I sent for to come to me to discourse about my Lord Sandwich's business; (for whom I am in some pain lest the Accounts of the Wardrobe may not be in so good order as may please the new Lords' Treasurers, who are quick-sighted, and under obligations of recommending themselves to the King and the world by their finding and mending of faults, and are most of them not the best friends to my Lord).

8th. Up, and to the office, where all the news this morning is that the Dutch are come with a fleet of eighty sail to Harwich, and that guns were heard plain by Sir W. Rider's people at Bednall-greene all yesterday even. The news is confirmed that the Dutch are off Harwich, but had done nothing last night. The King hath sent down my Lord of Oxford to raise the countries there; and all the Western barges are taken up to make a bridge over the River about the Hope for horse to cross the River, if there be occasion.

9th. I hear that the Duke of Cambridge, who was given over long since by the Doctors, is now likely to recover; for which God be praised! To Sir W. Coventry, and there talked with him a great while; and mighty glad I was of my good fortune to visit him, for it keeps in my acquaintance with him, and the world sees it, and reckons my interest accordingly. In comes my Lord Barkeley, who is going down to Harwich also to look after the militia there: and there is also the Duke of Monmouth, and with him a great many young Hectors, the Lord Chesterfield, my Lord Mandeville, and others; but to little purpose, I fear, but to debauch the country women thereabouts. My Lord Barkeley wanting some maps, and Sir W. Coventry recommending the six maps of England that are bound up for the pocket, I did offer to present my Lord with them, which he accepted; and so I will send them him. I find an order come for the getting some fire-ships presently to annoy the Dutch, who are in the King's Channel, and expected up higher.

10th. Up; and news brought us that the Dutch are come up as high as the Nore; and more pressing orders for fire-ships. W. Batten, W. Pen, and I to St James's; whence the Duke of York gone this morning betimes, to send away some men down to Chatham. So we then to White Hall, and meet Sir W. Coventry, who presses all that is possible for fire-ships. So we three to the office presently; and thither comes Sir Fretcheville Hollis,[64] who is to command them all in some exploits he is to do with them on the enemy in the River. So we all down to Deptford, and pitched upon ships and set men at work: but, Lord! to see how backwardly things move at this pinch, notwithstanding that by the enemy's being now come up as high as almost the Hope, Sir J. Minnes, who was gone down to pay some ships there, hath sent up the money; and so we are possessed of money to do what we will with. Yet partly ourselves, being used to be idle and in despair, and partly people that have been used to be deceived by us

64 Son of Fretcheville Hollis, of Grimsby (Colonel of a regiment on the King's side during the Civil Wars, in which he acquired considerable credit,) by his second wife Elizabeth Molesworth, and himself a distinguished naval officer. He lost an arm in the sea-fight 1665, and afterwards served as Rear-Admiral under Sir R. Holmes, when they attacked the Smyrna fleet. He fell in the battle of Southwold Bay, 1672, on board the *Cambridge*. Although Mr Pepys speaks slightingly of Sir F. H. he was a man of high spirit and enterprise, and is thus eulogised by Dryden in his *Annus Mirabilis*.

> Young Hollis on a Muse by Mars begot,
> Born, Caesar-like, to write and act great deeds,
> Impatient to revenge his fatal shot,
> His right hand doubly to his left succeeds.

as to money won't believe us; and we know not, though we have it, how almost to promise it; and our wants such, and men out of the way, that it is an admirable thing to consider how much the King suffers, and how necessary it is in a State to keep the King's service always in a good posture and credit. Down to Gravesend, where I find the Duke of Albemarle just come, with a great many idle lords and gentlemen, with their pistols and fooleries; and the bulworke not able to have stood half an hour had they come up; but the Dutch are fallen down from the Hope and Shell-haven as low as Sheerenesse, and we do plainly at this time hear the guns play. Yet I do not find the Duke of Albemarle intends to go thither, but stays here to-night, and hath (though the Dutch are gone) ordered our frigates to be brought to a line between the two block-houses; which I took then to be a ridiculous thing. I find the town had removed most of their goods out of the town, for fear of the Dutch coming up to them; and from Sir John Griffen, that last night there was not twelve men to be got in the town to defend it: which the master of the house tells me is not true, but that the men of the town did intend to stay, though they did indeed, and so had he (at the Ship,) removed their goods. Thence went to an Ostend man-of-war just now come up, who met the Dutch fleet, who took three ships that he came convoying hither from him: says they are as low as the Nore, or thereabouts.

11th. Brouncker come to us, who is just now going to Chatham upon a desire of Commissioner Pett's, who is very fearful of the Dutch, and desires help for God and the King and kingdom's sake. So Brouncker goes down, and Sir J. Minnes also from Gravesend. This morning Pett writes us word that Sheerenesse is lost last night, after two or three hours' dispute. The enemy hath possessed himself of that place; which is very sad, and puts us into great fears of Chatham. Home, and there to our business, hiring some fire-ships, and receiving every hour almost letters from Sir W. Coventry, calling for more fireships: and an order from Council to enable us to take any man's ships; and Sir W. Coventry, in his letter to us, says he do not doubt but at this time (under an invasion, as he owns it to be) the King may by law take any man's goods. At this business late, and then home; where a great deal of serious talk with my wife about the sad state we are in, and especially from the beating up of drums this night for the trainbands upon pain of death to appear in arms to-morrow morning, with bullet and powder, and money to supply themselves with victuals for a fortnight: which, considering the soldiers drawn out to Chatham and elsewhere, looks as if they had a design to ruin the City and give it up to be undone; which, I hear, makes the sober citizens to think very sadly of things.

12th. Up very betimes to our business at the office, there hiring of more fire-ships; and at it close all the morning. At noon home, and Sir W. Pen dined with us. By and by after dinner my wife out by coach to see her mother; and I in another (being afraid at this busy time to be seen with a woman in a coach, as if I were idle) towards The. Turner's: but met Sir W. Coventry's boy; and there in a letter find that the Dutch had made no motion since their taking Sheerenesse, and the Duke of Albemarle writes that all is safe as to the great ships against any assault, the bomb and chaine being so fortified: which put my heart into great joy. When I come to Sir W. Coventry's chamber, I find him abroad; but his clerk, Powell, do tell me that ill news is come to Court of the Dutch breaking the Chaine at Chatham; which struck me to the heart. And to White Hall to hear the truth of it; and there going up the Park-stairs I did hear some lacquies speaking of sad news come to Court, saying, there is hardly any body in the Court but do look as if he cried. I met Roger Pepys, newly come out of the country: in discourse he told me that his grandfather, my great grandfather, had £800 per annum in Queene Elizabeth's time in the very town of Cottenham; and that we did certainly come out of Scotland with the Abbot of Crowland. Home, where all our hearts do now ake; for the news is true that the Dutch have broke the chaine and burned our ships, and particularly the *Royal Charles*: other particulars I know not, but it is said to be so. And the truth is I do fear so much that the whole kingdom is undone, that I do this night resolve to study with my father and wife what to do with the little that I have in money by me, for I give all the rest that I have in the King's hands for Tangier for lost. So God help us! and God knows what disorders we may fall into, and whether any violence on this office, or perhaps some severity on our persons, as being reckoned by the silly people, or perhaps may by policy of State be thought fit to be condemned by the King and Duke of York, and so put to trouble; though, God knows I have in my own person done my full duty, I am sure.

13th. No sooner up but hear the sad news confirmed of the *Royal Charles* being taken by them, and now in fitting by them, (which Pett should have carried up higher by our several orders, and deserves therefore to be hanged for not doing it,) and burning several others; and that another fleet is come up into the Hope. Upon which news the King and Duke of York have been below since four o'clock in the morning, to command the sinking of ships at Barking-Creeke and other places, to stop their coming up higher: which put me into such a fear, that I presently resolved of my father's and wife's going into the country; and at two hours' warning they did go by the coach this day, with about £1300 in gold in their night-bag. Pray God give them good passage, and good care to hide it when they come home! but my heart is full of fear. They gone, I continued in frights and fear what to do with the rest. W. Hewer hath been at the banker's, and hath got £500 out of Blackwell's hands of his own money; but they are so called upon that they will be all broke, hundreds coming to them for money and they answer him, 'It is payable at twenty days – when the days are out we will pay you;' and those that are not so they make tell over their money, and make their bags false on purpose to give cause to retell it, and so spend time. I cannot have my 200 pieces of gold again for silver, all being bought up last night that were to be had, and sold for 24 and 25s. a-piece. Every minute some one or other calls for this or that order; and so I forced to be at the office most of the day about the fire-ships which are to be suddenly fitted out. And it's a most strange thing that we hear nothing from any of my brethren at Chatham: so that we are wholly in the dark, various being the reports of what is done there; insomuch, that I sent Mr Clapham express thither to see how matters go. I did about noon resolve to send Mr Gibson away after my wife with another 1000 pieces, under colour of an express to Sir Jeremy Smith, who is, as I hear, with some ships at Newcastle; which I did really send to him, and may possibly prove of good use to the King, for it is possible in the hurry of business they may not think of it at Court, and the charge of express is not considerable to the King. The King and Duke of York up and down all the day here and there: some time on Tower Hill, where the City militia was; where the King did make a speech to them, that they should venture themselves no further than he would himself. I also sent (my mind being in pain) Saunders after my wife and father, to overtake them at their night's lodging, to see

how matters go with them. In the evening I sent for my cousin Sarah
and her husband, who come; and I did deliver them my chest of
writings about Brampton, and my brother Tom's papers, and my
journalls, which I value much: and did send my two silver flagons to
Kate Joyce's: that so being scattered what I have, something might be
saved. I have also made a girdle, by which with some trouble I do
carry about me £300 in gold about my body, that I may not be
without something in case I should be surprised; for I think, in any
nation but our's, people that appear (for we are not indeed so) so
faulty as we, would have their throats cut. In the evening comes Mr
Pelling and several others to the office, and tell me that never were
people so dejected as they are in the City all over at this day; and do
talk most loudly, even treason; as, that we are bought and sold, that
we are betrayed by the Papists and others about the King: cry out that
the office of the Ordnance hath been so backward as no powder to
have been at Chatham nor Upner Castle till such a time, and the
carriages all broken: that Legg[65] is a Papist; that Upner, the old good
castle built by Queen Elizabeth, should be lately slighted; that the
ships at Chatham should not be carried up higher. They look upon us
as lost, and remove their families and rich goods in the City; and do
think verily that the French being come down with an army to
Dunkirke, it is to invade us, and that we shall be invaded. Mr Clerke,
the solicitor, comes to me about business, and tells me that he hears
that the King hath chosen Mr Pierpoint and Vaughan of the West,
Privy-councillors; that my Lord Chancellor was affronted in the Hall
this day, by people telling him of his Dunkirke House; and that there
are regiments ordered to be got together, whereof to be commanders
my Lord Fairfax, Ingolsby, Bethell, Norton, and Birch, and other
Presbyterians; and that Dr Bates will have liberty to preach. Now,
whether this be true or not, I know not; but do think that nothing
but this will unite us together. Late at night comes Mr Hudson the
cooper, my neighbour, and tells me that he come from Chatham this
evening at five o'clock, and saw this afternoon the *Royal James*, *Oake*,
and *London*, burnt by the enemy with their fire-ships: that two or
three men-of-war come up with them, and made no more of Upner
Castle's shooting than of a fly; that those ships lay below Upner

65 William Legge, mentioned before. He was Treasurer and Superintendent of the
Ordnance, with General's pay.

Castle, (but therein, I conceive, he is in an error;) that the Dutch are fitting out the *Royall Charles*; that we shot so far as from the Yard thither, so that the shot did no good, for the bullets grazed on the water; that Upner played hard with their guns at first, but slowly afterwards, either from the men's being beat off, or their powder spent. But we hear that the fleet in the Hope is not come up any higher the last flood. And Sir W. Batten tells me that ships are provided to sink in the River, about Woolwich, that will prevent their coming up higher if they should attempt it. I made my will also this day, and did give all I had equally between my father and wife.

14th. Up, and to the office; where Mr Fryer comes and tells me that there are several Frenchman and Flemish ships in the River with passes from the Duke of York for carrying of prisoners, that ought to be parted from the rest of the ships, and their powder taken, lest they do fire themselves when the enemy comes, and so spoil us; which is good advice, and I think I will give notice of it; and did so. But it is pretty odd to see how every body, even at this high time of danger, puts business off of their own hands! He says that he told this to the Lieutenant of the Tower, (to whom I, for the same reason, was directing him to go); and the Lieutenant of the Tower bade him come to us, for he had nothing to do with it. And yesterday comes Captain Crew, of one of the fireships, and told me that the officers of the Ordnance would deliver his gunner's materials, but not compound them, but that we must do it; whereupon I was forced to write to them about it: and one that like a great many come to me this morning. By and by comes Mr Willson, and, by direction of his, a man of Mr Gauden's; who are come from Chatham last night, and saw the three ships burnt, they lying all dry, and boats going from the men-of-war to fire them. But that that he tells me of worst consequence is, that he himself (I think he said) did hear many Englishmen on board the Dutch ships speaking to one another in English; and that they did cry and say, 'We did heretofore fight for tickets; now we fight for dollars!' and did ask how such and such a one did, and would commend themselves to them: which is a sad consideration. And Mr Lewes (who was present at this fellow's discourse to me) did tell me, that he is told that when they took the *Royal Charles*, they said that they had their tickets signed (and showed some), and that now they come to have them paid, and would have them paid before they parted. And several seamen come this morning to me, to tell me that if I would get their tickets paid they would go and do all they could against the Dutch; but otherwise they would not venture being killed, and lose all they have already fought for: so that I was forced to try what I could do to get them paid. This man tells me that the ships burnt last night did lie above Upner Castle, over against the Docke; and the boats come from the ships of war and burnt them: all which is very sad. And masters of ships that are lately taken up, do keep from their ships all their stores, or as much as they can, so that we can dispatch them, having not time to appraise them, nor secure their payment. Only some little money we have, which we are fain to pay the men we have with every night, or they will not work. And indeed the hearts as well as affections of the seamen are turned away; and in the open streets in Wapping, and up and down, the wives have cried publickly, 'This comes of your not paying our husbands; and now your work is undone, or done by hands that understand it not.' And Sir W. Batten told me that he was himself affronted with a woman, in language of this kind, on Tower Hill publickly yesterday; and we are fain to bear it, and to keep one at the office-door to let no idle people in, for fear of firing of the office and doing us mischief. The City is troubled at their being put upon duty: summoned one hour, and discharged two hours after: and then again summoned two hours after that; to their great charge as well as trouble. And Pelling, the Potticary, tells me the world says all over, that less charge than what the kingdom is put to, of one kind or other, by this business, would have set out all our great ships. It is said they did in open streets yesterday, at Westminster, cry, 'A Parliament! a Parliament!' and I do believe it will cost blood to answer for these miscarriages. We do not hear that the Dutch are come to Gravesend; which is a wonder. But a wonderful thing it is that to this day we have not one word yet from Brouncker, or Peter Pett, or J. Minnes, of any thing at Chatham. The people that come hither to hear how things go, make me ashamed to be found unable to answer them: for I am left alone here at the office; and the truth is, I am glad my station is to be here, near my own home and out of danger, yet in a place of doing the King good service. I have this morning good news from Gibson; three letters from three several stages, that he was safe last night as far as Royston, at between nine and ten at night. The dismay that is upon us all, in the business of the kingdom and Navy at this day, is not to be expressed otherwise than by the condition the citizens were in when the City was on fire, nobody knowing which way to turn themselves, while every thing concurred to greaten the fire; as here the easterly gale and spring-tides for coming up both rivers, and enabling them to break the chaine. D. Gauden did tell me yesterday, that the day before at the Council they were ready to fall together by the ears at the Council-table, arraigning one another of being guilty of the counsel that brought us into this misery, by laying up all the great ships. Mr Hater tells me at noon that some rude people have been, as he hears, at my Lord Chancellor's, where they have cut down the trees before his house and broke his windows; and a gibbet either set up before or painted upon his gate, and these three words writ: 'Three sights to be seen; Dunkirke, Tangier, and a barren Queene.' It gives great matter of talk that it is said there is at this hour, in the Exchequer, as much money as is ready to break down the floor. This arises, I believe, from Sir G. Downing's late talk of the greatness of the sum lying there of people's money that they would not fetch away, which he showed me and a great many others. Most people that I speak with are in doubt how we shall do to secure our seamen from running over to the Dutch; which is a sad but very true consideration at this day. At noon I am told that my Lord Duke of Albemarle is made Lord High Constable; the meaning whereof at this time I know not, nor whether it be true or no. Dined, and Mr Hater and W. Hewer with me; where they do speak very sorrowfully of the posture of the times, and how people do cry out in the streets of their being bought and sold; and both they and every body that come to me do tell me that people make nothing of talking treason in the streets openly; as, that they are bought and sold, and governed by Papists, and that we are betrayed by people about the King, and shall be delivered up to the French, and I know not what. At dinner we discoursed of Tom of the Wood, a fellow that lives like a hermit near Woolwich, who, as they say (and Mr Bodham, they tell me, affirms that he was by at the Justice's when some did accuse him there for it) did foretell the burning of the City, and now says that a greater desolation is at hand. Thence we read and laughed at Lilly's prophecies this month, in his Almanack this year. So to the office after dinner; and thither comes Mr Pierce, who tells me his condition, how he cannot get his money (about £500, which, he says, is a very great part of what he hath for his family and children) out of Viner's hand: and indeed it is to be feared that this will wholly undo the bankers. He says he knows nothing of the late affronts to my Lord Chancellor's house, as is said, nor hears of the Duke of Albemarle's being made High Constable; but says that they are in great distraction at White Hall, and that every where people do speak high against Sir W. Coventry,[66] but he agrees with me, that he is the best Minister of State the King hath, and so from my heart I believe. At night come home Sir W. Batten and W. Pen, who only can tell me that they have placed guns at Woolwich and Deptford, and sunk some ships below Woolwich and Blackwall, and are in hopes that they will stop the enemy's coming up. But strange our confusion! that among them that are sunk they have gone and sunk without consideration the *Franclin*, one of the King's ships with stores to a very considerable value, that hath been long loaded for supply of the ships; and the new ship at Bristoll, and much wanted there. And nobody will own that they directed it, but do lay it on Sir W. Rider. They speak also of another ship loaded to the value of £80,000 sunk with the goods in her, or at least was mightily contended for by him and a foreign ship that had the faith of the nation for her security: this Sir R. Ford tells us. And it is too plain a truth, that both here and at Chatham the ships that we have sunk have many, and the first of them, been ships completely fitted for fire-ships at great charge. But most strange the backwardness and disorder of all people, especially the King's people in pay, to do any work, (Sir W. Pen tells me), all crying out for money. And it was so at Chatham that this night comes an order from Sir W. Coventry to stop the pay of the wages of that Yard, the Duke of Albemarle having related, that not above three of 1100 in pay there, did attend to do any work there. This evening having sent a messenger to Chatham on purpose, we have received a dull letter from my Lord Brouncker and Peter Pett, how matters have gone there this week; but not so much, or so particularly, as we knew it by common talk before, and as true. I doubt they will be found to have been but slow men in this business; and they say the Duke of Albemarle did tell my Lord Brouncker to his face that his discharging of the great ships there was the cause of all this; and I am told that it is become common talk against my Lord Brouncker. But in that he is to be justified, for he did it by verbal

66 Evelyn says it was owing to Sir W. C. that no fleet was fitted out in 1667.

order from Sir W. Coventry, and with good intent; and it was to good purpose, whatever the success be, for the men would have but spent the King so much the more in wages, and yet not attended on board to have done the King any service. And as an evidence of that, just now, being the 15th day in the morning that I am writing yesterday's passages, one is with me, Jacob Bryan, Purser of the *Princesse*, who confesses to me that he hath but 180 men borne at this day in victuals and wages on that ship lying at Chatham, being lately brought in thither; of which 180 there was not above five appeared to do the King any service at this late business. And this morning also, some of the *Cambridge*'s men come up from Portsmouth by order from Sir Fretcheville Hollis, who boasted to us the other day that he had sent for 50, and would be hanged if 100 did not come up that would do as much as twice the number of other men: I say some of them, instead of being at work at Deptford, where they were intended, do come to the office this morning to demand the payment of their tickets; for otherwise they would, they said, do no more work; and are, as I understand from every body that has to do with them, the most debauched, damning, swearing rogues that ever were in the Navy, just like their prophane commander.

15th. All the morning at the office. No news more than last night; only Purser Tyler comes and tells me that he being at all the passages in this business at Chatham, he says there have been horrible miscarriages, such as we shall shortly hear of: that the want of boats hath undone us; and it is commonly said, and Sir J. Minnes under his hand tells us, that they were employed by the men of the Yard to carry away their goods; and I hear that Commissioner Pett will be found the first man that began to remove: he is much spoken against, and Brouncker is complained of, and reproached for discharging the men of the great ships heretofore. At noon Mr Hater dined with me; and tells me he believes that it will hardly be the want of money alone that will excuse to the Parliament the neglect of not setting out a fleet, it having never been done in our greatest straits, but however unlikely it appeared, yet when it was gone about, the State or King did compass it; and there is something in it.

16th. Roger Pepys told me, that when I come to his house he will show me a decree in Chancery, wherein there was 26 men all house-keepers in the town of Cottenham, in Queene Elizabeth's time, of our name. By and by occasion offered for my writing to Sir W. Coventry a plain bold letter touching lack of money; which, when it was gone, I was afraid might give offence; but upon two or three readings over again the copy of it, I was satisfied it was a good letter; only Sir W. Batten signed it with me, which I could wish I had done alone.

17th. Every moment business of one kind or other about the fire-ships and other businesses, most of them vexatious for want of money, the commanders all complaining that if they miss to pay their men a night, they run away; seamen demanding money of them by way of advance, and some of Sir Fretcheville Hollis's men, that he so bragged of, demanding their tickets to be paid, or they would not work: this Hollis, Sir W. Batten and Mr Pen say, proves a conceited, idle, prating, lying fellow. Captain Cocke tells me there have been great endeavours of bringing in the Presbyterian interest, but that it will not do. He named to me several of the insipid lords that are to command the armies that are to be raised. He says the King and Court are all troubled, and the gates of the Court were shut up upon the first coming of the Dutch to us, but they do mind the business no more than ever: that the bankers, he fears, are broke as to ready-money, though Viner had £100,000 by him when our trouble begun: that he and the Duke of Albemarle have received into their own hands, of Viner, the former £10,000, and the latter £12,000, in tallies or assignments to secure what was in his hands of theirs; and many other great men of our masters have done the like; which is no good sign, when they begin to fear the main. He and every body cries out of the office of the Ordnance, for their neglects, both at Gravesend and Upner, and every where else.

18th. To the office, and by and by word was brought me that Commissioner Pett is brought to the Tower, and there laid up close prisoner; which puts me into a fright, lest they may do the same with us as they do with him. Great news to-night of the blowing up of one of the Dutch's greatest ships, while a Council of War was on board: the latter part, I doubt, is not so, it not being confirmed since; but the former, that they had a ship blown up, is said to be true. This evening comes Sir G. Carteret to the office, to talk of business at Sir W. Batten's; where all to be undone for want of money, there being none to pay the chest at their public pay the 24th of this month, which will make us a scorn to the world. After he had done there, he and I into the garden, and walked; and the greatest of our discourse is, his sense of the requisiteness of his parting with his being Treasurer of the Navy, if he can on any good terms. He do harp upon getting my Lord Brouncker to take it on half profit, but that he is not able to secure him in paying him so much. He tells me now the great question is, whether a Parliament or no Parliament; and says the Parliament itself cannot be thought able at present to raise money, and therefore it will be to no purpose to call one.

19th. Comes an order from Sir R. Browne, commanding me this afternoon to attend the Council-board with all my books and papers, touching the Medway. I was ready to fear some mischief to myself, though it appears most reasonable that it is to inform them about Commissioner Pett. I am called in to a large Committee of the Council: present, the Duke of Albemarle, Anglesy, Arlington, Ashly, Carteret, Duncomb, Coventry, Ingram, Clifford, Lauderdale, Morrice, Manchester, Craven, Carlisle, Bridgewater.[67] And after Sir W. Coventry's telling them what orders his Royal Highness had made for the safety of the Medway, I told them to their full content what we had done, and showed them our letters. Then was Peter Pett called in, with the Lieutenant of the Tower. He is in his old clothes, and looked most sillily. His charge was chiefly the not carrying up of the great ships, and the using of the boats in carrying away his goods; to which he answered very sillily, though his faults to me seem only great omissions. Lord Arlington and Coventry very severe against him; the former saying that, if he was not guilty the world would think them all guilty. The latter urged, that there must be some faults, and that the Admiral must be found to have done his part. I did say an unhappy word, which I was sorry for, when he complained of want of oares for the boats: and there was, it seems, enough, and good enough, to carry away all the boats with from the King's occasions. He said he used never a boat till they were all gone but one; and that was to carry away things of great value, and these were his models of ships; which, when the Council, some of them, had said they wished that the Dutch had had them instead of the King's ships, he answered, he did believe the Dutch would have made more advantage of the

67 John, second Earl of Bridgewater. Died 1686.

models than of the ships, and that the King had had greater loss thereby: this they all laughed at. After having heard him for an hour or more, they bid him withdraw. He being gone, they caused Sir Richard Browne to read over his minutes; and then my Lord Arlington moved that they might be put into my hands to put into form, I being more acquainted with such business; and they were so. So I away back with my books and papers; and when I got into the Court it was pretty to see how people gazed upon me, that I thought myself obliged to salute people and to smile, lest they should think I was a prisoner too: but afterwards I found that most did take me to be there to bear evidence against P. Pett. My wife did give me so bad an account of her and my father's method in burying of our gold, that made me mad: and she herself is not pleased with it, she believing that my sister knows of it. My father and she did it on Sunday, when they were gone to church, in open daylight, in the midst of the garden; where, for aught they knew, many eyes might see them: which put me into trouble, and presently cast about how to have it back again to secure it here, the times being a little better now.

20th. Mr Barber told me that all the discourse yesterday, about that part of the town where he was, was that Mr Pett and I were in the Tower; and I did hear the same before. Busy all the afternoon: in the evening did treat with, and in the end agree, but by some kind of compulsion, with the owners of six merchant-ships, to serve the King as men-of-war. But, Lord! to see how against the hair it is with these men, and everybody, to trust us and the King; and how unreasonable it is to expect they should be willing to lend their ships, and lay out 2 or £300 a man to fit their ships for the new voyages, when we have not paid them half of what we owe them for their old services! I did write so to Sir W. Coventry this night.

21st. This day comes news from Harwich that the Dutch fleet are all in sight, near 100 sail great and small, they think, coming towards them; where, they think, they shall be able to oppose them; but do cry out of the falling back of the seamen, few standing by them, and those with much faintness. The like they write from Portsmouth, and their letters this post are worth reading. Sir H. Cholmly come to me this day, and tells me the Court is as mad as ever; and that the night the Dutch burned our ships the King did sup with my Lady Castlemaine, at the Duchesse of Monmouth's, and there were all mad in hunting of a poor moth. All the Court afraid of a Parliament; but he thinks nothing can save us but the King's giving up all to a Parliament.

22nd. In the evening come Captain Hart and Hayward to me about the six merchant-ships now taken up for men-of-war; and in talking they told me about the taking of the *Royal Charles*; that nothing but carelessness lost the ship, for they might have saved her the very tide that the Dutch came up, if they would have but used means and had had but boats; and that the want of boats plainly lost all the other ships. That the Dutch did take her with a boat of nine men, who found not a man on board her, (and her laying so near them was a main temptation to them to come on;) and presently a man went up and struck her flag and jacke, and a trumpeter sounded upon her 'Joan's placket is torn':[68] that they did carry her down at a time, both for tides and wind, when the best pilot in Chatham would not have undertaken it, they heeling her on one side to make her draw little water: and so carried her away safe. They being gone, by and by comes Sir W. Pen, who hath been at Court; and in the first place I hear the Duke of Cambridge is dead; which is a great loss to the nation, having, I think, never an heyre male now of the King's or Duke's to succeed to the Crown. He tells me that they do begin already to damn the Dutch and call them cowards at White Hall, and think of them and their business no better than they used to do; which is very sad. The King did tell him himself, (which is so, I was told, here in the City,) that the City hath lent him £10,000 to be laid out towards securing of the River of Thames; which, methinks, is a very poor thing, that we should be induced to borrow by such mean sums.

23rd. To Woolwich, and there called on Mr Bodham: and he and I to see the batterys newly raised; which, indeed, are good works to command the River below the ships that are sunk, but not above them. It is a sad sight to see so many good ships there sunk in the River, while we would be thought to be masters of the sea. Cocke says the bankers cannot, till peace returns, ever hope to have credit again; so that they can pay no more money, but people must be contented to take publick security such as they can give them; and if so, and they do live to receive the money thereupon, the bankers will be happy men. Fenn read me an Order of Council passed the 17th

68 Placket: the open part of a woman's petticoat.

instant, directing all the Treasurers of any part of the King's revenue to make no payments but such as shall be approved by the present Lords Commissioners; which will, I think, spoil the credit of all his Majesty's service, when people cannot depend upon payment anywhere. But the King's declaration in behalf of the bankers, to make good their assignments for money, is very good, and will, I hope, secure me. Cocke says, that he hears it is come to it now that the King will try what he can soon do for a peace; and if he cannot, that then he will cast all upon the Parliament to do as they see fit: and in doing so, perhaps, it may save us all. The King of France, it is believed, is engaged for this year; so that we shall be safe as to him. The great misery the City and kingdom is like to suffer for want of coals in a little time is very visible, and, is feared, will breed a mutiny; for we are not in any prospect to command the sea for our colliers to come, but rather, it is feared, the Dutch may go and burn all our colliers at Newcastle; though others do say that they lie safe enough there. No news at all of late from Bredagh what our treaters do. In the evening comes Mr Povy about business; and he and I to walk in the garden an hour or two, and to talk of State matters. He tells me his opinion that it is out of possibility for us to escape being undone, there being nothing in our power to do that is necessary for the saving us: a lazy Prince, no Council, no money, no reputation at home or abroad. He says that to this day the King do follow the women as much as ever he did; that the Duke of York hath not got Mrs Middleton, as I was told the other day: but says that he wants not her, for he hath others, and hath always had, and that he hath known them brought through the Matted Gallery at White Hall into his closet; nay, he hath come out of his wife's bed, and gone to others laid in bed for him: that Mr Brouncker is not the only pimp, but that the whole family are of the same strain, and will do any thing to please him: that, besides the death of the two Princes lately, the family is in horrible disorder by being in debt by spending above £60,000 per annum, when he hath not £40,000: that the Duchesse is not only the proudest woman in the world, but the most expensefull; and that the Duke of York's marriage with her hath undone the kingdom, by making the Chancellor so great above reach, who otherwise would have been but an ordinary man to have been dealt with by other people; and he would have been careful of managing things well, for fear of being called to account; whereas now he is secure, and hath let things run to rack, as they now appear. That at a certain time Mr Povy did carry him an account of the state of the Duke of York's estate, showing in faithfullness how he spent more than his estate would bear, by above £20,000 per annum, and asked my Lord's opinion of it; to which he answered, that no man that loved the King or kingdom durst own the writing of that paper: at which Povy was started, and reckoned himself undone for this good service, and found it necessary then to show it to the Duke of York's Commissioners; who read, examined, and approved of it, so as to cause it to be put into form, and signed it, and gave it to the Duke. Now the end of the Chancellor was, for fear that his daughter's ill housewifery should be condemned. He tells me that the other day, upon this ill news of the Dutch being upon us, White Hall was shut up, and the Council called and sat close; (and, by the way, he do assure me, from the mouth of some Privy-councillors, that at this day the Privy-council in general do know no more what the state of the kingdom as to peace and war is, than he or I; nor who manages it, nor upon whom it depends;) and there my Lord Chancellor did make a speech to them, saying that they knew well that he was no friend to the war from the beginning, and therefore had concerned himself little in, nor could say much to it; and a great deal of that kind to discharge himself of the fault of the war. Upon which my Lord Anglesy rose up and told his Majesty that he thought their coming now together was not to enquire who was or was not the cause of the war, but to enquire what was or could be done in the business of making a peace, and in whose hands that was, and where it was stopped or forwarded; and went on very highly to have all made open to them: (and, by the way, I remember that Captain Cocke did the other day tell me that this Lord Anglesy hath said within few days, that he would willingly give £10,000 of his estate that he was well secured of the rest, such apprehensions he hath of the sequel of things, as giving all over for lost). He tells me, (speaking of the horrid effeminacy of the King,) that the King hath taken ten times more care and pains in making friends between my Lady Castlemaine and Mrs Stewart, when they have fallen out, than ever he did to save his kingdom; nay, that upon any falling out between my Lady Castlemaine's nurse and her woman, my Lady hath often said she would make the King to make them friends, and they would be friends and be quiet; which the King hath been fain to do: that the King is, at this day, every night in Hyde Park with the Duchesse of Monmouth, or with my Lady Castlemaine: that he is concerned of late by my Lord Arlington in the looking after some buildings that he is about in Norfolke,[69] where my Lord is laying out a great deal of money; and that he (Mr Povy,) considering the unsafeness of laying out money at such a time as this, and, besides, the enviousness of the particular county as well as all the kingdom to find him building and employing workmen, while all the ordinary people of the country are carried down to the sea-sides for securing the land, he thought it becoming him to go to my Lord Arlington (Sir Thomas Clifford by) and give it as his advice to hold his hands a little; but my Lord would not, but would have him go on, and so Sir Thomas Clifford advised also, which one would think (if he were a statesman) should be a sign of his foreseeing that all shall do well. He tells me that there is not so great confidence between any two men of power in the nation at this day, that he knows of, as between my Lord Arlington and Sir Thomas Clifford; and that it arises by accident only, there being no relation nor acquaintance between them, but only Sir Thomas Clifford's coming to him and applying himself to him for favours, when he came first up to town to be a Parliament-man.

25th. Up, and with Sir W. Pen in his new chariot (which indeed is plain, but pretty and more fashionable in shape than any coach he hath, and yet do not cost him, harness and all, above £32) to White Hall; where staid a very little: and thence to St James's to Sir W. Coventry, whom I have not seen since before the coming of the Dutch into the River, nor did indeed know how well to go to see him, for shame either to him or me, or both of us, to find ourselves in so much misery. I find that he and his fellow-Treasurers are in the utmost want of money, and do find fault with Sir G. Carteret, that having kept the mystery of borrowing money to himself so long, (to the ruin of the nation, as Sir W. Coventry said in words to Sir W. Pen and me,) he should now lay it aside and come to them for money for every penny he hath, declaring that he can raise no more: which, I confess do appear to me the most like ill-will of any thing that I have observed of Sir W. Coventry, when he himself did tell us on another occasion at the same time, that the bankers who used to furnish them money are not able to lend a farthing, and he knows

69 At Euston Hall in Suffolk, on the borders of Norfolk.

well enough that that was all the mystery Sir G. Carteret did use, that is, only his credit with them. He told us the masters and owners of two ships that I had complained of, for not readily setting forth their ships which we had taken up to make men-of-war, had been yesterday with the King and Council, and had made their case so well understood, that the King did owe them for what they had earned the last year, and that they could not set them out again without some money or stores out of the King's Yard; the latter of which Sir W. Coventry said must be done, for that they were not able to raise money for them, though it was but £200 a ship: which do show us our condition to be so bad, that I am in a total despair of ever having the nation do well. After that talking awhile, and all out of heart with stories of want of seamen, and seamen's running away, and their demanding a month's advance, and our being forced to give seamen 3s. a-day to go hence to work at Chatham, and other things that show nothing but destruction upon us; for it is certain that, as it now is, the seamen of England, in my conscience, would, if they could, go over and serve the King of France or Holland rather than us. Up to the Duke of York to his chamber, where he seems to be pretty easy, and now and then merry; but yet one may perceive in all their minds there is something of trouble and care, and with good reason. Thence to White Hall, with Sir W. Pen, by chariot; and there in the Court met with my Lord Anglesy: and he to talk with Sir W. Pen, and told him of the masters of ships being with the Council yesterday, and that we were not in condition, though the men were willing, to furnish them with £200 of money (already due to them as earned by them the last year) to enable them to set out their ships again this year for the King: which he is amazed at; and when I told him, 'My Lord, this is a sad instance of the condition we are in,' he answered that it was so indeed, and sighed; and so parted: and he up to the Council-chamber, where I perceive they sit every morning. It is worth noting that the King and Council in their order of the 23rd instant, for unloading three merchant-ships taken up for the King's service for men-of-war, do call the late coming of the Dutch 'an invasion'. I was told yesterday, that Mr Oldenburg,[70] our Secretary at Gresham College, is put into the Tower, for writing news to a virtuoso in France, with whom he constantly corresponds in philosophical

70 Henry Oldenburgh, Secretary to the Royal Society.

matters; which makes it very unsafe at this time to write, or almost do any thing. Several captains come to the office yesterday and to-day, complaining that their men come and go when they will, and will not be commanded, though they are paid every night, or may be. Nay, this afternoon comes Harry Russell from Gravesend, telling us that the money carried down yesterday for the Chest at Chatham had like to have been seized upon yesterday in the barge there by seamen, who did beat our waterman: and what men should these be but the boats' crew of Sir Fretcheville Hollis, who used to brag so much of the goodness and order of his men, and his command over them? Sir H. Cholmly tells me great news; that this day in Council the King hath declared that he will call his Parliament in thirty days: which is the best news I have heard a great while, and will, if any thing, save the kingdom. How the King come to be advised to this, I know not; but he tells me that it was against the Duke of York's mind flatly, who did rather advise the King to raise money as he pleased; and against the Chancellor's, who told the King that Queene Elizabeth did do all her business in eighty-eight without calling a Parliament, and so might he do for anything he saw. But, blessed be God, it is done; and pray God it may hold, though some of us must surely go to the pot, for all must be flung up to them, or nothing will be done.

26th. The Parliament is ordered to meet the 25th of July, being, as they say, St James's day; which every creature is glad of. Colonel Reymes[71] tells me of a letter come last night or the day before from my Lord St Albans out of France, wherein he says that the King of France did lately fall out with him, giving him ill names, saying that he had belied him to our King, by saying that he had promised to assist our King, and to forward the peace; saying that indeed he had offered to forward the peace at such a time, but it was not accepted of, and so he thinks himself not obliged, and would do what was fit for him; and so made him to go out of his sight in great displeasure: and he hath given this account to the King, which, Colonel Reymes tells me, puts them into new melancholy at Court, and he believes hath forwarded the resolution of calling the Parliament. At White Hall spied Mr Povy, who tells me as a great secret, which none knows but himself, that Sir G. Carteret hath parted with his place of Treasurer of the

71 Bullen Reymes, MP for Melcombe Regis.

Navy by consent to my Lord Anglesy, and is to be Treasurer of Ireland in his stead; but upon what terms it is, I know not: and that it is in his power to bring me to as great a friendship and confidence in my Lord Anglesy, as ever I was with Sir W. Coventry. Such is the want already of coals, and the despair of having any supply, by reason of the enemy's being abroad, and no fleet of ours to secure them, that they are come this day to £5 10s. per chaldron.

27th. Proclamations come out this day for the Parliament to meet the 25th of next month: for which God be praised! And another to invite seamen to bring in their complaints, of their being ill used in the getting their tickets and money. Pierce tells me that he hears for certain fresh at Court, that France and we shall agree; and more, that yesterday was damned at the Council the Canary Company; and also that my Lord Mordaunt hath laid down his Commission. News this tide that about 80 sail of Dutch, great and small, were seen coming up the River this morning; and this tide some of them to the upper end of the Hope.

28th. We find the Duke of York and Sir W. Coventry gone this morning by two o'clock to Chatham, to come home tonight: and it is fine to observe how both the King and Duke of York have in their several late journeys to and again done them in the night for coolnesse. They tell me that the Duke of Buckingham hath surrendered himself to Secretary Morrice, and is going to the Tower. Mr Fenn, at the table, says that he hath been taken by the watch two or three times of late, at unseasonable hours, but so disguised that they could not know him: and when I come home by and by, Mr Lowther tells me that the Duke of Buckingham do dine publickly this day at Wadlow's, at the Sun Tavern; and is mighty merry, and sent word to the Lieutenant of the Tower that he would come to him as soon as he had dined. It is said that the King of France do make a sport of us now; and says, that he knows no reason why his cosen the King of England should not be as willing to let him have his kingdom, as that the Dutch should take it from him. Sir G. Carteret did tell me, that the business was done between him and my Lord Anglesy; that himself is to have the other's place of Deputy Treasurer of Ireland (which is a place of honour and great profit, being far better than the Treasurer's, my Lord of Corke's,) and to give the other his of Treasurer of the Navy; that the King, at his earnest entreaty, did with much unwillingness, but with owing of great obligations to him for his faithfulness and long service to him and his father, grant his desire. My Lord Chancellor, I perceive, is his friend in it. I remember I did in the morning tell Sir H. Cholmly of this business: and he answered me, he was sorry for it; for whatever Sir G. Carteret was, he is confident my Lord Anglesy is one of the greatest knaves in the world. Home, and there find my wife making of tea; a drink which Mr Pelling, the Potticary, tells her is good for her cold and defluxions. To Sir W. Batten's to see how he did; and he is better than he was. He told me how Mrs Lowther had her train held up yesterday by her page at his house in the country; which is ridiculous. Mr Pelling told us the news of the town; how the officers of the Navy are cried out upon, and a great many greater men; but do think that I shall do well enough- and I think, if I have justice, I shall. We hear that the Dutch are gone down again; and, thanks be to God, the trouble they give us this second time is not very considerable!

30th. To Rochester about ten of the clock. At the landing-place I met my Lord Brouncker and my Lord Douglas, and all the officers of the soldiers in the town, waiting there for the Duke of York, whom they heard was coming. By and by comes my Lord Middleton, well mounted: he seems a fine soldier, and so every body says he is; and a man like my Lord Tiviott, and indeed most of the Scotch gentry (as I observe,) of few words. After seeing the boats come up from Chatham with them that rowed with bandeleeres about their shoulders, and muskets in their boats; they being the workmen of the Yard, who have promised to redeem their credit, lost by their deserting the service when the Dutch were there; I and Creed down by boat to Chatham-yard. Thence to see the batteries made; which indeed are very fine, and guns placed so as one would think the River should be very secure. Here I was told that in all the late attempt there was but one man that they knew killed on shore; and that was a man that had laid upon his belly upon one of the hills on the other side of the River, to see the action; and a bullet come, and so he was killed. Thence by barge, it raining hard, down to the chaine; and in our way did see the sad wrackes of the poor *Royall Oake, James,* and *London*; and several other of our ships by us sunk, and several of the enemy's, whereof three men-of-war that they could not get off, and so burned. I do not see that Upner Castle hath received any hurt by them, though they played long against it; and they themselves shot till they had hardly a gun left upon the carriages, so badly provided they were: they have now made two batteries on that side, which will be very good, and do good service. So to the chaine, and there saw it fast at the end on Upner side of the River; very fast, and borne up upon the several stages across the River; and where it is broke nobody can tell me. I went on shore on Upner side to look upon the end of the chaine; and caused the link to be measured, and it was six inches and one-fourth in circumference. It seems very remarkable to me, and of great honour to the Dutch, that those of them that did go on shore to Gillingham, though they went in fear of their lives, and were some of them killed, and notwithstanding their provocation at Scelling, yet killed none of our people nor plundered their houses, but did take some things of easy carriage and left the rest, and not a house burned; and, which is to our eternal disgrace, that what my Lord Douglas's men, who come after them, found there, they plundered and took all away: and the watermen that carried us did further tell us, that our own soldiers are far more terrible to those people of the country-towns than the Dutch themselves. We were told at the batteries, upon my seeing of the field-guns that were there, that had they come a day sooner they had been able to have saved all; but they had no orders, and lay lingering upon the way. Several complaints, I hear, of the *Monmouth*'s coming away too soon from the chaine, where she was placed with the two guard-ships to secure it; and Captain Robert Clerke, my friend, is blamed for so doing there, but I hear nothing of him at London about it; but Captain Brookes's running aground with the *Sancta Maria*, which was one of the three ships that were ordered to be sunk to have dammed up the River at the chaine, is mightily cried against, and with reason. It is a strange thing to see, that while my Lords Douglas and Middleton do ride up and down upon single horses, my Lord Brouncker do go up and down with his hackney coach and six horses at the King's charge, and is not able to do so much good as a good boatswain in this business.

July 2nd. To the office, where W. Pen and myself and Sir T. Harvey met, the first time we have had a meeting since the coming of the Dutch upon this coast.

3rd. Sir Richard Ford tells us how he hath been at the Sessions-house, and there it is plain that there is a combination of rogues in the town that do make it their business to set houses on fire, and that one house they did set on fire in Aldersgate-street last Easter; and that this is proved by two young men, whom one of them debauched by degrees to steal their fathers' plate and clothes, and at last to be of their company. One of these boys is a son of a Montagu, of my Lord Manchester's family. To the Council-chamber, to deliver a letter to their Lordships about the state of the six merchantmen which we have been so long fitting out. When I come, the King and the whole table full of Lords were hearing of a pitifull cause of a complaint of an old man with a great grey beard against his son, for not allowing him something to live on; and at last come to the ordering the son to allow his father £10 a-year. This cause lasted them near two hours; which, methinks, at this time to be the work of the Council-board of England, is a scandalous thing. Here I find all the news is the enemy's landing 3000 men near Harwich, and attacking Landguard Fort, and being beat off thence with our great guns, killing some of their men, and they leaving their ladders behind them; but we had no horse in the way on Suffolke side, otherwise we might have galled their foot. The Duke of York is gone down thither this day, while the Generall sat sleeping this afternoon at the Council-table.

4th. To the Sessions-house, where I have a mind to hear Bazill Fielding's case tried; and so got up to the Bench, my Lord Chief-Justice Keeling[72] being Judge. Here I stood bare, not challenging, though I might well enough, to be covered. But here were several fine trials; among others, several brought in for making it their trade to set houses on fire merely to get plunder; and all proved by the two little boys spoken of yesterday by Sir R. Ford, who did give so good account of particulars that I never heard children in my life. One my Lady Montagu's (I know not what Lady Montagu) son, and the other of good condition, were playing in Moorefields, and one rogue, Gabriel Holmes, did come to them and teach them to drink, and then to bring him plate and clothes from their fathers' houses: and this Gabriel Holmes did advise to have had two houses set on fire, one after another, that while they were quenching of one they might be burning another. The boys did swear against one of them, that he had

72 Sir John Keeling, Knight, King's Serjeant 1661, Chief Justice of the King's Bench 1665.

made it his part to pull out the plug out of the engine while it was a-playing; and it really was so. Well, this fellow Holmes was found guilty of the act of burning the house, and other things that he stood indicted for. It was time very well spent to be here. Here I saw how favourable the Judge was to a young gentleman that struck one of the officers, for not making him room: told him he had endangered the loss of his hand, but that he hoped he had not struck him, and would suppose that he had not struck him. The Court then rose, and I to dinner with my Lord Mayor and Sheriffs; where a good dinner and good discourse, the Judge being there. There was also tried this morning Fielding (which I thought had been Bazill, but it proved the other, and Bazill was killed,) that killed his brother, who was found guilty of murder, and nobody pitied him. The Judge seems to be a worthy man, and able; and do intend for these rogues that burned this house to be hung in some conspicuous place in the town, for an example.

6th. Mr Williamson told me that Mr Coventry is coming over with a project of a peace; which, if the States agree to, and our King when their Ministers on both sides have showed it them, we shall agree, and that is all: but the King, I hear, do give it out plain that the peace is concluded. This day with great satisfaction I hear that my Lady Jemimah is brought to bed, at Hinchingbroke, of a boy.[73]

7th (Lord's day). Mr Moor tells me that the discontented Parliament-men are fearful that the next sitting the King will try for a general excise by which to raise him money, and then to fling off the Parliament, and raise a land-army and keep them all down like slaves; and it is gotten among them that Bab. May, the Privy-purse, hath been heard to say that £300 a-year is enough for any country-gentleman; which makes them mad, and they do talk of 6 or £800,000 gone into the Privy-purse this war, when in King James's time it arose but to £5000, and in King Charles's but £10,000 in a year. He tells me that a goldsmith in town told him, that being with some plate with my Lady Castlemaine lately, she directed her woman (the great beauty,) 'Willson,' says she, 'make a note for this and for that to the Privy-purse for money.' He tells me a little more of the

73 In 1681 created Baron Carteret of Hawnes, co. Bedford, in consideration of the eminent services rendered by his grandfather and father to Charles II.

basenesse of the courses taken at Court in the case of Mr Moyer, who is at liberty, and is to give £500 for his liberty; but now the great ones are divided who shall have the money, the Duke of Albemarle on one hand, and another Lord on the other; and that it is fain to be decided by having the person's name put into the King's warrant for his liberty, at whose intercession the King shall own that he is set at liberty: which is a most lamentable thing, that we do professedly own that we do these things, not for right and justice' sake, but only to gratify this or that person about the King. God forgive us all!

8th. Mr Coventry is come from Bredah, as was expected; but, contrary to expectation, brings with him two or three articles which do not please the King: as to retrench the Act of Navigation, and then to ascertain what are contraband goods; and then that those exiled persons, who are or shall take refuge in their country, may be secure from any further prosecution. Whether these will be enough to break the peace upon, or no, he cannot tell; but I perceive the certainty of peace is blown over. To Charing Cross, there to see the great boy and girle that are lately come out of Ireland, the latter eight, the former but four years old, of most prodigious bigness for their age. I tried to weigh them in my arms, and find them twice as heavy as people almost twice their age; and yet I am apt to believe they are very young. Their father a little sorry fellow, and their mother an old Irish woman. They have had four children of this bigness, and four of ordinary growth, whereof two of each are dead. If (as my Lord Ormond certifies) it be true that they are no older, it is very monstrous.

9th. This evening news comes for certain that the Dutch are with their fleet before Dover, and that it is expected they will attempt something there. The business of the peace is quite dashed again.

12th. The Duke of Buckingham was before the Council the other day, and there did carry it very submissively and pleasingly to the King; but to my Lord Arlington, who do prosecute the business, he was most bitter and sharp, and very slighting. As to the letter about his employing a man to cast the King's nativity, says he to the King, 'Sir, this is none of my hand, and I refer it to your Majesty whether you do not know this hand.' The King answered, that it was indeed none of his, and that he knew whose it was, but could not recall it presently. 'Why,' says he, 'it is my sister of Richmond's,[74] some frolick or other of hers about some certain person; and there is nothing of the King's name in it, but it is only said to be his by supposition, as is said.' The King, it seems, was not very much displeased with what the Duke had said; but however, he is still in the Tower, and no discourse of his being out in haste, though my Lady Castlemaine hath so far solicited for him that the King and she are quite fallen out: he comes not to her, nor hath for some three or four days; and parted with very foul words, the King calling her a jade that meddled with things she had nothing to do with at all: and she calling him fool; and told him if he was not a fool he would not suffer his businesses to be carried on by fools that did not understand them, and cause his best subjects, and those best able to serve him, to be imprisoned; meaning the Duke of Buckingham. And it seems she was not only for his liberty, but to be restored to all his places; which, it is thought, he will never be. It was computed that the Parliament had given the King for this war only, besides all prizes, and besides the £200,000 which he was to spend of his own revenue, to guard the sea above £5,000,000 and odd £100,000; which is a most prodigious sum. It is strange how everybody do now-a-days reflect upon Oliver, and commend him, what brave things he did, and made all the neighbour princes fear him; while here a prince, come in with all the love and prayers and good liking of his people, who have given greater signs of loyalty and willingness to serve him with their estates than ever was done by any people, hath lost all so soon, that it is a miracle what way a man could devise to lose so much in so little time. Sir Thomas Crewe tells me how I am mightily in esteem with the Parliament: there being harangues made in the House to the Speaker, of Mr Pepys's readiness and civility to show them everything.

13th. Mr Pierce tells us what troubles me, that my Lord Buckhurst hath got Nell away from the King's house, and gives her £100 a-year, so as she hath sent her parts to the house, and will act no more. And yesterday Sir Thomas Crewe told me that Lacy lies a-dying; nor

74 Mary, daughter of George Villiers first Duke of Buckingham; married, first, to Charles Lord Herbert; secondly, to James Duke of Richmond and Lenox; and thirdly, to Thomas Howard, brother to Charles Earl of Carlisle. She left no issue by any of her husbands.

will receive any ghostly advice from a bishop, an old acquaintance of his, that went to see him. It is an odd and sad thing to say, that though this be a peace worse than we had before, yet every body's fear almost is, that the Dutch will not stand by their promise, now the King hath consented to all they would have. And yet no wise man that I meet with, when he comes to think of it, but wishes with all his heart a war; but that the King is not a man to be trusted with the management of it. It was pleasantly said by a man in this City, a stranger, to one that told him the peace was concluded, 'Well,' says he, 'and have you a peace?' 'Yes,' says the other. 'Why then,' says he, 'hold your peace!' Partly reproaching us with the disgracefulness of it, that it is not fit to be mentioned; and next, that we are not able to make the Dutch keep it, when they have a mind to break it.

14th. To Epsum, by eight o'clock, to the well; where much company. And to the towne to the King's Head; and hear that my Lord Buckhurst and Nelly are lodged at the next house, and Sir Charles Sedley with them: and keep a merry house. Poor girl! I pity her; but more the loss of her at the King's house. Here Tom Wilson come to see me, and sat and talked an hour: and I perceive he hath been much acquainted with Dr Fuller (Tom) and Dr Pierson, and several of the great cavalier parsons during the late troubles; and I was glad to hear him talk of them, which he did very ingenuously, and very much of Dr Fuller's art of memory, which he did tell me several instances of. By and by he parted, and I talked with the two women that farm the well at £12 per annum of the lord of the manor. Mr Evelyn with his lady, and also my Lord George Barkeley's lady,[75] and their fine daughter, that the King of France liked so well, and did dance so rich in jewells before the King at the Ball I was at at our Court last winter, and also their son,[76] a Knight of the Bath, were at church this morning. I walked upon the Downes, where a flock of sheep was; and the most pleasant and innocent sight that ever I saw in my life. We found a shepherd and his little boy reading, far from any houses or sight of people, the Bible to him; and we took notice of his wooling knit stockings, of two colours mixed. Mrs Turner mightily pleased with my resolution, which, I tell her, is never to keep a

75 Elizabeth, daughter and co-heir of John Massingberd, Esq.
76 Charles, eldest son, summoned to Parliament as Baron Berkeley, *vita patris,* 1680. Died 1710, having succeeded his father in the Earldom 1698.

country-house, but to keep a coach, and with my wife on the Saturday to go sometimes for a day to this place, and then quit to another place; and there is more variety and as little charge, and no trouble, as there is in a country-house.

17th. Home, where I was saluted with the news of Hogg's bringing a rich Canary prize to Hull: and Sir W. Batten do offer me £1000 down for my particular share, beside Sir Richard Ford's part; which do tempt me; but yet I would not take it, but will stand and fall with the company. He and two more, the Panther and Fanfan, did enter into consortship; and so they have all brought in each a prize, though ours worth as much as both theirs, and more. However, it will be well worth having, God be thanked for it! This news makes us all very glad. I at Sir W. Batten's did hear the particulars of it; and there for joy he did give the company that were there a bottle or two of his own last year's wine growing at Walthamstow, than which the whole company said they never drank better foreign wine in their lives. The Duke of Buckingham is, it seems, set at liberty without any further charge against him or other clearing of him, but let to go out; which is one of the strangest instances of the fool's play, with which all publick things are done in this age, that is to be apprehended. And it is said that when he was charged with making himself popular, (as indeed he is, for many of the discontented Parliament, Sir Robert Howard, and Sir Thomas Meres, and others, did attend at the Council-chamber when he was examined,) he should answer, that whoever was committed to prison by my Lord Chancellor or my Lord Arlington, could not want being popular. But it is worth considering the ill state a Minister of State is in, under such a Prince as ours is; for, undoubtedly, neither of those two great men would have been so fierce against the Duke of Buckingham at the Council-table the other day, had they not been assured of the King's good liking, and supporting them therein: whereas, perhaps at the desire of my Lady Castlemaine, (who, I suppose, hath at last overcome the King,) the Duke of Buckingham is well received again, and now these men delivered up to the interest he can make for his revenge. He told me over the story of Mrs Stewart, much after the manner which I was told it by Mr Evelyn: only he says it is verily believed that the King did never intend to marry her to any but himself, and that the Duke of York and Lord Chancellor were jealous of it: and that Mrs Stewart might be got with child by the King, or somebody else, and the King own a marriage before his contract (for it is but a contract, as he tells me to this day,) with the Queene, and so wipe their noses of the Crown; and that, therefore, the Duke of York and Chancellor did do all they could to forward the match with my Lord Duke of Richmond, that she might be married out of the way: but above all, it is a worthy part that this good lady hath acted. My sister Michell[77] come from Lee to see us; but do tattle so much of the late business of the Dutch coming thither that I am weary of it. Yet it is worth remembering what she says: that she hath heard both seamen and soldiers swear they would rather serve the Dutch than the King, for they should be better used. She saw the *Royal Charles* brought into the river by them; and how they shot off their great guns for joy, when they got her out of Chatham river.

19th. One tells me that, by letter from Holland, the people there are made to believe that our condition in England is such as they may have whatever they will ask; and that so they are mighty high, and despise us, or a peace with us: and there is too much reason for them to do so. The Dutch fleet are in great squadrons everywhere still about Harwich, and were lately at Portsmouth; and the last letters say at Plymouth, and now gone to Dartmouth to destroy our Streights' fleet lately got in thither: but God knows whether they can do it any hurt, or no.

22nd. Up to my Lord Chancellor's, where was a Committee of Tangier in my Lord's roome, where he sits to hear causes, and where all the Judges' pictures hung up, very fine. But to see how Sir W. Coventry did oppose both my Lord Chancellor and the Duke of York himself, about the Order of the Commissioners of the Treasury to me for not paying of pensions, and with so much reason, and eloquence so natural, was admirable. And another thing, about his pressing for the reduction of the charge of Tangier, which they would have put off to another time; 'But,' says he, 'the King suffers so much by the putting off of the consideration of reductions of charge, that he is undone; and therefore I do pray you, Sir, (to his Royal Highness,) that when any thing offers of the kind, you will not let it escape you.' Here was a great bundle of letters brought

77 The wife of Balthazar St Michel, Mrs Pepys's brother.

hither, sent up from sea, from a vessel of ours that hath taken them after they had been flung over by a Dutchman; wherein, among others, the Duke of York did read the superscription of one to De Witt, thus – 'To the most wise, foreseeing, and discreet, These, &c.;' which, I thought with myself, I could have been glad might have been duly directed to any one of them at the table, though the greatest men in this kingdom. The Duke of York, the Lord Chancellor, my Lord Duke of Albemarle, Arlington, Ashly, Peterborough, and Coventry, (the best of them all for parts,) I perceive they do all profess their expectation of a peace, and that suddenly. Sir W. Coventry did declare his opinion that if Tangier were offered us now, as the King's condition is, he would advise against the taking it; saying, that the King's charge is too great, and must be brought down, it being like the fire of this City, never to be mastered till you have brought it under you; and that these places abroad are but so much charge to the King, and we do rather herein strive to greaten them than lessen them; and then the King is forced to part with them, 'as,' says he, 'he did with Dunkirke, by my Lord Tiviott's making it so chargeable to the King as he did that, and would have done Tangier, if he had lived.' I perceive he is the only man that do seek the King's profit, and is bold to deliver what he thinks on every occasion. With much pleasure reflecting upon our discourse to-day at the Tangier meeting, and crying up the worth of Sir W. Coventry. Creed tells me of the fray between the Duke of Buckingham at the Duke's play-house the last Saturday, (and it is the first day I have heard that they have acted at either the King's or Duke's houses this month or six weeks), and Henry Killigrew, whom the Duke of Buckingham did soundly beat and take away his sword, and make a fool of, till the fellony prayed him to spare his life; and I am glad of it, for it seems in this business the Duke of Buckingham did carry himself very innocently and well, and I wish he had paid this fellow's coat well. I heard something of this at the 'Change to-day: and it is pretty to hear how people do speak kindly of the Duke of Buckingham, as one that will enquire into faults; and therefore they do mightily favour him. And it puts me in mind that, this afternoon, Billing the Quaker meeting me in the Hall, come to me, and after a little discourse did say, 'Well,' says he, 'now you will be all called to an account'; meaning the Parliament is drawing near.

23rd. By and by comes sudden news to me by letter from the Clerke of the Cheque at Gravesend, that there were thirty sail of Dutch men-of-war coming up into the Hope this last tide: which I told Sir W. Pen of; but he would not believe it, but laughed, and said it was a fleet of Billanders, and that the guns that were heard was the salutation of the Swede's Embassador that comes over with them. But within half an hour comes another letter from Captain Proud, that eight of them were come into the Hope, and thirty more following them, at ten this morning. By and by comes an order from White Hall to send down one of our number to Chatham, fearing that, as they did before, they may make a show first up hither, but then go to Chatham: so my Lord Brouncker do go, and we here are ordered to give notice to the merchant men-of-war, gone below the barricado at Woolwich, to come up again.

24th. Betimes this morning comes a letter from the Clerk of the Cheque at Gravesend to me, to tell me that the Dutch fleet did come all into the Hope yesterday noon, and held a fight with our ships from thence till seven at night; that they had burned twelve fire-ships, and we took one of theirs, and burned five of our fire-ships. But then rising and going to Sir W. Batten, he tells me that we have burned one of their men-of-war, and another of theirs is blown up: but how true this is, I know not. But these fellows are mighty bold and have had the fortune of the wind easterly this time to bring them up, and prevent our troubling them with our fire-ships; and, indeed, have had the winds at their command from the beginning, and now do take the beginning of the spring, as if they had some great design to do. About five o'clock down to Gravesend; and as we come nearer Gravesend, we hear the Dutch fleet and ours a-firing their guns most distinctly and loud. So I landed and discoursed with the landlord of the Ship, who undeceives me in what I heard this morning about the Dutch having lost two men-of-war, for it is not so, but several of their fireships. He do say, that this afternoon they did force our ships to retreat, but that now they are gone down as far as Shield-haven: but what the event hath been of this evening's guns they know not, but suppose not much, for they have all this while shot at good distance one from another. They seem confident of the security of this town and the River above it, if ever the enemy should come up so high; their fortifications being so good, and guns many. But he do say that people do complain of Sir Edward Spragg, that he hath not done extraordinary; and more of Sir W. Jenings, that he came up with his tamkins[78] in his guns.

25th. I demanded of Sir R. Ford and the rest, what passed to-day at the meeting of Parliament: who told me that, contrary to all expectation by the King that there would be but a thin meeting, there met above 300 this first day, and all the discontented party; and, indeed, the whole House seems to be no other almost. The Speaker told them, as soon as they were sat, that he was ordered by the King to let them know he was hindered by some important business to come to them and speak to them, as he intended; and, therefore, ordered him to move that they would adjourn themselves till Monday next, (it being very plain to all the House that he expects to hear by that time of the sealing of the peace, which by letters, it seems, from my Lord Hollis was to be sealed the last Sunday.) But before they would come to the question whether they would adjourn, Sir Thomas Tomkins steps up and tells them, that all the country is grieved at this new-raised standing-army; and that they thought themselves safe enough in their trayn-bands: and that, therefore, he desired the King might be moved to disband them. Then rises Garraway and seconds him, only with this explanation, (which he said he believed the other meant;) that, as soon as peace should be concluded, they might be disbanded. Then rose Sir W. Coventry, and told them that he did approve of what the last gentleman said; but also, that at the same time he did no more than what he durst be bold to say he knew to be the King's mind, that as soon as peace was concluded he would do it of himself. Then rose Sir Thomas Littleton, and did give several reasons from the uncertainty of their meeting again but to adjourne, (in case news comes of the peace being ended before Monday next,) and the possibility of the King's having some about him that may endeavour to alter his own, and the good part of his Council's advice, for the keeping up of the land-army: and, therefore, it was fit that they did present it to the King as their desire, that as soon as peace was concluded the land-army might be laid down, and that this their request might be carried to the King by them of their House that were Privy-councillors;

78 Tamkin, or tompion, the stopple of a great gun.

which was put to the vote, and carried *nemine contradicente*. So after this vote passed, they adjourned: but it is plain what the effects of this Parliament will be, if they be suffered to sit, that they will fall foul upon the faults of the Government; and I pray God they may be permitted to do it, for nothing else, I fear, will save the King and kingdom than the doing it betimes.

27th. To the office, where I hear that Sir John Coventry[79] is come over from Bredagh, (a nephew, I think, of Sir W. Coventry's); but what message he brings I know not. This morning news is come that Sir Jos. Jordan is come from Harwich, with sixteen fire-ships and four other little ships of war; and did attempt to do some execution upon the enemy, but did it without discretion, as most do say, so as they have been able to do no good, but have lost four of their fire-ships. They attempted this, it seems, when the wind was too strong, that our grapplings could not hold: others say we came to leeward of them, but all condemn it as a foolish management. They are come to Sir Edward Spragg about Lee, and the Dutch are below at the Nore. At the office all the morning: and at noon to the 'Change, where I met Fenn. And he tells me that Sir John Coventry do bring the confirmation of the peace; but I do not find the 'Change at all glad of it, but rather the worse, they looking upon it as a peace made only to preserve the King for a time in his lusts and ease, and to sacrifice trade and his kingdoms only to his own pleasures; so that the hearts of merchants are quite down. He tells me that the King and my Lady Castlemaine are quite broke off, and she is gone away, and is with child, and swears the King shall own it; and she will have it christened in the Chapel at White Hall so, and owned for the King's, as other Kings have done; or she will bring it into White Hall gallery, and dash the brains of it out before the King's face. He tells me that the King and Court were never in the world so bad as they are now for gaming, swearing, women, and drinking, and the most abominable vices that ever were in the world; so that all must come to nought. He told me that Sir G. Carteret was at this end of the town: so I went to visit him in Broad-street. And there he and I together: and he is

79 Nephew to Sir William and Henry Coventry; created KB at Charles II's coronation, and MP for Weymouth in several Parliaments. The outrage committed on his person by Sir Thomas Sandys, O'Bryan, and others, who cut his nose to the bone, gave rise to the passing a Bill still known by the name of the Coventry Act.

mightily pleased with my Lady Jem's having a son; and a mighty glad man he is. He tells me, as to news, that the peace is now confirmed, and all that over. He says it was a very unhappy motion in the House the other day about the land-army; for whether the King hath a mind of his own to do the thing desired, or no, his doing it will be looked upon as a thing done only in fear of the Parliament. He says that the Duke of York is suspected to be the great man that is for raising this army, and bringing things to be commanded by an army; but that he do know that he is wronged therein. He do say that the Court is in a way to ruin all for their pleasures; and says that he himself hath once taken the liberty to tell the King the necessity of having at least a show of religion in the Government, and sobriety; and that it was that that did set up and keep up Oliver, though he was the greatest rogue in the world. He tells me the King adheres to no man, but this day delivers himself up to this and the next to that, to the ruin of himself and business: that he is at the command of any woman like a slave, though he be the best man to the Queene in the world, with so much respect, and never lies a night from her; but yet cannot command himself in the presence of a woman he likes. It raining this day all day to our great joy, it having not rained, I think, this month before, so as the ground was every where so burned and dry as could be; and no travelling in the road or streets in London, for dust.

28th. All the morning close to draw up a letter to Sir W. Coventry upon the tidings of peace, taking occasion (before I am forced to it) to resign up to his Royall Highness my place of the Victualling, and to recommend myself to him by promise of doing my utmost to improve this peace in the best manner we may, to save the kingdom from ruin.

29th. Up, and with Sir W. Batten to St James's, to Sir W. Coventry's chamber; where, among other things, he came to me and told me that he had received my yesterday's letters, and that we concurred very well in our notions; and that as to my place which I had offered to resign of the Victualling, he had drawn up a letter at the same time for the Duke of York's signing for the like places in general raised during this war; and that he had done me right to the Duke of York, to let him know that I had of my own accord offered to resign mine. The letter do bid us to do all things, particularizing several, for the laying up of the ships and easing the King of charge;

so that the war is now professedly over. By and by up to the Duke of York's chamber; and there all the talk was about Jordan's coming with so much indiscretion, with his four little frigates and sixteen fire-ships from Harwich, to annoy the enemy. His failures were of several sorts, I know not which the truest: that he came with so strong a gale of wind that his grapplings would not hold; that he did come by their lee, whereas if he had come athwart their hawse, they would have held; that they did not stop a tide, and ebb up with a windward tide, and then they would have come so fast. Now there happened to be Captain Jenifer by, who commanded the *Lily* in this business, and thus says: that finding the Dutch not so many as they expected, they did not know that there were more of them above, and so were not so earnest to the setting upon these; that they did do what they could to make the fire-ships fall in among the enemy; and for their lives Sir J. Jordan nor others could, by shooting several times at them, make them go in: and it seems they were commanded by some idle fellows, such as they could of a sudden gather up at Harwich; which is a sad consideration, that at such a time as this, where the saving the reputation of the whole nation lay at stake, and after so long a war, the King had not credit to gather a few able men to command these vessels. He says, that if they had come up slower, the enemy would (with their boats and their great sloops, which they have to row with a great many men,) and did come and cut up several of our fire-ships, and would certainly have taken most of them, for they do come with a great provision of these boats on purpose, and to save their men, which is bravely done of them, though they did on this very occasion show great fear, as they say, by some men leaping overboard out of a great ship (as these were all of them of sixty and seventy guns a-piece) which one of our fire-ships laid on board, though the fire did not take. But yet it is brave to see what care they do take to encourage their men to provide great stores of boats to save them, while we have not credit to find one boat for a ship. And further, he told us that this new way used by Deane (and this Sir W. Coventry observed several times) of preparing of fireships do not do the work; for the fire not being strong and quick enough to flame up, so as to take the rigging and sails, lies smothering a great while, half an hour before it flames, in which time they can get the fire-ship off safely, though (which is uncertain, and did fail in one or two this bout) it do serve to burn our own ships. But what a shame it is to consider how two of our ships' companies did desert their ships for fear of being taken by their boats, our little frigates being forced to leave them, being chased by their greater! And one more company did set their ship on fire, and leave her; which afterwards a Feversham fisherman came up to, and put out the fire, and carried safe into Feversham, where she now is. Which was observed by the Duke of York, and all the company with him, that it was only want of courage, and a general dismay and abjectness of spirit upon all our men; and others did observe our ill management, and God Almighty's curse upon all that we have in hand, for never such an opportunity was of destroying so many good ships of theirs as we now had. But to see how negligent we were in this business, that our fleet of Jordan's should not have any notice where Spragg was, nor Spragg of Jordan's so as to be able to meet and join in the business, and help one another; but Jordan, when he saw Spragg's fleet above, did think them to be another part of the enemy's fleet! While, on the other side, notwithstanding our people at Court made such a secret of Jordan's design that nobody must know it, and even this office itself must not know it; nor for my part I did not, though Sir W. Batten says by others' discourse to him he had heard something of it; yet De Ruyter (or he that commanded this fleet) had notice of it, and told it to a fisherman of ours that he took and released on Thursday last, which was the day before our fleet came to him. But then, that that seems most to our disgrace, and which the Duke of York did take special and vehement notice of, is, that when the Dutch saw so many fire-ships provided for them, themselves lying, I think, about the Nore, they did with all their great ships, with a North-east wind, (as I take it they said, but whatever it was, it was a wind that we should not have done it with,) turn down to the Middleground; which, the Duke of York observed, never was nor would have been undertaken by ourselves. And whereas some of the company answered, it was their great fear, not their choice, that made them do it, the Duke of York answered, that it was, it may be, their fear and wisdom that made them do it; but yet their fear did not make them mistake, as we should have done, when we have had no fear upon us, and have run our ships on ground. And this brought it into my mind, that they managed their retreat down this difficult passage, with all their fear, better than we could do ourselves in the main sea, when the Duke of Albemarle ran away from the Dutch, when the Prince was lost, and the *Royal Charles* and the other great ships came on ground upon the Galloper. Thus in all things, in wisdom, courage, force, knowledge of our own streams, and success, the Dutch have the best of us, and do end the war with victory on their side. One thing extraordinary was this day: a man, a Quaker, came naked through the Hall, only very civilly tied about the loins to avoid scandal, and with a chafing-dish of fire and brimstone burning upon his head, did pass through the Hall, crying, 'Repent! repent!' Presently comes down the House of Commons, the King having made a very short and no pleasing speech to them at all, not at all giving them thanks for their readiness to come up to town at this busy time; but told them that he did think he should have had occasion for them, but had none, and therefore did dismiss them to look after their own occasions till October; and that he did wonder any should offer to bring in a suspicion that he intended to rule by an army, or otherwise than by the laws of the land, which he promised them he would do; and so bade them go home and settle the minds of the country in that particular; and only added, that he had made a peace which he did believe they would find reasonable, and a good peace, but did give them none of the particulars thereof. Thus they are dismissed again to their general great distaste, I believe the greatest that ever Parliament was, to see themselves so fooled, and the nation in certain condition of ruin, while the King, they see, is only governed by his lust, and women, and rogues about him. The Speaker, they found, was kept from coming in the morning to the House on purpose till after the King was come to the House of Lords, for fear they should be doing any thing in the House of Commons to the further dissatisfaction of the King and his courtiers. They do all give up the kingdom for lost, that I speak to; and do hear what the King says, how he and the Duke of York do do what they can to get up an army, that they may need no more Parliaments: and how my Lady Castlemaine hath, before the late breach between her and the King, said to the King, that he must rule by an army, or all would be lost. I am told that many petitions were provided for the Parliament, complaining of the wrongs they have received from the Court and courtiers, in city and country, if the Parliament had but sat: and I do perceive they all do resolve to have a good account of the money spent before ever they give a farthing more; and the whole kingdom is every where sensible of their being abused, insomuch that they forced their Parliament-men to come up to sit; and my cozen Roger told me that (but that was in mirth) he believed, if he had not come up he should have had his house burned. The kingdom never in so troubled a condition in this world as now; nobody pleased with the peace, and yet nobody daring to wish for the continuance of the war, it being plain that nothing do nor can thrive under us. Here I saw old good Mr Vaughan, and several of the great men of the Commons, and some of them old men, that are come 200 miles and more to attend this session of Parliament; and have been at great charge and disappointments in their other private business; and now all to no purpose, neither to serve their country, content themselves, nor receive any thanks from the King. It is verily expected by many of them that the King will continue the prorogation in October, so as, if it be possible, never to have this Parliament more. My Lord Bristoll took his place in the House of Lords this day, but not in his robes; and when the King came in he withdrew: but my Lord of Buckingham was there as brisk as ever, and sat in his robes; which is a monstrous thing, that a man should be proclaimed against, and put in the Tower, and released without any trial, and yet not restored to his places. But above all, I saw my Lord Mordaunt[80] as merry as the best, that it seems hath done such further indignities to Mr Taylor since the last sitting of Parliament as would hang him, if there were nothing else, would the King do what were fit for him; but nothing of that is now likely to be. Cozen Roger and Creed to dinner with me, and very merry: but among other things they told me of the strange, bold sermon of Dr Creeton[81] yesterday before the King; how he preached against the sins of the Court, and particularly against adultery, over and over instancing how for that single sin in David the whole nation was undone; and of our negligence in having our castles without ammunition and powder when the Dutch came upon us; and how we have no courage now-a-days, but let our ships be taken out of our harbour. Here Creed did tell us the story of the duell last night, in Covent-garden, between Sir H. Bellasses and Tom Porter. It is worth remembering the silliness of the quarrel, and

80 See note, November 26, 1666.
81 Probably Robert Creyghton of Trinity College, Cambridge, AM 1662. Regius Professor of Greek 1672/73.

is a kind of emblem of the general complexion of this whole
kingdom at present. They two dined yesterday at Sir Robert Carr's[82]
where it seems people do drink high, all that come. It happened that
these two, the greatest friends in the world, were talking together:
and Sir H. Bellasses talked a little louder than ordinary to Tom
Porter, giving of him some advice. Some of the company standing
by said, 'What! are they quarrelling, that they talk so high?' Sir H.
Bellasses hearing it, said, 'No!' says he: 'I would have you know I
never quarrel, but I strike; and take that as a rule of mine!' – 'How?'
says Tom Porter, 'strike! I would I could see the man in England that
durst give me a blow!' with that Sir H. Bellasses did give him a box
of the eare; and so they were going to fight there, but were
hindered. And by and by Tom Porter went out, and meeting
Dryden the poet, told him of the business, and that he was resolved
to fight Sir H. Bellasses presently; for he knew, if he did not, they
should be friends to-morrow, and then the blow would rest upon
him; which he would prevent, and desired Dryden to let him have
his boy to bring him notice which way Sir H. Bellasses goes. By and
by he is informed that Sir H. Bellasses's coach was coming: so Tom
Porter went down out of the Coffee-house where he stayed for the
tidings, and stopped the coach, and bade Sir H. Bellasses come out.
'Why,' says H. Bellasses, 'you will not hurt me coming out – will
you?' 'No,' says Tom Porter. So out he went, and both drew: and
H. Bellasses having drawn and flung away his scabbard, Tom Porter
asked him whether he was ready? The other answering him he was,
they fell to fight, some of their acquaintance by. They wounded one
another, and H. Bellasses so much that it is feared he will die: and
finding himself severely wounded, he called to Tom Porter, and
kissed him and bade him shift for himself; 'for,' says he, 'Tom, thou
hast hurt me; but I will make shift to stand upon my legs till thou
mayest withdraw, and the world not take notice of you, for I would
not have thee troubled for what thou hast done.' And so whether he
did fly or no I cannot tell; but Tom Porter showed H. Bellasses that
he was wounded too: and they are both ill, but H. Bellasses to fear of
life. And this is a fine example; and H. Bellasses a Parliament-man
too, and both of them extraordinary friends! Among other discourse

82 MP, Knight and Baronet, of Sleaford, Lincolnshire, and one of the proposed
Knights of the Royal Oak for that county.

my cosen Roger told us a thing certain, that my Lady Castlemaine hath made a Bishop lately, namely, her uncle Dr Glenham,[83] who, I think they say, is Bishop of Carlisle; a drunken, swearing rascal, and a scandal to the Church; and do now pretend to be Bishop of Lincoln, in competition with Dr Raynbow,[84] who is reckoned as worthy a man as most in the Church for piety and learning: which are things so scandalous to consider, that no man can doubt but we must be undone that hears of them. Cosen Roger did acquaint me in private with an offer made of his marrying of Mrs Elizabeth Wiles, whom I know; a kinswoman of Mr Honiwood's, an ugly old maid, but good housewife, and is said to have £2500 to her portion; though I am against it in my heart, she being not handsome at all: and it hath been the very bad fortune of the Pepyses that ever I knew, never to marry an handsome woman, excepting Ned Pepys. To White Hall; and looking out of the window into the garden, I saw the King (whom I have not had any desire to see since the Dutch came upon the coast first to Sheerness, for shame that I should see him, or he me, methinks, after such a dishonour) come upon the garden; with him two or three idle Lords; and instantly after him, in another walk, my Lady Castlemaine, led by Bab. May: at which I was surprised, having but newly heard the stories of the King and her being parted for ever. So I took Mr Povy, who was there, aside, and he told me all, – how imperious this woman is, and hectors the King to whatever she will. It seems she is with child, and the King says he did not get it: with that she made a slighting puh with her mouth, and went out of the house, and never came in again till the King went to Sir Daniel Harvy's to pray her; and so she is come to-day, when one would think his mind should be full of some other cares, having but this morning broken up such a Parliament with so much discontent and so many wants upon him, and but yesterday heard such a sermon against adultery. But it seems she hath told the King, that whoever did get it, he should own it. And the bottom of the quarrel is this: – She is fallen in love with young Jermin, who hath of late been with her oftener than the King, and is now going to marry my Lady Falmouth;[85] the King is mad at her entertaining Jermin, and she is

83 Henry Glenham, DD, was Dean of Bristol, 1661: but, I believe, never raised to the Bench.
84 Dr Rainbow was Bishop of Carlisle from 1664 to 1684.
85 Lady Falmouth married the Earl of Dorset.

mad at Jermin's going to marry from her: so they are all mad; and thus the kingdom is governed! But he tells me for certain that nothing is more sure than that the King, and Duke of York, and the Chancellor, are desirous and labouring all they can to get an army, whatever the King says to the Parliament; and he believes that they are at last resolved to stand and fall all three together: so that he says in terms that the match of the Duke of York with the Chancellor's daughter hath undone the nation. He tells me also that the King hath not greater enemies in the world than those of his own family; for there is not an officer in the house almost but curses him for letting them starve, and there is not a farthing of money to be raised for the buying them bread.

30th. To the Treasury-chamber, where I did speak with the Lords. Here I do hear that there are three Lords more to be added to them; my Lord Bridgewater, my Lord Anglesy, and my Lord Chamberlaine. Mr Cooling told us how the King, once speaking of the Duke of York's being mastered by his wife, said to some of the company by, that he would go no more abroad with this Tom Otter[86] (meaning the Duke of York) and his wife. Tom Killigrew being by, said, 'Sir, pray which is the best for a man, to be a Tom Otter to his wife or to his mistress?' meaning the King's being so to my Lady Castlemaine.

31st. To Marrowbone, where my Lord Mayor and Aldermen, it seems, dined to-day; and were just now going away, methought, in a disconsolate condition, compared with their splendour they formerly had when the City was standing.

August 1st. Home, the gates of the City shut, it being so late; and at Newgate we find them in trouble, some thieves having this night broke open prison.

3rd. To the office, there to enable myself, by finishing our great account, to give it to the Lords Commissioners of the Treasury; which I did, and there was called in to them, to tell them only the total of our debt of the Navy on the 25th of May last, which is above

86 See the play of *Epicoene, or the Silent Woman*, in which Mrs Otter thus addresses her henpecked husband, Thomas Otter – 'Is this according to the instrument when I married you, that I would be princess and reign in my own house, and you would be my subject, and obey me ?' – Act III, Scene i.

£950,000. Here I find them mighty hot in their answer to the Council-board about our Treasurer's threepences of the Victualling, and also against the present farm of the Customes, which they do most highly inveigh against.

5th. I hear the ill news of our loss lately of four rich ships, two from Guinea, one from Gallipoly, all with rich oyles, and the other from Barbadoes, worth, as is guessed, £80,000. But here is strong talk as if Harman had taken some of the Dutch East India ships, (but I dare not yet believe it,) and brought them into Lisbon. To the Duke of York's house, and there saw *Love Trickes, or the School of Compliments*;[87] a silly play, only Miss Davis, dancing in a shepherd's clothes, did please us mightily.

6th. A full Board. Here, talking of news, my Lord Anglesy did tell us that the Dutch do make a further bogle with us about two or three things, which they will be satisfied in, he says, by us easily, but only in one, it seems, they do demand that we shall not interrupt their East Indiamen coming home, and of which they are in some fear; and we are full of hopes that we have light upon some of them and carried them into Lisbon by Harman; which God send! But they (which do show the low esteem they have of us) have the confidence to demand that we shall have a cessation on our parts, and yet they at liberty to take what they will; which is such an affront, as another cannot be devised greater.

7th. Though the King and my Lady Castlemaine are friends again, she is not at White Hall, but at Sir D. Harvy's, whither the King goes to her; and he says she made him ask her forgiveness upon his knees, and promised to offend her no more so: and that, indeed, she did threaten to bring all his bastards to his closet-door, and hath nearly hectored him out of his wits.

8th. Sir Henry Bellasses is dead of the duell he fought about ten days ago with Tom Porter; and it is pretty to see how the world talk of them as of a couple of fools that killed one another out of love. I to my bookseller's; where by and by I met Mr Evelyn, and talked of several things, but particularly of the times: and he tells me that wise men do prepare to remove abroad what they have, for that we must

87 A comedy, by James Shirley.

be ruined, our case being past relief, the kingdom so much in debt, and the King minding nothing but his lust, going two days a-week to see my Lady Castlemaine at Sir D. Harvy's.

9th. To St James's, and there met Sir W. Coventry; and he and I walked in the Park an hour. And then to his chamber, where he read to me the heads of the late great dispute between him and the rest of the Commissioners of the Treasury, and our new Treasurer of the Navy; where they have overthrown him the last Wednesday, in the great dispute touching his having the payment of the Victualler, which is now settled by Council that he is not to have it: and, indeed, they have been most just as well as most severe and bold in the doing this against a man of his quality: but I perceive he does really make no difference between any man. He tells me this day it is supposed the peace is ratified at Bredah, and all that matter over. We did talk of many retrenchments of charge of the Navy which he will put in practice, and every where else; though, he tells me, he despairs of being able to do what ought to be done for the saving of the kingdom, (which I tell him, indeed, all the world is almost in hopes of, upon the proceeding of these gentlemen for the regulating of the Treasury,) it being so late, and our poverty grown so great, that they want where to set their feet to begin to do any thing. He tells me how weary he hath for this year and a half been of the warr; and how in the Duke of York's bedchamber at Christ Church, at Oxford, when the Court was there, he did labour to persuade the Duke to fling off the care of the Navy, and get it committed to other hands; which, if he had done, would have been much to his honour, being just come home with so much honour from sea as he was. I took notice of the sharp letter he wrote (which he sent us to read) to Sir Edward Spragg, where he is very plain about his leaving his charge of the ships at Gravesend, when the enemy came last up, and several other things; a copy whereof I have kept. But it is done like a most worthy man, and he says it is good now and then to tell these gentlemen their duty, for they need it. And it seems, as he tells me, all our Knights are fallen out one with another, he and Jenings and Hollis, and (his words were) they are disputing which is the coward among them; and yet men that take the greatest liberty of censuring others! Here with him very late, till I could hardly get a coach or link willing to go through the ruines; but I do, but will not do it again, being indeed very dangerous.

10th. Sir John Denham's Poems are going to be all printed together; and, among others, some new things; and among them he showed me a copy of verses of his upon Sir John Minnes's going heretofore to Bullogne to eat a pig. Cowly, he tells me, is dead; who, it seems, was a mighty civil, serious man; which I did not know before.

11th. To the Wells at Barnett, by seven o'clock; and there found many people a-drinking; but the morning is a very cold morning, so as we were very cold all the way in the coach. And so to Hatfield, to the inn next my Lord Salisbury's house; and there rested ourselves, and drank, and bespoke dinner: and so to church. In this church lies the former Lord of Salisbury (Cecil), buried in a noble tomb. Then we to our inn, and there dined very well, and mighty merry; and walked out into the Park through the fine walk of trees, and to the Vineyard, and there showed them that which is in good order, and indeed a place of great delight; which, together with our fine walk through the Park, was of as much pleasure as could be desired in the world for country pleasure and good ayre. Being come back and weary with the walk, the women had pleasure in putting on some straw-hats, which are much worn in this country, and did become them mightily, but especially my wife.

12th. To my bookseller's, and did buy Scott's *Discourse of Witches*; and to hear Mr Cowly mightily lamented (his death) by Dr Ward, the Bishop of Winchester, and Dr Bates, who were standing there, as the best poet of our nation, and as good a man.

13th. Attended the Duke of York, with our usual business; who upon occasion told us that he did expect this night or tomorrow to hear from Bredah of the consummation of the peace.

15th. Sir W. Pen and I to the Duke's house; where a new play. The King and Court there: the house full, and an act begun. And so we went to the King's, and there saw *The Merry Wives of Windsor*, which did not please me at all, in no part of it.

16th. My wife and I to the Duke's playhouse, where we saw the new play acted yesterday, *The Feign Innocence, or Sir Martin Marall*; a play made by my Lord Duke of Newcastle, but, as every body says, corrected by Dryden. It is the most entire piece of mirth, a complete farce from one end to the other, that certainly was ever writ. I never laughed so in all my life, and at very good wit therein, not fooling. The House full, and in all things of mighty content to me. Every body wonders that we have no news from Bredah of the ratification of the peace; and do suspect that there is some stop in it.

17th. To the King's playhouse, where the house extraordinary full; and there the King and Duke of York to see the new play, *Queene Elizabeth's Troubles, and the history of Eighty Eight*. I confess I have sucked in so much of the sad story of Queene Elizabeth from my cradle, that I was ready to weep for her sometimes; but the play is the most ridiculous that sure ever came upon stage, and, indeed, is merely a show, only shows the true garbe of the Queene in those days, just as we see Queene Mary and Queene Elizabeth painted: but the play is merely a puppet play, acted by living puppets. Neither the design nor language better; and one stands by and tells us the meaning of things: only I was pleased to see Knipp dance among the milkmaids, and to hear her sing a song to Queene Elizabeth; and to see her come out in her night-gowne with no lockes on, but her bare face and hair only tied up in a knot behind; which is the comeliest dress that ever I saw her in to her advantage.

18th. To Cree Church, to see it how it is; but I find no alteration there, as they say there was, for my Lord Mayor and Aldermen to come to sermon, as they do every Sunday, as they did formerly to Paul's.

20th. Sir W. Coventry fell to discourse of retrenchments: and therein he tells how he would have but only one Clerk of the Acts. He do tell me he hath propounded how the charge of the Navy in peace shall come within £200,000, by keeping out twenty-four ships in summer, and ten in the winter. And several other particulars we went over of retrenchment: and I find I must provide some things to offer, that I may be found studious to lessen the King's charge. Sir W. Coventry did single Sir W. Pen and me, and desired us to lend the King some money, out of the prizes we have taken by Hogg. He did not much press it, and we made but a merry answer thereto: but I perceive he did ask it seriously, and did tell us that there never was so much need of it in the world as now, we being brought to the lowest straits that can be in the world.

22nd. Up, and to the office: whence Lord Brouncker, J. Minnes, and W. Pen, and I went to examine some men that are put in there for rescuing of men that were pressed into the service: and we do plainly see that the desperate condition that we put men into for want of their pay makes them mad, they being as good men as ever were in the world, and would as readily serve the King again, were they but paid. Two men leapt overboard, among others, into the Thames out of the vessel into which they were pressed, and were shot by the soldiers placed there to keep them, two days since; so much people do avoid the King's service! And then these men are pressed without money, and so we cannot punish them for any thing, so that we are forced only to make a show of severity[88] by keeping them in prison, but are unable to punish them. Returning to the office, I did ask whether we might visit Commissioner Pett (to which, I confess, I have no great mind); and it was answered that he was close prisoner, and we could not; but the Lieutenant of the Tower would send for him to his lodgings, if we would: so we put it off to another time. To Captain Cocke's to dinner; where Lord Brouncker and his lady, Matt. Wren, and Bulteale, and Sir Allan Apsly; the last of whom did make good sport, he being already fallen under the retrenchments of the new Committee, as he is Master Falconer; which makes him mad. With my Lord Brouncker and his mistress to the King's playhouse, and there saw *The Indian Emperour*:[89] where I find Nell come again, which I am glad of; but was most infinitely displeased with her being put to act the Emperour's daughter, which is a great and serious part, which she does most basely. This evening Mr Pelling comes to me, and tells me that this night the Dutch letters are come, and that the peace was proclaimed there the 19th inst. and that all is finished: which for my life I know not whether to be glad or sorry for, a peace being so necessary, and yet so bad in its terms.

23rd. To White Hall, to attend the Council. The King there: and it was about considering how the fleet might be discharged at their coming in shortly, the peace being now ratified, and it takes place on Monday next. To the Treasury-chamber, where I waited talking with Sir G. Downing till the Lords met. He tells me how he will

88 Shooting the men was rather more than a show of severity.
89 A tragi-comedy, by Dryden.

make all the Exchequer officers, of one side and the other, to lend the King money upon the Act; and that the least Clerk shall lend money, and he believes the least will £100: but this I do not believe. He made me almost ashamed that we of the Navy had not in all this time lent any; so that I find it necessary I should, and so will speedily do it before any of my fellows begin and lead me to a bigger sum. By and by the Lords come; and I perceive Sir W. Coventry is the man, and nothing done till he comes. Among other things I heard him observe, looking over a paper, that Sir John Shaw is a miracle of a man, for he thinks he executes more places than any man in England: for there he finds him a Surveyor of some of the King's woods, and so reckoned up many other places, the most inconsistent in the world. Their business with me was to consider how to assigne such of our commanders as will take assignements upon the Act for their wages; and the consideration thereof was referred to me to give them an answer the next sitting: which is a horrid poor thing; but they scruple at nothing of honour in the case. I find most people pleased with their being at ease, and safe of a peace, that they may know no more charge or hazard of an ill-managed war; but nobody speaking of the peace with any content or pleasure, but are silent in it, as of a thing they are ashamed of; no, not at Court, much less in the City.

24th. St Bartholomew's Day. This morning was proclaimed the peace between us and the States of the United Provinces, and also of the King of France and Denmarke; and in the afternoon the Proclamations were printed and came out; and at night the bells rung, but no bonfires that I hear of any where, partly from the dearness of firing, but principally from the little content most people have in the peace. This day comes a letter from the Duke of York to the Board, to invite us, which is as much as to fright us, into the lending the King money; which is a poor thing, and most dishonourable, and shows in what a case we are at the end of the war to our neighbours. And the King do now declare publickly to give 10 per cent. to all lenders; which make some think that the Dutch themselves will send over money, and lend it upon our publick faith, the Act of Parliament.

26th. To the office, where we sat upon a particular business all the morning: and my Lord Anglesy with us; who, and my Lord Brouncker, do bring us news how my Lord Chancellor's seal is to be taken away from him to-day. The thing is so great and sudden to me, that it put me into a very great admiration what should be the meaning of it; and they do not own that they know what it should be; but this is certain, that the King did resolve it on Saturday, and did yesterday send the Duke of Albemarle (the only man fit for those works) to him for his purse: to which the Chancellor answered, that he received it from the King, and would deliver it to the King's own hand, and so civilly returned the Duke of Albemarle without it; and this morning my Lord Chancellor is to be with the King, to come to an end in the business. Dined at Sir W. Batten's, where Mr Boreman was, who came from White Hall; who tells us that he saw my Lord Chancellor come in his coach with some of his men, without his seal, to White Hall to his chamber; and thither the King and Duke of York came and staid together alone an hour or more: and it is said that the King do say that he will have the Parliament meet, and that it will prevent much trouble by having of him out of their enmity by his place being taken away; for that all their enmity will be at him. It is said also that my Lord Chancellor answers, that he desires he may be brought to his trial, if he have done anything to lose his office; and that he will be willing and is most desirous to lose that and his head both together. Upon what terms they parted nobody knows; but the Chancellor looked sad, he says. Then in comes Sir Richard Ford, and says he hears that there is nobody more presses to reconcile the King and Chancellor than the Duke of Albemarle and Duke of Buckingham: the latter of which is very strange, not only that he who was so lately his enemy should do it, but that this man, that but the other day was in danger of losing his own head, should so soon come to be a mediator for others: it shows a wise Government. They all say that he is but a poor man, not worth above £3000 a-year in land; but this I cannot believe: and all do blame him for having built so great a house, till he had got a better estate. Sir W. Pen and I had a great deal of discourse with Mall;[90] who tells us that Nell is already left by Lord Buckhurst, and that he makes sport of her and swears she hath had all she could get of him; and Hart[91] her great admirer now hates her; and that she is very poor, and hath lost my Lady Castlemaine, who was her great friend also: but she is come to the playhouse, but is neglected by them all.

90 Orange Moll, mentioned before.
91 The celebrated actor.

27th. To White Hall; and there hear how it is like to go well enough with my Lord Chancellor; that he is like to keep his Seal, desiring that he may stand his trial in Parliament, if they will accuse him of any thing. This day Mr Pierce, the surgeon, was with me; and tells me how this business of my Lord Chancellor's was certainly designed in my Lady Castlemaine's chamber; and that when he went from the King on Monday morning she was in bed (though about twelve o'clock), and ran out in her smock into her aviary looking into White Hall garden; and thither her woman brought her her nightgown, and stood blessing herself at the old man's going away: and several of the gallants of White Hall (of which there were many staying to see the Chancellor's return) did talk to her in her bird-cage; among others Blancford, telling her she was the bird of passage.

28th. To White Hall: till past twelve in a crowd of people in the lobby, expecting the hearing of the great cause of Alderman Barker against my Lord Deputy of Ireland for his ill usage in his business of land there; but the King and Council sat so long as they neither heard them nor me. Went twice round Bartholomew fayre; which I was glad to see again, after two years missing it by the plague.

29th. I find at Sir G. Carteret's that they do mightily joy themselves in the hopes of my Lord Chancellor's getting over this trouble; and I make them believe (and so, indeed, I do believe he will) that my Lord Chancellor is become popular by it. I find by all hands that the Court is at this day all to pieces, every man of a faction of one sort or other, so as it is to be feared what it will come to. But that that pleases me is, I hear to-night that Mr Brouncker is turned away yesterday by the Duke of York, for some bold words he was heard by Colonel Werden to say in the garden the day the Chancellor was with the King – that he believed the King would be hectored out of every thing. For this the Duke of York, who all say hath been very strong for his father-in-law at this trial, hath turned him away: and every body, I think, is glad of it; for he was a pestilent rogue, an atheist, that would have sold his King and country for 6d. almost, so corrupt and wicked a rogue he is by all men's report. But one observed to me, that there never was the occasion of men's holding their tongues at Court and every where else as there is at this day, for nobody knows which side will be uppermost.

30th. At White Hall I met with Sir G. Downing, who tells me of Sir W. Pen's offering to lend £500; and I tell him of my £300 which he would have me to lend upon the credit of the latter part of the Act; saying, that by that means my 10 per cent. will continue to me the longer. But I understand better, and will do it upon the £380,000 which will come to be paid the sooner; there being no delight in lending money now, to be paid by the King two years hence. But here he and Sir William Doyly were attending the Council as Commissioners for sick and wounded, and prisoners: and they told me their business, which was to know how we shall do to release our prisoners; for it seems the Dutch have got us to agree in the treaty (as they fool us in any thing), that the dyet of the prisoners on both sides shall be paid for before they be released: which they have done, knowing ours to run high, they having more prisoners of ours than we have of theirs; so they are able and most ready to discharge the debt of theirs, but we are neither able nor willing to do that for ours, the debt of those in Zeland only amounting to above £5000 for men taken in the King's own ships, besides others taken in merchantmen, who expect, as is usual, that the King should redeem them; but I think he will not, by what Sir G. Downing says. This our prisoners complain of there; and say in their letters, which Sir G. Downing showed me, that they have made a good feat that they should be taken in the service of the King, and the King not pay for their victuals while prisoners for him. But so far they are from doing thus with their men as we do to discourage ours, that I find in the letters of some of our prisoners there, which he showed me, that they have with money got our men, that they took, to work and carry their ships home for them; and they have been well rewarded, and released when they come into Holland: which is done like a noble, brave, and wise people. I to Bartholomew fayre to walk up and down; and there among other things find my Lady Castlemaine at a puppet-play (*Patient Grizell*), and the street full of people expecting her coming out. I confess I did wonder at her courage to come abroad, thinking the people would abuse her: but they, silly people! do not know the work she makes, and therefore suffered her with great respect to take coach, and she away without any trouble at all. Captain Cocke tells me that there is yet expectation that the Chancellor will lose the Seal; and assures me that there have been high words between the Duke of York and Sir W. Coventry, for his being so high against the

Chancellor; so as the Duke of York would not sign some papers that he brought, saying that he could not endure the sight of him: and that Sir W. Coventry answered, that what he did was in obedience to the King's commands; and that he did not think any man fit to serve a prince, that did not know how to retire and live a country life.

31st. At the office all the morning; where by Sir W. Pen I do hear that the Seal was fetched away to the King yesterday from the Lord Chancellor by Secretary Morrice; which puts me into a great horror. In the evening Mr Ball of the Excise-office tells me that the Seal is delivered to Sir Orlando Bridgeman; the man of the whole nation that is the best spoken of, and will please most people; and therefore I am mighty glad of it. He was then at my Lord Arlington's, whither I went, expecting to see him come out; but staid so long, and Sir W. Coventry coming there, whom I had not a mind should see me there idle upon a post-night, I went home without seeing him; but he is there with his Seal in his hand.

September 1st. Our new Lord-keeper Bridgeman, did this day, the first time, attend the King to chapel with his Seal. Sir H. Cholmly tells me there are hopes that the women also will have a rout, and particularly that my Lady Castlemaine is coming to a composition with the King to be gone; but how true this is, I know not. Blancfort is made Privy-purse to the Duke of York; the Attorney-General[92] is made Chief Justice in the room of my Lord Bridgeman; the Solicitor-generall is made Attorney-general; and Sir Edward Turner made Solicitor-general.[92] It is pretty to see how strange every body looks, nobody knowing whence this arises; whether from my Lady Castlemaine, Bab. May, and their faction; or from the Duke of York, notwithstanding his great appearing of defence of the Chancellor; or from Sir William Coventry, and some few with him. But greater changes are yet expected.

2nd. This day is kept in the City as a publick fast for the fire this day twelve months: but I was not at church, being commanded with the rest to attend the Duke of York; and therefore with Sir J. Minnes to St James's, where we had much business before the Duke of York, and observed all things to be very kind between the Duke of York

92 According to Beatson, no change took place in these officers at this time.

and Sir W. Coventry; which did mightily joy me. When we had
done, Sir W. Coventry called me down with him to his chamber,
and there told me that he is leaving the Duke of York's service;
which I was amazed at. But he tells me that it is not with the least
unkindness on the Duke of York's side, though he expects (and I told
him he was in the right) it will be interpreted otherwise, because
done just at this time; 'but,' says he, 'I did desire it a good while since,
and the Duke of York did with much entreaty grant it, desiring that I
would say nothing of it, that he might have time and liberty to
choose his successor, without being importuned for others whom he
should not like': and that he hath chosen Mr Wren, which I am glad
of, he being a very ingenious man; and so Sir W. Coventry says of
him, though he knows him little; but particularly commends him for
the book he writ in answer to Harrington's *Oceana*, which for that
reason I intend to buy. He tells me the true reason is, that he being a
man not willing to undertake more business than he can go through,
and being desirous to have his whole time to spend upon the business
of the Treasury, and a little for his own ease, he did desire this of the
Duke of York. He assures me that the kindness with which he goes
away from the Duke of York, is one of the greatest joys that ever he
had in the world. I used some freedom with him, telling him how
the world hath discoursed of his having offended the Duke of York,
about the late business of the Chancellor. He does not deny it, but
says that perhaps the Duke of York might have some reason for it, he
opposing him in a thing wherein he was so earnest: but tells me, that
notwithstanding all that, the Duke of York does not now, nor can
blame him; for he was the man that did propose the removal of the
Chancellor; and that he did still persist in it, and at this day publickly
owns it, and is glad of it: but that the Duke of York knows that he
did first speak of it to the Duke of York before he spoke to any
mortal creature besides, which was fair dealing: and the Duke of
York was then of the same mind with him, and did speak of it to the
King, though since, for reasons best known to himself, he afterwards
altered. I did then desire to know, what was the great matter that
grounded his desire of the Chancellor's removal? He told me many
things not fit to be spoken, and yet not any thing of his being
unfaithful to the King, but, *instar omnium*, he told me that while he
was so great at the Council-board, and in the administration of
matters, there was no room for any body to propose any remedy to

what was amiss, or to compass any thing, though never so good, for the kingdom, unless approved of by the Chancellor, he managing all things with that greatness, which now will be removed, that the King may have the benefit of others' advice. I then told him that the world hath an opinion that he hath joined himself with my Lady Castlemaine's faction: but in this business, he told me, he cannot help it, but says they are in an errour; for he will never, while he lives, truckle under any body or any faction, but do just as his own reason and judgment directs; and when he cannot use that freedom, he will have nothing to do in public affairs: but then he added that he never was the man that ever had any discourse with my Lady Castlemaine, or with others from her, about this or any public business, or ever made her a visit, or at least not this twelve-month, or been in her lodgings but when called on any business to attend the King there, nor hath had any thing to do in knowing her mind in this business. He ended all with telling me that he knows that he that serves a prince must expect and be contented to stand all fortunes, and be provided to retreat; and that he is most willing to do whatever the King shall please. And so we parted, he setting me down out of his coach at Charing Cross, and desired me to tell Sir W. Pen what he had told me of his leaving the Duke of York's service, that his friends might not be the last that know it. I took a coach and went homewards; but then turned again, and to White Hall, where I met with many people; and among other things do learn that there is some fear that Mr Brouncker is got into the King's favour, and will be cherished there; which will breed ill will between the King and Duke of York, he lodging at this time in White Hall since he was put away from the Duke of York; and he is great with Bab. May, my Lady Castlemaine, and that wicked crew. But I find this denied by Sir G. Carteret, who tells me that he is sure he hath no kindness from the King; that the King at first, indeed, did endeavour to persuade the Duke of York from putting him away; but when, besides this business of his ill words concerning his Majesty in the business of the Chancellor, he told him that he hath had a long time a mind to put him away for his ill offices, done between him and his wife, the King held his peace, and said no more, but wished him to do what he pleased with him; which was very noble. I met with Fenn; and he tells me, as I do hear from some others, that the business of the Chancellor's had proceeded from something of a mistake, for the Duke of York did first tell the King that the

Chancellor had a desire to be eased of his great trouble: and that the King, when the Chancellor came to him, did wonder to hear him deny it, and the Duke of York was forced to deny to the King that ever he did tell him so in those terms: but the King did answer that he was sure that he did say some such things to him; but, however, since it had gone so far, did desire him to be contented with it as a thing very convenient for him as well as for himself (the King:) and so matters proceeded, as we find. Now it is likely the Chancellor might some time or other, in a compliment or vanity, say to the Duke of York, that he was weary of this burden, and I know not what; and this comes of it. Some people, and myself among them, are of good hope from this change that things are reforming; but there are others that do think it is a hit of chance, as all other our greatest matters are, and that there is no general plot or contrivance in any number of people what to do next, (though, I believe, Sir W. Coventry may in himself have further designs;) and so that though other changes may come, yet they shall be accidental and not laid upon good principles of doing good. Mr May showed me the King's new buildings, in order to their having of some old sails for the closing of the windows this winter. I dined with Sir G. Carteret, with whom dined Mr Jack Ashburnham and Dr Creeton, who I observe to be a most good man and scholar. In discourse at dinner concerning the change of men's humours and fashions touching meats, Mr Ashburnham told us, that he remembers since the only fruit in request, and eaten by the King and Queene at table as the best fruit, was the Katharine payre, though they knew at the time other fruits of France and our own country. After dinner comes in Mr Townsend: and there I was witness of a horrid rateing which Mr Ashburnham, as one of the Grooms of the King's Bedchamber, did give him for want of linen for the King's person; which he swore was not to be endured, and that the King would not endure it, and that the King his father would have hanged his Wardrobe-man should he have been served so; the King having at this day no hankerchers, and but three bands to his neck, he swore. Mr Townsend pleaded want of money and the owing of the linendraper £5000; and that he hath of late got many rich things made, beds and sheets and saddles, without money; and that he can go no further: but still this old man (indeed like an old loving servant) did cry out for the King's person to be neglected. But when he was gone, Townsend told me that it is the Grooms taking away the

King's linen at the quarter's end, as their fees, which makes this great want; for whether the King can get it or no, they will run away at the quarter's end with what he hath had, let the King get more as he can. All the company gone, Sir G. Carteret and I to talk: and it is pretty to observe how already he says that he did always look upon the Chancellor indeed as his friend, though he never did do him any service at all, nor ever got any thing by, nor was a man apt (and that, I think, is true) to do any man any kindness of his own nature; though I do know he was believed by all the world to be the greatest support of Sir G. Carteret with the King of any man in England: but so little is now made of it! He observes that my Lord Sandwich will lose a great friend in him; and I think so too, my Lord Hinchingbroke being about a match calculated purely out of respect to my Lord Chancellor's family. By and by Sir G. Carteret, and Townsend, and I to consider of an answer to the Commissioners of the Treasury about my Lord Sandwich's profits in the Wardrobe; which seem as we make them to be very small, not £1000 a-year, but only the difference in measure at which he buys and delivers out to the King, and then 6d. in the pound from the tradesman for what money he receives for him; but this, it is believed, these Commissioners will endeavour to take away. From him I went to see a great match at tennis, between Prince Rupert and one Captain Cooke against Bab. May and the elder Chichly; where the King was, and Court; and it seems they are the best players at tennis in the nation. But this puts me in mind of what I observed in the morning, that the King playing at tennis had a steele-yard carried to him; and I was told it was to weigh him after he had done playing; and at noon Mr Ashburnham told me that it is only the King's curiosity, which he usually hath of weighing himself before and after his play, to see how much he loses in weight by playing; and this day he lost 4½ lbs. I to Sir W. Batten and Sir W. Pen, and there discoursed of Sir W. Coventry's leaving the Duke of York, and Mr Wren's succeeding him. They told me both seriously that they had long cut me out for Secretary to the Duke of York, if ever Sir W. Coventry left him; which agreeing with what I have heard from other hands heretofore, do make me not only think that something of that kind hath been thought on, but do comfort me to see that the world hath such an esteem of my qualities as to think me fit for any such thing: though I am glad with all my heart that I am not so; for it would never please me to be forced to the attendance that that would require, and leave my wife and family to themselves, as I must do in such a case; thinking myself now in the best place that ever man was in to please his own mind in, and therefore I will take to preserve it.

3rd. Attended the Duke of York about the list of ships that we propose to sell: and here there attended Mr Wren the first time, who hath not yet, I think, received the Duke of York's seal and papers. At our coming hither we found the Duke and Duchesse all alone at dinner, methought melancholy: or else I thought so, from the late occasion of the Chancellor's fall, who, they say, however, takes it very contentedly.

4th. By coach to White Hall to the Council-chamber; and there met with Sir W. Coventry going in, who took me aside, and told me that he was just come from delivering up his seal and papers to Mr Wren; and told me he must now take his leave of me as a naval man, but that he shall always bear respect to his friends there,[93] and particularly to myself with great kindness; which I returned to him with thanks, and so with much kindness parted; and he into the Council. Staid and heard Alderman Barker's case of his being abused by the Council of Ireland, touching his lands there. All I observed there is the silliness of the King, playing with his dog all the while, and not minding the business; and what he said was mighty weak: but my Lord Keeper I observed to be a mighty able man. To the Duke of York's playhouse, and there saw *Mustapha*; which the more I see the more I like; and is a most admirable poem, and bravely acted; only both Betterton and Harris could not contain from laughing in the midst of a most serious part, from the ridiculous mistake of one of the men upon the stage; which I did not like. This morning was told by Sir W. Batten that he do hear from Mr Grey, who hath good intelligence, that our Queene is to go into a nunnery, there to spend her days; and that my Lady Castlemaine is going into France, and is to have a pension of £4000 a-year. This latter I do more believe than the other, it being very wise in her to do it and save all she hath, besides easing the King and kingdom of a burden and reproach.

8th. Lord Brouncker says he do believe that my Lady Castlemaine is compounding with the King for a pension, and to leave the Court;

93 The officers of the Navy.

but that her demands are mighty high: but he believes the King is resolved, and so do everybody else I speak with, to do all possible to please the Parliament; and he do declare that he will deliver every body up to give an account of their actions: and that last Friday, it seems, there was an Act of Council passed, to put out all Papists in office, and to keep out any from coming in. Sir G. Downing told he had been seven years finding out a man that could dress English sheep-skin as it should be; and indeed it is now as good in all respects as kidd; and, he says, will save £100,000 a-year that goes out to France for kidds'-skins. He tells me that at this day the King in familiar talk do call the Chancellor 'the insolent man,' and says that he would not let him speak himself in Council: which is very high, and do show that the Chancellor is like to be in a bad state, unless he can defend himself better than people think. And yet Creed tells me that he do hear that my Lord Cornbury[94] do say that his father do long for the coming of the Parliament, in order to his own vindication, more than any one of his enemies. And here it comes into my head to set down what Mr Rawlinson (whom I met in Fenchurch-street on Friday last looking over his ruines there) told me that he was told by one of my Lord Chancellor's gentlemen lately, that a grant coming to him to be sealed, wherein the King hath given my Lady Castlemaine, or somebody by her means, a place which he did not like well of, he did stop the grant; saying, that he thought this woman would sell every thing shortly: which she hearing of, she sent to let him know that she had disposed of this place, and did not doubt in a little time to dispose of his. To White Hall, and saw the King and Queene at dinner; and observed (which I never did before) the formality, but it is but a formality, of putting a bit of bread wiped upon each dish into the mouth of every man that brings a dish; but it should be in the sauce. Here were some Russes come to see the King at dinner; among others the interpreter, a comely Englishman, in the Envoy's own clothes; which the Envoy, it seems, in vanity did send to show his fine clothes upon this man's back, he being one, it seems, of a comelier presence than himself: and yet it is said that none of their clothes are their own, but taken out of the King's own Wardrobe; and which they dare not bring back dirty or spotted, but clean, or are in danger of being beaten, as they say: inasmuch that, Sir Charles

94 Henry, afterwards second Earl of Clarendon.

Cotterell[95] says, when they are to have an audience they never venture to put on their clothes till he appears to come and fetch them; and as soon as ever they come home, put them off again. I to Sir G. Carteret's to dinner; where Mr Cofferer Ashburnham; who told a good story of a prisoner's being condemned at Salisbury for a small matter. While he was on the bench with his father-in-law Judge Richardson,[96] and while they were considering to transport him to save his life, the fellow flung a great stone at the Judge, that missed him, but broke through the wainscoat. Upon this he had his hand cut off, and was hanged presently.

9th. To White Hall; and here do hear, by Tom Killigrew and Mr Progers, that for certain news is come of Harman's having spoiled nineteen of twenty-two French ships, somewhere about the Barbadoes, I think they said; but wherever it is, it is a good service and very welcome. To the Bear-garden, where now the yard was full of people, and those most of them seamen, striving by force to get in. I got into the common pit; and there, with my cloak about my face, I stood and saw the prize fought, till one of them, a shoemaker, was so cut in both his wrists that he could not fight any longer, and then they broke off: his enemy was a butcher. The sport very good, and various humours to be seen among the rabble that is there.

10th. To St James's, where we all met and did our usual weekly business with the Duke of York. But, Lord! methinks both he and we are mighty flat and dull to what we used to be when Sir W. Coventry was among us. Met Mr Povy; and he and I to walk an hour or more in the Pell Mell, talking of the times. He tells me among other things, that this business of the Chancellor do breed a kind of inward distance between the King and the Duke of York, and that it cannot be

95 Knight, and Master of the Ceremonies from 1641 to 1686, when he resigned in favour of his son.
96 Sir Thomas Richardson, Knight; appointed Chief Justice of the Common Pleas 1626. This anecdote is thus confirmed in Chief Justice Treby's *Notes to Dyers' Reports,* folio edition, p. 188, b. 'Richardson, Ch. Just. de C. Banc. al Assises at Salisbury, in Summer 1631, fuit assault per prisoner la condemne pur felony; que puis son condemnation ject un brickbat a le dit Justice, qui narrowly mist; et pur ceo immediately fuit indictment drawn, per Noy, envers le prisoner, et son dexter manus ampute, and fix at gibbet, sur que luy meme immediatement hange in presence de Court.'

avoided; for though the latter did at first move it through his folly, yet he is made to see that he is wounded by it, and is become much a less man than he was, and so will be: but he tells me that they are, and have always been, great dissemblers one towards another; and that their parting heretofore in France is never to be thoroughly reconciled between them. He tells me that he believes there is no such thing likely to be as a composition with my Lady Castlemaine, and that she shall be got out of the way before the Parliament comes; for he says she is as high as ever she was, though he believes the King is as weary of her as is possible; and would give any thing to remove her, but he is so weak in his passion that he dare not do it: that he do believe that my Lord Chancellor will be doing some acts in the Parliament which shall render him popular; and that there are many people now do speak kindly of him that did not before; but that if he do do this, it must provoke the King and that party that removed him. He seems to doubt what the King of France will do, in case an accommodation shall be made between Spain and him for Flanders, for then he will have nothing more easy to do with his army than to subdue us.

11th. Come to dine with me Sir W. Batten and his lady, and Mr Griffith their Ward, and Sir W. Pen and his lady, and Mrs Lowther, (who is grown either through pride or want of manners a fool, having not a word to say; and, as a further mark of a beggarly proud fool, hath a bracelet of diamonds and rubies about her wrist, and a sixpenny necklace about her neck, and not one good rag of clothes upon her back;) and Sir John Chichly in their company, and Mr Turner. Here I had an extraordinary good and handsome dinner for them, better than any of them deserve or understand (saving Sir John Chichly and Mr Turner.) To the Duke of York's playhouse, and there saw part of the *Ungrateful Lovers*; and sat by Beck Marshall, whose hand is very handsome. Here came Mr Moore, and sat and discoursed with me of public matters: the sum of which is, that he do doubt that there is more at the bottom than the removal of the Chancellor; that is, he do verily believe that the King do resolve to declare the Duke of Monmouth legitimate, and that we shall soon see it. This I do not think the Duke of York will endure without blows; but his poverty, and being lessened by having the Chancellor fallen and Sir W. Coventry gone from him, will disable him from being able to do any thing almost, he being himself almost lost in the esteem of people; and will be more and more, unless my Lord Chancellor (who is already begun to be pitied by some people, and to be better thought of than was expected) do recover himself in Parliament. He do say that that is very true, that my Lord Chancellor did lately make some stop of some grants of £2000 a-year to my Lord Grandison,[97] which was only in his name, for the use of my Lady Castlemaine's children; and that this did incense her, and she did speak very scornful words and sent a scornful message to him about it.

14th. The King and Duke of York and the whole Court is mighty joyful at the Duchesse of York's being brought to bed this day, or yesterday, of a son; which will settle men's minds mightily. And Pierce tells me that he do think that what the King do, of giving the Duke of Monmouth the command of his Guards, and giving my Lord Gerard £12,000 for it, is merely to find an employment for him upon which he may live, and not out of any design to bring him into any title to the Crowne; which Mr Moore did the other day put me into great fear of. To the King's playhouse to see The Northerne Castle, which I think I never did see before. Knipp acted in it, and did her part very extraordinary well; but the play is but a mean, sorry play. Sir H. Cholmly was with me a good while; who tells me that the Duke of York's child is christened, the Duke of Albemarle and the Marquis of Worcester[98] godfathers, and my Lady Suffolke godmother; and they have named it Edgar, which is a brave name. But it seems they are more joyful in the Chancellor's family, at the birth of this Prince, than in wisdom they should, for fear it should give the King cause of jealousy. Sir H. Cholmly thinks there may possibly be some persons that would be glad to have the Queene removed to some monastery, or somewhere or other, to make room for a new wife; for they will all be unsafe under the Duke of York. He says the King and Parliament will agree; that is, that the King will do any thing that they will have him. I met with 'a fourth Advice[99] to the Painter upon the

97 George Villiers, fourth Viscount Grandison, and younger brother of Lady Castlemaine's father, who had died without issue male.

98 Edward, second Marquis of Worcester, author of The Century of Inventions.

99 In the Collection of Poems on Affairs of State, there are four pieces called 'Directions to a Painter'; the first of them 'concerning the Dutch War, 1667, by Sir John Denham'. The same book also contains 'The Last Instructions to a Painter about the Dutch Wars', by Andrew Marvel, Esq., which from its severity I suppose to be the work here alluded to.

coming in of the Dutch to the River and end of the war', that made my heart ake to read, it being too sharp and so true. Here I also saw a printed account of the examinations taken touching the burning of the City of London, showing the plot of the Papists therein; which, it seems, hath been ordered to be burnt by the hands of the common hangman, in Westminster Palace. My wife and Mercer and I away to the King's Playhouse, to see *The Scornfull Lady*; but it being now three o'clock there was not one soul in the pit; whereupon, for shame we could not go in, but, against our wills, went all to see *Tu quoque* again, where there was pretty store of company. Here we saw Madam Morland,[100] who is grown mighty fat, but is very comely. Thence to the King's house, upon a wager of mine with my wife that there would be no acting there to-day, there being no company: so I went in and found a pretty good company there, and saw their dance at the end of the play.

18th. I walked in the Exchange; which is now made mighty pretty, by having windows and doors before all their shops, to keep out the cold.

20th. By coach to the King's playhouse, and there saw *The Mad Couple*,[101] my wife having been at the same play with Jane in the 18d. seat.

21st. The King, Duke of York, and the men of the Court have been these four or five days a-hunting at Bagshot.

22nd. At noon comes Mr Sheres, whom I find a good, ingenious man, but do talk a little too much of his travels. He left my Lord Sandwich well, but in pain to be at home for want of money, which comes very hardly. I have indulged myself more in pleasure for these last two months than ever I did in my life before, since I came to be a person concerned in business; and I doubt, when I come to make up my accounts, I shall find it so by the expence.

23rd. At my Lord Ashly's by invitation to dine there. At table it is worth remembering that my Lord tells us that the House of Lords is the last appeal that a man can make upon a point of interpretation of

---

100 Sir Samuel Morland's first wife.
101 Probably *A Mad Couple well Matched*, a comedy by Richard Brome, printed in 1653.

the law, and that therein they are above the Judges; and that he did assert this in the Lords' House upon the late occasion of the quarrel between my Lord Bristoll and the Chancellor, when the former did accuse the latter of treason, and the Judges did bring it in not to be treason: my Lord Ashly did declare that the judgement of the Judges was nothing in the presence of their Lordships, but only as far as they were the properest men to bring precedents; but not to interpret the law to their Lordships, but only the inducements of their persuasions: and this the Lords did concur in. Another pretty thing was my Lady Ashly's speaking of the bad qualities of glass-coaches; among others, the flying open of the doors upon any great shake: but another was, that my Lady Peterborough being in her glass-coach with the glass up, and seeing a lady pass by in a coach whom she would salute, the glass was so clear that she thought it had been open, and so ran her head through the glass! We were put into my Lord's room before he could come to us, and there had opportunity to look over his state of his accounts of the prizes; and there saw how bountiful the King hath been to several people: and hardly any man almost, commander of the Navy of any note, but hath had some reward or other out of them; and many sums to the Privy-purse, but not so many, I see, as I thought there had been: but we could not look quite through it. But several Bed-chambermen and people about the Court had good sums; and, among others, Sir John Minnes and Lord Brouncker have £200 a-piece for looking to the East India prizes, while I did their work for them. By and by my Lord came, and we did look over Yeabsly's business a little; and I find how prettily this cunning Lord can be partial and dissemble it in this case, being privy to the bribe he is to receive. With Sir H. Cholmly to Westminster; who by the way told me how merry the King and Duke of York and Court were the other day when they were abroad a-hunting. They came to Sir G. Carteret's house at Cranbourne, and there were entertained, and all made drunk; and being all drunk, Armerer did come to the King, and swore to him by God, 'Sir,' says he, 'you are not so kind to the Duke of York of late as you used to be.' — 'Not I?' says the King. 'Why so?' 'Why,' says he, 'if you are, let us drink his health.' 'Why let us,' says the King. Then he fell on his knees and drank it; and having done, the King began to drink it. 'Nay, Sir,' says Armerer, 'by God you must do it on your knees!' So he did, and then all the company: and having done it, all fell a-crying for joy, being all maudlin and kissing one another, the King the Duke of York, and the Duke of York the King: and in such a maudlin pickle as never people were: and so passed the day. But Sir H. Cholmly tells me, that the King hath this good luck: that the next day he hates to have any body mention what he had done the day before, nor will suffer any body to gain upon him that way; which is a good quality. By and by comes Captain Cocke about business; who tells me that Mr Brouncker is lost for ever, notwithstanding that my Lord Brouncker hath advised with him (Cocke) how he might make a peace with the Duke of York and Chancellor, upon promise of serving him in the Parliament: but Cocke says that is base to offer, and will have no success there. He says that Mr Wren hath refused a present of Tom Wilson's for his place of Store-keeper at Chatham, and is resolved never to take any thing: which is both wise in him, and good to the King's service

25th. With Sir H. Cholmly (who came to me about his business) to White Hall: and thither came also my Lord Brouncker. And we by and by called in, and our paper read; and much discourse thereon by Sir G. Carteret, my Lord Anglesy, Sir W. Coventry, and my Lord Ashly, and myself: but I could easily discern that they none of them understood the business; and the King at last ended it with saying lazily, 'Why,' says he, 'after all this discourse I now come to understand it; and that is, that there can nothing be done in this more than is possible,' (which was so silly as I never heard): 'and therefore,' says he, 'I would have these gentlemen do as much as possible to hasten the Treasurer's accounts; and that is all.' And so we broke up: and I confess I went away ashamed, to see how slightly things are advised upon there. Here I saw the Duke of Buckingham sit in Council again, where he was re-admitted, it seems, the last Council-day: and it is wonderful to see how this man is come again to his places, all of them, after the reproach and disgrace done him; so that things are done in a most foolish manner quite through. The Duke of Buckingham did second Sir W. Coventry in the advising the King that he would not concern himself in the evening or not evening any man's accounts, or any thing else, wherein he had not the same satisfaction that would satisfy the Parliament; saying, that nothing would displease the Parliament more than to find him defending any thing that is not right nor justifiable to the utmost degree: but methought he spoke it but very poorly. After this I walked up and down the Gallery till noon: and here I met with Bishop Fuller, who, to my great joy, is made (which I did not hear before) Bishop of Lincolne. At noon I took coach, and to Sir G. Carteret's in Lincoln's-inn-fields, to the house that is my Lord's, which my Lord lets him have: and this is the first day of dining there. And there dined with him and his lady my Lord Privy-seale,[102] who is indeed a very sober man: who, among other talk, did mightily wonder at the reason of the growth of the credit of bankers, (since it is so ordinary a thing for citizens to break out of knavery). Upon this we had much discourse; and I observed therein, to the honour of this City, that I have not heard of one citizen of London broke in all this war, this plague, or this fire, and this coming up of the enemy among us; which he owned to be very considerable. I to the King's playhouse, my eyes being so bad since last night's straining of them that I am hardly able to see, besides the pain which I have in them. The play was a new play: and infinitely full; the King and all the Court almost there. It is *The Storme*, a play of Fletcher's; which is but so-so, methinks; only there is a most admirable dance at the end, of the ladies, in a military manner, which indeed did please me mightily.

27th. Creed and Sheres come and dined with me; and we had a great deal of pretty discourse of the ceremoniousness of the Spaniards, whose ceremonies are so many and so known, that, he tells me, upon all occasions of joy or sorrow in a Grandee's family, my Lord Embassador is fain to send one with an *en hora buena* (if it be upon a marriage or birth of a child), or a *pesa me,* if it be upon the death of a child, or so. And these ceremonies are so set, and the words of the compliment, that he hath been sent from my Lord when he hath done no more than send in word to the Grandee that one was there from the Embassador; and he knowing what was his errand, that hath been enough, and he never spoken with him; nay, several Grandees having been to marry a daughter, have wrote letters to my Lord to give him notice, and out of the greatness of his wisdom to desire his advice, though people he never saw; and then my Lord he answers by commending the greatness of his discretion in making so good an alliance, &c. and so ends. He says that it is so far from dishonour to a man to give private revenge for an affront,

102 John Lord Roberts, afterwards Earl of Radnor, filled this office from 1661 to 1669.

that the contrary is a disgrace; they holding that he that receives an affront is not fit to appear in the sight of the world till he hath revenged himself; and therefore, that a gentleman there that receives an affront oftentimes never appears again in the world till he hath, by some private way or other, revenged himself: and that, on this account, several have followed their enemies privately to the Indys, thence to Italy, thence to France and back again, waiting for an opportunity to be revenged. He says my Lord was fain to keep a letter from the Duke of York to the Queene of Spain a great while in his hands, before he could think fit to deliver it, till he had learnt whether the Queene could receive it, it being directed to his cosen. He says that many ladies in Spain, after they are found to be with child, do never stir out of their beds or chambers till they are brought to bed: so ceremonious they are in that point also. He tells me of their wooing by serenades at the window, and that their friends do always make the match; but yet they have opportunities to meet at masse at church, and there they make love: that the Court there hath no dancing nor visits at night to see the King or Queene, but is always just like a cloyster, nobody stirring in it; that my Lord Sandwich wears a beard now, turned up in the Spanish manner. But that which pleases me most indeed is, that the peace which he hath made with Spain is now printed here, and is acknowledged by all the merchants to be the best peace that ever England had with them; and it appears that the King thinks it so, for this is printed before the ratification is gone over: whereas that with France and Holland was not in a good while after, till copys came over of it in English out of Holland and France, that it was a reproach not to have it printed here. This I am mighty glad of; and is the first and only piece of good news, or thing fit to be owned, that this nation hath done several years.

28th. All the morning at the office busy upon an Order of Council, wherein they are mightily at a loss what to advise about our discharging of seamen by ticket, there being no money to pay their wages before January. After dinner comes Sir Fr. Hollis to me about business; and I with him by coach to the Temple, and there I light; all the way he telling me romantic lies of himself and his family, how they have been Parliament-men for Grimsby, he and his forefathers, this 140 years; and his father is now: and himself, at this day, stands for to be with his father,[103] by the death of his fellow burgess; and that he believes it will cost him as much as it did his predecessor, which was £300 in ale, and £52 in buttered ale; which I believe is one of his devilish lies.

30th. To the Duke of York to Council, where the officers of the Navy did attend; and my Lord Ashly did move that an assignment for money on the Act might be put into the hands of the East India Company, or City of London, which he thought the seamen would believe. But this my Lord Anglesy did very handsomely oppose, and I think did carry it that it will not be: and it is indeed a mean thing that the King should so far own his own want of credit as to borrow theirs in this manner. My Lord Anglesy told him that this was the way indeed to teach the Parliament to trust the King no more for the time to come, but to have a kingdom's Treasurer distinct from the King's.

October 1st. To White Hall; and there in the Boarded Gallery did hear the musick with which the King is presented this night by Monsieur Grebus, the Master of his Musick: both instrumental (I think twenty-four violins) and vocall: an English song upon Peace. But, God forgive me! I never was so little pleased with a concert of music in my life. The manner of setting of words and repeating them out of order, and that with a number of voices, makes me sick, the whole design of vocall musick being lost by it. Here was a great press of people; but I did not see many pleased with it, only the instrumental musick he had brought by practice to play very just.

3rd. To St James's, where Sir W. Coventry took me into the Gallery and walked with me an hour, discoursing of Navy business, and with much kindness to and confidence in me still; which I must endeavour to preserve, and will do. And, good man! all his care how to get the Navy paid off, and that all other things therein may go well. He gone, I thence to my Lady Peterborough, who sent for me: and with her an hour talking about her husband's pension, and how she hath got an order for its being paid again; though I believe, for all that order, it will hardly be; but of that I said nothing; but her design is to get it paid again: and how to raise money upon it to clear it from the engagement which lies upon it to some citizens, who lent her

103 Jervas Hollis and Sir Frecheville Hollis represented Grimsby in 1669. – Chamberlayne's *Angliae Notitia*.

husband money (without her knowledge) upon it, to vast loss. She intends to force them to take their money again, and release her husband of those hard terms. The woman is a very wise woman, and is very plain in telling me how her plate and jewels are at pawne for money, and how they are forced to live beyond their estate, and do get nothing by his being a courtier. The lady I pity, and her family.

4th. To my Lord Crewe's, and there did stay with him an hour till almost night, discoursing about the ill state of my Lord Sandwich, that he can neither be got to be called home, nor money got to maintain him there;[104] which will ruin his family. And the truth is, he do almost deserve it, for by all relation he hath, in little more than a year and half, spent £20,000 of the King's money, and the best part of £10,000 of his own; which is a most prodigious expence, more than ever Embassador spent there, and more than these Commissioners of the Treasury will or do allow. And they demand an account before they will give him any more money; which puts all his friends to a loss what to answer. But more money we must get him, or to be called home. I offer to speak to Sir W. Coventry about it; but my Lord will not advise to it, without consent of Sir G. Carteret.

5th. Up, and to the office; and there all the morning; none but my Lord Anglesy and myself. But much surprized with the news of the death of Sir W. Batten, who died this morning, having been but two days sick. Sir W. Pen and I did dispatch a letter this morning to Sir W. Coventry, to recommend Colonell Middleton, who we think a most honest and understanding man, and fit for that place. Sir G. Carteret did also come this morning, and walked with me in the garden; and concluded not to concern or have any advice made to Sir W. Coventry in behalf of my Lord Sandwich's business: so I do rest satisfied, though I do think they are all mad, that they will judge Sir W. Coventry an enemy, when he is indeed no such man to any body, but is severe and just, as he ought to be, where he sees things ill done. To the King's house; and there going in met with Knipp, and she took us up into the tireing-rooms; and to the women's shift, where Nell was dressing herself, and was all unready, and is very pretty, prettier than I thought. And into the scene-room, and there sat down, and she gave us fruit: and here I read the questions to

104 In Spain.

Knipp, while she answered me, through all her part of *Flora's Figarys*, which was acted to-day. But, Lord! to see how they were both painted, would make a man mad, and did make me loath them; and what base company of men comes among them, and how lewdly they talk! And how poor the men are in clothes, and yet what a show they make on the stage by candle-light, is very observable. But to see how Nell cursed, for having so few people in the pit, was strange; the other house carrying away all the people at the new play, and is said now-a-days to have generally most company, as being better players. By and by into the pit, and there saw the play, which is pretty good.

7th. I and my wife, and Willet,[105] set out in a coach I have hired with four horses; and W. Hewer and Murford rode by us on horseback; and before night come to Bishop-Stafford.[106] Took coach to Audly-End, and did go all over the house and garden; and mighty merry we were. The house indeed do appear very fine, but not so fine as it hath heretofore to me; particularly the ceilings are not so good as I always took them to be, being nothing so well wrought as my Lord Chancellor's are; and though the figure of the house without be very extraordinary good, yet the stayre-case is exceeding poor; and a great many pictures, and not one good one in the house but one of Harry the Eighth, done by Holben; and not one good suit of hangings in all the house, but all most ancient things, such as I would not give the hanging-up of in my house; and the other furniture, beds and other things, accordingly. Only the gallery is good, and above all things the cellars, where we went down and drank of much good liquor. And indeed the cellars are fine: and here my wife and I did sing to my great content. And then to the garden, and there eat many grapes, and took some with us: and so away thence exceeding well satisfied, though not to that degree that by my old esteem of the house I ought and did expect to have done, the situation of it not pleasing me. Thence away to Cambridge, and did take up at the Rose.

9th. Up, and got ready, and eat our breakfast; and then took coach; and the poor, as they did yesterday, did stand at the coach to have something given them, as they do to all great persons; and I did give

105 Mrs Pepys's maid.
106 Stortford.

them something: and the town musick did also come and play; but, Lord! what sad musick they made! So through the town, and observed at our College of Magdalene the posts new painted, and understand that the Vice Chancellor is there this year. And so away for Huntingdon; and come to Brampton at about noon, and there find my father and sister and brother all well: and up and down to see the garden with my father, and the house, and do altogether find it very pretty; and I bless God that I am like to have such a pretty place to retire to. After dinner I walked up to Hinchingbroke, where my Lady expected me; and there spent all the afternoon with her: the same most excellent, good, discreet lady that ever she was; and, among other things, is mightily pleased with the lady that is like to be her son Hinchingbroke's wife. I am pleased with my Lady Paulina[107] and Anne, who are both grown very proper ladies, and handsome enough. But I do find by my Lady that they are reduced to great straits for money, having been forced to sell her plate, 8 or £900 worth; and she is now going to sell a suit of her best hangings, of which I could almost wish to buy a piece or two, if the pieces will be broke. But the house is most excellently furnished, and brave rooms and good pictures, so that it do please me infinitely beyond Audley End.

10th. Up, to walk up and down in the garden with my father, to talk of all our concernments: about a husband for my sister, whereof there is at present no appearance; but we must endeavour to find her one now, for she grows old and ugly. My father and I with a dark lantern, it being now night, into the garden with my wife, and there went about our great work to dig up my gold. But, Lord! what a tosse I was for some time in, that they could not justly tell where it was: but by and by poking with a spit we found it, and then begun with a spudd to lift up the ground. But, good God! to see how sillily they did it, not half a foot under ground, and in the sight of the world from a hundred places, if any body by accident were near hand, and within sight of a neighbour's window: only my father says that he saw them all gone to church before he began the work, when he laid the money. But I was out of my wits almost, and the more from that, upon my lifting up the earth with the spudd, I did discern that I had scattered the pieces of gold round about the ground among the grass

107 A mistake for Lady Catherine, Lady Paulina being dead.

and loose earth: and taking up the iron head-pieces wherein they were put, I perceived the earth was got among the gold, and wet so that the bags were all rotten, and all the notes, that I could not tell what in the world to say to it, not knowing how to judge what was wanting, or what had been lost by Gibson in his coming down: which, all put together, did make me mad; and at last I was forced to take up the head-pieces, dirt and all, and as many of the scattered pieces as I could with the dirt discern by candle light, and carry them up into my brother's chamber, and there locke them up till I had eat a little supper: and then, all people going to bed, W. Hewer and I did all alone with several pails of water and besoms at last wash the dirt off the pieces, and parted the pieces and the dirt, and then began to tell them by a note which I had of the value of the whole (in my pocket.) And do find that there was short above a hundred pieces: which did make me mad; and considering that the neighbour's house was so near that we could not possibly speak one to another in the garden at that place where the gold lay (especially my father being deaf) but they must know what we had been doing, I feared that they might in the night come and gather some pieces and prevent us the next morning; so W. Hewer and I out again about midnight (for it was now grown so late) and there by candle-light did make shift to gather forty-five pieces more. And so in and to cleanse them: and by this time it was past two in the morning; and so to bed, and there lay in some disquiet all night telling of the clock till it was day-light.

11th. And then W. Hewer and I, with pails and a sieve, did lock ourselves into the garden, and there gather all the earth about the place into pails, and then sift those pails in one of the summer-houses (just as they do for dyamonds in other parts of the world); and there to our great content did by nine o'clock make the last night's forty-five up seventy-nine: so that we are come to about twenty or thirty of what I think the true number should be. So do leave my father to make a second examination of the dirt; and my mind at rest in it, being but an accident: and so give me some kind of content to remember how painful it is sometimes to keep money, as well as to get it, and how doubtful I was to keep it all night, and how to secure it to London. About ten o'clock took coach, my wife and I, and Willett, and W. Hewer, and Murford and Bowles (whom my Lady lent me to go along with me my journey, not telling her the reason, but it was only to secure my gold,) and my brother John on horseback; and with these four I thought myself pretty safe. My gold I put into a basket and set under one of the seats; and so my work every quarter of an hour was to look to see whether all was well; and I did ride in great fear all the day.

12th. By five o'clock got home, where I find all well; and did bring my gold to my heart's content very safe, having not this day carried it in a basket, but in our hands: the girl took care of one, and my wife another bag, and I the rest, I being afraid of the bottom of the coach, lest it should break. At home we find that Sir W. Batten's body was to-day carried from hence, with a hundred or two of coaches, to Walthamstow, and there buried. The Parliament met on Thursday last, and adjourned to Monday next. The King did make them a very kind speech, promising them to leave all to them to do, and call to account what and whom they pleased; and declared by my Lord Keeper how many (thirty-six) actes he had done since he saw them: among others, disbanding the army, and putting all Papists out of employment, and displacing persons that had managed their business ill. The Parliament is mightily pleased with the King's speech, and voted giving him thanks for what he said and hath done; and among other things, would by name thank him for displacing my Lord Chancellor, for which a great many did speak in the House, but it was opposed by some, and particularly Harry Coventry, who got that it should be put to a Committee to consider what particulars to mention in their thanks to the King, saying that it was too soon to give thanks for the displacing of a man, before they knew or had examined what was the cause of his displacing. And so it rested: but this do show that they are and will be very high. And Mr Pierce do tell me that he fears and do hear that it hath been said among them, that they will move for the calling my Lord Sandwich home, to bring him to account; which do trouble me mightily, but I trust it will not be so. Anon comes home Sir W. Pen from the buriall; and he says that Lady Batten and her children-in-law are all broke in pieces, and that there is but £800 found in the world of money; and is in great doubt what we shall do towards the doing ourselves right with them, about the prize-money.

13th. To St James's; and there to the Duke of York's chamber: and there he was dressing; and many Lords and Parliament-men, come to kiss his hands, they being newly come to town. And there the Duke of York did of himself call me to him and tell me that he had spoke to the King, and that the King had granted me the ship I asked for; and did moreover say that he was mightily pleased with my service, and that he would be willing to do any thing that was in his power for me: which he said with mighty kindness; which I did return him thanks for, and departed with mighty joy, more than I did expect. And so walked over the Park to White Hall, and then met Sir H. Cholmly, who walked with me and told me most of the news I heard last night of the Parliament; and thinks they will do all things very well, only they will be revenged of My Lord Chancellor; and says, however, that he thinks there will be but two things proved on him; and that one is, that he may have said to the King and to others words to breed in the King an ill opinion of the Parliament – that they were factious, and that it was better to dissolve them: and this he thinks they will be able to prove; but what this will amount to, he knows not. And next, that he hath taken money for several bargains that have been made with the Crown; and did instance one that is already complained of: but there are so many more involved in it, that should they unravel things of this sort, every body almost will be more or less concerned. But these are the two great points which he thinks they will insist on, and prove against him.

14th. To Mr Wren's; and he told me that my business was done about my warrant on the Maybolt Galliott; which I did see, and thought it was not so full in the reciting of my services as the other was in that of Sir W. Pen's; yet I was well pleased with it, and do intend to fetch it away anon. To visit Sir G. Carteret, and from him do understand that the King himself (but this he told me as a great secret) is satisfied that these thanks which he expects from the House, for the laying aside of my Lord Chancellor, are a thing irregular; but since it is come into the House, he do think it necessary to carry it on, and will have it, and hath made his mind known to be so to some of the House. But Sir G. Carteret do say he knows nothing of what my Lord Brouncker told us to-day, that the King was angry with the Duke of York yesterday, and advised him not to hinder what he had a mind to have done touching this business; which is news very bad, if true. He tells me also that the King will have the thanks of the House go on: and commends my Lord Keeper's speech for all but what he was forced to say about the reason of the King's sending away the House so soon the last time, when they were met.

16th. At home most of the morning with Sir H. Cholmly, about some accounts of his: and for news he tells me that the Commons and Lords have concurred and delivered the King their thanks, among other things, for his removal of the Chancellor; who took their thanks very well, and, among other things, promised them (in these words) never in any degree to give the Chancellor any employment again. And he tells me that it is very true, he hath it from one that was by, that the King did give the Duke of York a sound reprimande; told him that he had lived with him with more kindness than ever any brother King lived with a brother, and that he lived as much like a monarch as himself, but advised him not to cross him in his designs about the Chancellor; in which the Duke of York do very wisely acquiesce, and will be quiet as the King bade him, but presently commands all his friends to be silent in the business of the Chancellor, and they were so: but that the Chancellor hath done all that is possible to provoke the King, and to bring himself to lose his head, by enraging of people. To the Duke of York's house; and I was vexed to see Young (who is but a bad actor at best) act Macbeth, in the room of Betterton, who, poor man! is sick

17th. The Parliament run on mighty furiously, having yesterday been almost all the morning complaining against some high proceedings of my Lord Chief Justice Keeling, that the gentlemen of the country did complain against him in the House, and run very high. It is the man that did fall out with my cosen Roger Pepys, once at the Assizes there, and would have laid him by the heels; but, it seems, a very able lawyer. This afternoon my Lord Anglesy tells us that the House of Commons have this morning run into the enquiry in many things; as, the sale of Dunkirke, the dividing of the fleet the last year, the business of the prizes with my Lord Sandwich, and many other things: so that now they begin to fall close upon it, and God knows what will be the end of it, but a Committee they have chosen to enquire into the miscarriages of the war.

18th. To White Hall, and there attended the Duke of York; but first we find him to spend above an hour in private in his closet with Sir W. Coventry; which I was glad to see, that there is so much confidence between them. By and by we were called in. The Duke of York considering that the King had a mind for Spragg to command the *Rupert*, which would not be well, by turning out Hubbard, who is a good man, said he did not know whether he did so well conforme as at this time to please the people and Parliament. Sir W. Coventry answered, and the Duke of York merrily agreed to it, that it was very hard to know what it was that the Parliament would call conformity at this time.

19th. Full of my desire of seeing my Lord Orrery's new play this afternoon at the King's house, *The Black Prince*, the first time it is acted; where, though we came by two o'clock, yet there was no room in the pit, but were forced to go into one of the upper boxes, at 4s. a piece, which is the first time I ever sat in a box in my life. And in the same box came by and by, behind me, my Lord Barkeley and his lady; but I did not turn my face to them to be known, so that I was excused from giving them my seat. And this pleasure I had, that from this place the scenes do appear very fine indeed, and much better than in the pit. The house infinite full, and the King and Duke of York there. The whole house was mightily pleased all along till the reading of a letter, which was so long and so unnecessary that they frequently began to laugh, and to hiss twenty times, that had it not been for the King's being there, they had certainly hissed it off the stage.

20th (Lord's day). Up, and put on my new tunique of velvett; which is very plain, but good. This morning is brought to me an order for the presenting the Committee of Parliament to-morrow with a list of the commanders and ships' names of all the fleets set out since the war, and particularly of those ships which are divided from the fleet with Prince Rupert; which gives me occasion to see that they are busy after that business, and I am glad of it. This afternoon comes to me Captain O'Bryan, about a ship that the King hath given him; and he and I to talk of the Parliament. And he tells me that the business of the Duke of York's slackening sail in the first fight, at the beginning of the war, is brought into question, and Sir W. Penn and Captain Cox are to appear to-morrow about it; and it is thought will at last be laid upon Mr Brouncker's giving orders from the Duke of York (which the Duke of York do not own) to Captain Cox to do it; but it seems they do resent this very highly, and are mad in going through all business, where they can lay any fault. I am glad to hear that in the world I am as kindly spoke of as any body; for, for aught I see, there is bloody work like to be, Sir W. Coventry having been forced to produce a letter in Parliament, wherein the Duke of Albemarle did from Sheernesse write in what good posture all things were at Chatham, and that they were so well placed that he feared no attempt of the enemy: so that, among other things, I do see every body is upon his own defence, and spares not to blame another to defend himself; and the same course I shall take. But God knows where it will end! Pelling tells me that my Lady Duchesse Albemarle was at Mrs Turner's this afternoon (she being ill,) and did there publickly talk of business, and of our office; and that she believed that I was safe, and had done well; and so, I thank God, I hear every body speaks of me; and indeed I think, without vanity, I may expect to be profited rather than injured by this enquiry which the Parliament makes into business.

21st. To Westminster, and up to the lobby, where many command-ers of the fleet were, and Captain Cox, and Mr Pierce the Surgeon; the last of whom hath been in the House, and declared that he heard Brouncker advise and give arguments to Cox for the safety of the Duke of York's person to shorten sail, that they might not be in the middle of the enemy in the morning alone; and Cox denying to observe his advice, having received the Duke of York's commands over night to keep within gun-shot (as they then were) of the enemy, Brouncker did go to Harman, and used the same arguments, and told him that he was sure it would be well pleasing to the King that care should be taken of not endangering the Duke of York; and, after much persuasion, Harman was heard to say, 'Why, if it must be, then lower the topsail.' And so did shorten sail, to the loss, as the Parliament will have it, of the greatest victory that ever was, and which would have saved all the expence of blood and money, and honour, that followed; and this they do resent, so as to put it to the question, whether Brouncker should not be carried to the Tower: who do confess that, out of kindness to the Duke of York's safety, he did advise that they should do so, but did not use the Duke of York's name therein; and so it was only his error in advising it, but the greatest theirs in taking it contrary to order. At last it ended that it should be suspended till Harman comes home; and then the Parliament-men do all tell me that it will fall heavy, and, they think, be fatal to Brouncker or him. Sir W. Pen tells me he was gone to bed, having been all day labouring, and then not able to stand, of the gout, and did give order for the keeping the sails standing as they then were all night. But, which I wonder at, he tells me that he did not know the next day that they had shortened sail, nor ever did enquire into it till about ten days ago, that this began to be mentioned; and indeed it is charged privately as a fault on the Duke of York, that he did not presently examine the reason of the breach of his orders, and punish it. But Cox tells me that he did finally refuse it; and what prevailed with Harman he knows not, and do think that we might have done considerable service on the enemy the next day, if this had not been done. Thus this business ended to-day, having kept them till almost two o'clock: and then I by coach with Sir W. Pen as far as St Clement's talking of this matter, and there set down; and I walked to Sir G. Carteret's, and there dined with him and several Parliament-men, who, I perceive, do all look upon it as a thing certain that the Parliament will enquire into every thing, and will be very severe where they can find any fault. Sir W. Coventry, I hear, did this day make a speech, in apology for his reading the letter of the Duke of Albemarle, concerning the good condition which Chatham was in before the enemy came thither; declaring his simple intention therein without prejudice to my Lord. And I am told that he was also with the Duke of Albemarle yesterday to excuse it; but this day I do hear, by some of Sir W. Coventry's friends, that they think he hath done himself much injury by making this man and his interest so much his enemy. After dinner I away to Westminster, and up to the Parliament house, and there did wait with great patience till seven at night to be called in to the Committee, who sat all this afternoon examining the business of Chatham; and at last was called in, and told that the least they expected from us Mr Wren had promised them, and only bade me to bring all my fellow-officers thither to-morrow afternoon. Sir Robert Brookes in the chair: methinks a sorry fellow to be there, because a young man; and yet he seems to speak very well. I gone thence, my cosen Pepys comes out to me, and walks in the Hall with me, and bids me prepare to answer to every thing; for they do seem to lay the business of Chatham upon the Commissioners of the Navy, and they are resolved to lay the fault heavy somewhere, and to punish it: and prays me to prepare to save myself, and gives me hints what to prepare against; which I am obliged to him for. This day I did get a list of the fourteen particular miscarriages which are already before the

Committee to be examined; wherein, besides two or three that will concern this office much, there are those of the prizes, and that of Bergen, and not following the Dutch ships, against my Lord Sandwich; that I fear will ruin him, unless he hath very good luck, or they may be in better temper before he can come to be charged: but my heart is full of fear for him and his family. I hear that they do prosecute the business against my Lord Chief Justice Keeling with great severity.

22nd. Slept but ill all the last part of the night, for fear of this day's success in Parliament: therefore up, and all of us all the morning close, till almost two o'clock, collecting all we had to say and had done from the beginning, touching the safety of the River Medway and Chatham. And having done this, and put it into order, we away, I not having time to eat my dinner; and so all in my Lord Brouncker's coach, (that is to say, Brouncker, W. Pen, T. Hater, and myself,) talking of the other great matter with which they charge us, that is, of discharging men by ticket, in order to our defence in case that should be asked. We came to the Parliament-door, and there, after a little waiting till the Committee was sat, we were, the House being very full, called in: (Sir W. Pen went in and sat as a Member: and my Lord Brouncker would not at first go in, expecting to have a chair set for him, and his brother had bid him not go in till he was called for; but, after a few words, I had occasion to mention him, and so he was called in, but without any more chair or respect paid him than myself:) and so Brouncker, and T. Hater, and I were there to answer: and I had a chair brought me to lean my books upon; and so did give them such an account, in a series of the whole business that had passed the office touching the matter, and so answered all questions given me about it, that I did not perceive but they were fully satisfied with me and the business as to our office: and then Commissioner Pett (who was by at all my discourse, and this held till within an hour after candle-light, for I had candles brought in to read my papers by) was to answer for himself, we having lodged all matters with him for execution. But, Lord! what a tumultuous thing this Committee is, for all the reputation they have of a great council, is a strange consideration; there being as impertinent questions, and as disorderly proposed, as any man could make. But Commissioner Pett of all men living did make the weakest defence of himself: nothing to the purpose, nor to satisfaction, nor certain; but sometimes one thing and sometimes another, sometimes for himself and sometimes against him; and his greatest failure was (that I observed) from his considering whether the question propounded was his part to answer or no, and the thing to be done was his work to do: the want of which distinction will overthrow him; for he concerns himself in giving an account of the disposal of the boats, which he had no reason at all to do, or take any blame upon him for them. He charged the not carrying up of the *Charles* upon the Tuesday to the Duke of Albemarle; but I see the House is mighty favourable to the Duke of Albemarle, and would give little weight to it. And something of want of armes he spoke, which Sir J. Duncomb answered with great imperiousness and earnestness; but, for all that, I do see the House is resolved to be better satisfied in the business of the unreadiness of Sheernesse, and want of armes and ammunition there and every where; and all their officers were here to-day attending, but only one called in, about armes for boats to answer Commissioner Pett. None of my brethren said anything but me there: but only two or three silly words my Lord Brouncker gave in answer to one question about the number of men that were in the King's Yard at the time. At last the House dismissed us, and shortly after did adjourn the debate till Friday next: and my cosen Pepys did come out and joy me in my acquitting myself so well, and so did several others, and my fellow officers all very briske to see themselves so well acquitted; which makes me a little proud, but yet not secure but we may yet meet with a back-blow which we see not.

23rd. To White Hall, there to attend the Duke of York; but came a little too late, and so missed it: only spoke with him, and heard him correct my Lord Barkeley, who fell foul on Sir Edward Spragg, (who, it seems, said yesterday to the House, that if the officers of the Ordnance had done as much work at Sheernesse in ten weeks as the Prince did in ten days, he could have defended the place against the Dutch): but the Duke of York told him that every body must have liberty at this time to make their own defence, though it be to the charging of the fault upon any other, so it be true; so I perceive the whole world is at work in blaming one another. Thence Sir W. Pen and I back into London; and there saw the King, with his kettle-drums and trumpets, going to the Exchange to lay the first stone of the first pillar of the new building of the Exchange; which, the gates being shut, I could not get in to see; so with Sir W. Pen to Captain Cocke's, and then again toward Westminster; but in my way stopped at the Exchange and got in, the King being newly gone; and there find the bottom of the first pillar laid. And here was a shed set up, and hung with tapestry, and a canopy of state, and some good victuals and wine, for the King, who, it seems, did it;[108] and so a great many people, as Tom Killigrew and others of the Court, there. I do find Mr Gauden in his gowne as Sheriffe, and understand that the King hath this morning knighted him upon the place (which I am mightily pleased with); and I think the other Sheriffe, who is Davis,[109] the little fellow, my schoolfellow the bookseller, who was one of Audley's executors, and now become Sheriffe; which is a strange turn, methinks. To Westminster Hall, where I came just as the House rose; and there in the Hall met with Sir W. Coventry, who is in pain to defend himself in the business of tickets, it being said that the paying of the ships at Chatham by ticket was by his direction. He says the House was well satisfied with my Report yesterday; and so several others told me in the Hall that my Report was very good and satisfactory, and that I have got advantage by it in the House: I pray God it may prove so! To the King's playhouse, and saw *The Black Prince*; which is now mightily bettered by that long letter being printed, and so delivered to every body at their going in, and some short reference made to it in the play. But here to my great satisfaction I did see my Lord Hinchingbroke and his mistress (with her father and mother); and I am mightily pleased with the young lady, being handsome enough, and indeed to my great liking, as I would have her. This day it was moved in the House that a day might be appointed to bring in an impeachment against the Chancellor, but it was decried as being irregular; but that if there was ground for complaint, it might be brought to the Committee for miscarriages, and, if they thought good, to present it to the House; and so it was carried. They did also vote this day thanks to be given to the Prince and Duke of Albemarle, for their care and conduct in the last year's war; which is a strange act: but, I know not how, the blockhead Albemarle hath strange luck to be loved, though he be (and every man must know it) the heaviest man in the world, but stout and honest to his country. This evening late, Mr Moore

108 i.e., laid the stone.
109 He became afterwards Lord Mayor.

come to me to prepare matters for my Lord Sandwich's defence; wherein I can little assist, but will do all I can; and am in great fear of nothing but the damned business of the prizes, but I fear my Lord will receive a cursed deal of trouble by it.

25th. Up, and to make our answer ready for the Parliament this afternoon, to show how Commissioner Pett was singly concerned in the execution of all orders at Chatham, and that we did properly lodge all orders with him. Thence with Sir W. Pen to the Parliament Committee, and there I had no more matters asked me. The Commissioners of the Ordnance, being examined with all severity and hardly used, did go away with mighty blame; and I am told by every body that it is likely to stick mighty hard upon them: at which every body is glad, because of Duncomb's pride, and their expecting to have the thanks of the House; whereas they have deserved, as the Parliament apprehends, as bad as bad can be. Here is great talk of an impeachment brought in against my Lord Mordaunt, and that another will be brought in against my Lord Chancellor in a few days. Here I understand for certain that they have ordered that my Lord Arlington's letters, and Secretary Morrice's letters of intelligence, be consulted about the business of the Dutch fleet's coming abroad; and I do hear how Birch is the man that do examine and trouble every body with his questions.

26th. Mrs Pierce tells me that the two Marshalls at the King's house are Stephen Marshall's the great Presbyterian's daughters: and that Nelly and Beck Marshall falling out the other day, the latter called the other my Lord Buckhurst's mistress. Nell answered her, 'I was but one man's mistress, though I was brought up in a brothel to fill strong water to the gentlemen; and you are a mistress to three or four, though a Presbyter's praying daughter!'

27th. This evening come Sir J. Minnes to me, to let me know that a Parliament-man hath been with him to tell him that the Parliament intend to examine him particularly about Sir W. Coventry's selling of places, and about my Lord Brouncker's discharging the ships at Chatham by ticket: for the former of which I am more particularly sorry, that that business of Sir W. Coventry should come up again; though this old man tells me, and I believe, that he can say nothing to it.

28th. Sir W. Coventry says he is so well armed to justify himself in every thing, unless in the old business of selling places, when he says every body did; and he will now not be forward to tell his own story, as he hath been; but tells me he is grown wiser, and will put them to prove any thing, and he will defend himself: that he is weary of public employment; and neither ever designed, nor will ever, if his commission were brought to him wrapt in gold, accept of any single place in the State, as particularly Secretary of State: which, he says, the world discourses Morrice is willing to resign.

29th. To Westminster Hall, the House sitting all this day about the method of bringing in the charge against my Lord Chancellor; and at last resolved for a Committee to draw up the heads.

30th. To the Parliament-house: where, after the Committee was sat, I was called in: and the first thing was upon the complaint of a dirty slut that was there, about a ticket which she had lost, and had applied herself to me for another. I did give them a short and satisfactory answer to that; and so they sent her away, and were ashamed of their foolery, in giving occasion to 500 seamen and seamen's wives to come before them, as there were this afternoon.

31st. I to Westminster; and there at the lobby do hear by Commissioner Pett, to my great amazement, that he is in worse condition than before, by the coming in of the Duke of Albemarle's and Prince Rupert's Narratives this day; wherein the former do most severely lay matters upon him, so as the House this day have, I think, ordered him to the Tower again, or something like it: so that the poor man is likely to be overthrown, I doubt, right or wrong, so infinite fond they are of any thing the Duke of Albemarle says or writes to them! I did then go down, and there met with Colonell Reames and cosen Roger Pepys: and there they do tell me how the Duke of Albemarle and the Prince have laid blame on a great many, and particularly on our office in general; and particularly for want of provision, wherein I shall come to be questioned again in that business myself; which do trouble me. But my cosen Pepys and I had much discourse alone: and he do bewail the constitution of this House, and says there is a direct caball and faction as much as is possible between those for and against the Chancellor, and so in other factions, that there is nothing almost done honestly and with integrity; only some few, he says, there are, that do keep out of all plots and combinations, and when their time comes will speak and see right done if possible; and that he himself is looked upon to be a man that will be of no faction, and so they do shun to make him: and I am glad of it. He tells me that he thanks God that he never knew what it was to be tempted to be a knave in his life, till he did come into the House of Commons, where there is nothing done but by passion, and faction, and private interest. I espied Sir D. Gauden's coach, and so went out of mine into his; and there had opportunity to talk of the business of victuals, which the Duke of Albemarle and Prince did complain that they were in want of the last year: but we do conclude we shall be able to show quite the contrary of that; only it troubles me that we must come to contend with these great persons, which will overrun us.

November 1st. I this morning before chapel visited Sir G. Carteret, who is vexed to see how things are likely to go, but cannot help it, and yet seems to think himself mighty safe. I also visited my Lord Hinchingbroke, at his chamber at White Hall; where I found Mr Turner, Moore, and Creed talking of my Lord Sandwich, whose case I doubt is but bad, and, I fear, will not escape being worse. To the King's playhouse, and there saw a silly play and an old one, *The Taming of a Shrew.*

2nd. To the King's playhouse, and there saw *Henry the Fourth;* and, contrary to expectation, was pleased in nothing more than in Cartwright's[110] speaking of Falstaffe's speech about 'What is Honour?' The house full of Parliament-men, it being holyday with them: and it was observable how a gentleman of good habit sitting just before us, eating of some fruit in the midst of the play, did drop down as dead, being choked; but with much ado Orange Mall did thrust her finger down his throat, and brought him to life again.

4th. To Westminster; and there landing at the New Exchange stairs, I to Sir W. Coventry: and there he read over to me the Prince's and Duke of Albemarle's Narratives; wherein they are very severe against him and our office. But Sir W. Coventry do contemn them; only that their persons and qualities are great, and so I do perceive he is

110 William Cartwright, one of Killigrew's Company at the original establishment of Drury-lane. By his will, dated 1686, he left his books, pictures, and furniture to Dulwich College, where his portrait still remains.

afraid of them, though he will not confess it. But he do say that, if he can get out of these briars, he will never trouble himself with Princes nor Dukes again. He finds several things in their Narratives which are both inconsistent and foolish, as well as untrue. Sir H. Cholmly owns Sir W. Coventry, in his opinion, to be one of the worthiest men in the nation, as I do really think he is. He tells me he do think really that they will cut off my Lord Chancellor's head, the Chancellor at this day having as much pride as is possible to those few that venture their fortunes by coming to see him; and that the Duke of York is troubled much, knowing that those that fling down the Chancellor cannot stop there, but will do something to him, to prevent his having it in his power hereafter to avenge himself and father-in-law upon them. And this Sir H. Cholmly fears may be by divorcing the Queene and getting another, or declaring the Duke of Monmouth legitimate: which God forbid! He tells me he do verily believe that there will come in an impeachment of High Treason against my Lord of Ormond; among other things, for ordering the quartering of soldiers in Ireland on free quarters; which, it seems, is High Treason in that country, and was one of the things that lost the Lord Strafford his head, and the law is not yet repealed; which, he says, was a mighty oversight of him not to have repealed (which he might with ease have done), or have justified himself by an Act.

7th. At noon resolved with Sir W. Pen to go to see *The Tempest*, an old play of Shakespeare's, acted, I hear, the first day. And so my wife, and girl, and W. Hewer by themselves, and Sir W. Pen and I afterwards by ourselves: and forced to sit in the side balcony over against the musique-room at the Duke's House, close by my Lady Dorset[111] and a great many great ones. The house mighty full; the King and Court there: and the most innocent play that ever I saw; and a curious piece of musique in an echo of half sentences, the echo repeating the former half, while the man goes on to the latter; which is mighty pretty. The play has no great wit, but yet good above ordinary plays.

9th. The House very busy, and like to be so all day, about my Lord Chancellor's impeachment, whether Treason or not.

111 Frances, daughter of Lionel Earl of Middlesex, wife of Richard fifth Earl of Dorset.

10th. To White Hall, to speak with Sir W. Coventry; and there, beyond all we looked for do hear that the Duke of York hath got and is full of the small-pox. And so we to his lodgings; and there find most of the family going to St James's, and the gallery-doors locked up, that nobody might pass to nor fro: and so a sad house, I am sorry to see. I am sad to consider the effects of his death if he should miscarry; but Dr Frazier tells me that he is in as good condition as a man can be in his case. They appeared last night: it seems he was let blood on Friday.

11th. Sir G. Carteret and I towards the Temple in coach together; and there he did tell me how the King do all he can in the world to overthrow my Lord Chancellor, and that notice is taken of every man about the King that is not seen to promote the ruine of the Chancellor; and that this being another great day in his business, he dares not but be there. He tells me that as soon as Secretary Morrice brought the Great Seale from my Lord Chancellor, Bab. May fell upon his knees and catched the King about the legs, and joyed him, and said that this was the first time that ever he could call him King of England, being freed from this great man: which was a most ridiculous saying. And he told me that when first my Lord Gerard, a great while ago, came to the King, and told him that the Chancellor did say openly that the King was a lazy person and not fit to govern (which is now made one of the things in people's mouths against the Chancellor,) 'Why,' says the King, 'that is no news, for he hath told me so twenty times, and but the other day he told me so'; and made matter of mirth at it: but yet this light discourse is likely to prove bad to him.

12th. Up, and to the office, where sat all the morning; and there hear that the Duke of York do yet do very well with his small-pox: pray God he may continue to do so! This morning also, to my astonishment, I hear that yesterday my Lord Chancellor, to another of his Articles, that of betraying the King's councils to his enemies, is voted to have matter against him for an impeachment of High Treason, and that this day the impeachment is to be carried up to the House of Lords: which is very high, and I am troubled at it; for God knows what will follow, since they that do this must do more to secure themselves against any that will revenge this, if it ever come in their power!

13th. To Westminster: where I find the House sitting, and in a mighty heat about Commissioner Pett, that they would have him impeached, though the Committee have yet brought in but part of their Report: and this heat of the House is much heightened by Sir Thomas Clifford telling them, that he was the man that did, out of his own purse, employ people at the out-ports to prevent the King of Scotts to escape after the battle of Worcester. The house was in a great heat all this day about it; and at last it was carried, however, that it should be referred back to the Committee to make further enquiry. By and by I met with Mr Wren, who tells me that the Duke of York is in as good condition as is possible for a man in his condition of the small-pox. He, I perceive, is mightily concerned in the business of my Lord Chancellor, the impeachment against whom is gone up to the House of Lords; and great differences there are in the Lords' House about it, and the Lords are very high one against another. This day Mr Chichly told me, with a seeming trouble, that the House have stopped his son Jack (Sir John) his going to France, that he may be a witness against my Lord Sandwich: which do trouble me, though he can, I think, say little.

15th. A conference between the two Houses to-day; so I stayed: and it was only to tell the Commons that the Lords cannot agree to the confining or sequestring of the Earle of Clarendon from the Parliament, forasmuch as they do not specify any particular crime which they lay upon him and call Treason. This the House did receive, and so parted: at which, I hear the Commons are like to grow very high, and will insist upon their privileges, and the Lords will own theirs, though the Duke of Buckingham, Bristoll, and others have been very high in the House of Lords to have had him committed. This is likely to breed ill blood. The King hath (as Mr Moore says Sir Thomas Crewe told him) been heard to say that the quarrel is not between my Lord Chancellor and him, but his brother and him; which will make sad work among us if that be once promoted, as to be sure it will, Buckingham and Bristoll being now the only counsel the King follows, so as Arlington and Coventry are come to signify little. He tells me they are likely to fall upon my Lord Sandwich; but for my part sometimes I am apt to think they cannot do him much harm, he telling me that there is no great fear of the business of Resumption. This day Poundy the waterman was with me, to let me know that he was summoned to bear witness against me to Prince Rupert's people (who have a commission to look after the business of prize-goods), about the business of the prize-goods I was concerned in: but I did desire him to speak all he knew, and not to spare me, nor did promise nor give him any thing, but sent him away with good words.

16th. Met Mr Gregory, my old acquaintance, an understanding gentleman; and he and I walked an hour together, talking of the bad prospect of the times. And the sum of what I learn from him is this: That the King is the most concerned in the world against the Chancellor and all people that do not appear against him, and therefore is angry with the Bishops, having said that he had one Bishop on his side (Crofts),[112] and but one: that Buckingham and Bristoll are now his only Cabinet Counsel; and that, before the Duke of York fell sick, Buckingham was admitted to the King of his Cabinet, and there stayed with him several hours, and the Duke of York shut out. That it is plain that there is dislike between the King and Duke of York, and that it is to be feared that the House will go so far against the Chancellor, that they must do something to undo the Duke of York, or will not think themselves safe. That this Lord Vaughan[113] that is so great against the Chancellor, is one of the lewdest fellows of the age, worse than Sir Charles Sedley; and that he was heard to swear he would do my Lord Clarendon's business. That he do find that my Lord Clarendon hath more friends in both Houses than he believes he would have, by reason that they do see what are the hands that pull him down; which they do not like. That Harry Coventry was scolded at by the King severely the other day; and that his answer was, that if he must not speak what he thought in this business in Parliament, he must not come thither. And he says that by this very business Harry Coventry hath got more fame and common esteem than any gentleman in England hath at this day, and is an excellent and able person. That the King, who not long ago did say of Bristoll, that he was a man able in three years to get himself a fortune

---

112 Herbert Croft, Dean of Hereford, elected Bishop of that see 1661.

113 John Lord Vaughan, eldest surviving son to Richard Earl of Carbery, whom he succeeded. He was well versed in literature, and President of the Royal Society from 1686 to 1689, and had been Governor of Jamaica. He was amongst Dryden's earliest patrons. Died 1712/13.

in any kingdom in the world, and lose all again in three months, do now hug him and commend his parts every where, above all the world. How fickle is this man, and how unhappy we like to be! That he fears some furious courses will be taken against the Duke of York; and that he hath heard that it was designed, if they cannot carry matters against the Chancellor, to impeach the Duke of York himself; which God forbid! That Sir Edward Nicholas, whom he served while Secretary, is one of the best men in the world, but hated by the Queene-Mother, (for a service he did the old King against her mind and her favourites;) and that she and my Lady Castlemaine did make the King to lay him aside: but this man says that he is one of the most heavenly and charitable men in the whole world. That the House of Commons resolve to stand by their proceedings, and have chosen a Committee to draw up the reason thereof to carry to the Lords; which is likely to breed great heat between them. That the Parliament, after all this, is likely to give the King no money; and therefore, that it is to be wondered what makes the King give way to so great extravagancies, which do all tend to the making him less than he is, and so will every day more and more: and by this means every creature is divided against the other, that there never was so great an uncertainty in England, of what would be the event of things, as at this day; nobody being at ease, or safe. To White Hall; and there got into the theatre-room, and there heard both the vocall and instrumentall musick. Here was the King and Queene, and some of the ladies; among whom none more jolly than my Lady Buckingham, her Lord being once more a great man.

19th. I was told this day that Lory Hide,[114] second son of my Lord Chancellor, did some time since in the House say, that if he thought his father was guilty but of one of the things then said against him, he would be the first that should call for judgement against him: which Mr Waller the poet did say was spoke like the old Roman, like Brutus, for its greatness and worthiness.

20th. This afternoon Mr Mills told me how fully satisfactory my first Report was to the House in the business of Chatham: which I am glad to hear; and the more, for that I know that he is a great creature of Sir R. Brookes's.

114 Laurence Hyde, Master of the Robes, afterwards created Earl of Rochester.

21st. Among other things of news I do hear, that upon the reading of the House of Commons' Reasons of the manner of their proceedings in the business of my Lord Chancellor, the Reasons were so bad, that my Lord Bristoll himself did declare that he would not stand to what he had and did still advise the Lords to concur to, upon any of the Reasons of the House of Commons; but if it was put to the question whether it should be done on their Reasons, he would be against them: and indeed it seems the Reasons, however they come to escape the House of Commons (which shows how slightly the greatest matters are done in this world, and even in Parliaments), were none of them of strength, but the principle of them untrue; they saying, that where any man is brought before a Judge accused of Treason in general, without specifying the particular, the Judge is obliged to commit him. The question being put by the Lords to my Lord Keeper, he said that quite the contrary was true. And then in the Sixth Article (I will get a copy of them if I can) there are two or three things strangely asserted to the diminishing of the King's power, as is said at least; things that heretofore would not have been heard of. But then the question being put among the Lords, as my Lord Bristoll advised, whether, upon the whole matter and Reasons that had been laid before them, they would commit my Lord Clarendon, it was carried five to one against it; there being but three Bishops against him, of whom Cosens[115] and Dr Reynolds[116] were two, and I know not the third. This made the opposite Lords, as Bristoll and Buckingham, so mad that they declared and protested against it, speaking very broad that there was mutiny and rebellion in the hearts of the Lords, and that they desired they might enter their dissents, which they did do in great fury. So that upon the Lords sending to the Commons, as I am told, to have a conference for them to give their answer to the Commons' Reasons, the Commons did desire a free conference: but the Lords do deny it; and the reason is, that they hold not the Commons any Court, but that themselves only are a Court, and the Chief Court of Judicature, and therefore are not to dispute the laws and method of their own Court with them that are none, and so will not submit so much as to have their power

115 John Cosins, Master of Peterhouse and Dean of Peterborough in the time of Charles I; afterwards Bishop of Durham. Died 1671/72, aged 78.
116 Edward Reynolds, Bishop of Norwich. Died 1676.

disputed. And it is conceived that much of this eagerness among the Lords do arise from the fear some of them have that they may be dealt with in the same manner themselves, and therefore do stand upon it now. It seems my Lord Clarendon hath, as is said and believed, had his coach and horses several times in his coach, ready to carry him to the Tower, expecting a message to that purpose; but by this means his case is like to be laid by. With Creed to a Tavern, where Dean Wilkins and others: and good discourse; among the rest, of a man that is a little frantic (that hath been a kind of Minister, Dr Wilkins saying that he hath read for him in his church), that is poor and a debauched man, that the College have hired for 20s. to have some of the blood of a sheep let into his body; and it is to be done on Saturday next. They purpose to let in about twelve ounces; which, they compute, is what will be let in in a minute's time by a watch. On this occasion Dr Whistler told a pretty story related by Muffett, a good author, of Dr Cayus that built Caius College; that being very old, and living only at that time upon woman's milk, he, while he fed upon the milk of an angry fretful woman, was so himself; and then being advised to take it of a good-natured patient woman, he did become so beyond the common temper of his age.

22nd. Met with Cooling, my Lord Chamberlain's Secretary, and from him learn the truth of all I heard last night; and understand further, that this stiffness of the Lords is in no manner of kindness to my Lord Chancellor, for he neither hath, nor do, nor for the future can oblige any of them, but rather the contrary; but that they do fear what the consequence may be to themselves, should they yield in his case, as many of them have reason. And more, he showed me how this is rather to the wrong and prejudice of my Lord Chancellor, for that it is better for him to come to be tried before the Lords, where he can have right and make interest, than, when the Parliament is up, be committed by the King, and tried by a Court on purpose made by the King of what Lords the King pleases, who have a mind to have his head. So that my Lord Cornbury himself, his son, (he tells me,) hath moved that if they have Treason against my Lord of Clarendon, that they would specify it and send it up to the Lords, that he might come to his trial; so full of intrigues this business is! Walked a good while in the Temple church, observing the plainness of Selden's tomb, and how much better one of his executors hath, who is buried by him.

23rd. Busy till late preparing things to fortify myself and fellows against the Parliament; and particularly myself against what I fear is thought, that I have suppressed the Order of the Board by which the discharging the great ships at Chatham by tickets was directed; whereas, indeed, there was no such Order.

25th. This morning Sir W. Pen tells me that the house was very hot on Saturday last upon the business of liberty of speech in the House, and damned the vote in the beginning of the Long-Parliament against it; so that he fears that there may be some bad thing which they have a mind to broach, which they dare not do without more security than they now have. God keep us, for things look mighty ill!

26th. This evening comes to me to my closet at the office Sir John Chichly, of his own accord, to tell me what he shall answer to the Committee, when, as he expects, he shall be examined about my Lord Sandwich; which is so little as will not hurt my Lord at all, I know.

27th. Mr Pierce comes to me, and there in general tells me, how the King is now fallen in and become a slave to the Duke of Buckingham, led by none but him, whom he (Mr Pierce) swears he knows do hate the very person of the King, and would as well, as will certainly, ruin him. He do say, and I think is right, that the King do in this do the most ungrateful part of a master to a servant that ever was done, in this carriage of his to my Lord Chancellor: that it may be the Chancellor may have faults, but none such as these they speak of; that he do now really fear that all is going to ruin, for he says he hears that Sir W. Coventry hath been just before his sickness with the Duke of York, to ask his forgiveness and peace for what he had done; for that he never could foresee that what he meant so well, in the counselling to lay by the Chancellor, should come to this.

30th. To Arundell House, to the election of officers[117] for the next year; where I was near being chosen of the Council, but am glad I was not, for I could not have attended, though above all things I could wish it; and do take it as a mighty respect to have been named there. Then to Cary House, a house now of entertainment, next my Lord Ashly's; where I have heretofore heard Common Prayer in the time

117 Of the Royal Society.

of Dr Mossum.[118] I was pleased to see the person who had his blood taken out. He speaks well, and did this day give the Society a relation thereof in Latin, saying that he finds himself much better since, and as a new man; but he is cracked a little in his head, though he speaks very reasonably, and very well. He had but 20s. for his suffering it, and is to have the same again tried upon him: the first sound man that ever had it tried on him in England, and but one that we hear of in France. My Lord Anglesy told me this day that he did believe the House of Commons would the next week yield to the Lords; but speaking with others this day, they conclude they will not, but that rather the King will accommodate it by committing my Lord Clarendon himself. I remember what Mr Evelyn said, that he did believe we should soon see ourselves fall into a Commonwealth again.

December 1st. I to church: and in our pew there sat a great lady, whom I afterwards understood to be my Lady Carlisle,[119] a very fine woman indeed in person.

2nd. The Lords' answer is come down to the Commons, that they are not satisfied in the Commons' reasons; and so the Commons are hot, and like to sit all day upon the business what to do herein, most thinking that they will remonstrate against the Lords. Thence to Lord Crewe's, and there dined with him; where, after dinner, he took me aside and bewailed the condition of the nation, now the King and his brother are at a distance about this business of the Chancellor, and the two houses differing: and he do believe that there are so many about the King like to be concerned and troubled by the Parliament, that they will get him to dissolve or prorogue the Parliament; and the rather, for that the King is likely by this good husbandry of the Treasury to get out of debt, and the Parliament is likely to give no money. Among other things, my Lord Crewe did tell me with grief that he hears that the King of late hath not dined nor supped with the Queene, as he used of late to do. To Westminster Hall, where my cosen Roger tells me of the high vote of the Commons this afternoon, that the proceedings of the Lords in

118 Probably Robert Messum, DD, Dean of Christ Church, Dublin; and in 1666 made Bishop of Derry.
119 Anne, daughter of Edward Lord Howard of Escrick, wife to Charles first Earl of Carlisle.

the case of my Lord Clarendon are an obstruction to justice, and of ill precedent to future times.

3rd. To Sir W. Coventry's, the first time I have seen him at his new house since he came to lodge there. He tells me of the vote for none of the House to be of the Commission for the Bill of Accounts; which he thinks is so great a disappointment to Birch and others that expected to be of it, that he thinks, could it have been seen, there would not have been any Bill at all. We hope it will be the better for all that are to account; it being likely that the men, being few and not of the House will hear reason. The main business I went about was about Gilsthrop, Sir W. Batten's clerk; who being upon his death-bed, and now dead, hath offered to make discoveries of the disorders of the Navy and of £65,000 damage to the King: which made mighty noise in the Commons' House; and members appointed to go to him, which they did; but nothing to the purpose got from him, but complaints of false musters, and ships being refitted with victuals and stores at Plymouth after they were fitted from other ports. But all this to no purpose, nor more than we know and will owne. But the best is, that this loggerhead should say this, that understands nothing of the Navy, nor ever would; and hath particularly blemished his master by name among us. I told Sir W. Coventry of my letter to Sir R. Brookes, and his answer to me. He advises me, in what I write to him, to be as short as I can, and obscure, saving in things fully plain; for that all that he do is to make mischief; and that the greatest wisdom in dealing with the Parliament in the world is to say little, and let them get out what they can by force: which I shall observe. He declared to me much of his mind to be ruled by his own measures, and not to go so far as many would have him to the ruin of my Lord Chancellor, and for which they do endeavour to do what they can against Sir W. Coventry. 'But,' says he, 'I have done my do in helping to get him out of the administration of things, for which he is not fit; but for his life or estate I will have nothing to say to it: besides that, my duty to my master the Duke of York is such, that I will perish before I will do any thing to displease or disoblige him, where the very necessity of the kingdom do not in my judgment call me.' Home; and there met W. Batelier, who tells me the first great news, that my Lord Chancellor is fled this day, and left a paper behind him for the House of Lords, telling them the reason of his retiring, complaining of a design for his ruin. But the paper I must get: only the thing at present is great, and will put the King and Commons to some new counsels certainly. Sir Richard Ford told us this evening an odd story of the basenesse of the Lord Mayor, Sir W. Bolton, in cheating the poor of the City (out of the collections made for the people that were burned) of £1800; of which he can give no account, and in which he hath forsworn himself plainly, so as the Court of Aldermen have sequestered him from their Court till he do bring in an account. He says also that this day hath been made appear to them that the Keeper of Newgate hath at this day made his house the only nursery of rogues, prostitutes, pickpockets and thieves, in the world; where they were bred and entertained, and the whole society met: and that for the sake of the Sheriffes they durst not this day commit him, for fear of making him let out the prisoners, but are fain to go by artifice to deal with him. He tells me also, speaking of the new street that is to be made from Guild Hall down to Cheapside, that the ground is already most of it bought. And tells me of one particular, of a man that hath a piece of ground lying in the very middle of the street that must be; which, when the street is cut out of it, there will remain ground enough, of each side, to build a house to front the street. He demanded £700 for the ground, and to be excused paying any thing for the melioration of the rest of his ground that he was to keep. The Court consented to give him £700, only not to abate him the consideration: which the man denied; but told them, and so they agreed, that he would excuse the City the £700, that he might have the benefit of the melioration without paying any thing for it. So much some will get by having the City burned! Ground by this means, that was not worth 4d. a-foot before, will now, when houses are built, be worth 15s. a-foot. But he tells me of the common standard now reckoned on between man and man, in places where there is no alteration of circumstances, but only the houses burnt, there the ground, which with a house on it did yield £1000 a year, is now reputed worth £33 6s. 8d.; and that this is the common market-price between one man and another, made upon a good and moderate medium.

4th. I hear that the House of Lords did send down the paper which my Lord Clarendon left behind him, directed to the Lords, to be seditious and scandalous; and the Commons have voted that it be burned by the hands of the hangman, and that the King be desired to agree to it. I do hear also that they have desired the King to use means to stop his escape out of the nation. This day Gilsthrop is buried, who hath made all the late discourse of the great discovery of £65,000 of which the King hath been wronged.

6th. With Sir J. Minnes to the Duke of York, the first time that I have seen him, or we waited on him, since his sickness: and blessed be God, he is not at all the worse for the smallpox, but is only a little weak yet. We did much business with him, and so parted. My Lord Anglesy told me how my Lord Northampton[120] brought in a Bill into the House of Lords yesterday, under the name of a Bill for the Honour and Privilege of the House, and Mercy to my Lord Clarendon: which, he told me, he opposed, saying that he was a man accused of treason by the House of Commons, and mercy was not proper for him, having not been tried yet, and so no mercy needful for him. However, the Duke of Buckingham and others did desire that the Bill might be read; and it was for banishing my Lord Clarendon from all his Majesty's dominions, and that it should be treason to have him found in any of them: the thing is only a thing of vanity, and to insult over him. By and by home with Sir J. Minnes, who tells me that my Lord Clarendon did go away in a Custom-house boat, and is now at Callis: and, I confess, nothing seems to hang more heavy than his leaving of this unfortunate paper behind him, that hath angered both Houses, and hath, I think, reconciled them in that which otherwise would have broke them in pieces: so that I do hence, and from Sir W. Coventry's late example and doctrine to me, learn that on these sorts of occasions there is nothing like silence; it being seldom any wrong to a man to say nothing, but for the most part it is to say any thing. Sir J. Minnes told me a story of my Lord Cottington, who, wanting a son, intended to make his nephew his heir, a country boy; but did alter his mind upon the boy's being persuaded by another young heir (in roguery) to crow like a cock at my Lord's table, much company being there, and the boy having a great trick at doing that perfectly. My Lord bade them take away that fool from the table, and so gave over the thoughts of making him his heir from this piece of folly. Captain Cocke comes to

120 James third Earl of Northampton, Lord Lieutenant of Warwickshire, and Constable of the Tower. Died 1681.

me; and, among other discourse, tells me that he is told that an impeachment against Sir W. Coventry will be brought in very soon. He tells me that even those that are against my Lord Chancellor and the Court in the House, do not trust nor agree one with another. He tells me that my Lord Chancellor went away about ten at night, on Saturday last, at Westminster; and took boat at Westminster, and thence by a vessel to Callis, where he believes he now is; and that the Duke of York and Mr Wren knew of it, and that himself did know of it on Sunday morning: that on Sunday his coach, and people about it, went to Twittenham, and the world thought that he had been there: that nothing but this unhappy paper hath undone him, and that he doubts that this paper hath lost him every where: that his withdrawing do reconcile things so far as, he thinks, the heat of their fury will be over, and that all will be made well between the two brothers: that Holland do endeavour to persuade the King of France to break peace with us: that the Dutch will, without doubt, have sixty sail of ships out the next year: so knows not what will become of us, but hopes the Parliament will find money for us to have a fleet.

7th. Somebody told me this day that they hear that Thomson with the wooden leg, and Wildman, the Fifth-Monarchy man (a great creature of the Duke of Buckingham's), are in nomination to be Commissioners, among others, upon the Bill of Accounts.

8th. To White Hall, where I saw the Duchess of York (in a fine dress of second mourning for her mother, being black edged with ermin) go to make her first visit to the Queene since the Duke of York's being sick; and by and by she being returned, the Queene came and visited her. But it was pretty to observe that Sir W. Coventry and I walking an hour and more together in the Matted Gallery, he observed, and so did I, how the Duchesse, soon as she spied him, turned her head a' one side. Here he and I walked thus long, which we have not done a great while before. Our discourse was upon every thing: the unhappiness of having our matters examined by people that understand them not; that it is better for us in the Navy to have men that do understand the whole, and that are not passionate; that we that have taken the most pains are called upon to answer for all crimes, while those that, like Sir W. Batten and Sir J. Minnes, did sit and do nothing, do lie still without any trouble: that if it were to serve the King and kingdom again in a war, neither of us could do more, though upon this experience we might do better than we did: that the commanders, the gentlemen that could never be brought to order, but undid all, are now the men that find fault and abuse others: that it had been much better for the King to have given Sir J. Minnes and Sir W. Batten £1000 a-year to have sat still, than to have had them in this business this war: that the serving a prince that minds not his business is most unhappy for them that serve him well, and an unhappiness so great that he declares he will never have more to do with a war under him. That he hath papers which do flatly contradict the Duke of Albemarle's Narrative; and that he hath been with the Duke of Albemarle and showed him them, to prevent his falling into another like fault: that the Duke of Albemarle seems to be able to answer them; but he thinks that the Duke of Albemarle and the Prince are contented to let their Narratives sleep, they being not only contradictory in some things (as he observed about the business of the Duke of Albemarle's being to follow the Prince upon the dividing the fleet in case the enemy come out), but neither of them to be maintained in others. That the business the other night of my Lord Anglesy at the Council was happily got over for my Lord, by his dexterous silencing it, and the rest not urging it further; forasmuch as had the Duke of Buckingham come in time enough and had got it by the end, he would have toused him in it; Sir W. Coventry telling me that my Lord Anglesy did with such impudence maintain the quarrel against the Commons and some of the Lords, in the business of my Lord Clarendon, that he believes there are enough would be glad but of this occasion to be revenged of him. He tells me that he hears some of the Thomsons are like to be of the Commission for the Accounts, and Wildman, which he much wonders at, as having been a false fellow to every body, and in prison most of the time since the King's coming in. But he do tell me that the House is in such a condition that nobody can tell what to make of them, and, he thinks, they were never in before; that every body leads, and nobody follows; and that he do now think that, since a great many are defeated in their expectation of being of the Commission, now they would put it into such hands as it shall get no credit from: for if they do look to the bottom and see the King's case, they think they are then bound to give the King money; whereas they would be excused from that, and therefore endeavour to make this business of the Accounts to signify little. Comes Captain Cocke to me; and there he tells me, to my great satisfaction, that Sir Robert Brookes did dine with him to-day; and that he told him, speaking of me, that he would make me the darling of the House of Commons, so much he is satisfied concerning me. And this Cocke did tell me that I might give him thanks for it; and I do think it may do me good, for he do happen to be held a considerable person, of a young man, both for sobriety and ability.

9th. Comes Sir G. Carteret to talk with me; who seems to think himself safe as to his particular, but do doubt what will become of the whole kingdom, things being so broke in pieces. He tells me that the King himself did the other day very particularly tell the whole story of my Lord Sandwich's not following the Dutch ships, with which he is charged; and shows the reasons of it to be the only good course he could have taken, and do discourse it very knowingly. This I am glad of, though, as the King is now, his favour for aught I see, serves very little in stead at this day, but rather is an argument against a man; and the King do not concern himself to relieve or justify any body, but is wholly negligent of every body's concernment.

10th. The King did send a message to the House to-day that he would adjourn them on the 17th instant to February; by which time, at least, I shall have more respite to prepare things on my own behalf and the office, against their return.

11th. I met Harris the player, and talked of *Catiline*, which is to be suddenly acted at the King's house; and there all agree that it cannot be well done at that house, there not being good actors enough: and Burt[121] acts Cicero, which they all conclude he will not be able to do well. The King gives them £500 for robes, there being, as they say, to be sixteen scarlet robes. Comes Sir W. Warren[122] to talk about some business of his and mine: and he, I find, would have me not to think that the Parliament, in the mind they are in, and having so many good offices in their view to dispose of, will leave any of the

---

121 Davies says Burt ranked in the list of good actors without possessing superior talents – *Dramatic Miscellanies*.

122 I have been recently informed that Charles II, April 12, 1662, knighted a rich tradesman of Wapping, named William Warren, and there is still in that parish a place called 'Sir William Warren's Square,' perhaps built on the site of the knight's residence.

King's officers in, but will rout all, though I am likely to escape as well as any, if any can escape. And I think he is in the right, and I do look for it accordingly.

12th. My bookseller did give me a list of the twenty who were mentioned for the Commission in Parliament for the Accounts: and it is strange that of the twenty the Parliament could not think fit to choose their nine, but were fain to add three that were not in the list of the twenty, they being many of them factious people and ringleaders in the late troubles; so that Sir John Talbot did fly out and was very hot in the business of Wildman's being named, and took notice how he was entertained in the bosom of the Duke of Buckingham, a Privy counsellor; and that it was fit to be observed by the House, and punished. The men that I know of the nine I like very well; that is, Mr Pierrepoint, Lord Brereton,[123] and Sir William Turner; and I do think the rest are so too, but such as will not be able to do this business as it ought to be to do any good with. Here I did also see their votes against my Lord Chief Justice Keeling, that his proceedings were illegal, and that he was a contemner of Magna Charta, the great preserver of our lives, freedoms and properties, and an introduction to arbitrary government; which is very high language, and of the same sound with that in the year 1640. This day my Lord Chancellor's letter was burned at the 'Change.

13th. To Westminster, to the Parliament-door, to speak with Roger: and here I saw my Lord Keeling go into the House to the bar, to have his business heard by the whole House to-day; and a great crowd of people to stare upon him. Here I hear that the Lord's Bill for banishing and disabling my Lord Clarendon from bearing any office, or being in the King's dominions, and it being made felony for any to correspond with him but his own children, is brought to the Commons; but they will not agree to it, being not satisfied with that as sufficient, but will have a Bill of Attainder brought in against him: but they make use of this against the Lords, that they that would not think there was cause

---

123 William, third Lord Brereton, of Leaghlin in Ireland, MP for Cheshire, where he possessed an estate which he disposed of on account of the exigencies of the times, and his father's losses in the cause of Charles I. He was educated at Breda, and was an accomplished and amiable nobleman, and one of the Founders of the Royal Society. Died 1679.

enough to commit him without hearing, will have him banished without hearing. By and by comes out my cosen Roger to me, he being not willing to be in the House at the business of my Lord Keeling, lest he should be called upon to complain against him for his abusing him at Cambridge. Among other news it is now fresh that the King of Portugall is deposed, and his brother made King; and that my Lord Sandwich is gone from Madrid with great honour to Lisbon, to make up at this juncture a peace to the advantage, as the Spaniard would have it, of Spain. I wish it may be for my Lord's honour, if it be so; but it seems my Lord is in mighty estimation in Spain. With my cosen Roger to Westminster Hall; and there we met the House rising: and they have voted my Lord Chief Justice Keeling's proceedings illegal; but that out of particular respect to him and the mediation of a great many, they have resolved to proceed no further against him.

16th. To Westminster, where I find the House mighty busy upon a petition against my Lord Gerard, which lays heavy things to his charge, of his abusing the King in his Guards; and very hot the House is upon it.

17th. This day I do hear at White Hall that the Duke of Monmouth is sick, and in danger of the small-pox.

19th. To the office, where Commissioner Middleton first took his place at the Board as Surveyor of the Navy; and indeed I think will be an excellent officer, I am sure much beyond what his predecessor was. This evening the King by message (which he never did before) hath passed several Bills, among others that for the Accounts and for banishing my Lord Chancellor, and hath adjourned the House to February; at which I am glad, hoping in this time to get leisure to state my Tangier Accounts, and to prepare better for the Parliament's enquiries. Here I hear how the House of Lords with great severity, if not tyranny, have proceeded against poor Carr, who only erred in the manner of the presenting his petition against my Lord Gerard, it being first printed before it was presented: which was, it seems, by Colonell Sands's going into the country, into whose hands he had put it: the poor man is ordered to stand in the pillory two or three times, and to have his eares cut, and be imprisoned I know not how long. But it is believed that the Commons, when they meet, will not be well pleased with it; and they have no reason, I think.

21st. The Nonconformists are mighty high, and their meetings frequented and connived at; and they do expect to have their day now soon; for my Lord of Buckingham is a declared friend to them, and even to the Quakers, who had very good words the other day from the King himself: and, what is more, the Archbishop of Canterbury[124] is called no more to the Caball, nor, by the way, Sir W. Coventry: which I am sorry for, the Caball at present being, as he says, the King, and Duke of Buckingham, and Lord Keeper, the Duke of Albemarle, and Privy Seale. The Bishops differing from the King in the late business in the House of Lords, have caused this and what is like to follow, for every body is encouraged now-a-days to speak, and even to preach (as I have heard one of them), as bad things against them as ever in the year 1640; which is a strange change.

23rd. I to the Exchange; and there I saw Carr stand in the pillory for the business of my Lord Gerard; and there hear by Creed that the Bishops of Winchester[125] and of Rochester,[126] and the Dean of the Chapel, and some other great prelates, are suspended: and a cloud upon the Archbishop ever since the late business in the House of Lords; and I believe it will be a heavy blow to the Clergy.

24th. By coach to St James's, it being about six at night; my design being to see the ceremonys, this night being the eve of Christmas, at the Queene's chapel. I got in almost up to the rail, and with a great deal of patience staid from nine at night to two in the morning in a very great crowd: and there expected but found nothing extraordinary, there being nothing but a high masse. The Queene was there, and some high ladies. All being done, I was sorry for my coming, and missing of what I expected; which was, to have had a child born and dressed there, and a great deal of do: but we broke up, and nothing like it done. And there I left people receiving the Sacrament: and the Queene gone, and ladies; only my Lady Castlemaine, who looked prettily in her night-clothes. And so took my coach, which waited; and drank some burnt wine at the Rose Tavern door while the constables came, and two or three bellmen went by, it being a fine light moonshine morning: and so home round the City.

124 Gilbert Sheldon.
125 George Morley.
126 John Dolben.

26th. With my wife to the King's playhouse, and there saw *The Surprizall*;[127] which did not please me to-day, the actors not pleasing me; and especially Nell's acting of a serious part, which she spoils. I hear this day that Mrs Stewart do at this day keep a great court at Somerset House with her husband the Duke of Richmond, she being visited for her beauty's sake by people as the Queene is at nights; and they say also that she is likely to go to Court again, and there put my Lady Castlemaine's nose out of joynt.

27th. A Committee of Tangier met: the Duke of York there. And there I did discourse over to them their condition as to money; which they were all mightily as I could desire satisfied with, but the Duke of Albemarle, who takes the part of the Guards against us in our supplies of money; which is an odd consideration for a dull, heavy blockhead as he is, understanding no more of either than a goose: but the ability and integrity of Sir W. Coventry, in all the King's concernments, I do and must admire. After the Committee, Sir W. Coventry tells me that the businesse of getting the Duchesse of Richmond to Court is broke off, the Duke not suffering it; and thereby great trouble is brought among the people that endeavoured it, and thought they had compassed it. And Lord! to think that at this time the King should mind no other cares but these! He tells me that my Lord of Canterbury is a mighty stout man, and a man of a brave, high spirit, and cares not for this disfavour that he is under at Court, knowing that the King cannot take away his profits during his life, and therefore do not value it.

28th. To the King's house, and there saw *The Mad Couple*; which is but an ordinary play; but only Nell's and Hart's mad parts are most excellent done, but especially her's: which makes it a miracle to me to think how ill she do any serious part, as the other day, just like a fool or changeling; and, in a mad part, do beyond all imitation almost. It pleased us mightily to see the natural affection of a poor woman, the mother of one of the children brought on the stage: the child crying, she by force got upon the stage, and took up her child and carried it away off of the stage from Hart. Many fine faces here to-day. I am told to-day, which troubles me, that great complaint is made upon the 'Change among our merchants, that the very Ostend little

127 A comedy, by Sir Robert Howard.

pickaroon men-of-war do offer violence to our merchant-men and search them, beat our masters, and plunder them, upon pretence of carrying Frenchmen's goods.

29th. At night comes Mrs Turner to see us; and there, among other talk, she tells me that Mr William Pen, who is lately come over from Ireland, is a Quaker again, or some very melancholy thing; that he cares for no company, nor comes into any: which is a pleasant thing, after his being abroad so long, and his father such a hypocritical rogue, and at this time an Atheist.

30th. Sir G. Carteret and I alone did talk of the ruinous condition we are in, the King being going to put out of the Council so many able men; such as my Lord Anglesy, Ashly, Hollis, Secretary Morrice (to bring in Mr Trevor[128]) and the Archbishop of Canterbury and my Lord Bridgewater. He tells me that this is true, only the Duke of York do endeavour to hinder it, and the Duke of York himself did tell him so; that the King and the Duke of York do not in company disagree, but are friendly; but that there is a core in their hearts, he doubts, which is not to be easily removed; for these men so suffer only for their constancy to the Chancellor, or at least from the King's ill-will against him. He do suggest that something is intended for the Duke of Monmouth, and, it may be, against the Queene also: that we are in no manner sure against an invasion the next year: that the Duke of Buckingham do rule all now, and the Duke of York comes indeed to the Caball, but signifies little there. That this new faction do not endure, nor the King, Sir W. Coventry; but yet that he is so usefull that they cannot be without him; but that he is not now called to the Caball. That my Lord of Buckingham, Bristoll, and Arlington do seem to agree in these things; but that they do not in their hearts trust one another, but do drive several ways all of them. In short, he do bless himself that he is no more concerned in matters now; and the hopes he hath of being at liberty, when his accounts are over, to retire into the country. That he do give over the kingdom for wholly lost. This day I got a little rent in my new fine camlett cloak with the latch of Sir G. Carteret's door; but it is darned up at my tailor's, that it will be no great blemish to it; but it troubled me. I could not but

128 John Trevor, knighted by Charles II who made him Secretary of State, 1668, which office he held till his death in 1672.

observe that Sir Philip Carteret[129] would fain have given me my going into a play; but yet when he came to the door he had no money to pay for himself, I having refused to accept of it for myself, but was fain; and I perceive he is known there, and do run upon the score for plays, which is a shame; but I perceive always he is in want of money. In the pit I met with Sir Ch. North (formerly Mr North, who was with my Lord at sea); and he, of his own accord, was so silly as to tell me he is married; and for her quality, being a Lord's daughter,[130] (my Lord Grey) and person and beauty, and years and estate and disposition, he is the happiest man in the world. I am sure he is an ugly fellow; but a good scholar and sober gentleman; and heir to his father, now Lord North, the old Lord being dead.

31st. Thus ends the year, with great happiness to myself and family as to health and good condition in the world, blessed be God for it! only with great trouble to my mind in reference to the publick, there being little hopes left but that the whole nation must in a very little time be lost, either by troubles at home, the Parliament being dissatisfied, and the King led into unsettled councils by some about him, himself considering little, and divisions growing between the King and Duke of York; or else by foreign invasion, to which we must submit if any at this bad point of time should come upon us, which the King of France is well able to do. These thoughts, and some cares upon me, concerning my standing in this office when the Committee of Parliament shall come to examine our Navy matters, which they will now shortly do. I pray God they may do the kingdom service therein, as they will have sufficient opportunity of doing it.

1667/68. January 1st. Dined with my Lord Crewe, with whom was Mr Browne, Clerk of the House of Lords, and Mr John Crewe. Here was mighty good discourse, as there is always: and among other things my Lord Crewe did turn to a place in the *Life of Sir Philip Sidney*, wrote by Sir Fulke Greville, which do foretell the present condition of this nation, in relation to the Dutch, to the very degree of a prophecy; and is so remarkable that I am resolved to buy one of

129 Sir G. Carteret's eldest son, mentioned before, who had been knighted.
130 Catherine, daughter to William Lord Grey of Warke, and widow of Sir Edward Moseley.

them, it being quite through a good discourse. Here they did talk much of the present cheapness of corne, even to a miracle; so as their farmers can pay no rent, but do fling up their lands; and would pay in corne: but (which I did observe to my Lord, and he liked well of it) our gentry are grown so ignorant in every thing of good husbandry that they know not how to bestow this corne; which, did they understand but a little trade, they would be able to joyne together and know what markets there are abroad, and send it thither, and thereby ease their tenants and be able to pay themselves. They did talk much of the disgrace the Archbishop is fallen under with the King, and the rest of the Bishops also. Thence I after dinner to the Duke of York's playhouse, and there saw *Sir Martin Mar-all*; which I have seen so often, and yet am mightily pleased with it, and think it mighty witty, and the fullest of proper matter for mirth that ever was writ; and I do clearly see that they do improve in their acting of it. Here a mighty company of citizens, prentices, and others; and it makes me observe, that when I began first to be able to bestow a play on myself, I do not remember that I saw so many by half of the ordinary prentices and mean people in the pit at 2s. 6d. a-piece as now; I going for several years no higher than the 12d. and then the 18d. places, though I strained hard to go in then when I did: so much the vanity and prodigality of the age is to be observed in this particular. Thence I to White Hall, and there walked up and down the house a while, and do hear nothing of any thing done further in this business of the change of Privy-counsellors: only I hear that Sir G. Savile,[1] one of the Parliament Committee of nine for examining the Accounts, is by the King made a Lord, the Lord Halifax; which, I believe, will displease the Parliament. By and by I met with Mr Brisband; and having it in my mind this Christmas to do (what I never can remember that I did) go to see the gaming at the groome-porter's (I having in my coming from the playhouse stepped into the two Temple-halls, and there saw the dirty prentices and idle people playing; wherein I was mistaken, in thinking to have seen gentlemen of quality playing there), he did lead me thither; where, after staying an hour, they began to play, at about eight at night. And to see the formality of the groome-porter, who is their judge of all disputes in play and all quarrels that may arise

1 Of Rufford, co. Notts, Bart; created Lord Savile of Eland, and Viscount Halifax, 1668, Earl of Halifax, 1679, and Marquis of Halifax, 1682. Died 1695.

therein, and how his under-officers are there to observe true play at each table, and to give new dice, is a consideration I never could have thought had been in the world, had I not now seen it. And so I having enough for once, refusing to venture, though Brisband pressed me hard, went away.

2nd. Attended the King and the Duke of York in the Duke of York's lodgings, with the rest of the officers and many of the commanders of the fleet, and some of our master shipwrights, to discourse the business of having the topmasts of ships made to lower abaft of the mainmast; a business I understand not, and so can give no good account; but I do see that by how much greater the Council and the number of counsellors is, the more confused the issue is of their councils; so that little was said to the purpose regularly, and but little use was made of it, they coming to a very broken conclusion upon it, to make trial in a ship or two. From this they fell to other talk about the fleet's fighting this late war, and how the King's ships have been shattered; though the King said that the world would not have it that above ten or twenty ships in any fight did do any service, and that this hath been told so to him himself by ignorant people. The Prince, who was there, was mightily surprised at it, and seemed troubled; but the King told him that it was only discourse of the world. But Mr Wren whispered me in the eare, and said that the Duke of Albemarle had put it into his Narrative for the House, that not above twenty-five ships fought in the engagement wherein he was, but that he was advised to leave it out; but this he did write from sea, I am sure, or words to that effect: and did displease many commanders, among others Captain Batts, who the Duke of York said was a very stout man, all the world knew; and that another was brought into his ship that had been turned out of his place when he was a boatswain, not long before, for being a drunkard. This the Prince[2] took notice of, and would have been angry, I think, but they let their discourse fall: but the Duke of York was earnest in it. And the Prince said to me, standing by me, 'If they will turn out every man that will be drunk, they must turn out all the commanders in the fleet. What is the matter if he be drunk, so when he comes to fight he do his work? At least, let him be punished for his drunkenness, and

2 Rupert.

not put out of his command presently.' This he spoke very much concerned for this idle fellow, one Greene. After this the King began to tell stories of the cowardize of the Spaniards in Flanders, when he was there, at the siege of Mardike and Dunkirke; which was very pretty, though he tells them but meanly. To Westminster Hall, and there staid a little: and then home, and by the way did find with difficulty the *Life of Sir Philip Sidney*. And the bookseller told me that he had sold four within this week or two, which is more than ever he sold in all his life of them; and he could not imagine what should be the reason of it: but I suppose it is from the same reason of people's observing of this part therein, touching his prophecying our present condition here in England in relation to the Dutch, which is very remarkable. It is generally believed that France is endeavouring a firmer league with us than the former, in order to his going on with his business against Spain the next year; which I am, and so every body else is, I think, very glad of, for all our fear is of his invading us. This day at White Hall I overheard Sir W. Coventry propose to the King his ordering of some particular thing in the Wardrobe, which was of no great value; but yet, as much as it was, it was of profit to the King and saving to his purse. The King answered to it with great indifferency, as a thing that it was no great matter whether it was done or no. Sir W. Coventry answered; 'I see your Majesty do not remember the old English proverb, "He that will not stoop for a pin, will never be worth a pound." ' And so they parted, the King bidding him do as he would; which, methought, was an answer not like a King that did intend ever to do well.

4th. It seems worth remembering that this day I did hear my Lord Anglesy at the table, speaking touching this new Act for Accounts, say that the House of Lords did pass it because it was a senseless, impracticable, ineffectual, and foolish Act; and that my Lord Ashly having shown that it was so to the House of Lords, the Duke of Buckingham did stand up and told the Lords that they were beholden to my Lord Ashly, that having first commended them for a most grave and honourable assembly, he thought it fit for the House to pass this Act for Accounts because it was a foolish and simple Act; and it seems it was passed with but a few in the House, when it was intended to have met in a grand Committee upon it. And it seems that in itself it is not to be practised till after this session of Parliament, by the very words of the Act, which nobody regarded, and therefore cannot come in force yet, unless the next meeting they do make a new Act for the bringing it into force sooner; which is a strange omission. But I perceive my Lord Anglesy do make a mere laughing-stock of this Act, as a thing that can do nothing considerable, for all its great noise.

5th. The business of putting out of some of the Privy-council is over, the King being at last advised to forbear it; for whereas he did design it to make room for some of the House of Commons that are against him, thereby to gratify them, it is believed that it will but so much the more fret the rest that are not provided for, and raise a new stock of enemies by them that are displeased; and it goes for a pretty saying of my Lord Anglesy's up and down the Court, that he should lately say to one of the great promoters of this putting him and others out of the Council, 'Well, and what are we to look for when we are outed? Will all things be set right in the nation?' The other said that he did believe that many things would be mended; 'But,' says my Lord, 'will you and the rest of you be contented to be hanged if you do not redeem all our misfortunes and set all right, if the power be put into your hands?' The other answered, No, he would not undertake that. 'Why then,' says my Lord, 'I and the rest of us that you are labouring to put out will be contented to be hanged if we do not recover all that is past, if the King will put the power into our hands and adhere wholly to our advice.'

7th. To the Nursery; but the house did not act to-day; and so I to the other two playhouses into the pit to gaze up and down, and there did by this means for nothing see an act in *The Schoole of Compliments* at the Duke of York's house, and *Henry the Fourth* at the King's house; but not liking either of the plays, I took my coach again, and home.

8th. To White Hall, and by coach home, taking up Mr Prin at the Court gate (it raining), and setting him down at the Temple; and by the way did ask him about the manner of holding of Parliaments, and whether the number of Knights and Burgesses were always the same? And he says that the latter were not; but that, for aught he can find, they were sent up at the discretion at first of the Sheriffes, to whom the writs are sent to send up generally the Burgesses and citizens of their county; and he do find that heretofore the Parliament-men being paid by the country, several burroughs have complained of the Sheriffes putting them to the charge of sending up Burgesses; which is a very extraordinary thing to me, that knew not this, but thought that the number had been known, and always the same.

10th. To White Hall; and there to wait on the Duke of York with the rest of my brethren, which we did a little in the King's green-room while the King was in Council: and in this room we found my Lord Bristoll walking alone; which wondering at while the Council was sitting, I was answered that as being a Catholique he could not be of the Council; which I did not consider before. This day I received a letter from my father and another from my cosen Roger Pepys, who have had a view of Jackson's evidences of his estate, and do mightily like of the man and his condition and estate, and do advise me to accept of the match for my sister, and to finish it soon as I can; and he do it so as I confess I am contented to have it done, and so give her her portion.

11th. To the King's house, to see *The Wildgoose Chase*.[3] In this play I met with nothing extraordinary at all, but very dull inventions and designs. Knipp came and sat by us, and her talk pleased me a little, she tells me how Miss Davis is for certain going away from the Duke's house, the King being in love with her; and a house is taken for her, and furnishing; and she hath a ring given her already worth £600: that the King did send several times for Nelly, and she was with him; and I am sorry for it, and can hope for no good to the State from having a Prince so devoted to his pleasure. She told me also of a play shortly coming upon the stage of Sir Charles Sedley's, which, she thinks, will be called *The Wandering Ladys*, a comedy that she thinks will be most pleasant; and also another play, called *The Duke of Lorane*: besides *Catiline*, which she thinks, for want of the clothes which the King promised them, will not be acted for a good while.

14th. To my bookseller, Martin, and there did receive my book I expected of China, a most excellent book with rare cuts; and there fell into discourse with him about the burning of Paul's when the City was burned, his house being in the church-yard. And he tells me that it took fire first upon the end of a board that among others was laid upon the roof instead of lead, the lead being broke off, and

3 By Beaumont and Fletcher.

thence down lower and lower: but that the burning of the goods under St Fayth's arose from the goods taking fire in the church-yard, and so got into St Fayth's church; and that they first took fire from the Draper's side, by some timber of the houses that were burned falling into the church. He says that one warehouse of books was saved under Paul's; and there were several dogs found burned among the goods in the church-yard, and but one man, which was an old man, that said he would go and save a blanket which he had in the church, and being weak the fire overcame him. He says that most of the booksellers do design to fall a-building again the next year; but that the Bishop of London do use them most basely, worse than any other landlords, and says he will be paid to this day the rent, or else he will not come to treat with them for the time to come; and will not, on that condition either, promise them in any thing how he will use them; and the Parliament sitting, he claims his privilege, and will not be cited before the Lord Chief Justice, as others are there, to be forced to a fair dealing. Thence by coach to Mrs Pierce's, where my wife is; and there they fell to discourse of the last night's work at Court, where the ladies and Duke of Monmouth and others acted *The Indian Emperour*; wherein they told me these things most remarkable: That not any woman but the Duchesse of Monmouth and Mrs Cornwallis did any thing but like fools and stocks, but that these two did do most extraordinary well: that not any man did any thing well but Captain Olrigran,[4] who spoke and did well, but above all things did dance most incomparably. That she did sit near the players of the Duke's house; among the rest Miss Davis, who is the most impertinent slut, she says, in the world; and the more, now the King do show her countenance; and is reckoned his mistress, even to the scorne of the whole world; the King gazing on her, and my Lady Castlemaine being melancholy and out of humour, all the play not smiling once. The King, it seems, hath given her a ring of £700 which she shows to every body, and owns that the King did give it her; and he hath furnished a house in Suffolke-street most richly for her; which is a most infinite shame. It seems she is a bastard of Colonell Howard, my Lord Berkshire, and that he hath got her for the King: but Pierce says that she is a most homely jade as ever she saw, though she dances beyond any thing in the world. She tells me

4 *Sic.*

that the Duchesse of Richmond do not yet come to the Court, nor hath seen the King, nor will not, nor do he own his desire of seeing her; but hath used means to get her to Court, but they do not take.

15th. This afternoon my Lord Anglesy tells us that it is voted in Council to have a fleet of 50 ships out: but it is only a disguise for the Parliament to get some money by; but it will not take, I believe.

16th. Lord Anglesy tells us again that a fleet is to be set out; and that it is generally, he hears, said that it is but a Spanish rhodomontado; and that he saying so just now to the Duke of Albemarle, who came to town last night (after the thing was ordered,) he told him a story of two seamen: one wished all the guns of the ship were his, and that they were silver; and says the other, 'You are a fool, for if you can have it for wishing, why do you not wish them gold?' 'So,' says he, 'if a rhodomontado will do any good, why do you not say 100 ships?' And it is true; for the Dutch and French are said to make such preparations as 50 sail will do no good. Mightily pleased with Mr Gibson's talking; he telling me so many good stories relating to the war and practices of commanders which I will find a time to recollect; and he will be an admirable help to my writing a history of the Navy, if ever I do.

17th. Much discourse of the duell yesterday between the Duke of Buckingham, Holmes, and one Jenkins, on one side, and my Lord of Shrewsbury,[5] Sir John Talbot,[6] and one Bernard Howard,[7] on the other side: and all about my Lady Shrewsbury,[8] who is at this time, and hath for a great while been, a mistress to the Duke of Buckingham. And so her husband challenged him, and they met yesterday in a close near Barne-Elmes and there fought: and my Lord Shrewsbury is run through the body, from the right breast through the shoulder; and Sir John Talbot all along up one of his armes; and Jenkins killed upon the place, and the rest all in a little measure

5 Francis, eleventh Earl of Shrewsbury, died of his wounds March 16th following.
6 Sir John Talbot, a Gentleman of the Privy Chamber, MP for Knaresborough.
7 Bernard Howard, eighth son of Henry Frederic Earl of Arundel.
8 Anna Maria, daughter of Robert Earl of Cardigan, the Duke of Buckingham's mistress, and said to have held his horse, in the habit of a page, while he was fighting with her husband. She married, secondly, George Rodney Bridges, son of Sir Thomas Bridges of Keynsham, Somerset, and died April 20, 1702.

wounded. This will make the world think that the King hath good counsellors about him, when the Duke of Buckingham, the greatest man about him, is a fellow of no more sobriety than to fight about a mistress. And this may prove a very bad accident to the Duke of Buckingham, but that my Lady Castlemaine do rule all at this time as much as ever she did, and she will, it is believed, keep all matters well with the Duke of Buckingham: though this is a time that the King will be very backward, I suppose, to appear in such a business. And it is pretty to hear how the King had some notice of this challenge a week or two ago, and did give it to my Lord Generall to confine the Duke, or take security that he should not do any such thing as fight: and the Generall trusted to the King that he, sending for him, would do it; and the King trusted to the Generall. And it is said that my Lord Shrewsbury's case is to be feared, that he may die too; and that may make it much worse for the Duke of Buckingham: and I shall not be much sorry for it, that we may have some sober man come in his room to assist in the Government. Creed tells me of Mr Harry Howard's giving the Royall Society a piece of ground next to his house to build a college on: which is a most generous act. And he tells me he is a very fine person, and understands and speaks well; and no rigid Papist neither, but one that would not have a Protestant servant leave his religion, which he was going to do, thinking to recommend himself to his master by it; saying, that he had rather have an honest Protestant than a knavish Catholique. I was not called in to the Council; and therefore home, first informing myself that my Lord Hinchingbroke hath been married this week to my Lord Burlington's daughter: so that that great business is over; and I am mighty glad of it, though I am not satisfied that I have not a favour sent me.

19th. Lord Shrewsbury is likely to do well.

20th. To Drumbleby's the pipe-maker, there to advise about the making of a flageolet to go low and soft; and he do show me a way which do do, and also a fashion of having two pipes of the same note fastened together, so as I can play on one, and then echo it upon the other; which is mighty pretty. So to my Lord Crewe's to dinner; where we hear all the good news of our making a league now with Holland against the French Power coming over them or us: which is the first good act that hath been done a great while, and done secretly and with great seeming wisdom; and is certainly good for us at this time, while we are in no condition to resist the French, if he should come over hither: and then a little time of peace will give us time to lay up something, which these Commissioners of the Treasury are doing; and the world do begin to see that they will do the King's work for him, if he will let them. My Lord told a good story of Mr Newman, the Minister in New England, who wrote the Concordance, of his foretelling his death and preaching a funeral sermon, and did at last bid the angels do their office, and died. It seems there is great presumption that there will be a Toleration granted: so that the Presbyterians do hold up their heads; but they will hardly trust the King or the Parliament what to yield them, though most of the sober party be for some kind of allowance to be given them. Lord Gerard is likely to meet with ill, the next sitting of Parliament, about Carr being set in the pillory; and I am glad of it. And it is mighty acceptable to the world to hear, that among other reductions the King do reduce his Guards: which do please mightily.

21st. Comes news from Kate Joyce that, if I would see her husband alive, I must come presently. So I to him, and find his breath rattled in the throate; and they did lay pigeons to his feet, and all despair of him. It seems on Thursday last he went sober and quiet to Islington, and behind one of the inns (the White Lion) did fling himself into a pond: was spied by a poor woman, and got out by some people, and set on his head and got to life: and so his wife and friends sent for. He confessed his doing the thing, being led by the Devil; and do declare his reason to be his trouble in having forgot to serve God as he ought since he came to his new employment:[9] and I believe that, and the sense of his great loss by the fire, did bring him to it; for he grew sick, and worse and worse to this day. The friends that were there being now in fear that the goods and estate would be seized on, though he lived all this while, because of his endeavouring to drown himself, my cosen did endeavour to remove what she could of plate out of the house, and desired me to take my flagons; which I did, but in great fear all the way of being seized; though there was no reason for it, he not being dead. So with Sir D. Gauden to Guild Hall to advise with the Towne-Clerke about the practice of the City and nation in this

9 He kept a tavern.

case: and he thinks it cannot be found selfe-murder; but if it be, it will fall, all the estate, to the King. So I to my cosen's again; where I no sooner come but find that he was departed. So at their entreaty I presently to White Hall, and there find Sir W. Coventry; and he carried me to the King, the Duke of York being with him, and there told my story which I had told him; and the King, without more ado, granted that, if it was found, the estate should be to the widow and children: which indeed was a very great courtesy, for people are looking out for the estate.

22nd. At noon with my Lord Brouncker to Sir D. Gauden's, at the Victualling-office, to dinner, where I have not dined since he was Sheriffe. He expected us: and a good dinner, and much good company; and a fine house, and especially two rooms very fine, he hath built there. His lady a good lady; but my Lord led himself and me to a great absurdity in kissing all the ladies, but the finest of all the company, leaving her out I know not how; and I was loath to do it, since he omitted it. Here little Chaplin dined, who is like to be Sheriffe the next year; and a pretty humoured little man he is: and Mr Talents the younger, of Magdalene College, Chaplain to the Sheriffe; which I was glad to see, though not much acquainted with him.

23rd. At the office all the morning; and at noon find the Bishop of Lincolne[10] come to dine with us; and after him comes Mr Brisband. And there mighty good company. But the Bishop a very extraordinary good-natured man, and one that is mightily pleased, as well as I am, that I live so near Bugden,[11] the seat of his bishopricke, where he is like to reside; and indeed I am glad of it. In discourse we think ourselves safe for this year, by this league with Holland; which pleases every body, and, they say, vexes France; insomuch that De l'Estrade, the French Embassador in Holland, when he heard it, told the States that he would have them not forget that his master is in the head of 100,000 men, and is but 28 years old; which was a great speech. The Bishop tells me he thinks that the great business of Toleration will not, notwithstanding this talk, be carried this Parliament; nor for the King's taking away the Deans' and Chapters' lands to supply his wants, they signifying little to him if he had them for his present service.

10 Dr William Fuller, translated from Limerick 1667.
11 At Brampton.

27th. Mr Povy do tell me how he is like to lose his £400 a-year pension of the Duke of York, which he took in consideration of his place that was taken from him. He tells me the Duchesse is a devil against him, and do now come like Queene Elizabeth, and sits with the Duke of York's Council, and sees what they do; and she crosses out this man's wages and prices as she sees fit for saving money: but yet, he tells me, she reserves £5000 a-year for her own spending; and my Lady Peterborough by and by tells me that the Duchesse do lay up mightily jewells.

28th. To White Hall; and by and by the Duke of York comes, and we had a little meeting, Anglesy, W. Pen, and I there, and none else: and, among other things, did discourse of the want of discipline in the fleet; which the Duke of York confessed, and yet said that he while he was there did keep it in a good measure, but that it was now lost when he was absent; but he will endeavour to have it again. That he did tell the Prince and Duke of Albemarle they would lose all order by making such and such men commanders, which they would because they were stout men: he told them it was a reproach to the nation, as if there were no sober men among us, that were stout, to be had. That they did put out some men for cowards that the Duke of York had put in, but little before, for stout men; and would now, were he to go to sea again, entertain them in his own division to choose: and did put in an idle fellow, Greene, who was hardly thought fit for a boatswain by him; they did put him from being a lieutenant to a captain's place of a second-rate ship; as idle a drunken fellow, he said, as any was in the fleet. That he will now desire the King to let him be what he is, that is, Admirall; and he will put in none but those that he hath great reason to think well of: and particularly says that though he likes Colonel Legg well, yet his son that was, he knows not how, made a captain after he had been but one voyage at sea, he should go to sea another apprenticeship before ever he gives him a command. We did tell him of the many defects and disorders among the captains, and I prayed we might do it in writing to him; which he liked; and I am glad of an opportunity of doing it. My wife this day hears from her father and mother: they are in France, at Paris; he, poor good man! thankful for my small charities to him.

29th. To Sir W. Coventry. He tells me he hath no friends in the whole Court but my Lord Keeper and Sir John Duncomb. They have reduced the charges of Ireland about £70,000 a-year, and thereby cut off good profits from my Lord Lieutenant; which will make a new enemy, but he cares not. He tells me that Townsend, of the Wardrobe, is the veriest knave and bufflehead that ever he saw.

30th. I first heard that my cosen Pepys, of Salisbury Court, was Marshall to my Lord Coke when he was Lord Chief Justice; which beginning of his I did not know to be so low; but so it was, it seems.

31st. Up; and by coach, with W. Griffin with me, and our Contract-books, to Durham Yard, to the Commissioners for Accounts; the first time I ever was there; and staid awhile before I was admitted to them. I did observe a great many people attending about complaints of seamen concerning tickets, and among others Mr Carcasse, and Mr Martin my purser. And I observe a fellow, one Collins, is there, who is employed by these Commissioners particularly to hold an office in Bishopsgate-street, or somewhere thereabouts, to receive complaints of all people about tickets: and I believe he will have work enough. Presently I was called in; where I found the whole number of Commissioners, and was there received with great respect and kindness; and did give them great satisfaction, making it my endeavour to inform them what it was they were to expect from me, and what was the duty of other people; this being my only way to preserve myself, after all my pains and trouble. They did ask many questions, and demanded other books of me, which I did give them very ready and acceptable answers to; and, upon the whole, I do observe they do go about their business like men resolved to go through with it, and in a very good method, like men of understanding. They have Mr Jessop their secretary: and it is pretty to see that they are fain to find out an old-fashioned man of Cromwell's to do their business for them, as well as the Parliament to pitch upon such for the most part in the lowest of people that were brought into the House for Commissioners. I went away giving and receiving great satisfaction: and so to White Hall, to the Commissioners of the Treasury; where waiting some time, I there met with Colonell Birch: and he and I fell into discourse; and I did give him thanks for his kindness to me in the Parliament-house, both before my face and behind my back. He told me that he knew me to be a man of the old way of taking pains, and did always endeavour to do me right, and prevent any thing that was moved that might tend to my injury;

which I was obliged to him for, and thanked him. Thence to talk of other things, and the want of money: and he told me of the general want of money in the country; that land sold for nothing, and the many pennyworths he knows of lands and houses upon them, with good titles in his country, at 16 years' purchase: 'And,' says he, 'though I am in debt, yet I have a mind to one thing, and that is a Bishop's lease': but said, 'I will yet choose such a lease before any other, because I know they cannot stand, and then it will fall into the King's hands, and I in possession shall have an advantage by it.' Says he, 'I know they must fall, and they are now near it, taking all the ways they can to undo themselves, and showing us the way': and thereupon told me a story of the present quarrel between the Bishop[12] and Dean[13] of Coventry and Lichfield; the former of whom did excommunicate the latter, and caused his excommunication to be read in the church while he was there; and after it was read, the Dean made the service be gone through with, though himself an excommunicate was present (which is contrary to the Canon), and said he would justify the quire therein against the Bishop: and so they are at law in the Arches about it; which is a very pretty story. He tells me that the King is for Toleration, though the Bishops be against it; and that he do not doubt but it will be carried in Parliament: but that he fears some will stand for the tolerating of Papists with the rest; and that he knows not what to say, but rather thinks that the sober party will be without it rather than have it upon those terms; and I do believe so. It is observed, and is true, in the late fire of London, that the fire burned just as many parish-churches as there were hours from the beginning to the end of the fire; and next, that there were just as many churches left standing as there were taverns left standing in the rest of the City that was not burned, being, I think, thirteen in all of each: which is pretty to observe.

February 1st. To the office till past two o'clock; where at the Board some high words passed between Sir W. Pen and I, begun by me, and yielded to by him, I being in the right in finding fault with him for his neglect of duty. Home, my head mighty full of business now on my hands: viz. of finishing my Tangier Accounts; of auditing my last year's Accounts; of preparing answers to the Commissioners of

12 John Hacket.
13 Henry Greswold, AM.

Accounts; of drawing up several important letters to the Duke of York and the Commissioners of the Treasury; the marrying of my sister; the building of a coach and stables against summer, and the setting many things in the office right: and the drawing up a new form of Contract with the Victualler of the Navy, and several other things, which pains, however, will go through with.

5th. Mr Moore mightily commends my Lord Hinchingbroke's match and Lady, though he buys her £10,000 dear, by the jointure and settlement his father makes her; and says that the Duke of York and Duchesse of York did come to see them in bed together on their wedding-night, and how my Lord had fifty pieces of gold taken out of his pocket that night after he was in bed. He tells me that an Act of Comprehension is likely to pass this Parliament for admitting of all persuasions in religion to the public observation of their particular worship, but in certain places, and the persons therein concerned to be listed of this or that church; which, it is thought, will do them more hurt than good, and make them not own their persuasion. He tells me that there is a pardon passed to the Duke of Buckingham, my Lord of Shrewsbury and the rest, for the late duell and murder; which he thinks a worse fault than any ill use my late Lord Chancellor ever put the great Seal to, and will be so thought by the Parliament, for them to be pardoned without bringing them to any trial: and that my Lord Privy-seale therefore would not have it pass his hand, but made it go by immediate warrant; or at least they knew that he would not pass it, and so did direct it to go by immediate warrant, that it might not come to him. He tells me what a character my Lord Sandwich hath sent over of Mr Godolphin;[14] as the worthiest man, and such a friend to him as he may be trusted in any thing relating to him in the world; as one whom, he says, he hath infallible assurances that he will remaine his friend: which is very high, but indeed they say the gentleman is a fine man.

6th. Sir H. Cholmly tells me how the Parliament (which is to meet again to-day) are likely to fall heavy on the business of the Duke of Buckingham's pardon; and I shall be glad of it: and that the King hath put out of the Court the two Hides, my Lord Chancellor's two sons,

14 Sidney Godolphin, Groom of the Bedchamber to Charles II; made a Commissioner of the Treasury 1678/79, and in 1684 created Baron Godolphin.

and also the Bishops of Rochester[15] and Winchester,[16] the latter of whom should have preached before him yesterday, being Ash-Wednesday, and had his sermon ready, but was put by; which is great news. My wife being gone before, I to the Duke of York's playhouse; where a new play of Etheridge's, called *She would if she could*; and though I was there by two o'clock, there was 1000 people put back that could not have room in the pit; and I at last, because my wife was there, made shift to get into the 18d. box, and there saw: but, Lord! how full was the house, and how silly the play, there being nothing in the world good in it, and few people pleased in it. The King was there; but I sat mightily behind, and could see but little, and hear not all. The play being done, I into the pit to look for my wife, it being dark and raining; but could not find her, and so staid going between the two doors and through the pit an hour and half, I think, after the play was done; the people staying there till the rain was over, and to talk one with another. And among the rest here was the Duke of Buckingham to-day openly sat in the pit; and there I found him with my Lord Buckhurst, and Sedley, and Etheridge the poet; the last of whom I did hear mightily find fault with the actors, that they were out of humour and had not their parts perfect, and that Harris did do nothing, nor could so much as sing a ketch in it; and so was mightily concerned: while all the rest did through the whole pit blame the play as a silly, dull thing though there was something very roguish and witty; but the design of the play and end mighty insipid. At last I did find my wife.

7th. Met my cosen Roger Pepys, (the Parliament meeting yesterday and adjourned to Monday next;) and here he tells me that Mr Jackson my sister's servant is come to town, and hath this day suffered a recovery on his estate in order to the making her a settlement. There is a great triall between my Lord Gerard and Carr to-day, who is indicted for his life at the King's Bench for running from his colours; but all do say that my Lord Gerard, though he designs the ruin of this man, will not get any thing by it. Met my cosen Roger again, and Mr Jackson, who is a plain young man, handsome enough for her,[17] one of no education nor discourse, but of few words, and one altogether

15 John Dolben.
16 George Morley.
17 Paulina Pepys.

that, I think, will please me well enough. My cosen had got me to give the odd sixth £100 presently, which I intended to keep to the birth of the first child: and let it go – I shall be eased of the care. So there parted, my mind pretty well satisfied with this plain fellow for my sister; though I shall, I see, have no pleasure nor content in him, as if he had been a man of reading and parts, like Cumberland.

8th. The great talk is of Carr's coming off in all his trials, to the disgrace of my Lord Gerard to that degree, and the ripping up of so many notorious rogueries and cheats of my Lord's, that my Lord, it is thought, will be ruined: and above all do show the madness of the House of Commons, who rejected the petition of this poor man by a combination of a few in the House; and, much more, the base proceedings (just the epitome of all our publick managements in this age) of the House of Lords, that ordered him to stand in the pillory for those very things, without hearing and examining what he hath now, by the seeking of my Lord Gerard himself, cleared himself of in open Court, to the gaining himself the pity of all the world, and shame for ever to my Lord Gerard.

10th. Made a visit to Mr Godolphin at his chamber; and I do find him a very pretty and able person, a man of very fine parts, and of infinite zeal to my Lord Sandwich; and one that says, he is (he believes) as wise and able a person as any prince in the world hath. He tells me that he meets with unmannerly usage by Sir Robert Southwell,[18] in Portugall, who would sign with him in his negociations there, being a forward young man; but that my Lord mastered him in that point, it being ruled for my Lord here at a hearing of a Committee of the Council. He says that if my Lord can compass a peace between Spain and Portugall, and hath the doing of it and the honour himself, it will be a thing of more honour than ever any man had, and of as much advantage. Thence to Westminster Hall, where the Hall mighty full: and, among other things, the House begins to sit to-day, and the King came. But before the King's coming the House of Commons met; and upon information given them of a Bill intended to be brought in, as common report said, for Comprehension,

18 He was knighted and sent as Envoy Extraordinary to Portugal 1665, and with the same rank to Brussels in 1671. He became afterwards Clerk to the Privy Council, and was five times elected President of the Royal Society. Died 1702, aged 60.

they did mightily and generally inveigh against it, and did vote that the King should be desired by the House, and the message delivered by the Privy-counsellors of the House, that the laws against breakers of the Act for Uniformity should be put in execution: and it was moved in the House that if any people had a mind to bring any new laws into the House about religion, they might come as a proposer of new laws did in Athens, with ropes about their necks. By and by the King comes to the Lords' House, and there tells them of his league with Holland, and the necessity of a fleet, and his debts; and, therefore, want of money; and his desire that they would think of some way to bring in all his Protestant subjects to a right understanding and peace one with another; meaning the Bill of Comprehension. The Commons coming to their House, it was moved that the vote passed this morning might be suspended, because of the King's Speech, till the House was full and called over, two days hence: but it was denied, so furious they are against this Bill; and thereby a great blow either given to the King or Presbyters, or, which is the rather of the two, to the House itself, by denying a thing desired by the King, and so much desired by much the greater part of the nation. Whatever the consequence be, if the King be a man of any stomach and heat, all do believe that he will resent this vote. Read over and agreed upon the deed of settlement to our minds: my sister to have £600 presently, and she to be joyntured in £60 per annum; wherein I am very well satisfied.

11th. To Pemberton's[19] chamber. It was pretty here to see the heaps of money upon this lawyer's table; and more, to see how he had not since last night spent any time upon our business, but begun with telling us that we were not at all concerned in that Act; which was a total mistake, by his not having read over the Act at all.

12th. My cosen Roger told me the pleasant passage of a fellow's bringing a bag of letters to-day into the lobby of the House, where he left them, and withdrew himself without observation. The bag being opened, the letters were found all of one size, and directed with one hand: a letter to most of the Members of the House. The House was acquainted with it, and voted they should be brought in and one

19 Francis Pemberton, afterwards knighted, and made Lord Chief Justice of the King's Bench 1679.

opened by the Speaker; wherein if he found any thing unfit to communicate, to propose a Committee to be chosen for it. The Speaker opening one, found it only a case with a libell in it, printed: a satire most sober and bitter as ever I read; and every letter was the same. So the House fell a-scrambling for them like boys; and my cosen Roger had one directed to him, which he lent me to read.

13th. Mr Brisband tells me in discourse that Tom Killigrew hath a fee out of the Wardrobe for cap and bells, under the title of the King's Foole or Jester; and may revile or jeere any body, the greatest person, without offence, by the privilege of his place. This morning Sir G. Carteret come to the office to see and talk with me: and he assures me that to this day the King is the most kind man to my Lord Sandwich in the whole world; that he himself do not now mind any publick business, but suffers things to go on at Court as they will, he seeing all likely to come to ruin: that this morning the Duke of York sent to him to come to make up one of a Committee of the Council for Navy Affairs; upon which, when he came, he told the Duke of York that he was none of them: which shows how things are now-a-days ordered, that there should be a Committee for the Navy, and the Lord Admirall knows not the persons of it; and that Sir G. Carteret and my Lord Anglesy should be left out of it, and men wholly improper put into it. I do hear of all hands that there is great difference at this day between my Lord Arlington and Sir W. Coventry; which I am sorry for.

14th. I to my office to perfect my Narrative about prize-goods; and did carry it to the Commissioners of Accounts, who did receive it with great kindness, and express great value of and respect to me: and my heart is at rest that it is lodged there in so full truth and plainness, though it may hereafter prove some loss to me. But here I do see they are entered into many enquiries about prizes, by the great attendance of commanders and others before them; which is a work I am not sorry for. Thence I away, with my head busy but my heart at pretty good ease, to visit Colonell Thomson, one of the Committee of Accounts; who among the rest is mighty kind to me, and is likely to mind our business more than any; and I would be glad to have a good understanding with him. Thence after dinner to White Hall to attend the Duke of York; where I did let him know too the troublesome life we lead, and particularly myself, by being obliged to such attendances every day as I am, on one Committee or other. And I do find the Duke of York himself troubled, and willing not to be troubled with occasions of having his name used among the Parliament; though he himself do declare that he did give directions to Lord Brouncker to discharge the men at Chatham by ticket, and will own it if the House call for it, but not else. Thence I attended the King and Council, and some of the rest of us, in a business to be heard about the value of a ship of one Dorrington's. And it was pretty to observe how Sir W. Pen, making use of this argument against the validity of an oath, against the King, being made by the master's mate of the ship, who was but a fellow of about 23 years of age; the master of the ship, against whom we pleaded, did say that he did think himself at that age capable of being master's mate of any ship; and do know that he, Sir W. Pen, was so himself, and in no better degree at that age himself: which word did strike Sir W. Pen mad, and made him open his mouth no more; and I saw the King and Duke of York wink at one another at it. This done, we into the Gallery; and there I walked with several people, and among others my Lord Brouncker; who I do find under much trouble still about the business of the tickets, his very case being brought in, as is said, this day in the Report of the Miscarriages. And he seems to lay much of it on me, which I did clear and satisfy him in; and would be glad with all my heart to serve him in, and have done it more than he hath done for himself, he not deserving the least blame, but commendations, for this. I met with my cosen Roger Pepys and Creed; and from them understand that the Report was read to-day of the Miscarriages, wherein my Lord Sandwich is named about the business I mentioned this morning; but I will be at rest, for it can do him no hurt. Our business of tickets is soundly up, and many others; so they went over them again, and spent all the morning on the first, which is the dividing of the fleet; wherein hot work was, and that among great men, Privy-counsellors, and, they say, Sir W. Coventry; but I do not much fear it, but do hope that it will show a little of the Duke of Albemarle and the Prince to have been advisers in it: but whereas they ordered that the King's Speech should be considered to-day, they took no notice of it at all, but are really come to despise the King in all possible ways of showing it. And it was the other day a strange saying, as I am told by my cosen Roger Pepys, in the House, when it was moved that the King's Speech should be considered, that though the first part of the Speech, meaning the league that is there talked of, be the only good publick thing that hath been done since the King come into England, yet it might bear with being put off to consider till Friday next, which was this day. Secretary Morrice did this day in the House, when they talked of intelligence, say that he was allowed but £700 a-year for intelligence; whereas in Cromwell's time he did allow £70,000 a-year for it; and was confirmed therein by Colonell Birch, who said that thereby Cromwell carried the secrets of all the princes of Europe at his girdle. The House is in a most broken condition; nobody adhering to any thing, but reviling and finding fault: and now quite mad at the Undertakers, as they are commonly called, Littleton, Lord Vaughan, Sir R. Howard, and others that are brought over to the Court, and did undertake to get the King money: but they despise and will not hear them in the House; and the Court do as much, seeing that they cannot be useful to them, as was expected. In short, it is plain that the King will never be able to do any thing with this Parliament; and that the only likely way to do better (for it cannot do worse) is to break this and call another Parliament; and some do think that it is intended. I was told to-night that my Lady Castlemaine is so great a gamester as to have won £15,000 in one night, and lost £25,000 in another night at play, and hath played £1000 and £1500 at a cast.

16th. Mr Hollier[20] dined with my wife and me. Much discourse about the bad state of the Church, and how the Clergy are come to be men of no worth in the world; and, as the world do now generally discourse, they must be reformed: and I believe the Hierarchy will in a little time be shaken, whether they will or no; the King being offended with them and set upon it, as I hear.

17th. Great high words in the House on Saturday last upon the first part of the Committee's Report about the dividing of the fleet; wherein some would have the counsels of the King to be declared, and the reasons of them, and who did give them; where Sir W. Coventry laid open to them the consequences of doing that, that the King would never have any honest and wise men ever to be of his Council. They did here in the House talk boldly of the King's bad Counsellors, and how they must all be turned out, and many others, and better brought in: and the proceedings of the Long-Parliament in

20 He was a surgeon.

the beginning of the war were called to memory; and the King's bad intelligence was mentioned, wherein they were bitter against my Lord Arlington, saying, among other things, that whatever Morrice's was, who declared he had but £750 a-year allowed him for intelligence, the King paid too dear for my Lord Arlington's in giving him £10,000 and a Barony for it. Sir W. Coventry did here come to his defence in the business of the letter that was sent to call back Prince Rupert after he was divided from the fleet, wherein great delay was objected; but he did show that he sent it at one in the morning, when the Duke of York did give him the instructions after supper that night, and did clear himself well of it; only it was laid as a fault, which I know not how he removes, of not sending it by an express, but by the ordinary post; it coming not to Sir Philip Honiwood's hand at Portsmouth till four in the afternoon that day, being about fifteen or sixteen hours in going. The dividing of the fleet however is, I hear, voted a miscarriage, and the not building a fortification at Sheernesse; and I have reason every hour to expect that they will vote the like of our paying men off by ticket; and what the consequence of that will be, I know not.

18th. Sir W. Coventry and I did look over the list of commanders, and found that we could presently recollect thirty-seven commanders that have been killed in actuall service this war. He tells me that Sir Fr. Hollis is the main man that hath prosecuted him hitherto in the business of dividing the fleet, saying vainly that the want of that letter to the Prince hath given him that that he shall remember it by to his grave, meaning the loss of his arme;[21] when, God knows, he is as idle and insignificant a fellow as ever came into the fleet. I well remember what in mirth he said to me this morning, when upon this discourse he said if ever there was another Dutch war they should not find a Secretary; 'Nor,' said I, 'a Clerk of the Acts, for I see the reward of it; and, thank God, I have enough of my own to buy me a book and a good fiddle, and I have a good wife;' – 'Why,' says he, 'I have enough to buy me a good book, and shall not need a fiddle, because I have never a one of your good wives.' This morning the House is upon a Bill, brought in to-day by Sir Richard Temple, for obliging the King to call Parliaments every three years; or if he fail, for others

21 See note, June 10, 1667.

to be obliged to do it, and to keep him from a power of dissolving any Parliament in less than forty days after their first day of sitting: which is such a Bill as do speak very high proceedings to the lessening of the King; and this they will carry, and whatever else they desire, before they will give any money; and the King must have money, whatever it cost him. I to see Kate Joyce; where I find her and her friends in great ease of mind, the Jury having this day given in their verdict that her husband died of a fever. Some opposition there was, the foreman pressing them to declare the cause of the fever, thinking thereby to obstruct it; but they did adhere to their verdict, and would give no reason: so all trouble is now over, and she safe in her estate.

19th. In the evening to White Hall; where I find Sir W. Coventry a great while with the Duke of York in the King's drawing-room, they two talking together all alone; which did mightily please me. I do hear how La Roche, a French captain, who was once prisoner here, being with his ship at Plymouth, hath played some freakes there, for which his men being beat out of the town, he hath put up a flag of defiance, and also somewhere there about did land with his men and go a mile into the country, and did some prank; which sounds pretty odd to our disgrace, but we are in condition now to bear any thing. But, blessed be God! all the Court is full of good news of my Lord Sandwich's having made a peace between Spain and Portugall; which is mighty great news, and above all to my Lord's honour more than any thing he ever did; and yet I do fear it will not prevail to secure him in Parliament against incivilities there.

20th. The House most of the morning upon the business of not prosecuting the first victory: which they have voted one of the greatest miscarriages of the whole war, though they cannot lay the fault any where yet, because Harman is not come home. Dined, and by one o'clock to the King's house: a new play, *The Duke of Lerma*, of Sir Robert Howard's: where the King and Court was; and Knipp and Nell spoke the prologue most excellently, especially Knipp, who spoke beyond any creature I ever heard. The play designed to reproach our King with his mistresses, that I was troubled for it, and expected it should be interrupted; but it ended all well, which salved all.

21st. The House this day is still as backward for giving any money as ever, and do declare they will first have an account of the disposals of the last Poll-bill, and eleven months' tax. And it is pretty odde that the very first sum mentioned in the account brought in by Sir Robert Long of the disposal of the Poll-bill money is £5000 to my Lord Arlington for intelligence; which was mighty unseasonable, so soon after they had so much cried out against his want of intelligence. The King do also own but £250,000 or thereabouts yet paid on the Poll-bill, and that he hath charged £350,000 upon it. This makes them mad; for that the former Poll-bill, that was so much less in its extent than the last, which took in all sexes and qualities, did come to £350,000. Upon the whole, I perceive they are like to do nothing in this matter to please the King, or relieve the State, be the case never so pressing; and therefore it is thought by a great many that the King cannot be worse if he should dissolve them; but there is nobody dares advise it, nor do he consider any thing himself. My cosen Roger Pepys showed me Granger's written confession, of his being forced by imprisonment, &c. by my Lord Gerard, most barbarously to confess his forging of a deed in behalf of Fitton, in the great case between him and my Lord Gerard; which business is under examination, and is the foulest against my Lord Gerard that ever any thing in the world was, and will, all do believe, ruine him; and I shall be glad of it.

22nd. To the Duke's playhouse, and there saw *Alblemanazar*,[22] an old play, this the second time of acting. It is said to have been the ground of B. Jonson's *Alchymist*; but, saving the ridiculousnesse of Angell's part, which is called Trinkilo, I do not see any thing extraordinary in it, but was indeed weary of it before it was done. The King here; and indeed all of us pretty merry at the mimique tricks of Trinkilo.

23rd. I met with Sir W. Coventry, and he and I walked awhile together in the Matted Gallery; and there he told me all the proceedings yesterday: that the matter is found in general a miscarriage, but no persons named; and so there is no great matter to our prejudice yet, till, if ever, they come to particular persons. He told me Birch was very industrious to do what he could, and did like a friend; but they were resolved to find the thing in general a miscarriage: and says, that when we shall think fit to desire its being heard, as to our

22 *Albulmazar*, a comedy, by Tomkins of Trinity College, Cambridge.

own defence, it will be granted. He tells me how he hath with advantage cleared himself in what concerns himself therein, by his servant Robson; which I am glad of. He tells me that there is a letter sent by conspiracy to some of the House, which he hath seen, about the manner of selling of places; which he do believe he shall be called upon to-morrow for: and thinks himself well prepared to defend himself in it; and then neither he nor his friends for him are afraid of any thing to his prejudice. Thence by coach with Brisband to Sir G. Carteret's, in Lincoln's Inn-fields, and there dined: a good dinner and good company. And after dinner he and I alone, discoursing of my Lord Sandwich's matters; who hath, in the first business before the House, been very kindly used beyond expectation, the matter being laid by till his coming home: and old Sir Vaughan did speak for my Lord; which I am mighty glad of. The business of the prizes is the worst that can be said, and therein I do fear something may lie hard upon him; but against this we must prepare the best we can for his defence. Thence with Sir G. Carteret to White Hall; where finding a meeting of the Committee of the Council for the Navy, his Royal Highness there, and Sir W. Pen, and some of the Brethren of the Trinity House to attend, I did go in with them. And it was to be informed of the practice heretofore, for all foreign nations at enmity one with another to forbear any acts of hostility to one another in the presence of any of the King of England's ships; of which several instances were given: and it is referred to their further enquiry, in order to the giving instructions accordingly to our ships now during the war between Spain and France. Would to God we were in the same condition as heretofore, to challenge and maintain this our dominion! Thence with W. Pen homeward, and quite through to Mile End for a little ayre; the days being now pretty long, but the ways mighty dirty. Going back again, Sir R. Brookes overtook us coming to town; who played the jacke with us all, and is a fellow that I must trust no more, he quoting me for all he hath said in this business of tickets; though I have told him nothing that either is not true, or I afraid to own. But here talking he did discourse in this stile: 'We,' and We all along, 'will not give any money, be the pretence never so great, nay, though the enemy was in the River of Thames again, till we know what is become of the last money given.' And I do believe he do speak the mind of his fellows; and so let him. This evening my wife did with great pleasure show me her stock of jewells, encreased by the ring she hath made lately as my Valentine's gift this year, a Turky stone set with diamonds: and with this, and what she had, she reckons that she hath above £150 worth of jewells of one kind or other; and I am glad of it, for it is fit the wretch should have something to content herself with.

24th. Meeting Dr Gibbons,[23] he and I to see an organ at the Dean of Westminster's lodgings at the Abby, the Bishop of Rochester's;[24] where he lives like a great prelate, his lodgings being very good; though at present under great disgrace at Court, being put by his Clerk of the Closet's place. I saw his lady, of whom the *Terrae Filius* of Oxford was once so merry; and two children, whereof one a very pretty little boy, like him, so fat and black. Here I saw the organ; but it is too big for my house, and the fashion do not please me enough; and therefore I will not have it. To the Nursery, where none of us ever were before; where the house is better and the musique better than we looked for, and the acting not much worse because I expected as bad as could be: and I was not much mistaken, for it was so. I was prettily served this day at the playhouse-door; where, giving six shillings into the fellow's hand for three of us, the fellow by legerdemain did convey one away, and with so much grace faced me down that I did give him but five, that, though I knew the contrary, yet I was overpowered by his so grave and serious demanding the other shilling, that I could not deny him, but was forced by myself to give it him.

26th. To Westminster Hall, where, it being now about six o'clock, I find the House just risen; and met with Sir W. Coventry and the Lieutenant of the Tower, they having sat all day; and with great difficulty have got a vote for giving the King £300,000, not to be raised by any land-tax. The sum is much smaller than I expected, and than the King needs; but is grounded upon Mr Wren's reading our estimates the other day of £270,000 to keep the fleet abroad, wherein we demanded nothing for setting and fitting of them out, which will cost almost £200,000 I do verily believe: and do believe that the King hath no cause to thank Wren for this motion. I home

---

23 Christopher Gibbons, Organist to the King and of Westminster Abbey. He was admitted Doctor of Music at Oxford 1664, and died 1676.
24 John Dolben; afterwards translated to York.

to Sir W. Coventry's lodgings with him and the Lieutenant of the Tower, where also was Sir John Coventry, and Sir John Duncomb, and Sir Job Charleton.[25] And here a great deal of good discourse: and they seem mighty glad to have this vote pass; which I did wonder at, to see them so well satisfied with so small a sum, Sir John Duncomb swearing (as I perceive he will freely do) that it was as much as the nation could beare.

27th. With my wife to the King's House to see *The Virgin Martyr*,[26] the first time it hath been acted a great while: and it is mighty pleasant; not that the play is worth much, but it is finely acted by Beck Marshall. But that which did please me beyond any thing in the whole world, was the wind-musique when the angel comes down; which is so sweet that it ravished me, and indeed, in a word, did wrap up my soul so that it made me really sick, just as I have formerly been when in love with my wife; that neither then, nor all the evening going home, and at home, I was able to think of any thing, but remained all night transported, so as I could not believe that ever any musique hath that real command over the soul of a man as this did upon me; and makes me resolve to practice wind-musique, and to make my wife do the like.

28th. After dinner with Sir W. Pen to White Hall, where we and the rest of us presented a great letter of the state of our want of money to his Royal Highness. I did also present a demand of mine for consideration for my travelling-charges of coach and boat-hire during the war: which, although his Royal Highness and the company did all like of, yet, contrary to my expectation, I find him so jealous now of doing any thing extraordinary, that he desired the gentlemen that they would consider it, and report their minds in it to him. This did unsettle my mind a great while, not expecting this stop: but, however, I shall do as well, I know, though it causes me a little stop. But that that troubles me most is, that while we were thus together with the Duke of York, comes in Mr Wren from the House; where, he tells us, another storm hath been all this day almost against the

25 MP for Ludlow; and in 1663 elected Speaker, which office he resigned on account of ill health. He was successively King's Serjeant, Chief Justice of Chester, and a Justice of the Common Pleas; created a Baronet 1686, and died 1697.
26 A tragedy, by Massinger.

officers of the Navy upon this complaint, – that though they have made good rules for payment of tickets, yet that they have not observed them themselves; which was driven so high as to have it urged that we should presently be put out of our places: and so they have at last ordered that we shall be heard at the bar of the House upon this business on Thursday next. This did mightily trouble me and us all; but me particularly, who am least able to bear these troubles, though I have the least cause to be concerned in it. Thence therefore to visit Sir H. Cholmly, who hath for some time been ill of a cold; and thence walked towards Westminster, and met Colonell Birch, who took me back to walk with him, and did give me an account of this day's heat against the Navy-officers, and an account of his speech on our behalf, which was very good. And indeed we are much beholden to him, as I, after I parted with him, did find by my cosen Roger, whom I went to: and he and I to his lodgings. And there he did tell me the same over again; and how Birch did stand up in our defence; and that he do see that there are many desirous to have us out of the office; and the House is so furious and passionate that he thinks nobody can be secure, let him deserve never so well. But now, he tells me, we shall have a fair hearing of the House, and he hopes justice of them: but upon the whole, he do agree with me that I should hold my hand as to making any purchase of land, which I had formerly discoursed with him about, till we see a little further how matters go. He tells me that what made them so mad to-day first was, several letters in the House about the Fanatickes in several places coming in great bodies and turning people out of the churches, and there preaching themselves, and pulling the surplice over the parsons' heads: this was confirmed from several places; which makes them stark mad, especially the hectors and bravadoes of the House, who show all the zeal on this occasion.

29th. They tell me how Sir Thomas Allen hath taken the English-men out of La Roche's ship, and taken from him an Ostend prize which La Roche had fetched out of our harbours. And at this day La Roche keeps upon our coasts; and had the boldness to land some men and go a mile up into the country, and there took some goods belonging to this prize out of a house there: which our King resents, and, they say, hath wrote to the King of France about. And every body do think a war will follow; and then in what a case we shall be for want of money, nobody knows. Wrote to my father, and sent him Colvill's note for £600 for my sister's portion.

March 1st. Lord's day. Up very betimes, and by coach to Sir W. Coventry's; and there largely carrying with me all my notes and papers, did run over our whole defence in the business of tickets, in order to the answering the House on Thursday next; and I do think, unless they be set without reason to ruin us, we shall make a good defence. I find him in great anxiety, though he will not discover it, in the business of the proceedings of Parliament; and would as little as is possible have his name mentioned in our discourse to them. And particularly the business of selling places is now upon his hand to defend himself in; wherein I did help him in his defence about the flag-maker's place, which is named in the House. We did here do the like about the complaint of want of victuals in the fleet in the year 1666, which will lie upon me to defend also.

2nd. Mr Moore was with me, and do tell me, and so W. Hewer tells me, he hears this morning that all the town is full of the discourse that the officers of the Navy shall be all turned out, but honest Sir John Minnes; who, God knows, is fitter to have been turned out himself than any of us, doing the King more hurt by his dotage and folly than all the rest can do by their knavery, if they had a mind to it. This day I have the news that my sister was married on Thursday last to Mr Jackson; so that work is, I hope, well over.

3rd. Up betimes to work again, and then met at the office, where to our great business of this answer to the Parliament; where to my great vexation I find my Lord Brouncker prepared only to excuse himself, while I, that have least reason to trouble myself, am preparing with great pains to defend them all: and more, I perceive he would lodge the beginning of discharging ships by ticket upon me; but I care not, for I believe I shall get more honour by it when the Parliament against my will shall see how the whole business of the office was done by me. Down by water to Deptford; where the King, Queene, and Court are to see launched the new ship built by Mr Shish, called the *Charles*. God send her better luck than the former! Here some of our brethren, who went in a boat a little before my boat, did by appointment take opportunity of asking the King's leave that we might make full use of the want of money in our excuse to the

Parliament for the business of tickets and other things they will lay to our charge, all which arise from nothing else: and this the King did readily agree to, and did give us leave to make our full use of it. The ship being well launched, I back again by boat.

5th. To Westminster; where I found myself come time enough, and my brethren all ready. But I full of thoughts and trouble touching the issue of this day: and to comfort myself did go to the Dog and drink half-a-pint of mulled sack, and in the hall did drink a dram of brandy at Mrs Hewlett's; and with the warmth of this did find myself in better order as to courage, truly. So we all up to the lobby; and between eleven and twelve o'clock were called in, with the mace before us, into the House; where a mighty full House: and we stood at the bar; namely, Brouncker, Sir J. Minnes, Sir T. Harvey, and myself, W. Pen being in the House as a Member. I perceive the whole House was full of expectation of our defence what it would be, and with great prejudice. After the Speaker had told us the dissatisfaction of the House, and read the Report of the Committee, I began our defence most acceptably and smoothly, and continued at it without any hesitation or losse, but with full scope, and all my reason free about me, as if it had been at my own table, from that time till past three in the afternoon; and so ended, without any interruption from the Speaker; but we withdrew. And there all my fellow officers, and all the world that was within hearing, did congratulate me, and cry up my speech as the best thing they ever heard; and my fellow-officers were overjoyed in it. And we were called in again by and by to answer only one question touching our paying tickets to ticket-mongers; and so out. And we were in hopes to have had a vote this day in our favour, and so the generality of the House was; but my speech being so long, many had gone out to dinner and come in again half-drunk. And then there are two or three that are professed enemies to us and every body else; among others, Sir T. Littleton, Sir Thomas Lee,[27] Mr Wiles (the coxcomb whom I saw heretofore at the cock-fighting), and a few others: I say, these did rise up and speak against the coming to a vote now, the House not being full by reason of several being at dinner, but most because that the House was to attend the King this afternoon about the business of religion (wherein they pray him to put in force all the laws against Nonconformists and

27 Of Hartwell, Bucks; created a Baronet 1660.

Papists): and this prevented it, so that they put it off to to-morrow come se'nnight. However, it is plain we have got great ground; and every body says I have got the most honour that any could have had opportunity of getting: and so our hearts mightily overjoyed at this success. After dinner to the King's house, and there saw part of *The Discontented Colonell.*[28]

6th. Up betimes, and with Sir D. Gauden to Sir W. Coventry's chamber; where the first word he said to me was, 'Good-morrow, Mr Pepys, that must be Speaker of the Parliament-house': and did protest I had got honour for ever in Parliament. He said that his brother, that sat by him, admires me; and another gentleman said that I could not get less than £1000 a-year, if I would put on a gown and plead at the Chancery-bar. But, what pleases me most, he tells me that the Solicitor-generall did protest that he thought I spoke the best of any man in England. After several talks with him alone touching his own businesses, he carried me to White Hall; and there parted. And I to the Duke of York's lodgings, and find him going to the Parke, it being a very fine morning; and I after him: and as soon as he saw me, he told me with great satisfaction that I had converted a great many yesterday, and did with great praise of me go on with the discourse with me. And by and by overtaking the King, the King and Duke of York came to me both; and he[29] said, 'Mr Pepys, I am very glad of your success yesterday': and fell to talk of my well speaking. And many of the Lords there. My Lord Barkeley did cry me up for what they had heard of it; and others, Parliament-men there about the King, did say that they never heard such a speech in their lives delivered in that manner. Progers of the Bedchamber swore to me afterwards before Brouncker, in the afternoon, that he did tell the King that he thought I might match the Solicitor-generall. Every body that saw me almost came to me, as Joseph Williamson and others, with such eulogys as cannot be expressed. From thence I went to Westminster Hall; where I met Mr G. Montagu, who came to me and kissed me, and told me that he had often heretofore kissed my hands, but now he would kiss my lips; protesting that I was another Cicero, and said, all the world said the same of me. Mr Ashburnham,

28 *Brennoralt, or The Discontented Colonel*; a tragedy, by Sir John Suckling.
29 The King.

and every creature I met there of the Parliament, or that knew any thing of the Parliament's actings, did salute me with this honour: Mr Godolphin; Mr Sands, who swore he would go twenty miles at any time to hear the like again, and that he never saw so many sit four hours together to hear any man in his life as there did to hear me. Mr Chichly, Sir John Duncomb, and every body do say that the kingdom will ring of my abilities, and that I have done myself right for my whole life; and so Captain Cocke and others of my friends say that no man had ever such an opportunity of making his abilities known. And that I may cite all at once, Mr Lieutenant of the Tower did tell me that Mr Vaughan did protest to him, and that in his hearing it said so to the Duke of Albemarle, and afterwards to Sir W. Coventry, that he had sat twenty-six years in Parliament and never heard such a speech there before: for which the Lord God make me thankful; and that I may make use of it, not to pride and vain-glory, but that, now I have this esteem, I may do nothing that may lessen it! To White Hall to wait on the Duke of York; where he again and all the company magnified me, and several in the Gallery: among others, my Lord Gerard, who never knew me before nor spoke to me, desires his being better acquainted with me: and that, at table where he was, he never heard so much said of any man as of me in his whole life. So waited on the Duke of York, and thence into the Gallery, where the House of Lords waited the King's coming out of the Park; which he did by and by. And there in the Vane-roome my Lord Keeper delivered a Message to the King, the Lords being about him, wherein the Barons of England, from many good arguments very well expressed in the part he read out of, do demand precedence in England of all noblemen of either of the King's other two kingdoms, be their title what it will; and did show that they were in England reputed but as Commoners, and sat in the House of Commons, and at conferences with the Lords did stand bare. It was mighty worth my hearing; but the King did say only that he would consider of it, and so dismissed them.

8th. With Sir W. Coventry, who I find full of care in his own business, how to defend himself against those that have a mind to choque him; and though I believe not for honour and for the keeping his employment, but for safety and reputation's sake, is desirous to preserve himself free from blame.

9th. By coach to White Hall, and there met Lord Brouncker: and he and I to the Commissioners of the Treasury; where I find them mighty kind to me, more, I think, than was wont. And here I also met Colvill the goldsmith; who tells me, with great joy, how the world upon the 'Change talks of me; and how several Parliament-men, viz. Boscawen[30] and Major Walden of Huntingdon, who it seems do deal with him, do say how bravely I did speak, and that the House was ready to have given me thanks for it: but that, I think, is a vanity.

10th. With Sir D. Gauden homewards, calling at Lincolne's Inn-fields. But my Lady Jemimah was not within: and so to Newgate, where he stopped to give directions to the jaylor about a Knight, one Sir Thomas Halford,[31] brought in yesterday for killing one Colonell Temple, falling out at a taverne. Home; and there comes Mr Moore to me; who tells me that he fears my Lord Sandwich will meet with very great difficulties to go through about the prizes, it being found that he did give orders for more than the King's letter do justify; and then for the Act of Resumption, which he fears will go on, and is designed only to do him hurt; which troubles me much. He tells me he believes the Parliament will not be brought to do any thing in matters of religion, but will adhere to the Bishops.

11th. Meeting Mr Colvill I walked with him to his building, where he is building a fine house, where he formerly lived, in Lumbard-street: and it will be a very fine street. So to Westminster; and there walked, till by and by comes Sir W. Coventry, and with him Mr Chichly and Mr Andrew Newport. I to dinner with them to Mr Chichly's in Queene-street, in Covent Garden. A very fine house, and a man that lives in mighty great fashion, with all things in a most extraordinary manner noble and rich about him, and eats in the French fashion all; and mighty nobly served with his servants, and very civilly; that I was mighty pleased with it: and good discourse. He is a great defender of the Church of England and against the Act for Comprehension; which is the work of this day, about which the House is like to sit till night. After dinner with them back to Westminster. Captain Cocke told me that the Speaker says he never

30 Edward Boscawen, MP for Truro.
31 Of Welham, Leicestershire, Baronet.

heard such a defence made in all his life in the House, and that the Solicitor-generall do commend me even to envy.

12th. To Gresham College, there to show myself; and was there greeted by Dr Wilkins, Whistler, and others, as the patron of the Navy-office, and one that got great fame by my late speech to the Parliament.

13th. At noon, all of us to Chatelin, the French house in Covent Garden, to dinner; Brouncker, J. Minnes, W. Pen, T. Harvey, and myself; and there had a dinner cost us 8s. 6d. a-piece, a base dinner, which did not please us at all. My head being full of to-morrow's dinner, I to my Lord Crewe's, there to invite Sir Thomas Crewe; and there met with my Lord Hinchingbroke and his lady, the first time I spoke to her. I saluted her; and she mighty civil: and, with my Lady Jemimah, do all resolve to be very merry to-morrow at my house. My Lady Hinchingbroke I cannot say is a beauty, nor ugly; but is altogether a comely lady enough, and seems very good-humoured. Thence home; and there I find one laying of my napkins against to-morrow in figures of all sorts; which is mighty pretty, and it seems it is his trade, and he gets much money by it.

14th. Up very betimes, and with Jane to Lovett's, there to conclude upon our dinner; and thence to the pewterer's, to buy a pewter sesterne, which I have ever hitherto been without. Anon comes my company, viz. my Lord Hinchingbroke and his lady, Sir Philip Carteret and his lady, Godolphin and my cosen Roger, and Creed: and mighty merry; and by and by to dinner, which was very good and plentifull: (and I should have said, and Mr George Montagu, who came at a very little warning, which was exceeding kind of him.) And there, among other things, my Lord had Sir Samuel Morland's late invention for casting up of sums of £. s. d.; which is very pretty, but not very useful. Most of our discourse was of my Lord Sandwich and his family, as being all of us of the family. And with extraordinary pleasure all the afternoon, thus together eating and looking over my closet; and my Lady Hinchingbroke I find a very sweet-natured and well-disposed lady, a lover of books and pictures, and of good understanding. About five o'clock they went; and then my wife and I abroad by coach into Moore-fields, only for a little ayre.

15th. Walked with Sir W. Coventry into the Park, and there met the King and the Duke of York, and walked a good while with them: and here met Sir Jer. Smith, who tells me he is like to get the better of Holmes, and that when he is come to an end of that he will do Hollis's business for him in the House for his blasphemies; which I shall be glad of. So to White Hall, and there walked with this man and that man till chapel done and the King dined: and then Sir Thomas Clifford the Comptroller took me with him to dinner to his lodgings, where my Lord Arlington and a great deal of good and great company; where I very civilly used by them, and had a most excellent dinner. And good discourse of Spain, Mr Godolphin being there; particularly of the removal of the bodies of all the dead kings of Spain that could be got together, and brought to the Pantheon at the Escuriall (when it was finished) and there placed before the altar, there to lie for ever: and there was a sermon made to them upon this text, *'Arida ossa, audite verbum Dei'*; and a most eloquent sermon, as they say.

17th. To the Excise-office, where I met Mr Ball, and did receive my paper I went for; and there fell in talk with him, who being an old cavalier do swear and curse at the present state of things, that we should be brought to this, that we must be undone and cannot be saved; that the Parliament is sitting now, and will till midnight, to find how to raise this £300,000 and doubts they will not do it so as to be seasonable for the King: but do cry out against all our great men at Court; how it is a fine thing for a Secretary of State to dance a jigg, and that it was not so heretofore; and, above all, do curse my Lord of Bristoll, saying the worst news that ever he heard in his life, or that the Devil could ever bring us, was this Lord's coming to prayers the other day in the House of Lords, by which he is coming about again from being a Papist, which will undo this nation; and he says he ever did say at the King's first coming in, that this nation could not be safe while that man was alive. The house, I hear, have this day concluded upon raising £100,000 of the £300,000 by wine, and the rest by poll, and have resolved to excuse the Church, in expectation that they will do the more of themselves at this juncture; and I do hear that Sir W. Coventry did make a speech in behalf of the clergy.

18th. To White Hall, where we and my Lord Brouncket attended the Council, to discourse about the fitness of entering of men presently for the manning of the fleet, before one ship is in condition to receive them. Sir W. Coventry did argue against it: I was wholly silent, because I saw the King upon the earnestness of the Prince was willing to it, crying very civilly, 'If ever you intend to man the fleet without being cheated by the captains and pursers, you may go to bed and resolve never to have it manned.' And so it was, like other things, over-ruled that all volunteers should be presently entered. Then there was another great business about our signing of certificates to the Exchequer for goods upon the £1,250,000 Act; which the Commissioners of the Treasury did all oppose, and to the laying fault upon us. But I did then speak to the justifying what we had done even to the angering of Duncomb and Clifford; which I was vexed at: but for all that, I did set the office and myself right, and went away with the victory, my Lord Keeper saying that he would not advise the Council to order us to sign more certificates. But before I began to say any thing in this matter, the King and the Duke of York talking at the Council-table before all the Lords of the Committee of Miscarriages, how this entering of men before the ships could be ready would be reckoned a miscarriage; 'Why,' says the King, 'it is then but Mr Pepys making of another speech to them'; which made all the Lords (and there were by also the Atturny and Solicitor-generall) look upon me. Thence Sir W. Coventry, W. Pen, and I by hackney-coach to take a little ayre in Hyde Parke, the first time that I have been there this year; and we did meet many coaches going and coming, it being mighty pleasant weather. And so coming back again I light in the Pell Mell; and there went to see Sir H. Cholmly, who continues very ill of his cold. And there came in Sir H. Yelverton, and Sir H. Cholmly commended to me his acquaintance which the other received, but without remembering to me, or I him, of our being school-fellows together; and I said nothing of it. But he took notice of my speech the other day at the bar of the House; and indeed I perceive he is a wise man. Here he do say that the town is full of it; that now the Parliament hath resolved upon £300,000; the King instead of fifty will set out but twenty-five ships; and the Dutch as many, and that Smith is to command them, who is allowed to have the better of Holmes in the late dispute, and is in good esteem in the Parliament above the other. Thence home, and there in favour to my eyes staid at home reading the ridiculous *History of my Lord Newcastle*, wrote by his wife; which shows her to be a mad, conceited, ridiculous woman, and he an asse to suffer her to write what she writes to him and of him. So to bed, my eyes being very bad; and I know not how in the world to abstain from reading.

19th. Walked all along Thames-street, which I have not done since it was burned, as far as Billingsgate; and there do see a brave street likely to be, many brave houses being built, and of them a great many by Mr Jaggard; but the raising of the street will make it mighty fine.

20th. All the evening pricking down some things and trying some conclusions upon my viall, in order to the inventing a better theory of musique than hath yet been abroad; and I think verily I shall do it. This day at Court I do hear that Sir W. Pen do command this summer's fleet; and Mr Progers of the Bedchamber as a secret told me that the Prince Rupert is troubled at it, and several friends of his have been with him to know the reason of it; so that he do pity Sir W. Pen, whom he hath a great kindness for, that he should not at any desire of his be put to this service, and thereby make the Prince his enemy and contract more envy from other people.

24th. From the Duke's chamber Sir W. Coventry and I to walk in the Matted Gallery; and there, among other things, he tells me of the wicked design that now is at last contriving against him, to get a petition presented from people, that the money they have paid to Sir W. Coventry for their places may be repaid them back: and that this is set on by Temple and Hollis of the Parliament, and, among other mean people in it, by Captain Tatnell: and he prays me that I will use some effectual way to sift Tatnell what he do and who puts him on in this business: which I do undertake, and will do with all my skill for his service, being troubled that he is still under this difficulty. Thence back to White Hall: where great talk of the tumult at the other end of the town, about Moore-fields, among the prentices taking the liberty of these holydays to pull down brothels. And Lord! to see the apprehensions which this did give to all people at Court, that presently order was given for all the soldiers, horse and foot, to be in armes; and forthwith alarmes were beat by drum and trumpet through Westminster, and all to their colours and to horse, as if the French were coming into the town. So Creed, whom I met here, and I to Lincolne's Inn-fields, thinking to have gone into the fields to have seen the prentices; but here we found these fields full of soldiers all in a body, and my Lord Craven commanding of them, and riding up and down to give orders like a madman. And some young men we saw brought by soldiers to the guard at White Hall, and overheard others that stood by say that it was only for pulling down the brothels; and none of the bystanders finding fault with them, but rather of the soldiers for hindering them. And we heard a Justice of Peace this morning say to the King, that he had been endeavouring to suppress this tumult, but could not; and that imprisoning some of them in the new prison at Clerkenwell, the rest did come and break open the prison and release them; and that they do give out that they are for pulling down the brothels, which is one of the great grievances of the nation. To which the King made a very poor, cold, insipid answer: 'Why, why do they go to them, then?' – and that was all, and had no mind to go on with the discourse. This evening I came home from White Hall with Sir W. Pen, who fell in talk about his going to sea this year, and the difficulties that arise to him by it, by giving offence to the Prince and occasioning envy to him, and many other things that make it a bad matter at this time of want of money and necessaries, and bad and uneven counsels at home, for him to go abroad: and did tell me how much with the King and Duke of York he had endeavoured to be excused, desiring the Prince might be satisfied in it who hath a mind to go; but he tells me they will not excuse him, and I believe it, and truly do judge it a piece of bad fortune to W. Pen.

25th. Up, and walked to White Hall, there to wait on the Duke of York; which I did: and in his chamber there, first by hearing the Duke of York call me by my name, my Lord Burlington did come to me and with great respect take notice of me and my relation to my Lord Sandwich, and express great kindness to me; and so to talk of my Lord Sandwich's concernments. By and by the Duke of York is ready; and I did wait for an opportunity of speaking my mind to him about Sir J. Minnes, his being unable to do the King any service. The Duke of York and all with him this morning were full of the talk of the prentices, who are not yet put down, though the guards and militia of the town have been in armes all this night and the night before; and the prentices have made fools of them, sometimes by running from them and flinging stones at them. Some blood hath been spilt, but a great many houses pulled down; and, among others, the Duke of York was mighty merry at that of Daman Page's, the great bawd of the seamen; and the Duke of York complained merrily that he hath lost two tenants by their houses being pulled down, who paid him for their wine-licences £15 a-year. But these idle fellows have had the confidence to say that they did ill in contenting themselves in pulling down the little brothels, and did not go and pull down the great one at White Hall. And some of them have the last night had a word among them, and it was 'Reformation and Reducement'. This do make the courtiers ill at ease to see this spirit among people, though they think this matter will not come to much: but it speakes people's minds; and then they do say that there are men of understanding among them, that have been of Cromwell's army: but how true that is, I know not.

26th. To the Duke of York's house to see the new play, called *The Man is the Master*;[32] where the house was, it being not one o'clock, very full. By and by the King came; and we sat just under him, so that I durst not turn my back all the play. The most of the mirth was sorry, poor stuffe, of eating of sack posset and slabbering themselves, and mirth fit for clownes; the prologue but poor, and the epilogue little in it but the extraordinariness of it, it being sung by Harris and another in the form of a ballet. My wife extraordinary fine to-day in her flower tabby suit, bought a year and more ago, before my mother's death put her into mourning, and so not worn till this day: and every body in love with it; and indeed she is very fine and handsome in it. Home in a coach round by the wall; where we met so many stops by the watches, that it cost us much time and some trouble, and more money, to every watch to them to drink; this being encreased by the trouble the prentices did lately give the City, so that the militia and watches are very strict at this time; and we had like to have met with a stop for all night at the constable's watch at Mooregate by a pragmatical constable; but we came well home at about two in the morning. This noon from Mrs Williams's my Lord Brouncker sent to Somerset House to hear how the Duchesse of Richmond do; and word was brought him that she is pretty well, but mighty full of the small pox, by which all do conclude she will be wholly spoiled; which is the greatest instance of the uncertainty of

32 A comedy, by Sir Wm. Davenant, taken from Molière's *Joddelet*.

beauty that could be in this age; but then she hath had the benefit of it to be first married, and to have kept it so long under the greatest temptations in the world from a King, and yet without the least imputation. This afternoon, at the play, Sir Fr. Hollis spoke to me as a secret and matter of confidence in me, and friendship to Sir W. Pen, who is now out of town, that it were well he were made acquainted that he finds in the House of Commons, which met this day, several motions made for the calling strictly again upon the miscarriages, and particularly in the business of the prizes and the not prosecuting of the first victory, only to give an affront to Sir W. Pen, whose going to sea this year does give them matter of great dislike.

27th. This day at noon comes Mr Pelling to me, and shows me the stone cut lately out of Sir Thomas Adams's[33] (the old comely Alderman) body; which is very large indeed, bigger I think than my fist, and weighs above twenty-five ounces: and which is very miraculous, he never in all his life had any fit of it, but lived to a great age without pain, and died at last of something else, without any sense of this in all his life. This day Creed at White Hall in discourse told me what information he hath had from very good hands, of the cowardize and ill-government of Sir Jer. Smith and Sir Thomas Allen, and the repute they have both of them abroad in the Streights, from their deportment when they did at several times command there; and that, above all Englishmen that ever were there, there never was any man that behaved himself like poor Charles Wager, whom the very Moores do mention with tears sometimes.

29th. To church; and there did first find a strange reader, who could not find in the Service-book the place for churching women, but was fain to change books with the clerke: and then a stranger preached, a seeming able man; but said in his pulpit that God did a greater work in raising of an oake-tree from an acorn, than a man's body raising it at the last day from his dust (showing the possibility of the Resurrection): which was, methought, a strange saying. Harris do so commend my wife's picture of Mr Hales's, that I shall have him draw Harris's head; and he hath also persuaded me to have Cooper draw my wife's, which though it cost £30 yet I will have done. I do hear

33 Knight and Bart. Alderman of London; died 1667. He founded an Arabic Professorship at Cambridge,

by several that Sir W. Pen's going to sea do dislike the Parliament mightily, and that they have revived the Committee of Miscarriages to find something to prevent it; and that he being the other day with the Duke of Albemarle to ask his opinion touching his going to sea, the Duchesse overheard and came in to him, and asked W. Pen how he durst have the confidence to offer to go to sea again to the endangering the nation, when he knew himself such a coward as he was; which, if true, is very severe.

30th. By coach to Common-garden Coffee-house, where by appointment I was to meet Harris; which I did, and also Mr Cooper the great painter, and Mr Hales. And thence presently to Mr Cooper's house to see some of his work; which is all in little, but so excellent as, though I must confess I do think the colouring of the flesh to be a little forced, yet the painting is so extraordinary as I do never expect to see the like again. Here I did see Mrs Stewart's picture as when a young maid, and now just done before her having the small-pox: and it would make a man weep to see what she was then, and what she is like to be by people's discourse now. Here I saw my Lord Generall's picture, and my Lord Arlington and Ashly's, and several others: but among the rest one Swinfen that was Secretary to my Lord Manchester, Lord Chamberlain (with Cooling), done so admirably as I never saw any thing: but the misery was, this fellow died in debt and never paid Cooper for his picture; but it being seized on by his creditors among his other goods after his death, Cooper himself says that he did buy it and give £25 out of his purse for it, for what he was to have had but £30. To White Hall and Westminster, where I find the Parliament still bogling about the raising of this money. And every body's mouth full now; and Mr Wren himself tells me that the Duke of York declares to go to sea himself this year; and I perceive it is only on this occasion of distaste of the Parliament against W. Pen's going, and to prevent the Prince's: but I think it is mighty hot counsel for the Duke of York at this time to go out of the way; but, Lord! what pass are all our matters come to! At noon by appointment to Cursitor's-alley in Chancery-lane, to meet Captain Cocke and some other creditors of the Navy, and their Counsel (Pemberton, North, Offly, and Charles Porter); and there dined and talked of the business of the assignments on the Exchequer of the £1,250,000 on behalf of our creditors; and there I do perceive that the Counsel had heard of my performance in the Parliament-house lately, and did value me and what I said accordingly. At dinner we had a great deal of good discourse about Parliament; their number being uncertain, and always at the will of the King to encrease as he saw reason to erect a new borough. But all concluded that the bane of the Parliament hath been the leaving off the old custom of the places allowing wages to those that served them in Parliament, by which they chose men that understood their business and would attend it, and they could expect an account from; which now they cannot: and so the Parliament is become a company of men unable to give account for the interest of the place they serve for. Thence, the meeting of the Counsel with the King's Counsel this afternoon being put off by reason of the death of Serjeant Maynard's[34] lady, I to White Hall, where the Parliament was to wait on the King; and they did: and he did think fit to tell them that they might expect to be adjourned at Whitsuntide, and that they might make haste to raise their money; but this, I fear, will displease them, who did expect to sit as long as they pleased.

April 2nd. With Lord Brouncker to the Royall Society, where they had just done; but there I was forced to subscribe to the building of a college, and did give £40; and several others did subscribe, some greater and some less sums; but several I saw hang off: and I doubt it will spoil the Society, for it breeds faction and ill-will, and becomes burdensome to some that cannot or would not do it.

3rd. As soon as we had done with the Duke of York we did attend the Council; and were there called in, and did hear Mr Sollicitor make his Report to the Council in the business of a complaint against us, for having prepared certificates on the Exchequer for the further sum of £50,000; which he did in a most excellent manner of words, but most cruelly severe against us, and so were some of the Lords Commissioners of the Treasury, as men guilty of a practice with the tradesmen, to the King's prejudice. I was unwilling to enter into a contest with them; but took advantage of two or three words last spoke, and brought it to a short issue in good words, that if we had

34 John Maynard, an eminent lawyer; made Serjeant to Cromwell in 1653, and afterwards King's Serjeant by Charles II, who knighted him. In 1661 he was chosen Member for Berealston, and sat in every Parliament till the Revolution. Died 1690, aged 88.

APRIL 1668   683

the King's order to hold our hands, we would; which did end the
matter: and they all resolved we should have it, and so it ended. And
so we away; I vexed that I did not speak more in a cause so fit to be
spoke in, and wherein we had so much advantage; but perhaps I
might have provoked the Sollicitor and the Commissioners of the
Treasury, and therefore since I am not sorry that I forebore. This day
I hear that Prince Rupert and Holmes do go to sea: and by this there
is a seeming friendship and peace among our great seamen; but the
devil a bit there is any love among them, or can be.

4th. I did attend the Duke of York, and he did carry us to the King's
lodgings: but he was asleep in his closet; so we stayed in the green-
roome; where the Duke of York did tell us what rules he had of
knowing the weather, and did now tell us we should have rain before
to-morrow (it having been a dry season for some time), and so it did
rain all night almost; and pretty rules he hath, and told Brouncker and
me some of them, which were such as no reason can readily be given
for them. By and by the King comes out: and then to talk of other
things; about the Quakers not swearing, and how they do swear in
the business of a late election of a Knight of the Shire of Hartfordshire
in behalf of one they have a mind to have; and how my Lord of
Pembroke says he hath heard the Quaker at the tennis-court swear to
himself when he loses; and told us what pretty notions my Lord
Pembroke hath of the first chapter of Genesis, and a great deal of such
fooleries; which the King made mighty mockery at.

5th. I hear that eight of the ringleaders in the late tumults of the
prentices at Easter are condemned to die.

6th. The King and Duke of York themselves in my absence did call
for some of the Commissioners of the Treasury and give them
directions about the business of the certificates; which I, despairing to
do any thing on a Sunday, and not thinking that they would think of
it themselves, did rest satisfied with, and stayed at home all yesterday,
leaving it to do something in this day: but I find that the King and
Duke of York had been so pressing in it, that my Lord Ashly was
more forward with the doing of it this day than I could have been.
And so I to White Hall with Alderman Backewell in his coach, with
Mr Blany, my Lord's Secretary; and there did draw up a rough
draught of what order I would have, and did carry it in, and had it

read twice and approved of before my Lord Ashly and three more of the Commissioners of the Treasury; and then went up to the Council-chamber, where the Duke of York and Prince Rupert, and the rest of the Committee of the Navy, were sitting: and I did get some of them to read it there; and they would have had it passed presently, but Sir John Nichollas desired they would first have it approved by a full Council; and therefore a Council extraordinary was readily summoned against the afternoon, and the Duke of York run presently to the King, as if now they were really set to mind their business; which God grant! Mr Montagu did tell me how Mr Vaughan in that very room did say that I was a great man, and had great understanding, and I know not what; which, I confess, I was a little proud of, if I may believe him. Here I do hear as a great secret that the King, and Duke of York and Duchesse, and my Lady Castlemaine, are now all agreed in a strict league, and all things like to go very current, and that it is not impossible to have my Lord Clarendon in time here again. But I do hear that my Lady Castlemaine is horribly vexed at the late libell, the petition of the poor prostitutes about the town whose houses were pulled down the other day. I have got one of them; and it is not very witty, but devilish severe against her and the King: and I wonder how it durst be printed and spread abroad; which shows that the times are loose, and come to a great disregard of the King, or Court, or Government. To the Park; and then to the House, and there at the door eat and drank whither came my Lady Kerneagy,[35] of whom Creed tells me more particulars: how her Lord, finding her and the Duke of York at the King's first coming in, too kind, did get it out of her that he did dishonour him; and did take the most pernicious and full piece of revenge that ever I heard of; and he at this day owns it with great glory, and looks upon the Duke of York and the world with great content in the ampleness of his revenge.[36] This day in the afternoon, stepping with the Duke of York into St James's Park, it rained; and I was forced to lend the Duke of York my cloak, which he wore through the Park.

7th. To the King's playhouse, and there saw *The English Monsieur*[37] (sitting for privacy sake in an upper box): the play hath much mirth in

35 Carnegie.
36 See *Mémoires de Grammont*.
37 A comedy, by James Howard.

it as to that particular humour. After the play done I down to Knipp, and did stay her undressing herself: and there saw the several players, men and women, go by; and pretty to see how strange they are all, one to another, after the play is done. Here I hear Sir W. Davenant is just now dead; and so who will succeed him in the mastership of the House is not yet known. The eldest Davenport is, it seems, gone from this house to be kept by somebody; which I am glad of, she being a very bad actor. Mrs Knipp tells me that my Lady Castlemaine is mightily in love with Hart of their house; and he is much with her in private, and she goes to him and do give him many presents; and that the thing is most certain, and Beck Marshall only privy to it, and the means of bringing them together: which is a very odd thing; and by this means she is even with the King's love to Mrs Davis.

8th. To Drumbleby's, and there did talk a great deal about pipes; and did buy a recorder, which I do intend to learn to play on, the sound of it being, of all sounds in the world, most pleasing to me.

9th. I up and down to the Duke of York's playhouse, there to see, which I did, Sir W. Davenant's corpse, carried out towards Westminster, there to be buried. Here were many coaches and six horses, and many hacknies, that made it look, methought, as if it were the buriall of a poor poet. He seemed to have many children, by five or six in the first mourning-coach, all boys. To my office, where is come a packet from the Downes from my brother Balty, who with Harman are arrived there, of which this day comes the first news. And now the Parliament will be satisfied, I suppose, about the business they have so long desired between Brouncker[38] and Harman, about not prosecuting the first victory.

16th. To Westminster Hall, where I hear W. Pen is ordered to be impeached. There spoke with many, and particularly with G. Montagu; and went with him and Creed to his house, where he told how Sir W. Pen hath been severe to Lord Sandwich; but the Coventrys both labouring to save him by laying it on Lord Sandwich; which our friends cry out upon, and I am silent, but do believe they did it as the only way to save him. It could not be carried to commit him. It is thought the House do cool: Sir W. Coventry's being for him provoked Sir R. Howard and his party: Court all for W. Pen.

38 Henry Brouncker.

17th. I hear that the House is upon the business of Harman, who, they say, takes all on himself.

18th. Do hear this morning that Harman is committed by the Parliament last night, the day he came up; which is hard: but he took all upon himself first, and then, when a witness came in to say otherwise, he would have retracted; and the House took it so ill, they would commit him.

19th. Roger Pepys did tell me the whole story of Harman, how he prevaricated, and hath undoubtedly been imposed on and wheedled; and he is like the miller's man that in Richard the Third's time was hanged for his master.

20th. To White Hall, and there hear how Brouncker is fled, which I think will undo him; but what good it will do Harman I know not, he hath so befouled himself; but it will be good sport to my Lord Chancellor to hear how his great enemy is fain to take the same course that he is. There met Robinson, who tells me that he fears his master, Sir W. Coventry, will this week have his business brought upon the stage again about selling of places; which I shall be sorry for, though the less since I hear his standing up for Pen the other day, to the prejudice, though not to the ruin, of my Lord Sandwich; and yet I do think what he did, he did out of a principle of honesty. Meeting Sir William Hooker the Alderman, he did cry out mighty high against Sir W. Pen for his getting such an estate and giving £15,000 with his daughter; which is more by half than ever he did give; but this the world believes, and so let them.

21st. I hear how Sir W. Pen's impeachment was read and agreed to in the House this day, and ordered to be engrossed; and he suspended the House: Harman set at liberty; and Brouncker put out of the House, and a writ[39] for a new election, and an impeachment ordered to be brought in against him, he being fled.

22nd. To White Hall; and there we attended the Duke of York as usual; and I did present Mrs Pett the widow and her petition to the Duke of York, for some relief from the King. Here was to-day a proposition made to the Duke of York by Captain Von Hemskirke

39 At Romney, which Brouncker represented.

for £20,000 to discover an art how to make a ship go two feet for one what any ship do now: which the King inclines to try, it costing him nothing to try; and it is referred to us to contract with the man. Then by water from the Privy-stairs to Westminster Hall: and taking water the King and the Duke of York were in the new buildings; and the Duke of York called to me whither I was going? And I answered aloud, 'To wait on our masters at Westminster'; at which he and all the company laughed: but I was sorry and troubled for it afterwards, for fear any Parliament-man should have been there; and it will be a caution to me for the time to come.

24th. I did hear the Duke of York tell how Sir W. Pen's impeachment was brought into the House of Lords to-day; and he spoke with great kindness of him: and that the Lords would not commit him till they could find precedent for it, and did incline to favour him.

25th. To Westminster Hall, and there met with Roger Pepys; and he tells me that nothing hath lately passed about my Lord Sandwich, but only Sir Robert Carr did speak hardly of him. But it is hoped that nothing will be done more this meeting of Parliament, which the King did by a message yesterday declare again should rise the 4th of May, and then only adjourne for three months; and this message being only about an adjournment did please them mightily, for they are desirous of their power mightily.

27th. To Westminster Hall, and up to the Lords' House; and there saw Sir W. Pen go into the House of Lords, where his impeachment was read to him and he used mighty civilly, the Duke of York being there; and two days hence, at his desire, he is to bring in his answer, and a day then to be appointed for his being heard with Counsel. Thence down into the Hall, and with Creed and Godolphin walked; and do hear that to-morrow is appointed, upon a motion on Friday last, to discourse the business of my Lord Sandwich, moved by Sir R. Howard, that he should be sent for home; and I fear it will be ordered. Certain news come, I hear, this day, that the Spanish Plenipotentiary in Flanders will not agree to the peace and terms we and the Dutch have made for him and the King of France; and by this means the face of things may be altered, and we forced to join with the French against Spain; which will be an odd thing.

28th. By coach to Westminster Hall, and there do understand that the business of religion and the Act against Conventicles have so taken them up all this morning, and do still, that my Lord Sandwich's business is not like to come on to-day; which I am heartily glad of. This law against Conventicles is very severe; but Creed, whom I meet here, do tell me that it being moved that Papists' meetings might be included, the House was divided upon it, and it was carried in the negative; which will give great disgust to the people, I doubt. To the King's house, and there did see *Love in a Maze*; wherein very good mirth of Lacy the clown, and Wintershell the country-knight, his master.

29th. To White Hall, and there do hear how Sir W. Pen hath delivered in his answer; and the Lords have sent it down to the Commons, but they have not yet read it nor taken notice of it, so as I believe they will by design defer it till they rise, that so he by lying under an impeachment may be prevented in his going to sea; which will vex him, and trouble the Duke of York. To Westminster Hall, and there met Mr G. Montagu, and walked and talked; who tells me that the best fence against the Parliament's present fury is delay, and recommended it to me in my friends' business and my own, if I have any; and is that that Sir W. Coventry do take, and will secure himself: that the King will deliver up all to the Parliament; and being petitioned the other day by Mr Brouncker to protect him, with teares in his eyes the King did say he could not, and bid him shift for himself, at least till the House is up.

30th. To the Dolphin Tavern, there to meet our neighbours all of the parish, this being Procession-day, to dine. And did: and much very good discourse; they being most of them very able merchants, as any in the City: Sir Andrew Rickard, Mr Vandeputt, Sir John Fredericke, Harrington, and others. They talked with Mr Mills about the meaning of this day, and the good uses of it; and how heretofore, and yet in several places, they do whip a boy at each place they stop at in their procession. I stopped to talk with Mr Brisband, who gives me an account of the rough usage Sir G. Carteret and his Counsel had the other day before the Commissioners of Accounts, and what I do believe we shall all of us have in a greater degree than any he hath had yet with them, before their three years are out; which are not yet begun, nor God knows when they will, this being like to be no session of Parliament when they now rise. Thus ends this month; my wife in the country, myself full of pleasure and expence; in some trouble for my friends, and my Lord Sandwich by the Parliament, and more for my eyes, which are daily worse and worse, that I dare not write or read almost any thing. The Parliament going in a few days to rise: myself so long without accounting now (for seven or eight months, I think, or more,) that I know not what condition almost I am in as to getting or spending for all that time; which troubles me, but I will soon do it. The kingdom in an ill state through poverty: a fleet going out, and no money to maintain it or set it out; seamen yet unpaid, and mutinous when pressed to go out again; our office able to do little, nobody trusting us, nor we desiring any to trust us, and yet have not money for any thing, but only what particularly belongs to this fleet going out, and that but lamely too. The Parliament several months upon an Act for £300,000 but cannot or will not agree upon it, but do keep it back, in spite of the King's desires to hasten it, till they can obtain what they have a mind in revenge upon some men for the late ill managements: and he is forced to submit to what they please, knowing that without it he shall have no money, and they as well that if they give the money the King will suffer them to do little more: and then the business of religion do disquiet every body, the Parliament being vehement against the Nonconformists, while the King seems to be willing to countenance them. So we are all poor and in pieces, God help us! while the peace is like to go on between Spain and France; and then the French may be apprehended able to attack us. So God help us!

May 1st. Met my cosen Thomas Pepys of Deptford, and took some turns with him; and he is mightily troubled for this Act now passed against Conventicles, and in a few words and sober do lament the condition we are in by a negligent prince and a mad Parliament. To the King's playhouse, and there saw *The Surprizall*; and a disorder in the pit by its raining in from the cupola at top. I understand how the Houses of Commons and Lords are like to disagree very much about the business of the East India Company, and one Skinner; to the latter of which the Lords have awarded £5000 from the former, for some wrong done him heretofore; and the former appealing to the Commons, the Lords vote their petition a libell; and so there is like to follow very hot work.

3rd. To church, where I saw Sir A. Rickard, though he be under the Black Rod, by order of the Lords' House, upon the quarrel between the East India Company and Skinner; which is like to come to a very great heat between the two Houses. To Old Street, to see Sir Thomas Teddiman, who is very ill in bed of a fever, got, I believe, by the fright the Parliament have put him into of late.

5th. Creed and I to the Duke of York's playhouse; and there coming late, up to the balcony-box, where we find my Lady Castlemaine and several great ladies; and there we sat with them, and I saw *The Impertinents* once more, now three times, and the three only days it hath been acted. And to see the folly how the house do this day cry up the play more than yesterday! and I for that reason like it, I find, the better too. By Sir Positive At-all, I understand is meant Sir Robert Howard. My Lady pretty well pleased with it: but here I sat close to her fine woman, Willson, who indeed is very handsome, but, they say, with child by the King. I asked, and she told me this was the first time her Lady had seen it, I having a mind to say something to her. One thing of familiarity I observed in my Lady Castlemaine: she called to one of her women, another that sat by this, for a little patch off of her face, and put it into her mouth and wetted it, and so clapped it upon her own by the side of her mouth, I suppose she feeling a pimple rising there. Thence with Creed to Westminster Hall, and there met with cosen Roger, who tells me of the great conference this day between the Lords and Commons about the business of the East India Company, as being one of the weightiest conferences that hath been, and maintained as weightily. I am heartily sorry I was not there, it being upon a mighty point of the privileges of the subjects of England in regard to the authority of the House of Lords, and their being condemned by them as the Supreme Court, which we say ought not to be but by appeal from other Courts. And he tells me that the Commons had much the better of them in reason and history there quoted, and believes the Lords will let it fall.

6th. I understand that my Lord St John is meant by Mr Woodcocke in *The Impertinents*. Home to put up things against to-morrow's carrier for my wife; and, among others, a very fine salmon-pie sent me by Mr Steventon, W. Hewer's uncle.

7th. To the King's house; where going in for Knipp, the play being done, I did see Beck Marshall come dressed off the stage, and look mighty fine and pretty, and noble: and also Nell in her boy's clothes, mighty pretty. But Lord! their confidence, and how many men do hover about them as soon as they come off the stage, and how confident they are in their talk! Here was also Haynes, the incomparable dancer of the King's house. Then we abroad to Marrowbone, and there walked in the garden, the first time I ever was there; and a pretty place it is.

8th. The Lords' House did sit till eleven o'clock last night about the business of difference between them and the Commons in the matter of the East India Company. To my Lord Crewe's, and there dined; where Mr Case the minister, a dull fellow in his talk, and all in the Presbyterian manner; a great deal of noise and a kind of religious tone, but very dull. After dinner my Lord and I together. He tells me he hears that there are great disputes like to be at Court between the factions of the two women, my Lady Castlemaine and Mrs Stewart, who is now well again, (the King having made several public visits to her,) and like to come to Court: the other is to go to Barkeshire-house, which is taken for her, and they say a Privy-seal is passed for £5000 for it. He believes all will come to ruin. Thence I to White Hall; where the Duke of York gone to the Lords' House, where there is to be a conference on the Lords' side with the Commons this afternoon, giving in their Reasons, which I would have been at, but could not; for going by direction to the Prince's chamber, there Brouncker, W. Pen, and Mr Wren and I met, and did our business with the Duke of York. But, Lord! to see how this play of Sir Positive At-all in abuse of Sir Robert Howard do take, all the Duke's and every body's talk being of that, and telling more stories of him of the like nature, that it is now the town and country talk, and, they say, is most exactly true. The Duke of York himself said that of his playing at trap-ball is true, and told several other stories of him. Then to Brouncker's house, and there sat and talked, I asking many questions in mathematics to my Lord, which he do me the pleasure to satisfy me in.

9th. I hear that the Queene hath miscarryed of a perfect child, being gone about ten weeks; which do show that she can conceive, though it be unfortunate that she cannot bring forth. We are told also that last night the Duchesse of Monmouth, dancing at her lodgings, hath sprained her thigh. We are told also that the House of Commons sat till five o'clock this morning upon the business of the difference between the Lords and them, resolving to do something therein before they rise to assert their privileges. So I at noon by water to Westminster, and there find the King hath waited in the Prince's chamber these two hours, and the Houses are not ready for him. The Commons having sent this morning, after their long debate therein the last night, to the Lords, that they do think the only expedient left to preserve unity between the two Houses is, that they do put a stop to any proceedings upon their late judgement against the East India Company, till their next meeting; to which the Lords returned answer, that they would return answer to them by a messenger of their own; which they not presently doing, they were all inflamed, and thought it was only a trick to keep them in suspense till the King come to adjourne them; and so rather than lose the opportunity of doing themselves right, they presently with great fury come to this vote: 'That whoever should assist in the execution of the judgement of the Lords against the Company should be held betrayers of the liberties of the people of England, and of the privileges of that House.' This the Lords had notice of, and were mad at it; and so continued debating without any design to yield to the Commons, till the King came in and sent for the Commons: where the Speaker made a short but silly speech about their giving him £300,000; and then the several Bills their titles were read, and the King's assent signified in the proper terms, according to the nature of the Bills; of which about three or four were public Bills, and seven or eight private ones, (the additional Bills for the building of the City and the Bill against Conventicles being none of them.) The King did make a short silly speech, which he read, giving them thanks for the money, which now, he said, he did believe would be sufficient, because there was peace between his neighbours; which was a kind of a slur, methought, to the Commons: and that he was sorry for what he heard of difference between the two Houses, but that he hoped their recess would put them into a way of accommodation; and so adjourned them to the 9th of August, and then recollected himself and told them the 11th; so imperfect a speaker he is. So the Commons went to their House, and forthwith adjourned; and the Lords resumed their House, the King being gone, and sat an hour or two after: but what they did, I cannot tell; but every body expected they would commit Sir Andrew Rickard, Sir Samuel Barnardiston,[40] Mr Boone, and Mr Wynne, who were all there, and called in upon their knees to the bar of the House: and Sir John Robinson I left there, endeavouring to prevent their being committed to the Tower, lest he should thereby be forced to deny their order, because of this vote of the Commons, whereof he is one; which is an odde case.

12th. Lord Anglesy, in talk about the late difference between the two Houses, do tell us that he thinks the House of Lords may be in an error, at least it is possible they may, in this matter of Skinner; and did declare his judgement in the House of Lords against their proceedings therein, he having hindered 100 originall causes being brought into their House, notwithstanding that he was put upon defending their proceedings: but that he is confident that the House of Commons are in the wrong, in the method they take to remedy an error of the Lords, for no vote of theirs can do it; but in all like cases the Commons have done it by petition to the King, sent up to the Lords, and by them agreed to and so redressed, as they did in the petition of Right. He says that he did tell them indeed, which is talked of, and which did vex the Commons, that the Lords were *Judices nati et Conciliarii nati*; but all other Judges among us are under salary, and the Commons themselves served for wages; and therefore the Lords, in reason, the freer Judges.

13th. To attend the Council about the business of Hemskirke's project of building a ship that sails two feet for one of any other ship; which the Council did agree to be put in practice, the King to give him, if it proves good, £5000 in hand, and £15,000 more in seven years: which for my part I think a piece of folly for them to meddle with, because the secret cannot be long kept. This morning I hear that last night Sir Thomas Teddiman, poor man! did die by a thrush in his mouth: a good man, and stout and able, and much lamented, though people do make a little mirth, and say, as I believe it did in good part, that the business of the Parliament did break his heart, or at least put him into this fever and disorder that caused his death.

15th. To a Committee for Tangier; where God knows how my Lord Bellasses' accounts passed: understood by nobody but my Lord

40 Wood mentions Sir S. Barnadiston as a leading Fanatic, *c.* 1683.

Ashly, who, I believe, was allowed to let them go as he pleased. But here Sir H. Cholmly had his propositions read about a greater price for his work of the Molle, or to do it upon account; which being read, he was bid to withdraw. But, Lord! to see how unlucky a man may be by chance! for, making an unfortunate motion when they were almost tired with the other business, the Duke of York did find fault with it, and that made all the rest, that I believe he had better have given a great deal and had nothing said to it to-day; whereas I have seen other things more extravagant passed at first hearing, without any difficulty. To Loriner's-hall, by Mooregate, (a hall I never heard of before,) to Sir Thomas Teddiman's burial, where most people belonging to the sea were. And here we had rings: and here I do hear that some of the last words that he said were, that he had a very good King, God bless him! but that the Parliament had very ill rewarded him for all the service he had endeavoured to do them and his country: so that for certain this did go far towards his death. But, Lord! to see among the company the young command-ers, and Thomas Killigrew and others that came, how unlike a burial this was, O'Brian taking out some ballads out of his pocket, which I read, and the rest come about me to hear! And there very merry we were all, they being new ballads. By and by the corpse went; and I, with my Lord Brouncker, and Dr Clerke, and Mr Pierce, as far as the foot of London-bridge; and there we struck off into Thames-street, the rest going to Redriffe, where he is to be buried. The Duchesse of Monmouth's hip is, I hear, now set again, after much pain. I am told also that the Countesse of Shrewsbery is brought home by the Duke of Buckingham to his house; where his Duchesse saying that it was not for her and the other to live together in a house, he answered, 'Why, Madam, I did think so, and therefore have ordered your coach to be ready to carry you to your father's;' which was a devilish speech, but, they say, true; and my Lady Shrewsbery is there, it seems.

16th. To the King's playhouse, and there saw the best part of *The Sea Voyage*,[41] where Knipp did her part of sorrow very well.

17th (Lord's day). Up, and put on my new stuff-suit, with a shoulder-belt according to the new fashion, and the hands of my vest

41 A comedy, by Beaumont and Fletcher.

and tunique laced with silk-lace of the colour of my suit: and so very handsome to church.

28th. To my Lord Bellasses, at his new house by my late Lord Treasurer's; which indeed is mighty noble, and good pictures, indeed not one bad one in it. It being almost twelve o'clock, or little more, to the King's playhouse, where the doors were not then open; but presently they did open; and we in, and find many people already come in by private ways into the pit, it being the first day of Sir Charles Sedley's new play so long expected, *The Mulberry Garden*; of whom, being so reputed a wit, all the world do expect great matters. I having sat here awhile and eat nothing to-day, did slip out, getting a boy to keep my place; and to the Rose Tavern, and there got half a breast of mutton off of the spit, and dined all alone. And so to the play again; where the King and Queene by and by come, and all the Court; and the house infinitely full. But the play, when it come, though there was here and there a pretty saying, and that not very many neither, yet the whole of the play had nothing extraordinary in it all, neither of language nor design; insomuch that the King I did not see laugh nor pleased from the beginning to the end, nor the company; insomuch that I have not been less pleased at a new play in my life, I think.

19th. Pierce tells me that for certain Mr Vaughan is made Lord Chief Justice; which I am glad of. He tells me too, that since my Lord of Ormond's coming over, the King begins to be mightily reclaimed, and sups every night with great pleasure with the Queene: and yet, it seems, he is mighty hot upon the Duchesse of Richmond; insomuch that, upon Sunday was se'nnight at night, after he had ordered his Guards and coach to be ready to carry him to the Park, he did on a sudden take a pair of oars or sculler, and all alone, or but one with him, go to Somerset House, and there, the garden-door not being open, himself clamber over the wall to make a visit to her; which is a horrid shame.

20th. To the Council-chamber, where the Committee of the Navy sat; and here we discoursed several things, but, Lord! like fools, so as it was a shame to see things of this importance managed by a Council that understand nothing of them. And, among other things, one was about this building of a ship with Hemskirke's secret, to sail a third faster than any other ship; but he hath got Prince Rupert on his side, and by that means, I believe, will get his conditions made better than he would otherwise, or ought indeed. To the Mulbery-garden,[42] where I never was before; and find it a very silly place, worse than Spring-garden, and but little company, only a wilderness here that is somewhat pretty.

21st. To the office, where meets me Sir Richard Ford; who among other things congratulates me, as one or two did yesterday, on my great purchase; and he advises me rather to forbear, if it be not done, as a thing that the world will envy me in: and what is it but my cosen Tom Pepys's buying of Martin Abbey,[43] in Surrey? All the town is full of the talk of a meteor, or some fire, that did on Saturday last fly over the City at night; which do put me in mind that, being then walking in the dark an hour or more myself in the garden after I had done writing, I did see a light before me come from behind me, which made me turn back my head; and I did see a sudden fire or light running in the sky, as it were towards Cheapside-ward, and vanished very quick; which did make me bethink myself what holyday it was, and took it for some rocket, though it was much brighter: and the world do make much discourse of it, their apprehensions being mighty full of the rest of the City to be burned, and the Papists to cut our throats.

22nd. I fitted myself for my journey to Brampton tomorrow, which I fear will not be pleasant because of the wet weather, it rained very hard all this day; but the less it troubles me, because the King and Duke of York and Court are at this day at Newmarket at a great horse-race, and proposed great pleasure for two or three days, but are in the same wet.

23rd. To the Bull in Bishopsgate Street; and there about six took coach, and so away to Bishop's Stafford.[44] The ways are mighty full of water, so as hardly to be passed. After dinner to Cambridge, about nine at night: and there I met my father's horses.

42 On the site of which Buckingham-house was erected.
43 In 1668 the site of Murton, *alias* Martin Priory, was conveyed by Ellis Crispe to Thomas Pepys, Esq., of Hatcham Barns, Master of the Jewel-office to Charles II and James II – Manning's *Surrey*.
44 Bishop Stortford, in Hertfordshire.

24th. We set out by three o'clock to Brampton. Here I saw my brother and sister Jackson. After dinner my Lady Sandwich sending to see whether I was come, I presently took horse, and find her and her family at chapel: and thither I went in to them, and sat out the sermon; where I heard Jervas Fulwood, now their chaplain, preach a very good and civantick kind of sermon, too good for an ordinary congregation. After sermon I with my Lady, and my Lady Hinchingbroke, and Paulina, and Lord Hinchingbroke.

25th. To Cambridge, the waters not being now so high as before. Here lighting, I took my boy and two brothers, and walked to Magdalene College; and there into the butterys as a stranger, and there drank of their beer, which pleased me, as the best I ever drank; and hear by the butler's man, who was son to Goody Mulliner over-against the College, that we used to buy stewed prunes of, concerning the College and persons in it; and find very few, only Mr Hollins[45] and Pechell, I think, that were of my time.

26th. To the coach; where about six o'clock we set out, and got to Bishopsgate-street before eight o'clock, the waters being now most of them down, and we avoiding the bad way in the forest by a privy way, which brought us to Hodsden; and so to Tibald's that road; which was mighty pleasant.

27th. Met Mr Sawyer, my old chamber-fellow; and he and I by water together to the Temple, he giving me an account of the base, rude usage, which he and Sir G. Carteret had lately before the Commissioners of Accounts, where he was as Counsel to Sir G. Carteret; which I was sorry to hear, they behaving themselves like most insolent and ill-mannered men. To see Sir W. Pen; whom I find still very ill of the gout, sitting in his great chair, made on purpose for persons sick of that disease for their ease; and this very chair, he tells me, was made for my Lady Lambert.

29th. Received some directions from the Duke of York and the Committee of the Navy about casting up the charge of the present summer's fleet, that so they may come within the bounds of the sum given by the Parliament. But it is pretty to see how Prince Rupert

45 John Hollins of Medley, in Yorkshire; admitted a Pensioner of Magdalene College, March 1651.

and other mad silly people are for setting out but a little fleet, there being no occasion for it: and say it will be best to save the money for better uses. But Sir G. Carteret did declare that in wisdom it was better to do so; but that, in obedience to the Parliament, he was for setting out the fifty sail talked on, though it spent all the money, and to little purpose; and that this was better than to leave it to the Parliament to make bad constructions of their thrift, if any trouble should happen. Thus wary the world is grown! Thence back again presently home, and did business till noon. And then to Sir G. Carteret's to dinner with much good company, it being the King's birthday, and many healths drunk. And here I did receive another letter from my Lord Sandwich; which troubles me to see how I have neglected him in not writing, or but once, all this time of his being abroad; and I see he takes notice, but yet gently, of it.

30th. Up, and put on a new summer black bombazin suit; and being come now to an agreement with my barber to keep my perriwig in good order at 20s. a-year, I am like to go very spruce, more than I used to do. To the King's playhouse, and there saw *Philaster*;[46] where it is pretty to see how I could remember almost all along, ever since I was a boy, Arethusa, the part which I was to have acted at Sir Robert Cooke's; and it was very pleasant to me, but more to think what a ridiculous thing it would have been for me to have acted a beautiful woman. To Fox Hall, and there fell into the company of Harry Killigrew, a rogue newly come back out of France, but still in disgrace at our Court, and young Newport and others, as very rogues as any in the town, who were ready to take hold of every woman that come by them. And so to supper in an arbour: but, Lord! their mad talk did make my heart ake. And here I first understood by their talk the meaning of the company that lately were called Ballers; Harris telling how it was by a meeting of some young blades, where he was among them, and my Lady Bennet and her ladies; and there dancing naked, and all the roguish things in the world. But, Lord! what loose company was this that I was in to-night, though full of wit; and worth a man's being in for once to know the nature of it, and their manner of talk and lives.

---

46 A tragedy, by Beaumont and Fletcher.

31st. I hear that Mrs Davis is quite gone from the Duke of York's house, and Gosnell comes in her room; which I am glad of. At the play at Court the other night Mrs Davis was there; and when she was to come to dance her jigg, the Queene would not stay to see it; which people do think was out of displeasure at her being the King's mistress, that she could not bear it. My Lady Castlemaine is, it seems, now mightily out of request, the King coming little to her, and then she mighty melancholy and discontented.

June 1st. Alone to Fox Hall, and walked and saw young Newport and two more rogues of the town seize on two ladies, who walked with them an hour with their masks on; (perhaps civil ladies;) and there I left them.

3rd. To White Hall to the Council-chamber, where I did present the Duke of York with an account of the charge of the present fleet to his satisfaction; and this being done, did ask his leave for my going out of town five or six days, which he did give me, saying, that my diligence in the King's business was such that I ought not to be denied when my own business called me any whither. To my Lord Crewe's to visit him; from whom I learn nothing but that there hath been some controversy at the Council-table about my Lord Sandwich's signing, where some would not have had him, in the treaty with Portugall; but all, I think, is over in it.

4th. Mr Clerke the solicitor dined with me and my clerks. After dinner I carried and set him down at the Temple, he observing to me how St Sepulchre's church steeple is repaired already a good deal, and the Fleet-bridge is contracted for by the City to begin to be built this summer; which do please me mightily. I to White Hall, and walked through the Park for a little ayre; and so back to the Council-chamber to the Committee of the Navy, about the business of fitting the present fleet suitable to the money given; which, as the King orders it and by what appears, will be very little, and so as I perceive the Duke of York will have nothing to command, nor can intend to go abroad. But it is pretty to see how careful these great men are to do every thing so as they may answer it to the Parliament, thinking themselves safe in nothing but where the Judges (with whom they often advise) do say the matter is doubtful; and so they take upon themselves then to be the chief persons to interpret what is doubtful.

Thence home, and all the evening to set matters in order against my going to Brampton to-morrow, being resolved upon my journey, and having the Duke of York's leave again to-day; though I do plainly see that I can very ill be spared now, there being much business, especially about this which I have attended the Council about, and I the man that am alone consulted with; and besides, my Lord Brouncker is at this time ill, and Sir W. Pen. So things being put in order at the office, I home to do the like there; and so to bed.

5th. Friday.[47] At Barnet for milk, 6d. On the highway, to menders of the highway, 6d. Dinner at Stevenage, 5s. 6d.

6th. Saturday. Spent at Huntingdon with Bowles and Appleyard, and Shepley, 2s.

7th. Sunday. My father, for money lent, and horse hire, £1 11s.

8th. Monday. Father's servants (father having in the garden told me bad stories of my wife's ill words), 14s.; one that helped at the horses, 1s.; menders of the highway, 2s. Pleasant country to Bedford; where, while they stay, I rode through the town; and a good country town; and there drinking, 1s. We on to Newport; and there I and W. Hewer to the church, and there give the boy 1s. So to Buckingham, a good old town. Here I to see the church; which very good, and the leads, and a school in it: did give the sexton's boy 1s. A fair bridge here, with many arches: vexed at my people's making me lose so much time: reckoning, 13s. 4d. Mightily pleased with the pleasure of the ground all the day. At night to Newport Pagnell; and there a good pleasant country-town, but few people in it. A very fair and like a cathedral-church; and I saw the leads, and a vault that goes far under ground: the town, and so most of this country, well watered. Lay here well, and rose next day by four o'clock: few people in the town: and so away. Reckoning for supper, 19s. 6d.; poor, 6d. Mischance to the coach, but no time lost.

9th. Tuesday. We came to Oxford, a very sweet place: paid our guide £1 2s. 6d.; barber, 2s. 6d.; book (Stonhenge) 4s.; boy that showed me the colleges before dinner, 1s. To dinner; and then out with my wife and people, and landlord: and to him that showed us

47 The journal from this time to the 17th of June is contained on five leaves, inserted in the book; and after them follow several blank pages.

the schools and library, 10s.; to him that showed us All Souls' College and Chichly's picture, 5s. So to see Christ Church with my wife, I seeing several others very fine alone before dinner, and did give the boy that went with me, 1s. Strawberries, 1s. 2d. Dinner and servants, £1 0s. 6d. After coming home from the schools, I out with the landlord to Brazennose College to the butteries, and in the cellar find the hand[48] of the child of Hales, . . . long. Butler, 2s. Thence with coach and people to Physic-garden, 1s. So to Friar Bacon's study: I up and saw it, and gave the man 1s. – Bottle of sack for landlord, 2s. Oxford mighty fine place; and well seated, and cheap entertainment. At night came to Abingdon, where had been a fair of custard; and met many people and scholars going home; and there did get some pretty good musick, and sang and danced till supper: 5s.

10th. Wednesday. Up, and walked to the hospitall: very large and fine, and pictures of founders and the History of the hospitall; and is said to be worth £700 per annum, and that Mr Foly was here lately to see how their lands were settled. And here, in old English, the story of the occasion of it, and a rebus at the bottom. So did give the poor, which they would not take but in their box, 2s. 6d. So to the inn, and paid the reckoning and what not, 13s. So forth towards Hungerford. Led this good way by our landlord, one Heart, an old but very civil and well-spoken man, more than I ever heard, of his quality. He gone, we forward; and I vexed at my people's not minding the way. So come to Hungerford, where very good trouts, eels, and cray-fish. Dinner: a mean town. At dinner there, 12s. Thence set out with a guide, who saw us to Newmarket-heath, and then left us, 3s. 6d. So all over the plain by the sight of the steeple (the plain high and low) to Salisbury by night; but before I came to the town, I saw a great fortification, and there light, and to it and in it; and find it prodigious, so as to fright me to be in it all alone at that time of night, it being dark. I understand since it to be that that is called Old Sarum. Come to the George Inne, where lay in a silk bed; and very good diet. To supper; then to bed.

11th. Thursday. Up, and W. Hewer and I up and down the town,

48 John Middleton, a giant from Lancashire known as the 'Child of Hale', was born 1578, died 1623. He visited Brasenose College, and the outline of his enormous hand was cut in stone in the cellar there. The blank in Pepys's text before the word 'long' was presumably left for the dimensions of the hand to be inserted.

and find it a very brave place. The river goes through every street; and a most capacious marketplace. The city great, I think greater than Hereford. But the minster most admirable; as big, I think, and handsomer than Westminster: and a most large close about it, and houses for the officers thereof, and a fine palace for the Bishop. So to my lodging back, and took out my wife and people to show them the town and church; but they being at prayers, we could not be shown the quire. A very good organ; and I looked in and saw the Bishop, my friend Dr Ward. Thence to the inne; and there not being able to hire coach-horses, and not willing to use our own, we got saddle-horses, very dear. Boy that went to look for them 6d. So the three women behind W. Hewer, Murford, and our guide, and I single to Stonehenge, over the plain and some great hills, even to fright us. Come thither, and find them as prodigious as any tales I ever heard of them, and worth going this journey to see. God knows what their use was: they are hard to tell, but yet may be told. Gave the shepherd-woman, for leading our horses, 4d. So back by Wilton, my Lord Pembroke's house, which we could not see, he being just coming to town; but the situation I do not like, nor the house at present much, it being in a low but rich valley. So back home; and there being light we to the church, and there find them at prayers again, so could not see the quire; but I sent the women home, and I did go in and saw very many fine tombs, and among the rest some very ancient of the Montagus. So home to dinner; and that being done, paid the reckoning, which was so exorbitant, and particular in rate of my horses, and 7s. 6d. for bread and beer, that I was mad, and resolve to trouble the mistress about it, and get something for the poor; and come away in that humour; £2 5s. 6d. Servants, 1s. 6d.; poor 1s.; guide to the Stones, 2s.; poor woman in the street, 1s.; ribbands, 9d.; wash-woman, 1s.; sempstress for W. Hewer, 3s.; lent W. Hewer, 2s. Thence about six o'clock, and with a guide went over the smooth plain indeed till night; and then by a happy mistake, and that looked like an adventure, we were carried out of our way to a town where we would lie, since we could not go as far as we would. By and by to bed, glad of this mistake, because it seems, had we gone on as we pretended, we could not have passed with our coach, and must have lain on the plain all night. This day from Salisbury I wrote by the post my excuse for not coming home, which I hope will do, for I am resolved to see the Bath, and, it may be, Bristol.

12th. Friday. Up, finding our beds good, but lousy: which made us merry. We set out, the reckoning and servants coming to 9s. 6d.; my guide thither, 2s.; coachman advanced, 10s. So rode a very good way, led to my great content by our landlord to Philips-Norton, with great pleasure, being now come into Somersetshire; where my wife and Deb. mightily joyed thereat,[49] I commending the country, as indeed it deserves. And the first town we came to was Brekington; where we stopping for something for the horses, we called two or three little boys to us, and pleased ourselves with their manner of speech. At Philips-Norton I walked to the church and there saw a very ancient tomb of some Knight Templar, I think; and here saw the tombstone whereon there were only two heads cut, which the story goes, and creditably, were two sisters, called the Fair Maids of Foscott, that had two bodies upward and one belly, and there lie buried. Here is also a very fine ring of six bells, and they mighty tuneable. Having dined very well, 10s., we come before night to the Bath; where I presently stepped out with my landlord, and saw the baths with people in them. They are not so large as I expected, but yet pleasant; and the town most of stone, and clean, though the streets generally narrow. I home, and being weary, went to bed without supper; the rest supping.

13th. Saturday. Up at four o'clock, being by appointment called up to the Cross Bath; where we were carried after one another, myself and wife and Betty Turner, Willet, and W. Hewer. And by and by, though we designed to have done before company come, much company come; very fine ladies; and the manner pretty enough, only methinks it cannot be clean to go so many bodies together in the same water. Good conversation among them that are acquainted here, and stay together. Strange to see how hot the water is; and in some places, though this is the most temperate bath, the springs so hot as the feet not able to endure. But strange to see, when women and men here, that live all the season in these waters, cannot but be parboiled and look like the creatures of the bath! Carried away wrapped in a sheet, and in a chair home; and there one after another thus carried (I staying above two hours in the water) home to bed, sweating for an hour. And by and by comes musick to play to me, extraordinary good as ever I heard at London almost any where: 5s. Up to go to Bristoll about eleven o'clock, and paying my landlord

49 They were natives of that county.

that was our guide from Chiltren 10s., and the serjeant of the bath 10s., and the man that carried us in chairs 3s. 6d., set out toward Bristoll, and come thither, the way bad, (in coach hired to spare our own horses,) but country good, about two o'clock; where set down at the Horse-shoe, and there being trimmed by a very handsome fellow, 2s., walked with my wife and people through the city, which is in every respect another London, that one can hardly know it to stand in the country no more than that. No carts, it standing generally on vaults, only dog-carts. So to the Three Crowns Tavern I was directed; but when I came in, the master told me that he had newly given over the selling of wine; it seems grown rich: and so went to the Sun; and there Deb. going with W. Hewer and Betty Turner to see her uncle, and leaving my wife with the mistress of the house, I to see the quay, which is a most large and noble place; and to see the new ship building by Bally, neither he nor Furzer[50] being in town. It will be a fine ship. Spoke with the foreman, and did give the boys that kept the cabin 2s. Walked back to the Sun, where I find Deb. come back, and with her, her uncle, a sober merchant, very good company, and so like one of our sober wealthy London merchants as pleased me mightily. Here we dined, and much good talk with him, 7s. 6d.; a messenger to Sir John Knight,[51] who was not at home, 6d. Then walked with him and my wife and company round the quay, and to the ship; and he showed me the Custom-house, and made me understand many things of the place, and led us through Marsh-street, where our girl was born. But, Lord! the joy that was among the old poor people of the place, to see Mrs Willet's daughter, it seems her mother being a brave woman and mightily beloved! And so brought us a back way by surprize to his house; where a substantial good house, and well furnished; and did give us good entertainment of strawberries, a whole venison-pasty cold, and plenty of brave wine, and above all Bristol milk: where comes in another poor woman, who hearing that Deb. was here did come running hither, and with her eyes so full of tears and heart so full of joy that she could not speak when she come in, that it made me weep too: I protest that I was not able to speak to her, which I would have done, to have diverted her tears. His wife a good woman, and so sober and substantiall as I was

50 Daniel Furzer, Surveyor to the Navy.
51 Mayor of Bristol 1663, and MP for that city.

never more pleased any where. Servant-maid, 2s. So thence took leave and he with us through the city; where in walking I find the city pay him great respect, and he the like to the meanest, which pleased me mightily. He showed us the place where the merchants meet here, and a fine cross yet standing, like Cheapside. And so to the Horse-shoe, where paid the reckoning, 2s. 6d. We back, and by moonshine to the Bath again about ten o'clock: bad way; and giving the coachman 1s. went all of us to bed.

14th (Sunday). Up, and walked up and down the town, and saw a pretty good market-place, and many good streets, and very fair stone-houses. And so to the great church, and there saw Bishop Montagu's tomb; and, when placed, did there see many brave people come, and among others two men brought in litters, and set down in the chancel to hear: but I did not know one face. Here a good organ; but a vain pragmatical fellow preached a ridiculous, affected sermon, that made me angry, and some gentlemen that sat next me, and sang well. So home, walking round the walls of the City, which are good, and the battlements all whole. To this church again, to see it and look over the monuments; where, among others, Dr Venner and Pelling, and a lady of Sir W. Waller's;[52] he lying with his face broken. My landlord did give me a good account of the antiquity of this town and Wells; and of two heads, on two pillars, in Wells church.

15th. Monday. Looked into the baths, and find the King and Queene's full of a mixed sort of good and bad, and the Cross only almost for the gentry. So home with my wife, and did pay my guides, two women, 5s.; one man, 2s. 6d.; poor, 6d.; woman to lay my foot-cloth, 1s. So to our inne, and there eat and paid reckoning, £1 8s. 6d.; servants, 3s.; poor, 1s.; lent the coachman, 10s. Before I took coach, I went to make a boy dive in the King's bath, 1s. I paid also for my coach and a horse to Bristoll, £1 1s. 6d. Took coach, and away without any of the company of the other stage-coaches that go out of this town to-day; and rode all day with some trouble, for fear of our being out of our way, over the Downes, (where the life of the shepherds is, in fair weather only, pretty). In the afternoon come to Abury; where seeing great stones like those of Stonehenge standing up, I stopped and took a countryman of that town, and he carried

52 Jane, sole daughter of Sir Richard Reynell.

me and showed me a place trenched in, like Old Sarum almost, with great stones pitched in it, some bigger than those at Stonehenge in figure, to my great admiration: and he told me that most people of learning coming by do come and view them, and that the King did so; and the mount cast hard by is called Selbury, from one King Seall buried there, as tradition says. I did give this man 1s. So took coach again, seeing one place with great high stones pitched round, which I believe was once some particular building, in some measure like that of Stonehenge. But, about a mile off, it was prodigious to see how full the Downes are of great stones, and all along the vallies stones of considerable bigness, most of them growing certainly out of the ground, so thick as to cover the ground; which makes me think the less of the wonder of Stonehenge, for hence they might undoubtedly supply themselves with stones, as well as those at Abury. In my way did give to the poor and menders of the highway 3s. Before night come to Marlborough, and lay at the Hart; a good house, and a pretty fair town for a street or two; and what is most singular is, their houses on one side having their penthouses supported with pillars, which makes it a good walk. All the five coaches that come this day from Bath, as well as we, were gone out of the town before six.

16th. Tuesday. After paying the reckoning, 14s. 4d. and servants 2s., poor 1s., set out; and passing through a good part of this country of Wiltshire, saw a good house[53] of Alexander Popham's,[54] and another of my Lord Craven's,[55] I think, in Barkeshire. Come to Newbery, and there dined; and musick: a song of the old courtier of Queene Elizabeth's, and how he was changed upon the coming in of the King, did please me mightily, and I did cause W. Hewer to write it out. Then comes the reckoning, (forced to change gold,) 8s. 7d.; servants and poor, 1s. 6d. So out, and lost our way, but come into it again; and in the evening betimes come to Reding; and I to walk about the town, which is a very great one, I think bigger than Salisbury: a river runs through it in seven branches, (which unite in one, in one part of the town,) and runs into the Thames half-a-mile off: one odd sign of the Broad Face. Then to my inn, and so to bed.

53 Littlecote.
54 MP for Bath.
55 Hampstead Marshal, since destroyed by fire.

17th (Wednesday). Rose, and paying the reckoning 12s. 6d.; servants and poor, 2s. 6d.; musick, the worst we have had, coming to our chamber-door, but calling us by wrong names; so set out with one coach in company, and through Maydenhead, which I never saw before, to Colebrooke by noon; the way mighty good; and there dined, and fitted ourselves a little to go through London anon. Thence pleasant way to London before night, and find all very well to great content; and saw Sir W. Pen, who is well again. I hear of the illness by the great fire at Barbadoes.

18th. I did receive a hint or two from my Lord Anglesy, as if he thought much of my taking the ayre as I have done; but I care not: but whatever the matter is, I think he hath some ill-will to me, or at least an opinion that I am more the servant of the Board than I am. To my Lady Peterborough's; who tells me, among other things, her Lord's good words to the Duke of York lately about my Lord Sandwich, and that the Duke of York is kind to my Lord Sandwich; which I am glad to hear.

19th. Between two and three in the morning we were waked with the maids crying out, 'Fire, fire, in Marke-lane!' So I rose and looked out, and it was dreadful; and strange apprehensions in me and us all of being presently burnt. So we all rose; and my care presently was to secure my gold and plate and papers, and could quickly have done it, but I went forth to see where it was; and the whole town was presently in the streets and I found it in a new-built house that stood alone in Minchin-lane, over-against the Cloth-workers'-hall, which burned furiously: the house not yet quite finished; and the benefit of brick was well seen, for it burnt all inward and fell down within itself; so no fear of doing more hurt. Yesterday I heard how my Lord Ashly is like to die, having some imposthume in his breast, that he hath been fain to be cut into the body. To White Hall, where we attended the Duke of York in his closet upon our usual business. And thence out, and did see many of the Knights of the Garter with the King and Duke of York going into the Privy-chamber to elect the Elector of Saxony in that Order; who, I did hear the Duke of York say, was a good drinker: I know not upon what score this compliment is done him.

22nd. With Balty to St James's, and there presented him to Mr Wren about his being Muster-master this year; which will be done. So up to wait on the Duke of York, and thence with Sir W. Coventry walked to White Hall: good discourse about the Navy, where want of money undoes us. Thence to the Coffee-house in Covent-garden; but met with nobody but Sir Philip Howard, who shamed me before the whole house there in commendation of my speech in Parliament. To the King's playhouse, and saw an act or two of the new play, *Evening Love*,[56] again, but like it not. Calling this day at Herringman's,[57] he tells me Dryden do himself call it but a fifth-rate play. From thence to my Lord Brouncker's, where a Council of the Royall Society; and there heard Mr Harry Howard's noble offers about ground for our college, and his intentions of building his own house there, most nobly. My business was to meet Mr Boyle; which I did, and discoursed about my eyes; and he did give me the best advice he could, but refers me to one Turberville[58] of Salisbury lately come to town, who I will go to. Thence home; where the streets full at our end of the town, removing their wine against the Act begins, which will be two days hence, to raise the price.

23rd. To Dr Turberville about my eyes; whom I met with: and he did discourse, I thought, learnedly about them; and takes time, before he did prescribe me any thing, to think of it.

24th. Creed and Colonel Atkins come to me about sending coals to Tangier; and upon that most of the morning.

28th. Much talk of the French setting out their fleet afresh; but I hear nothing that our King is alarmed at it at all, but rather making his fleet less.

29th. To Dr Turberville's, and there did receive a direction for some physic, and also a glass of something to drop into my eyes: he gives me hopes that I may do well. Then to White Hall; where I find the Duke of York in the Council-chamber; and the officers of the Navy were called in about Navy business, about calling in of more ships; the King of France having, as the Duke of York says, ordered his fleet to come in, notwithstanding what he had lately ordered for their staying abroad. Thence to the chapel, it being St Peter's day,

---

56 *An Evening's Love, or The Mock Astrologer*, a comedy by Dryden.
57 H. Herringman, a printer and publisher in the New Exchange.
58 Daubigney Turberville, of Oriel College; created MD at Oxford 1660.

and did hear an anthem of Silas Taylor's making; a dull, old-fashioned thing of six and seven parts, that nobody could understand: and the Duke of York, when he came out, told me that he was a better storekeeper than anthem-maker, and that was bad enough too. This morning Mr May showed me the King's new buildings at White Hall, very fine; and among other things, his cielings and his houses of office.

July 1st. To White Hall, and so to St James's where we met; and much business with the Duke of York. And I find the Duke of York very hot for regulations in the Navy; and I believe is put on it by Sir W. Coventry; and I am glad of it: and particularly he falls heavy on Chatham-yard, and is vexed that Lord Anglesy did the other day complain at the Council-table of disorders in the Navy, and not to him. So I to White Hall to a Committee of Tangier; and there vexed with the importunity and clamours of Alderman Backewell for my aquittance for money by him supplied to the garrison, before I have any order for paying it. So home, calling at several places, among others the 'Change, and on Cooper, to know when my wife shall come and sit for her picture.

3rd. To Commissioners of Accounts at Brooke-house, the first time I was ever there: and found Sir W. Turner in the chair; and present, Lord Halifax, Thomas Gregory, Dunster, and Osborne. I long with them, and see them hot set on this matter; but I did give them proper and safe answers. Halifax, I perceive, was industrious on my side on behalf of his uncle Coventry, it being the business of Sir W. Warren. Vexed only at their denial of a copy of what I set my hand to and swore. To an alehouse: met Mr Pierce the surgeon, and Dr Clerke, Waldron,[59] Turberville my physician for the eyes, and Lowre,[60] to dissect several eyes of sheep and oxen, with great pleasure and to my great information. But strange that this Turberville should be so great a man, and yet to this day had seen no eyes dissected, or but once, but desired this Dr Lowre to give him the opportunity to see him dissect some.

59 Thomas Waldron, of Balliol College; created MD at Oxford 1653; afterwards Physician in Ordinary to Charles II.
60 Probably Richard Lower, of Christ Church; admitted Bachelor of Physic at Oxford 1665.

4th. Up, and to see Sir W. Coventry, and give him an account of my doings yesterday; which he well liked of, and was told thereof by my Lord Halifax before; but I do perceive he is much concerned for this business. Gives me advice to write a smart letter to the Duke of York about the want of money in the Navy, and desire him to communicate it to the Commissioners of the Treasury; for he tells me he hath hot work sometimes to contend with the rest for the Navy, they being all concerned for some other part of the King's expenses, which they would prefer to this of the Navy. He showed me his closet, with his round-table for him to sit in the middle, very convenient; and I borrowed several books of him, to collect things out of the Navy, which I have not.

6th. With Sir W. Coventry; and we walked in the Park together a good while. He mighty kind to me; and hear many pretty stories of my Lord Chancellor's being heretofore made sport of by Peter Talbot the priest, in his story of the death of Cardinal Bleau; by Lord Cottington, in his *Dolor de las Tripas*; and Tom Killigrew, in his being bred in Ram-ally, and now bound prentice to Lord Cottington, going to Spain with £1000 and two suits of clothes. Thence to Mr Cooper's, and there met my wife and W. Hewer and Deb.; and there my wife first sat for her picture: but he is a most admirable workman, and good company. Here comes Harris, and first told us how Betterton is come again upon the stage: whereupon my wife and company to the house to see *Henry the Fifth*; while I to attend the Duke of York at the Committee of the Navy at the Council, where some high dispute between him and W. Coventry about settling pensions upon all flag-officers while unemployed; W. Coventry against it, and, I think, with reason. Great doings at Paris, I hear, with their triumphs for their late conquests. The Duchesse of Richmond sworn last week of the Queene's Bedchamber, and the King minding little else but what he used to do – about his women.

7th. We are fain to go round by Newgate because of Fleet-bridge being under rebuilding.

8th. To Sir W. Coventry, and there discoursed of several things; and I find him much concerned in the present enquiries now on foot of the Commissioners of Accounts, though he reckons himself and the rest very safe, but vexed to see us liable to these troubles in things wherein we have laboured to do best. Thence, he being to go out of town to-morrow to drink Banbury waters, I to the Duke of York to attend him about business of the office; and find him mighty free to me, and how he is concerned to mend things in the Navy himself, and not leave it to other people. So home to dinner; and then with my wife to Cooper's, and there saw her sit; and he do extraordinary things indeed. So to White Hall; and there by and by the Duke of York comes to the Robe-chamber and spent with us three hours till night, in hearing the business of the Masters-attendants of Chatham, and the Store-keeper of Woolwich; and resolves to displace them all; so hot he is of giving proofs of his justice at this time, that it is their great fate now to come to be questioned at such a time as this.

10th. To Cooper's; and there find my wife (and W. Hewer and Deb.), sitting, and painting: and here he do work finely, though I fear it will not be so like as I expected: but now I understand his great skill in musick, his playing and setting to the French lute most excellently: and he speaks French, and indeed is an excellent man.

11th. To the King's Playhouse to see an old play of Shirly's, called *Hide Parke*; the first day acted; where horses are brought upon the stage: but it is but a very moderate play, only an excellent epilogue spoke by Beck Marshall.

13th. To Cooper's and spent the afternoon with them; and it will be an excellent picture. This morning I was let blood, and did bleed about fourteen ounces, towards curing my eyes.

14th. This day Bosse finished his copy of my picture, which I confess I do not admire, though my wife prefers him to Browne; nor do I think it like. He does it for W. Hewer, who hath my wife's also, which I like less.

15th. At noon is brought home the espinette I bought the other day of Haward; cost me £5. My Lady Duchesse of Monmouth is still lame, and likely always to be so; which is a sad chance for a young lady to get only by trying of tricks in dancing.

17th. To White Hall, where waited on the Duke of York and then the Council about the business of tickets; and I did discourse to their liking, only was too high to assert that nothing could be invented to secure the King more in the business of tickets than there is, which the Duke of Buckingham did except against, and I could have answered, but forbore, but all liked very well.

18th. They say the King of France is making a war again in Flanders with the King of Spain; the King of Spain refusing to give him all that he says was promised him in that treaty.

19th. Come Mr Cooper, Hales, Harris, Mr Butler that wrote *Hudibras*, and Mr Cooper's cosen Jacke; and by and by come Mr Reeves and his wife, whom I never saw before. And there we dined: a good dinner, and company that pleased me mightily, being all eminent men in their way. Spent all the afternoon in talk and mirth, and in the evening parted.

20th. To visit my Lord Crewe, who is very sick, to great danger, by an erisypelas; the first day I heard of it.

21st. Went to my plate-maker's, and there spent an hour about contriving my little plates for my books of the King's four Yards.

22nd. Attending at the Committee of the Navy about the old business of tickets; where the only expedient they have found is to bind the commanders and officers by oaths. The Duke of York told me how the Duke of Buckingham, after the Council the other day, did make mirth at my position about the sufficiency of present rules in the business of tickets; and here I took occasion to desire a private discourse with the Duke of York, and he granted it me on Friday next.

24th. Up, and by water to St James's (having by the way shown Symson Sir W. Coventry's chimney-pieces, in order to the making me one;) and there, after the Duke of York was ready, he called me to his closet; and there I did long and largely show him the weakness of our office, and did give him advice to call us to account for our duties; which he did take mighty well, and desired me to draw up what I would have him write to the office. I did lay open the whole failings of the office, and how it was his duty to fine them and to find fault with them as Admiral, especially at this time; which he agreed to, and seemed much to rely on what I said.

27th. To see my Lord Crewe, whom I find up; and did wait on him; but his face sore, but in hopes to do now very well again. Thence to

Cooper's, where my wife's picture almost done, and mighty fine indeed. So over the water with my wife and Deb. and Mercer to Spring-garden, and there eat and walked; and observe how rude some of the young gallants of the town are become, to go into people's arbors where there are not men, and almost force the women; which troubled me, to see the confidence of the vice of the age: and so we away by water with much pleasure home.

30th. To White Hall. There met with Mr May, who was giving directions about making a close way for people to go dry from the gate up into the House, to prevent their going through the galleries; which will be very good. I staid and talked with him about the state of the King's offices in general, and how ill he is served, and do still find him an excellent person.

31st. With Mr Ashburnham; and I made him admire my drawing a thing presently in shorthand; but, God knows, I have paid dear for it in my eyes. To the King's house, to see the first day of Lacy's *Monsieur Ragou*, now new acted. The King and Court all there, and mighty merry: a farce. The month ends mighty sadly with me, my eyes being now past all use almost; and I am mighty hot upon trying the late printed experiment of paper tubes.

August 5th. To the Duke of York's playhouse, and there saw *The Guardian*; formerly the same, I find, that was called *Cutter of Coleman Street*; a silly play. And thence to Westminster Hall, where I met Fitzgerald; and with him to a tavern to consider of the instructions for Sir Thomas Allen, against his going to Algier; he and I being designed to go down to Portsmouth by the Council's order to-morrow morning. So I away home, and there bespeak a coach; and so home, and to bed.

6th. Waked betimes, and my wife at an hour's warning is resolved to go with me; which pleases me, her readiness. But before ready comes a letter from Fitzgerald, that he is seized upon last night by an order of the General's by a file of musqueteers, and kept prisoner in his chamber. The Duke of York did tell me of it to-day: it is about a quarrel between him and Witham, and they fear a challenge. So I to him, and sent my wife by the coach round to Lambeth. I lost my labour going to his lodgings; and he in bed: and staying a great while for him I at last grew impatient, and would stay no longer; but to St

James's to Mr Wren, to bid him 'God be with you!' and so over the water to Fox Hall; and there my wife and Deb. took me up, and we away to Gilford, losing our way for three or four miles about Cobham. At Gilford we dined; and I showed them the hospitall there of Bishop Abbot's,[61] and his tomb in the church; which, and the rest of the tombs there, are kept mighty clean and neat, with curtains before them. So to coach again, and got to Lippook, late over Hindhead, having an old man a guide in the coach with us; but got thither with great fear of being out of our way, it being ten at night. Here good, honest people; and after supper to bed.

7th. To coach, and with a guide to Petersfield, where I find Sir Thomas Allen and Mr Tippets[62] come; the first about the business, the latter only in respect to me; as also Fitzgerald, who came post all last night, and newly arrived here. We four sat down presently to our business, and in an hour despatched all our talk; and did inform Sir Thomas Allen well in it, who, I perceive, in serious matters is a serious man: and tells me he wishes all we are told be true, in our defence; for he finds by all that the Turkes have to this day been very civil to our merchantmen every where; and if they would have broke with us, they never had such an opportunity over our rich merchantmen as lately coming out of the Streights. Then to dinner; and pretty merry: and here was Mr Martin the purser, who dined with us, and wrote some things for us. And so took coach again back: Fitzgerald with us, whom I was pleased with all the day, with his discourse of his observations abroad, as being a great soldier and of long standing abroad; and knows all things and persons abroad very well, – I mean the great soldiers of France and Spain and Germany; and talkes very well. Came at night to Gilford; where the Red Lyon so full of people, and a wedding, that the master of the house did get us a lodging over the way, at a private house, his landlord's, mighty neat and fine: and there supped; and so bed.

8th. I hear that Colbert the French Ambassador is come, and hath been at Court *incognito*. When he hath his audience, I know not.

9th. Waited on the Duke of York; and both by him and several of the Privy-council, beyond expectation, I find that my going to Sir

---

61 George Abbot, Archbishop of Canterbury. Died 1633.
62 John Tippet, a Surveyor of the Navy; afterwards knighted.

Thomas Allen was looked upon as a thing necessary; and I have got some advantage by it among them.

10th. To my Lord Arlington's house, the first time since he came thither, at Goring-house, a very fine, noble place; and there he received me in sight of several Lords with great respect. I did give him an account of my journey. And here, while I waited for him a little, my Lord Orrery took notice of me, and begun discourse of hangings, and of the improvement of shipping; I not thinking that he knew me, but did then discover it was a mighty compliment of my abilities and ingenuity; which I am mighty proud of; and he do speak most excellently. To Cooper's, where I spent all the afternoon with my wife and girl, seeing him make an end of her picture; which he did to my great content, though not so great as I confess I expected, being not satisfied in the greatness of the resemblance, nor in the blue garment; but it is most certainly a most rare piece of work as to the painting. He hath £30 for his work, and the chrystal and case and gold case comes to £8 3s. 4d.; and which I sent him this night, that I might be out of his debt.

11th. The Parliament met enough to adjourne to the 10th of November next. At the office all the afternoon till night, being mightily pleased with a trial I have made of the use of a tube-spectacall of paper, tried with my right eye. This day I hear that, to the great joy of the Nonconformists, the time is out of the Act against them; so that they may meet: and they have declared that they will have a morning lecture up again, which is pretty strange; and they are connived at by the King every where, I hear, in the City and country. This afternoon my wife and Mercer and Deb. went with Pelling to see the gypsies at Lambeth, and have their fortunes told; but what they did, I did not enquire.

12th. Captain Cocke tells me that he hears for certain the Duke of York will lose the authority of an Admirall, and be governed by a Committee: and all our office changed; only they are in dispute whether I shall continue or no; which puts new thoughts in me, but I know not whether to be glad or sorry.

14th. I with Mr Wren, by invitation, to Sir Stephen Fox's to dinner: where the Cofferer and Sir Edward Savage; where many good stories of the antiquity and estates of many families at this day in Cheshire,

and that part of the kingdom, more than what is on this side near
London. My Lady dining with us; a very good lady, and a family
governed so nobly and neatly as do me good to see it. Thence the
Cofferer, Sir Stephen, and I to the Commissioners of the Treasury
about business: and so I up to the Duke of York, who enquired for
what I had promised him, about my observations of the miscarriages of
our office; and I told him he should have it next week, being glad he
called for it; for I find he is concerned to do something, and to secure
himself thereby, I believe: for the world is labouring to eclipse him, I
doubt; I mean the factious part of the Parliament. The office met this
afternoon as usual, and waited on him; where, among other things, he
talked a great while of his intentions of going to Dover soon, to be
sworn as Lord Warden; which is a matter of great ceremony and state.

16th. All the morning at my office with W. Hewer; there drawing
up my Report to the Duke of York, as I have promised, about the
faults of this office.

17th. To Hamstead, to speak with the Atturny-generall; whom we
met in the fields, by his old rout and house. And after a little talk
about our business of Ackeworth, went and saw the Lord Wotton's[63]
house[64] and garden, which is wonderfull fine: too good for the house
the gardens are, being indeed the most noble that ever I saw, and
brave orange and lemon-trees. Thence to Mr Chichly's by invitation,
and there dined with Sir John, his father not coming home. And
while at dinner comes by the French Ambassador Colbert's mules
(the first I ever saw,) with their sumpter-clothes mighty rich, and his
coaches, he being to have his entry to-day: but his things, though
rich, are not new; supposed to be the same his brother had the other
day at the treaty at Aix-la-Chapelle, in Flanders.

18th. Alone to the Park; but there were few coaches: among the few
there were our two great beauties, my Lady Castlemaine and
Richmond; the first time I saw the latter since she had the small pox.
I had much pleasure to see them, but I thought they were strange one
to another.

63 Henry de Kirkhoven, Lord of Denfleet in Holland, married Katherine widow of
Henry Lord Stanhope, and daughter of Lord Wotton; and her second husband, the
person here mentioned, was created Lord Wotton, of Wotton in Kent, 1651.
64 Belsize House, pulled down long ago.

20th. To work till past twelve at night, that I might get my great letter to the Duke of York ready against tomorrow; which I shall do, to my great content.

21st. Up betimes, and with my people again to work, and finished all before noon: and then I by water to White Hall, and there did tell the Duke of York that I had done; and he hath desired me to come to him at Sunday next in the afternoon, to read it over; by which I have more time to consider and correct it. To St James's: and by and by comes Monsieur Colbert the French Ambassador, to make his first visit to the Duke of York, and then to the Duchesse. And I saw it: a silly piece of ceremony, he saying only a few formal words. A comely man, and in a black suit and cloak of silk; which is a strange fashion now it hath been so long left off. This day I did first see the Duke of York's room of pictures of some Maids of Honour, done by Lilly: good, but not like.

22nd. To the 'Change, and thence home, and took London-bridge in my way; walking down Fish-street and Gracious-street, to see how very fine a descent they have now made down the hill, that it is become very easy and pleasant.

23rd. To church, and heard a good sermon of Mr Gifford's at our church, upon 'Seek ye first the kingdom of Heaven and its righteousness, and all things shall be added to you.' A very excellent and persuasive, good and moral sermon. He showed, like a wise man, that righteousness is a surer moral way of being rich, than sin and villany. After dinner to the office, Mr Gibson and I, to examine my letter to the Duke of York; which, to my great joy, I did very well by my paper tube, without pain to my eyes. And I do mightily like what I have therein done; and did according to the Duke of York's order make haste to St James's, and about four o'clock got thither: and there the Duke of York was ready expecting me, and did hear it all over with extraordinary content; and did give me many and hearty thanks, and in words the most expressive tell me his sense of my good endeavours, and that he would have a care of me on all occasions: and did with much inwardness tell me what was doing, suitable almost to what Captain Cocke tells me, of designs to make alterations in the Navy: and is most open to me in them, and with utmost confidence desires my further advice on all occasions: and he resolves to have my letter transcribed and sent forthwith to the office. So with as much satisfaction as I could possibly or did hope for, and obligation on the Duke of York's side professed to me, I away.

25th. Up, and by water to St James's; and there with Mr Wren did discourse about my great letter, which the Duke of York hath given him; and he hath set it to be transcribed by Billings his man, whom, as he tells me, he can most confide in for secresy; and is much pleased with it, and earnest to have it be: and he and I are like to be much together in the considering how to reform the office, and that by the Duke of York's command. Thence I, mightily pleased with this success, away to the office; where all the morning, my head full of this business. And it is pretty how Lord Brouncker this day did tell me how he hears that a design is on foot to remove us out of the office; and proposes that we two do agree to draw up a form of new constitution of the office, there to provide remedies for the evils we are now under, that so we may be beforehand with the world; which I agreed to, saying nothing of my design: and the truth is, he is the best man of them all, and I would be glad next myself to save him; for as he deserves best, so I doubt he needs his place most.

26th. It is strange to see with what speed the people employed do pull down Paul's steeple, and with what ease: it is said that it and the quire are to be taken down this year, and another church begun in the room thereof the next. Home by coach with Sir D. Gauden; who by the way tells me how the City do go on in several things towards the building of the public places, which I am glad to hear; and gives hope that in a few years it will be a glorious place. But we met with several stops and troubles in the way in the streets, so as makes it bad to travel in the dark now through the City. So I to Mr Batelier's by appointment, where I find my wife and Deb. and Mercer; Mrs Pierce and her husband, son, and daughter; and Knipp and Harris, and W. Batelier and his sister Mary and cosen Gumbleton, a good-humoured fat young gentleman, son to the Jeweller, that dances well. And here danced all night long, with a noble supper; and about two in the morning the table spread again for a noble breakfast beyond all moderation; and then broke up.

27th. To St James's; and there with Mr Wren did correct his copy of my letter, which the Duke of York hath signed in my very words, without alteration of a syllable. And so, pleased therewith, I to my

Lord Brouncker, who I find within, but hath business, and so comes not to the office to-day. And so I by water to the office, where we sat all the morning: and just as the Board rises comes the Duke of York's letter; which I knowing, and the Board not being full, and desiring rather to have the Duke of York deliver it himself to us, I suppressed it for this day, my heart beginning to falsify in this business, as being doubtful of the trouble it may give me by provoking them; but, however, I am resolved to go through it, and it is too late to help it now. At noon to dinner to Captain Cocke's, where I met with Mr Wren; my going being to tell him what I have done, which he likes, and to confer with Cocke about our office; who tells me that he is confident the design of removing our officers do hold, but that he is sure that I am safe enough. So away home; and there met at Sir Richard Ford's with the Duke of York's Commissioners about our prizes, with whom we shall have some trouble before we make an end with them.

28th. To White Hall; where the Duke of York did call me aside, and told me that he must speak with me in the afternoon and with Mr Wren, for that now he hath got the paper from my Lord Keeper about the exceptions taken against the management of the Navy; and so we are to debate upon answering them. At noon I home with Sir W. Coventry to his house; and there dined with him, and talked freely with him; and did acquaint him with what I have done, which he is well pleased with and glad of: and do tell me that there are endeavours on foot to bring the Navy into new, but, he fears, worse hands. The Duke of York fell to work with us (the Committee being gone) in the Council-chamber; and there with his own hand did give us his long letter, telling us that he had received several from us, and now did give us one from him, taking notice of our several doubts and failures, and desired answer to it as he therein desired: this pleased me well. And so fell to other business, and then parted. And the Duke of York and Wren and I, it being now candle-light, into the Duke of York's closet in White Hall; and there read over this paper of my Lord Keeper's, wherein are laid down the faults of the Navy, so silly, and the remedies so ridiculous, or else the same that are now already provided, that we thought it not to need any answer, the Duke of York being able himself to do it: that so it makes us admire the confidence of these men to offer things so silly in a business of such moment. But it is a most perfect instance of the complexion of the times! And so the Duke of York said himself; who, I perceive, is mightily concerned in it, and do again and again recommend it to Mr Wren and me together, to consider upon remedies fit to provide for him to propound to the King, before the rest of the world, and particularly the Commissioners of Accounts, who are men of understanding and order, to find our faults, and offer remedies of their own: which I am glad of, and will endeavour to do something in it. So parted, and with much difficulty by candle-light walked over the Matted Gallery, as it is now with the mats and boards all taken up, so that we walked over the rafters. But strange to see how hard matter the plaister of Paris is that is there taken up, as hard as stone! And pity to see Holben's work in the ceiling blotted on and only whited over! My wife this day with Hales, to sit for her hand to be mended in her picture.

29th. Up, and all the morning at the office; where the Duke of York's long letter was read to their great trouble, and their suspecting me to have been the writer of it. And at noon comes by appointment Harris to dine with me: and after dinner he and I to Chyrurgeons'- hall, where they are building it new, very fine; and there to see their theatre, which stood all the fire, and (which was our business) their great picture of Holben's, thinking to have bought it by the help of Mr Pierce for a little money: I did think to give £200 for it, it being said to be worth £1000; but it is so spoiled that I have no mind to it, and is not a pleasant though a good picture. Thence carried Harris to his playhouse; where, though four o'clock, so few people there are at *The Impertinents*, as I went out; and do believe they did not act, though there was my Lord Arlington and his company there. So I out, and met my wife in a coach, and stopped her going thither to meet me; and took her and Mercer and Deb. to Bartholomew fair, and there did see a ridiculous, obscene little stage-play, called *Marry Andrey*; a foolish thing, but seen by every body: and so to Jacob Hall's[65] dancing on the ropes; a thing worth seeing, and mightily followed.

30th. Lord's day. Walked to St James's and Pell Mell, and read over with Sir W. Coventry my long letter to the Duke of York, and which the Duke of York hath from mine wrote to the Board,

65 Jacob Hall, the famous rope-dancer, was said to have received a salary from Lady Castlemaine, who had become enamoured of him.

wherein he is mightily pleased, and I perceive do put great value upon me, and did talk very openly on all matters of State, and how some people have got the Bill into their mouths (meaning the Duke of Buckingham and his party), and would likely run away with all. But what pleased me mightily was to hear the good character he did give of my Lord Falmouth for his generosity, good-nature, desire of public good, and low thoughts of his own wisdom; his employing his interest in the King to do good offices to all people, without any other fault than the freedom he do learn in France of thinking himself obliged to serve his King in his pleasures; and was Sir W. Coventry's particular friend; and Sir W. Coventry do tell me very odde circumstances about the fatality of his death, which are very strange.[66] Thence to White Hall to chapel, and heard the anthem, and did dine with the Duke of Albemarle in a dirty manner as ever. All the afternoon I sauntered up and down the house and Park. And there was a Committee for Tangier met; wherein Lord Middleton would, I think, have found fault with me for want of coles; but I slighted it, and he made nothing of it, but was thought to be drunk; and I see that he hath a mind to find fault with me and Creed, neither of us having yet applied ourselves to him about any thing: but do talk of his profits and perquisites taken from him, and garrison reduced, and that it must be increased, and such things as I fear he will be just such another as my Lord Tiviott and the rest to ruin that place. So I to the Park, and there walk an hour or two; and in the King's garden, and saw the Queene and ladies walk; and I did steal some apples of the trees; and here did see my Lady Richmond, who is of a noble person as ever I did see, but her face worse than it was considerably by the smallpox; her sister is also very handsome. So to White Hall in the evening to the Queene's side, and there met the Duke of York; and he did tell me and Sir W. Coventry, who was with me, how the Lord Anglesy did take notice of our reading his long and sharp letter to the Board; but that it was the better, at least he said so. The Duke of York, I perceive, is earnest in it, and will have good effects of it; telling Sir W. Coventry that it was a letter that might have come from the Commissioners of Accounts, but it was better it should come first from him. I met Lord Brouncker; who, I perceive, and the

66 I have read the particulars of this prediction in a manuscript in the Pepysian Collection, but the reference to it is unfortunately mislaid.

rest, do smell that it comes from me, but dare not find fault with me; and I am glad of it, it being my glory and defence that I did occasion and write it. So by water home; and did spend the evening with W. Hewer, telling him how we are all like to be turned out, Lord Brouncker telling me this evening that the Duke of Buckingham did within few hours say that he had enough to turn us all out: which I am not sorry for at all, for I know the world will judge me to go for company; and my eyes are such as I am not able to do the business of my office as I used, and would desire to do while I am in it.

31st. To the Duke of York's playhouse, and saw *Hamlet*, which we have not seen this year before, or more; and mightily pleased with it, but above all with Betterton, the best part, I believe that ever man acted.

September 1st. To the fair, and there saw several sights; among others, the mare that tells money and many things to admiration.

2nd. Fast-day for the burning of London strictly observed.

3rd. To my bookseller's for Hobbs's *Leviathan*, which is now mightily called for: and what was heretofore sold for 8s. I now give 24s. at the second hand, and is sold for 30s., it being a book the Bishops will not let be printed again.

4th. To the fair to see the play *Bartholomew-fair*, with puppets. And it is an excellent play; the more I see it, the more I love the wit of it; only the business of abusing the Puritans begins to grow stale and of no use, they being the people that at last will be found the wisest. This night Knipp tells us that there is a Spanish woman lately come over that pretends to sing as well as Mrs Knight;[67] both of whom I must endeavour to hear.

5th. To Mr Hales's new house, where I find he hath finished my wife's hand, which is better than the other. And here I find Harris's picture done in his habit of *Henry the Fifth*, mighty like a player, but I do not think the picture near so good as any yet he hath made for me; however, it is pretty well.

---

67 A celebrated singer and favourite of Charles II. Her portrait was engraved in 1749 by Faber, after Kneller. There is in Waller's poems a song, sung by Mrs Knight to the Queen on her birthday.

7th. With my Lord Brouncker (who was this day in unusual manner merry, I believe with drink), J. Minnes, and W. Pen to Bartholomew-fair; and there saw the dancing mare again (which to-day I find to act much worse than the other day, she forgetting many things, which her master beat her for, and was mightily vexed,) and then the dancing of the ropes, and also the little stage-play, which is very ridiculous.

8th. This day I received so earnest an invitation again from Roger Pepys to come to Stourbridge-fair, that I resolve to let my wife go; which she shall do the next week.

9th. To the Duke of Richmond's lodgings by his desire by letter yesterday. I find him at his lodgings in the little building in the bowling-green at White Hall, that was begun to be built by Captain Rolt. They are fine rooms. I did hope to see his lady; but she, I hear, is in the country. His business was about his yacht; and he seems a mighty good-natured man, and did presently write me a warrant for a doe from Cobham, when the season comes, buck season being past. I shall make much of this acquaintance, that I may live to see his lady near. Thence to Westminster, to Sir R. Long's office; and going, met Mr George Montagu, who talked and complimented me mightily; and a long discourse I had with him: who, for news, tells me for certain that Trevor do come to be Secretary at Michaelmas, and that Morrice goes out, and, he believes, without any compensation. He tells me that now Buckingham do rule all; and the other day, in the King's journey he is now in, at Bagshot and that way, he caused Prince Rupert's horses to be turned out of an inne, and caused his own to be kept there; which the Prince complained of to the King, and the Duke of York seconded the complaint; but the King did over-rule it for Buckingham, by which there are high displeasures among them: and Buckingham and Arlington rule all. To White Hall; where Brouncker, W. Pen, and I attended the Commissioners of the Treasury about the victualling contract; where high words between Sir Thomas Clifford and us, and myself more particularly, who told him that something, that he said was told him about this business, was a flat untruth. However, we went on to our business in the examination of the draught, and so parted, and I vexed at what happened.

13th (Lord's day). By coach to St James's, and met, to my wish, the Duke of York and Mr Wren: and understand the Duke of York hath received answers from Brouncker, W. Pen, and J. Minnes; and as soon as he saw me, he bid Mr Wren read them over with me. So having no opportunity of talk with the Duke of York, and Mr Wren some business to do, he put them into my hands like an idle companion, to take home with me before himself had read them; which do give me great opportunity of altering my answering, if there was cause. After supper made my wife to read them all over, wherein she is mighty useful to me: and I find them all evasions, and in many things false, and in few to the full purpose. Little said reflective on me; though W. Pen and J. Minnes do mean me in one or two places, and J. Minnes a little more plainly would lead the Duke of York to question the exactness of my keeping my records; but all to no purpose. My mind is mightily pleased by this, if I can but get time to have a copy taken of them for my future use; but I must return them to-morrow. So to bed.

14th. Up betimes, and walked to the Temple, and stopped, viewing the Exchange and Paul's and St Fayth's; where strange how the very sight of the stones falling from the top of the steeple do make me sea-sick! But no hurt, I hear, hath yet happened in all this work of the steeple; which is very much. So from the Temple I by coach to St James's; where I find Sir W. Pen and Lord Anglesy, who delivered this morning his answer to the Duke of York, but I could not see it. But after being above with the Duke of York, I down with Mr Wren; and he and I read all over that I had, and I expounded them to him, and did so order it that I had them home with me, so that I shall to my heart's wish be able to take a copy of them. After dinner I by water to White Hall; and there, with the Cofferer and Sir Stephen Fox, attended the Commissioners of the Treasury about bettering our fund; and are promised it speedily.

15th. To the King's playhouse to see a new play, acted but yesterday, a translation out of French by Dryden, called *The Ladys à la Mode*: so mean a thing as, when they come to say it would be acted again to-morrow, both he that said it (Beeson)[68] and the pit fell a-laughing.

---

68 Probably Beeston, who had been Manager of the Cockpit Theatre.

16th. Walking it to the Temple, and in my way observe that the stockes are now pulled quite down: and it will make the coming into Cornhill and Lumber-street mighty noble. I stopped too at Paul's, and there did go into St Fayth's church, and also in the body of the west part of the church; and do see a hideous sight of the walls of the church ready to fall, that I was in fear as long as I was in it; and here I saw the great vaults underneath the body of the church. No hurt, I hear, is done yet, since their going to pull down the church and steeple; but one man, one Mound, this week fell from the top of the roof of the east end that stands next the steeple, and there broke himself all to pieces. It is pretty here to see how the late church was but a case wrought over the old church; for you may see the very old pillars standing whole within the wall of this. When I come to St James's, I find the Duke of York gone with the King to see the muster of the Guards in Hide Park; and their Colonell, the Duke of Monmouth, to take his command this day of the King's Life-guard, by surrender of my Lord Gerard. So I took a hackney-coach and saw it all: and indeed it was mighty noble, and their firing mighty fine, and the Duke of Monmouth in mighty rich clothes; but the well ordering of the men I understand not. Here, among a thousand coaches that were there, I saw and spoke to Mrs Pierce: and by and by Mr Wren hunts me out and gives me my Lord Anglesy's answer to the Duke of York's letter: where, I perceive, he do do what he can to hurt me, by bidding the Duke of York call for my books: but this will do me all the right in the world, and yet I am troubled at it. So away out of the Park, and home; and there Mr Gibson and I to dinner: and all the afternoon with him writing over anew and a little altering my answer to the Duke of York, which I have not yet delivered, and so have the opportunity of doing it after seeing all their answers, though this do give me occasion to alter very little. This done, he to write it over, and I to the office; where late, and then home, and he had finished it. And then he to read to me the *Life of Archbishop Laud*, wrote by Dr Heylin; which is a shrewd book, but that which I believe will do the Bishops in general no great good, but hurt, it pleads so much for Popery.

18th. To St James's, and there took a turn or two in the Park; and then up to the Duke of York, and there had opportunity of delivering my answer to his late letter, which he did not read, but give to Mr Wren, as looking on it as a thing I needed not have done, but only that I might not give occasion to the rest to suspect my communication with the Duke of York against them. So now I am at rest in that matter, and shall be more when my copies are finished of their answers.

19th. To the King's playhouse, and there saw *The Silent Woman*; the best comedy, I think, that ever was wrote: and sitting by Shadwell[69] the poet, he was big with admiration of it. Here was my Lord Brouncker and W. Pen and their ladies in the box, being grown mighty kind of a sudden; but, God knows, it will last but a little while, I dare swear. Knipp did her part mighty well. All the news now is that Mr Trevor is for certain to be Secretary in Morrice's place, which the Duke of York did himself tell me yesterday; and also that Parliament is to be adjourned to the 1st of March, which do please me well, hoping thereby to get my things in a little better order than I should have done; and the less attendances at that end of the town in winter.

20th. To church, and thence home to dinner, staying till past one o'clock for Harris, whom I invited, and to bring Shadwell the poet with him; but they came not, and so a good dinner lost through my own folly. And so to dinner alone, having since church heard the boy read over Dryden's Reply to Sir R. Howard's Answer about his Essay of Poesy, and a Letter in answer to that; the last whereof is mighty silly, in behalf of Howard. The Duchesse of Monmouth is at this time in great trouble of the shortness of her lame leg, which is likely to grow shorter and shorter, that she will never recover it.

21st. To St James's, and there the Duke of York did of his own accord come to me and tell me that he had read and do like of my answers to the objections which he did give me the other day about the Navy: and so did Sir W. Coventry too, who told me that the Duke of York had shown him them. To Southwarke-fair, very dirty, and there saw the puppet-show of Whittington, which was pretty to see: and how that idle thing do work upon people that see it, and even myself too! And thence to Jacob Hall's dancing on the ropes, where I saw such action as I never saw before, and mightily worth

69 Thomas Shadwell, the dramatic writer. Died 1692.

seeing; and here took acquaintance with a fellow that carried me to a tavern, whither come the musick of this booth, and by and by Jacob Hall himself, with whom I had a mind to speak, to hear whether he had ever any mischief by falls in his time. He told me, 'Yes, many, but never to the breaking of a limb.' He seems a mighty strong man. So giving them a bottle or two of wine, I away. So by water by link-light through the bridge, it being mighty dark, but still weather; and so home. This day came out first the new five-pieces in gold, coined by the Guiny Company; and I did get two pieces of Mr Holder.

22nd. This day Mr Wren did give me at the Board Commissioner Middleton's answer to the Duke of York's great letter; so that now I have all of them.

23rd. At noon comes Mr Evelyn to me about some business with the office, and there in discourse tells me of his loss to the value of £500 which he hath met with in a late attempt of making of bricks upon an adventure with others, by which he presumed to have got a great deal of money: so that I see the most ingenious men may sometimes be mistaken.

27th. In the Park, where I met Mr Wren; and he and I walked together in the Pell-Mell, it being most summer weather that ever was seen. And here talking of several things; of the corruption of the Court, and how unfit it is for ingenuous men, and himself particularly, to live in it, where a man cannot live but he must spend, and cannot get suitably without breach of his honour: and he did thereupon tell me of the basest thing of my Lord Barkeley that ever was heard of any man – which was this: – how the Duke of York's Commissioners do let his wine-licenses at a bad rate, and being offered a better, they did persuade the Duke of York to give some satisfaction to the former to quit it, and let it to the latter; which being done, my Lord Barkeley did make the bargain for the former to have £1500 a-year to quit it; whereof since it is come to light that they were to have but £800 and himself £700, which the Duke of York hath ever since for some years paid, though the second bargain hath been broken, and the Duke of York lost by it half of what the first was. He told me that there had been a seeming accommodation between the Duke of York and the Duke of Buckingham and Lord Arlington, the two latter desiring it; but yet that there is not true agreement between them, but they do labour to bring in all new creatures into play, and the Duke of York do oppose it. Thence, he gone, I to the Queene's chapel, and there heard some good singing; and so to White Hall, and saw the King and Queene at dnner: and thence with Sir Stephen Fox to dinner; and the Cofferer with us; and there mighty kind usage and good discourse. Thence spent all the afternoon walking in the Park, and then in the evening at Court on the Queene's side; and there met Mr Godolphin, who tells me that the news is true we heard yesterday of my Lord Sandwich's being come to Mount's-bay, in Cornwall. This night, in the Queene's drawing-room, my Lord Brouncker told me the difference that is now between the three Embassadors here, the Venetian, French, and Spaniard; the third not being willing to make a visit to the first, because he would not receive him at the door; who is willing to give him as much respect as he did to the French, who was used no otherwise, and who refuses now to take more of him, upon being desired thereto in order to the making an accommodation in this matter.

28th. Knipp's maid comes to me to tell me that the women's day at the playhouse is to-day, and that therefore I must be there to encrease their profit. By water to St James's, and there had good opportunity of speaking with the Duke of York; who desires me again, talking on that matter, to prepare something for him to do for the better managing of our office; telling me that my Lord Keeper and he talking about it yesterday, my Lord Keeper did advise him to do so, it being better to come from him than otherwise; which I have promised to do. Thence to my Lord Burlington's house, the first time I ever was there, it being the house built by Sir John Denham, next to Clarendon-house. And here I visited my Lord Hinchingbroke and his lady; Mr Sidney Montagu being last night come to town unexpectedly from Mount's-bay, where he left my Lord well eight days since, so as we now hourly expect to hear of his arrivall at Portsmouth. Sidney is mighty grown; and I am glad I am here to see him at his first coming, though it cost me dear, for here I come to be necessitated to supply them with £500 for my Lord. He sent him up with a declaration to his friends, of the necessity of his being presently supplied with £2000; but I do not think he will get £1000: however, I think it becomes my duty to my Lord to do something extraordinary in this, and the rather because I have been remiss in writing to him during this voyage, more than ever I did in my life, and more indeed than was fit for me. By and by comes Sir W. Godolphin to see Mr Sidney, who, I perceive, is much dissatisfied that he should come to town last night, and not yet be with my Lord Arlington; who, and all the town, hear of his being come, and he did, it seems, take notice of it to Godolphin this morning. So that I perceive this remissness in affairs do continue in my Lord's managements still: which I am sorry for; but, above all, to see in what a condition my Lord is for money, that I dare swear he do not know where to take up £500 of any man in England at this time upon his word but of myself, as I believe by the sequel hereof it will appear. Here I first saw and saluted my Lady Burlington,[70] a very fine-speaking lady, and a good woman, but old and not handsome; but a brave woman. Here I also, standing by a candle that was brought for sealing a letter, do set my periwigg a-fire; which made such an odd noise nobody could tell what it was till they saw the flame, my back being to the candle. To the King's playhouse, and there saw *The City Match*,[71] not acted these thirty years, and but a silly play: the King and Court there; the house for the women's sake mighty full. So I to White Hall, and there all the evening on the Queene's side; and it being a most summer-like day, and a fine warm evening, the Italians came in a barge under the leads before the Queene's drawing-room; and so the Queene and ladies went out and heard them for almost an hour: and the singing was indeed very good together; but yet there was but one voice that alone did appear considerable, and that was Signior Joanni. This done, by and by they went in: and here I saw Mr Sidney Montagu kiss the Queene's hand, who was mighty kind to him, and the ladies looked mightily on him; and the King came by and by, and did talk to him. So I away by coach with Alderman Backewell home, who is mighty kind to me, more than ordinary, in his expressions. But I do hear this day what troubles me, that Sir W. Coventry is quite out of play, the King seldom speaking to him; and that there is a design of making a Lord Treasurer, and that my Lord Arlington shall be the man; but I cannot believe it. But yet the Duke of Buckingham hath it in his mind, and

---

70 Elizabeth, sole daughter and heir to Henry Earl of Cumberland, wife of Richard first Earl of Burlington.
71 A comedy, by Jasper Mayne, DD.

those with him, to make a thorough alteration in things; and, among the rest, Coventry to be out.

October 12th.[72] To White Hall to enquire when the Duke of York will be in town, in order to Mr Turner's going down to Audley End about his place; and here I met in St James's Park with one that told me that the Duke of York would be in town to-morrow. Home, where I find Sir H. Cholmly come to town; and is come hither to see me: and he is a man that I love mightily, as being of a gentleman the most industrious that ever I saw. He staid with me awhile talking and telling me his obligations to my Lord Sandwich, which I was glad of; and that the Duke of Buckingham is now chief of all men in this kingdom, which I knew before; and that he do think the Parliament will hardly ever meet again; which is a great many men's thoughts, and I shall not be sorry for it. Read a ridiculous nonsensical book set out by Will. Pen for the Quakers; but so full of nothing but nonsense, that I was ashamed to read in it.

13th. With my Lord Brouncker, and did get his ready assent to T. Hater's having of Mr Turner's place, and so Sir J. Minnes's also: but when we come to sit down at the Board comes to us Mr Wren this day to town, and tells me that James Southern do petition the Duke of York for the Store-keeper's place of Deptford; which did trouble me much, and also the Board; though upon discourse after he was gone we did resolve to move hard for our Clerks, and that places of preferment may go according to seniority and merit. At my Lord Middleton's; and I did this day find by discourse with somebody that this gentleman was the great Major-general Middleton that was of the Scots army in the beginning of the late war against the King.

14th. To White Hall, and there walked to St James's, where I find the Court mighty full, it being the Duke of York's birthday; and he mighty fine, and all the musick, one after another, to my great content. Here I met with Sir H. Cholmly; and he and I to walk, and to my Lord Barkeley's new house, there to see a new experiment of a

72 A hiatus occurs in the Diary at this period for thirteen days; during which Mr Pepys went into the country, as he subsequently alludes to his having been at Saxham whilst the King was there. He had probably been to Impington to fetch his wife, and perhaps omitted copying his rough notes into the blank pages evidently left for them in the journal.

cart, which, by having two little wheeles fastened to the axle-tree, is said to make it go with half the ease and more than another cart; but we did not see the trial made. To the King's playhouse, and saw *The Faithful Shepherdess*,[73] that I might hear the French eunuch sing; which I did to my great content; though I do admire his action as much as his singing, being both beyond all I ever saw or heard.

15th. This day at the Board came unexpected the warrants from the Duke of York for Mr Turner and Hater, for the places they desire; which contents me mightily.

17th. Mr Moore and Seamour were with me this afternoon; who tell me that my Lord Sandwich was received mighty kindly by the King, and is in exceeding great esteem with him and the rest about him; but I doubt it will be hard for him to please both the King and the Duke of York, which I shall be sorry for. Mr Moore tells me the sad condition my Lord is in in his estate and debts; and the way he now lives in so high, and so many vain servants about him, that he must be ruined if he do not take up; which, by the grace of God, I will put him upon when I come to see him.

18th. With Lord Brouncker to Lincolne's Inn, and Mr Ball, to visit Dr Wilkins, now newly Bishop of Chester: and he received us mighty kindly; and had most excellent discourse from him about his book of Reall Character. And so I with Lord Brouncker to White Hall, and there saw the Queene and some ladies.

19th. To the Duke of York's playhouse; and there saw, the first time acted, *The Queene of Arragon*,[74] an old Blackfriars' play, but an admirable one, so good that I am astonished at it, and wonder where it hath lain asleep all this while that I have never heard of it before.

20th. At this time my wife and I mighty busy laying out money in dressing up our best chamber, and thinking of a coach and coachman and horses, &c.; and the more because of Creed's being now married to Mrs Pickering;[75] a thing I could never have expected, but it is

73 A dramatic pastoral, by J. Fletcher.
74 A tragi-comedy, by William Habington. Upon its revival, the prologue and epilogue were written by Butler, the author of *Hudibras*.
75 Elizabeth, daughter of Sir Gilbert Pickering, Bart., became the wife of John Creed, Esq., of Oundle, and had issue by him Major Richard Creed, killed at the battle of Blenheim.

done about seven or ten days since. I walked out to look for a coach, and saw many; and did light on one for which I bid £50 which do please me mightily.

21st. Dining with Mr Batelier, I rose from table before the rest, because under an obligation to go to my Lord Brouncker's, where to meet several gentlemen of the Royal Society, to go and make a visit to the French Embassador Colbert at Leicester-house, he having endeavoured to make one or two to my Lord Brouncker as our President: but he was not within, but I came too late. To my Lord Sandwich's lodgings; who came to town the last night, and is come thither to lie: and met with him within: and among others my new cosen Creed, who looks mighty soberly; and he and I saluted one another with mighty gravity, till we came to a little more freedom of talk about it. But here I hear that Sir Gilbert Pickering is lately dead, about three days since; which makes some sorrow there, though not much, because of his being long expected to die, having been in a lethargy long. So waited on my Lord to Court, and there staid and saw the ladies awhile: and thence to my wife, and took them up; and so home, and to supper and bed.

23rd. To my Lord Sandwich's, where I find my Lord within, but busy private; and so I staid a little talking with the young gentlemen, and so away with Mr Pierce the surgeon towards Tyburne, to see the people executed; but came too late, it being done: two men and a woman hanged. Pierce do tell me, among other news, the late frolick and debauchery of Sir Charles Sedley and Buckhurst running up and down all the night, almost naked, through the streets; and at last fighting, and being beat by the watch and clapped up all night; and how the King takes their parts; and my Lord Chief Justice Keeling hath laid the constable by the heels to answer it next Sessions: which is a horrid shame. How the King and these gentlemen did made the fiddlers of Thetford this last progress to sing them all the obscene songs they could think of. How Sir W. Coventry was brought the other day to the Duchesse of York by the Duke of York, to kiss her hand; who did acknowledge his unhappiness to occasion her so much sorrow, declaring his intentions in it, and praying her pardon; which she did give him upon his promise to make good his pretences of innocence to her family by his faithfulness to his master the Duke of York. That the Duke of Buckingham is now all in all, and will ruin

Coventry, if he can: and that W. Coventry do now rest wholly upon the Duke of York for his standing; which is a great turn. He tells me that my Lady Castlemaine, however, is a mortal enemy to the Duke of Buckingham; which I understand not, but it seems she is disgusted with his greatness and his ill usage of her. That the King was drunk at Saxam[76] with Sedley, Buckhurst &c. the night that my Lord Arlington came thither, and would not give him audience, or could not; which is true, for it was the night that I was there and saw the King go up to his chamber, and was told that the King had been drinking. He tells me too that the Duke of York did the next day chide Bab. May for his occasioning the King's giving himself up to these gentlemen, to the neglecting of my Lord Arlington: to which he answered merrily, that there was no man in England that had a head to lose durst do what they do every day with the King, and asked the Duke of York's pardon; which is a sign of a mad world; God bless us out of it!

24th. This morning comes to me the coachmaker, and agreed with me for £53 and to stand to the courtesy of what more I should give him upon the finishing of it. He is likely also to fit me with a coachman.

26th. I was obliged to attend the Duke of York, thinking to have had a meeting of Tangier to-day, but had not: but he did take me and Mr Wren into his closet, and there did press me to prepare what I had to say upon the answers of my fellow-officers to his great letter; which I promised to do against his coming to town again the next week: and so to other discourse, finding plainly that he is in trouble and apprehensions of the Reformers, and would be found to do what he can towards reforming himself. And so thence to my Lord Sandwich's; where after long stay, he being in talk with others privately, I to him; and there, he taking physic and keeping his chamber, I had an hour's talk with him about the ill posture of things at this time, while the King gives countenance to Sir Charles Sedley and Lord Buckhurst. He tells me that he thinks his matters do stand well with the King, and hopes to have dispatch to his mind; but I doubt it, and do see that he do fear it too. He told me of my Lady

76 Saxham, near Newmarket, in Suffolk, a seat of William Baron Crofts, long since pulled down.

Carteret's trouble about my writing of that letter of the Duke of York's lately to the office; which I did not own, but declared to be of no injury to G. Carteret, and that I would write a letter to him to satisfy him therein. But this I am in pain how to do without doing myself wrong, and the end I had of preparing a justification to myself hereafter, when the faults of the Navy come to be found out: however I will do it in the best manner I can.

29th. Mr Wren first tells us of the order from the King, come last night to the Duke of York, for signifying his pleasure to the Solicitor-generall for drawing up a Commission for suspending of my Lord Anglesy, and putting in Sir Thomas Littleton and Sir Thomas Osborne[77] (the former a creature of Arlington's, and the latter of the Duke of Buckingham's) during the suspension. The Duke of York was forced to obey, and did grant it, he being to go to Newmarket this day with the King, and so the King pressed for it. But Mr Wren do own that the Duke of York is the most wounded in this in the world, for it is done and concluded without his privity, after his appearing for him; and that it is plain that they do ayme to bring the Admiralty into Commission too, and lessen the Duke of York. This do put strange apprehensions into all our Board; only I think I am the least troubled at it, for I care not at all for it: but my Lord Brouncker and Pen do seem to think much of it.

30th. Up betimes; and Mr Povy comes to even accounts with me; which we did, and then fell to other talk. He tells me, in short, how the King is made a child of by Buckingham and Arlington, to the lessening of the Duke of York, whom they cannot suffer to be great, for fear of my Lord Chancellor's return, which therefore they make the King violent against. That he believes it is impossible these two great men can hold together long; or, at least, that the ambition of the former is so great that he will endeavour to master all, and bring into play as many as he can. That Anglesy will not lose his place easily, but will contend in law with whoever comes to execute it. That the Duke of York, in all things but in his amours, is led by the nose by his wife. That Sir W. Coventry is now by the Duke of York made

77 Eldest son of Sir Edward Osborne, Bart.; made a Privy-counsellor 1672, and the following year constituted Lord High Treasurer, and elected KG in 1677. He was created Baron Kiveton and Viscount Latimer 1673, Earl of Danby 1674, Marquis of Caermarthen 1689, and Duke of Leeds 1694. Died 1712, aged 81.

friends with the Duchesse; and that he is often there, and waits on her. That he do believe that these present great men will break in time, and that Sir W. Coventry will be a great man again; for he do labour to have nothing to do in matters of the State, and is so usefull to the side that he is on, that he will stand, though at present he is quite out of play. That my Lady Castlemaine hates the Duke of Buckingham. That the Duke of York hath expressed himself very kind to my Lord Sandwich; which I am mighty glad of. That we are to expect more changes if these men stand.

31st. This day my Lord Anglesy was at the office, and do seem to make nothing of this business of his suspension, resolving to bring it into Council; where he seems not to doubt to have right, he standing upon his defence and patent; and hath put in his caveats to the several offices; so as soon as the King comes back again, which will be on Tuesday next, he will bring it into the Council.

November 2nd. To Mr Povy's; and there I find my Lords Sandwich, Peterborough, and Hinchingbroke, Charles Harbord, and Sidney Montagu; and there I was stopped, and dined mighty nobly at a good table with one little dish at a time upon it; but mighty merry. I was glad to see it; but sorry, methought, to see my Lord have so little reason to be merry, and yet glad for his sake to have him cheerful. After dinner up, and looked up and down the house, and so to the cellar; and thence I slipt away without taking leave.

4th. To White Hall; and there I find the King and Duke of York came the last night, and every body's mouth full of my Lord Anglesy's suspension being sealed, which it was, it seems, yesterday; so that he is prevented in his remedy at the Council. And, it seems, the two new Treasurers did kiss the King's hand this morning, brought in by my Lord Arlington. They walked up and down together in the Court this day, and several people joyed them; but I avoided it, that I might not be seen to look either way. This day also I hear that my Lord Ormond is to be declared in Council no more Deputy Governor of Ireland, his commission being expired: and the King is prevailed with to take it out of his hands; which people do mightily admire, saying that he is the greatest subject of any prince in Christendome, and hath more acres of land than any, and hath done more for his Prince than ever any yet did. But all will not do; he must down, it seems, the Duke of Buckingham carrying all before him. But that that troubles me most is that they begin to talk that the Duke of York's regiment is ordered to be disbanded; and more that undoubtedly his Admiralty will follow: which do shake me mightily, and I fear will have ill consequences in the nation, for these counsels are very mad. The Duke of York do, by all men's report, carry himself wonderfull submissive to the King, in the most humble manner in the world; but yet, it seems, nothing must be spared that tends to the keeping out the Chancellor; and that is the reason of all this. The great discourse now is, that the Parliament shall be dissolved and another called, which shall give the King the Dean and Chapter's lands; and that will put him out of debt. And it is said that Buckingham do knowingly meet daily with Wildman and other Commonwealth-men; and that when he is with them he makes the King believe that he is with his wenches. And something looks like the Parliament's being dissolved, by Harry Brouncker's being now come back, and appearing this day the first day at White Hall; but he hath not been yet with the King, but is secure that he shall be well received, I hear. God bless us when such men as he shall be restored! But that that pleases me most is, that several do tell me that Pen is to be removed; and others that he hath resigned his place; and particularly Spragg tells me for certain that he hath resigned it, and is become a partner with Gauden in the Victualling: in which I think he hath done a very cunning thing; but I am sure I am glad of it; and it will be well for the King to have him out of this office. Sir John Talbot talks mighty high for my Lord of Ormond: and I perceive this family of the Talbots hath been raised by my Lord.

5th. The Duke of York did call me and Mr Wren; and my paper that I have lately taken pains to draw up was read, and the Duke of York pleased therewith; and we did all along conclude upon answers to my mind for the Board, and that that, if put in execution, will do the King's business. But I do now more and more perceive the Duke of York's trouble, and that he do lie under great weight of mind from the Duke of Buckingham's carrying things against him; and particularly when I advised that he would use his interest that a seaman might come into the room of Sir W. Pen, who is now declared to be gone from us to that of the Victualling, and did show how the office would now be left without one seaman in it but the Surveyor and the

Controller, who is so old as to be able to do nothing. He told me plainly that I knew his mind well enough as to seamen, but that it must be as others will. And Wren did tell it me as a secret, that when the Duke of York did first tell the King about Sir W. Pen's leaving of the place, and that when the Duke of York did move the King that either Captain Cox or Sir Jer. Smith might succeed him, the King did tell him that that was a matter fit to be considered of, and would not agree to either presently: and so the Duke of York could not prevail for either, nor knows who it shall be. The Duke of York did tell me himself, that if he had not carried it privately when first he mentioned Pen's leaving his place to the King, it had not been done: for the Duke of Buckingham and those of his party do cry out upon it as a strange thing to trust such a thing into the hands of one that stands accused in Parliament: and that they have so far prevailed upon the King that he would not have him named in Council, but only take his name to the Board; but I think he said that only D. Gauden's name shall go in the patent; at least, at the time when Sir Richard Browne asked the King the names of D. Gauden's security, the King told him it was not yet necessary for him to declare them. And by and by, when the Duke of York and we had done, Wren brought into the closet Captain Cox and James Temple about business of the Guinea Company; and talking something of the Duke of Buckingham's concernment therein, says the Duke of York, 'I shall give the Devil his due,' as they say the Duke of Buckingham hath paid in his money to the Company, or something of that kind, wherein he would do right to him. The Duke of York told me how these people do begin to cast dirt upon the business that passed the Council lately touching Supernumeraries, as passed by virtue of his authority there, there being not liberty for any man to withstand what the Duke of York advises there; which, he told me, they bring only as an argument to insinuate the putting of the Admiralty into Commission, which by all men's discourse is now designed, and I perceive the same by him. This being done, and going from him, I up and down the house to hear news: and there every body's mouth full of changes; and among others, the Duke of York's regiment of Guards that was raised during the late war at sea it is to be disbanded: and also, that this day the King do intend to declare that the Duke of Ormond is no more Deputy of Ireland, but that he will put it into Commission. This day our new Treasurers did kiss the King's hand;

who complimented them, as they say, very highly, – that he had for a long time been abused in his Treasury, and that he was now safe in their hands. I saw them walk up and down the Court together all this morning; the first time I ever saw Osborne, who is a comely gentleman. This day I was told that my Lord Anglesy did deliver a petition on Wednesday in Council to the King, laying open, that whereas he had heard that his Majesty had made such a disposal of his place, which he had formerly granted him for life upon a valuable consideration, and that without any thing laid to his charge, and during a Parliament's sessions, he prayed that his Majesty would be pleased to let his case be heard before the Council and the Judges of the land, who were his proper Counsel in all matters of right: to which, I am told, the King, after my Lord's being withdrawn, concluded upon his giving him an answer some few days hence; and so he was called in and told so. At the Treasurer's, Sir Thomas Clifford, where I did eat some oysters; which while we were at, in comes my Lord Keeper and much company; and so I thought it best to withdraw. And so away, and to the Swedes Agent's, and there met Mr Povy; where the Agent would have me stay and dine, there being only them and Joseph Williamson, and Sir Thomas Clayton;[78] but what he is I know not. Here much extraordinary noble discourse of foreign princes, and particularly the greatness of the King of France, and of his being fallen into the right way of making the kingdom great. I was mightily pleased with this company and their discourse.

6th. To see Roger Pepys at his lodgings next door to Arundell-house, a barber's. And there I did see a book, which my Lord Sandwich hath promised one to me of, *A Description of the Escuriall in Spain*; which I have a great desire to have, though I took it for a finer book when he promised it me.

9th. The Duke of York told me that Sir W. Pen had been with him this morning to ask whether it would be fit for him to sit at the office now, because of his resolution to be gone and to become concerned in the Victualling. The Duke of York answered, Yes, till his contract was signed. Thence I to Lord Sandwich's, and there to see him; but

78 Thomas Clayton, MD, Professor of Physic, and Anatomy Lecturer at Oxford, for which University he was chosen Member 1660, and afterwards knighted and made Warden of Merton College.

was made to stay very long, as his best friends are, and when I came to him had little pleasure, his head being full of his own business, I think. Thence to White Hall with him to a Committee of Tangier; a day appointed for him to give an account of Tangier, and what he did and found there; which, though he had admirable matter for it, and his doings there were good, and would have afforded a noble account, yet he did it with a mind so low and mean, and delivered in so poor a manner, that it appeared nothing at all, nor any body seemed to value it; whereas he might have shown himself to have merited extraordinary thanks, and been held to have done a very great service: whereas now, all that cost the King hath been at for his journey through Spain thither, seems to be almost lost. After we were up, Creed and I walked together, and did talk a good while of the weak Report my Lord made, and were troubled for it; I fearing that either his mind and judgment are depressed, or that he do it out of his great neglect, and so that he do all the rest of his affairs accordingly.

11th. To the office; where by a speciall desire the new Treasurers came, and there did show their Patent and the Great Seal for the suspension of my Lord Anglesy: and here did sit and discourse of the business of the office; and brought Mr Hutchinson with them, who, I hear, is to be their Paymaster, in the room of Mr Waith. For it seems they do turn out every servant that belongs to the present Treasurer; and so for Fenn do bring in Mr Littleton, Sir Thomas's brother, and oust all the rest. But Mr Hutchinson do already see that his work now will be another kind of thing than before, as to the trouble of it.

13th. Up, and with Sir W. Pen by coach to White Hall; where to the Duke of York, and there did our usual business. And thence I to the Commissioners of the Treasury; where I staid and heard an excellent case argued between my Lord Gerard and the town of Newcastle, about a piece of ground which that Lord hath got a grant of under the Exchequer Seal, which they were endeavouring to get of the King under the Great Seal. I liked mightily the Counsel for the town, Shaftow their Recorder, and Mr Offly. But I was troubled, and so were the Lords,[79] to hear my Lord fly out against their[80] great pretence of merit from the King for their sufferings and loyalty;

79 The Lords Commissioners.
80 The inhabitants of Newcastle.

telling them that they might thank him for that repute which they have for their loyalty, for that it was he that forced them to be so against their wills, when he was there: and, moreover, did offer a paper to the Lords to read from the town, sent in 1648; but the Lords would not read it; but I believe it was something about bringing the King to trial, or some such thing, in that year. Thence I to the Three Tuns Tavern by Charing Cross, and there dined with W. Pen, Sir J. Minnes, and Commissioner Middleton; and as merry as my mind could be, that hath so much trouble upon it at home. And thence to White Hall, and there staid in Mr Wren's chamber with him reading over my draught of a letter, which Mr Gibson then attended me with; and there he did like all, but doubted whether it would be necessary for the Duke to write in so sharp a style to the office as I had drawn it in; which I yield to him, to consider the present posture of the times and the Duke of York, and whether it were not better to err on that hand than the other. He told me that he did not think it was necessary for the Duke of York to do, and that it would not suit so well with his nature nor greatness; which last perhaps is true, but then do too truly show the effects of having princes in places where order and discipline should be. I left it to him to do as the Duke of York pleases; and so fell to other talk, and with great freedom, of public things. And he told me, upon my several inquiries to that purpose, that he did believe it was not yet resolved whether the Parliament should ever meet more or no, the three great rulers of things now standing thus: – The Duke of Buckingham is absolutely against their meeting, as moved thereto by his people that he advises with, the people of the late times, who do never expect to have any thing done by this Parliament for their religion, and who do propose that, by the sale of the Church-lands, they shall be able to put the King out of debt: my Lord Keeper is utterly against putting away this and choosing another Parliament, lest they prove worse than this, and will make all the King's friends, and the King himself, in a desperate condition: my Lord Arlington knows not which is best for him, being to seek whether this or the next will use him worst. He tells me that he believes that it is intended to call this Parliament, and try them with a sum of money; and if they do not like it, then to send them going, and call another who will, at the ruin of the Church perhaps, please the King with what he will have for a time. And he tells me, therefore, that he do believe that this policy will be endeavoured by the Church and their friends, – to seem to promise the King money when it shall be propounded, but make the King and these great men buy it dear before they have it. He tells me that he is really persuaded that the design of the Duke of Buckingham is, by bringing the State into such a condition as, if the King do die without issue, it shall upon his death break into pieces again; and so put by the Duke of York, whom they have disobliged, they know, to that degree as to despair of his pardon. He tells me that there is no way to rule the King but by brisknesse, which the Duke of Buckingham hath above all men; and that the Duke of York having it not, his best way is what he practices, that is to say, a good temper, which will support him till the Duke of Buckingham and Lord Arlington fall out, which cannot be long first, the former knowing that the latter did, in the time of the Chancellor, endeavour with the Chancellor to hang him at that time, when he was proclaimed against. And here, by the by, he told me that the Duke of Buckingham did by his friends treat with my Lord Chancellor, by the mediation of Matt. Wren and Clifford, to fall in with my Lord Chancellor; which, he tells me, he did advise my Lord Chancellor to accept of, as that, that with his own interest and the Duke of York's, would undoubtedly have secured all to him and his family; but that my Lord Chancellor was a man not to be advised, thinking himself too high to be counselled: and so all is come to nothing; for by that means the Duke of Buckingham became desperate, and was forced to fall in with Arlington, to his ruin. This morning at the Treasury-chamber I did meet Jack Fenn, and there he did show me my Lord Anglesy's petition and the King's answer: the former good and stout, as I before did hear it; but the latter short and weak, saying that he was not by what the King had done hindered from taking the benefit of his laws, and that the reason he had to suspect his mismanagement of his money in Ireland did make him think it unfit to trust him with his Treasury in England till he was satisfied in the former.

15th. After dinner, W. How to tell me what hath happened between him and the Commissioners of late, who are hot again, more than ever, about my Lord Sandwich's business of prizes; which I am troubled for, and the more because of the great security and neglect with which I think my Lord do look upon this matter, that may yet, for aught I know, undo him.

17th. To the office all the morning, where the new Treasurers come their second time, and before they sat down did discourse with the Board, and particularly my Lord Brouncker, about their place, which they challenge as having been heretofore due and given to their predecessor; which, at last, my Lord did own hath been given him only out of courtesy to his quality, and that he did not take it as of right at the Board: so they, for the present, sat down and did give him the place, but I think with an intent to have the Duke of York's directions about it.

20th. This evening comes Mr Billup to me, to read over Mr Wren's alterations of my draught of a letter for the Duke of York to sign to the Board; which I like mighty well, they being not considerable, only in mollifying some hard terms which I had thought fit to put in. From this to other discourse; and do find that the Duke of York and his master, Mr Wren, do look upon this service of mine as a very seasonable service to the Duke of York, as that which he will have to show to his enemies in his own justification of his care of the King's business: and I am sure I am heartily glad of it, both for the King's sake and the Duke of York's, and my own also; for if I continue, my work by this means will be the less, and my share in the blame also.

22nd. This day my boy's livery is come home, the first I ever had, of greene lined with red; and it likes me well enough.

23rd. To visit my Lord Sandwich, who is now so reserved, or moped rather I think with his own business, that he bids welcome to no man, I think, to his satisfaction. I met with Mr Povy; who tells me that this discourse which I told him of, of the Duke of Monmouth being made Prince of Wales, hath nothing in it; though he thinks there are all the endeavours used in the world to overthrow the Duke of York. He would not have me doubt of my safety in the Navy, which I am doubtful of, from the reports of a general removal: but he will endeavour to inform me what he can gather from my Lord Arlington. That he do think that the Duke of Buckingham hath a mind rather to overthrow all the kingdom, and bring in a Commonwealth, wherein he may think to be General of their Army, or to make himself King; which, he believes, he may be led to by some advice he hath had with conjurors, which he do affect.

25th. Mr Wren and I to his chamber, and there talked: and he seems to hope that these people, the Duke of Buckingham and Arlington, will run themselves off of their legs; they being forced to be always putting the King upon one idle thing or other, against the easiness of his nature, which he will never be able to bear nor they to keep him to, and so will lose themselves. And, for instance of their little progress, he tells me that my Lord of Ormond is like yet to carry it, and to continue in his command in Ireland; at least, they cannot get the better of him yet. But he tells me that the Keeper is wrought upon, as they say, to give his opinion for the dissolving of the Parliament; which, he thinks, will undo him in the eyes of the people. He do not seem to own the hearing or fearing of any thing to be done in the Admiralty to the lessening of the Duke of York, though he hears how the town-talk is full of it.

26th. Troubled at W. Hewer's losing of a tally of £1000, which I sent him this day to receive of the Commissioners of Excise.

27th. Comes Mr Povey by appointment to dine with me; and much pleasant discourse with him, and some serious: and he tells me that he would by all means have me get to be a Parliament-man the next Parliament. By and by comes my cosen Roger, and dines with us; and, after dinner, did seal his mortgage, wherein I do wholly rely on his honesty, not having so much as read over what he hath given me for it, nor minded it, but do trust to his integrity therein.

28th. This day presented to the Board the Duke of York's letter; which, I perceive, troubled Sir W. Pen, he declaring himself meant in that part that concerned excuse by sickness; but I do not care, but am mightily glad that it is done, and now I shall begin to be at pretty good ease in the office. This morning, to my great content, W. Hewer tells me that a porter is come who found my tally in Holborn, and brings it him, for which he gives him 20s.

29th. My wife lately frighted me about her being a Catholique; and I dare not, therefore, move her to go to church, for fear she should deny me. But this morning, of her own accord, she spoke of going to church the next Sunday: which pleases me mightily.

30th. My wife after dinner went the first time abroad in her coach, calling on Roger Pepys, and visiting Mrs Creed and my cosen

Turner. Thus ended this month with very good content, but most expenseful to my purse on things of pleasure, having furnished my wife's closet, and the best chamber, and a coach and horses, that ever I knew in the world; and I am put into the greatest condition of outward state that ever I was in, or hoped ever to be, or desired: and this at a time when we do daily expect great changes in this office; and by all reports we must all of us turn out. But my eyes are come to that condition that I am not able to work; and therefore that and my wife's desire make me have no manner of trouble in my thoughts about it. So God do his will in it!

December 2nd. Abroad with my wife, the first time that ever I rode in my own coach, which do make my heart rejoice and praise God, and pray him to bless it to me and continue it. So she and I to the King's playhouse, and there saw *The Usurper*:[81] a pretty good play in all but what is designed to resemble Cromwell and Hugh Peters, which is mighty silly. The play done, we to White Hall; where my wife staid while I up to the Duchesse and Queene's side, to speak with the Duke of York: and here saw all the ladies, and heard the silly discourse of the King with his people about him, telling a story of my Lord Rochester's having of his clothes stole while he was with a wench; and his gold all gone, but his clothes found afterwards stuffed into a featherbed by the wench that stole them. I spoke with the Duke of York, just as he was set down to supper with the King, about our sending of victuals to Sir Thomas Allen's fleet hence to Cales, to meet him.

3rd. Sir Jer. Smith with me; who is a silly, prating, talking man; but he tells me what he hears, – that Holmes and Spragg now rule all with the Duke of Buckingham as to sea-business, and will be great men: but he do prophecy what will be the fruit of it; so I do. So to the office, where we sat all the morning; and at noon home to dinner, and then abroad again with my wife to the Duke of York's playhouse, and saw *The Unfortunate Lovers*:[82] a mean play I think, but some parts very good, and excellently acted. We sat under the boxes, and saw the fine ladies; among others, my Lady Kerneguy, who is most devilishly painted. And so home, it being mighty pleasure to go

81 A tragedy, by Edward Howard.
82 A tragedy, by Sir Wm. Davenant.

alone with my poor wife in a coach of our own to a play, and makes us appear mighty great, I think, in the world; at least, greater than ever I could, or my friends for me, have once expected; or, I think, than ever any of my family ever yet lived in my memory, but my cosen Pepys in Salisbury Court.

4th. Did wait as usual upon the Duke of York, where, upon discoursing something touching the Ticket-office, which by letter the Board did give the Duke of York their advice to be put upon Lord Brouncker, Sir J. Minnes did foolishly rise up and complain of the office, and his being made nothing of; and this before Sir Thomas Littleton, who would be glad of this difference among us: which did trouble me mightily; and therefore I did forbear to say what I otherwise would have thought fit for me to say on this occasion, upon so impertinent a speech as this doating fool made — but, I say, I let it alone, and contented myself that it went as I advised, as to the Duke of York's judgment in the thing disputed. Mr Pickering, who meets me at Smithfield, and I, and W. Hewer, and a friend (a jockey) of his, did go about to see several pairs of horses for my coach; but it was late, and we agreed on none, but left it to another time: but here I do see instances of a piece of craft and cunning that I never dreamed of, concerning the buying and choosing of horses. To the office, where vexed to see how ill all the Controller's business is likely to go, as long as ever Sir J. Minnes lives; and so troubled I was that I thought it a good occasion for me to give my thoughts of it in writing, and therefore wrote a letter at the Board, by the help of a tube, to Lord Brouncker, and did give it him, which I kept a copy of, and it may be of use to me hereafter to show in this matter. This being done, I home to my aunt, who supped with us, and my uncle also: and a good-humoured woman she is, so that I think we shall keep her acquaintance; but mighty proud she is of her wedding-ring, being lately set with diamonds; cost her about £12: and I did commend it mightily to her, but do not think it very suitable for one of our quality.

5th. No news stirring, but that my Lord of Ormond is likely to go to Ireland again, which do show that the Duke of Buckingham do not rule all so absolutely; and that, however, we shall speedily have more changes in the Navy: and it is certain that the Nonconformists do now preach openly in houses in many places, and among others the house that was heretofore Sir G. Carteret's in Leadenhall-streete, and have ready access to the King. And now the great dispute is, whether this Parliament or another; and my great design, if I continue in the Navy, is to get myself to be a Parliament-man.

6th (Lord's day). Up, and with my wife to church; which pleases me mightily, I being full of fear that she would never go to church again, after she had declared to me that she was a Roman Catholique. But though I do verily think she fears God, and is truly and sincerely righteous, yet I do see she is not so strictly a Catholique as not to go to church with me; which pleases me mightily.

7th. Sir W. Coventry says that he hath no more mind to be found meddling with the Navy, lest it should do it hurt as well as him. So to talk of general things: and telling him that with all these doings he, I thanked God, stood yet; he told me, Yes, but that he thought his continuing in did arise from his enemies my Lord of Buckingham and Arlington's seeing that he cared so little if he was out; and he do protest to me that he is as weary of the Treasury as ever he was of the Navy. He tells me that he do believe that their heat is over almost as to the Navy, there being now none left of the old stock but my Lord Brouncker, J. Minnes (who is ready to leave the world), and myself. But he tells me that he do foresee very great wants and great disorders by reason thereof; insomuch, as he is represented to the King by his enemies as a melancholy man, and one that is still prophecying ill events, so as the King called him Visionaire; which being told him, he said he answered the party, that, whatever he foresaw, he was not afraid as to himself of any thing, nor particularly of my Lord Arlington so much as the Duke of Buckingham hath been, nor of the Duke of Buckingham so much as my Lord Arlington at this time is. But he tells me that he hath been always looked upon as a melancholy man; whereas others that would please the King do make him believe that all is safe: and so he hath heard my Lord Chancellor openly say to the King, that he was now a glorious prince, and in a glorious condition, because of some one accident that hath happened, or some one rut that hath been removed; 'when,' says Sir W. Coventry, 'they reckoned their one good meal, without considering that there was nothing left in the cupboard for to-morrow.' After this discourse to my Lord Sandwich's, and took a quarter of an hour's walk in the garden with him, which I have not done for so much time with him since his coming into England; and talking of his own condition, and particularly of the world's talk of his going to Tangier. I find if his conditions can be made profitable and safe as to money, he would go, but not else; but, however, will seem not averse to it, because of facilitating his other accounts now depending; which he finds hard to get through, but yet hath some hopes, the King, he says, speaking very kindly to him.

8th. Up, and Sir H. Cholmly betimes with me, about some accounts and monies due to him: and he gone, I to the office, where sat all the morning. And here, among other things, breaks out the storm W. Hewer and I have long expected from the Surveyor, about W. Hewer's conspiring to get a contract to the burdening of the stores with kerseys and cottons, of which he hath often complained, and lately more than ever, and now he did by a most scandalous letter to the Board reflecting on my office: and by discourse it fell to such high words between him and me as can hardly ever be forgot; I declaring I would believe W. Hewer as soon as him, and laying the fault, if there be any, upon himself; he, on the other hand, vilifying of my word and W. Hewer's, calling him knave, and that if he were his clerk he should lose his ears. At last I closed the business for this morning with making the thing ridiculous, as it is, and he swearing that the King should have right in it, or he would lose his place. The office was cleared of all but ourselves and W. Hewer; but, however, the world did by the beginning see what it meant, and it will, I believe, come to high terms between us; which I am sorry for, to have any blemish laid upon me or mine at this time, though never so unjustly, for fear of giving occasion to my real discredit: and therefore I was not only all the rest of the morning vexed, but so went home to dinner; where my wife tells me of my Lord Orrery's new play *Tryphon*,[83] at the Duke of York's house, which, however, I would see, and therefore put a bit of meat in our mouths and went thither; where, with much ado, at half-past one, we got into a blind hole in the 18d. place above stairs, where we could not hear well. The house infinite full, but the prologue most silly, and the play, though admirable, yet no pleasure almost in it, because just the very same design, and words, and sense, and plot, as every one of his plays have, any one of which

83 A tragedy, taken from the first book of Maccabees, and performed with great success.

alone would be held admirable, whereas so many of the same design and fancy do but dull one another; and this, I perceive, is the sense of every body else as well as myself, who therefore showed but little pleasure in it. So home mighty hot, and my mind mightily out of order, so as I could not eat my supper, or sleep almost all night; though I spent till twelve at night with W. Hewer to consider of our business: and we find it not only most free from any blame of our side, but so horrid scandalous on the other, to make so groundless a complaint, and one so shameful to him, that it could not but let me see that there is no need of my being troubled; but such is the weakness of my nature that I could not help it, which vexes me, showing me how unable I am to live with difficulties.

10th. Up, and to the office, where busy all the morning: Middleton not there, so no words or looks of him. At noon home to dinner; and so to the office, and there all the afternoon busy. And at night W. Hewer home with me; and we think we have got matter enough to make Middleton appear a coxcomb. But it troubled me to have Sir W. Warren meet me at night going out of the office home, and tell me that Middleton do intend to complain to the Duke of York: but, upon consideration of the business, I did go to bed satisfied that it was best for me that he should; and so my trouble was over, and to bed and slept well.

11th. Up, and with W. Hewer by water to Somerset-house; and there I to my Lord Brouncker before he went forth to the Duke of York, and there told him my confidence that I should make Middleton appear a fool, and that it was, I thought, best for me to complain of the wrong he hath done; but brought it about that my Lord desired me I would forbear, and promised that he would prevent Middleton till I had given in my answer to the Board, which I desired. And so away to White Hall, and there did our usual attendance: and no word spoke before the Duke of York by Middleton at all; at which I was glad to my heart, because by this means I have time to draw up my answer to my mind. Concluded upon giving £50 for a fine pair of black horses we saw this day se'nnight; and so set Mr Pickering down near his house (whom I am much beholden to for his care herein, and he hath admirable skill, I perceive, in this business), and so home.

12th. I hear this day that there is fallen down a new house not quite finished in Lumbard-street, and that there have been several so, they making use of bad mortar and bricks; but no hurt yet, as God hath ordered it. This day was brought home my pair of black coach-horses, the first I ever was master of, a fine pair.

14th. This day I hear, and am glad, that the King hath prorogued the Parliament to October next; and, among other reasons, it will give me time to go to France, I hope.

15th. Up, and to the office, where sat all the morning, and the new Treasurers there; and, for my life, I cannot keep Sir J. Minnes and others of the Board from showing our weakness, to the dishonour of the Board, though I am not concerned; but it do vex me to the heart to have it before these people, that would be glad to find out all our weaknesses.

18th. To Lord Brouncker, and got him to read over my paper, who owns most absolute content in it, and the advantage I have in it, and the folly of the Surveyor. At noon home to dinner; and then to Brooke-house, and there spoke with Colonell Thomson, I by order carrying them our Contract-books, from the beginning to the end of the late war. I found him finding of errors in a ship's book, where he showed me many; which must end in the ruin, I doubt, of the Controller, who found them not out in the pay of the ship, or the whole office. To the office, and after some other business done we fell to mine. The Surveyor began to be a little brisk at the beginning; but when I came to the point to touch him, which I had all the advantages in the world to do, he became as calm as a lamb, and owned, as the whole Board did, their satisfaction, and cried excuse: and so all made friends; and their acknowledgment put into writing and delivered into Sir J. Minnes's hand, to be kept there for the use of the board or me, when I shall call for it; they desiring it might be so, that I might not make use of it to the prejudice of the Surveyor, whom I had an advantage over by his extraordinary folly in this matter. So Middleton desiring to be friends, I forgave him; and all mighty quiet, and fell to talk of other stories, and there staid all of us till nine or ten at night (more than ever we did in our lives before together).

19th. My wife and I by Hackney to the King's playhouse, and there, the pit being full, sat in the box above, and saw *Catiline's Conspiracy*, yesterday being the first day: a play of much good sense and words to read, but that do appear the worst upon the stage, I mean the least diverting, that ever I saw any, though most fine in clothes; and a fine scene of the Senate and of a fight as ever I saw in my life. We sat next to Betty Hall, that did belong to this house, and was Sir Philip Howard's mistress; a mighty pretty wench.

20th. The Duke of York in good humour did fall to tell us many fine stories of the wars in Flanders, and how the Spaniards are the best disciplined foot in the world; will refuse no extraordinary service if commanded, but scorn to be paid for it as in other countries, though at the same time they will beg in the streets: not a soldier will carry you a cloak-bag for money for the world, though he will beg a penny, and will do the thing if commanded by his commander. That in the citadel of Antwerp a soldier hath not a liberty of begging till he hath served three years. They will cry out against their King and commanders and generals, none like them in the world, and yet will not hear a stranger say a word of them but they will cut his throat. That upon a time some of the commanders of their army exclaiming against their generals, and particularly the Marquis de Caranen, the Confessor of the Marquis coming by and hearing them, he stops and gravely tells them that the three great trades of the world are, the lawyers, who govern the world; the churchmen, who enjoy the world; and a sort of fellows whom they call soldiers, who make it their work to defend the world. He told us too, that Turenne being now become a Catholique, he is likely to get over the head of Colbert, their interests being contrary; the latter to promote trade and the sea (which, says the Duke of York, is that we have most cause to fear), and Turenne to employ the King and his forces by land to encrease his conquests. W. Hewer tells me to-day that he hears that the King of France hath declared in print, that he do intend this next summer to forbid his commanders to strike to us, but that both we and the Dutch shall strike to him, and that he hath made his captains swear it already that they will observe it: which is a great thing if he do it, as I know nothing to hinder him.

21st. Went into Holborne, and there saw the woman that is to be seen with a beard. She is a little plain woman, a Dane; her name, Ursula Dyan; about forty years old; her voice like a little girl's; with a beard as much as any man I ever saw, black almost and grizly: it began to grow at about seven years old, and was shaved not above seven months ago, and is now so big as any man's almost that ever I saw; I say, bushy and thick. It was a strange sight to me, I confess, and what pleased me mightily. Thence to the Duke's playhouse, and saw *Macbeth*. The King and Court there; and we sat just under them and my Lady Castlemaine, and close to a woman that comes into the pit, a kind of a loose gossip, that pretends to be like her, and is so something. And my wife, by my troth, appeared, I think, as pretty as any of them; I never thought so much before; and so did Talbot and W. Hewer, as they said, I heard, to one another. The King and Duke of York minded me, and smiled upon me, at the handsome woman near me: but it vexed me to see Moll Davis, in the box over the King's and my Lady Castlemaine, look down upon the King, and he up to her; and so did my Lady Castlemaine once, to see who it was; but when she saw Moll Davis, she looked like fire; which troubled me.

23rd. Discoursed with Sir John Bankes; who thinks this prorogation will please all but the Parliament itself, which will, if ever they meet, be vexed at Buckingham, who yet governs all. He says the Nonconformists are glad of it, and, he believes, will get the upper-hand in a little time, for the King must trust to them or nobody; and he thinks the King will be forced to it. He says that Sir D. Gauden is mighty troubled at Pen's being put upon him by the Duke of York, and that he believes he will get clear of it; which, though it will trouble me to have Pen still at the office, yet I shall think D. Gauden do well in it, and what I would advise him to, because I love him. I up to my Lord Brouncker at his lodgings; and sat with him an hour on purpose to talk over the wretched state of this office at present, according to the present hands it is made up of; wherein he do fully concur with me, and that it is our part not only to prepare for defending it and ourselves against the consequences of it, but to take the best ways we can to make it known to the Duke of York; for, till Sir J. Minnes be removed, and a sufficient man brought into W. Pen's place when he is gone, it is impossible for this office to support itself.

25th. Christmas day. To dinner alone with my wife, who, poor wretch! sat undressed all day till ten at night, altering and lacing of a noble petticoat; while I by her making the boy read to me the *Life of Julius Caesar*, and Des Cartes' book of Musick.

27th. Lord's day. Saw the King at chapel; but staid not to hear any thing, but went to walk in the Park with W. Hewer; and there, among others, met with Sir G. Downing, and walked with him an hour talking of business, and how the late war was managed, there being nobody to take care of it: and he telling, when he was in Holland, what he offered the King to do if he might have power, and then upon the least word, perhaps of a woman, to the King, he was contradicted again, and particularly to the loss of all that we lost in Guinny. He told me that he had so good spies, that he hath had the keys taken out of De Witt's pocket when he was a-bed, and his closet opened and papers brought to him and left in his hands for an hour, and carried back and laid in the place again, and keys put into his pocket again. He says he hath always had their most private debates, that have been but between two or three of the chief of them, brought to him in an hour after, and an hour after that hath sent word thereof to the King, but nobody here regarded them. But he tells me the sad news that he is out of all expectations that ever the debts of the Navy will be paid, if the Parliament do not enable the King to do it by money; all they can hope for to do out of the King's revenue being but to keep our wheels a-going on present services, and, if they can, to cut off the growing interest: which is a sad story, and grieves me to the heart.

28th. Called up by drums and trumpets; these things and boxes having cost me much money this Christmas already, and will do more.

1668/69. January 1st. Presented from Captain Beckford with a noble silver warming-pan.

4th. W. Hewer and I went and saw the great tall woman that is to be seen, who is but twenty-one years old, and I do easily stand under her arms. To White Hall, where a Committee of Tangier met; and I did receive an instance of the Duke of York's kindness to me, and the whole Committee, that they would not order any thing about the Treasury for the Corporation now in establishing, without my assent and considering whether it would be to my wrong or no. Thence up and down the house, and to the Duke of York's side, and there in the Duchesse's presence: and was mightily complimented by my Lady Peterborough in my Lord Sandwich's presence, whom she engaged to thank me for my kindness to her and her Lord. We also declared our minds together to the Duke of York about Sir John Minnes's incapacity to do any service in the office: he promised to speak to the King about it.

7th. My wife and I to the King's playhouse, and there saw *The Island Princesse*,[1] the first time I ever saw it; and it is a pretty good play, many good things being in it, and a good scene of a town on fire. We sat in an upper box, and the jade Nell came and sat in the next box; a bold merry slut, who lay laughing there upon people: and with a comrade of hers, of the Duke's house, that came in to see the play.

11th. Abroad with my wife to the King's playhouse, and there saw *The Joviall Crew*; but ill acted to what it was heretofore in Clun's time, and when Lacy could dance. Thence to the New Exchange, to buy some things; and, among others, my wife did give me my pair of gloves, which by contract she is to give me in her £30 a-year. Here Mrs Smith tells us of the great murder thereabouts on Saturday last, of one Captain Bumbridge, by one Symons, both of her acquaintance; and hectors that were at play, and in drink: the former is killed, and is kinsman to my Lord of Ormond, which made him speak of it with so much passion.

12th. Mr Pierce, I asking him whither he was going, told me as a great secret that he was going to his master's mistress, Mrs Churchill,[2] with some physic; meaning, I suppose, that she is with child.

15th. To Sir W. Coventry; where with him a good while in his chamber, talking of the great factions at Court at this day, even to the sober engaging of great persons, and differences, and making the King cheap and ridiculous. It is about my Lady Harvy's being offended at Doll Common's acting of Sempronia to imitate her; for which she got my Lord Chamberlain, her kinsman, to imprison Doll: upon which my Lady Castlemaine made the King to release her, and to order her to act it again worse than ever, the other day where the King himself was; and since it was acted again, and my Lady Harvy provided people

1 A tragi-comedy, by Beaumont and Fletcher.
2 Arabella Churchill, sister to John Duke of Marlborough, one of the Maids of Honour to the Duchess of York. James Duke of Berwick and three other children were the fruits of this intrigue. She married subsequently Colonel Godfrey, Comptroller of the Household, and died 1730, aged 82.

to hiss her and fling oranges at her: but it seems the heat is come to a great height, and real troubles at Court about it. Through the Park, where I met the King and the Duke of York, and so walked with them; and I did give the Duke of York thanks for his favour to me yesterday, at the Committee of Tangier, in my absence, (where some business was brought forward which the Duke of York would not suffer to go on without my presence at the debate). And he answered me just thus: that he ought to have a care of him that do the King's business in the manner that I do, and words of more force than that. Then down with Lord Brouncker to Sir R. Murray, into the King's little elaboratory under his closet; a pretty place; and there saw a great many chymical glasses and things, but understood none of them.

16th. Mr Wren thinks that the Parliament is likely to meet again, the King being frighted with what the Speaker hath put him in mind of, – his promise not to prorogue, but only to adjourn them. They speak mighty freely of the folly of the King in this foolish woman's business of my Lady Harvy. Povy tells me that Sir W. Coventry was with the King alone an hour this day; and that my Lady Castlemaine is now in a higher command over the King than ever – not as a mistress, for she scorns him, but as a tyrant, to command him: and says that the Duchesse of York and the Duke of York are mighty great with her, which is a great interest to my Lord Chancellor's family; and that they do agree to hinder all they can the proceedings of the Duke of Buckingham and Arlington. And so we are in the old mad condition, or rather worse than any; no man knowing what the French intend to do next summer.

17th. Spoke with my Lord Bellasses and Peterborough about the business now in dispute about my deputing a Treasurer to pay the garrison at Tangier; which I would avoid and not be accountable, and they will serve me therein. Here I met Hugh May, and he brings me to the knowledge of Sir Harry Capell,[3] a member of Parliament and brother of my Lord Essex,[4] who hath a great value it seems for me, and they appoint a day to come and dine with me, and see my books and papers of the office; which I shall be glad to show them,

---

3 Made KB at the Coronation of Charles II and created Lord Capel 1692; died at Dublin, while Lord Lieutenant of Ireland, 1696.
4 Arthur Capel, created Earl of Essex 1661; found dead in the Tower 1683.

and have opportunity to satisfy them therein. Here all the discourse is, that now the King is of opinion to have the Parliament called, notwithstanding his late resolutions for proroguing them; so unstable are his councils and those about him.

18th. To Sir W. Coventry's, and there discourse the business of my Treasurer's place at Tangier; wherein he consents to my desire, and concurs therein: which I am glad of, that I may not be accountable for a man so far off. And so I to my Lord Sandwich's, and there walk with him through the garden to White Hall; where he tells me what he hath done about this Treasurer's place, (and I perceive the whole thing did proceed from him:) that finding it would be best to have the Governor have nothing to do with the pay of the garrison, he did propose to the Duke of York alone that a paymaster should be there; and that being desirous to do a courtesy to Sir Charles Harbord,[5] and to prevent the Duke of York's looking out for any body else, he did name him to the Duke of York. That when he came the other day to move this to the board of Tangier, the Duke of York it seems did readily reply, that it was fit to have Mr Pepys satisfied therein first, and that it was not good to make places for persons. This my Lord in great confidence tells me that he do take very ill from the Duke of York, though nobody knew the meaning of these words but him; and that he did take no notice of them, but bit his lip, being satisfied that the Duke of York's care of me was as desirable to him as it could be to have Sir Charles Harbord; and did seem industrious to let me see that he was glad that the Duke of York and he might come to contend who shall be the kindest to me; which I owned as his great love, and so I hope and believe it is; though my Lord did go a little too far in this business, to move it so far without consulting me. But I took no notice of that, but was glad to see this competition come about, that my Lord Sandwich is apparently jealous of my thinking that the Duke of York do mean me more kindness than him. So we walked together, and I took this occasion to invite him to dinner to my house, and he readily appointed Friday next; which I shall be glad to have over to his content, he having never yet eat a bit of my bread. Thence to the Duke of York on the King's side, and meeting Mr Sidney Montagu and Sheres, a small invitation served their turn to carry them to London, where I paid Sheres his £100 given him for

5 Sir Charles Harbord, MP for Launceston.

his pains in drawing the plate of Tangier fortifications. At White Hall, and there in the Queene's withdrawing-room invited my Lord Peterborough to dine with me with my Lord Sandwich, who readily accepted it.

19th. To the King's house, to see *Horace*;[6] this the third day of its acting: a silly tragedy; but Lacy hath made a farce of several dances – between each act one: but his words are but silly, and invention not extraordinary as to the dances; only some Dutchmen come out of the mouth and tail of a Hamburgh sow.

20th. Heard at the Council-board the City, by their single Counsel Symson, and the Company of Strangers Merchants, debate the business of water-baylage; a tax demanded upon all goods, by the City, imported and exported: which these merchants oppose; and demanding leave to try the justice of the City's demand by a Quo Warranto, which the City opposed, the Merchants did quite lay the City on their backs with great triumph, the City's cause being apparently too weak: but here I observed Mr Gold, the merchant, to speak very well and very sharply against the City. This afternoon before the play I called with my wife at Dancre's,[7] the great landscape-painter, by Mr Povy's advice; and have bespoke him to come to take measure of my dining-room panels.

22nd. At the 'Change I met with Mr Dancre, with whom I was on Wednesday; and he took measure of my panels in my dining-room, where, in the four, I intend to have the four houses of the King, White Hall, Hampton Court, Greenwich, and Windsor. Mightily pleased with the fellow that came to lay the cloth and fold the napkins; which I like so well as that I am resolved to give him 40s. to teach my wife to do it.

23rd. To the office till noon, when word brought me that my Lord Sandwich was come; so I presently rose, and there I found my Lords Sandwich, Peterborough, and Sir Charles Harbord; and presently after them comes my Lord Hinchingbroke, Mr Sidney, and Sir

6 There were two translations about this period of the *Horace* of P. Corneille; one by Charles Cotton, the other (which was performed at Court,) by Catherine Phillips, the fifth act being added by Sir John Denham.
7 Henry Dankers, born at the Hague, employed by Charles II to paint views of his sea-ports and palaces. He followed his profession for some years in London.

William Godolphin. And after greeting them and some time spent in talk, dinner was brought up, one dish after another, but a dish at a time; but all so good: but, above all things, the variety of wines and excellent of their kind I had for them, and all in so good order, that they were mightily pleased, and myself full of content at it: and indeed it was, of a dinner of about six or eight dishes, as noble as any man need to have, I think; at least, all was done in the noblest manner that ever I had any, and I have rarely seen in my life better any where else, even at the Court. After dinner my Lords to cards, and the rest of us sitting about them and talking, and looking on my books and pictures, and my wife's drawings, which they commended mightily: and mighty merry all day long with exceeding great content, and so till seven at night; and so took their leaves, it being dark and foul weather. Thus was this entertainment over, the best of its kind and the fullest of honour and content to me that ever I had in my life; and I shall not easily have so good again.

24th (Lord's day). An order brought me in bed, for the principal officers to attend the King at my Lord Keeper's this afternoon, it being resolved late the last night; and by the warrant I find my Lord Keeper did not then know the cause of it, the messenger being ordered to call upon him to tell it him by the way, as he came to us. I to White Hall; and here I met Will. Batelier, newly come post from France, his boots all dirty. He brought letters to the King; and I glad to see him, it having been reported that he was drowned for some days past. By and by the King comes out, and so I took coach and followed his coaches to my Lord Keeper's at Essex-house, where I never was before, since I saw my old Lord Essex lie in state when he was dead. A large, but ugly house. Here all the officers of the Navy attended, and by and by were called in to the King and Cabinet, where my Lord, who was ill, did lie upon the bed, as my old Lord Treasurer or Chancellor heretofore used to do. And the business was to know in what time all the King's ships might be repaired fit for service. The Surveyor answered, in two years, and not sooner. I did give them hopes that, with supplies of money suitable, we might have them all fit for sea some part of the summer after this. Then they demanded in what time we could set out forty ships. It was answered, as they might be chosen of the newest and most ready, we could with money get forty ready against May. The King seemed mighty full that we should have money to do all that we desired, and satisfied that without it nothing could be done: and so without determining any thing we were dismissed; and I doubt all will end in some little fleet this year, and that of hired merchantmen, which would indeed be cheaper to the King and have many conveniences attending it, more than to fit out the King's own. And this, I perceive, is designed, springing from Sir W. Coventry's counsel; and the King and most of the Lords, I perceive, full of it, to get the King's fleet all at once in condition for service. Thence with Mr Wren in his coach, for discourse' sake: and he told me how the business of the Parliament is wholly laid aside, it being over-ruled now that they shall not meet, but must be prorogued, upon this argument chiefly: that all the differences between the two Houses, and things on foot that were matters of difference and discontent, may be laid aside, and must begin again if ever the House shall have a mind to pursue them.

25th. My wife showed me many excellent prints of Nantueil's and others, which W. Batelier hath at my desire brought me out of France, of the King's and Colbert's and others, most excellent, to my great content.

26th. To the office, and then to White Hall, leaving my wife at Unthanke's; and I to the Secretary's chamber, where I was by particular order this day summonsed to attend, as I find Sir D. Gauden also was. And here was the King and the Cabinet met; and being called in, among the rest I find my Lord Privy Seale, whom I never before knew to be in so much play as to be of the Cabinet. The business is that the Algerines have broke the peace with us by taking out some Spaniards and goods out of an English ship which had the Duke of York's pass, of which advice came this day; and the King is resolved to stop Sir Thomas Allen's fleet from coming home till he hath amends made him for this affront, and therefore sent for us to advise about victuals to be sent to that fleet, and some more ships: wherein I answered them to what they demanded of me, which was but some few mean things; but I see that on all these occasions they seem to rely most upon me.

27th. To the Duke of York's playhouse, and there saw *The Five Hours' Adventure*, which hath not been acted a good while before, but once, and is a most excellent play I must confess.

28th. Going home to supper with my wife, and to get her to read to me, I did find that Mr Sheres hath beyond his promise not only got me a candlestick made me, after a form he remembers to have seen in Spain, for keeping the light from one's eyes, but hath got it done in silver very neat, and designs to give it me in thanks for my paying him his £100 in money for his service at Tangier, which was ordered him; but I do intend to force him to make me pay for it. But I yet, without his direction, cannot tell how it is to be made use of.

29th. To the Duke of York, where I did give a severe account of our proceedings, and what we found in the business of Sir W. Jenings's demand of Supernumeraries. I thought it a good occasion to make an example of him, for he is a proud idle fellow; and it did meet with the Duke of York's acceptance and well-liking; and he did call him in after I had done, and did not only give him a soft rebuke, but condemns him to pay both their victuals and wages, or right himself of the purser. This I was glad of, and so were all the rest of us; though I know I have made myself an immortal enemy by it.

31st (Lord's day). To church, and there did hear the Doctor that is lately turned Divine, Dr Waterhouse. He preaches in a devout manner, not elegant nor very persuasive, but seems to mean well, and that he would preach holily; and was mighty passionate against people that made a scoff of religion.

February 1st. Meeting Mr Povy, he and I away to Dancre's to speak something touching the pictures I am getting him to make for me. And thence he carried me to Mr Streeter's[8] the famous history-painter over the way, whom I have often heard of, but did never see him before; and there I found him and Dr Wren and several virtuosos looking upon the paintings which he is making for the new Theatre at Oxford: and indeed they look as if they would be very fine, and the rest think better than those of Rubens in the Banqueting-house at White Hall, but I do not so fully think so. But they will certainly be very noble; and I am mightily pleased to have the fortune to see this man and his work, which is very famous. And he a very civil little man, and lame, but lives very handsomely. So thence to my Lord Bellasses, and met him within: my business only to see a chimney-piece of Dancres doing in distemper, with egg to keep off the glaring

8 Robert Streater, appointed Serjeant Painter at the Restoration. Died 1680.

of the light, which I must have done for my room: and indeed it is pretty, but I must confess I do think it is not altogether so beautiful as the oyle pictures; but I will have some of one and some of another. So to the King's playhouse, thinking to have seen *The Heyresse*, first acted on Saturday last: but when we come thither we find no play there; Kinaston, that did act a part therein in abuse to Sir Charles Sedley, being last night exceedingly beaten with sticks by two or three that saluted him, so as he is mightily bruised and forced to keep his bed.

2nd. To dinner at noon, where I find Mr Sheres; and there made a short dinner, and carried him with us to the King's playhouse, where *The Heyresse*, notwithstanding Kinaston's being beaten, is acted: and they say the King is very angry with Sir Charles Sedley for his being beaten, but he do deny it. But his part is done by Beeston, who is fain to read it out of a book all the while, and thereby spoils the part, and almost the play, it being one of the best parts in it: and though the design is in the first conception of it pretty good, yet it is but an indifferent play; wrote, they say, by my Lord Newcastle.[9] But it was pleasant to see Beeston come in with others, supposing it to be dark, and yet he is forced to read his part by the light of the candles: and this I observing to a gentleman that sat by me, he was mightily pleased therewith, and spread it up and down. But that that pleased me most in the play is the first song that Knipp sings (she singing three or four); and indeed it was very finely sung, so as to make the whole house clap her.

5th. Betimes to Sir W. Coventry's, meaning by my visit to keep fresh my interest in him. And he tells me how it hath been talked that he was to go one of the Commissioners to Ireland, which he was resolved never to do unless directly commanded: for that to go thither while the Chief Secretary of State was his professed enemy, was to undo himself; and therefore it were better for him to venture being unhappy here, than to go further off to be undone by some obscure instructions, or whatever other way of mischief his enemy should cut out for him. He mighty kind to me; and so parted.

6th. To the King's playhouse, and there in an upper box (where come in Colonell Poynton and Doll Stacey, who is very fine, and by

9 *The Heiress* does not appear in the list of the Duke of Newcastle's works, nor can I find any mention of it elsewhere.

her wedding-ring I suppose he hath married her at last,) did see *The Moor of Venice*: but ill acted in most parts, Moone (which did a little surprize me) not acting Iago's part by much so well as Clun used to do: nor another Hart's, which was Cassio's; nor indeed Burt doing the Moor's so well as I once thought he did. Thence home; and just at Holborne-conduit the bolt broke that holds the fore-wheels to the perch, and so the horses went away with them and left the coachman and us: but being near our coach-maker's, and we staying in a little ironmonger's shop, we were presently supplied with another.

8th. To visit my Lord Sandwich; and there, while my Lord was dressing himself, did see a young Spaniard that he hath brought over with him dance, which he is admired for as the best dancer in Spain, and indeed he do with mighty mastery; but I do not like his dancing as well as the English, though my Lord commends it mightily. But I will have him to my house, and show it my wife. Here I met with Mr Moore, who tells me the state of my Lord's accounts of his embassy, which I find not so good as I thought: for though it be passed the King and his Caball (the Committee for Foreign Affairs, as they are called,) yet they have cut off from £19,000 full £8000 and have now sent it to the Lords of the Treasury, who, though the Committee have allowed the rest, yet they are not obliged to abide by it. So that I do fear this account may yet be long ere it be passed, – much more ere that sum be paid. I am sorry for the family.

9th. To the King's playhouse, and there saw *The Island Princesse*, which I like mighty well as an excellent play: and here we find Kinaston to be well enough to act again; which he do very well, after his beating by Sir Charles Sedley's appointment.

10th. To the plaisterer's at Charing Cross that casts heads and bodies in plaister; and there I had my whole face done; but I was vexed first to be forced to daub all my face over with pomatum. Thus was the mold made; but when it came off there was little pleasure in it as it looks in the mold, nor any resemblance whatever there will be in the figure when I come to see it cast off. To White Hall, where I staid till the Duke of York came from hunting, which he did by and by, and when dressed did come out to dinner; and there I waited. And he did mightily magnify his sauce, which he did then eat with every thing, and said it was the best universal sauce in the world, it being taught him by the Spanish Embassador; made of some parsley and a dry toast, beat in a mortar together with vinegar, salt, and a little pepper: he eats it with flesh, or fowl, or fish. And then he did now mightily commend some new sort of wine lately found out, called Navarr wine; which I tasted, and is, I think, good wine: but I did like better the notion of the sauce, and by and by did taste it, and liked it mightily. After dinner I did what I went for; which was to get his consent that Balty might hold his Muster-master's place by deputy in his new employment which I design for him, about the Storekeeper's accounts; which the Duke of York did grant me, and I was mightily glad of it.

12th. To wait on the Duke of York with the rest of us at the Robes; where the Duke of York did tell us that the King would have us prepare a draught of the present administration of the Navy, and what it was in the late times, in order to his being able to distinguish between the good and the bad; which I shall do, but to do it well will give me a great deal of trouble. Here we showed him Sir J. Minnes's propositions about balancing Storekeeper's accounts; and I did show him Hosier's, which did please him mightily, and he will have it showed the Council and King anon to be put in practice. Thence to the Treasurer's; and I and Sir J. Minnes and Mr Tippets down to the Lords Commissioners of the Treasury, and there had a hot debate from Sir Thomas Clifford and my Lord Ashly (the latter of whom, I hear, is turning about as fast as he can to the Duke of Buckingham's side, being in danger, it seems, of being otherwise out of play, which would not be convenient for him,) against Sir W. Coventry and Sir J. Duncomb; who did uphold our office against an accusation of our Treasurers, who told the Lords that they found that we had run the King in debt £50,000 or more, more than the money appointed for the year would defray; which they declared like fools, and with design to hurt us, though the thing is in itself ridiculous. But my Lord Ashly and Clifford did most horribly cry out against the want of method in the office. At last it came that it should be put in writing what they had to object; but I was devilish mad at it, to see us thus wounded by our own members. Attended with Lord Brouncker the King and Council about the proposition of balancing Store-keeper's accounts; and there presented Hosier's book, and it was mighty well resented[10] and approved of. So the Council being up, we to the

10 Resent, to take well or ill. – Johnson.

Queene's side with the King and Duke of York: and the Duke of York did take me out to talk of our Treasurers, whom he is mighty angry with; and I perceive he is mighty desirous to bring in as many good motions of profit and reformation in the Navy as he can before the Treasurers do light upon them, they being desirous, it seems, to be thought the great reformers: and the Duke of York do well. But to my great joy he is mighty open to me in every thing; and by this means I know his whole mind, and shall be able to secure myself if he stands. Here to-night I understand by my Lord Brouncker, that at last it is concluded on by the King and Buckingham that my Lord of Ormond shall not hold his government of Ireland; which is a great stroke to show the power of Buckingham and the poor spirit of the King, and little hold that any man can have of him. Home, and there Pelling hath got W. Pen's book against the Trinity. I got my wife to read it to me; and I find it so well writ as, I think, it is too good for him ever to have writ it; and it is a serious sort of book, and not fit for every body to read.

14th (Lord's day). Up, and by coach to Sir W. Coventry: and there he tells me he takes no more care for any thing more than in the Treasury; and that that being done, he goes to cards and other delights, as plays, and in the summer-time to bowles. But here he did show me two or three old books of the Navy of my Lord Northumberland's[11] times, which he hath taken many good notes out of, for justifying the Duke of York and us in many things, wherein perhaps precedent will be necessary to produce. Thence to White Hall, where the Duke of York expected me; and in his closet Wren and I. He did tell me how the King hath been acquainted with the Treasurers' discourse at the Lords Commissioners of the Treasury the other day, and is dissatisfied with our running him in debt; which I removed. And he did carry me to the King, and I did satisfy him also: but his satisfaction is nothing worth, it being easily got and easily removed. But I do purpose to put it in writing, that shall make the Treasurers ashamed. But the Duke of York is horrid angry against them; and he hath cause, for they do work all they can to bring dishonour upon his management, as do plainly appear in all they do. Having done with the Duke of York, who do repose all in me, I with

11 Algernon Percy, tenth Earl of Northumberland, made Lord High Admiral, 1635.

Mr Wren to his chamber to talk; where he observed, that these people are all of them a broken sort of people that have not much to lose, and therefore will venture all to make their fortunes better: that Sir Thomas Osborne is a beggar, having 11 or £1200 a-year, but owes above £10,000. The Duke of Buckingham's condition is shortly this: that he hath about £19,600 a-year, of which he pays away about £7000 a-year in interest, about £2000 in fee-farm rents to the King, about £6000 in wages and pensions, and the rest to live upon and pay taxes for the whole. Wren says, that for the Duke of York to stir in this matter, as his quality might justify, would but make all things worse, and that therefore he must bend and suffer all till time works it out: that he fears they will sacrifice the Church, and that the King will take any thing (and so he holds up his head a little longer), and then break in pieces. But Sir W. Coventry did to-day mightily magnify my late Lord Treasurer for a wise and solid, though infirm man: and among other things, that when he hath said it was impossible in nature to find this or that sum of money, and my Lord Chancellor hath made sport of it, and told the King that when my Lord hath said it was impossible, yet he hath made shift to find it, and that was by Sir G. Carteret's getting credit, my Lord did once in his hearing say thus, which he magnifies as a great saying – that impossible would be found impossible at last; meaning that the King would run himself out beyond all his credit and funds, and then we should too late find it impossible; which is, he says, now come to pass.

15th. To the plaisterer's, and there saw the figure of my face taken from the mould; and it is most admirably like, and I will have another made before I take it away. At the 'Change I did at my bookseller's shop accidentally fall into talk with Sir Samuel Tuke[12] about trees and Mr Evelyn's garden; and I do find him, I think, a little conceited, but a man of very fine discourse as any I ever heard almost; which I was mighty glad of. In Suffolk-street lives Moll Davies; and we did see her coach come for her to her door, a mighty pretty fine coach. To White Hall; and there, by means of Mr Cooling, did get into the play, the only one we have seen this winter: it was *The Five Hours' Adventure*: but I sat so far I could not hear well, nor was there any pretty woman that I did see but my wife, who sat in my Lady Fox's

---

12 Sir Samuel Tuke, of Cressing Temple, Essex, Bart., was a Colonel in Charles I's army, and cosen to Mr Evelyn. He died at Somerset-house, January 1673.

pew with her. The house very full; and late before done, so that it was past eleven before we got home.

17th. The King dining yesterday at the Dutch Embassador's, after dinner they drank and were pretty merry; and among the rest of the King's company there was that worthy fellow my Lord of Rochester, and Tom Killigrew, whose mirth and raillery offended the former so much, that he did give Tom Killigrew a box on the ear in the King's presence; which do give much offence to the people here at Court to see how cheap the King makes himself, and the more, for that the King hath not only passed by the thing and pardoned it to Rochester already, but this very morning the King did publicly walk up and down, and Rochester I saw with him as free as ever, to the King's everlasting shame to have so idle a rogue his companion. How Tom Killigrew takes it, I do not hear. I do also this day hear that my Lord Privy-Seale do accept to go Lieutenant into Ireland; but whether it be true or no, I cannot tell. To Colonel Middleton's to the burial of his wife, where we were all invited, and much more company, and had each of us a ring. At church there was my Lord Brouncker and Mrs Williams in our pew, the first time they were ever there, or that I knew that either of them would go to church.

19th. This morning, among other things, talking with Sir W. Coventry, I did propose to him my putting in to serve in Parliament, if there should, as the world begins to expect, be a new one chose. He likes it mightily, both for the King's and service's sake, and the Duke of York's, and will propound it to the Duke of York: and I confess, if there be one, I would be glad to be in.

22nd. In the evening to White Hall, and there did without much trouble get into the playhouse, finding a good place among the Ladies of Honour, and all of us sitting in the pit; and then by and by came the King and Queene, and they began *Bartholomew-fair*. But I like no play here so well as at the common playhouse; besides that, my eyes being very ill since last Sunday and this day se'nnight, I was in mighty pain to defend myself now from the light of the candles. After the play done, we met with W. Batelier and W. Hewer and Talbot Pepys,[13] and they followed us in a hackney-coach: and we all stopped at Hercules' Pillars; and there I did give them the best supper

13 Of Impington. Died 1681, aged 35.

I could, and pretty merry; and so home between eleven and twelve at night.

23rd. To Westminster Abbey, and there did see all the tombs very finely, having one with us alone (there being other company this day to see the tombs, it being Shrove-Tuesday:) and here we did see, by particular favour, the body of Queen Katherine of Valois; and I had the upper part of her body in my hands, and I did kiss her mouth, reflecting upon it that I did kiss a queene, and that this was my birth-day, thirty-six years old, that I did kiss a queene. But here this man, who seems to understand well, tells me that the saying is not true that she was never buried, for she was buried; only when Henry the Seventh built his chapel, she was taken up and laid in this wooden coffin; but I did there see that in it the body was buried in a leaden one, which remains under the body to this day.

25th. To the Duke of York's house, and there before one, but the house infinite full; where by and by the King and Court come, it being a new play, or an old one new vamped by Shadwell, called *The Royall Shepherdesse;*[14] but the silliest for words and design, and every thing, that ever I saw in my whole life, there being nothing in the world pleasing in it, but a good martiall dance of pikemen, where Harris and another do handle their pikes in a dance to admiration; but never less satisfied with a play in my life.

26th. To the King's playhouse, and saw *The Faithfull Shepherdesse.* But, Lord! what an empty house, there not being, as I could tell the people, so many as to make up above £10 in the whole house! But I plainly discern the musick is the better, by how much the house the emptier.

March 1st. I do hear that my Lady Paulina Montagu did die yesterday! at which I went to my Lord's lodgings, but he is shut up with sorrow, and so not to be spoken with: and therefore I returned, and to Westminster Hall, where I have not been, I think, in some months. And here the Hall was very full, the King having by Commission to some Lords this day prorogued the Parliament till the 19th of October next; at which I am glad, hoping to have time to go over to France this

14 A tragi-comedy, altered by Thomas Shadwell from a comedy written by Mr Fountain, called *The Rewards of Virtue.*

year. But I was most of all surprised this morning by my Lord Bellasses, who by appointment met me at Auditor Wood's at the Temple, and tells me of a duell designed between the Duke of Buckingham and my Lord Halifax, or Sir W. Coventry; the challenge being carried by Harry Saville, but prevented by my Lord Arlington, and the King told of it: and this was all the discourse at Court this day. But I meeting Sir W. Coventry in the Duke of York's chamber, he would not own it to me, but told me he was a man of too much peace to meddle with fighting; and so it rested: but the talk is full in the town of the business. Thence, having walked some turns with my cosen Pepys, and most people by their discourse believing that this Parliament will never sit more, I away. I did bring home a piece of my face cast in plaister, for to make a vizard upon for my eyes.

2nd. My wife this day put on first her French gown, called a Sac, which becomes her very well.

3rd. To White Hall, where W. Hewer met me; and he and I took a turn in St James's Park, and in the Mall did meet Sir W. Coventry and Sir J. Duncomb, and did speak with them about some business, before the Lords of the Treasury: but I did find them more than usually busy, though I knew not then the reason of it, though I guessed it by what followed next day. Thence to Dancre's the painter's and there saw my picture of Greenwich, finished to my very good content, though this manner of distemper do make the figures not so pleasing as in oyle. To the Duke of York's playhouse, and there saw an old play, the first time acted these forty years, called *The Lady's Tryall*,[15] acted only by the young people of the house; but the house very full. To the New Exchange, and so called at my cousin Turner's; and there meeting Mr Bellwood, did hear how my Lord Mayor being invited this day to dinner at the Reader's at the Temple, and endeavouring to carry his sword up, the students did pull it down, and forced him to go and stay all the day in a private Counsellor's chamber until the Reader himself could get the young gentlemen to dinner; and then my Lord Mayor did retreat out of the Temple by stealth, with his sword up. This do make great heat among the students; and my Lord Mayor did send to the King, and also I hear that Sir Richard Browne did cause the drums to beat for

15 A tragedy, by John Ford.

the Train-bands; but all is over, only I hear that the students do resolve to try the Charter of the City. So we home, and betimes to bed, and slept well all night.

4th. To White Hall, where in the first Court I did meet Sir Jeremy Smith, who did tell me that Sir W. Coventry was just now sent to the Tower, about the business of the challenging the Duke of Buckingham, and so was also Harry Saville to the Gate-house; which, as he is a gentleman, and of the Duke of York's Bedchamber, I heard afterwards that the Duke of York is mightily incensed at, and do appear very high to the King that he might not be sent thither, but to the Tower, this being done only in contempt to him. This news of Sir W. Coventry did strike me to the heart, and with reason, for by this and my Lord of Ormond's business I do doubt that the Duke of Buckingham will be so flushed that he will not stop at any thing, but be forced to do any thing now, as thinking it not safe to end here; and, Sir W. Coventry being gone, the King will have no good Counsellor left, nor the Duke of York any sure friend to stick to him; nor any good man will remain to advise what is good. This, therefore, do heartily trouble me, as any thing that ever I heard. So up into the House, and met with several people; but the Committee did not meet. And the whole House I find full of the business of Sir W. Coventry's, and most men very sensible of the cause and effects of it. So, meeting with my Lord Bellasses, he told me the particulars of this matter; that it arises about a quarrel which Sir W. Coventry had with the Duke of Buckingham, about a design between him and Sir Robert Howard to bring him into a play at the King's house; which W. Coventry not enduring, did by H. Saville send a letter to the Duke of Buckingham, that he had a desire to speak with him. Upon which the Duke of Buckingham did bid Holmes (his champion ever since my Lord Shrewsbury's business) go to him to do the business; but H. Saville would not tell it to any but himself, and therefore did go presently to the Duke of Buckingham, and told him that his uncle Coventry was a person of honour, and was sensible of his Grace's liberty taken of abusing him, and that he had a desire of satisfaction, and would fight with him. But that here they were interrupted by my Lord Chamberlain's coming in, who was commanded to go to bid the Duke of Buckingham to come to the King, Holmes having discovered it. He told me that the King did last night at the Council

ask the Duke of Buckingham, upon his honour, whether he received
any challenge from W. Coventry? which he confessed that he had;
and then the King asking W. Coventry, he told him that he did not
owne what the Duke of Buckingham had said, though it was not fit
for him to give him a direct contradiction. But, being by the King
put upon declaring the truth upon his honour, he answered that he
had understood that many hard questions had upon this business been
moved to some lawyers, and that therefore he was unwilling to
declare any thing that might from his own mouth render him
obnoxious to his Majesty's displeasure, and therefore prayed to be
excused: which the King did think fit to interpret to be a confession,
and so gave warrant that night for his commitment to the Tower.
Being very much troubled at this, I away by coach homewards, and
directly to the Tower, where I find him in one Mr Bennet's house,
son to Major Bayly, one of the Officers of the Ordnance, in the
Bricke Tower: where I find him busy with my Lord Halifax and his
brother; so I would not stay to interrupt them, but only to give him
comfort and offer my service to him, which he kindly and cheerfully
received, only owning his being troubled for the King his master's
displeasure, which I suppose is the ordinary form and will of persons
in this condition. And so I parted with great content that I had so
earlily seen him there; and so, going out, did meet Sir Jer. Smith
going to meet me, who had newly been with Sir W. Coventry. And
so he and I by water to Redriffe, and so walked to Deptford, where I
have not been, I think, these twelve months: and there to the
Treasurer's house, where the Duke of York is, and his Duchesse; and
there we find them at dinner in the great room, unhung: and there
was with them my Lady Duchesse of Monmouth, the Countess of
Falmouth, Castlemaine, Henrietta Hide,[16] my Lady Hinchingbroke's
sister, and my Lady Peterborough. And after dinner Sir Jer. Smith and
I were invited down to dinner with some of the Maids of Honour,
namely, Mrs Ogle,[17] Blake,[18] and Howard,[19] (which did me good to
have the honour to dine with and look on); and the mother of the

16 Henrietta, fifth daughter to the Earl of Burlington, married Laurence Hyde,
afterwards Earl of Rochester.
17 Anne Ogle.
18 Mary, daughter of Colonel Blague, married Sir Thomas Yarborough. See
Mémoires de Grammont.
19 Dorothy Howard.

Maids, and Mrs Howard, the mother of the Maid of Honour of that name, and the Duke's housekeeper here. Here was also Monsieur Blancfort, Sir Richard Powell, Colonell Villers, Sir Jonathan Trelawny,[20] and others. And here drank most excellent, and great variety, and plenty of wines, more than I have drank at once these seven years, but yet did me no great hurt. Having dined very merrily, and understanding by Blancfort how angry the Duke of York was about their offering to send Saville to the Gate-house among the rogues; and then, observing how this company, both the ladies and all, are of a gang, and did drink a health to the union of the two brothers, and talking of others as their enemies, they parted, and so we up: and there I did find the Duke of York and Duchesse with all the great ladies sitting upon a carpet on the ground, there being no chairs, playing at 'I love my love with an A, because he is so and so; and I hate him with an A, because of this and that': and some of them, but particularly the Duchesse herself and my Lady Castlemaine, were very witty. This done, they took barge, and I with Sir J. Smith to Captain Cox's; and there to talk, and left them.

5th. After dinner I to the Tower, where I find Sir W. Coventry with abundance of company with him; and after sitting awhile and hearing some merry discourse, and, among others, of Mr Brouncker's being this day summoned to Sir William Morton,[21] one of the Judges, to give in security for his good behaviour upon his words the other day to Sir John Morton,[22] a Parliament-man, at White Hall, who had heretofore spoke very highly against Brouncker in the House, I away, and to Aldgate.

6th. Before the office I stepped to Sir W. Coventry at the Tower, and there had a great deal of discourse with him; among others, of the King's putting him out of the Council yesterday, with which he is well contented, as with what else they can strip him of, he telling me, and so hath long, that he is weary and surfeited of business. But he joins with me in his fears that all will go to naught, as matters are now managed. He told me the matter of the play that was intended for his

20 Eldest son of Sir John Trelawney, who was created a Baronet 1628. He served with credit in 1672 under Marshal Turenne, and was afterwards made Governor of Plymouth by King William, for his good conduct in Ireland.
21 Made a Justice of the King's Bench 1665. Died 1672.
22 MP for Weymouth in 1680.

abuse, wherein they foolishly and sillily bring in two tables like that
which he hath made with a round hole in the middle in his closet to
turn himself in;[23] and he is to be in one of them as master, and Sir J.
Duncomb in the other, as his man or imitator: and their discourse in
those tables about the disposing of their books and papers very foolish.
But that that he is offended with, is his being made so contemptible, as
that any should dare to make a gentleman a subject for the mirth of
the world: and that therefore he had told Tom Killigrew that he
should tell his actors, whoever they were, that did offer at any thing
like representing him, that he would not complain to my Lord
Chamberlain, which was too weak, nor get him beaten, as Sir Charles
Sedley is said to have done; but that he would cause his nose to be cut.
He told me how that the Duke of Buckingham did himself some time
since desire to join with him, of all men in England, and did bid him
propound to himself to be Chief Minister of State, saying that he
would bring it about, but that he refused to have any thing to do with
any faction; and that the Duke of Buckingham did, within these few
days, say that, of all men in England, he would have chosen Sir W.
Coventry to have joined entire with. He tells me that he fears their
prevailing against the Duke of York; and that their violence will force
them to it, as being already beyond his pardon. He repeated to me
many examples of challengings of Privy-counsellors and others; but
never any proceeded against with that severity which he is, it never
amounting with others to more than a little confinement. He tells me
of his being weary of the Treasury, and of the folly, ambition, and
desire of popularity of Sir Thomas Clifford; and yet the rudeness of his
tongue and passions, when angry.

7th (Lord's day). To the Tower to see Sir W. Coventry, who had H.
Jermin and a great many more with him, and more while I was there
came in: so that I do hear that there was not less than sixty coaches
there yesterday and the other day; which I hear also that there is great
exception taken at by the King, and the Duke of Buckingham, but it
cannot be helped. I to White Hall, and there hear that there are letters
come from Sir Thomas Allen, that he hath made some kind of peace
with Argier; upon which the King and Duke of York, being to go
out of town tomorrow, are met at my Lord Arlington's: so I there,
and by Mr Wren was desired to stay to see if there were occasion for

23 See Diary, July 4, 1668, where Sir W. C.'s round table is described.

their speaking with me, which I did, walking without, with Charles Porter, talking of a great many things: and I perceive all the world is against the Duke of Buckingham's acting thus high, and do prophecy nothing but ruin from it. But he do well observe that the Church lands cannot certainly come to much, if the King shall be persuaded to take them, they being leased out for long leases. By and by after two hours' stay they rose, having, as Wren tells me, resolved upon sending six ships to the Streights forthwith, not being contented with the peace upon the terms they demand; which are, that all our ships, where any Turks or Moores shall be found slaves, shall be prizes; which will imply that they must be searched. I hear that to-morrow the King and Duke of York set out for Newmarket, by three in the morning, to some foot and horse-races; to be abroad ten or twelve days. So I without seeing the Duke of York; but Mr Wren showed me the order of Council about the balancing Store-keeper's accounts, passed the Council in the very terms I drew it, only I did put in my name as he that presented the book of Hosier's preparing, and that is left out, I mean my name; which is no great matter.

8th. To White Hall, from whence the King and the Duke of York went by three in the morning, and had the misfortune to be overset with the Duke of York, the Duke of Monmouth, and the Prince,[24] at the King's gate in Holborne; and the King all dirty, but no hurt. How it come to pass I know not, but only it was dark, and the torches did not, they say, light the coach as they should do. I thought this morning to have seen my Lord Sandwich before he went out of town, but I came half an hour too late; which troubles me, I having not seen him since my Lady Pall died. And so to the Privy-Seal office, to examine what records I could find there for my help in the great business I am put upon of defending the present constitution of the Navy; but there could not have liberty without order from him that is in present waiting, Mr Bickerstaffe, who is out of town.

9th. Up, and to the Tower; and there find Sir W. Coventry alone writing down his journall, which, he tells me, he now keeps of the material things; upon which I told him, (and he is the only man I ever told it to, I think,) that I kept it most strictly these eight or ten years; and I am sorry almost that I told it him, it not being necessary,

24 Rupert.

nor maybe convenient, to have it known. Here he showed me the petition he had sent to the King by my Lord Keeper; which was not to desire any admittance to employment, but submitting himself therein humbly to his Majesty; but prayed the removal of his displeasure, and that he might be set free. He tells me that my Lord Keeper did acquaint the King with the substance of it, not showing him the petition; who answered, that he was disposing of his employments, and when that was done he might be led to discharge him: and this is what he expects, and what he seems to desire. But by this discourse he was pleased to take occasion to show me and read to me his account, which he hath kept by him under his own hand, of all his discourse and the King's answers to him upon the great business of my Lord Clarendon, and how he had first moved the Duke of York with it twice at good distance, one after another, but without success; showing me thereby the simplicity and reasons of his so doing, and the manner of it; and the King's accepting it, telling him that he was not satisfied in his management, and did discover some dissatisfaction against him for his opposing the laying aside of my Lord Treasurer at Oxford, which was a secret the King had not discovered. And really I was mighty proud to be privy to this great transaction, it giving me great conviction of the noble nature and ends of Sir W. Coventry in it, and considerations in general of the consequences of great men's actions, and the uncertainty of their estates, and other very serious considerations.

11th. Up, and to Sir W. Coventry to the Tower; who tells me that he hears that the Commission is gone down to the King with a blank to fill for his place in the Treasury: and he believes it will be filled with one of our Treasurers of the Navy, but which he knows not, but he believes it will be Osborne. We walked down to the stonewalk, which is called, it seems, my Lord of Northumberland's walk, being paved by some one of that title that was prisoner there; and at the end of it there is a piece of iron upon the wall with his arms upon it, and holes to put in a peg for every turn they make upon that walk.

12th. With great content spent all the morning looking over the Navy accounts of several years, and the several patents of the Treasurers. W. Hewer carried me to Nott's, the famous bookbinder that bound for my Lord Chancellor's library: and here I did take occasion for curiosity to bespeak a book to be bound, only that I might have one of his binding.

13th. That which put me in good humour both at noon and night, is the fancy that I am this day made a captain of one of the King's ships, Mr Wren having this day sent me the Duke of York's commission to be Captain of the *Jerzy*, in order to my being of a Court-martiall for examining the loss of the *Defyance*, and other things; which do give me occasion of much mirth, and may be of some use to me, at least I shall get a little money for the time I have it; it being designed that I must really be a captain to be able to sit in this Court.

15th. Up, and by water with W. Hewer to the Temple; and thence to the Rolls, where I made enquiry for several rolls, and was soon informed in the manner of it: and so spent the whole morning with W. Hewer, he taking little notes in short hand, while I hired a clerk there to read to me about twelve or more several rolls which I did call for. And it was great pleasure to me to see the method wherein their rolls are kept; that when the master of the office, one Mr Case, do call for them, (who is a man that I have heretofore known by coming to my Lord Sandwich's,) he did most readily turn to them. At noon they shut up; and W. Hewer and I did walk to the Cocke, at the end of Suffolke-street, where I never was, a great ordinary mightily cried up, and there bespoke a pullet: which, while dressing, he and I walked into St James's Park, and thence back and dined very handsome with a good soup and a pullet for 4s. 6d. the whole. Thence back to the Rolls, and did a little more business: and so by water to White Hall, whither I went to speak with Mr Williamson (that if he hath any papers relating to the Navy I might see them, which he promises me). And so by water home with great content for what I have this day found, having got almost as much as I desire of the history of the Navy, from 1618 to 1642, when the King and Parliament fell out.

16th. Comes to me Mr Evelyn of Deptford, a worthy good man, and dined with me (but a bad dinner): who is grieved for and speaks openly to me his thoughts of the times, and our ruin approaching; and all by the folly of the King. His business to me was about some ground of his at Deptford, next to the King's yard: and after dinner we parted. To Woolwich, where I saw, but did not go on board, my ship the *Jerzy*, she lying at the wharf under repair. But my business was to speak with Ackworth about some old things and passages in the Navy, for my information therein, in order to my great business now of stating the history of the Navy. This I did; and upon the whole do find that the late times, in all their management, were not more husbandly than we; and other things of good content to me. Thence to Greenwich by water, and there landed at the King's house, which goes on slow, but is very pretty. I to the Park, there to see the prospect of the hill, to judge of Dancre's picture which he hath made thereof for me; and I do like it very well: and it is a very pretty place. Thence to Deptford, but staid not, Unthwayte being out of the way. And so home, and then to the King's Tavern (Morrice's) and staid till W. Hewer fetched his uncle Blackburn by appointment to me, to discourse of the business of the Navy in the late times; and he did do it by giving me a most exact account in writing of the several turns in the Admiralty and Navy of the persons employed therein, from the beginning of the King's leaving the Parliament to his son's coming in, to my great content; and now I am fully informed in all I at present desire. We fell to other talk; and I find by him that the Bishops must certainly fall, and their hierarchy; these people have got so much ground upon the King and kingdom as is not to be got again from them: and the Bishops do well deserve it. But it is all the talk, I find, that Dr Wilkins, my friend, Bishop of Chester shall be removed to Winchester and be Lord Treasurer. Though this be foolish talk, yet I do gather that he is a mighty rising man, as being a Latitudinarian, and the Duke of Buckingham his great friend.

18th. Up, and to see Sir W. Coventry, and walked with him a good while in the stone-walk: and brave discourse about my Lord Chancellor and his ill managements and mistakes, and several things of the Navy.

19th. Sir Thomas Clifford did speak to me, as desirous that I would some time come and confer with him about the Navy; which I am glad of, but will take the direction of the Duke of York before I do it, though I would be glad to do something to secure myself, if I could, in my employment. Thence to the plaisterer's, and took my face and my Lord Duke of Albemarle's home with me by coach, they being done to my mind; and mighty glad I am of understanding this way of having the pictures of any friends. After dinner with Commissioner Middleton and Kempthorne to a Court-martiall, to

which, by virtue of my late captainship, I am called, the first I was
ever at; where many commanders, and Kempthorne president. Here
was tried a difference between Sir L. Van Hemskirke, the Dutch
captain who commands the *Nonsuch*, built by his direction, and his
lieutenant; a drunken kind of silly business. We ordered the
lieutenant to ask him pardon, and have resolved to lay before the
Duke of York what concerns the captain, which was striking of his
lieutenant and challenging him to fight, which comes not within any
article of the laws martiall. But upon discourse the other day with Sir
W. Coventry I did advise Middleton, and he and I did forbear to
give judgment, but after the debate did withdraw into another cabin,
(the Court being held in one of the yachts, which was on purpose
brought up over against St Katherine's) it being to be feared that this
precedent of our being made captains in order to the trying of the
loss of the *Defyance*, wherein we are the proper persons to enquire
into the want of instructions while ships do lie in harbour, might be
hereafter made of evil use, by putting the Duke of Buckingham, or
any of these rude fellows that now are uppermost, to make packed
Courts by captains made on purpose to serve their turns. The other
cause was of the loss of the *Providence* at Tangier, where the captain's
being by chance on shore may prove very inconvenient to him, for
example's sake, though the man be a good man, and one whom for
Norwood's sake I would be kind to; but I will not offer any thing to
the excusing such a miscarriage. He is at present confined till he can
bring better proofs on his behalf of the reasons of his being on shore.
So Middleton and I away to the office; and there I late busy, making
my people, as I have done lately, to read Mr Holland's *Discourse of the
Navy*, and what other things I can get to inform me fully in all. And
here late, about eight at night, comes Mr Wren to me, who had
been at the Tower to visit Sir W. Coventry. He came only to see
how matters go, and tells me as a secret, that the last night the Duke
of York's closet was broken open, and his cabinets, and shut again
one of them; that the rogue that did it hath left plate and a watch
behind him, and therefore they fear that it was only for papers,
which looks like a very malicious business in design to hurt the Duke
of York; but they cannot know that till the Duke of York comes to
town about the papers, and therefore make no words of it. He gone,
I to work again, and then to supper home, and to bed.

20th. Up, and to the Tower to Sir W. Coventry, and there walked with him alone on the stone-walk till company came to him; and there about the business of the Navy discoursed with him, and about my Lord Chancellor and Treasurer; that they were against the war at first, declaring, as wise men and statesmen, at first to the King, that they thought it fit to have a war with them at some time or other, but that it ought not to be till we found the Crowns of Spain and France together by the eares, the want of which did ruin our war. But then he told me that a great while before the war my Lord Chancellor did speak of a war with some heat as a thing to be desired, and did it upon a belief that he could with his own speeches make the Parliament give what money he pleased, and do what he would, or would make the King desire; but he found himself soon deceived of the Parliament, they having a long time before his removal been cloyed with his speeches and good words, and being come to hate him. Sir W. Coventry did tell me it as the wisest thing that ever was said to the King by any statesman of his time, and it was by my Lord Treasurer that is dead, whom, I find, he takes for a very great statesman, – that when the King did show himself forward for passing the Act of Indemnity, he did advise the King that he would hold his hand in doing it till he had got his power restored that had been diminished by the late times, and his revenue settled in such a manner as he might depend on himself without resting upon Parliaments, and then pass it. But my Lord Chancellor, who thought he could have the command of Parliaments for ever, because for the King's sake they were awhile willing to grant all the King desired, did press for its being done; and so it was, and the King from that time able to do nothing with the Parliament almost. Mightily pleased with the news brought me to-night that the King and Duke of York are come back this afternoon, and no sooner come but a warrant was sent to the Tower for the releasing Sir W. Coventry: which do put me in some hopes that there may be in this absence some accommodation made between the Duke of York and the Duke of Buckingham and Lord Arlington.

21st. To White Hall, in a scull; where to the Duke of York's dressing-room, and there met Harry Saville, and do understand that Sir W. Coventry is come to his house last night. I understand by Mr Wren that his friends having by Secretary Trevor and my Lord Keeper applied to the King upon his first coming home, and a promise made that he should be discharged this day, my Lord Arlington did anticipate them by sending a warrant presently for his discharge; which looks a little like kindness, or a desire of it; which God send! though I fear the contrary. However, my heart is glad that he is out. Thence up and down the House. Met Mr May, who tells me the story of his being put by Sir John Denham's place (of Surveyor of the King's Works, who, it seems, is lately dead) by the unkindness of the Duke of Buckingham, who hath brought in Dr Wren. Though, he tells me, he hath been his servant for twenty years together in all his wants and dangers, saving him from want of bread by his care and management, and with a promise of having his help in his advancement, and an engagement under his hand for £1000 not yet paid, and yet the Duke of Buckingham is so ungrateful as to put him by: which is an ill thing, though Dr Wren is a worthy man. But he tells me that the King is kind to him, and hath promised him a pension of £300 a year out of the Works; which will be of more content to him than the place, which under their present wants of money is a place that disobliges most people, being not able to do what they desire to their lodgings. Here meeting with Sir H. Cholmly and Povy, they tell me that my Lord Middleton is resolved in the caball that he shall not go to Tangier; and that Sir Edward Harlow, whom I know not, is propounded to go, who was Governor of Dunkirke, and, they say, a most worthy brave man; which I shall be very glad of. News lately come of the Algerines taking £13,000 in money out of one of our Company's East India ships outward-bound, which will certainly make the war last; which I am sorry for, being so poor as we are, and broken in pieces.

22nd. Up, and by water with W. Hewer to White Hall, there to attend the Lords of the Treasury; but before they sat, I did make a step to see Sir W. Coventry at his house, where, I bless God, he is come again; but in my way I met him, and so he took me into his coach and carried me to White Hall, and there set me down, where he ought not, at least he hath not yet leave to come, nor hath thought fit yet to ask it, hearing that Harry Saville is not only denied to kiss the King's hand, but the King being asked it by the Duke of York, the King did deny it, and directed that he shall not receive him to wait upon him in his chamber till further orders. Sir W. Coventry told me that he was going to visit Sir John Trevor, who hath been kind to him; and he showed me a long list of all his friends that he must this week make visits to, that came to visit him in the Tower: and seems mighty well satisfied with his being out of business, but I hope he will not long be so; at least, I do believe that all must go to rack if the King do not come to see the want of such a servant. Thence to the Treasury-chamber, and there all the morning to my great grief put to do Sir G. Downing's work of dividing the Customes for this year between the Navy, the Ordnance, and Tangier: but it did so trouble my eyes, that I had rather have given £20 than have had it to do; but I did thereby oblige Sir Thomas Clifford and Sir J. Duncomb, and so am glad of the opportunity to recommend myself to the former, for the latter I need not, he loving me well already. At it till noon, here being several of my brethren with me, but doing nothing, but I all. But this day I did also represent to our Treasurers, which was read here, a state of the charge of the Navy, and what the expence of it this year would likely be; which is done so as will appear well done and to my honour, for so the Lords did take it; and I oblige the Treasurers by doing it at their request. I to look over my papers for the East India Company against the afternoon: which done, I with them to White Hall, and there to the Treasury-chamber, where the East India Company and three Counsellors pleaded against me alone for three or four hours, till seven at night; before the Lords; and the Lords did give me the conquest on behalf of the King, but could not come to any conclusion, the Company being stiff; and so I think we shall go to law with them. This done, and my eyes mighty bad with this day's work, I to Mr Wren's, and then up to the Duke of York, and there with Mr Wren did propound to him my going to Chatham tomorrow with Commissioner Middleton, and so this week to make the pay there, and examine the business of the *Defyance* being lost.

23rd. I took coach with Commissioner Middleton, Captain Tinker, and Mr Huchinson, and out towards Chatham, and dined at Dartford, where we staid an hour or two, it being a cold day; and so on, and got to Chatham just at night, with very good discourse by the way, but mostly of matters of religion, wherein Huchinson his vein lies.

24th. To the Hill-house, and there did give order for a coach to be made ready; and got Mr Gibson, whom I carried with me, to go with me and Mr Coney, the surgeon, towards Maydstone; which I had a mighty mind to see. A mighty cold and windy, but clear day; and had the pleasure of seeing the Medway running winding up and down mightily, and a very fine country: and I went a little out of the way to have visited Sir John Bankes, but he at London; but here I had a sight of his seat and house,[25] the outside, which is an old abbey just like Hinchingbroke, and as good at least, and mightily finely placed by the river; and he keeps the grounds about it, and walls and the house, very handsome: I was mightily pleased with the sight of it. Thence to Maydstone, which I had a mighty mind to see, having never been there; and walked all up and down the town, and up to the top of the steeple and had a noble view, and then down again: and in the town did see an old man beating of flax, and did step into the barn and give him money, and saw that piece of husbandry, which I never saw; and it is very pretty. In the street also I did buy and send to our inne, the Bell, a dish of fresh fish. And so having walked all round the town, and found it very pretty as most towns I ever saw, though not very big, and people of good fashion in it, we to our inne and had a good dinner; and a barber came to me and there trimmed me, that I might be clean against night to go to Mrs Allen. And so staying till four o'clock we set out, I alone in the coach going and coming: and in our way back I light out of the way to see a Saxon monument, as they say, of a King, which is of three stones standing upright, and a great round one lying on them, of great bigness, although not so big as those on Salisbury plain. But certainly it is a thing of great antiquity, and I am mightily glad to see it: it is near to Alesford, where Sir John Bankes lives. So homeward to Chatham, Captain Allen's, and there light.

25th. Up, and by and by, about eight o'clock, came Rear-Admirall Kempthorne and seven captains more, by the Duke of York's order, as we expected, to hold the Court-martiall about the loss of the *Defyance*. And so presently we by boat to the *Charles*, which lies over-against Upner Castle; and there I did manage the business, the Duke of York having by special order directed them to take the assistance of Commissioner Middleton and me, forasmuch as there might be need of advice in what relates to the government of the ships in harbour. And so I did lay the law open to them, and rattle the master-

25 The Friary in Aylesford parish, now the property of the Earl of Aylesford, whose ancestor Heneage Finch married the eldest daughter and co-heiress of Sir John Bankes.

attendants out of their wits almost; and made the trial last till seven at night, not eating a bit all the day; only when he had done examination, and I given my thoughts that the neglect of the gunner of the ship was as great as I thought any neglect could be, which might by the law deserve death, but Commissioner Middleton did declare that he was against giving the sentence of death, we withdrew, as not being of the Court, and so left them to do what they pleased: and while they were debating it, the boatswain of the ship did bring us out of the kettle a piece of hot salt beef, and some brown bread and brandy; and there we did make a little meal, but so good as I never would desire to eat better meat while I live, only I would have cleaner dishes. By and by they had done, and called us down from the quarterdeck; and there we find they do sentence that the gunner of the *Defyance* should stand upon the *Charles* three hours with his fault writ upon his breast, and with a halter about his neck, and so be made incapable of any service. The truth is, the man do seem, and is, I believe, a good man; but his neglect, in trusting a girl to carry fire into his cabin, is not to be pardoned. This being done, we took boat and home; and there a good supper was ready for us, which should have been our dinner. The captains, desirous to be at London, went away presently for Gravesend, to get thither by this night's tide. And so we to supper, it having been a great snowy and mighty cold, foul day; and so after supper to bed.

26th. Up, and with Middleton all the morning at the Docke, looking over the store-houses and Commissioner Pett's house, in order to Captain Cox's coming to live there in his stead as Commissioner. But it is a mighty pretty house; and pretty to see how every thing is said to be out of repair for this new man, though £10 would put it into as good condition in every thing as it ever was in, so free every body is of the King's money! And so to dinner at the Hill-house; and after dinner till eight at night close, Middleton and I, examining the business of Mr Pett about selling a boat; and we find him a very knave; and some other quarrels of his, wherein to justify himself he hath made complaints of others. This being done, we to supper, and so to talk, Commissioner Middleton being mighty good company upon a journey; and so to bed.

27th. We took coach again, and got home about six at night.

29th. Up, and by water to White Hall; and there to the Duke of

York to show myself after my journey to Chatham, but did no business to-day with him: only after gone from him, I to Sir T. Clifford's; and there, after an hour's waiting, he being alone in his closet, I did speak with him, and give him the account he gave me to draw up, and he did like it very well: and then fell to talk of the business of the Navy; and giving me good words, did fall foul of the constitution, and did then discover his thoughts, that Sir J. Minnes was too old, and so was Colonell Middleton, and that my Lord Brouncker did mind his mathematics too much. I did not give much encouragement to that of finding fault with my fellow-officers; but did stand up for the constitution, and did say that what faults there were in our office would be found not to arise from the constitution, but from the failures of the officers in whose hands it was. This he did seem to give good ear to; but did give me of myself very good words, which pleased me well, though I shall not build upon them any thing. Thence home; and after dinner by water with Tom down to Greenwich, he reading to me all the way coming and going my collections out of the Duke of York's old manuscript of the Navy, which I have bound up, and do please me mightily. At Greenwich I came to Captain Cocke's, where the house full of company at the burial of James Temple, who it seems hath been dead these five days. Here I had a very good ring, which I did give my wife as soon as I came home. I spent my time there walking in the garden talking with James Pierce; who tells me that he is certain that the Duke of Buckingham had been with his wenches all the time that he was absent, which was all the last week, nobody knowing where he was. The great talk is of the King's being hot of late against Conventicles, and to see whether the Duke of Buckingham's being returned will turn the King, which will make him very popular; and some think it is his plot to make the King thus, to show his power in the making him change his mind. But Pierce did tell me that the King did certainly say, that he that took one stone from the Church did take two from his Crown. By and by the corpse came out; and I with Sir Richard Browne and Mr Evelyn in their coach to the church, where Mr Plume[26] preached.

30th. Up, and to Sir W. Coventry, to see and discourse with him;

26 Thomas Plume, DD, Vicar of Greenwich 1662, and installed Archdeacon of Rochester 1679. Died 1704.

and he tells me that he hath lately been with my Lord Keeper, and had much discourse about the Navy: and particularly he tells me that he finds they are divided touching me and my Lord Brouncker; some are for removing, and some for keeping us. He told my Lord Keeper that it should cost the King £10,000 before he had made another as fit to serve him in the Navy as I am; which though I believe it is true, yet I am much pleased to have that character given me by Sir W. Coventry, whatever be the success of it. But I perceive they do think that I know too much, and shall impose upon whomever shall come next, and therefore must be removed; though he tells me that Sir T. Clifford is inclined well enough to me, and Sir T. Osborne, by what I have lately done, I suppose. This news is but what I ought not to be much troubled for, considering my incapacity, in regard to my eyes, to continue long at this work.

31st. Up, and by water to Sir W. Coventry's, there to talk with him about business of the Navy, and received from him direction what to advise the Duke of York at this time; which was to submit and give way to the King's naming a man or two that the people about him have a mind should be brought into the Navy, and perhaps that may stop their fury in running further against the whole: and this, he believes, will do it. After much discourse with him, I walked out with him into St James's Park; where, being afraid to be seen with him, (he having not leave yet to kiss the King's hand, but notice taken, as I hear, of all that go to him,) I did take the pretence of my attending the Tangier Committee to take my leave, though to serve him I should, I think, stick at nothing. At the Committee this morning my Lord Middleton declares at last his being ready to go, as soon as ever money can be made ready to pay the garrison: and so I have orders to get money, but how soon I know not. Thence to Dancre's, and there saw our pictures which are in doing: and I did choose a view of Rome instead of Hampton Court; and mightily pleased I shall be in them. Here were Sir Charles Cotterell and his son bespeaking something: both ingenious men, I hear. Thence my wife and I to the Park; and pretty store of company; and so home with great content. And so ends the month, my mind in pretty good content for all things but the designs on foot to bring alterations in the office, which trouble me.

April 1st. Up, and with Colonell Middleton (at the desire of Rear-

Admirall Kempthorne the president, for our assisting them) to the Court-martiall on board a yacht in the River here to try the business of the purser's complaints, (Baker against Trevanion, his commander, of the *Dartmouth*). But, Lord! to see what wretched doings there were among all the commanders to ruin the purser, and defend the captain in all his rogueries, be it to the prejudice of the King or purser, no good man could bear! I confess I was pretty high, which the young gentlemen commanders did not like: and Middleton did the same. But could not bring it to any issue this day, sitting till two o'clock; and therefore we, being sent for, went to Sir W. Pen's by invitation to dine. At my cosen Turner's, and there we staid awhile and talked: and particularly here we met with Dr Ball, the parson of the Temple, who did tell me a great many pretty stories about the manner of the parsons being paid for their preaching at Paul's heretofore and now, and the ground of the lecture; and heretofore for the names of the founders thereof, which were many, at some 5s. some 6s. per annum towards it: and had their names read in the pulpit every sermon among those holy persons that the Church do order a collect for giving God thanks for.

2nd. To White Hall, and there to the Duke of York's lodgings; whither he, by and by, by his appointment came: and alone with him an hour in his closet, telling him mine and Sir W. Coventry's advice touching the present posture of the Navy, as the Duke of Buckingham and the rest do now labour to make changes therein; and that it were best for him to suffer the King to be satisfied with the bringing in of a man or two whom they desire. I did also give the Duke of York a short account of the history of the Navy as to our office, wherewith he was very well satisfied: but I do find that he is pretty stiff against their bringing in of men against his mind, as the Treasurers were, and particularly against Child's coming in, because he is a merchant. After much discourse with him we parted: and the Council sat while I staid waiting for his telling me when I should be ready to give him a written account of the administration of the Navy, which caused me to wait the whole afternoon, till night. In the mean time, stepping to the Duchesse of York's side to speak with Lady Peterborough, I did see the young Duchesse, a little child in hanging sleeves, dance most finely, so as almost to ravish me, her ears were so good. Taught by a Frenchman that did heretofore teach the

King, and all the King's children, and the Queene-Mother herself, who do still dance well.

3rd. Up, and to the Council of War again with Middleton: but the proceedings of the commanders so devilishly bad, and so professedly partial to the captain, that I could endure it no longer, but took occasion to pretend business at the office, and away, and Colonell Middleton with me, who was of the same mind, and resolved to declare our minds freely to the Duke of York about it.

4th. After dinner with Sir J. Minnes and T. Middleton to White Hall, by appointment; and at my Lord Arlington's the office did attend the King and caball, to discourse of the further quantity of victuals fit to be declared for, which was 2000 men for six months; and so without more ado or stay there, hearing no news but that Sir Thomas Allen is to be expected every hour at home with his fleet, or news of his being gone back to Algier. The Queene-Mother hath been of late mighty ill, and some fears of her death.

5th. Went five or six miles towards Branford, where the Prince of Tuscany,[27] who comes into England only to spend money and see our country, comes into the town to-day, and is much expected; and we met him, but the coach passing by apace we could not see much of him, but he seems a very jolly and good comely man.

6th. Middleton and I did in plain terms acquaint the Duke of York what we thought and had observed in the late Court-martiall; which the Duke of York did give ear to, and though he thinks not fit to revoke what is already done in this case by a Court-martiall, yet it shall bring forth some good laws in the behaviour of captains to their under-officers for the time to come.

7th. To the Lords of the Treasury, where all the morning, and settled matters to their liking about the assignments on the Customes between the Navy-office and Victualler, and to that end spent most of the morning there with D. Gauden. I to the Council-chamber, and there heard the great complaint of the City, tried against the gentlemen of the Temple for the late riot, as they would have it, when my Lord Mayor was there. But, upon hearing the whole business, the City was

27 Cosmo de' Medici, who succeeded his father Ferdinand in the Dukedom of Tuscany 1670.

certainly to blame to charge them in this manner as with a riot; but the King and Council did forbear to determine any thing in it, till the other business of the title and privilege be decided, which is now under dispute at law between them, – whether the Temple be within the liberty of the City or no. But I was sorry to see the City so ill advised as to complain in a thing where their proofs were so weak.

8th. Up, and to White Hall to the King's side to find Sir T. Clifford, where the Duke of York came and found me; which I was sorry for, for fear he should think I was making friends on that side. But I did put it off the best I could, my being there; and so by and by had opportunity alone to show Sir T. Clifford the fair account I had drawn up of the Customes, which he liked, and seemed mightily pleased with me: and so away to the Excise-office, to do a little business there: and so to the office, where all the morning.

9th. Up, and by water to White Hall, and there with the Board attended the Duke of York, and Sir Thomas Allen with us (who came to town yesterday;) and it is resolved another fleet shall go to the Streights forthwith, and he command it. But his coming home is mighty hardly talked on by the merchants, for leaving their ships there to the mercy of the Turks: but of this more in my White-book. To the Excise-office, and to several places; among others to Mr Faythorne's, to have seen an instrument which he was said to have of drawing perspectives, but he had it not; but here I did see his workhouse, and the best things of his doing he had by him.

10th. After dinner comes Mr Seamour to visit me, a talking fellow; but I hear by him that Captain Trevanion do give it out every where that I did over-rule the whole Court-martiall against him, so long as I was there. And perhaps I may receive at this time some wrong by it; but I care not, for what I did was out of my desire to do justice.

11th. To Loton the landscape-drawer, a Dutchman, living in St James's Market; but there saw no good pictures. But by accident he did direct us to a painter that was then in the house with him, a Dutchman, newly come over, one Evereest,[28] who took us to his lodging close by, and did show us a little flowerpot of his drawing,

28 Probably Simon Varelst, a Dutch flower-painter, who practised his art with much success in England about this time.

the finest thing that ever, I think, I saw in my life; the drops of dew hanging on the leaves, so as I was forced again and again to put my finger to it, to feel whether my eyes were deceived or no. He do ask £70 for it: I had the vanity to bid him £20. But a better picture I never saw in my whole life; and it is worth going twenty miles to see it. Thence, leaving Balty there, I took my wife to St James's, and there carried her to the Queene's chapel, the first time I ever did it; and heard excellent musick, but not so good as by accident I did hear there yesterday as I went through the Park from White Hall to see Sir W. Coventry, which I have forgot to set down in my Journal yesterday. And going out of the chapel I did see the Prince of Tuscany come out, a comely black fat man, in a mourning-suit; and my wife and I did see him this afternoon through a window in this chapel. All that Sir W. Coventry yesterday did tell me new was, that the King would not yet give him leave to come to kiss his hand; and he do believe that he will not in a great while do it, till those about him shall see fit: which I am sorry for. Thence to the Park, my wife and I: and here Sir W. Coventry did first see me and my wife in a coach of our own; and so did also this night the Duke of York, who did eye my wife mightily. But I begin to doubt that my being so much seen in my own coach at this time may be observed to my prejudice; but I must venture it now. So home, and so set down my Journal, with the help of my left eye through my tube, for fourteen days past; which is so much as I hope I shall not run in arrear again, but the badness of my eyes do force me to it.

12th. The whole office attended the Duke of York at his meeting with Sir Thomas Allen and several flag-officers, to consider of the manner of managing the war with Algier; and it being a thing I was wholly silent in, I did only observe; and find that their manner of discourse on this weighty affair was very mean and disorderly, the Duke of York himself being the man that I thought spoke most to the purpose. By water to the Bear-garden, and there happened to sit by Sir Fretcheville Hollis, who is still full of his vain-glorious and prophane talk. Here we saw a prize fought between a soldier and a country-fellow, one Warrel, who promised the least in his looks, and performed the most of valour in his boldness and evenness of mind, and smiles in all he did, that ever I saw; and we were all both deceived and infinitely taken with him. He did soundly beat the soldier, and cut him over the head. Thence back to White Hall, mightily pleased all of us with this sight, and particularly this fellow, as a most extraordinary man for his temper and evenness in fighting. This evening coming home we overtook Alderman Backewell's coach and his lady, and followed them to their house, and there made them the first visit, where they received us with extraordinary civility, and owning the obligation. But I do, contrary to my expectation, find her something a proud and vainglorious woman, in telling the number of her servants and family and expences. He is also so, but he was ever of that strain. But here he showed me the model of his houses that he is going to build in Cornhill and Lumbard-street; but he hath purchased so much there that it looks like a little town, and must have cost him a great deal of money.

13th. I by hackney-coach to the Spittle, and heard a piece of a dull sermon to my Lord Mayor and Aldermen and thence saw them all take horse and ride away, which I have not seen together many a day: their wives also went in their coaches. And indeed the sight was mighty pleasing. Thence took occasion to go back to a milliner's in Fenchurch-street, whose name I understand to be Clerke; and there her husband inviting me up to the balcony to see the show go by to dinner at Clothworkers'-hall, I did go up, and there saw it go by.

14th. To the Duke of York's playhouse, and there saw *The Impertinents*, a play which pleases me well still; but it is with great trouble that I now see a play because of my eyes, the light of the candles making it very troublesome to me. After the play to Creed's. They do here talk mightily of my Lady Paulina making a very good end, and being mightily religious in her life-time; and she hath left many good notes of sermons and religion wrote with her own hand, which nobody ever knew of: which I am glad of; but she was always a peevish lady.

17th. To Sir W. Coventry's, reading over first my draught of the Administration of the Navy, which he do like very well; and so fell to talk of his late disgrace and how basely and in what a mean manner the Duke of Buckingham hath proceeded against him, – not like a man of honour. He tells me that the King will not give other answer, about his coming to kiss his hands, than 'Not yet.' But he says that this that he desires of kissing the King's hand is only to show to the world that he is not a discontent, and not in any desire to come again into play, though I do perceive that he speaks this with less earnestness than heretofore: and this it may be is, from what he told me lately, that the King is offended at what is talked, that he hath declared himself desirous not to have to do with any employment more. But he do tell me that the leisure he hath yet had do not at all begin to be burdensome to him, he knowing how to spend his time with content to himself; and that he hopes shortly to contract his expence, so as that he shall not be under any straits in that respect neither; and so seems to be in very good condition of content. Thence I away over the Park, it being now night, to White Hall: and there in the Duchesse's chamber do find the Duke of York; and upon my offer to speak with him, he did come to me and withdrew to his closet, and there did hear and approve my paper of the Administration of the Navy, only did bid me alter these words, 'upon the rupture between the late King and the Parliament,' to these, 'the beginning of the late Rebellion'; giving it me as but reason to show that it was with the Rebellion that the Navy was put by out of its old good course into that of a Commission. Having done this, we fell to other talk; he with great confidence telling me how matters go among our adversaries, in reference to the Navy, and that he thinks they do begin to flag: but then beginning to talk in general of the excellency of old constitutions, he did bring out of his cabinet, and made me read it, an extract out of a book of my late Lord of Northumberland's, so prophetic of the business of Chatham as is almost miraculous. I did desire, and he did give it me to copy out: which pleased me mightily.

18th. To my office again to examine the fair draught: and so borrowing Sir J. Minnes's coach, he going with Colonell Middleton, I to White Hall, where we all met and did sign it. And then to my Lord Arlington's, where the King and the Duke of York and Prince Rupert, as also Ormond and the two secretaries, with my Lord Ashly and Sir T. Clifford, were. And there by and by being called in, Mr Williamson did read over our paper, which was in a letter to the Duke of York, bound up in a book with the Duke of York's Book of Instructions. He read it well; and after read, we were bid to withdraw, nothing being at all said to it. And by and by we were called in again, and nothing said to that business; but another begun about the state of this year's action and our wants of money, as I had stated the same lately to our Treasurers; which I was bid, and did largely, and with great content open. And having so done, we all withdrew, and left them to debate our supply of money; to which being called in, and referred to attend on the Lords of the Treasury, we all departed. And I only staid in the House till the Council rose; and then to the Duke of York in the Duchesse's chamber, where he told me that the book was there left with my Lord Arlington for any of the Lords to view that had a mind, and to prepare and present to the King what they had to say in writing to any part of it; which is all we can desire, and so that rested. The Duke of York then went to other talk; and by and by comes the Prince of Tuscany to visit him and the Duchesse; and I find that he do still remain *incognito*, and so intends to do all the time he stays here, for avoiding trouble to the King and himself, and expence also to both.

20th. At noon comes my guest Mr Hugh May, and with him Sir Henry Capell, my old Lord Capell's son, and Mr Parker. And I had a pretty dinner for them; and both before and after dinner had excellent discourse; and showed them my closet and my office, and the method of it, to their great content: and more extraordinary manly discourse and opportunity of showing myself, and learning from others, I have not in ordinary discourse had in my life, they being all persons of worth, but especially Sir H. Capell, whose being a Parliament-man, and hearing my discourse in the Parliament-house, hath, as May tells me, given him a long desire to know and discourse with me. In the afternoon we walked to the Old Artillery-ground near the Spitalfields, where I never was before, but now by Captain Deane's invitation did go to see his new gun tryed, this being the place where the officers of the Ordnance do try all their great guns: and when we came, did find that the trial had been made, and they going away, with extraordinary report of the proof of his gun, which, from the shortness and bigness, they do call Punchinello. But I desired Colonell Legg to stay and give us a sight of her performance; which he did, and there, in short, against a gun more than as long and as heavy again, and charged with as much powder again, she carried the same bullet as strong to the mark, and nearer and above the mark at a point blank than theirs, and is more easily managed, and recoyles no more than that; which is a thing so extraordinary as to be admired for the happiness of his invention, and to the great regret of the old gunners and officers of the Ordnance that were there, only Colonell Legg did do her much right in his report of her. And so having seen this great and first experiment we all parted, I seeing my guests into a hackney-coach, and myself, with Captain Deane, taking a hackney-coach, did go out towards Bow, and went as far as Stratford, and all the way talking of this invention, and he offering me a third of the profit of it; which, for aught I know, or do at present think, may prove matter considerable to us; for either the King will give him a reward for it if he keeps it to himself, or he will give us a patent to make our profit of it; and no doubt but it will be of profit to merchantmen and others to have guns of the same force at half the charge. This was our talk; and then to talk of other things, of the Navy in general: and, among other things, he did tell me that he do hear how the Duke of Buckingham hath a spite at me, which I knew before, but value it not; and he tells me that Sir T. Allen is not my friend: but for all this I am not much troubled, for I know myself so usefull that, as I believe, they will not part with me; so I thank God my condition is such that I can retire and be able to live with comfort, though not with abundance.

21st. To Auditor Wood's, and met my Lord Bellasses upon some business of his accounts. Attended the Duke of York a little, being the first time of my waiting on him at St James's this summer, whither he is now newly gone. And thence walked to White Hall; and so by and by to the Council-chamber, and heard a remarkable cause pleaded between the Farmers of the Excise of Wiltshire, in complaint against the Justices of Peace of Salisbury: and Sir H. Finch was for the former. But, Lord! to see how he did with his admirable eloquence order the matter, is not to be conceived almost: so pleasant a thing it is to hear him plead! After dinner by water to White Hall, where the Duke of York did meet our office, and went with us to the Lords Commission-ers of the Treasury: and there we did go over all the business of the state I had drawn up of this year's action and expence; which I did do to their satisfaction, and convincing them of the necessity of providing more money, if possible, for us. Thence the Duke of York being gone, I did there stay walking with Sir H. Cholmly in the Court, talking of news; where he told me that now the great design of the Duke of Buckingham is to prevent the meeting, since he cannot bring about with the King the dissolving of this Parliament, that the King may not need it; and therefore my Lord St Alban's is hourly expected with great offers of a million of money to buy our breach with the Dutch; and this, they do think, may tempt the King to take the money, and thereby be out of a necessity of calling the Parliament again, which these people dare not suffer to meet again: but this he doubts, and so do I, that it will be the ruin of the nation if we fall out with Holland.

22nd. Up, and to the office, where all the morning. At noon home to dinner, and Captain Deane with us; and very good discourse, and particularly about my getting a book for him to draw up his whole theory of shipping; which at my desire he hath gone far in, and hath shown me what he hath done therein to admiration. I did give him a parallelogram, which he is mightily taken with. And so after dinner to the office, where all the afternoon till night late, and then home.

23rd. To the Council-chamber, and heard two or three causes; among others that of the complaint of Sir Philip Howard and Watson, the inventors, as they pretend, of the business of varnishing and lackerworke, against the Company of Painters, who take upon them to do the same thing; where I saw a great instance of the weakness of a young Counsel they used to such an audience, against the Solicitor-generall and two more able Counsel used to it. Though he had the right of his side, and did prevail for what he pretended to against the rest, yet it was with much disadvantage and hazard. Here I also heard Mr Papillion make his defence to the King against some complaints of the Farmers of Excise; but it was so weak, and done only by his own seeking, that it was to his injury more than profit, and made his case the worse, being ill-managed, and in a cause against the King.

25th (Lord's day). Up, and to my office awhile, and thither comes Lead with my vizard, with a tube fastened within both eyes; which, with the help which he prompts me to, of a glass in the tube, do content me mightily. W. How came and dined with us; and then I to my office, he being gone, to write down my Journal for the last twelve days: and did it with the help of my vizard and tube fixed to it, and do find it mighty manageable, but how helpfull to my eyes this trial will show me. So abroad with my wife in the afternoon to the Park, where very much company, and the weather very pleasant. I carried my wife to the Lodge, the first time this year, and there in our coach eat a cheesecake and drank a tankard of milk. I showed her this day also first the Prince of Tuscany, who was in the Park, and many very fine ladies.

26th. After dinner comes Colonell Macknachan, one that I see often at Court, a Scotchman, but know him not; only he brings me a letter from my Lord Middleton, who, he says, is in great distress for £500 to relieve my Lord Morton[29] with (but upon what account I know not;) and he would have me advance it without order upon his pay for Tangier; which I was astonished at, but had the grace to deny him with an excuse. And so he went away, leaving me a little troubled that I was thus driven on a sudden to do any thing herein: but Creed coming just now to see me, he approves of what I have done. A great fire happened in Durham-yard last night, burning the house of one Lady Hungerford, who was to come to town to it this night; and so the house is burned, new furnished, by carelessness of the girl sent to take off a candle from a bunch of candles, which she did by burning it off, and left the rest, as is supposed, on fire. The King and Court were here, it seems, and stopped the fire by blowing up of the next house. The King and Court went out of town to Newmarket this morning betimes, for a week.

28th. Up, and was called upon by Sir H. Cholmly to discourse about some accounts of his of Tangier: and then to other talk. And I find by him that it is brought almost to effect, the late endeavours of the Duke of York and Duchesse, the Queene-Mother, and my Lord St Alban's together with some of the contrary faction, as my Lord Arlington, that for a sum of money we shall enter into a league with the King of France, wherein, he says, my Lord Chancellor is also concerned; and that he believes that in the doing hereof it is meant that he shall come in again, and that this sum of money will so help the King as that he will not need the Parliament; and that in that regard it will be forwarded by the Duke of Buckingham and his faction, who dread the Parliament. But hereby must leave the Dutch, and that I doubt will undo us; and Sir H. Cholmly says he finds W. Coventry do think the like. My Lady Castlemaine is instrumental in this matter, and, he says, never more great with the King than she is

29 William, ninth Earl of Morton, who had married Lord Middleton's daughter Grizel.

now. But this is a thing that will make the Parliament and kingdom mad, and will turn to our ruine; for with this money the King shall wanton away his time in pleasures, and think nothing of the main till it be too late. This morning Mr Sheres sent me in two volumes, Marian his *History of Spaine* in Spanish, an excellent book; and I am much obliged to him for it.

30th. Up, and by coach to the coachmaker's; and there I do find a great many ladies sitting in the body of a coach that must be ended by to-morrow, (they were my Lady Marquess of Winchester,[30] Bellasses,[31] and other great ladies,) eating of bread and butter, and drinking ale. I to my coach, which is silvered over, but no varnish yet laid on, so I put it in a way of doing; and myself about other business, and particularly to see Sir W. Coventry, with whom I talked a good while to my great content: and so to other places, among others, to my tailor's; and then to the belt-maker's, where my belt cost me 55s. of the colour of my new suit; and here understanding that the mistress of the house, an oldish woman in a hat, hath some water good for the eyes, she did dress me, making my eyes smart most horribly, and did give me a little glass of it, which I will use, and hope it will do me good. So to the cutler's, and there did give Tom, who was with me all day, a sword cost me 12s. and a belt of my owne; and sent my own silver-hilt sword agilding against to-morrow. This morning I did visit Mr Oldenburgh, and did see the instrument for perspective made by Dr Wren, of which I have one making by Browne; and the sight of this do please me mightily. At noon my wife came to me at my tailor's, and I sent her home, and myself and Tom dined at Hercules Pillars; and so about our business again, and particularly to Lilly's, the varnisher, about my prints, whereof some of them are pasted upon the boards, and to my full content. Thence to the frame-maker's, one Norris, in Long Acre; who showed me several forms of frames, which were pretty, in little bits of mouldings to choose patterns by. This done, I to my coachmaker's, and there vexed to see nothing yet

30 Isabella, daughter of William Viscount Stafford, third wife to James fifth Marquis of Winchester.

31 John Lord Bellassis was thrice married: first, to Jane, daughter of Sir Robert Boteler, of Woodhall, Knt.; secondly, to Ann, daughter of Sir Robert Crane, of Chilton, Suffolk; thirdly, to Lady Anne Powlet, daughter of John, fourth Marquis of Winchester. The lady here mentioned was the second or third wife; probably the latter.

done to my coach, at three in the afternoon; but I set it in doing, and stood by till eight at night, and saw the painter varnish it, which is pretty to see how every doing it over do make it more and more yellow: and it dries as fast in the sun as it can be laid on almost; and most coaches are now-a-days done so, and it is very pretty when laid on well, and not too pale as some are, even to show the silver. Here I did make the workmen drink, and saw my coach cleaned and oyled; and staying among poor people there in the ally, did hear them call their fat child Punch, which pleased me mightily, that word being become a word of common use for all that is thick and short.

May 1st. Up betimes. My wife extraordinary fine with her flowered tabby gown that she made two years ago, now laced exceeding pretty; and indeed was fine all over. And mighty earnest to go, though the day was very lowering; and she would have me put on my fine suit, which I did. And so anon we went alone through the town with our new liveries of serge, and the horses' manes and tails tied with red ribbons, and the standards thus gilt with varnish, and all clean, and green reines, that people did mightily look upon us; and the truth is, I did not see any coach more pretty, though more gay, than ours all the day; the day being unpleasing, though the Park full of coaches, but dusty, and windy, and cold, and now and then a little dribbling of rain; and what made it worse, there were so many hackney coaches as spoiled the sight of the gentlemen's; and so we had little pleasure.

2nd (Lord's day). Up, and by water to White Hall, and there visited my Lord Sandwich, who, after about two months' absence at Hinchingbroke, came to town last night. I saw him; and he was very kind: and I am glad he is so, I having not wrote to him all the time, my eyes indeed not letting me. Here with Sir Charles Harbord and my Lord Hinchingbroke and Sidney, and we looked upon the picture of Tangier, designed by Charles Harbord and drawn by Dancre, which my Lord Sandwich admires, as being the truest picture that ever he saw in his life: and it is indeed very pretty, and I will be at the cost of having one of them. Thence with them to White Hall, and there walked out the sermon with one or other; and then saw the Duke of York, and he talked to me a little; and so away back by water home.

3rd. Up, and by coach to my Lord Brouncker's, where Sir G.

Carteret did meet Sir J. Minnes and me, to discourse upon Mr Deering's business, who was directed in the time of the war to provide provisions at Hamburgh, by Sir G. Carteret's direction; and now Sir G. Carteret is afraid to own it, it being done without written order. But by our meeting we do all begin to recollect enough to preserve Mr Deering, which I think, poor silly man! I shall be glad of, it being too much he should suffer for endeavouring to serve us. Thence to St James's, where the Duke of York was playing in the Pell Mell; and so he called me to him most part of the time that he played which was an hour, and talked alone to me; and, among other things, tells me how the King will not yet be got to name any body in the room of Pen, but puts it off for three or four days: from whence he do collect that they are brewing something for the Navy, but what he knows not; but I perceive is vexed that things should go so, and he hath reason; for he told me that it is likely they will do in this as in other things – resolve first, and consider it and the fitness of it afterwards. Thence to White Hall, and met with Creed, and discoursed of matters; and I perceive by him that he makes no doubt but that all will turn to the old religion, for these people cannot hold things in their hands, nor prevent its coming to that; and by his discourse he fits himself for it, and would have my Lord Sandwich do so too, and me. After a little talk with him, and particularly about the ruinous condition of Tangier, which I have a great mind to lay before the Duke of York, but dare not because of his great kindness to Lord Middleton, before it be too late, we parted, and I homeward; but called at Povy's, and there he stopped me to dinner, there being Mr Williamson, the Lieutenant of the Tower, Mr Child, and several others. And after dinner Povy and I together to talk of Tangier; and he would have me move the Duke of York in it, for it concerns him particularly more than any, as being the head of us; and I do think to do it.

5th. To St James's, and thence with the Duke of York to White Hall, where the Board waited on him all the morning; and so at noon with Sir Thomas Allen, and Sir Edward Scott[32] and Lord Carlingford, to the Spanish Embassador's, where I dined the first time. The olio not so good as Shere's. There was at the table himself and a Spanish Countess, a good, comely, and witty lady; three Fathers, and us. Discourse good and pleasant. And here was an Oxford scholar, in a

32 Sir Edward Scott, made LL.D. at Oxford 1677.

Doctor of Laws' gowne, sent from the College where the Embassador lay when the Court was there, to salute him before his return to Spain. This man, though a gentle sort of scholar, yet sat like a fool for want of French or Spanish, but knew only Latin, which he spoke like an Englishman, to one of the Fathers. And by and by he and I to talk; and the company very merry at my defending Cambridge against Oxford; and I made much use of my French and Spanish here, to my great content. But the dinner not extraordinary at all, either for quantity or quality.

7th. Up, and by coach to Sir W. Coventry's; and there to talk with him a great deal with great content. And so to the Duke of York, having a great mind to speak to him about Tangier; but when I came to it, his interest for my Lord Middleton is such that I dared not.

8th. After dinner all the afternoon within, with Mr Hater, Gibson, and W. Hewer, reading over and drawing up new things in the Instructions of Commanders, which will be good, and I hope to get them confirmed by the Duke of York; though I perceive nothing will effectually perfect them but to look over the whole body of the Instructions of all the officers of a ship, and make them all perfect together. This being done, comes my bookseller, and brings me home bound my collection of papers, about my Addresse to the Duke of York in August, which makes me glad, it being that which shall do me more right many years hence than perhaps all I ever did in my life: and therefore I do, both for my own and the King's sake, value it much. By and by also comes Browne, the mathematical instrument-maker, and brings me home my instrument for perspective, made according to the description of Dr Wren's in the late Transactions; and he hath made it, I think, very well, and that I believe will do the thing, and therein gives me great content; but I have, I fear, all the content that must be received by my eyes, which are almost lost.

10th. To White Hall, where the Duke of York met the office, and there discoursed of several things, particularly the Instructions of Commanders of ships. But here happened by chance a discourse of the Council of Trade, against which the Duke of York is mightily displeased, and particularly Mr Child, against whom he speaking hardly, Captain Cox did second the Duke of York, by saying that he was talked on for an unfayre dealer with masters of ships about freight: to which Sir T. Littleton very hotly and foolishly replied presently, that he never heard any honest man speak ill of Child; to which the Duke of York did make a smart reply, and was angry: so as I was sorry to hear it come so far, and that I, by seeming to assent to Cox, might be observed too much by Littleton, though I said nothing aloud, for this must breed great heart-burnings. After this meeting done, the Duke of York took the Treasurers into his closet to chide them, as Mr Wren tells me; for that my Lord Keeper did last night at the Council say, when nobody was ready to say anything against the constitution of the Navy, that he did believe the Treasurers of the Navy had something to say; which was very foul on their part, to be parties against us. They being gone, Mr Wren took boat, thinking to dine with my Lord of Canterbury;[33] but when we came to Lambeth, the gate was shut, which is strictly done at twelve o'clock, and nobody comes in afterwards; so we lost our labour, and therefore back to White Hall, and thence walked to my Lord Crewe, whom I have not seen since he was sick, which is eight months ago, I think; and there dined with him. He is mightily broke. A stranger, a country gentleman, was with him; and he pleased with my discourse accidentally about the decay of gentlemen's families in the country, telling us that the old rule was, that a family might remain fifty miles from London one hundred years, one hundred miles from London two hundred years, and so farther or nearer London more or less years. He also told us that he hath heard his father say, that in his time it was so rare for a country gentleman to come to London, that when he did come, he used to make his will before he set out. Thence to St James's, and there met the Duke of York; who told me with great content that he did now think he should master our adversaries, for that the King did tell him that he was satisfied in the constitution of the Navy, but that it was well to give these people leave to object against it, which they having not done, he did give order to give warrant to the Duke of York to direct Sir Jeremy Smith to be a Commissioner of the Navy in the room of Pen; which, though he be an impertinent fellow, yet I am glad of it, it showing that the other side is not so strong as it was: and so in plain terms the Duke of York did tell me, that they were every day losing ground; and particularly

33 Gilbert Sheldon.

that he would take care to keep out Child: at all which I am glad, though yet I dare not think myself secure: but the King may yet be wrought upon by these people to bring changes in our office, and remove us ere it be long. To White Hall to a Committee of Tangier, where I see all things going to rack in the business of the Corporation, and consequently in the place, by Middleton's going. Thence walked a little with Creed, who tells me he hears how fine my horses and coach are, and advises me to avoid being noted for it; which I was vexed to hear taken notice of, being what I feared; and Povy told me of my gold-laced sleeves in the Park yesterday, which vexed me also, so as to resolve never to appear in Court with them, but presently to have them taken off, as it is fit I should.

11th. My wife up by four o'clock, to go to gather May-dew. Some trouble at Court for fear of the Queene's miscarrying; she being, as they all conclude, far gone with child.

12th. My brother John tells me the first news that my sister Jackson is with child and far gone.

13th. At noon comes my Lord Hinchingbroke, and Sidney, and Sir Charles Harbord, and Roger Pepys, and dined with me; and had a good dinner, and very merry with us all the afternoon, it being a farewell to Sidney.

14th. At noon to dinner with Mr Wren to Lambeth, with the Archbishop of Canterbury; the first time I was ever there, and I have long longed for it. Where a noble house, and well furnished with good pictures and furniture, and noble attendance in good order, and a great deal of company though an ordinary day; and exceeding great cheer, no where better, or so much, that ever I think I saw for an ordinary table: and the Bishop mighty kind to me particularly, desiring my company another time when less company there. Most of the company gone, and I going, I heard by a gentleman of a sermon that was to be there; and so I staid to hear it, thinking it serious, till by and by the gentleman told me it was a mockery, by one Cornet Bolton, a very gentlemanlike man, that behind a chair did pray and preach like a Presbyter Scot, with all the possible imitation in grimaces and voice. And his text about the hanging up their harps upon the willows: and a serious good sermon too, exclaiming against Bishops, and crying up of my good Lord

Eglington, till it made us all burst; but I did wonder to have the Bishop at this time to make himself sport with things of this kind, but I perceive it was shown him as a rarity. And he took care to have the room-door shut, but there were about twenty gentlemen there: and myself infinitely pleased with the novelty. So over to White Hall to a little Committee of Tangier; and thence walking in the Gallery, I met Sir Thomas Osborne, who, to my great content, did of his own accord fall into discourse with me, with such professions of value and respect, placing the whole virtue of the office of the Navy upon me, and that for the Controller's place no man in England was fit for it but me, when Sir J. Minnes, as he says it is necessary, is removed: but then knows not what to do for a man in my place; and in discourse, though I have no mind to the other, did bring in Tom Hater to be the fittest man in the world for it, which he took good notice of. But in the whole I was mightily pleased, reckoning myself fifty per cent. securer in my place than I did before think myself to be. By water with my brother as high as Fulham, talking and singing, and playing the rogue with the Western bargemen about the women of Woolwich; which mads them.

16th. I all the afternoon drawing up a foul draught of my petition to the Duke of York about my eyes, for leave to spend three or four months out of the office, drawing it so as to give occasion to a voyage abroad; which I did to my pretty good liking. And then with my wife to Hyde Park, where a good deal of company and good weather.

17th. Great news now of the French taking St Domingo, in Spaniola, from the Spaniards; which troubles us, that they should have got it, and have the honour of taking it, when we could not.

19th. With my coach to St James's; and there finding the Duke of York gone to muster his men in Hyde Park, I alone with my boy thither, and there saw more, walking out of my coach as other gentlemen did, of a soldier's trade than ever I did in my life: the men being mighty fine, and their Commanders, particularly the Duke of Monmouth; but methought their trade but very easy as to the mustering of their men, and the men but indifferently ready to perform what was commanded in the handling of their arms. Here the news was first talked of Harry Killigrew's being wounded in nine places last night by footmen in the highway, going from the Park in a

hackney-coach towards Hammersmith, to his house at Turnham
Greene: they being supposed to be my Lady Shrewsbury's men, she
being by in her coach with six horses; upon an old grudge of his
saying openly that he had intrigued with her. Thence by and by to
White Hall, and there I waited upon the King and Queene all dinner
time in the Queene's lodgings, she being in her white pinner, and
appearing like a woman with child; and she seemed handsomer plain
so than dressed. And by and by dinner done, I out and to walk in the
Gallery, for the Duke of York's coming out; and there meeting Mr
May, he took me down about four o'clock to Mr Chevin's lodgings,
and all alone did get me a dish of cold chickens and good wine; and I
dined like a prince, being before very hungry and empty. By and by
the Duke of York comes, and readily took me to his closet, and
received my petition, and discoursed about my eyes, and pitied me,
and with much kindness did give me his consent to be absent, and
approved of my proposition to go into Holland to observe things
there of the Navy; but would first ask the King's leave, which he
anon did, and did tell me that the King would be a good master to
me, (these were his words about my eyes,) and do like of my going
into Holland, but do advise that nobody should know of my going
thither, and that I should pretend to go into the country somewhere;
which I liked well. In discourse this afternoon, the Duke of York did
tell me that he was the most amazed at one thing just now that ever
he was in his life; which was, that the Duke of Buckingham did just
now come into the Queene's bedchamber, where the King was, with
much mixed company, and, among others, Tom Killigrew, the father
of Harry, who was last night wounded so as to be in danger of death,
and his man is quite dead; and there did say that he had spoke with
some one that was by, (which person all the world must know must
be his mistress, my Lady Shrewsbury,) who says that they did not
mean to hurt, but beat him, and that he did run first at them with his
sword; so that he do hereby clearly discover that he knows who did
it, and is of conspiracy with them, being of known conspiracy with
her; which the Duke of York did seem to be pleased with, and said it
might perhaps cost him his life in the House of Lords; and I find was
mightily pleased with it, saying it was the most impudent thing, as
well as the most foolish, that ever he knew man do in all his life.

20th. With my eyes mighty weary, and my head full of care how to get my accounts and business settled against my journey, home to supper, and to bed.

24th. To White Hall, where I attended the Duke of York and was by him led to the King, who expressed great sense of my misfortune in my eyes, and concernment for their recovery; and accordingly signified, not only his assent to my desire therein, but commanded me to give them rest this summer, according to my late petition to the Duke of York.

27th. To White Hall, where all the morning. Dined with Mr Chevins, with Alderman Backewell, and Spragg. The Court full of the news from Captain Hubbert of the *Milford*, touching his being affronted in the Streights, shot at, and having eight men killed him by a French man-of-war, calling him 'English dog', and commanding him to strike; which he refused, and, as knowing himself much too weak for him, made away from him. The Queen, as being supposed with child, fell ill, so as to call for Madam Nun, Mr Chevins' sister, and one of her women, from dinner from us; this being the last day of their doubtfulness touching her being with child, and they were therein well confirmed by her Majesty's being well again before night. One Sir Edmund Bury Godfry,[34] a woodmonger and Justice of Peace in Westminster, having two days since arrested Sir Alexander Frazier for about £30 in firing, the bailiffs were apprehended, committed to the porter's lodge, and there, by the King's command, the last night severely whipped; from which the Justice himself very hardly escaped, (to such an unusual degree was the King moved therein). But he lies now in the lodge justifying his act, as grounded upon the opinion of several of the Judges, and, among others, my Lord Chief-Justice: which makes the King very angry with the Chief-Justice, as they say; and the Justice do lie and justify his act, and says he will suffer in the cause for the people, and do refuse to receive almost any nutriment. The effects of it may be bad to the Court.

28th. To St James's, where the king's being with the Duke of York prevented a meeting of the Tangier Commission. But Lord! what a deal of sorry discourse did I hear between the King and several Lords

34 Supposed to have been murdered by the Papists, October 17th, 1678, when he was found pierced with his own sword, and with several marks of violence on his body.

about him here! but very mean, methought. So with Creed to the Excise-office, and back to White Hall, where, in the Park, Sir G. Carteret did give an account of his discourse lately with the Commissioners of Accounts, who except against many things, but none that I find considerable; among others, that of the officers of the Navy selling of the King's goods, and particularly my providing him with calico flags; which having been by order, and but once, when necessity and the King's apparent profit justified it as conformable to my particular duty, it will prove to my advantage that it be enquired into. Nevertheless, having this morning received from them a demand of an account of all monies within their cognizance received and issued by me, I was willing upon this hint to give myself rest, by knowing whether their meaning therein might reach only to my Treasurership for Tangier, or the monies employed on this occasion. I went therefore to them this afternoon to understand what monies they meant; where they answered me by saying, 'The eleven months' tax, customs, and prize money', without mentioning (any more or than I demanding) the service they respected therein: and so without further discourse we parted upon very good terms of respect, and with few words, but my mind not fully satisfied about the monies they mean.

29th. The King's birth-day. To White Hall, where all very gay; and particularly the Prince of Tuscany very fine, and is the first day of his appearing out of mourning since he came. I heard the Bishop of Peterborough[35] preach but dully; but a good anthem of Pelham's. Home to dinner, and then with my wife to Hyde Park, where all the evening: great store of company, and great preparations by the Prince of Tuscany to celebrate the night with fire-works, for the King's birthday. And so home.

30th (Whitsunday). By water to White Hall, and thence to Sir W. Coventry, where all the morning by his bed-side, he being indisposed. Our discourse was upon the notes I have lately prepared for Commanders' Instructions; but concluded that nothing will render them effectual without an amendment in the choice of them, that they be seamen, and not gentlemen above the command of the Admiral, by the greatness of their relations at Court. Thence to

35 Joseph Henshaw. Died 1678.

White Hall, and dined with Mr Chevins and his sister: whither by and by came in Mr Progers and Sir Thomas Allen, and by and by fine Mrs Wells, who is a great beauty; and there I had my full gaze upon her, to my great content, she being a woman of pretty conversation. Thence to the Duke of York, who, with the officers of the Navy, made a good entrance on my draught of my new Instructions to Commanders, as well expressing his Generalls of a reformation among them, as liking of my humble offers towards it. Thence being called by my wife, we to the Park; whence the rain sent us suddenly home.

31st. Up very betimes, and continued all the morning with Dr Hewer, upon examining and stating my accounts, in order to the fitting myself to go abroad beyond sea, which the ill condition of my eyes and my neglect for a year or two hath kept me behind-hand in, and so as to render it very difficult now and troublesome to my mind to do it; but I this day made a satisfactory entrance therein. Had another meeting with the Duke of York at White Hall on yesterday's work, and made a good advance: and so being called by my wife, we to the Park, Mary Batelier, and a Dutch gentleman, a friend of hers, being with us. Thence to the World's End, a drinking house by the Park; and there merry, and so home late. And thus ends all that I doubt I shall ever be able to do with my own eyes in the keeping of my Journall, I being not able to do it any longer, having done now so long as to undo my eyes almost every time that I take a pen in my hand; and therefore, whatever comes of it, I must forbear: and therefore resolve, from this time forward to have it kept by my people in longhand, and must be contented to set down no more than is fit for them and all the world to know; or if there be any thing, I must endeavour to keep a margin in my book open, to add here and there a note in short-hand with my own hand. And so I betake myself to that course, which is almost as much as to see myself go into my grave: for which, and all the discomforts that will accompany my being blind, the good God prepare me!

S. P.
May 31, 1669